Intelligent Optimization and Control Modeling in Power and Energy System

Intelligent Optimization and Control Modeling in Power and Energy System

Guest Editors

Yuan Cao
Chunsheng Wang
Liqing Liao

MDPI

Basel • Beijing • Wuhan • Barcelona • Belgrade • Novi Sad • Cluj • Manchester

Guest Editors

Yuan Cao
School of Automation
Central South University
Changsha
China

Chunsheng Wang
School of Information Science and Engineering
Central South University
Changsha
China

Liqing Liao
School of Automation
Central South University
Changsha
China

Editorial Office
MDPI AG
Grosspeteranlage 5
4052 Basel, Switzerland

This is a reprint of the Special Issue, published open access by the journal *Mathematics* (ISSN 2227-7390), freely accessible at: https://www.mdpi.com/journal/mathematics/special_issues/823TWUZ6KY.

For citation purposes, cite each article independently as indicated on the article page online and as indicated below:

Lastname, A.A.; Lastname, B.B. Article Title. *Journal Name* **Year**, *Volume Number*, Page Range.

ISBN 978-3-7258-7444-6 (Hbk)
ISBN 978-3-7258-7445-3 (PDF)
https://doi.org/10.3390/books978-3-7258-7445-3

Contents

About the Editors

Yuan Cao

Yuan Cao is an Associate Professor with the School of Automation at Central South University, Changsha, China. He received the B.S. and M.S. degrees from Central South University in 2011 and 2014, respectively, and the Ph.D. degree from the Department of Electrical and Computer Engineering at the University of Alabama, USA, in 2019, all in electrical engineering. Before transitioning to academia, he gained significant industrial experience as a Senior Electrical Engineer at Baidu USA in Sunnyvale, CA, and Hyperloop in Los Angeles, CA.

He has authored more than 60 papers in scientific journals and holds over 20 patents. His research interests and current projects involve energy storage, advanced battery management systems (BMS), and wireless power transfer systems.

Chunsheng Wang

Chunsheng Wang received the B.S. degree in engineering from Beijing Jiaotong University (formerly known as Northern Jiaotong University), Beijing, China, in 1991, the M.S. degree in engineering from Southwest Jiaotong University, Chengdu, China, in 2004, and the Ph.D. degree in engineering from Central South University, Changsha, China, in 2008. In 2008, he joined the staff of Central South University, where he is currently a Professor with the School of Automation. His current research interests include optimization and control of multicarrier energy network modeling, energy management and integrated energy systems, and artificial intelligence and applications.

Liqing Liao

Liqing Liao was born in November 1965 in Wugang, Shaoyang, Hunan Province. Dr. Liao obtained a Doctor of Engineering degree in June 2010 and was appointed Professor in September 2003. He mainly teaches electrical and energy-related courses such as Principles of Microcomputers and Interface Technology, Power System Automation. A 2002 young backbone teacher in Hunan Province, Dr. Liao was a visiting scholar at the University of Essex, UK from 2011 to 2012. He participated in C919 brake control system design, presided over key jet wheel brake R&D, undertakes CR929 anti-skid control research, and led electrical control system development for the national 973 Project as a key researcher in the "2011 Plan" center.

Preface

Energy is the fundamental cornerstone of modern civilization, driving economic growth, technological innovation, and the enhancement of global living standards. As the world transitions toward a more sustainable and electrified future, the reliance on resilient, efficient, and clean energy systems has never been more critical. However, this transition introduces unprecedented complexities, such as the volatility of renewable energy sources, the decentralization of power generation, and the increasing demand for high-performance energy storage. To navigate these challenges, the development and application of intelligent control and optimization modeling have become indispensable. These mathematical and algorithmic tools serve as the "brain" of modern energy infrastructure, enabling the seamless integration of diverse technologies while ensuring stability and economic viability.

The primary purpose of this Reprint is to provide a comprehensive overview of the latest breakthroughs in mathematical modeling and intelligent control within the energy sector. By bridging the gap between theoretical mathematical frameworks and practical engineering applications, this work aims to offer a roadmap for researchers and practitioners striving to optimize the next generation of power systems. The scope of this volume is broad, encompassing critical areas such as the optimization and scheduling of microgrids, the advancement of distributed renewable energy generation, and the refinement of grid-optimization control mechanisms.

This collection places significant focus on the health and safety of energy assets. Several papers delve into the intricate modeling of energy system health states, particularly focusing on the estimation of State of Charge (SOC) and State of Health (SOH) for battery systems. Furthermore, the Reprint explores the integration of artificial intelligence and machine learning in load forecasting, demand response, and the optimization of electric vehicle (EV) charging infrastructures. These contributions highlight how data-driven modeling and advanced intelligent optimization strategies can transform raw energy data into actionable insights, facilitating more responsive and robust energy management systems.

This Reprint contains the 12 articles accepted and published in the Special Issue "Intelligent Optimization and Control Modeling in Power and Energy Systems" of the MDPI journal *Mathematics*. Each article underwent a rigorous peer-review process to ensure scientific excellence and technical relevance. The compilation of these works serves not only as a record of recent academic progress but also as a catalyst for future research in hybrid renewable systems and distributed optimization techniques for power networks.

As the Guest Editors of this Special Issue, we would like to express our sincere gratitude to the authors for their high-quality contributions and their dedication to advancing this field. We are also deeply thankful to the reviewers for their meticulous comments and valuable feedback, which significantly enhanced the clarity and impact of the research presented here. Finally, we extend the appreciation to the editorial and administrative staff at MDPI, particularly the Managing Editor, for their professional collaboration and support throughout the publication process. We hope that this Reprint will prove to be a valuable resource for those working at the intersection of applied mathematics, control theory, and energy engineering, inspiring continued innovation in the quest for a smarter and more sustainable energy future.

Yuan Cao, Chunsheng Wang, and Liqing Liao

Guest Editors

mathematics

MDPI

Article

Stochastic Optimal Control Problem and Sensitivity Analysis for a Residential Heating System

Maalvladédon Ganet Somé [1,2,*] and Japhet Niyobuhungiro [1,3]

1 Department of Mathematics, School of Science, College of Science and Technology, University of Rwanda, Kigali P.O. Box 4285, Rwanda
2 African Institute for Mathematical Sciences, Ghana, Legon, Accra, 1st Shoppers Street, Spintex, Accra P.O. Box LGDTD 20046, Ghana
3 National Council for Science and Technology, Kigali P.O. Box 2285, Rwanda; jniyobuhungiro@ncst.gov.rw
* Correspondence: maalvladedon@aims.edu.gh

Abstract

We consider a network of a residential heating system (RHS) composed of two types of agents: a prosumer and a consumer. Both are connected to a community heating system (CHS), which supplies non-intermittent thermal energy for space heating and domestic hot water. The prosumer utilizes a combination of solar thermal collectors and CHS heat, whereas the consumer depends entirely on the CHS. Any excess heat generated by the prosumer can either be stored on-site or fed back into the CHS. Weather conditions, modeled as a common noise term, affect both agents simultaneously. The prosumer's objective is to minimize the expected discounted total cost, taking into account storage charging and discharging losses as well as uncertainties in future heat production and demand. This leads to a stochastic optimal control problem addressed through dynamic programming techniques. Scenario-based analyses are then performed to examine how different parameters influence both the value function and the resulting optimal control strategies. For a common noise coefficient $\sigma_0 = 0.4$, the prosumer incurs an approximate 16.08% increase in the aggregated discounted cost from the case of no common noise. For a discharging efficiency $\eta_E = \frac{1}{0.9}$, the maximum aggregated discounted cost increases by approximately 1.85% as compared to the perfect discharging efficiency. Similarly, for a charging efficiency $\eta_E = 0.9$, we observe an approximate 1.94% increase in the aggregated discounted cost as compared to a perfect charging efficiency. Furthermore, we derive insights into the maximum expected discounted investment that a consumer would need to make in renewable technologies in order to transition into a prosumer.

Keywords: residential heating system; prosumer; stochastic optimal control; dynamic programming; storage efficiency; thermal energy storage

MSC: 93E20; 49L20; 91G80; 65N06

1. Introduction

In recent decades, global weather patterns have shifted markedly, largely due to human-driven factors such as extensive fossil fuel use and deforestation, both of which have significantly increased the global carbon footprint. Projections from the United Nations Department of Economic and Social Affairs indicate that, by 2050, urbanization will reach 68%, with more than 40 metropolitan areas exceeding 10 million inhabitants [1].

As noted in [1], cities currently account for over two-thirds of global CO_2 emissions and energy consumption. These combined pressures—accelerating urbanization, climate change, and rising energy demand—underscore the urgent need to transition away from a business-as-usual economic model toward one that prioritizes sustainability and energy efficiency across all sectors. According to the International Energy Agency (IEA), buildings contribute roughly 30% of global final energy use and 26% of energy-related emissions. Consistent with [2], in the United States and many European countries, 18–30% of total energy consumption is associated with the thermal energy needs of buildings. In this study, we consider a residential heating system (RHS) composed of two agents—a prosumer and a pure consumer (hereafter simply "consumer")—as illustrated in Figure 1. In this setting, a prosumer is an entity capable of producing and consuming thermal energy, whereas a consumer only uses energy supplied to it. The RHS provides heat for space heating and domestic hot water demands. The prosumer is equipped with a solar thermal collector for local heat generation, an internal storage (IS), and an external storage (ES), both modeled as water-based storage tanks for simplicity [2]. The IS serves short-term storage needs, while the ES accommodates longer-term storage. Because solar production and residual thermal demand are highly intermittent and weather-dependent, additional support is required to ensure a stable and sustainable thermal supply. To address this, both buildings are connected to a community heating system (CHS). In this work, we consider a low-temperature bidirectional CHS (LTB-CHS) [1,3–5] and assume, for simplicity, that the temperature in the distribution pipes remains constant. The LTB-CHS is a relatively recent concept in district energy networks, offering benefits such as improved integration of renewable heat sources, simplified coupling with distributed technologies, and reduced carbon emissions. Its bidirectional capability allows buildings to inject surplus heat into the network, lowering peak central production requirements and enabling economic incentives whereby building owners can sell excess heat. Since the supply temperature in an LTB-CHS is lower than that in conventional systems, a heat pump (HP) is required to upgrade the delivered heat to the desired level.

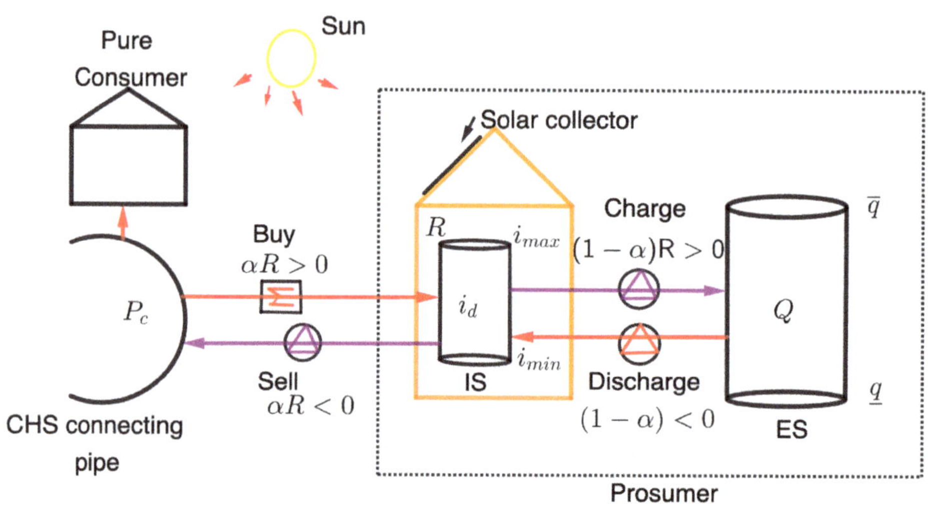

Figure 1. A model with a consumer and a prosumer connected to a community heating system.

In our modeling approach, daily temperature variations influence both the prosumer and consumer and are represented by a common noise process. Following [2,6,7], we define residual demand as the imbalance between thermal supply and demand. We assume that the prosumer can meet this residual demand either via the CHS or by using the ES,

https://doi.org/10.3390/math14030489

whereas the consumer relies solely on the CHS. When production falls short, the prosumer either purchases heat from the CHS or releases it from the ES. Conversely, during periods of surplus production, the prosumer may store the excess in the ES (subject to capacity limits) or sell it to the CHS. The consumer, lacking local production and storage, always faces unmet demand that must be satisfied exclusively through CHS purchases. Consistent with [2], we assume that the CHS is responsible for fulfilling the residual thermal demands of both agents, even though this demand fluctuates with respect to the common noise. Moreover, energy transfer between the IS and ES, as well as energy exports from the prosumer to the CHS, requires an ordinary pump (OP). The prosumer aims to minimize the expected total discounted cost associated with meeting its thermal demand, while accounting for uncertain weather conditions and variability in solar output. In contrast, the consumer—lacking local production or storage—continuously faces unmet thermal demand that must be supplied entirely from the CHS.

Including both agents in our framework enables us to determine the maximum expected investment that would make it economically reasonable for a consumer to adopt distributed renewable heating technologies and storage infrastructure, thereby transitioning into a prosumer.

Previous work, such as [2], has formulated an RHS model and solved a stochastic optimal control problem using semi-Lagrangian and dynamic programming approaches. In Ref. [7], the authors addressed a similar problem for a stand-alone system with geothermal storage. However, these studies did not explicitly model the dependence of residual demand on daily temperature variations via a common noise process, nor did they include ES charging and discharging inefficiencies. Our model fills this gap by incorporating these features, which increase realism. Models with common noise are advantageous because they reflect uncertainties that affect all agents simultaneously, potentially altering both qualitative and quantitative system behavior. Applications of common noise models in the energy sector include [6,8–13].

Unlike in [2,7], we incorporate ES charging and discharging efficiencies, which account for storage losses when heat is stored or released. For simplicity, we assume that these efficiency factors depend solely on the residual demand, as in [14].

Our contributions include first modeling a consumer connected to the CHS. We also motivate a common noise in the dynamics of the residual demands. This allows us to capture the impact of daily temperature variations on the residual demand. In addition, we include charging/discharging efficiencies in the dynamics of the ES temperature level. In reality, losses are observed during charging or discharging processes of the ES. Therefore, modeling these efficiencies is required. Furthermore, we perform a sensitivity analysis on the common noise, charging and discharging parameters to evaluate their impact on the expected total discounted cost. We also show that the value function is a viscosity solution of the associated partial differential equation (PDE). We derive the discrete-time state-dependent control set from the state constraint without imposing charging and discharging thresholds. In this work, the state-dependent control intervals depend on the charging/discharging efficiencies. We compare the costs of satisfying residual demands for both the consumer and the prosumer, and we estimate the expected investment that a consumer would need to undertake to transition into a prosumer. Finally, we perform extensive numerical experiments and provide economic interpretations.

The remainder of this paper is structured as follows: Section 2 introduces the model, including state variables, control variables, constraints, and the heat price specification. Section 3 presents the optimal control problems for both agents. Sections 4 and 5 describe the semi-Lagrangian discretization and numerical results, including sensitivity analysis. Section 6 concludes and outlines directions for future research.

https://doi.org/10.3390/math14030489

2. Model Formulation

In what follows, we study a model that includes both a prosumer and a consumer connected to a CHS. The prosumer is able to generate thermal energy locally while also drawing from, or supplying heat to, the CHS. In contrast, the consumer has neither local production capabilities nor on-site storage units. We present a mathematical framework and corresponding optimization problems for both agents. Throughout this paper, we work on a fixed probability space $(\Omega, \mathcal{F}, \mathbb{P})$ endowed with a filtration $\mathbb{F} = (\mathcal{F}_t)_{t\in[0,T]}$ that satisfies the usual conditions and supports two independent standard Brownian motions W_R and W^0. The parameter $T > 0$ denotes the finite planning horizon.

An RHS is designed to supply thermal energy for both space heating and domestic hot water in a building. The prosumer is equipped with a solar collector, two storage units, a heat pump, and ordinary pumps. Thermal energy generated by the solar collector is first directed to the internal storage (IS) to meet immediate demand, while the external storage (ES) serves as a long-term buffer to handle periods of insufficient or excess production. We describe the imbalance between thermal supply and demand, resulting from stochastic fluctuations in solar collector output, by a stochastic process $R = (R(t))_{t\in[0,T]}$. This process is decomposed as $R(t) = \mu^R(t) + Z^R(t)$, where $\mu^R(t)$ denotes the seasonal average and $Z^R(t)$ represents random deviations from this mean.

The IS is modeled as a cylindrical tank whose water temperature must remain within prescribed bounds, i_{min} and i_{max}. In this study, we treat the IS as a black box and do not model its internal thermodynamic behavior explicitly. The ES is also represented as a cylindrical water tank with a fixed mass of stored water, which can be heated up to a maximum temperature $\overline{q}$ through transfers of thermal energy from the IS. Conversely, it can be cooled to a minimum temperature $\underline{q}$ when heat is withdrawn to satisfy the residual demand. For simplicity, we assume that charging and discharging the ES involves only ordinary pumps.

At any time $t \in [0, T]$, the prosumer's state variables consist of the exogenous, deseasonalized residual demand Z^R and the endogenous ES temperature level Q. We therefore define the prosumer's state process as $X = (Z^R, Q)^\top$.

For the consumer, the state is given solely by the deseasonalized residual demand $\widetilde{Z}$, which is entirely exogenous.

Residual Demand: The deseasonalized residual demand processes Z^R and $\widetilde{Z}$, associated with the prosumer and the consumer, respectively, evolve according to

$$\mathrm{d}Z^R(t) = -\kappa_R Z^R(t)\mathrm{d}t + \sigma_R(t)\mathrm{d}W_R(t) + \sigma_0 \mathrm{d}W^0(t), \tag{1}$$

$$\mathrm{d}\widetilde{Z}(t) = -\kappa_0 \widetilde{Z}(t)\mathrm{d}t + \sigma_0 \mathrm{d}W^0(t), \tag{2}$$

where W_R represents the idiosyncratic noise capturing uncertainties specific to the prosumer's heat demand, and W^0 is the common noise accounting for shared weather-driven fluctuations.

The seasonal behavior of the residual demands is modeled by bounded and deterministic seasonality functions $\mu^R, \widetilde{\mu} : [0, T] \to \mathbb{R}$ for the prosumer and the consumer, respectively. Typical choices of $\widehat{\mu}(t) = \mu^R, \widetilde{\mu}$ include

$$\widehat{\mu}(t) = c_0 + ct + \sum_{j=1}^{m_1} \left(c_j \cos\left(\frac{2\pi}{\rho_j}(t - t_j)\right) + d_j \sin\left(\frac{2\pi}{\rho_j}(t - t_j)\right)\right), \tag{3}$$

where c_0 is the long-term mean residual demand; c_j, d_j represent the amplitudes of seasonality component j of the cosine and sine terms, respectively; ρ_j, t_j represent the length and a reference time of seasonality component j, respectively; c is the coefficient of the linear term; and m_1 is the number of seasonality components.

https://doi.org/10.3390/math14030489

Since the prosumer is equipped with a local production unit, which can lead to overproduction, the expression of $R(t)$ agrees with our modeling perspectives. Similarly, we model $\widetilde{R}(t) = \widetilde{\mu}(t) + \widetilde{Z}(t)$ and choose parameters of $\widetilde{\mu}(t)$ and $\widetilde{Z}(t)$ for which there exists $\nu \ll 1$ such that $\mathbb{P}(\widetilde{R}(t) < 0) < \nu$. Below, $R > 0$ is referred to as unsatisfied demand and $R < 0$ as overproduction.

The control $\alpha \in [0,1]$ denotes the proportion of residual demand satisfied by the CHS. As in Ref. [2], we assume the decomposition $R(t) = \alpha(t)R(t) + (1-\alpha(t))R(t)$, where $\alpha(t)R(t)$ is the residual demand satisfied by the ES, and $(1-\alpha(t))R(t)$ is the residual demand satisfied by the CHS. Satisfying the residual demand via the CHS suggests either buying (for $R > 0$) or selling (for $R < 0$). Likewise, satisfying the residual demand via the ES implies either discharging (for $R > 0$) or charging (for $R < 0$).

External Storage: In the following, we consider as storage a water tank where the water mass and specific heat capacity are given by $m_Q[kg]$ and $c_P[KWh/kg\ K]$, respectively. The surface area of the tank is denoted as $A[m^2]$. From the heat fluxes and the Newton cooling law with the heat transfer coefficient $\gamma\ [kW/m^2K]$, the change in the thermal energy of the water inside the ES is given by

$$\mathrm{d}Q(t) = \frac{-1}{m_Q c_P}(\eta_E(t)(1-\alpha(t))R(t) + A\gamma(Q(t) - \underline{q}))\mathrm{d}t, \quad Q(0) = Q_0. \tag{4}$$

The first term $\eta_E(t)(1-\alpha(t))R(t)$ represents the ES's charging or discharging rate. Indeed, for an unsatisfied demand ($R(t) > 0$) and for a non-empty ES ($Q(t) > \underline{q}$), the prosumer discharges the storage at a rate $\alpha(t) > 0$. For an overproduction ($R(t) < 0$) and for a non-full ES ($Q(t) < \overline{q}$), the prosumer can charge the storage at the rate $\alpha(t) < 0$. The second term $A\gamma(Q(t) - \underline{q})$ is the rate of heat transfer with the environment. η_E represents the charging or discharging efficiency of the ES. Letting $\eta_E^C, \eta_E^D \in (0,1)$, we model η_E for simplicity as in [14] by

$$\eta_E(t) := \eta_E(R(t)) = \begin{cases} \eta_E^C, & \text{if } R(t) < 0, \\ \\ 1/\eta_E^D, & \text{if } R(t) \geq 0. \end{cases} \tag{5}$$

Remark 1.

- *A large γ implies large losses per unit of time, prohibiting long-term storage. Similarly, a small γ implies small losses per unit of time, allowing for long-term storage.*
- *In the case $\alpha = 0$, the prosumer does not satisfy its residual demand via the CHS. In the event of an unsatisfied demand ($R(t) > 0$), $\alpha = 1$ implies that the prosumer satisfies all of the residual demand via the CHS. However, for an overproduction ($R(t) < 0$), $\alpha = 1$ implies that the prosumer sells all the residual demand to the CHS.*

State and Control Constraints: In order to reflect physical limitations of our external storage, we suggest that $Q(t) \in [\underline{q}, \overline{q}]$, where $\underline{q}$ and $\overline{q}$ are the minimum and maximum storage levels, respectively. $Q(t) = \underline{q}$ is referred to as an empty storage, while $Q(t) = \overline{q}$ is a full storage.

The operational limitations experienced by the prosumer give rise to state-dependent control constraints:

1. If $Q(t) = \underline{q}$, only charging is feasible. Therefore,
    - If $R(t) > 0$, all residual demand is satisfied by the CHS, implying $\alpha(t) = 1$.
    - If $R(t) < 0$, there are no control constraints other than the requirement $\alpha(t) \in [0,1]$.
2. If $Q(t) = \overline{q}$, we examine the following cases:

https://doi.org/10.3390/math14030489

- $R(t) > 0$, no control constraints other than the requirement $\alpha(t) \in [0,1]$.
- $R(t) < 0$ and (4) suggest that $\eta_E(1-\alpha(t))R(t) + A\gamma(Q(t) - \underline{q}) \geq 0$, hence implying that $\alpha(t) \geq 1 + \frac{A\gamma(\overline{q}-q)}{R(t)\eta_E^C} =: \widehat{\chi}(t, R(t))$. In the following, we define $\chi(t,R(t)) = \widehat{\chi}(t,R(t)) \vee 0$ and choose $\alpha(t) = \chi(t,R(t)) = \chi(t)$.

Hence, the state-dependent set of feasible controls, $\mathcal{U}(t, z^R, q)$, is defined by

$$\mathcal{U}(t,z^R,q) = \begin{cases} [0,1], & q > \underline{q}, \quad z^R \geq -\mu^R(t), \\ \{1\}, & q = \underline{q}, \quad z^R \geq -\mu^R(t), \\ [0,1], & q < \overline{q}, \quad z^R < -\mu^R(t), \\ [\chi(t),1], & q = \overline{q}, \quad z^R < -\mu^R(t). \end{cases}$$

Heat Price Formulation: We introduce time-varying heat buying and selling prices, denoted by $P_{buy}(t)$ and $P_{sell}(t)$, respectively, for all $t \in [0,T]$. We assume a contractual agreement between the prosumer and the CHS, binding the latter to always satisfy the residual demand of the former. To incentivize the CHS, it retains the right to determine the values of $P_{buy}(t)$ and $P_{sell}(t)$. We model P_{buy} as a deterministic function composed of a constant baseline and multiple seasonal fluctuations. P_{sell} is a fixed markdown from the buying price through the spread parameter $\xi > 0$. Therefore, we obtain

$$P_{buy}(t) = \ell_0 + \sum_{j=1}^{m_2} \ell_j \cos\left(\frac{2\pi}{\rho_j^S}(t - t_j^S)\right), \quad \text{and} \quad P_{sell}(t) = P_{buy}(t) - \xi. \tag{6}$$

The constant term ℓ_0 $[\frac{€}{kWh}]$ corresponds to the long-term average heat price, while each cosine term introduces a seasonal component with amplitude ℓ_j $[\frac{€}{kWh}]$, period ρ_j^S $[h]$, and phase shift t_j^S $[h]$; m_2 represents the number of seasonalities. The sum in the heat price model means that it is not driven by a simple seasonal pattern but by the combined effects of several independent and interpretable cycles, each corresponding to a different physical, operational, or economic rhythm of the heating system. The deterministic seasonal structure makes prices transparent and predictable for the prosumer, while the positive spread guarantees economic viability for the CHS. The bid–ask spread reflects transaction costs, operational constraints, or the market power of the CHS. It ensures that the CHS is compensated for providing balancing and backup services.

Assumption 1. *Let P_c and i_d denote the heat pump inlet and outlet temperatures, respectively. Similar to [2], we assume that the condition $\underline{q} > i_d > i_{min} > P_c$ holds.*

Assumption 1 suggests that no heat pumps are necessary when satisfying the residual demand via the ES. This justifies the use of ordinary pumps in our model.

3. Problem Formulation

In this section, we formulate both the prosumer's and consumer's problems. The prosumer's objective is to satisfy its heating and hot water demand while minimizing the cost of running the pumps and payments to the CHS.

3.1. Prosumer's Problem

In the following, we present a mathematical framework to determine both the value and the optimal control strategy for the prosumer's problem. This leads to the formulation of a stochastic optimal control problem for which the state process is defined as

https://doi.org/10.3390/math14030489

$X = (Z^R, Q) \in \mathcal{X} = \mathbb{R} \times [\underline{q}, \overline{q}]$, representing the relevant system variables. From the dynamics described in the first equation in (1) and (4), the state process evolves as follows:

$$\begin{aligned} dZ^R(t) &= f(Z^R(t))dt + \sigma_R dW_R(t) + \sigma_0 dW_0(t), \qquad & Z^R(0) &= Z_0^R \in \mathbb{R}, \\ dQ(t) &= h(Z^R(t), Q(t), \alpha(t))dt, & Q(0) &= Q_0 \in [\underline{q}, \overline{q}], \end{aligned} \tag{7}$$

where $f(z^R) = -\kappa_R z^R$ and $h(z^R, q, v) = \frac{-1}{m_Q c_P}(\eta_E(t)(1-v)(\mu^R(t) + z^R) + A\gamma(q - \underline{q}))$.

Assumption 2. *Let* $(z^R, q) \in \mathbb{R} \times [\underline{q}, \overline{q}]$ *and* $q_1, q_2 \in [\underline{q}, \overline{q}]$.

1. *The function* $h(z^R, q, v)$ *is* $\mathcal{F}$*-measurable.*
2. *The function* $h(z^R, q, v)$ *is continuous for almost all* z^R.
3. *For almost all* z^R, *there exists* $C \in \mathbb{R}$ *such that* $|h(z^R, q_1, v) - h(z^R, q_2, v)| \leq C|q_1 - q_2|$.

As in [15], this assumption ensures that the random ordinary differential equation (RODE) in (7) is well defined.

Cost Formulation

The costs incurred for operating the prosumer's system are divided into a running cost and a terminal cost. Together, they define the total cost that needs to be minimized.

Running Cost: This consists of the cost (revenue) of satisfying the residual demand via the CHS, along with the cost of electricity consumption for operating the pumps when interacting with both the CHS and the ES. At $t \in [0, T]$, the prosumer can either purchase or sell thermal energy from or to the CHS at prices $P_{buy}(t)$ and $P_{sell}(t)$, respectively, to satisfy its residual demand. Let φ_0 denote the cost (revenue) per unit of time of buying (selling) thermal energy from (to) the CHS, defined by

$$\varphi_0(t, z^R, v) = \begin{cases} v(\mu^R(t) + z^R)P_{buy}(t), & z^R \geq -\mu^R(t), \\ v(\mu^R(t) + z^R)P_{sell}(t), & z^R < -\mu^R(t). \end{cases}$$

Since we assume that the prosumer is connected to an LTB-CHS, we incur an additional cost for the electricity consumption due to the use of a heat pump when satisfying the residual demand via the CHS. Let b_1 and $b_2[K^{-1}]$ denote positive constants penalizing a high water flow rate and a high temperature difference between P_c and i_d, respectively. Letting S denote the electricity price, the cost of electricity consumption φ_1 incurred when interacting with the CHS is modeled by

$$\varphi_1(t, z^R, v) = \begin{cases} v(\mu^R(t) + z^R)(b_1 + b_2(i_d - P_c))S, & z^R \geq -\mu^R(t), \\ -v(\mu^R(t) + z^R)b_1 S, & z^R < -\mu^R(t), \end{cases}$$

For $z^R \geq -\mu^R(t)$, the first equation in φ_1 is the cost per unit of time of electricity consumption to run the heat pump to increase the temperature from P_c to i_d. On the other hand, for $z^R < -\mu^R(t)$, the last equation in φ_1 is the cost per unit of time of electricity consumption for operating the ordinary pump when selling thermal energy to the CHS.

The cost of satisfying the residual demand via the ES comes from the cost of electricity consumption to operate the ordinary pumps and is given by

$$\varphi_2(t, z^R, v) = (1 - v)|\mu^R(t) + z^R|b_1 S.$$

Therefore, the running cost $\Gamma(t, z^R, v)$ is given by $\Gamma(t, z^R, v) = \varphi_0(t, z^R, v) + \varphi_1(t, z^R, v) + \varphi_2(t, z^R, v)$.

https://doi.org/10.3390/math14030489

Terminal Cost: In the context of finite-time horizon models with terminal time $T > 0$, it is customary to incorporate a terminal cost. In our context, this depends on the ES storage level at time T and is denoted by $\Phi(Q(T))$. This terminal cost can reflect a contractual agreement for the ES temperature to be at an agreed level at T. Let P_{liq}, P_{pen} denote the liquidation price and penalty price, respectively. Indeed, at terminal time, the prosumer can sell the leftover thermal energy at P_{liq} per unit of thermal energy. Similarly, the prosumer can be penalized for failing to keep the ES at a certain level at T, where P_{pen} is the penalty price per unit of thermal energy. The liquidation price P_{liq} and penalty price P_{pen} satisfy the conditions $P_{liq} < P_{sell}(T)$ and $P_{pen} > P_{buy}(T)$, respectively. In the following, we let q_{ref} denote a pre-agreed temperature level in the ES, such that

$$\Phi(q) = \begin{cases} \frac{P_{pen} m_Q c_P (q_{ref} - q)}{\eta_E^C}, & q < q_{ref}, \\ -\eta_E^D P_{liq} m_Q c_P (q - q_{ref}), & q \geq q_{ref}. \end{cases} \tag{8}$$

In this model, the terminal cost $\Phi(q)$ now depends on the charging and discharging efficiency term $\eta_E(R(t))$.

The performance criterion J_P: $[0, T] \times \mathcal{X} \times \mathcal{U} \to \mathbb{R}$ denotes the expected aggregated total discounted cost over the time interval $[0, T]$ and is defined as follows:

$$J_P(t, x, \alpha) = \mathbb{E}_{t,x}\Big[\int_t^T e^{-\delta(s-t)} \Gamma(s, Z^R(s), \alpha(s)) \mathrm{d}s + e^{-\delta(T-t)} \Phi(Q(T)) \Big], \tag{9}$$

where $x = (z^R, q)$, $\delta \geq 0$ is a discount rate and $\mathbb{E}_{t,x}[\cdot]$ is the conditional expectation given that at initial time t, $X(t) = x$.

Assumption 3. *For any admissible control α, the functions Γ and Φ satisfy the condition*

$$\mathbb{E}\Big[\int_t^T |\Gamma(s, Z^R(s), \alpha(s))| \mathrm{d}s + |\Phi(Q(s))| \Big] < \infty. \tag{10}$$

Given that we want to use dynamic programming techniques, we restrict to Markov controls defined by $\alpha(t) = \theta(t, X(t))$, for all $t \in [0, T]$ with a measurable function θ: $[0, T] \times \mathcal{X} \to \mathcal{U}$, which is called a decision rule and is adapted to the filtration $\mathbb{F}$. We denote by $\mathcal{A}$ the class of admissible controls, defined as follows:

$$\begin{aligned} \mathcal{A} = \{ (\alpha(t))_{t \in [0,T]} \mid \quad & \alpha \text{ is } \mathbb{F} - \text{progressively measurable}, \alpha(t) = \theta(t, X(t)), \\ & \forall t \in [0, T], \theta(t, x) \in \mathcal{U}(t, x) \text{ and Equations (7) and (9) are well defined} \}. \end{aligned} \tag{11}$$

The prosumer seeks to minimize J_P over all admissible controls. The value of the prosumer's problem for all $(t, x) \in [0, T] \times \mathcal{X}$ is given by

$$V(t, x) = \inf_{\alpha \in \mathcal{A}} J_P(t, x, \alpha). \tag{12}$$

3.2. Consumer's Problem

We discuss the mathematical framework to determine the value of the consumer's problem. We recall that the consumer is not equipped with local production or storage units and is always subject to a positive residual demand. As a result, it always satisfies all residual demand via the CHS. The state process of the consumer is given by

$$\mathrm{d}\widetilde{Z}(t) = f_2(\widetilde{Z}(t)) \mathrm{d}t + \sigma_0 \mathrm{d}W_0(t), \qquad \widetilde{Z}(0) = \widetilde{Z}_0 \in \mathbb{R}, \tag{13}$$

where $f_2(\widetilde{z}) = -\kappa_0 \widetilde{z}$.

https://doi.org/10.3390/math14030489

Similar to the prosumer's case, the consumer's running cost consists of the cost of purchasing thermal energy from the CHS and the cost of operating the heat pump to raise the temperature from P_c to $\widetilde{i}_d$. Let $\widetilde{\varphi}_0$ and $\widetilde{\varphi}_1$ denote the cost per unit of time of purchasing thermal energy from the CHS and that of electricity consumption to run the heat pump, respectively, which are defined as follows:

$$\widetilde{\varphi}_0(t,\widetilde{z}) = \widetilde{R}(t)P_{buy}(t), \tag{14}$$
$$\widetilde{\varphi}_1(t,\widetilde{z}) = \widetilde{R}(t)(b_1 + b_2(\widetilde{i}_d - P_c))S, \tag{15}$$

where $\widetilde{R}(t) = \widetilde{\mu}(t) + \widetilde{Z}(t)$. Therefore, $\widetilde{\Gamma}(t,\widetilde{z}) = \widetilde{\varphi}_0(t,\widetilde{z}) + \widetilde{\varphi}_1(t,\widetilde{z})$.

Since the consumer is not equipped with a local storage unit, there is no terminal cost. The performance criterion $J_C : [0,T] \times \mathbb{R} \to \mathbb{R}^+$ denotes the expected aggregated total discounted cost over the time interval $[0,T]$ and is defined as follows:

$$J_C(t,\widetilde{z}) = \mathbb{E}_{t,\widetilde{z}}\Big[\int_t^T e^{-\delta(s-t)}\widetilde{\Gamma}(s,\widetilde{Z}(s))\mathrm{d}s\Big], \tag{16}$$

where $\delta \geq 0$ is a discount rate and $\mathbb{E}_{t,\widetilde{z}}[\cdot]$ is the conditional expectation given that at initial time t, $\widetilde{Z}(t) = \widetilde{z}$. The value of the consumer's problem for all $(t,\widetilde{z}) \in [0,T] \times \mathbb{R}$ is given by

$$\widetilde{V}(t,\widetilde{z}) = J_C(t,\widetilde{z}). \tag{17}$$

4. Semi-Lagrangian Discretization

In this section, we recall the discrete-time numerical scheme in [2]. We focus on the prosumer's problem, since the consumer's problem can be solved directly. We start by discussing the state discretization.

State Discretization: Let N_t, N_z, and N_q denote the number of grid points in the t-, z^R-, and q-directions, respectively. For computational reasons, we truncate the domain $\mathcal{X} = \mathbb{R} \times [\underline{q},\overline{q}]$ to $\widehat{\mathcal{X}} = [\underline{z}^R,\overline{z}^R] \times [\underline{q},\overline{q}]$, such that for a tolerance $\epsilon \ll 1, \mathbb{P}(Z^R(t) \in [\underline{z}^R,\overline{z}^R]) \geq 1-\epsilon$, for all $t \in [0,T]$. $\underline{z}^R$ and $\overline{z}^R$ represent the minimum and maximum values of the deseasonalized residual demand Z^R, respectively. Given the asymptotic standard deviation $s_0 = \sqrt{\frac{\sigma_R^2+\sigma_0^2}{2\kappa_R}}$ of Z^R, the 3-σ rule motivates $\underline{z}^R = -3s_0$ and $\overline{z}^R = 3s_0$.

Let $t_0 < t_1 < \cdots < t_{N_t}$, $z_0^R < z_1^R < \cdots < z_{N_z}^R$, and $q_0 < q_1 < \cdots < q_{N_q}$ be a finite number of grid points in the z^R and q-directions. We define

$$\widehat{\mathcal{G}} = \widehat{\mathcal{G}}_t \times \widehat{\mathcal{G}}_z \times \widehat{\mathcal{G}}_q = [t_0,\ldots,t_{N_t}] \times [z_0^R,\cdots,z_{N_z}^R] \times [q_0,\ldots,q_{N_q}],$$

where $t_n = t_0 + n\Delta t$, $z_i^R = \underline{z}^R + i\Delta z^R$, $q_k = \underline{q} + k\Delta q$, for $n \in \widehat{\mathcal{G}}_n = \{0,1,\ldots,N_t\}$, $i = 0,\ldots,N_z$ and $k = 0,\ldots,N_q$, as a 3-dimensional equidistant grid on $\widehat{\mathcal{X}}$ with the temporal and spatial step sizes

$$t_{n+1} - t_n =: \Delta t = \frac{T-t_0}{N_t}, \quad \Delta z^R = \frac{\overline{z}^R - \underline{z}^R}{N_z}, \quad \Delta q = \frac{\overline{q}-\underline{q}}{N_q}.$$

We now recall the discrete-time numerical scheme discussed in [2]. This is an alternative to the semi-Lagrangian approach introduced in [16] and extended in [17,18]. It is a finite difference scheme based on the theory presented in [19].

The control problem in (12) can be solved through dynamic programming techniques that rely on the following dynamic programming principle (DPP). The subsequent result is useful for solutions to the control problem in (12).

https://doi.org/10.3390/math14030489

Theorem 1 (DPP). *For all* $(t,x) \in [0,T) \times \mathcal{X}, h > 0$ *and* $t+h \leq T$, *the value function* $V(t,x)$, *satisfies the DPP*

$$V(t,x) = \inf_{\alpha \in \mathcal{A}} \mathbb{E}_{t,x}\Big[\int_t^{t+h} e^{-\delta(s-t)} \Gamma(s, Z^R(s), \alpha(s)) \mathrm{d}s + e^{-\delta h} V(t+h, X(t+h)) \Big]. \tag{18}$$

Proof. For a proof, we refer to [20]. □

The following result shows that the value function V, defined in (12), is a viscosity solution of an associated partial differential equation (PDE).

Proposition 1. *Let* $\Theta(t,x,v) = f(z^R),\ h(z^R,q,v),\ \Gamma(t,z^R,v),\ \Phi(q)$. *Thus, there exists* $L > 0$ *such that*

$$|\Theta(t,x,v) - \Theta(t,\widehat{x},v)| \leq L|x - \widehat{x}|, \quad \forall t \in [0,T], x, \widehat{x} \in \mathcal{X}, v \in \mathcal{U}, \tag{19}$$

$$|\Theta(t,0,v)| \leq L, \quad \forall (t,v) \in [0,T] \times \mathcal{U}. \tag{20}$$

Therefore, the value function V is a viscosity solution of the PDE

$$\frac{\partial V}{\partial t} + \mathcal{L}V + \inf_{v \in \mathcal{U}(t,z^R,q)} \{\mathcal{L}_q V + \Gamma(t,z^R,v)\} = 0, \tag{21}$$

with the terminal condition $V(T,q) = \Phi(q)$ *and* $\mathcal{L}V = f(z^R)\frac{\partial V}{\partial z^R} + \frac{1}{2}(\sigma_R^2(t) + \sigma_0^2)\frac{\partial^2 V}{\partial (z^R)^2} - \delta V$, $\mathcal{L}_q = h(z^R,q,v)\frac{\partial V}{\partial q}$.

Proof. First, we note that the functions $f(z^R),\ h(z^R,q,v),\ \Gamma(t,z^R,v),\ \Phi(q)$ are linear in the states z^R and q. Then, there exits $L > 0$, such that

$$|\Theta(t,x,v) - \Theta(t,\widehat{x},v)| \leq L|x - \widehat{x}|, \quad \forall t \in [0,T], x, \widehat{x} \in \mathcal{X}, v \in \mathcal{U}.$$

In addition, we have $|\Theta(t,0,v)| \leq L, \quad \forall (t,v) \in [0,T] \times \mathcal{U}$. Finally, the result follows from Theorem 2.3 in [21]. □

Idea of the Scheme: We begin by fixing the triple (t_n, z_i^R, q_k) and assume that, for $t \in [t_n, t_{n+1})$, the deseasonalized residual demand remains constant, i.e., $Z^R(t) = z_i^R$, where z_i^R is fixed and known. Next, we assume that the control is constant over this interval, i.e., $\alpha(t) = \alpha_{i,k}^n =: v$, which is fixed but unknown. Under these assumptions, and using the explicit solution, we compute the arrival point $\mathcal{Q}_{k(i,n)}^{v,n+1}$ of the ES temperature level, given that at time t_n, the storage level was q_k, the residual demand was $\mu^R(t_n) + z_i^R$, and constant action v was taken. We then apply the DPP in two steps: In the first step, using the above discretization, we obtain an approximation of the optimal control $\alpha_{i,k}^{*n} =: v^*$. In the second step, we substitute this approximate optimal control in the DPP and "release" the deseasonalized residual demand Z^R. Finally, by applying the Feynman–Kac formula to the second step, we derive a one-period PDE, which we discretize using finite difference methods to obtain a discrete-time scheme. This scheme is implemented in Algorithm 1.

From the above discussion, we formulate the following assumptions:

Assumption 4 (Piecewise Constant Control). *For* $n = 0, 1, \cdots, N_t - 1$ *and* $t \in [t_n, t_{n+1})$, *the control* α *and the associated decision rule* θ *are kept constant between two consecutive grid points of the time discretization. That is,*

$$\alpha(t) = \alpha(t_n) \quad \text{and} \quad \theta(t, X(t)) = \theta(t_n, X(t_n)).$$

https://doi.org/10.3390/math14030489

Algorithm 1 Backward Recursion Algorithm

Data: $\{t_n\}_{n=0,\cdots,N_t}$, $\{z_i^R\}_{i=0,\cdots,N_z}$, $\{q_k\}_{k=0,\cdots,N_q}$
Input: Γ, Φ, δ
Output: Approximation of the value function $V_{i,k}^n$ and optimal control $v_{i,k}^{*n}$
Step 1 At the terminal time $n := N_t$;
for $i := 0$ *to* N_z **do**
  for $k := 0$ *to* N_q **do**
    $V_{i,k}^{N_t} \leftarrow \Phi(q_k)$
  end
end
Step 2 Backward recursion in time
for $n := N_t - 1$ *to* 0 **do**
  Internal points
  for $k := 1$ *to* $N_q - 1$ **do**
    for $i := 1$ *to* $N_z - 1$ **do**
      Compute $V_{i,k}^n$ by solving the linear system (41),

$$v_{i,k}^{*n} \leftarrow \underset{v \in \mathcal{U}_d^n(t_n, z_i^R, q_k)}{\operatorname{argmin}} \left[\int_{t_n}^{t_{n+1}} e^{-\delta(t-t_n)} \Gamma(t, z_i^R, v) dt + e^{-\delta \Delta_t} V(t_{n+1}, z_i^R Q_{k(i,n)}^{v,n+1}) \right].$$

    end
  end
  Compute the boundary and corner value functions $V_{0,0}^n$, V_{0,N_q}^n, $V_{N_z,0}^n$, and V_{N_z,N_q}^n and their corresponding approximate controls.
end

Assumption 5 (Piecewise Constant Model Parameters). *For $n = 0, 1, \cdots, N_t - 1$ and $t \in [t_n, t_{n+1})$, the time-dependent seasonality μ^R and the efficiency parameter η_E are kept constant between two consecutive grid points of the time discretization. That is,*

$$\mu^R(t) = \mu^R(t_n) = \mu_n^R, \quad \mu^R(T) = \mu_{N_t}^R,$$
$$\eta_E(t) = \eta_E(t_n) = \eta_{E,n}, \quad \eta_E(T) = \eta_{E,N_t},$$

Assumptions 4 and 5 suggest that the system's time-dependent parameters are adjusted only at discrete-time points and remain constant within two consecutive discrete-time points. This situation is also consistent with reality.

Let $Q^v(t)$ denote the solution of the ODE (7) for the ES temperature level on the time interval $[t_n, t_{n+1})$ for a fixed but unknown control v, satisfying

$$\mathrm{d}Q^v(t) = h(Z^R(t), Q^v(t), v)\mathrm{d}t, \quad Q^v(t_n) = q_k, \quad t \in [t_n, t_{n+1}). \tag{22}$$

Lemma 1. *Let Assumptions 4 and 5 hold and $\lambda = \frac{A\gamma}{m_Q c_P}$. Then, for $n = 0, 1, \cdots, N_t, i = 0, 1, \cdots, N_z, k = 0, 1, \cdots, N_q, t \in [t_n, t_{n+1})$ and $Q^v(t_n) = q_k$, the closed-from solution of Q^v is given by*

$$Q^v(t) = q_k e^{-\lambda(t-t_n)} + \Big(\frac{\eta_{E,n}(v-1)(\mu_n^R + z_i^R)}{A\gamma} + \underline{q} \Big)(1 - e^{-\lambda(t-t_n)}). \tag{23}$$

Moreover, letting $t = t_{n+1}$ and $\theta_{i,k}^n = \frac{A\gamma q_k - [\eta_{E,n}(v-1)(\mu_n^R + z_i^R) - A\gamma \underline{q}]}{\Delta q} \frac{1-e^{-\lambda \Delta t}}{A\gamma}$, (23) *becomes*

$$Q_{k(i,n)}^{v,n+1} = q_k - \theta_{i,k}^n \Delta q. \tag{24}$$

Proof. Let $\lambda = \frac{A\gamma}{m_Q c_P}$. For $n = 0, 1, \cdots, N_t, i = 0, 1, \cdots, N_z$ and $k = 0, 1, \cdots, N_q$, assume that $Q^v(t_n) = q_k$. Under Assumptions 4 and 5, (22) is a linear first-order ODE with constant coefficients and source term, which is solved to obtain the desired result. Now, substituting $t = t_{n+1}$ in (23) yields

$$\mathcal{Q}^{v,n+1}_{k(i,n)} = q_k e^{-\lambda\Delta t} + \Big(\frac{\eta_{E,n}(v-1)(\mu^R_n + z^R_i)}{A\gamma} + \underline{q}\Big)(1 - e^{-\lambda\Delta t}) \tag{25}$$

Rearranging the terms in (25) yields (24). □

$\mathcal{Q}^{v,n+1}_{k(i,n)}$ denotes the ES temperature level at time t_{n+1} knowing that, at time t_n, the ES was at the level q_k with a residual demand $\mu^R_n + z^R_i$ and an action v was taken.

Discrete-Time State-Dependent Control Constraints: In order for $\mathcal{Q}^{v,n+1}_{k(i,n)}$ to always satisfy the condition $\mathcal{Q}^{v,n+1}_{k(i,n)} \in [\underline{q}, \overline{q}]$, we reformulate $\mathcal{U}$ to adapt to the discrete-time setting, where the control can only be adjusted at the end of the time interval $[t_n, t_{n+1})$. We obtain

$$\mathcal{U}^n_d(z^R_i, q_k) = \{v \in \mathcal{U}(t_n, z^R_i, q_k) \quad | \quad \mathcal{Q}^{v,n+1}_{k(i,n)} \in [\underline{q}, \overline{q}]\}. \tag{26}$$

In the following lemma, we give the full expression of $\mathcal{U}^n_d(z^R_i, q_k)$.

Lemma 2. *Under Assumptions 4 and 5, the set of discrete-time state-dependent constraints is*

$$\mathcal{U}^n_d(z^R_i, q_k) = \begin{cases} [\max(0, v^d_{min}), \min(1, v^d_{max})], & q_k > \underline{q}, \quad \mu^R_n + z^R_i \geq 0, \\ \{1\}, & q_k = \underline{q}, \quad \mu^R_n + z^R_i \geq 0, \\ [\max(0, v^c_{min}), \min(1, v^c_{max})], & q_k < \overline{q}, \quad \mu^R_n + z^R_i < 0, \\ [\max(\chi(t_n), v^c_{min}), \min(1, v^c_{max})], & q_k = \overline{q}, \quad \mu^R_n + z^R_i < 0, \end{cases}$$

where

$$\begin{aligned} v^d_{min} &= 1 + \frac{\eta^D_E[A\gamma(\underline{q} - q_k e^{-\lambda\Delta t}) - \underline{q}(1 - e^{-\lambda\Delta t})]}{(1 - e^{-\lambda\Delta t})(\mu^R_n + z^R_i)}, \\ v^d_{max} &= 1 + \frac{\eta^D_E[A\gamma(\overline{q} - q_k e^{-\lambda\Delta t}) - \underline{q}(1 - e^{-\lambda\Delta t})]}{(1 - e^{-\lambda\Delta t})(\mu^R_n + z^R_i)}, \\ v^c_{min} &= 1 + \frac{A\gamma(\overline{q} - q_k e^{-\lambda\Delta t}) - \underline{q}(1 - e^{-\lambda\Delta t})}{\eta^C_E(1 - e^{-\lambda\Delta t})(\mu^R_n + z^R_i)}, \\ v^c_{max} &= 1 + \frac{A\gamma(\underline{q} - q_k e^{-\lambda\Delta t}) - \underline{q}(1 - e^{-\lambda\Delta t})}{\eta^C_E(1 - e^{-\lambda\Delta t})(\mu^R_n + z^R_i)}. \end{aligned}$$

Proof. From the condition $\mathcal{Q}^{v,n+1}_{k(i,n)} \in [\underline{q}, \overline{q}]$, we obtain

$$\begin{aligned} \frac{A\gamma(\underline{q} - q_k e^{-\lambda\Delta t})}{1 - e^{-\lambda\Delta t}} - \underline{q} &\leq \eta_E(v-1)(\mu^R_n + z^R_i) \\ &\leq \frac{A\gamma(\overline{q} - q_k e^{-\lambda\Delta t})}{1 - e^{-\lambda\Delta t}} - \underline{q}. \end{aligned}$$

If $\mu^R_n + z^R_i \geq 0, \eta_E = \frac{1}{\eta^D_E}$, and we obtain $v \in [v^d_{min}, v^d_{max}]$. Similarly, if $\mu^R_n + z^R_i < 0, \eta_E = \eta^C_E$, and we have $v \in [v^c_{min}, v^c_{max}]$. Therefore, for $\mu^R_n + z^R_i \geq 0, \mathcal{U}^n_d(z^R_i, q_k) = \mathcal{U}(t_n, z^R_i, q_k) \cap [v^d_{min}, v^d_{max}]$, and for $\mu^R_n + z^R_i < 0, \mathcal{U}^n_d(z^R_i, q_k) = \mathcal{U}(t_n, z^R_i, q_k) \cap [v^c_{min}, v^c_{max}]$. □

One-Step Terminal Value Problem: Starting from the DPP as in [22], we derive the following proposition, which is analogous to Theorem 4.3 in [2]. This result provides the one-step approximate optimal control together with the associated terminal value problem.

https://doi.org/10.3390/math14030489

The latter is then solved numerically to determine the value and optimal strategy of the prosumer's optimization problem.

Proposition 2. *Let (t_n, z_i^R, q_k) be fixed, and suppose that Assumptions 4 and 5 hold. Then, starting from the DPP, the one-step approximate optimal control v^* is given by*

$$v^* = \underset{v \in \mathcal{U}_d^n(z_i^R, q_k)}{\arg\min} \left\{ \int_{t_n}^{t_{n+1}} e^{-\delta(t-t_n)} \Gamma(t, z_i^R, v) \mathrm{d}t + e^{-\delta \Delta t} V(t_{n+1}, z_i^R, \mathcal{Q}_{k(i,n)}^{v,n+1}) \right\}. \tag{27}$$

In addition, setting $H(t, z^R) = V(t, z^R, \mathcal{Q}^{v^*})$, we obtain the one-step terminal value problem

$$\begin{aligned} \frac{\partial H}{\partial t}(t, z^R) + \mathcal{L}H(t, z^R) + \Gamma(t, z^R, v^*) &= 0, \qquad \text{on } [t_n, t_{n+1}) \times \mathcal{X} \\ H(t_{n+1}, z^R) &= V(t_{n+1}, z^R, \mathcal{Q}_{k(i,n)}^{v^*,n+1}), \end{aligned} \tag{28}$$

where $\mathcal{L}H = f(z^R)\frac{\partial H}{\partial z^R} + \frac{1}{2}(\sigma_R^2(t) + \sigma_0^2)\frac{\partial^2 H}{\partial (z^R)^2} - \delta H$.

Proof. The proof is similar to that of Theorem 4.3 in [2], taking $\sigma^2 = \sigma^2(t) + \sigma_0^2$. □

Positivity Condition: In order to solve the one-step terminal value problem (28) using numerical techniques, we first discretize the differential operator $\mathcal{L}$. We let Λ denote the discretization operator of $\mathcal{L}$ and denote $\vartheta_i = -\kappa_R z_i^R$. Given that the sign of ϑ_i changes according to z_i^R and cannot easily be determined, we apply the upwind discretization for the convection term $\frac{\partial V}{\partial z^R}$. Subsequently, we apply the central second-order finite difference for the diffusion term $\frac{\partial^2 V}{\partial (z^R)^2}$. Letting $\sigma_R(t_n) = \sigma_{R,n}$, we obtain

$$\begin{aligned} \Lambda V_{i,k}^n &= \frac{1}{2}(\sigma_{R,n}^2 + \sigma_0^2)\frac{V_{i-1,k}^n - 2V_{i,k}^n + V_{i+1,k}^n}{(\Delta z^R)^2} - \delta V_{i,k}^n + \begin{cases} \vartheta_i \frac{V_{i,k}^n - V_{i-1,k}^n}{\Delta z^R}, & \vartheta_i \geq 0, \\ \vartheta_i \frac{V_{i+1,k}^n - V_{i,k}^n}{\Delta z^R}, & \vartheta_i < 0, \end{cases} \\ &= A_i V_{i+1,k}^n - B_i V_{i,k}^n + C_i V_{i-1,k}^n, \end{aligned} \tag{29}$$

where the expressions of A_i, B_i, and C_i change depending on the sign of ϑ_i. The following result gives us the upper bound for Δz^R and defines the positivity condition for the coefficients A_i, B_i, and C_i.

Lemma 3 (Positivity Condition). *For $i = 1, \ldots, N_z - 1$ and $n = 0, \ldots, N_t - 1$, the coefficients A_i, B_i, and C_i remain positive provided*

$$\Delta z^R \leq \frac{\sqrt{2\kappa_R(\sigma_{R,n}^2 + \sigma_0^2)}}{6\kappa_R}. \tag{30}$$

Proof. Similar to the proof of Proposition 4.4 in [2]. □

CFL Condition: In the following, we formulate the Courant–Friedrichs–Lewy (CFL) condition, as introduced in [23]. It relates the spatial step size Δq to the time step Δt and ensures that the arrival point $\mathcal{Q}_{k(i,n)}^{v,n+1}$ consistently lies within the interval defined by the neighboring grid points $q_{k-1} = q_k - \Delta q$ and $q_{k+1} = q_k + \Delta q$ adjacent to q_k. From this assumption, the following inequalities can be derived

https://doi.org/10.3390/math14030489

$$\begin{aligned} \underline{q} := q_0 \leq \underline{q} - \theta^n_{i,0}\Delta q \leq q_1 := \underline{q} + \Delta q, \qquad & \theta^n_{i,0} \leq 0, \\ q_{k-1} \leq q_k - \theta^n_{i,k}\Delta q \quad \leq q_{k+1}, \qquad & k = 1, \dots, N_q - 1, \\ \overline{q} - \Delta q := q_{N_q - 1} \leq \overline{q} - \theta^n_{i,N_q}\Delta q \leq q_{N_q} := \overline{q}, \qquad & \theta^n_{i,N_q} \geq 0, \end{aligned} \tag{31}$$

In the following, we obtain the Courant–Friedrichs–Lewy (CFL) condition ([23]) relating the time step size Δt to the ES step size Δq. This ensures the stability of the derived numerical scheme. Let $\underline{\mu}^R = \min_{n \in \{0,1,\cdots,N_t\}} \mu^R_n$, $\overline{\mu}^R = \max_{n \in \{0,1,\cdots,N_t\}} \mu^R_n$. Therefore, from the above inequalities and the state-dependent set of feasible controls, the CFL condition is given by

$$\Delta q \geq \frac{\Delta t}{m_Q c_P} \max\Big(-\eta^C_E(\underline{\mu}^R + \underline{z}^R), \frac{\overline{\mu}^R + \overline{z}^R}{\eta^D_E} + A\gamma(\overline{q} - \underline{q})\Big). \tag{32}$$

Interpolation: As noted in [2], the arrival point $\mathcal{Q}^{v,n+1}_{k(i,n)}$ does not necessarily coincide with a grid point $q_k \in \widehat{\mathcal{G}}_q$. This prompts an interpolation of $V(t_{n+1}, z^R_i, \mathcal{Q}^{v,n+1}_{k(i,n)})$ based on the function values $V^{n+1}_{i,k}$ at the grid points of $\widehat{\mathcal{G}}$. Following [17], a linear interpolation is sufficient to construct a monotone difference scheme. In what follows, we denote by $V^{n+1}_{k(i,n)}$, the interpolated values of $V(t_{n+1}, z^R_i, \mathcal{Q}^{v,n+1}_{k(i,n)})$ defined in the result below.

Proposition 3. *Let* $\theta^n_{i,k} = \frac{A\gamma q_k - [\eta_{E,n}(v-1)(\mu^R_n + z^R_i) - A\gamma \underline{q}]}{\Delta q} \frac{1 - e^{-\lambda \Delta t}}{A\gamma}$, *and assume that the CFL condition holds. Then, the interpolated value* $V^{n+1}_{k(i,n)}$ *is given by*

$$V^{n+1}_{k(i,n)} = \mathcal{D}^{(q,n)}_{i,k} V^{n+1}_{i,k} + \mathcal{F}^{(q,n)}_{i,k} V^{n+1}_{i,k-1} + \mathcal{H}^{(q,n)}_{i,k} V^{n+1}_{i,k+1}, \tag{33}$$

for $i = 0, \dots, N_{z^R}$, $k = 1, \dots, N_q - 1$, $n = 0, \dots, N_t - 1$ *and where*
$\mathcal{D}^{(q,n)}_{i,k} = 1 - |\theta^n_{i,k}|$, $\mathcal{F}^{(q,n)}_{i,k} = \frac{\theta^n_{i,k} + |\theta^n_{i,k}|}{2}$ *and* $\mathcal{H}^{(q,n)}_{i,k} = -\frac{\theta^n_{i,k} - |\theta^n_{i,k}|}{2}$.
Furthermore, we obtain that for $k = 0$ *and* $k = N_q$,

$$\begin{aligned} V^{n+1}_{0(i,n)} &= \mathcal{D}^{(q,n)}_{i,0} V^{n+1}_{i,0} + \mathcal{H}^{(q,n)}_{i,0} V^{n+1}_{i,1}, \\ V^{n+1}_{N_q(i,n)} &= \mathcal{D}^{(q,n)}_{i,N_q} V^{n+1}_{i,N_q} + \mathcal{F}^{(q,n)}_{i,N_q} V^{n+1}_{i,N_q-1}. \end{aligned}$$

Proof. See Appendix C.3 in [2]. □

Now, we discretize the one-step terminal value problem (28) to obtain

$$\frac{V^{n+1}_{i,k} - V^n_{i,k}}{\Delta t} + \Lambda V^n_{i,k} + \Gamma(t_n, z^R_i, v^*) = 0. \tag{34}$$

Finally, we obtain the fully implicit scheme given by

$$\begin{aligned} V^n_{i,k} - \Delta t\Big\{A_i V^n_{i+1,k} - B_i V^n_{i,k} + C_i V^n_{i-1,k}\Big\} &= V^{n+1}_{k(i,n)} + \Delta t \Gamma(t_n, z^R_i, v^*), \\ \mathcal{Q}^{v,n+1}_{k(i,n)} &= q_k - \theta^n_{i,k}\Delta q, \\ v^{*n}_{i,k} &= \underset{v \in \mathcal{U}^n_d(z^R_i, q_k)}{\arg\min} \Big\{ \int_{t_n}^{t_{n+1}} e^{-\delta(t-t_n)}\Gamma(t, z^R_i, v)\mathrm{d}t \\ &\qquad + e^{-\delta \Delta t} V^{n+1}_{k(i,n)} \Big\} \\ \mathcal{U}^n_d(z^R_i, q_k) &= \{v \in \mathcal{U}(t_n, z^R_i, q_k) \quad | \ \mathcal{Q}^{v,n+1}_{k(i,n)} \in [\underline{q}, \overline{q}]\} \\ V^{N_t}_{i,k} &= \Phi(q_k). \end{aligned} \tag{35}$$

https://doi.org/10.3390/math14030489

From the first equation in (35), we want to form a system of linear algebraic equations that are useful to obtain the values of $V_{i,k}^n$. In that regard, we set $\Gamma_{i,k}^{n+1} = \Gamma(t_n, z_i^R, v^*)$ and assume that, for fixed n and k, the optimal strategy $v^* = v_{i,k}^{*n}$, the CFL condition, and the terms in (33) for all i are known. We denote by $\Psi_{i,k}^{n+1}$ the known right-hand side of the difference equation (35) for fixed t_n, q_k and for all i. Hence, for $i = 1, \cdots, N_z - 1$, $k = 1, \cdots, N_q - 1, n = 0, 1, \cdots, N_t - 1$, we obtain

$$(1 + \Delta t B_i) V_{i,k}^n - \Delta t C_i V_{i-1,k}^n - \Delta t A_i V_{i+1,k}^n = \Psi_{i,k}^{n+1}, \tag{36}$$

At the boundary $q = \underline{q}$, i.e., $k = 0$, we recall that $\theta_{i,0}^n \leq 0$. Similarly, at the boundary $q = \overline{q}$, i.e., $k = N_q$, we have $\theta_{i,N_q}^n \geq 0$. Therefore, we have the following

$$V_{k(i,n)}^{n+1} = \begin{cases} \left(1 - \theta_{i,k}^n\right) V_{i,k}^{n+1} + \theta_{i,k}^n V_{i,k-1}^{n+1} & \theta_{i,k}^n \geq 0, \quad k = 1, \ldots, N_q, \\ \left(1 + \theta_{i,k}^n\right) V_{i,k}^{n+1} - \theta_{i,k}^n V_{i,k+1}^{n+1} & \theta_{i,k}^n < 0, \quad k = 0, \ldots, N_q - 1. \end{cases} \tag{37}$$

Boundary Conditions: To ensure that the one-step terminal value problem, formulated as a PDE, is well posed, we specify boundary conditions at $z^R = \underline{z}^R, \overline{z}^R$ and $q = \underline{q}, \overline{q}$. These conditions arise from truncating the computational domain of the PDE from $\mathcal{X}$ to a bounded domain $\widehat{\mathcal{X}}$. Accordingly, we require that

$$\frac{\partial^2 V}{\partial (z^R)^2}(t, \underline{z}^R, q) = 0, \quad \frac{\partial^2 V}{\partial (z^R)^2}(t, \overline{z}^R, q) = 0, \quad (t, q) \in (0, T) \times [\underline{q}, \overline{q}]. \tag{38}$$

$$\frac{\partial^2 V}{\partial q^2}(t, z^R, \underline{q}) = 0, \quad \frac{\partial^2 V}{\partial q^2}(t, z^R, \overline{q}) = 0, \quad (t, z^R) \in (0, T) \times [\underline{z}^R, \overline{z}^R]. \tag{39}$$

We note that the corner values $V_{0,0}^n, V_{0,N_q}^n, V_{N_z,0}^n$, and V_{N_z,N_q}^n are computed using previously obtained values $V_{i,k}^n$ for $i = 0, \cdots, N_z$, $k = 0, \cdots, N_q$, so that

$$\begin{aligned} V_{0,0}^n &= 2V_{1,0}^n - V_{2,0}^n, \\ V_{0,N_q}^n &= 2V_{0,N_q-1}^n - V_{0,N_q-2}^n, \\ V_{N_z,0}^n &= 2V_{N_z,1}^n - V_{N_z,2}^n, \\ V_{N_z,N_q}^n &= 2V_{N_z,N_q-1}^n - V_{N_z,N_q-2}^n. \end{aligned} \tag{40}$$

Combining (40), the boundary conditions, and the difference equation (35), we proceed to the matrix formulation below.

Matrix Formulation: Simultaneously varying the indices i, k, for n fixed in the difference equation (35), and using (40), we obtain the following system of linear equations:

$$G\mathbf{V}_k^n = \mathbf{\Psi}_k^{n+1}, \quad \text{for } n = 0, \ldots, N_t - 1, \quad k = 1, \ldots, N_q - 1, \tag{41}$$

where $\mathbf{V}_k^n = (V_{1,k}^n, \ldots, V_{N_z-1,k}^n)^T$, $\mathbf{\Psi}_k^{n+1} = (\Psi_{1,k}^{n+1}, \ldots, \Psi_{N_z-1,k}^{n+1})^T$, with G an $(N_z - 1) \times (N_z - 1)$ tridiagonal matrix given as

$$G = \begin{bmatrix} e_1 & p_1 & 0 & 0 & \ldots & 0 & 0 \\ h_2 & e_2 & p_2 & 0 & \ldots & 0 & 0 \\ 0 & h_3 & e_3 & p_3 & \ldots & 0 & 0 \\ \ldots & \ldots & \ldots & \ldots & \ldots & \ldots & \ldots \\ 0 & 0 & 0 & \ldots & h_{N_z-2} & e_{N_z-2} & p_{N_z-2} \\ 0 & 0 & 0 & \ldots & 0 & h_{N_z-1} & e_{N_z-1} \end{bmatrix} \tag{42}$$

https://doi.org/10.3390/math14030489

where

$$\begin{aligned} e_1 &= 1 + \Delta t B_1 - 2\Delta t C_1, & p_1 &= \Delta t(C_1 - A_1), \\ e_k &= 1 + \Delta t B_k, \quad h_k = -\Delta t C_k, & p_k &= -\Delta t A_k, \quad k = 2, \cdots, N_z - 2 \\ e_{N_z-1} &= 1 + \Delta t B_{N_z-1} - 2\Delta t A_{N_z-1} & h_{N_z-1} &= -\Delta t(C_{N_z-1} - A_{N_z-1}). \end{aligned}$$

It now remains to obtain the values $V^n_{0,k}$, $V^n_{N_z,k}$, $V^n_{i,0}$, and V^n_{i,N_q}. To do so, we substitute the boundary conditions (38) in the difference equation (35) to obtain

$$\frac{\partial V}{\partial t}(t, z^R, q) + \mathcal{L}_1 V(t, z^R, q) + \Gamma(t, z^R, v^*) = 0, \tag{43}$$

where for $i = 0, \mathcal{L}_1 V = -\kappa_R \underline{z}^R \frac{\partial V}{\partial z^R} - \delta V$, while for $i = N_z, \mathcal{L}_1 V = -\kappa_R \overline{z}^R \frac{\partial V}{\partial z^R} - \delta V$. Following similar steps as above, we obtain the following for $z^R = \underline{z}^R$:

$$K\mathbf{V}^n_0 = \mathbf{\Psi}^{n+1}_0 + \Delta t A_0 \mathbf{V}^n_1, \quad \text{for } n = 0, \ldots, N_t - 1, \tag{44}$$

$\mathbf{V}^n_0 = (V^n_{0,1}, \ldots, V^n_{0,N_q-1})^T$, $\mathbf{\Psi}^{n+1}_0 = (\Psi^{n+1}_{0,1}, \ldots, \Psi^{n+1}_{0,N_q-1})^T$, $\mathbf{V}^n_1 = (V^n_{1,1}, \ldots, V^n_{1,N_q-1})^T$.

Similarly, for $z^R = \overline{z}^R$, we have

$$M\mathbf{V}^n_{N_z} = \mathbf{\Psi}_{N_z} + \Delta t C_{N_z} \mathbf{V}^n_{N_z-1}, \quad \text{for } n = 0, \ldots, N_t - 1, \tag{45}$$

$\mathbf{V}^n_{N_z} = (V^n_{N_z,1}, \ldots, V^n_{N_z,N_q-1})^T$, $\mathbf{\Psi}^{n+1}_{N_z} = (\Psi^{n+1}_{N_z,1}, \ldots, \Psi^{n+1}_{N_z,N_q-1})^T$, $\mathbf{V}^n_{N_z-1} = (V^n_{N_z-1,1}, \ldots, V^n_{N_z-1,N_q-1})^T$. Letting I_{N_q-1} denote the $(N_q - 1) \times (N_q - 1)$ identity matrix, K and M are $(N_q - 1) \times (N_q - 1)$ diagonal matrices given by

$$K = (1 + \Delta t B_0) I_{N_q-1}, \quad M = (1 + \Delta t C_{N_z}) I_{N_q-1}. \tag{46}$$

Substituting $k = 0$ and $k = N_q$, respectively, in the difference equation (35), we obtain the following for $n = 0, \ldots, N_t - 1$:

$$\begin{aligned} G\mathbf{V}^n_0 &= \mathbf{\Psi}^{n+1}_0, \quad \text{for } i = 1, \ldots, N_z - 1, \\ G\mathbf{V}^n_{N_q} &= \mathbf{\Psi}^{n+1}_{N_q}, \quad \text{for } i = 1, \ldots, N_z - 1, \end{aligned} \tag{47}$$

$\mathbf{V}^n_0 = (V^n_{1,0}, \ldots, V^n_{N_z-1,0})^T$, $\mathbf{\Psi}^{n+1}_0 = (\Psi^{n+1}_{1,0}, \ldots, \Psi^{n+1}_{N_z-1,0})^T$, $\mathbf{V}^n_{N_q} = (V^n_{1,N_q}, \ldots, V^n_{N_z-1,N_q})^T$, $\mathbf{\Psi}^{n+1}_{N_q} = (\Psi^{n+1}_{1,N_q}, \ldots, \Psi^{n+1}_{N_z-1,N_q})^T$. Further details can be obtained in [2].

Backward Recursion Algorithm: The approximate optimal control presented in (27), along with the value functions in (41), (44), (45), and (47), can be computed using Algorithm 1, proceeding backward in time from the terminal time step N_t. To determine $v^* = v^{*n}_{i,k}$, we take into account the storage level and distinguish between scenarios of unsatisfied demand and overproduction. This classification indicates which subinterval of $\mathcal{U}^n_d$ should be evaluated. Subsequently, an optimization procedure is carried out to identify the control value that minimizes the objective function. The resulting control is then interpreted as the optimal decision for the given state variables at grid points z^R_i and q_k. This procedure is applied iteratively across all combinations of grid points to recover the complete set of optimal controls.

5. Numerical Results

In this section, we discuss the numerical solution for the prosumer's problem. The results are based on the implementation of Algorithm 1 to find the optimal strategies and the

https://doi.org/10.3390/math14030489

value functions as well as studying the properties of the obtained value functions. As the terminal condition, we consider a penalization problem modeled as

$$\Phi(q) = \begin{cases} \frac{P_{pen} m_Q c_P (q_{pen} - q)}{\eta_E^C}, & q < q_{pen}, \\ 0, & q \geq q_{pen}. \end{cases} \tag{48}$$

For the purpose of the numerical simulations, the seasonality function and heat price are modeled, respectively, by

$$\mu^R(t) = c_0 + c\cos\left(\frac{2\pi t}{\rho}\right), \quad P_{buy}(t) = \ell_0 + \ell\cos\left(\frac{2\pi t}{\rho}\right), \quad P_{sell}(t) = P_{buy}(t) - \xi. \tag{49}$$

The full description of the model parameter values is given in the Table 1 below.

Table 1. Model and discretization parameters.

Parameters	Values	Units	Parameters	Values	Units
κ_R	0.025	h^{-1}	S	0.335	$\frac{€}{kWh}$
σ_R, σ_0	0.005, 0.4	$\frac{kW}{\sqrt{h}}$	P_{pen}	0.325	$\frac{€}{kWh}$
c_0, c	0.37, 1.00	kW	ξ	0.02	$\frac{€}{kWh}$
			ℓ_0, ℓ	0.17, 0.15	$\frac{€}{kWh}$
ρ	8760	h	$\underline{z}^R, \overline{z}^R$	−5.37, 5.37	kW
b_1	0.01		$T, \Delta t$	8760, 1	h
b_2	0.012	K^{-1}	N_t	8760	
m_Q	7854	kg	η_E^D, η_E^C	0.95, 0.95	
c_P	0.0012	$\frac{kWh}{kg\ K}$	N_z, N_q	85, 60	
A	21.99	m^2	P_c, i_d	20, 25	°C
γ	2.34×10^{-4}	$\frac{kW}{m^2\ K}$	$\underline{q}, q_{pen}, \overline{q}$	25, 40, 85	°C

Parameters γ, c_0, c, b_1, and b_2 are calibrated to the model, and the idea for the calibration is provided in [2].

Terminal Cost: Figure 2 shows the terminal cost $\Phi(q)$ as a function of the residual demand r and the ES storage level q. Here, the terminal cost is formulated as a penalization problem. By construction as in (48), we observe that the value function is constant with respect to the residual demand at the terminal time. However, if the storage level falls below the reference temperature q_{ref} = 40 °C, the prosumer incurs a cost proportional to the deviation from q_{ref} and the charging efficiency η_E^C. This cost increases the further the storage temperature is below the reference. For temperatures above the reference, no additional cost is incurred, and the storage is effectively considered to have no residual value.

Value Function and Optimal Strategy for Time-Dependent Heat Buying and Selling Prices: Figure 3 depicts the value functions and optimal strategies of the prosumer at the initial time $t = 0$ and on day $t = 362$. From the top- and bottom-left panels, we can observe that as the ES temperature increases, the prosumer incurs lower costs. Conversely, as the residual demand increases, the prosumer incurs higher costs. The top-right panel shows that, for an unsatisfied demand ($r \geq 0$), the prosumer satisfies all residual demand via the CHS if the ES is empty; otherwise, it discharges the ES. In the case of overproduction ($r < 0$), all excess production is sold to the CHS. From the bottom-right panel, we can note that, for an unsatisfied demand, the prosumer satisfies all residual demand via the CHS when $q < 40$ °C. For $q \geq 40$ °C, all residual demand is satisfied by the ES. In the case of overproduction, the prosumer first stores some energy in the ES and subsequently sells any remaining excess to the CHS. Since the horizon is one year (365 days), with a penalization cost at the terminal time, we can observe that on day 362, the prosumer begins filling the storage close to the penalty temperature $q_{ref} = 40$ °C to avoid higher terminal costs.

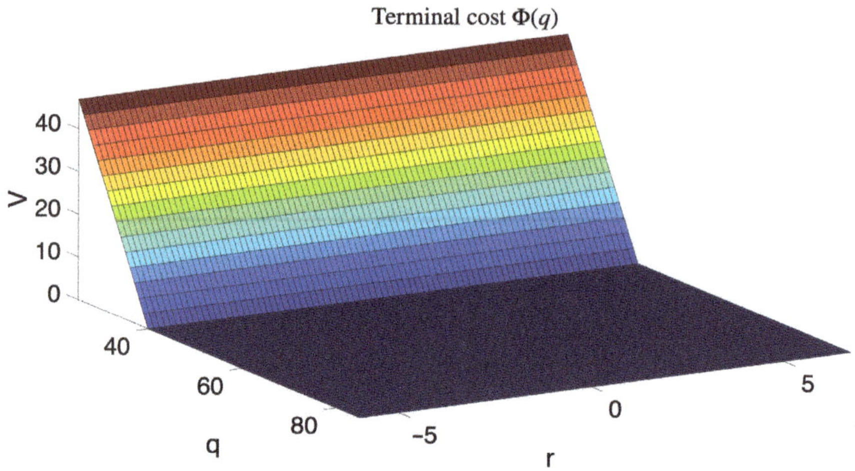

Figure 2. Terminal cost function $\Phi(q) = V(t_{N_t}, x)$ for a penalization problem.

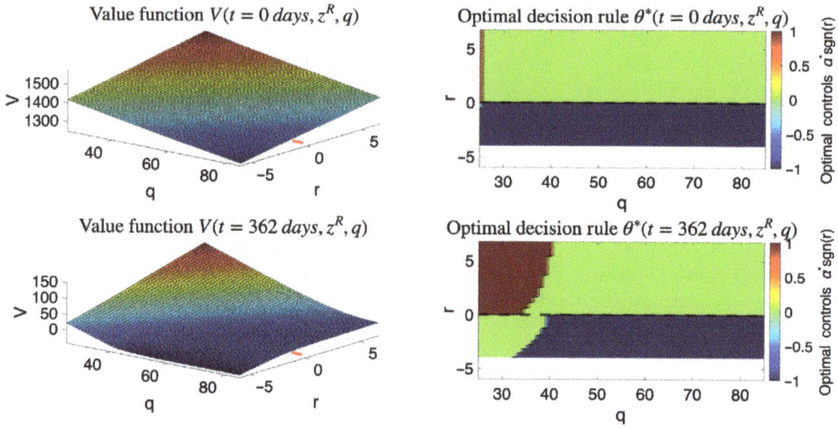

Figure 3. Value functions and optimal strategies of the prosumer at $t = 0, 362$ days for time-dependent heat buying and selling prices.

Figure 4 shows the prosumer's value functions and optimal strategies as functions of the residual demand r and the ES temperature level q on day $t = 230$. In the top-left panel, we can observe that, for a given residual demand, the prosumer incurs lower costs as the ES temperature increases. The expected aggregated discounted cost is higher for the strongest unsatisfied residual demand and lower for the strongest overproduction. On the other hand, the bottom-left panel shows that the cost increases with respect to the residual demand, with the highest cost incurred for an empty storage. The smallest cost is incurred for a full storage. In the top-right panel, we can observe that, for both the strongest and smallest unsatisfied demand, the prosumer first purchases thermal energy from the CHS. Afterwards, for a sufficiently filled ES, it discharges the storage to meet the unsatisfied demand. For the strongest overproduction, the prosumer stores all excess production in the ES and only sells to the CHS if the ES is full. In the bottom-right panel, for both an empty and 50%-full ES, the prosumer stores the excess production in the ES for an overproduction

https://doi.org/10.3390/math14030489

and satisfies all unsatisfied demand via the CHS for an unsatisfied residual demand. Now, for a full ES, the prosumer compensates the loss to the environment of the ES in the case of overproduction. For an unsatisfied demand, all residual demand is satisfied by the ES.

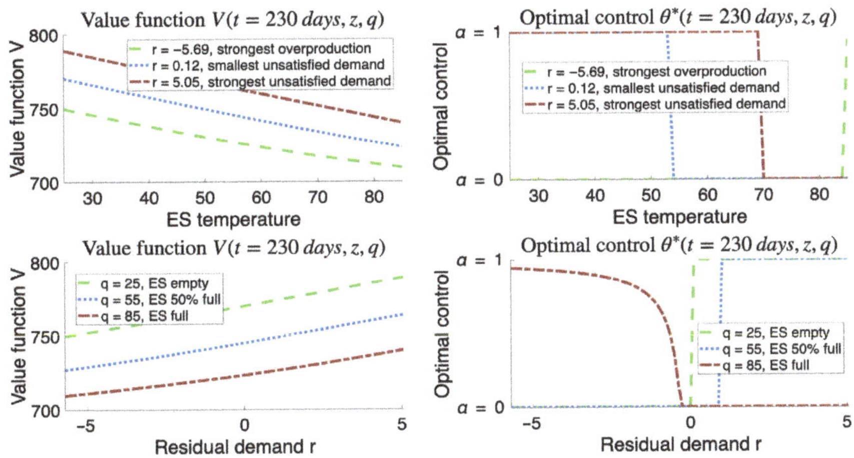

Figure 4. Value functions (**left**) and optimal strategies (**right**) as functions of the residual demand r and ES temperature level q at $t = 230$ days for time-dependent heat buying and selling prices.

Value Function and Optimal Strategy for Constant Heat Buying and Selling Prices: For the case of constant heat buying and selling prices, we focus on the value function and optimal strategies as functions of the residual demand r and the ES temperature level q. Let P^C_{buy} and P^C_{sell} denote the constant heat buying and selling prices, respectively. In the following, we model P^C_{buy} and P^C_{sell} as

$$P^C_{buy} = \max_{t\in[0,T]} P_{buy}(t) \quad P^C_{sell} = P^C_{buy} - \xi, \tag{50}$$

where P_{buy}, P_{sell}, and ξ are the same as in (49). In Figure 5, we focus on the top- and bottom-right panels since the top- and bottom-left panels have the same interpretation as in Figure 4. In the top-right panel of Figure 5, for both the strongest and the smallest unsatisfied demand, the prosumer discharges the ES if it is not empty; otherwise, all residual demand is satisfied by the CHS, at a higher cost. For the strongest overproduction, all excess thermal energy is sold to the CHS for revenue. As shown in the bottom-right panel, for an empty ES and overproduction, the prosumer sells all residual demand to the CHS. However, for an unsatisfied demand, all residual demand is satisfied by the CHS. For a half-full or full ES, the prosumer sells all residual demand to the CHS in the event of overproduction. For an unsatisfied demand, it discharges the ES.

Let V^{max} denote the maximum value function of the prosumer for time-dependent heat buying and selling prices. $V^{max}_{Constant}$ denotes the maximum value function of the prosumer for constant heat buying and selling prices, and $\widetilde{V}^{max}$ is the maximum value function of the consumer for time-dependent heat buying and selling prices.

In Table 2, we note that the prosumer incurs a higher expected aggregated discounted cost under the time-dependent heat prices model than with its constant counterpart. This is due to the fact that the time-dependent heat prices model reflects the changes in heat prices during cold and warm seasons, which is not observed in the constant pricing case. Since the consumer is not equipped with heat production and storage units, it relies solely on the CHS for its unsatisfied residual demand, hence leading to a much higher expected aggregated discounted cost. From the values of $\widetilde{V}^{max}$ and V^{max}, we can compute the expected consumer investment cost into heat production and storage units in order to reduce the cost of satisfying its heating and hot water demands. This investment cost is denoted by $\widetilde{C}_{invest} = \widetilde{V}^{max} - V^{max}$.

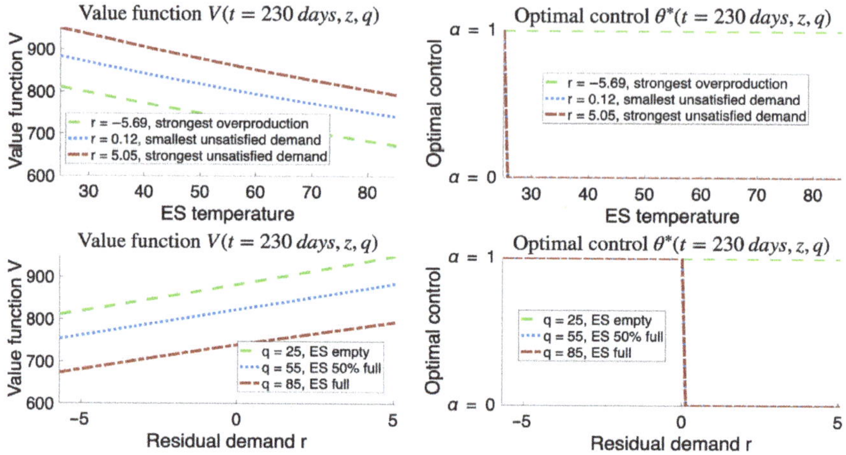

Figure 5. Value functions (**left**) and optimal strategies (**right**) as functions of the residual demand r and ES temperature level q at $t = 230$ days for constant heat buying and selling prices.

Table 2. Maximum value function for an imperfect efficiency with time-dependent and constant heat buying and selling prices, in EUR, for a prosumer and a consumer.

Value Function	Numerical Value
V^{max}	1562.9
$V^{max}_{Constant}$	1465.1
$\widetilde{V}^{max}$	40,474.0

5.1. Sensitivity Analysis

In this section, we perform a sensitivity analysis on σ_0, η_E^C, and η_C^D to study their impact on the expected aggregate discounted cost. The results presented correspond to the case of time-dependent heat buying and selling prices. All parameters are fixed, with values given in Table 1, except for σ_0, η_E^C and η_C^D, which are varied. Throughout this section, we let V^{max} denote the maximum value function, as in Table 2.

In Table 3, we can observe that as the impact of the weather conditions increases, the aggregated discounted cost becomes higher. This is the case because higher values of σ_0 increase the residual demand, which, in turn, increases the prosumer's cost. Thus, the more pronounced the impact of weather conditions is on the heating system, the higher the aggregated discounted cost the prosumer will incur. For example, for $\sigma_0 = 0$, the prosumer incurs a maximum cost of $V^{max} = 1346.4$ EUR whereas for $\sigma_0 = 0.4$, $V^{max} = 1562.9$ EUR, which is approximately a 16.08% increase from the case of no common noise.

Table 3. Maximum value function from varying common noise volatility coefficient σ_0 under time-dependent heat buying and selling prices, in EUR.

σ_0	0	0.1	0.15	0.25	0.35	0.4
V^{max}	1346.4	1377.3	1400.8	1459.4	1527.1	1562.9

https://doi.org/10.3390/math14030489

In Table 4, we can observe that the better the discharging efficiency, the smaller the cost incurred by the prosumer. This is due to the fact that, for a weak discharging efficiency, the prosumer, when satisfying residual demand via the ES, discharges more thermal energy to compensate for the loss during the process. Hence, a better discharging efficiency reduces losses during the discharge, hence contributing to the reduction in the prosumer's aggregated discounted cost. For a discharging efficiency $\eta_E = \frac{1}{0.9}$, we can observe an increase of approximately 1.85% in the aggregated discounted cost as compared to the case of a perfect discharging efficiency $\eta_E = 1$.

Table 4. Maximum value function for varying η_E^D under time-dependent heat buying and selling prices, in EUR.

η_E^D	0.90	0.92	0.94	0.96	1
V^{max}	1574.3	1570.2	1565.5	1559.9	1545.7

As the charging efficiency improves in Table 5, we can observe that the prosumer incurs a smaller aggregated discounted cost. For a weak charging efficiency, not all overproduction can be stored in the ES, due to the losses to the environment during charging. Therefore, as the charging efficiency improves, more thermal energy can be stored in the ES for further use. Hence, for a charging efficiency of 0.9, we observe an approximate 1.94% increase in the aggregated discounted cost as compared to a perfect charging efficiency.

Table 5. Maximum value function for varying η_E^C under time-dependent heat buying and selling prices, in EUR.

η_E^C	0.90	0.92	0.94	0.96	1
V^{max}	1575.2	1570.7	1565.7	1559.7	1545.2

5.2. Optimal Path of ES Level

In Figure 6, we show the optimal path of the ES temperature level Q together with the residual demand R, the seasonality function μ^R, and the absolute optimal control $\alpha^* R$ for a time-dependent heat price. At the initial time, we assume that the prosumer starts with a full storage. Hence, for an unsatisfied residual demand, the prosumer discharges the ES until it becomes empty. For overproduction, the prosumer slowly charges the ES and drives it almost full in late summer. We further observe that for $R > 0$, the prosumer discharges the ES to satisfy the unsatisfied demand and charges the ES for $R < 0$.

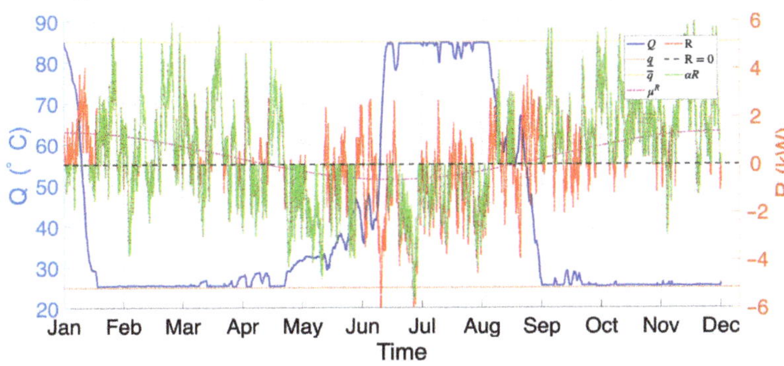

Figure 6. Optimal path of the ES Q (blue), seasonality function μ^R (magenta), residual demand R (red), and optimal absolute control $\alpha^* R$ (green). The minimum and maximum storage levels are represented by dotted lines (reddish orange and golden yellow, respectively).

https://doi.org/10.3390/math14030489

6. Summary and Outlook

In this work, we investigated a stochastic optimal control problem involving a prosumer and a consumer, both connected to a CHS. The prosumer is equipped with a local renewable heat production source (solar collector) and a local storage unit. The ES allows the prosumer to store excess thermal energy for future use. However, we assume that it is subject to charging and discharging efficiencies. In contrast, the consumer has no local production or storage unit and is therefore constantly subject to an unsatisfied demand. We focused primarily on the prosumer problem, as the consumer always satisfies all residual demand directly via the CHS. The prosumer's problem was formulated as a mathematical optimization problem, which we solved using semi-Lagrangian techniques. We presented the numerical results for both a time-dependent and a constant heat price formulation and observed that, under the former price formulation, the prosumer incurred a higher maximum expected aggregated discounted cost than in the latter price formulation. We further performed a sensitivity analysis on the common noise and charging/discharging efficiency parameters. For the case of the common noise, we noted that for $\sigma_0 = 0.4$, the maximum expected aggregated discounted cost increases by approximately 16.08% as compared to no common noise. Meanwhile, for the discharging efficiency, we observed that for $\eta_E = \frac{1}{0.9}$, the prosumer incurs a cost about 1.85% higher than in the case of a perfect discharging efficiency. Also, for the charging efficiency, we noted that for $\eta_E = 0.90$, the maximum expected aggregated discounted cost increases by approximately 1.94% as compared to the case of a perfect charging efficiency. Our numerical results also highlight the value function and the optimal strategies of the prosumer. Finally, for the consumer, we evaluated the maximum expected investment required in local heat production and storage to transform into a prosumer.

Looking ahead, it would be interesting to incorporate additional weather factors, such as ambient temperature, to better model the residual demand. Furthermore, modeling electricity prices as a stochastic differential equation (SDE) could provide more realistic dynamics. These extensions are currently under investigation in ongoing research.

Author Contributions: Conceptualization, M.G.S.; Methodology, M.G.S.; Software, M.G.S.; Validation, M.G.S.; Formal Analysis, M.G.S. and J.N.; Writing—Original Draft, M.G.S.; Writing—Review and Editing, M.G.S. and J.N.; Supervision, J.N.; Funding Acquisition, M.G.S. All authors have read and agreed to the published version of the manuscript.

Funding: This research was carried out with the aid of a grant from the International Development Research Centre, Ottawa, Canada, www.idrc.ca (accessed on 21 November 2025); and with financial support from the Government of Canada, provided through Global Affairs Canada (GAC), www.international.gc.ca (accessed on 21 November 2025).

Data Availability Statement: No new data were created or analyzed in this study.

Institutional Review Board Statement: Not applicable.

Informed Consent Statement: Not applicable.

Conflicts of Interest: The authors declare no conflict of interest.

References

1. Gjoka, K.; Rismanchi, B.; Crawford, R.H. Fifth-generation district heating and cooling systems: A review of recent advancements and implementation barriers. *Renew. Sustain. Energy Rev.* **2023**, *171*, 112997. [CrossRef]
2. Ganet Somé, M. Stochastic optimal control of prosumers in a district heating system. *arXiv* **2025**, arXiv:2501.09088. [CrossRef]
3. Bilardo, M.; Sandrone, F.; Zanzottera, G.; Fabrizio, E. Modelling a fifth generation bidirectional low temperature district heating and cooling (5gdhc) network for nearly zero energy district (nzed). *Energy Rep.* **2021**, *7*, 8390–8405. [CrossRef]

https://doi.org/10.3390/math14030489

4. Bünning, F.; Wetter, M.; Fuchs, M.; Müller, D. Bidirectional low temperature district energy systems with agent-based control: Performance comparison and operation optimization. *Appl. Energy* **2018**, *209*, 502–515. [CrossRef]
5. Li, H.; Wang, S.J. Challenges in smart low-temperature district heating development. *Energy Procedia* **2014**, *61*, 1472–1475. [CrossRef]
6. Alasseur, C.; Ben Taher, I.; Matoussi, A. An extended mean field game for storage in smart grids. *J. Optim. Theory Appl.* **2020**, *184*, 644–670. [CrossRef]
7. Takam, P.H.; Wunderlich, R. Cost-optimal management of a residential heating system with a geothermal energy storage under uncertainty. *Int. J. Dyn. Control* **2025**, *13*, 424. [CrossRef]
8. Djehiche, B.; Barreiro-Gomez, J.; Tembine, H. Price dynamics for electricity in smart grid via mean-field-type games. *Dyn. Games Appl.* **2020**, *10*, 798–818. [CrossRef]
9. Dumitrescu, R.; Leutscher, M.; Tankov, P. Energy transition under scenario uncertainty: A mean-field game of stopping with common noise. *Math. Financ. Econ.* **2024**, *18*, 233–274. [CrossRef]
10. Elie, R.; Hubert, E.; Mastrolia, T.; Possamaï, D. Mean–field moral hazard for optimal energy demand response management. *Math. Financ.* **2021**, *31*, 399–473. [CrossRef]
11. Escribe, C.; Garnier, J.; Gobet, E. A mean field game model for renewable investment under long-term uncertainty and risk aversion. *Dyn. Games Appl.* **2024**, *14*, 1093–1130. [CrossRef]
12. Frihi, Z.E.O.; Choutri, S.E.; Barreiro-Gomez, J.; Tembine, H. Hierarchical mean-field type control of price dynamics for electricity in smart grid. *J. Sys. Sci. Complex.* **2022**, *35*, 1–17. [CrossRef]
13. Fujii, M.; Takahashi, A. A mean field game approach to equilibrium pricing with market clearing condition. *SIAM J. Control Optim.* **2022**, *60*, 259–279. [CrossRef]
14. Verrilli, F.; Srinivasan, S.; Gambino, G.; Canelli, M.; Himanka, M.; Del Vecchio, C.; Sasso, M.; Glielmo, L. Model predictive control-based optimal operations of district heating system with thermal energy storage and flexible loads. *IEEE Trans. Autom. Sci. Eng.* **2016**, *14*, 547–557. [CrossRef]
15. Neckel, T.; Rupp, F. *Random Differential Equations in Scientific Computing*; Walter de Gruyter: Berlin, Germany, 2013.
16. D'Halluin, Y.; Forsyth, P.A.; Labahn, G. A semi-lagrangian approach for american asian options under jump diffusion. *SIAM J. Sci. Comput.* **2005**, *27*, 315–345. [CrossRef]
17. Chen, Z.; Forsyth, P.A. A semi-lagrangian approach for natural gas storage valuation and optimal operation. *SIAM J. Sci. Comput.* **2008**, *30*, 339–368. [CrossRef]
18. Ware, A. Accurate semi-lagrangian time stepping for stochastic optimal control problems with application to the valuation of natural gas storage. *SIAM J. Financ. Math.* **2013**, *4*, 427–451. [CrossRef]
19. Duffy, D.J. *Finite Difference Methods in Financial Engineering: A Partial Differential Equation Approach*; John Wiley & Sons: Hoboken, NJ, USA, 2013.
20. Yong, J.; Zhou, X.Y. *Stochastic Controls: Hamiltonian Systems and HJB Equations*; Springer Science & Business Media: Berlin/Heidelberg, Germany, 1999; Volume 43.
21. Touzi, N. *Stochastic Control Problems, Viscosity Solutions and Application to Finance*; Scuola normale Superiore; Springer: Berlin/Heidelberg, Germany, 2007.
22. Pham, H. *Continuous-Time Stochastic Control and Optimization with Financial Applications*; Springer Science & Business Media: Berlin/Heidelberg, Germany, 2009; Volume 61.
23. Courant, R.; Friedrichs, K.; Lewy, H. Über die partiellen differenzengleichungender mathematischen physik. *Math. Ann.* **1928**, *100*, 32–74. [CrossRef]

https://doi.org/10.3390/math14030489

mathematics

Article

Adaptive Iterative Algorithm for Optimizing the Load Profile of Charging Stations with Restrictions on the State of Charge of the Battery of Mining Dump Trucks

Nikita V. Martyushev [1,*], Boris V. Malozyomov [2], Vitaliy A. Gladkikh [3], Anton Y. Demin [1], Alexander V. Pogrebnoy [1], Elizaveta E. Kuleshova [1] and Yulia I. Karlina [3]

1 Department of Information Technology, Tomsk Polytechnic University, 634050 Tomsk, Russia; ad@tpu.ru (A.Y.D.); pogrebnoy@tpu.ru (A.V.P.); eek24@tpu.ru (E.E.K.)
2 Department of Electrotechnical Complexes, Novosibirsk State Technical University, 630073 Novosibirsk, Russia; borisnovel@mail.ru
3 Scientific Research and Testing Center "Stroytest", Moscow State University of Civil Engineering, 129337 Moscow, Russia; gladkich_87@mail.ru (V.A.G.); jul.karlina@gmail.com (Y.I.K.)
* Correspondence: martjushev@tpu.ru

Abstract: The development of electric quarry transport puts a significant strain on local power grids, leading to sharp peaks in consumption and degradation of power quality. Existing methods of peak smoothing, such as generation control, virtual power plants, or intelligent load management, have limited efficiency under the conditions of stochastic and high-power load profiles of industrial charging stations. A new strategy for direct charge and discharge management of a system for integrated battery energy storage (IBES) is based on dynamic iterative adjustment of load boundaries. The mathematical apparatus of the method includes the formalization of an optimization problem with constraints, which is solved using a nonlinear iterative filter with feedback. The key elements are adaptive algorithms that minimize the network power dispersion functionality (i.e., the variance of $P_{grid}(t)$ over the considered time interval) while respecting the constraints on the state of charge (SOC) and battery power. Numerical simulations and experimental studies demonstrate a 15 to 30% reduction in power dispersion compared to traditional constant power control methods. The results confirm the effectiveness of the proposed approach for optimizing energy consumption and increasing the stability of local power grids of quarry enterprises.

Keywords: optimal control; mathematical modeling; load peak smoothing; integrated battery energy storage system; dynamic optimization; iterative algorithms; nonlinear filtering; constrained problem; real-time control; adaptive systems; numerical methods

MSC: 93C10; 93D30; 90C26

1. Introduction

The rapid development of electric transport in the industrial sector, especially in the mining industry, leads to a significant increase in electricity consumption and the emergence of new load profiles that put pressure on the power system [1,2]. In recent years, large mining companies have been switching from diesel mining trucks to electric ones, reducing carbon emissions and operating costs. However, the mass introduction of such vehicles sharply increases peak loads in local power grids that supply charging stations, deteriorates the quality of electricity, increases losses, requiring modernization of distribution substations and power lines. The problem of smoothing peaks and filling in consumption dips is becoming a key area in the field of smart grids and flexible load management [3].

One of the most obvious ways to solve the problem of compensating peak loads is to regulate generation from energy sources, when power plants change the generated power depending on fluctuations in consumption. Similar approaches were actively used in thermal and hydropower engineering. For example, in [4] the authors proposed an algorithm for controlling thermal power plants to regulate load schedules by changing the modes of turbine generators. In [5], a system for optimizing gas turbine plants in the Shanghai energy system was developed, which reduced peaks by up to 12%. In [6], the authors studied the capabilities of hydroelectric units to compensate for daily load fluctuations and showed that increasing the flexibility of hydroelectric power plants requires significant operating costs. Despite certain successes, generation control methods have a number of drawbacks (long reaction time, low economic efficiency and high capital intensity) when expanding the capacity of plants. In addition, their use is limited in local power grids without generation, and the load is formed exclusively by consumers.

Another area is the use of renewable energy sources in conjunction with storage devices, accumulating excess electricity during periods of low demand and supplying it to the grid during peak consumption. In [7], the authors proposed a model for the market evaluation of energy storage systems taking into account the nonlinear characteristics of batteries, showing that optimizing the storage device parameters could increase the profitability of the project by 8–10%. The authors of [8] investigated the application of pumped storage systems in isolated island networks, where wind energy was used to pump water, providing up to 30% of fuel savings in diesel installations. However, for quarry enterprises remote from large sources of renewable energy, such solutions are not always feasible. The limited availability of wind and solar energy and the need for significant investment in infrastructure make this approach less suitable for off-grid industrial areas.

In recent years, special attention has been paid to virtual power plants (VPPs), which combine distributed energy sources, consumers and energy storage into a single control system. The authors of [9] performed an economic analysis of VPPs with large-scale battery systems and showed that their integration could increase the utilization rate of generating capacity and reduce the cost of electricity by 6–9%. However, the high complexity of prediction algorithms and the need for high-speed communication links limit the practical implementation of VPP in real-time, especially in industrial areas with unstable load profiles. In addition, the efficiency of virtual power plants decreases dramatically in the absence of reliable data on the state of grid elements.

Intelligent load management involving the system of integrated battery energy storage (IBES), which is connected to distribution networks or charging stations and acts as a buffer between the grid and consumers, is considered a promising area. In [10], a tool was developed for technical and economic analysis and optimization of small-scale photovoltaic systems with batteries, showing that the correct selection of the capacity and operating mode of the storage device can reduce peak loads by up to 18% and extend the service life of the battery by 25%. In [11], the authors demonstrated that the joint planning of household appliances and IBES reduced energy costs by up to 15% and load peaks by 20%. Despite these advances, most of the work is focused on the domestic or urban sector, where the load capacity is relatively low and temporary fluctuations in consumption are easily predictable. In the case of industrial charging systems for quarry transport, the load pattern is much more stochastic, and short-term peaks reach hundreds of kilowatts, making traditional strategies ineffective.

In summary, existing approaches show good results in residential or grid-connected environments but demonstrate limited transferability to quarry conditions. Generation control solutions require significant reserve capacity and have response times on the scale of minutes, which is insufficient for short spikes of 200–500 kW typical of haul truck charging [4–6]. VPP-based architectures depend on continuous high-speed communication and accurate forecasting that are difficult to maintain at remote sites with unstable power profiles [9]. Intelligent load-shifting methods with IBES buffers reported 15–20% of peak reduction in household and commercial studies [10,11], whereas quarry stations exhibit irregular multi-megawatt charging waves with poor predictability, reducing the effectiveness of rule-based scheduling. Therefore, the proposed approach specifically targets high-amplitude stochastic load patterns, where dynamic boundary adjustment provides faster response and does not rely on prediction accuracy.

Recent research has started to focus specifically on high-power charging infrastructure in industrial environments. The authors of [3] proposed a sequential decision-making process for the techno-economic operation of grid-connected traction substations with integrated solar PV and IBES, showing that the coordinated scheduling of storage and fast charging could significantly reduce demand peaks at traction nodes in the context of electric transport. In [4], the authors analyzed battery charging from a traction voltage inverter with an integrated charger and demonstrated the importance of matching charging profiles to the upstream network constraints and converter capabilities. For mining applications, the study [5] developed an optimal energy-efficiency control framework for a system of distributed energy-storage-based mining truck. These studies confirm that the electrification of heavy-duty vehicles creates highly concentrated and intermittent charging demand at industrial fast-charging stations, which in turn calls for dedicated peak-shaving strategies coordinated with the local grid. At the same time, a number of recent works have analyzed the use of battery energy storage systems for peak shaving in distribution grids and industrial consumers. The authors of [6] proposed a BESS-based scheme to reduce local and global peak loads in distribution networks, highlighting the role of storage placement and control strategy. The researchers of [7,8] formulated joint optimization problems for storage operation that simultaneously address peak shaving and ancillary services, obtaining super-linear economic benefits compared with independent operation. The scientists of [9] carried out techno-economic assessments of battery storage for peak demand management in smart grids and commercial facilities, while the research of [10] demonstrated that coordinated control of generation and storage could substantially improve reliability and peak-load handling capability in isolated or weak grids. However, most of these approaches rely on day-ahead optimization or model-predictive control with explicit forecasts of the load profile and electricity prices, which may be difficult to obtain in applications of stochastic industrial charging.

IBES distributed control systems based on machine learning algorithms are also of interest. In [12], a distributed control system was developed, using reinforcement learning to mitigate overvoltage during high penetration at solar power plants. The simulation results showed that voltage deviation was reduced by 35% while reducing load peaks. However, the use of such algorithms requires large computing resources and constant access to telemetry data, which makes it difficult to use them in conditions of limited communication channels at remote industrial facilities.

Another approach involves optimizing EV charging schedules based on network conditions and IBES parameters. In [13], the authors proposed a consistent decision-making algorithm for the optimal operation of traction substations integrated with solar photovoltaic systems and storage devices. Their model reduced peak loads by 22% and increased the use of renewable energy by up to 91% during the day. However, the method requires accurate prediction of the movement profile and consumption of electric dump trucks, which is extremely difficult in quarry conditions, where transportation cycles are irregular and depend on technological downtime.

A number of authors have considered hybrid energy storage schemes that combine lithium-ion batteries with supercapacitors or flywheels. In [13], the authors showed that combining systems can improve primary standby and load smoothing by 25% compared to single battery storage. In [14], the authors proposed a strategy for planning the work schedules of companies operating battery systems in the electricity market, which made it possible to increase the equipment utilization rate and to ensure the economic stability of the system. However, the use of hybrid schemes is associated with the complication of the control system, the need to synchronize the operating modes of various drives and an increase in the cost of installation.

Compared to state-filtered disturbance rejection and multilayer neuro-control algorithms, the proposed method has a simpler computational structure and does not require forecasting models, deep training datasets or high-performance processors. Active disturbance rejection controllers achieve high tracking quality but depend on internal observer tuning and may be sensitive to noise under stochastic load fluctuations. Neuro-control approaches provide strong generalization ability, but their implementation at remote industrial sites is limited by data availability and training stability.

The advantage of the present approach is real-time adaptability using iterative boundary adjustment applying only measurable variables (SOC, $P_{grid}(t)$, P_{load}), which reduce the variance by 15–30% without predictive models. The main limitation of our method is sub-optimality in long-horizon planning. In contrast to forecast-driven controllers, it operates reactively and does not anticipate future load surges. However, for isolated mine grid conditions with unpredictable duty cycles, this reactive robustness becomes a practical benefit.

In comparison with well-established strategies of energy storage control such as model predictive control (MPC), fuzzy logic controllers, and adaptive filtering approaches, the proposed method does not rely on a predictive model or rule base and does not require solving an optimization problem at each control step. MPC-based BESS controllers achieve high global optimality but require forecasting accuracy, matrix inversion, and horizon tuning, which limits their use in stochastic microgrids with rapidly varying loads. Fuzzy logic schemes ensure robustness to uncertainty but cannot guarantee variance minimization as a formal objective and require expert-defined membership functions. Adaptive filters smooth signals effectively, but do not incorporate physical battery constraints or allow boundary reconfiguration in response to SOC dynamics.

The novelty of the proposed approach lies in the dynamic iterative adjustment of the upper and lower power boundaries of *PH(t)* and *PL(t)* directly as a function of real-time energy capacity *(Ec, Ed)* and SOC, without prediction, rule tables or offline tuning. This makes the algorithm computationally lightweight and scalable for industrial stations where load uncertainty is high and predictive accuracy is limited.

Despite significant progress, all the considered approaches have common limitations. Generation control methods do not provide local load compensation in distribution networks; renewable energy solutions depend on weather conditions and require power redundancy [15]. Virtual power plants are difficult to implement in real time [16,17], and intelligent control algorithms and hybrid systems require high computing power and expensive components [18]. In mining environments where power is often supplied from isolated grids or loosely connected feeders, the greatest potential is to integrate the systems of battery energy storage directly into the charging stations of electric mining trucks. This approach makes it possible to locally smooth out peak loads [19], increase the stability of power supply and reduce the cost of reconstructing network equipment [20].

In contrast to the solutions considered earlier, this paper proposes using the strategy of direct charge and discharge control of IBES applying dynamic adjustment of load boundaries. This method is based on the continuous redistribution of energy between the grid and the storage device depending on the current consumption capacity [21]. Unlike traditional methods with fixed charging thresholds, the proposed algorithm allows for real-time adaptation of the charging and discharging boundaries. This provides a more accurate match to the load profile and extends the life of batteries by limiting the cycling depth [22]. This approach smooths peaks, fills troughs, increases the utilization rate of electrical equipment, savings in capital costs for the modernization of power grids [23].

The relevance of the chosen direction is conditioned by the combination of technological, economic and environmental significance. On the one hand, the transition of mining equipment to electric traction is a prerequisite for the decarbonization of the industry and is in line with global trends in sustainable development [24]. On the other hand, the increasing load on power systems requires intelligent solutions for adaptive energy flow management. The use of IBES as part of charging stations makes it possible to efficiently use the stored energy during periods of peak demand and create a buffer capacity without increasing transformer capacity. Moreover, the proposed direct control strategy can be implemented at the level of controllers of the local charging station without expensive data centers, which makes it especially attractive for industrial facilities with limited resources [25,26].

Therefore, this study is aimed at developing and experimentally testing a method for direct control of charge and discharge of a system of battery energy storage using dynamic adjustment of load boundaries integrated into an electric charging station for mining electric dump trucks. The main goal of this study is to develop and verify a mathematical model and algorithm for direct charge and discharge control IBES, integrated into a charging station for mining electric dump trucks. The algorithm is aimed at minimizing the target functional characterizing the dispersion of network power, while observing the system of differential and algebraic constraints describing the energy balance and physical limits of the storage battery. In what follows, we denote this objective as the dispersion functional DDD. A single mathematical definition of DDD is used throughout the work (see Equation (1) in Section 3, where DDD is given as the time variance of the network power ($P_{grid}(t)$) over the calculation interval TTT).

The algorithmic component is separated here from the general mathematical model to maintain clarity. The following text describes step-by-step boundary update rules, SOC-driven adaptation and convergence properties. The scientific novelty of the work lies in the following:

A new mathematical formalism of the problem of smoothing load peaks is proposed, representing it as a conditional optimization problem in continuous time with dynamically adaptable constraints.

An original iterative algorithm with dynamic adjustment of load boundary values (upper $PH(t)$ and lower $PL(t)$) have been developed, which is interpreted as a nonlinear adaptive filter. Unlike classical methods with fixed thresholds, this algorithm recalculates the boundaries in real time based on the current state of charge (SOC) and integral estimates of the charge/discharge energy (Ec, Ed).

The convergence of the iterative process to a quasi-stationary solution providing minimal power dispersion under conditions of a stochastic load profile is mathematically substantiated and experimentally confirmed.

Compared to existing adaptive BESS controllers, the key novelty of this work lies not in the use of iteration or feedback themselves, but in the mechanism of real-time boundary reconfiguration. Traditional strategies rely on fixed charging thresholds, predictive scheduling or model-based foresight, while the proposed method treats the upper and lower power limits (*PH(t)*, *PL(t)*) as continuously adjustable control variables. Their values evolve dynamically based on instantaneous grid power deviation and the integrated charge/discharge availability (*Ec*, *Ed*), enabling the controller to redistribute power without forecasting, optimization solvers or long-horizon planning. The system therefore adapts to stochastic load peaks using boundary migration rather than explicit trajectory tracking, which distinguishes the approach from gradient-based MPC, rule-driven battery dispatch and conventional constant-limit BESS operation reported in the literature.

Compared with existing optimization-based and model-predictive control strategies for load profile smoothing, the proposed dynamic boundary algorithm follows a different philosophy. Classical MPC or multi-time-scale optimal control formulations compute the storage power set-point by repeatedly solving a constrained optimization problem over a prediction horizon, which requires accurate forecasts of the load profile and relatively high computational resources. Advanced control schemes for BESS, including adaptive and distributed charge/discharge control, typically rely on detailed system models and communication between multiple agents, and their performance is sensitive to parameter tuning. In contrast, our approach embeds the minimization of network power variance into a nonlinear iterative filter that directly adjusts the admissible power band (*PH(t)*, *PL(t)*) in response to the measured SOC and cumulative charge/discharge energy. As a result, the controller operates without explicit load prediction, uses only local measurements available at the charging station, and can be implemented on low-cost industrial controllers while still providing a 15–30% of reduction in the power variance in the considered industrial fast-charging scenario.

The article structure: The article is organized as follows. Section 2 presents a mathematical formulation of the problem, including a system of power balance equations and constraints, a detailed description of an iterative algorithm for dynamic boundary tuning, illustrated by flowcharts. Section 3 demonstrates the quantification of the method effectiveness based on the introduced optimization criteria (variance, peak/trough difference) and visualizes the results of the algorithm for four typical operating modes. Section 4 provides a comparative analysis of the proposed strategy with the traditional constant-power method, supported by full-scale test data. Section 5 summarizes the main findings and outlines directions for future research.

2. Methods and Materials

The study is based on a combination of theoretical modeling and experimental verification aimed at analyzing the joint operation of an electric charging station for mining electric dump trucks [27] with a system of integrated battery energy storage (IBES). The study was carried out in two consecutive stages: at the first stage, a mathematical model of the interaction of the charging station, the power grid and the battery was created. At the second stage, full-scale tests were carried out on an experimental facility, including a charging module, an energy storage device, and a control system [28].

The experimental stand of the electric charging station was made in the form of a modular installation, including a converter part, a battery pack and a digital control system. To visualize the relationships between the components of the system, Figure 1 shows the structural diagram of the experimental test bench. The diagram shows the power supply network, the AC/DC converter, the battery energy storage system (IBES) with the BMS system, the load in the form of charging system modules for mining dump trucks, and a central controller that implements the proposed algorithm. The arrows show the power flows (P_{grid}, P_{bat}, P_{load}) and information feedback (SOC, power measurements) that close the control loop [29]. The following subsection formalizes the objective, constraints and stability criteria that define the IBES peak-shaving task. This part focuses strictly on the mathematical representation, without implementation-specific assumptions. The mathematical formulation of the problem was based on the representation of network power as $P_{grid}(t)$, load power as $P_{load}(t)$, and battery power as $P_{bat}(t)$. In this case, the power balance is implemented.

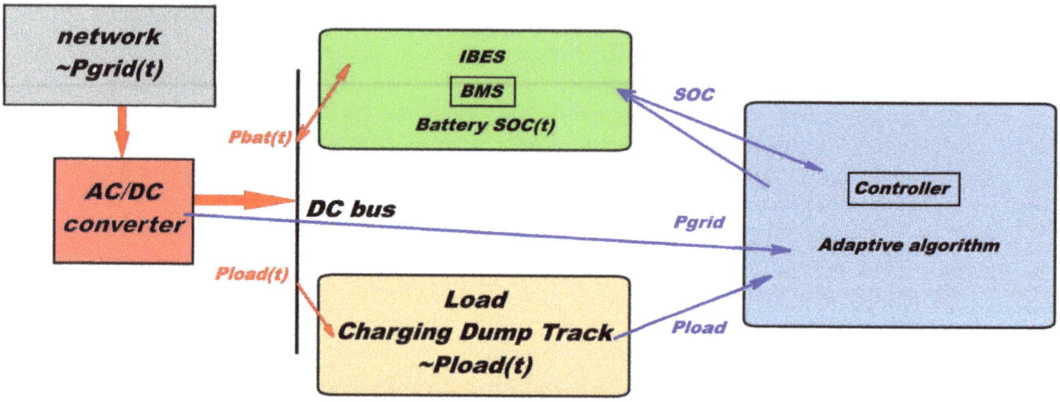

Figure 1. The structural diagram of the charging station system with a system of integrated battery energy storage (IBES).

Dotted lines indicate data flows (feedbacks); solid lines indicate power flows based on measurements of network power (P_{grid}), load power (P_{load}), and state of charge *(SOC)* of the battery. The main element of the energy part was an AC/DC converter, which provided a bidirectional energy conversion between the AC network and the DC bus. To protect against reverse currents, a diode barrier was used to prevent the flow of energy from the batteries to the grid in abnormal modes [30]. The battery module was a set of lithium-ion cells combined in a configuration with a rated power of up to 40 kW that was controlled by a BMS system that monitored currents, voltage, and state of charge (*SOC*). To simulate the load of an electric vehicle, a programmable active load was used, which made it possible to reproduce typical charging profiles for mining dump trucks [31]. All elements of the plant were controlled via the industrial CAN bus, which provided synchronization with the central controller and transmission of telemetry data to a personal computer. Using the PC, data were collected, power curves were visualized, and control algorithms were developed within the framework of a mathematical model [32].

For the reader's convenience, the main symbols and notations used in the mathematical formulation are summarized in Table 1.

Table 1. Main symbols and notations used in the mathematical model.

Symbol	Meaning	Units	Representative Values Used in Numerical Examples
$P_{grid}(t)$	Power drawn from the external grid by the charging station at t time	MW	(given by load-flow solution/measurement)
$P_{load}(t)$	Total load power of the fast-charging station (traction converters, auxiliaries, etc.) at t time	MW	Given by the measured load profile in Section 2
$P_{bat}(t)$	Power of the IBES battery at t time; positive for discharge, negative for charge	MW	–
R_{bat}	Sign indicator of the battery operating mode: $R_{bat} > 0$ for discharge, $R_{bat} < 0$ for charge	–	–
$SOC(t)$	State of charge of the battery at t time (the ratio of stored energy to nominal capacity)	p.u.	Typically, within 0.1–0.9 in simulations
SOC_{min}, SOC_{max}	Lower and upper admissible SOC limits	p.u.	$SOC_{min} = 0.1$, $SOC_{max} = 0.9$
E_{max}	Nominal (maximum) energy capacity of the battery	MWh	100 MWh (200 MWh in Mode 4)
E_0	Initial stored energy in the battery at the beginning of the simulation	MWh	10–40 MWh depending on the scenario
$E_c(t)$, $E_d(t)$	Cumulative charging and discharging energy of the battery over the current control interval	MWh	Reset to 0 at the beginning of each control interval
E_{cmax}, E_{dmax}	Admissible limits for cumulative charge and discharge energy, ensuring compliance with SOC bounds	MWh	Selected according to SOC_{min} and SOC_{max} in Section 2
$P_H(t)$, $P_L(t)$	Dynamic upper and lower boundaries of the admissible network power band used by the algorithm	MW	Adapted iteratively according to the dynamic boundary algorithm
γ	Iterative step coefficient in the dynamic boundary update law	–	Chosen empirically to ensure convergence (see Section 2)
λ	Filtering parameter that determines the smoothing of the dynamic boundaries and the sensitivity to random spikes	–	$0 < \lambda < 10$; the value used in simulations is given in Section 2
D	Variance (dispersion) of the network power of $P_{grid}(t)$ over the observation period	MW^2	Computed according to Equation (1)
ΔP_{load}	Difference between maximum and minimum values of the network power over the observation period	MW	Computed according to Equation (2)
β	Peak–Valley Coefficient characterizing the contrast between peak and valley loads	–	Computed according to Equation (4)
Δt	Time step of the discrete load and control profile	h or s, depending on data resolution)	Given by the sampling interval of the measured load profile
k	Iteration index of the dynamic boundary update algorithm	–	k = 0, 1, 2, . . .

The mathematical formulation of the problem was based on the representation of the power system of the charging station in the form of three interacting subsystems: the power supply network, the battery storage and the external load, whose role belongs to the electric car. Let the instantaneous power of load consumption be denoted as $P_{load}(t)$, the power output by the network as $P_{grid}(t)$, and the battery power as $P_{bat}(t)$. In this case, the power balance is achieved.

$$P_{\text{grid}}(t) = P_{\text{load}}(t) + P_{\text{bat}}(t), \tag{1}$$

where $R_{bat} > 0$ corresponds to the discharge of the battery (the transfer of energy to the load), and $R_{bat} < 0$ corresponds to its charge.

$$D = \frac{1}{T}\int_0^T [P_{\text{grid}}(t) = \overline{P}_{\text{grid}}]^2 dt, \tag{2}$$

where $\overline{P}_{\mathrm{grid}}$ is the average value of the network power for the time interval (T). This expression coincides with the dispersion functional D introduced in Equation (1). Minimization of this functional makes it possible to obtain an optimal distribution of charge and discharge modes, when network power fluctuations are minimal.

For the algorithm to work correctly, it is necessary to take into account the physical limitations of the battery. Firstly, the charging and discharging power is limited by $P_c^{\max}$ and $P_d^{\max}$ values, which is formalized by inequalities

$$-P_c^{\max} \leq P_{\mathrm{bat}}(t) \leq P_d^{\max}. \tag{3}$$

Secondly, the state of charge (the SOQ of the battery must remain within acceptable limits) is

$$SOC_{\min} \leq SOC(t) \leq SOC_{\max}. \tag{4}$$

The dynamics of the SOC change is described by the differential equation

$$\frac{dSOC(t)}{dt} = -\frac{\eta_c P_{\mathrm{bat}}(t)}{E_{\max}}, \tag{5}$$

where η_c is the energy conversion efficiency factor, and E_{max} is the nominal capacity of the battery. These dependencies form a system of constraints within which the charging and discharging modes are optimized [33].

In the developed model, the key element is the mechanism for dynamic adjustment of load boundary values, which ensures the adaptation of the control algorithm to current fluctuations in consumption [34]. In traditional methods, peak smoothing is carried out using fixed power thresholds, above which the battery charge or discharge is turned on [35]. However, this approach does not take into account the non-stationarity of the load and does not allow using the potential of the storage device efficiently. According to the proposed methodology, the boundary values of $P_H(t)$ and $P_L(t)$ are determined iteratively in the modeling process and change depending on the current levels of peaks and troughs of the consumption curve [36].

In this work, adaptivity means real-time modification of the control boundaries based on instantaneous feedback rather than on fixed thresholds. During every cycle of the Δt duration, the algorithm receives updated values of $P_{\mathrm{load}}(t)$, $P_{\mathrm{grid}}(t)$ and $SOC(t)$ and recalculates E_c and E_d. If the current boundary pair of ($P_H(t)$ and $P_L(t)$) leads to insufficient charge/discharge capability or violates SOC/power limits, the boundaries are shifted by $\pm\Delta P$ until a feasible state is reached. The adaptation therefore does not rely on forecasting or learning-based prediction; instead, it continuously tunes the boundaries according to the measured operating state of the system. In contrast to static tuning, where a fixed pair of ($P_H(t)$ and $P_L(t)$) cannot track rapid fluctuations, the dynamic update compensates stochastic peaks more effectively and prevents battery saturation by tightening or relaxing limits depending on available SOC reserve. This feedback-driven boundary update is the core mechanism that provides adaptability under highly variable industrial load conditions.

To find these limits, an iterative process is used, based on minimizing the discrepancy between the actual and desired charging or discharging capacity. Let Ec and Ed denote the energy stored and delivered by the battery per cycle (P_H^0,P_L^0):

$$P_H^0 = P_{\max} - P_d^{\max}, \ P_L^0 = P_{\min} - P_c^{\max}. \tag{6}$$

At each step of the iteration, the integral area under the load plot sections above and below these boundaries is calculated, which makes it possible to estimate the current values of E_c and E_d. If the calculated values are outside the permissible range of the battery's capacity, the boundaries are corrected by stepping ΔP up or down. Therefore, the algorithm tends to achieve a position of boundaries when the charge and discharge energy corresponds to the physical capabilities of the storage device [37], and the variance of network power is minimal.

Mathematically, this process can be considered as a problem of finding a quasi-stationary solution to a system of nonlinear equations that relate instantaneous values of power and accumulated energy [38]. The solution is found by iterative methods until the change in the load variance between adjacent iterations is less than that of the specified threshold (ε). To make the mathematical structure explicit, the control task can be written as a constrained optimization problem:

$$\min_{P_{bat}(t)} D = \frac{1}{T}\int_0^T \left(P_{grid}(t) - \overline{P_{grid}}\right)^2 \cdot dt \tag{7}$$

Subject to power constraints:

$$P_{bat}^{\min} \leq P_{\text{bat}}(t) \leq P_{bat}^{\max} \tag{8}$$

and SOC feasibility conditions:

$$SOC_{\min} \leq SOC(t) \leq SOC_{\max},\ \dot{SOC}(t) = -\frac{\eta_c P_{\text{bat}}(t)}{E_{\max}}, \tag{9}$$

The iterative nonlinear filter performs gradient-free adjustment of dynamic load boundaries ($P_H(t)$ and $P_L(t)$) to minimize D while ensuring that all candidate control actions remain inside the feasible domain defined above. At each iteration of k, the boundary is perturbed by $\pm\Delta P$, and the step is accepted only if both power and SOC constraints remain satisfied; otherwise, the change is rejected and the boundary is shifted in the opposite direction.

Convergence in simulation is demonstrated by the fact that for all 4 test modes the iteration count remained finite (10–35 iterations per cycle), and the stopping criterion of $|D_{k+1} - D_k| < 10^{-3}$ was consistently achieved. Numerical experiments and full-scale tests showed no divergence or boundary oscillations, confirming practical stability of the filter under stochastic load conditions.

This approach ensures the convergence of the algorithm even with sharp fluctuations in the consumption profile.

The logic of the proposed adaptive iterative algorithm for dynamic adjustment of the $P_H(t)$ and $P_L(t)$ load boundaries is presented in the form of a flowchart in Figure 2. The algorithm begins by measuring the current values of the load power and the state of IBES charge. Based on this data, the current energy capacitances of E_c and E_d are calculated. The key step is the condition check, which determines one of the four possible modes of operation of the system. Depending on the mode, the upper and/or lower limit of the load is adjusted by the value of ΔP. The iteration process continues until a balance is reached between the charge/discharge energy and capacitive capabilities of IBES, which minimizes the dispersion of network power. Figure 2 shows a flow diagram of an adaptive iterative algorithm for direct charge and discharge control of IBES.

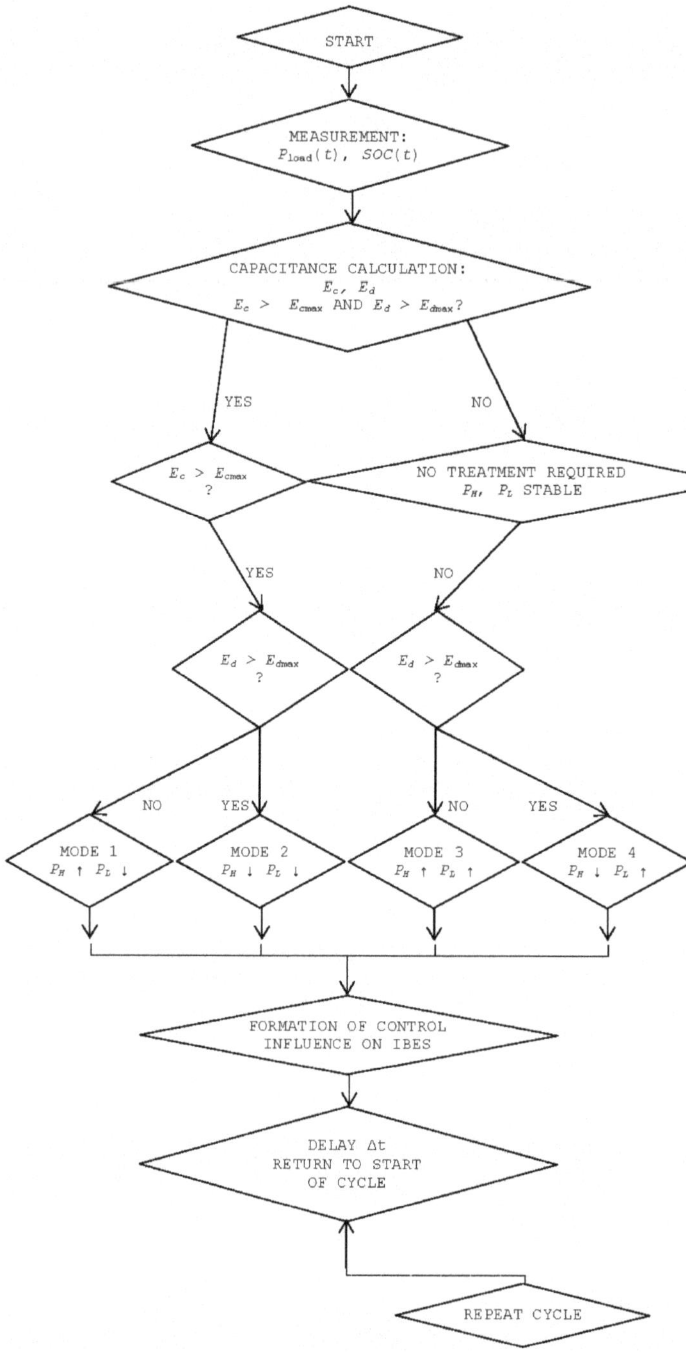

Figure 2. The block diagram of an adaptive iterative algorithm for direct charge and discharge control of IBES.

In real-time operation, the algorithm works as follows. First, the initial load boundaries of P_H^0 and P_L^0 are set based on a predicted or historically observed daily load curve and on the nominal charging/discharging capabilities of the battery (Equations (5)–(7)). Then, at each control step of the Δt duration (1 s in the numerical experiments), the controller receives updated measurements of the grid power ($P_{\text{grid}}(t)$), the load power ($P_{\text{load}}(t)$) and the battery state of charge ($SOC(t)$). Using these real-time inputs, the current charge and discharge energies per cycle (E_c and E_d) are recalculated as the areas of the load curve above and below the active boundaries of $P_H(t)$ and $P_L(t)$. If E_c and E_d satisfy the capacity constraints and the instantaneous power and SOC remain within the limits given by Equations (5) and (6), the boundaries are kept unchanged and the IBES charge/discharge power is determined directly from the position of $P_H(t)$ and $P_L(t)$. Otherwise, the algorithm slightly shifts one or both boundaries by a ΔP step up or down and repeats the calculation of E_c and E_d. In this way, each iteration first enforces the hard constraints on battery power and SOC, and it reduces the variance of the grid power (D) only within this feasible region. The cycle of measurement–update–correction is repeated at every time Δt step, which enables the system to track fast stochastic changes in the load without relying on long-horizon forecasts.

The algorithm functions in real time, calculating the current energy capacitances (E_c, E_d) at each step and adapting the load boundaries accordingly; a detailed description of the four operating modes will be provided later in this section.

In Figure 2, the following notations are adopted: $P_H\uparrow$ is an increase in the upper limit of power; $P_H\downarrow$ is a decrease in the upper limit of power; $P_L\uparrow$ is an increase in the lower limit of power. $P_L\downarrow$ is reducing the lower limit of power; E_c is the current energy capacity; E_d is the current energy dissipation; Δt is the time lag between iterations. Figure 2 shows the sequence of steps, logical branching (4 modes) and the closed nature of the algorithm. To clarify the link between the flowchart and the mathematical formulation, each block in Figure 2 directly corresponds to specific expressions introduced in Section 2. The calculation of E_c and E_d is based on integral evaluation of the areas defined in Equations (8) and (9), while SOC evolution follows the dynamic model (6). The decision node in the flowchart maps for the four conditional states is listed in Table 1, where each combination of (E_c,E_d) relative to (E_c^{max}, E_d^{max}) selects a specific update rule for $P_H(t)$ and $P_L(t)$. The adjustment step of ΔP shown in the diagram reflects the iterative boundary update mechanism formalized in Equations (25)–(27). In view of this, the flowchart is not abstract but represents a compact procedural form of the mathematical algorithm described earlier.

This visualizes the novelty of the proposed solutions: adaptive logic is based on dynamic boundaries rather than on static thresholds or predictions. A description of the characteristics of the operating modes of the above algorithm is given in Table 2.

Table 2. Modes Description.

No. Mode	Mode Options E_c, E_{cmax}, E_d, E_{dmax}	Parameters of the PH and PL Power Boundaries
1	$E_c > E_{cmax}$, $Ed \leq E_{dmax}$	– $P_H\uparrow$: Increasing the upper limit of power – $P_L\downarrow$: Reducing the lower limit of the capacity
2	$E_c > E_{cmax}$, $Ed > E_{dmax}$	– $P_H\downarrow$: Decreasing the upper limit of power – $P_L\downarrow$: Reducing the lower limit of the capacity
3	$E_c \leq E_{cmax}$, $Ed \leq E_{dmax}$	– $P_H\uparrow$: Increasing the upper limit of power – $P_L\uparrow$: Increasing the lower limit of the capacity
4	$E_c \leq E_{cmax}$, $Ed > E_{dmax}$	– $P_H\downarrow$: Decreasing the upper limit of power – $P_L\uparrow$: Increasing the lower limit of the capacity

For numerical modeling, experimental data of the daily consumption schedule of the experimental charging station were used, which are characterized by the presence of two pronounced peak sections and several zones of minimum load. In the considered dataset, the instantaneous load power ($P_{load}(t)$) varies between approximately 41.7 and 51.8 kW over a 24 h interval, with an average value of 46.9 kW. The most intensive charging periods correspond to clusters of high-power sessions when one or more dump trucks are connected, during which the power remains close to the upper level for several tens of minutes. Between these clusters, the station operates near the average power level, while shorter step-like changes caused by individual connection and disconnection events are superimposed in this trend. Such pattern reflects the stochastic nature of truck arrival times and leads to a sequence of peaks and troughs on time scales from several minutes up to a few hours.

Based on these data, different modes of IBES operation were compared. The computational experiments were performed in the MATLAB/Simulink R2020b software environment [39], where modules for modeling the network, battery and controller were implemented. In the numerical integration of the differential equations, the fourth-order Runge–Kutta scheme with a discretization step of 1 s was used, which provides stability under rapidly changing power profiles.

Laboratory tests were carried out to verify the adequacy of the model. Experimental data were taken using current and voltage sensors with a sampling rate of 10 Hz built into the converter, and data processing and algorithm implementation were performed in real time using an industrial controller with an ARM microprocessor. The obtained experimental power curves were compared with the results of modeling according to the standard deviation criterion and the peak-trough ratio coefficient. The discrepancy did not exceed 5%, which confirms the reliability of the proposed model and the mathematical transformations used.

From the point of view of the mathematical apparatus, the main transformation used in the study can be considered as the operation of the nonlinear filtering of the power time series [40]. In this case, a nonlinear iterative filter implies a feedback operator that maps the raw grid power signal ($P_{grid}(t)$) to a smoothed signal ($P_{grid}(t)$) by repeatedly updating the control boundaries of $P_H(t)$ and $P_L(t)$ so as to reduce the variance of $P_{grid}(t)$ under the battery constraints. At each time step, the filter computes correction increments for P_H and P_L based on the current power deviation, available charge/discharge energy and SOC limits and applies these corrections until the change in the dispersion measure between successive iterations becomes negligible. In contrast to the standard smoothing methods based on convolution of a signal with a fixed core, adaptive nonlinear filtering is used here, whose parameters are determined by the state of the battery and the dynamic limits of the load feedback and optimization algorithms in continuous time [41]. Essentially, the algorithm implements a discrete-continuum transformation in which the solution of the optimization problem is updated iteratively in time increments (Δt), and the load boundaries are recalculated as a function of the power deviations and the current SOC:

$$P_H^{(k+1)} = P_H^{(k)} + \gamma(E_d^{(k)} - E_d^*), \;\; P_L^{(k+1)} = P_L^{(k)} - \gamma(E_c^{(k)} - E_c^*), \tag{10}$$

where γ is the iterative step coefficient, and the asterisks indicate the target capacitance values. This transformation provides a quick approximation to a sustainable solution and allows the system to adapt to any changes in load without the need to predict its profile.

This subsection summarizes real-time execution settings, controller parameters, and a communication structure. Numerical examples remain in Sections 3 and 4 for separation between method and results. The developed algorithm was tested for four typical operating modes, differing in initial SOC values and battery power [42]. These four operating modes correspond exactly to the conditional branches shown in Figure 2, confirming that the flowchart reflects the executable control logic used in modeling and experiments. In each mode, the dispersion indicators, peak and trough differences, and a smoothing coefficient were evaluated. The results confirmed that the application of dynamic configuration of load boundaries could reduce the network power variance by 15–30% compared to traditional constant power management. This demonstrates the mathematical efficiency of an iterative approach that combines energy constraints with the principle of minimizing the functional of the variational type.

For clarity, the reported 15–30% reduction corresponds to measured decreases in the variance of $P_{grid}(t)$ over a 24 h operating cycle reproduced on a full-scale charging station test bench. The load profiles were derived from real operating data of mining haul trucks and replayed using a programmable active load to emulate quarry charging dynamics. The DDD variance was calculated according to (1) based on time-series measurements sampled at 10 Hz, and the baseline for comparison was the conventional constant-power charging strategy used in industrial charging stations. The experimental campaign covered four representative operating modes differing in initial SOC and power capacity, each evaluated in both baseline and adaptive-control configurations. In all modes, the adaptive method consistently yielded lower dispersion values, which confirms the quantitative improvement reported above.

It should be noted that the algorithm was implemented using numerical differentiation and integration methods that are resistant to measurement noise [43]. To eliminate the drift of the power signal, sliding averaging with exponential attenuation was used, which can be written as a recurrence relation:

$$\overline{P}_{\text{grid}}(t+\Delta t) = \lambda P_{\text{grid}}(t) + (1-\lambda)\overline{P}_{\text{grid}}(t), \tag{11}$$

where λ is the filtering parameter that determines the degree of averaging. This made it possible to ensure the stability of calculations and reduce the sensitivity of the algorithm to random load spikes.

Therefore, the proposed method combines the mathematical modeling of the dynamic processes of charge and discharge of IBES with experimental verification of the results. The central element of the study is the use of adaptive iterative transformations, which make it possible to adjust the boundaries of control in real time depending on the current state of the system [44]. From a mathematical point of view, this is a solution to the constraint optimization problem implemented by means of a nonlinear iterative feedback filter. Such formulation ensures high accuracy and stability of the algorithm, and experimental data confirm its applicability for industrial charging stations of mining electric dump trucks operating under conditions of variable load and limited power of the supply network [45].

3. Results and Discussion

In continuation of the presented method of modeling and experimental analysis, special attention is paid to the assessment of quantitative characteristics that make it possible to objectively determine the effectiveness of the proposed algorithm for direct control of the charge and discharge of the battery energy storage system. Since the developed approach is aimed at reducing dynamic fluctuations in power consumption and leveling the load profile, it is necessary to formalize the parameters that characterize the degree of power smoothing after the implementation of IBES. This section provides a mathematical basis for assessing the compensating properties of the energy storage device in various modes of operation of the charging station.

The basic idea is to compare the initial load profile without the drive and the corrected profile after applying a dynamic load boundary strategy. At the same time, the analysis is carried out not only for local fluctuations (within short time intervals), but also for the global trend of power change during the entire calculation period. The efficiency of IBES is evaluated by a number of indicators reflecting the degree of reduction of peaks and the leveling of thickness troughs [46].

The time series of network power ($P_{grid}(t)$), corresponding to the power mode of the charging station, and the power of the storage battery ($P_{bat}(t)$), which describes the energy exchange between the grid and the storage device, are used as initial data. The combination of these dependencies makes it possible to form a resultant load graph of the system with compensation, which serves as the basis for calculating integral estimates. The description of the degree of vibration compensation, four complementary indicators are introduced, covering the statistical and extreme properties of the power signal [47].

In what follows, we treat the variance of the series of grid power time as the dispersion functional of the network power. The first indicator is the dispersion (deviation) of power fluctuations, i.e., a value that characterizes the degree of dispersion of instantaneous power values relative to the average level. This parameter reflects the stability of energy consumption and is sensitive to short-term fluctuations. Mathematically, this dispersion functional (DDD) is expressed as:

$$D = \frac{1}{T}\int_{0}^{T} [P_{\text{grid}}(t) = \overline{P}_{\text{grid}}]^2 dt, \tag{12}$$

where $P_{grid}(t)$ is the power coming from the grid at t time; $\overline{P}_{\text{grid}}$ is its average value for the design period (T). The lower the value of D, the higher the system's ability to compensate for peak fluctuations and the more evenly the load is distributed over time.

The following indicator is the absolute difference between load peaks and troughs, defined as the difference between the maximum and minimum values of network power during the observation period:

$$\Delta P_{\text{load}} = P_{\text{max}} - P_{\text{min}}, \tag{13}$$

where P_{max} and P_{min} are the extreme values of the load graph, respectively. This parameter characterizes the total amplitude of oscillations and makes it possible to assess the efficiency of peak smoothing at the level of the power system [48].

For additional analysis of the relationship between local maximums and load minimums, the coefficient of the relative difference between peaks and bottoms is used:

$$\alpha = \frac{P_{\text{max}} - P_{\text{min}}}{P_{\text{max}}}, \tag{14}$$

which shows the relative magnitude of the uneven power distribution. When $\alpha \longrightarrow 0$, the load is almost uniform, while an increase in α indicates a significant power variation and the need to adjust the IBES modes.

The Peak–Valley Coefficient is defined as

$$\beta = \frac{P_{\text{min}}}{P_{\text{max}}}. \tag{15}$$

This parameter is inversely proportional to the contrast of the load graph and allows conveniently comparing the simulation results between different charging and discharging modes. The higher the β value, the closer the network load becomes to a constant one.

These indicators are used together, forming a mathematical system of criteria for quantitative analysis. Minimization of the D variance and the ΔP_{load} difference in combination with an increase in β serves as an indicator of successful compensation for fluctuations in consumption. In view of this, the developed estimation methodology integrates both integral statistical characteristics (variance) and extreme values that determine the real limits of the load. For the initial (uncompensated) daily profile of the experimental charging station these indicators take the following values: D = 50.7866 kW, ΔP_{load} = 159.1481 kW, α = 0.6798 and β = 0.3202. The corresponding standard deviation of the network power is $\sqrt{D} \approx 7.1$ kW, which is about 15% of the average load of 46.9 kW. These numerical characteristics quantify the stochastic high-power load of the quarry charging station and serve as a reference for assessing the performance of the proposed optimization strategy.

However, formal minimization of these parameters is impossible without taking into account the physical limitations of the battery system. The charging and discharging power of the battery is limited by limit values depending on its design and operating conditions. These limits are described by the ratio:

$$-P_c^{\max} \leq P_{\text{bat}}(t) \leq P_d^{\max}. \tag{16}$$

where $P_c^{\max}$ is the maximum charging power (with $P_{bat} < 0$), and $P_d^{\max}$ is the maximum discharge power (with $P_{bat} > 0$). To prevent the accelerated aging of batteries, charge efficiency factors (η_c) and discharge (η_d) are introduced, which are taken into account when calculating the energy balance. In future, we denote these bounds by $P_c^{\max}$ (maximum charging power) and $P_d^{\max}$ (maximum discharging power). These symbols are used consistently in all subsequent equations. For brevity, in the configuration of Table 2 below, the same quantities are shown as P_c and P_d, i.e., $P_c = P_c^{\max}$ and $P_d = P_d^{\max}$.

In addition to power limitation, the battery is characterized by a finite capacity that determines the range of change in the state of charge (SOC). To ensure safe and long-term operation, the SOC must remain within

$$SOC_{\min} \leq SOC(t) \leq SOC_{\max}. \tag{17}$$

where SOC_{min} and SOC_{max} are the lower and upper limits of the charge level. These limits prevent deep discharge and the overcharging of the battery, which lead to the degradation of electrochemical cells and a decrease in service life.

As part of the developed strategy for direct control of battery charge and discharge, dynamic power and capacity limits are used as active boundaries involved in the formation of the load profile. For this purpose, variable upper P_H and lower P_L load boundaries are introduced, which change over time depending on the current values of $P_{grid}(t)$, $SOC(t)$ and the maximum power of the battery [49]. In this context, the term *load boundaries* refers to two time-varying reference levels ($P_H(t)$ and $P_L(t)$) that delimit the admissible range of grid power. When the instantaneous load ($P_{load}(t)$) tends to exceed $P_H(t)$, IBES switches to a discharge mode to keep $P_{\text{grid}}(t)$ close to the upper boundary. Conversely, when $P_{load}(t)$ falls below $P_L(t)$, IBES is charged to prevent the grid power from dropping below the lower boundary. Therefore, $P_H(t)$ and $P_L(t)$ act as dynamic control thresholds shaping the effective load profile seen by the grid.

The initial values of these boundaries are determined based on the predicted load curve characteristic. Let the $\hat{P}_{\max}$ $\hat{P}_{\min}$ predicted consumption extremes be described; then the initial boundaries are chosen as

$$P_H^0 = \hat{P}_{\max} - P_d^{\text{nom}}, \quad P_L^0 = \hat{P}_{\min} - P_c^{\text{nom}}, \tag{18}$$

where P_d^{nom} and P_c^{nom} are the nominal discharge and charging powers, respectively. These parameters determine the initial limits of the area within which vibration compensation is carried out [50].

We denote these nominal powers by P_c^{nom} (nominal charging power) and P_d^{nom} (nominal discharging power). Together with $P_c^{\max}$ and $P_d^{\max}$ introduced after Equation (5), this provides a unique and unambiguous set of symbols used in the subsequent derivations.

Direct control of the IBES charge/discharge power is realized by means of dynamic load boundary control. In order to take full advantage of the effects of compensation for load peaks and consumption dips of battery energy storage systems, a strategy for direct control of the IBES charge/discharge power using dynamic adjustment of load boundaries is proposed. The strategy is presented below.

Initial parameter setting. As shown in Figure 3, the maximum load (P_{load}) and the minimum load ($P_{\max}$) can be determined as $P_{\min}$ from the predicted characteristic load curve, and the initial upper load limit (P_{H-ini}) and the initial lower load limit (P_{L-ini}) can be defined as

$$\begin{cases} P_{H-init} = P_{\max} - P_d \\ P_{L-init} = P_{\min} + P_c \end{cases} \tag{19}$$

where P_d and P_c are the rated discharge power and charge of the battery, respectively.

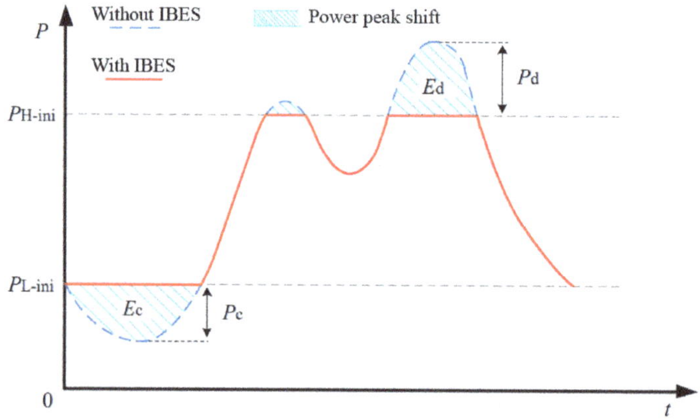

Figure 3. The diagram of initial load power time.

In addition, the area below P_{L-ini} bounded by P_{load} is defined as the initial charging capacity of E_{c-ini}. And the area above P_{H-ini} limited by P_{load} is defined as the initial discharge capacity of E_{d-ini}, E_{c-ini} and E_{d-ini} and can be expressed as

$$\begin{cases} E_{c-ini} = \int (P_{L-ini} - P_{load}(t))dt \\ E_{d-ini} = \int (P_{load}(t) - P_{H-ini})dt \end{cases} \tag{20}$$

The charge management strategy. Using the iterative process described above, it is possible to determine the time and power of charge and discharge. When the IBES power is low, areas of peaks and dips can be compensated. With high IBES power, using the maximum power, charging and discharging power of IBES, it is possible to improve the efficiency of compensation for load peaks and consumption dips.

A typical mode of operation of IBES for load power compensation is shown in Figure 4, where $E_c > E_{c\max}$ and $E_d > E_{d\max}$. The upper limit of the load of P_H needs to be iterated up and the lower limit of the load of P_L needs to be iterated down. This operating mode is suitable for scenarios with low IBES power, where the load curve is stable at the peak and trough points.

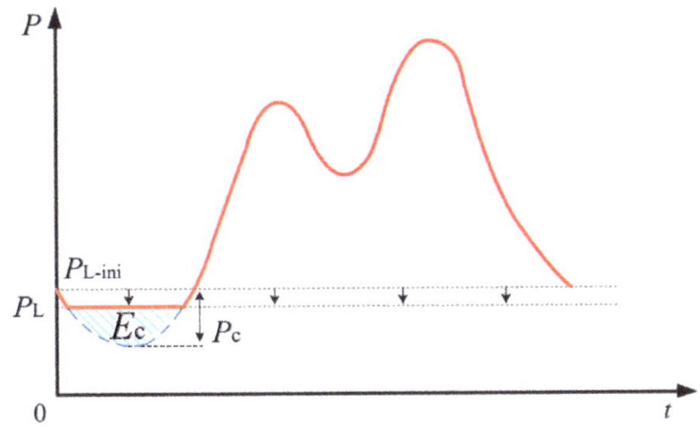

Figure 4. The iteration diagram when $E_{c-init} > E_{c\max}$.

When the initial charging capacity of E_{c-ini} exceeds the maximum rechargeable capacity of the $E_{c\max}$ battery, then the capacity limit cannot be met. If E_{c-ini} is less than $E_{c\max}$, the battery capacity cannot be fully utilized.

$E_{c\max}$ can be expressed as:

$$E_{c\max} = E_{\max} - E_0 \tag{21}$$

where $E_{c\max}$ is the maximum capacity of the battery, and E_0 is the initial capacity of the battery:

$$E_{c-init} > E_{c\max}$$

In order to reduce the charging capacity, E_c as the lower limit value of the load of P_L is repeated downwards. The iterative process is as follows:

$$\begin{cases} P_L = P_{L-init} - k\delta P \\ k = k+1 \end{cases} \tag{22}$$

Using δP in Figure 4, we determine the updated value of E_c according to Equations (9) and (11) and compare it to $E_{c\max}$. If $E_c > E_{c\max}$ at this point, we continue the iteration until the condition of $E_c < E_{c\max}$ is met. We determine the number of iterations when $k = k_n$ in order to determine the dynamically adjusted lower limit value of the load of P_L.

$$P_{load}(t) < P_L P_{bat}(t) = P_{load}(t) - P_L \tag{23}$$

When $E_{c-ini} < E_{c\max}$, a load curve is used to facilitate the calculation of the battery's rechargeable capacity. $P_{load}(t)$ shifts upwards by the amplitude of P_c and the auxiliary curve of $P_{net-c}(t)$ is plotted as shown in Figure 5.

$$P_{net-c}(t) = P_{load}(t) + P_c y \tag{24}$$

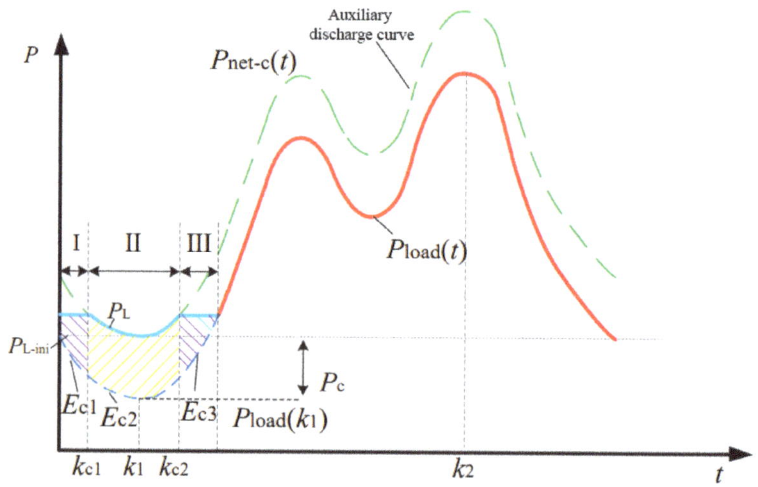

Figure 5. The iteration diagram when $E_{c-init} < E_{c\max}$.

At the same time $P_{\min}$ is defined as $P_{load}(k_1)$, which means that the sampling time corresponding to $P_{\min}$ is k_1. It is possible to define the initial power separation time as $k_{c1} - k_{c2} = k_1$. Then k_{c1} and k_{c2} will participate in the left and right iterations, respectively, depending on the size of the charging capacity, thereby dividing the charging area into three areas, as shown in Figure 5, namely:

- Domain I: When $t \in [0, k_{c1}]$, simultaneously satisfying $P_{load}(t) < P_{net-c}(k_{c1})$ and $P_{net-c}(t) > P_{net-c}(k_{c1})$.
- Domain II: When $t \in (k_{c1}, k_{c2})$ and $P_{net-c}(t) \leq P_{net-c}(k_{c2})$.
- Domain III: $t \in [k_{c2}, T]$, satisfying $P_{load}(t) < P_{net-c}(k_{c2})$ and $P_{net-c}(t) > P_{net-c}(k_{c2})$.

The charging capacities in the above three areas are E_{c1}, E_{c2} and E_{c3} accordingly, and they can be calculated as

$$\begin{cases} E_{c1} = \int_0^{k_{c1}} (P_{load}(k_{c1}) - P_{load}(t))dt \\ E_{c2} = \int_{k1}^{k_{c2}} P_c dt \\ E_{c3} = \int_{k_{c2}}^{T} (P_{load}(k_{c2}) - P_{load}(t))dt \end{cases} \tag{25}$$

Therefore, the total charging capacity will be equal to

$$E_c = E_{c1} + E_{c2} + E_{c3} \tag{26}$$

By increasing E_c, the maximum power load can be fully utilized, and the power sharing points must be iterated as k_{c1} k_{c2} both left and right, respectively. The iterative process is as follows:

$$\begin{cases} k_{c1} = k_1 - k \\ k = k + 1 \\ P_{load}(k_{c2}) = P_{load}(k_{c1}) \end{cases} \tag{27}$$

When $E_c < E_{c\max}$, we continue to repeat the iterations. When $E_c > E_{c\max}$, we stop the iterations. Next, we will fix the points of power sharing of k_{c1} and k_{c2} during the end of the iteration to obtain a dynamically adjusted lower k_{c1} limit value of the load of P_L

$$P_L = \begin{cases} P_{load}(k_{c1}) + P_c \\ P_{load}(t) + P_c \end{cases} \tag{28}$$

Therefore, the charging power of a battery is defined as:

$$P_{bat}(t) = P_{load}(t) - P_L \tag{29}$$

The strategy for controlling the discharge. The maximum discharge capacity is defined as $E_{d\max}$:

$$E_{d\max} = E_{\max} - E_{\min} \tag{30}$$

where $E_{\min}$ and $E_{\max}$ are the capacity of the battery at the minimum and maximum SOC levels, respectively.

Similar to the charging management method, the discharge methods must be considered: $E_{d-init} > E_{d\max}$ $E_{d-init} < E_{d\max}$.

(1) Under the $E_{d-init} > E_{d\max}$ condition, it is necessary to reduce the capacity of E_d to meet the capacity limitation, so it is necessary to repeat the upper limit value of the load of P_H. The iterative process is as follows:

$$\begin{cases} P_H = P_{H-init} + k\delta P \\ k = k+1 \end{cases} \tag{31}$$

As shown in Figure 6, we calculate and update the E_d value according to Equations (9) and (20). If $E_d > E_{d\max}$, we continue the iteration, and when $E_d < E_{d\max}$, we stop the iteration. We record the number of iterations of $k = k_{f2}$ to determine the dynamically adjusted upper G limit value of the P_H load. In view of this, the partial power of the battery when $P_{load}(t) > P_H$ is:

$$P_{bat}(t) = P_{load}(t) - P_H \tag{32}$$

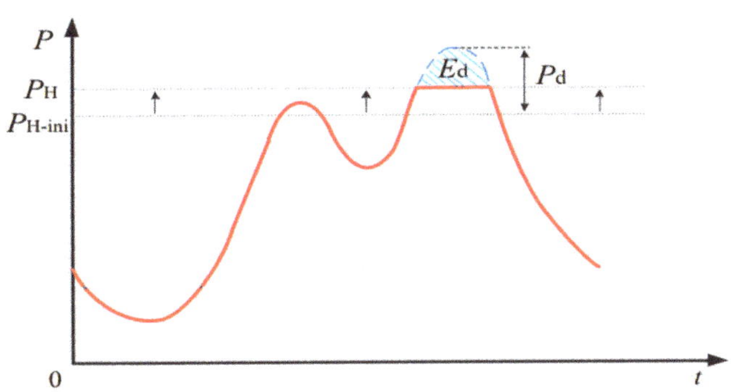

Figure 6. The iteration diagram when $E_{d-ini} > E_{d\max}$.

(2) When $E_{d-init} < E_{d\max}$, the curve of $P_{load}(t)$ shifts down by the amplitude of P_d and plot an auxiliary charging curve of $P_{net-d}(t)$ as shown in Figure 5. P_{net-d} can be expressed as:

$$P_{net-d}(t) = P_{load}(t) - P_d \tag{33}$$

Here, $P_{\max}$ is defined as $P_{load}(k_2)$, which means that the sampling time corresponding to $P_{\max}$ is k_2. We define the initial power sharing time as $k_{d1} = k_{d2} = k_2$. Among them, k_{d1} and k_{d2} will iterate left and right depending on the size of the charging capacity, thereby dividing the charging area into three domains, as shown in Figure 7, namely:

- Domain IV: when $t \in [0, k_{d1}]$, and it satisfies $P_{load}(t) > P_{net-c}(k_{d1})$ and $P_{net-d}(t) < P_{net-d}(k_{d1})$;
- Domain V: when $P_{net-d}(t) \geq P_{net-d}(k_{c2})$;
- Domain VI: when $t \in [k_{d2}, T]$, and it satisfies both $P_{load}(t) > P_{net-d}(k_{d2})$ and $P_{net-d}(t) < P_{net-d}(k_{d2})$.

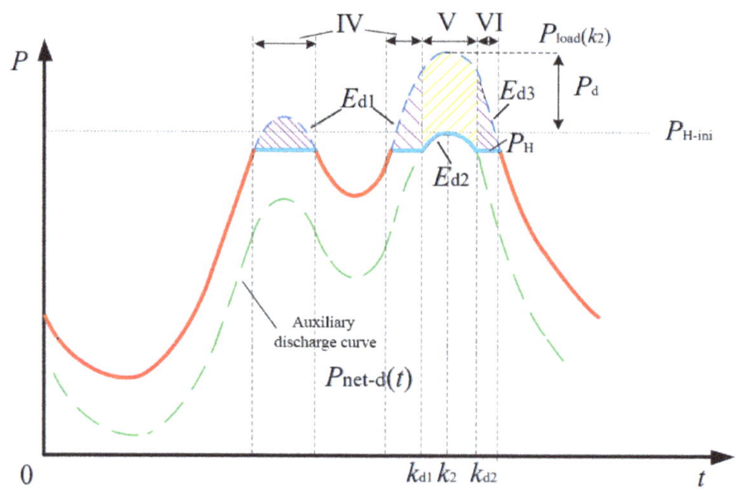

Figure 7. The iterative diagram for selecting the charging capacity of a battery pack.

The discharge capacity of the battery in the above three domains is E_{d1}, E_{d2} and E_{d3}, accordingly, and can be calculated as:

$$\begin{cases} E_{d1} = \int_0^{k_{d1}} (P_{load}(t) - P_{load}(k_{d1}))dt \\ E_{d2} = \int_{k_{d1}}^{k_{d2}} P_d dt \\ E_{d3} = \int_{k_{d2}}^{T} (P_{load}(t) - P_{load}(k_{d2}))dt \end{cases} \quad (34)$$

Total Discharge Energy:

$$E_d = E_{d1} + E_{d2} + E_{d3} \quad (35)$$

When increasing E_d in order to fully utilize the maximum power load, it is necessary to iterate the power sharing points of k_{d1} and k_{d2}, left and right, respectively, to dynamically adjust the upper limit value of the load of P_H. The iterative process is

$$\begin{cases} k_{d1} = k_2 - k \\ k = k + 1 \\ P_{load}(k_{d2}) = P_{load}(k_{d1}) \end{cases} \quad (36)$$

If $E_d < E_{d\max}$, it is still running; if we continue the iteration until $E_d > E_{d\max}$, it stops. By defining the power separation points of k_{d1} and k_{d2} at this time, the dynamically adjusted upper limit value of the load of P_H can be obtained as

$$P_H = \begin{cases} P_{load}(k_{d1}) - P_d \\ P_{load}(t) - P_d \end{cases} \quad (37)$$

Therefore, charging power can be expressed by the expression:

$$P_{bat}(t) = P_{load}(t) - P_H \quad (38)$$

When the IBES power is low, the peak and trough parts can be "filled"; when the IBES power is large, the peaks and troughs are converted into a "circular ring" in (k_{c1}, k_{c2}) and (k_{d1}, k_{d2}) intervals and "filled" in the remaining parts.

To program the IBES automatic control system, the algorithm shown in Figure 8 was synthesized. In the above algorithm, there are two iterative methods for dynamically adjusting the boundary value of the charging and discharging load [51] at the charging and discharging stage, based on the relationship between the initial value of the load and discharge and the maximum charging and discharging capacity of the load. Four charging and discharging control modes were proposed, as shown in Figure 9.

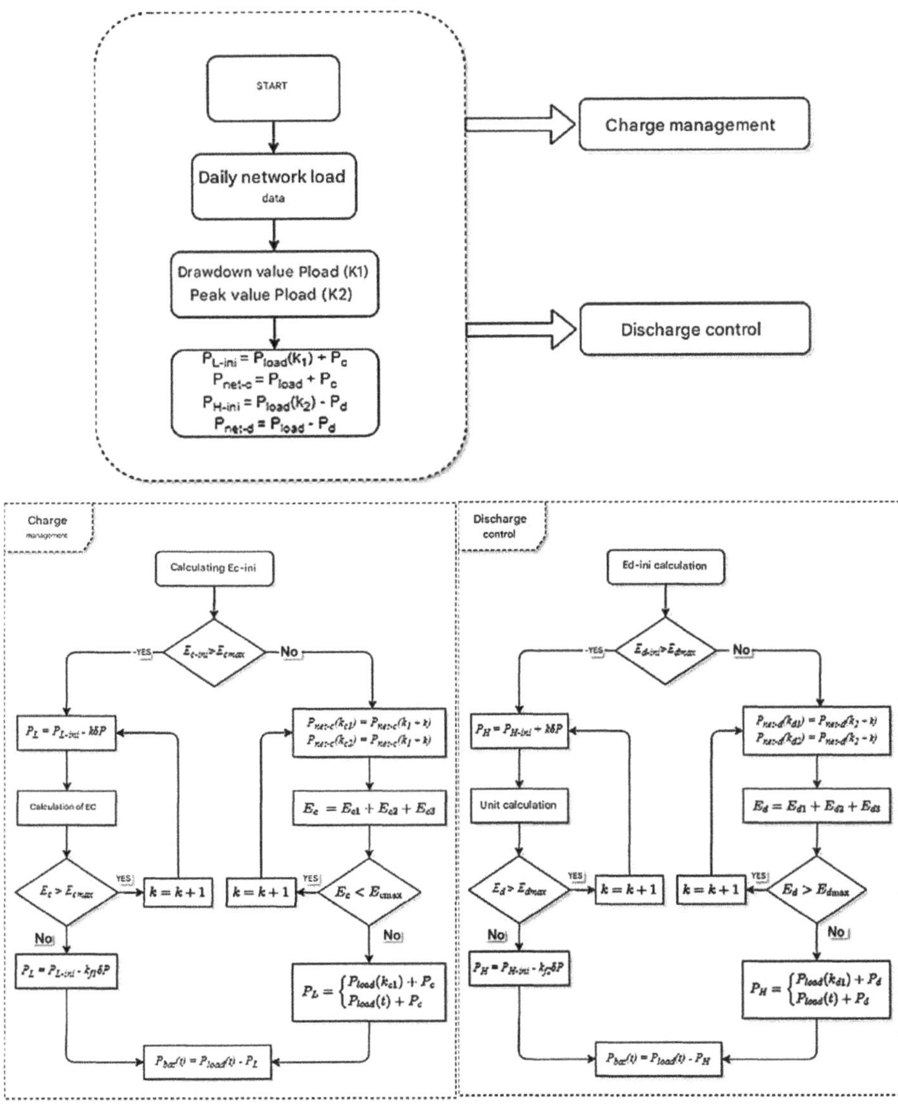

Figure 8. The charge–discharge algorithm for IBES automatic control system programming.

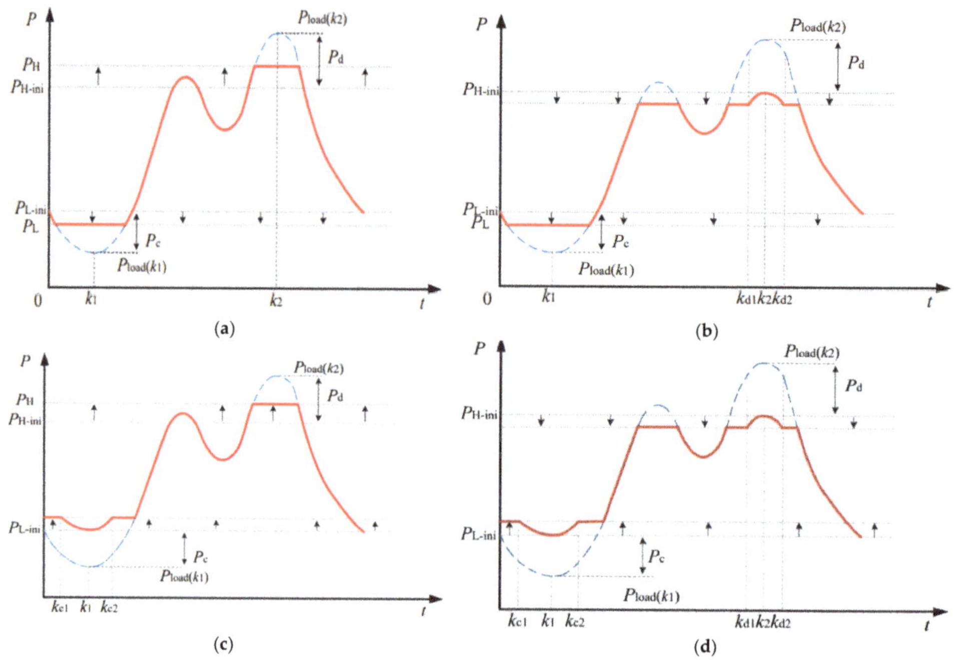

Figure 9. The temporary diagram of load power compensation using IBES of four types of charging/discharging modes: (**a**) mode 1, (**b**) mode 2, (**c**) mode 3, (**d**) mode 4.

Mode 1: As shown in Figure 9, when $E_c > E_{c\max}$ and $E_d > E_{d\max}$, the upper limit of the *PH* load needs to be iterated up and the lower bound of the *PL* load needs to be iterated down. This operating mode is suitable for scenarios with low IBES power where the load curve is stable at the peak and trough points.

Mode 2: As shown in Figure 9b, when $E_c > E_{c\max}$ and $E_d \leq E_{d\max}$, both the upper bounds of the *PH* load and the lower bound of the *PL* load need to be iterated down. This mode of operation is suitable for scenarios with high initial battery capacity in IBES. Due to the low $E_{c\max}$, the lower limit of the load can be shifted down to reduce the charging capacity. The discharge occurs at rated power, while other parts will be reduced to "flat-top waves".

Mode 3: As shown in Figure 9c, when $E_c \leq E_{c\max}$ and $E_d > E_{d\max}$, the upper limit of the *PH* load needs to be iterated up, and the lower limit of the *PL* load needs to be iterated up. This mode is suitable for high battery scenarios of $SoC_{\min}$. At this point, the battery cannot fully release the stored energy at the peak, so it is necessary to perform an upward iteration of the PH.

Mode 4: As shown in Figure 9d, when $E_c \leq E_{c\max}$ and $E_d \leq E_{d\max}$, the upper limit of the *PH* load needs to be iterated down, and the lower limit of the *PL* load needs to be iterated up. This mode is suitable for scenarios with high battery capacity and low SoC_0 capacity. In this way, it is possible to fully charge the IBES during the decline and release of the entire energy stored in the IBES at the peak.

4. Experimental Research and Analysis

As shown in Figure 10, using the example of the daily load curve of the consumption of an experimental charging station for charging an electric vehicle for a daily time interval.

At the same time, the maximum, minimum and average load values are 51.8, 41.7 and 46.9 kW, respectively.

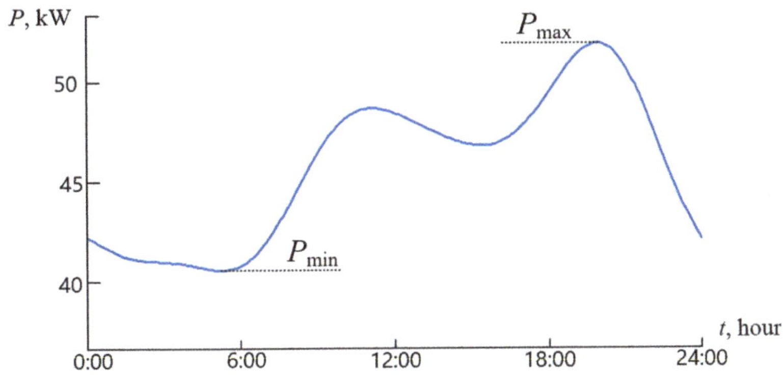

Figure 10. The daily load graph of the case under consideration.

In Table 3, E_{max} denotes the energy capacity of the storage system; P_c and P_d correspond to the maximum charging and discharging power limits introduced in Equation (5). $P_c \equiv P_c^{max}$ and $P_d \equiv P_d^{max}$, and E_0 are the initial energy content of the battery.

Table 3. The diagram of the energy storage configuration for four modes of operation.

Estimates	Mode 1	Mode 2	Mode 3	Mode 4
E_{max}, MWh	100	100	100	200
Pc, MW	20	20	15	20
Pd, MW	40	20	40	40
SOC, Range	0.1–0.9	0.1–0.9	0.1–0.9	0.1–0.9
E_0, MWh	40	10	10	20

Figure 11 shows the waveform for simulating battery charging and discharging control modes. Both dynamically adjustable upper and lower load boundary lines are horizontal lines. The basic waveform shown in Figure 9a corresponds to that in Figure 11. Table 2 presents the characteristics of the indicators for assessing the compensation of load peaks and consumption dips in comparison with the traditional constant power method.

To visually assess the effectiveness of the proposed method, Figure 12 shows the time power plots for mode 1. The graph allows one to directly compare the initial load profile ($P_{load}(t)$), the network power profile using the traditional constant power method, and the profile obtained using the developed adaptive algorithm and $P_L(t)$ during the day.

In Figure 12, the gray area shows the initial load profile. The dashed black line represents the operation of the system with the traditional constant power method. The solid blue line shows the network power profile using the proposed adaptive algorithm. The red and green dashed lines illustrate the dynamic adjustment of the top (P_H) and bottom (P_L) load limits, respectively. Visually, it is noticeable that the proposed method provides a significantly better smoothing of peaks and the filling of dips. Figure 12 demonstrates direct, visual evidence of the superiority of the new algorithm over the traditional approach. The figure shows how dynamic boundaries "trim" peaks and "raise" troughs. At the same time, the work of dynamic boundaries is visualized in real time, which is adapted to the shape of the load, in contrast to the static line of the traditional method.

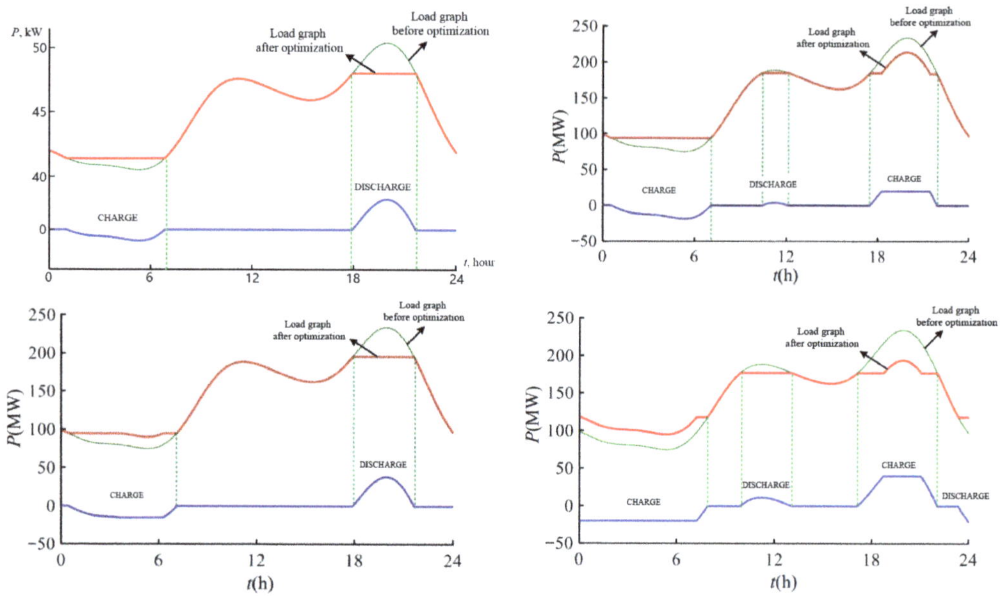

Figure 11. Results of simulation of charging/discharging modes.

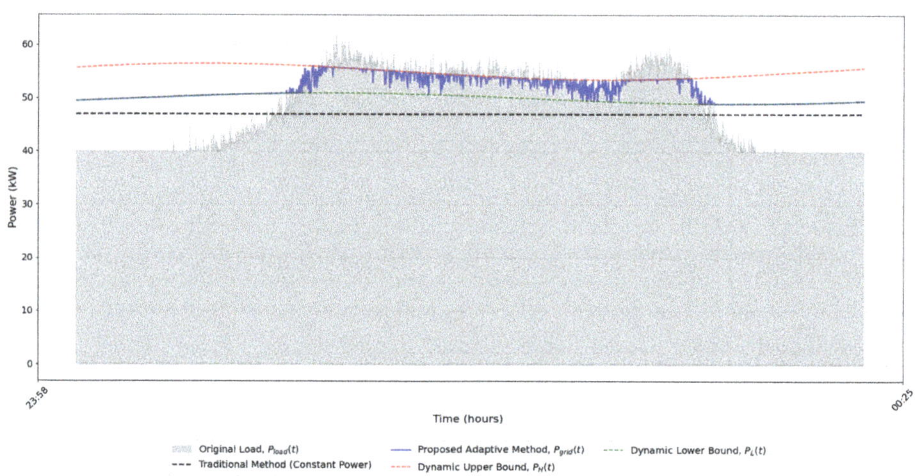

Figure 12. Comparative analysis of daily power profiles for mode 1.

The operation of the control algorithm is directly related to the state of the battery [52]. Figure 13 shows the dynamics of the IBES state of charge (SOC) for the same time interval as in Figure 12. The graph clearly demonstrates how energy is stored in the battery during periods of low load (when P_{grid} is close to P_L) and released to the grid during peak periods (when P_{grid} is limited by P_H).

Horizontal dotted lines indicate the permissible operating range of the SOC (20–90%). Charge cycles (SOC increase) in night and day hours with low power consumption and discharge cycles (SOC decrease) to compensate for morning and evening load peaks are clearly visible [53]. The algorithm ensures efficient use of IBES capacity within the set limits. Figure 13 demonstrates energy balance of the system and shows that the algorithm not only smooths the power but also does so while remaining within the safe and operational constraints of IBES. Therefore, it is emphasized that the adaptive strategy intelligently manages the energy buffer, preventing it from being overcharged or deeply discharged, which is critical for the longevity of the system [54].

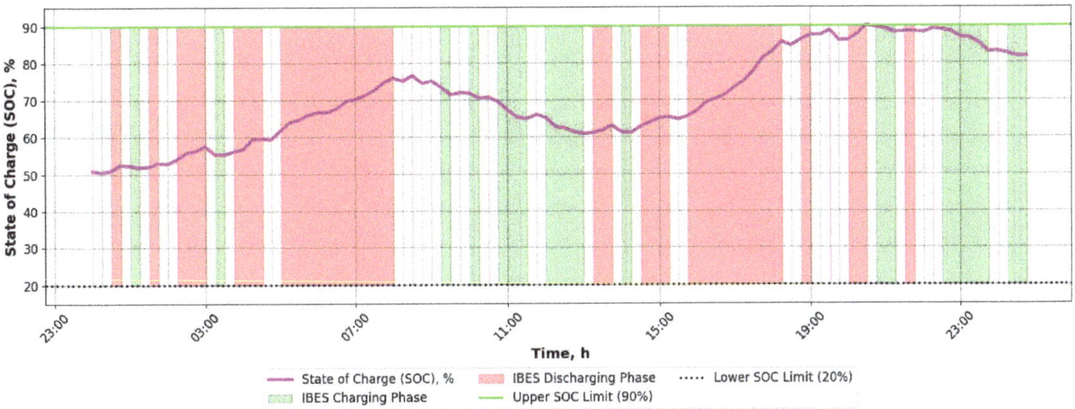

Figure 13. Dynamics of the state of charge (SOC) of the battery during the day when operating according to the proposed algorithm (Mode 1).

Both methods have specific features to compensate for load peaks and consumption dips. However, compared to the four deflection indicators, peak trough difference, a coefficient of peak trough difference and a peak trough coefficient in the charge and discharge mode, the proposed direct control strategy is significantly superior to the traditional constant power method, thus having better peak performance in the ability to compensate for load peaks and consumption dips (Table 4).

Table 4. Comparison of indicators in mode 1.

Estimates	Before Optimization	Power Control (Electricity Meter)	Suggested Method
D	50.7866	43.5259	42.8439
ΔP_{load}	159.1481	140.2782	107.1481
α	0.6798	0.6376	0.5467
β	0.3202	0.3624	0.4533

As shown in Figure 7, in mode 2, the upper limit of the PH load needs to be iterated down, and the lower bound of the PL load needs to be iterated down. The method of controlling the charge is the same as in mode 1 during load drop. However, at the peak end of the load, according to power constraints and iterative methods, there is a partially curved arc segment at the upper limit of the load, which will be discharged at rated power, and the rest will be flat-top waves. This feature is fully consistent with the basic waveform shown in Figure 7. Table 5 shows the characteristics of the peak smoothing and trough fill evaluation values compared to the traditional constant power method. It can be seen that the proposed strategy of direct power charging and discharging control can achieve less variance, peak trough difference, and a peak trough difference rate, but the peak trough coefficient is slightly higher. Therefore, the effect of peak smoothing and trough filling in mode 2 is still better than the traditional constant power method.

Table 5. Comparison of indicators in mode 2.

Estimates	Before Optimization	Power Control (Electricity Meter)	Suggested Method
D	50.7866	42.1240	42.0056
ΔP_{load}	159.1481	132.3654	120.4281
α	0.6798	0.6182	0.5624
β	0.3202	0.3818	0.4376

As shown in Figure 9c, in mode 3, the upper bound of the PH load must be iterated up, and the lower bound of the PL load must be iterated up. At this point, the peak load discharge management method is the same as in mode 1. When the load drops, based on power constraints and iterative methods, the lower boundary line is iteratively adjusted upwards. Therefore, at the lower limit of the load, there is a partially curved arc section that will be charged at rated power, and the rest will be flat-top waves and charged in the same way as in modes 1 and 2. Table 6 shows that the proposed strategy of direct power charge and discharge control can provide less dispersion, peak trough difference, and peak trough difference compared to the traditional constant power method. However, the peak trough ratio is slightly higher, so the effect of peak smoothing and trough filling in mode 3 is still better than the traditional constant power method.

Table 6. Comparison of indicators in mode 3.

Estimates	Before Optimization	Power Control (Electricity Meter)	Suggested Method
D	50.7866	41.9054	41.1882
ΔP_{load}	159.1481	134.3060	105.7481
α	0.6798	0.6084	0.5403
β	0.3202	0.3916	0.4597

As shown in Figure 9d, in mode 4, the upper bound of the PH load must be iterated down, and the lower bound of the PL load must be iterated up. The charging method in this mode in the minimum load area is completely similar to mode 3, and the discharge method in the peak load area is completely similar to mode 2. Table 7 shows that the proposed strategy of direct power charge and discharge control has less variance in load fluctuations compared to the traditional constant power method, indicating that this method is still superior to the traditional constant power method in convergence peaks and trough fills of Mode 4.

Table 7. Comparison of indicators in mode 4.

Estimates	Before Optimization	Power Control (Electricity Meter)	Suggested Method
D	50.7866	34.5819	33.9679
ΔP_{load}	159.1481	99.1481	99.1481
α	0.6798	0.5107	0.5107
β	0.3202	0.4893	0.4893

For a comprehensive comparison of the effectiveness of the management strategy proposed across all regimes, Figure 14 shows a summary bar chart showing the key indicator, i.e., network power variance (D). Although the performance comparison in this study is made relatively conventional constant power control, this reference baseline is relevant because it represents the default strategy currently implemented in industrial charging stations and thus reflects the real operational practice. More complex predictive and rule-based controllers are not used in quarry-grid environments due to communication restrictions and absence of reliable stochastic forecasting. The proposed approach is therefore positioned not only as theoretically novel, but as immediately deployable under current infrastructure limitations. The graph compares the variance values for the initial load profile, the system with traditional constant power management, and the system with the proposed adaptive algorithm for all four IBES modes of operation.

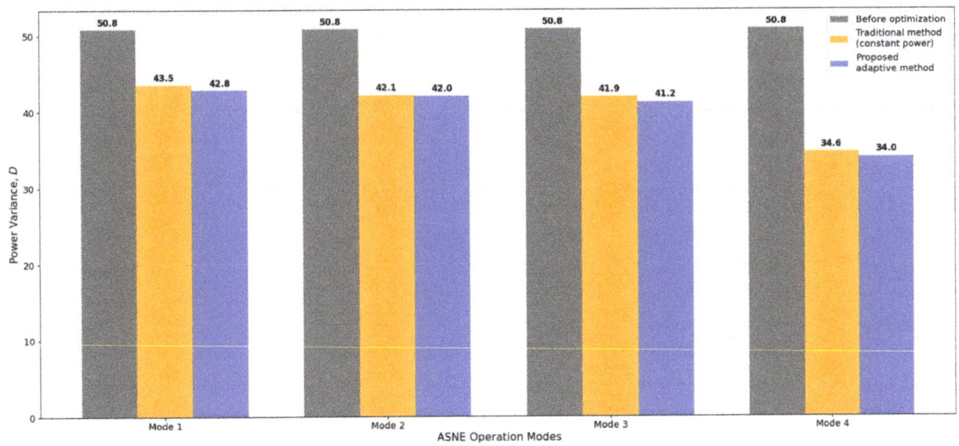

Figure 14. Comparative analysis of network power dispersion for different control methods and IBES operating modes.

In Figure 14, the columns clearly demonstrate that the proposed adaptive algorithm (dark blue) provides the least variance and, therefore, the best smoothing of the load profile in all four modes compared to the traditional method (orange) and the original profile (gray). The greatest relative efficiency is observed in Mode 4, where the capabilities of IBES are used to the fullest. Therefore, a summarized, quantitative picture of the effectiveness of the new method under various initial conditions (capacity, power) was obtained. The universality and robustness of the proposed algorithm is visually confirmed. It performs better in one scenario and consistently delivers superior performance in different system configurations.

5. Conclusions

In this paper, a new strategy for direct charge and discharge control of the system of integrated battery energy storage (IBES) based on dynamic iterative adjustment of load boundaries is proposed and investigated. The mathematical foundation of the method is the formalization of the problem of minimizing the dispersion of network power in the presence of nonlinear constraints related to the power and state of charge (SOC) of the battery. The developed adaptive algorithm demonstrates high efficiency for smoothing peaks and filling load dips in the power grids of industrial charging stations.

The results of theoretical analysis, numerical modeling, and experimental verification allow us to formulate the following main conclusions:

1. Mathematical efficiency and robustness. The proposed iterative algorithm with dynamic boundaries of $P_H(t)$ and $P_L(t)$ provides a steady reduction in network power dispersion by 15–30% compared to the traditional constant-power control method.
2. Optimal control and increased reliability. Dynamic adjustment of the load limits allows the charge and discharge energy to be optimally distributed in strict accordance with the current capacitive availability of the battery. This not only maximizes the utilization of IBES capacitance but also extends its lifespan by actively limiting the depth and number of charge–discharge cycles, thereby improving the overall reliability of the system.

3. Practical applicability. The algorithm is computationally simple, does not require complex predictive models, and can be implemented on local controllers with limited resources. This makes the proposed strategy particularly attractive for use at remote and isolated industrial sites, such as quarry plants.

Despite its advantages, several limitations should be acknowledged for realistic deployment. First, under tight SOC boundaries, the feasible region for boundary updates (P_H, P_L) becomes narrow, which may reduce smoothing performance in long-duration peak clusters. Second, the current implementation assumes observed rather than forecasted truck arrivals; therefore, large uncertainty in charging events can increase iteration count and delay convergence. Finally, although the iterative algorithm remains computationally lightweight, scaling to fleets with tens of chargers may require controller hardware with sufficient processing margin to maintain the 1 s update cycle. These aspects do not diminish the method's applicability but highlight conditions under which performance may degrade and where further research could be directed.

In terms of scalability, the proposed control approach can be extended to multi-charger configurations by assigning a shared IBES pool and applying the boundary update procedure independently for each charging port. Since the algorithm relies only on real-time measurements of $P_{load}(t)$, $P_{grid}(t)$ and $SOC(t)$, computational complexity grows linearly with the number of chargers, while the control step of $\Delta t = 1$ s remains sufficient for practical deployment. Increasing IBES capacity improves peak-shaving capability proportionally, as a larger energy buffer widens feasible ranges of $P_H(t)$ and $P_L(t)$, reducing boundary saturation and iteration count.

From an engineering perspective, the controller operates with modest communication requirements (10 Hz of telemetry exchange already validated in experiments) and reacts within one control cycle without the need for long-horizon forecasting. The integration into systems of quarry energy management may be achieved through standard CAN/MODBUS protocols, allowing the IBES controller to function as a supervisory layer above existing dispatch logic. These aspects support the applicability of the method to large-scale multi-vehicle charging stations and industrial operation scenarios.

Prospects for further research are seen in the following areas: an integration of stochastic load forecasting models for the implementation of predictive control, an extension of the mathematical model for the control of hybrid energy storage systems (IBES + supercapacitors), the development of multi-criteria optimization algorithms that simultaneously consider technical and economic indicators.

Author Contributions: Conceptualization, B.V.M. and N.V.M.; methodology, V.A.G. and Y.I.K.; software, E.E.K.; validation, A.Y.D. and A.V.P.; formal analysis, A.Y.D. and A.V.P.; investigation, A.Y.D. and A.V.P.; resources, E.E.K.; data curation, V.A.G. and Y.I.K.; writing—original drafting, B.V.M. and N.V.M.; writing—review and editing, V.A.G. and Y.I.K.; visualization, E.E.K. All authors have read and agreed to the published version of the manuscript.

Funding: This research received no external funding.

Data Availability Statement: The original contributions presented in this study are included in the article. Further inquiries can be directed to the corresponding author.

Conflicts of Interest: The authors declare no conflicts of interest.

References

1. Zahedmanesh, A.; Muttaqi, K.M.; Sutanto, D. A Sequential Decision-Making Process for Optimal Techno-Economic Operation of a Grid Connected Electrical Traction Substation Integrated with Solar PV and IBES. *IEEE Trans. Ind. Electron.* **2021**, *68*, 1353–1364. [CrossRef]
2. Nan, X.; Zhang, G.; Liu, W. Effects of typical energy storage systems participating in power grid peak-shaving on economy of power market: From multiple perspectives. *Therm. Power Gener.* **2019**, *48*, 13–21.
3. Liao, S.; Cheng, C.; Cai, H.; Cai, J.; Wu, D. Improved algorithm of adjusting discharge peak by thermal power plants. *Autom. Electr. Power Syst.* **2006**, *30*, 89–93.
4. Zhang, S.; Yan, M. Systematic planning and optimization for GAS turbine plants in Shanghai power system. *Power Syst. Technol.* **1996**, *20*, 27–32.
5. Wang, R.; Wang, J.; Zhang, H.; Bai, X. A cost analysis and practical compensation method for hydropower units peaking service. *Autom. Electr. Power Syst.* **2011**, *35*, 41–46.
6. Nguyen, T.A.; Copp, D.A.; Byrne, R.H.; Chalamala, B.R. Market Evaluation of Energy Storage Systems Incorporating Technology Specific Nonlinear Models. *IEEE Trans. Power Syst.* **2019**, *34*, 3706–3715. [CrossRef]
7. Matienko, O.I.; Kukartsev, V.V.; Antamoshkin, O.A.; Karlina, Y.I. Mathematical Model for the Study of Energy Storage Cycling in Electric Rail Transport. *World Electr. Veh. J.* **2025**, *16*, 357. [CrossRef]
8. Kaldellis, J.K.; Kapsali, M.; Kavadias, K.A. Energy balance analysis of wind-based pumped hydro storage systems in remote island electrical networks. *Appl. Energy* **2010**, *87*, 2427–2437. [CrossRef]
9. Yan, T.; Qu, Z.; Hui, D.; Liu, B.; Hu, J.; Jia, P. Economic analysis of the virtual power plants with large-scale battery energy storage systems. *Autom. Electr. Power Syst.* **2014**, *38*, 98–104.
10. Mohamed, A.A.; Best, R.J.; Liu, X.; Morrow, D.J. A Comprehensive Robust Techno-Economic Analysis and Sizing Tool for the Small-Scale PV and IBES. *IEEE Trans. Energy Convers.* **2022**, *37*, 560–572. [CrossRef]
11. Setlhaolo, D.; Xia, X. Optimal scheduling of household appliances with a battery storage system and coordination. *Energy Build.* **2015**, *94*, 61–70. [CrossRef]
12. Pryalukhin, A.F.; Daus, Y.V.; Konyukhov, V.Y.; Oparina, T.A.; Dubrovin, R.G. Simulation Modeling of Energy Efficiency of Electric Dump Truck Use Depending on the Operating Cycle. *World Electr. Veh. J.* **2025**, *16*, 217. [CrossRef]
13. Sigrist, L.; Lobato, E.; Rouco, L. Energy storage systems providing primary reserve and peak shaving in small isolated power systems: An economic assessment. *Int. J. Electr. Power* **2013**, *53*, 675–683. [CrossRef]
14. Al-Saffar, M.; Musilek, P. Reinforcement Learning-Based Distributed IBES Management for Mitigating Overvoltage Issues in Systems With High PV Penetration. *IEEE Trans. Smart Grid* **2020**, *11*, 2980–2994. [CrossRef]
15. Zhang, S.; Mishra, Y.; Ledwich, G.; Xue, Y. The operating schedule for battery energy storage companies in electricity market. *J. Mod. Power Syst. Clean. Energy* **2013**, *1*, 275–284. [CrossRef]
16. Garttan, G.; Alahakoon, S.; Emami, K.; Jayasinghe, S.G. Battery Energy Storage Systems: Energy Market Review, Challenges, and Opportunities in Frequency Control Ancillary Services. *Energies* **2025**, *18*, 4174. [CrossRef]
17. Chen, P.; Cui, W.; Shang, J.; Xu, B.; Li, C.; Lun, D. Control Strategy of Multiple Battery Energy Storage Stations for Power Grid Peak Shaving. *Appl. Sci.* **2025**, *15*, 8656. [CrossRef]
18. Eghtedarpour, N.; Farjah, E. Distributed charge/discharge control of energy storages in a micro-grid. *IET Renew. Power Gener.* **2014**, *8*, 498–506. [CrossRef]
19. Pogrebnoy, A.V.; Efremenkov, E.A.; Valuev, D.V.; Boltrushevich, A.E. Improving the Reliability of Current Collectors in Electric Vehicles. *Mathematics* **2025**, *13*, 2022. [CrossRef]
20. Kucevic, D.; Semmelmann, L.; Collath, N.; Jossen, A.; Hesse, H. Peak Shaving with Battery Energy Storage Systems in Distribution Grids: A Novel Approach to Reduce Local and Global Peak Loads. *Electricity* **2021**, *2*, 575–588. [CrossRef]
21. Nasir, N.N.; Hussin, S.M.; Hassan, M.Y.; Rosmin, N.; Md Rasid, M. Battery Energy Storage System in Peak Shaving Application. *Appl. Model. Simul.* **2018**, *2*, 84–88.
22. Wu, J.; Chen, Y.; Zhou, J.; Jiang, C.; Liu, W. Multi-timescale optimal control strategy for energy storage systems. *Front. Energy Res.* **2023**, *11*, 1240764. [CrossRef]
23. Hemmati, R.; Azizi, N. Advanced control strategy on battery energy storage system for bidirectional power control and stability improvement. *Appl. Energy* **2017**, *219*, 189–201.
24. Nussipali, R.; Konyukhov, V.Y.; Oparina, T.A.; Romanova, V.V.; Kononenko, R.V. Combined Power Generating Complex and Energy Storage System. *Electricity* **2024**, *5*, 931–946. [CrossRef]
25. Tang, Q.; Hu, M.; Bian, Y.; Wang, Y.; Lei, Z.; Peng, X.; Li, K. Optimal energy efficiency control framework for distributed energy-storage-based mining truck system. *Appl. Energy* **2024**, *350*, 121367.
26. Bao, H.; Knights, P.; Kizil, M.; Nehring, M. Energy Consumption and Battery Size of Battery Trolley Mining Truck Fleets. *Energies* **2024**, *17*, 1494. [CrossRef]

27. Shi, Y.; Xu, B.; Wang, D.; Zhang, B. Using Battery Storage for Peak Shaving and Frequency Regulation: Joint Optimization for Superlinear Gains. *IEEE Trans. Power Syst.* **2017**, *32*, 4469–4479.
28. Langenmayr, U.; Wang, W.; Jochem, P. Peak Demand is Shaved for Photovoltaic Battery Systems: Central Planner—Decentral Operator Approach. *Appl. Energy* **2020**, *266*, 114723.
29. Kirli, D.; Kiprakis, A. Techno-economic potential of battery energy storage systems in smart grids. *IET J. Energy Storage* **2020**, *1*, 103–112.
30. Martyushev, N.V.; Malozyomov, B.V.; Demin, A.Y.; Pogrebnoy, A.V.; Efremenkov, E.A.; Valuev, D.V.; Boltrushevich, A.E. Modeling the Reliability of an Electric Car Battery While Changing Its Charging and Discharge Characteristics. *Mathematics* **2025**, *13*, 1832. [CrossRef]
31. Mazumdar, J. All electric operation of ultraclass mining haultrucks. In Proceedings of the Conference Record—IAS Annual Meeting, Lake Buena Vista, FL, USA, 6–11 October 2013; pp. 1–5.
32. Khekert, E.V.; Chetverikova, V.V.; Golik, V.I.; Tynchenko, V.S. Improving the Reliability of the Protection of Electric Transport Networks. *World Electr. Veh. J.* **2025**, *16*, 477. [CrossRef]
33. Feng, Y.; Dong, Z.; Yang, J. Performance modeling and cost-benefit analysis of hybrid electric mining trucks. In Proceedings of the 12th IEEE/ASME International Conference on Mechatronic and Embedded Systems and Applications (MESA), Auckland, New Zealand, 29–31 August 2016; IEEE: Piscataway, NJ, USA, 2016; Volume 11, pp. 1–6.
34. Zou, Y.; Hu, X.; Ma, H.; Li, S. Combined State of Charge and State of Health estimation over lithium-ion battery cell cycle lifespan for electric vehicles. *J. Power Sources* **2016**, *273*, 793–803. [CrossRef]
35. Sarybayev, Y.Y.; Balgayev, D.Y.; Tkachenko, D.Y. Reliability-Oriented Modeling of Bellows Compensators: A Comparative PDE-Based Study Using Finite Difference and Finite Element Methods. *Mathematics* **2025**, *13*, 3452. [CrossRef]
36. Luo, X.; Wang, J.; Dooner, M.; Clarke, J. Overview of current development in electrical energy storage technologies and the application potential in power system operation. *Appl. Energy* **2015**, *137*, 511–536. [CrossRef]
37. Carlo, F.D. *Reliability and Maintainability in Operations Management*; Massimiliano, S., Ed.; InTech: London, UK, 2013.
38. Amy, H. What Is Equipment Reliability and How Do You Improve It? Available online: https://nonstopreliability.com/equipment-reliability/ (accessed on 15 October 2020).
39. Valuev, D.V.; Boltrushevich, A.E. Mathematical Modeling of Signals for Weight Control of Vehicles Using Seismic Sensors. *Mathematics* **2025**, *13*, 2083. [CrossRef]
40. Norris, G. The True Cost of Unplanned Equipment Downtime. Available online: https://www.forconstructionpros.com/equipment-management/article/21104195/the-true-cost-of-unplanned-equipment-downtime (accessed on 3 December 2019).
41. Kumar, U. Reliability Analysis of Load-Haul-Dump Machines. Ph.D. Thesis, Lulea Tekniska Universitet, Lulea, Sweden, 1990.
42. Nazarychev, A.N.; Dyachenok, G.V.; Sychev, Y.A. A reliability study of the traction drive system in haul trucks based on failure analysis of their functional parts. *J. Min. Inst.* **2023**, *261*, 363–373.
43. Yelemessov, K.; Baskanbayeva, D.; Sabirova, L. Algorithmic Optimal Control of Screw Compressors for Energy-Efficient Operation in Smart Power Systems. *Algorithms* **2025**, *18*, 583. [CrossRef]
44. Collins, E.W. Safety Evaluation of Coal Mine Power Systems. In Proceedings of the Annual Reliability and Maintainability Symposium, Philadelphia, PA, USA, 27–29 January 1987; Sandia National Labs.: Albuquerque, NM, USA, 1987.
45. Ivanov, V.V.; Dzyurich, D.O. Justification of the technological scheme parameters for the development of flooded deposits of construction sand. *J. Min. Inst.* **2022**, *253*, 33–40. [CrossRef]
46. Roy, S.K.; Bhattacharyya, M.M.; Naikan, V.N. Maintainability and reliability analysis of a fleet of shovels. *Min. Technol. Trans. Inst. Min. Metall. Sect. A* **2001**, *110*, 163–171. [CrossRef]
47. Khekert, E.V.; Klyuev, R.V.; Antamoshkin, O.A.; Remezov, I.S. Battery Charging Simulation of a Passenger Electric Vehicle from a Traction Voltage Inverter with an Integrated Charger. *World Electr. Veh. J.* **2025**, *16*, 391. [CrossRef]
48. Abdollahpour, P.; Tabatabaee Moradi, S.S.; Leusheva, E.; Morenov, V. A Numerical Study on the Application of Stress Cage Technology. *Energies* **2022**, *15*, 5439. [CrossRef]
49. Coetzee, J.L. The role of NHPP models in the practical analysis of maintenance failure data. *Reliab. Eng. Syst. Saf.* **1997**, *56*, 161–168. [CrossRef]
50. Gabov, V.V.; Zadkov, D.A.; Pryaluhin, A.F.; Sadovsky, M.V.; Molchanov, V.V. Mining combine screw executive body design. *MIAB Min. Inf. Anal. Bull.* **2023**, *11*, 51–71.
51. Skamyin, A.N.; Dobush, I.V.; Gurevich, I.A. Influence of nonlinear load on the measurement of harmonic impedance of the power supply system. In Proceedings of the 2023 5th International Youth Conference on Radio Electronics, Electrical and Power Engineering, Moscow, Russia, 16–18 March 2023.
52. Hall, R.A.; Daneshmend, L.K. Reliability Modelling of Surface Mining Equipment: Data Gathering and Analysis Methodologies. *Int. J. Surf. Min.* **2003**, *17*, 139–155. [CrossRef]

53. Abramovich, B.N.; Bogdanov, I.A. Improving the efficiency of autonomous electrical complexes of oil and gas enterprises. *J. Min. Inst.* **2021**, *249*, 408–416. [CrossRef]
54. Kondratiev, V.V.; Dorofeev, E.M.; Kononenko, R.V.; Vit'kina, G.Y. Optimization of Energy Balance and Powertrain for Electric Mining Dump Trucks in Coal Mine Reclamation Operations. *World Electr. Veh. J.* **2025**, *16*, 601. [CrossRef]

mathematics

MDPI

Article

Surrogate Model-Based Optimization of a Dual-Shield Total Temperature Probe for Aero-Engine Applications

Xuetao Zhang [1], Yufang Wang [1], Qi Lei [2,*], Jian Zhao [1] and Yudi Ai [2]

1 Beijing Changcheng Institute of Metrology and Measurement, Beijing 100095, China; zhangxt002@avic.com (X.Z.); wangyf076@avic.com (Y.W.); zhaoj028@avic.com (J.Z.)
2 School of Automation, Central South University, Changsha 410006, China; 254612104@csu.edu.cn
* Correspondence: aydaydayd2003@163.com or leiqi@csu.edu.cn

Abstract: The design of high-precision total temperature probes for aero-engines is constrained by the massive computational cost of high-fidelity simulations. This paper overcomes this barrier by introducing a surrogate model-based optimization framework for a dual-shield probe. A computationally efficient data-driven framework is established, merging conjugate-heat-transfer Computational Fluid Dynamics (CFDs), a Support Vector Regression (SVR) model, and a Genetic Algorithm (GA), which collectively replace the traditional costly design loop. The surrogate model's exceptional predictive fidelity is confirmed, and this approach obtains improvement in measurement accuracy, successfully reducing the temperature deviation and meeting the stringent requirement. Finally, the demonstrated framework is geometry-agnostic, establishing a generalizable and cost-effective strategy for the rapid design of high-performance thermometric components in gas turbine systems.

Keywords: total temperature probe; surrogate model; support vector regression; genetic algorithm; optimization

MSC: 65K10; 68T05; 76F60; 90C59

1. Introduction

The total temperature probe is a crucial sensor in testing aero engines and high-temperature airflows. Its measurement accuracy directly affects the engine's performance evaluation and safety control [1,2]. Much research has been conducted on improving measurement accuracy and calibrating probes in aircraft engines [3,4]. In practical applications, the coupling between thermodynamics and fluid mechanics under complex flow conditions leads to significant errors in total temperature measurements, primarily radiation, conduction, and velocity errors [5]. Meanwhile, due to issues with radiative heat dissipation and the limited installation space for dedicated temperature sensors, it is impossible to eliminate errors solely by designing a special head structure. Therefore, during the design stage, it is necessary to optimize the probe's shape as much as possible to improve its accuracy and to calibrate its measurement accuracy before use [6,7]. However, the inherent errors (e.g., radiation, conduction, and velocity) of standard probes, as well as the uneven airflow distribution caused by limited installation space, can pose challenges to probe design and calibration.

A large number of experiments have been carried out to optimize and calibrate probes [8,9]. These experimental results provide an essential basis for studying the total temperature error. However, the experimental methods are time-consuming. Especially, some repetitive work and the high cost in extreme cases have led to difficulties in experimental research. Furthermore, the source causing the total temperature thermocouple error cannot be accurately calibrated through experiments [10]. Numerical simulation offers an efficient means to optimize probe performance and analyze error mechanisms [11]. It can reveal the influence patterns of flow field interference, heat conduction, and radiation through multiphysics field-coupling simulation [12,13]. Compared to theoretical methods, numerical simulations have fewer assumptions and a broader range of applications. Unlike experimental methods, they do not require standard probes to measure flow field temperature, making them more efficient and cost-effective. They can also provide more physical phenomena and values within the flow field.

In recent years, with the advancement of CFD and conjugate heat transfer methods, an increasing number of scholars have applied numerical simulation technology to conduct extensive research on total temperature probes. Villafañe et al. [14] from the Von Karman Institute of Fluid Dynamics used numerical simulation methods for conjugate heat transfer to analyze probe response and various sources of temperature errors. Matas et al. [15] employed thermal network simulation methods and numerical simulation approaches to simulate multipoint total temperature probes for compressors and also compared the effects of different Reynolds-Averaged Navier–Stokes turbulence models on numerical simulation temperature measurement deviations. Wang et al. [16] designed a new shielded total temperature probe for relatively low-temperature gas measurement; the probe's characteristics and various error sources were analyzed using the conjugate heat transfer simulation method.

The gas flow and temperature fields in the engine are complex. To obtain a relatively accurate temperature field, probes are usually installed at different positions. Due to differences in installation locations, different flow field conditions, and temperature ranges, it is difficult for universal probes to achieve high-precision measurements in all situations. Therefore, it is usually necessary to separately design the structural parameters of probes for different working conditions and conduct calibration tests, which involves a significant amount of repetitive work. Wang et al. [7] combined numerical simulation with parametric design to streamline this process. The parametric method handles probe sizing, while numerical simulation conducts experimental analysis. This integration reduces repetitive design and calibration work, thereby enhancing the optimization of probe performance. Structural optimization represents a well-established approach for enhancing thermofluidic system performance, as similarly demonstrated in the optimization of porous cavity flow and heat transfer [17].

However, this method relies on high-precision CFD simulations, and each simulation takes considerable time. As the dimension of the optimization parameters increases, the computational cost rises significantly, making it challenging to meet the requirements for rapid iteration [18,19]. Meanwhile, this method relies on numerical simulation rather than experiments, making it difficult to fully utilize experimental data, such as wind tunnel calibration results, in the design and calibration of probes.

Surrogate modeling is a method for creating mathematical approximations of complex systems. Machine learning-based surrogate models can bypass computationally expensive simulations and have been widely adopted in CFD to accelerate design optimization and uncertainty quantification. They have been successfully applied across various domains, including turbulent modeling, flow control, and design optimization. Du et al. [20] proposed a deep learning-based surrogate for rapid prediction around complex 3D geometries, enabling efficient prediction of patient-specific aortic hemodynamics with a 100,000× speedup over traditional CFD simulations. Wilson et al. [21] built a surrogate model to predict wake-internal wind speeds from CFD data, achieving accurate interpolation of 3D wake velocities and extrapolation to novel wind speeds with low error, and Elkarii et al. [22] developed one for predicting pressure drop in slurry flow, proposing a new friction factor correlation based on 525 CFD data points with over 85% prediction accuracy. These methods are typically trained on data from high-fidelity numerical models, such as CFD. They can accurately predict outcomes with significantly less computational effort than the original simulations, making them an effective solution for scenarios requiring rapid analysis.

In the specific context of temperature measurement and sensor design, several studies demonstrate the potential of surrogate modeling. For instance, Jeon et al. [23] developed a Deep-Neural-Network-based surrogate model to optimize gas detector layouts, while Morozova et al. [24] created a CFD-driven surrogate model to predict flow parameters in mechanically ventilated rooms. These successful applications provide strong precedents and confidence for the present study to employ an SVR surrogate model to optimize total temperature probes.

In the design and optimization of instrumentation and precision sensors, machine learning surrogate models have demonstrated significant advantages for high-end equipment. For instance, Zhu et al. [25] applied an improved Back Propagation Neural Network (BPNN) and a genetic algorithm to optimize 11 thermal design parameters of a space telescope. Similarly, Zhang et al. [26] built a CatBoost surrogate to predict motor efficiency and torque for an aerospace system, and coupled it with the Non-dominated Sorting Genetic Algorithm-III algorithm to optimize 71 structural parameters, improving performance while reducing computational overhead. In microelectronic packaging, Shan et al. [27] used a Kriging surrogate model to rapidly evaluate how nozzle and backflow chamber structures affect jetting velocity and volume, and validated the optimized design experimentally via multi-objective genetic algorithm optimization.

To apply the surrogate model's predictive ability to the design of structural parameters, a powerful optimization method must work in conjunction with it. For such engineering optimization problems characterized by multivariate, nonlinear, and computationally expensive objective functions, population-based global optimization algorithms, such as GA, have been proven to be an ideal choice. Zhu et al. [25] used a Genetic Algorithm to optimize the parameters of their improved BP neural network surrogate model and to find the optimal thermal design parameters for a space telescope. Zhang et al. [26] employed the Non-dominated Sorting Genetic Algorithm-III algorithm, an advanced multi-objective Genetic Algorithm, to achieve rapid multi-objective optimization of 71 structural parameters for a complex electromechanical system. Shan et al. [27] applied a bi-objective Genetic Algorithm to concurrently optimize the dispensing velocity and the dispensed volume in their surrogate model-based study of a jetting system. Li et al. [28] utilized a Multi-Objective Genetic Algorithm to optimize the heat dissipation performance of an air-cooling battery pack based on a Kriging surrogate model. Gu et al. [29] adopted the Non-dominated Sorting Genetic Algorithm-II algorithm to solve the computationally expensive multi-objective optimization problem of a high-speed permanent magnet synchronous machine, leveraging surrogate models to reduce the FEM calculation burden. These algorithms can effectively avoid local optima and operate without gradient information, enabling them to collaborate efficiently with the surrogate model to jointly address challenges in probe optimization.

The shielded total temperature probe is typically used to measure the total temperature of high-temperature, high-speed gas flows, particularly to determine the exhaust temperature of aeroengine tail nozzles [5,30]. The key to improving the accuracy of flow field temperature measurement by probes lies in stopping the flow field. The probe's shielding cover plays an important role [31]. Different parameters of the shielding cover have varying degrees of hindrance to radiant heat transfer. Optimizing the design of the shielding cover is crucial for enhancing the temperature measurement accuracy of probes.

Despite the critical role of total temperature probes in aero-engine monitoring, their design optimization faces significant challenges. Traditional approaches, which rely heavily on experimental calibration or high-fidelity conjugate heat transfer CFD simulations, are often prohibitively time-consuming and computationally expensive for rapid design iterations. This is particularly true when dealing with multivariate geometric parameters under extreme operating conditions. Consequently, there is an urgent need for an efficient and automated optimization framework that can achieve high measurement accuracy for complex design spaces, significantly shorten the development cycle, and reduce computational costs. Therefore, this research aims to develop a design optimization framework based on surrogate models to address the limitations of traditional methods in the design of dual-shielded total temperature probes.

This study successfully developed and validated a surrogate model-based optimization framework for the design of a dual-shield total temperature probe. The main contributions are as follows:

(1) We have proposed an effective optimization methodology that integrates CFD, SVR surrogate model, and GA optimization. This framework effectively replaces traditional, expensive numerical simulation and experimental methods and can quickly achieve global optimization of probe structure parameters at relatively low computational cost.
(2) The framework delivers a substantial performance improvement. Through this approach, the probe's temperature measurement deviation was successfully reduced to within the acceptable range, demonstrating a significant improvement in accuracy. This optimized design meets the stringent accuracy requirement for critical aero-engine applications.
(3) The developed methodology is geometry-agnostic and extensible. The core workflow is not limited to the specific probe geometry presented here. It provides a cost-effective and generalizable framework for the optimized design of various temperature sensors and similar aerothermodynamic components across a wide range of operating conditions.

In Section 2, numerical simulations are used to generate a training dataset for a surrogate model. This enables the rapid prediction of temperature measurement errors under various structural parameters. In Section 3, a genetic algorithm based on a surrogate model is applied to efficiently find the optimal probe structure. This approach significantly reduces computational costs, enhances optimization efficiency, and provides a novel method for designing high-precision total temperature probes. Finally, the conclusion is given in Section 4.

2. Numerical Simulation Analysis

2.1. Research Object

The research object of this paper is the double-shielded water-cooled standard total temperature probe, whose structure comprises internal and external shields, a thermocouple wire, a flange, a water-cooled structure, and sealing components, as shown in Figure 1. The sensing part, indicated by the orange component in Figure 1, is made of precious metals, with the sensitive element being an iridium-rhodium alloy probe of 0.5 mm diameter. The support structure operating in the high-temperature airflow is divided into two sections: the portion supporting the sensing element is dry-fired and fabricated from precious metal, while the external section exposed to the high-temperature airflow is water-cooled and constructed from superalloy.

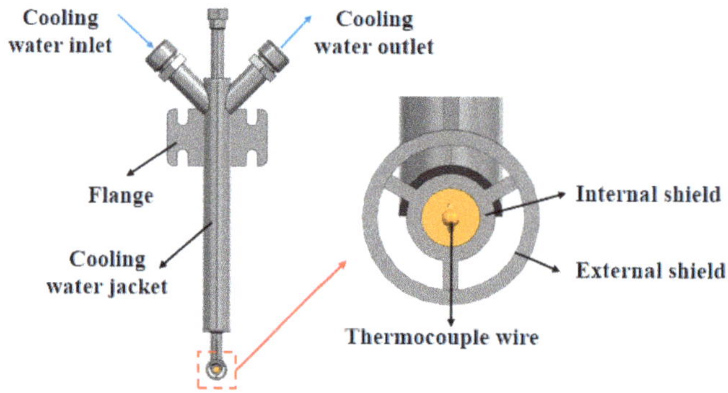

Figure 1. Total temperature probe structure.

According to the physical characteristics of the total temperature probe, the calculation domain is divided into three parts: the first part is the air fluid domain in contact with the sensing part of the probe, the second part is the cooling water domain involved in the total temperature probe cooling, and the third part is the solid domain of the total temperature probe structure. The structure diagram is shown in Figure 2, where the air fluid domain is consistent with the actual test environmental parameters of the total temperature probe.

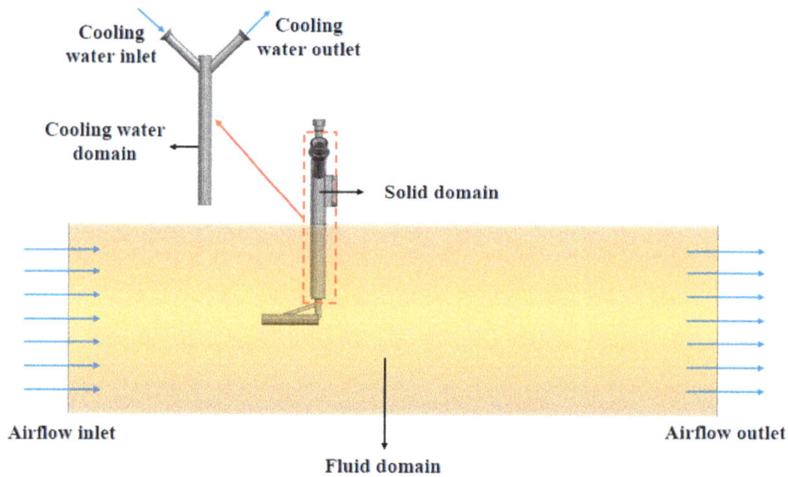

Figure 2. Simulation computational domain.

2.2. Numerical Method

Numerical simulations were performed using the commercial software ANSYS Fluent 2022R1. A conjugate heat transfer model was employed to solve the three-dimensional, steady-state Navier–Stokes equations using the Semi-Implicit Method for Pressure Linked Equations algorithm. For spatial discretization, the Least Squares Cell-Based scheme was utilized due to its accuracy and suitability for the polyhedral mesh employed in this study.

The Shear Stress Transport (SST) turbulence model was selected for its demonstrated accuracy in predicting flows with adverse pressure gradients and separation, which are anticipated around the probe geometry. This choice is supported by its proven capability in complex convective heat transfer simulations, as evidenced in the uncertainty and sensitivity analysis of [32]. The model maintains robustness throughout the boundary layer, making it particularly suited for the present conjugate heat transfer problem.

The fluid domain (air) was treated as an ideal gas to account for compressibility effects at the high Mach number (0.6) condition. The dynamic viscosity of air was calculated using Sutherland's formula, a standard semi-empirical relation for temperature-dependent viscosity [33]. The thermal conductivity was subsequently determined by the solver based on kinetic theory and its relation to the dynamic viscosity. Radiation heat transfer was modeled using the Discrete Ordinates model, which is capable of accounting for the participating media effects of the air within the computational domain.

Due to the complexity of the total temperature sensor model in this study, a polyhedral mesh was employed for grid generation. To ensure simulation accuracy, the mesh was refined around the total temperature probe, and boundary layers were generated on all fluid domain walls. The minimum grid size in the entire computational domain was set to one-tenth of the total temperature probe wire diameter, while the maximum grid size was set to one-fiftieth of the fluid domain diameter. Additionally, the entire computational region was refined with the total temperature probe as the center, using a growth rate of 1.05. Ultimately, the total number of grid cells was approximately 3 million, with about 200,000 in the solid domain, 300,000 in the cooling water fluid domain, and 2.5 million in the air fluid domain. The resulting mesh is shown in Figure 3.

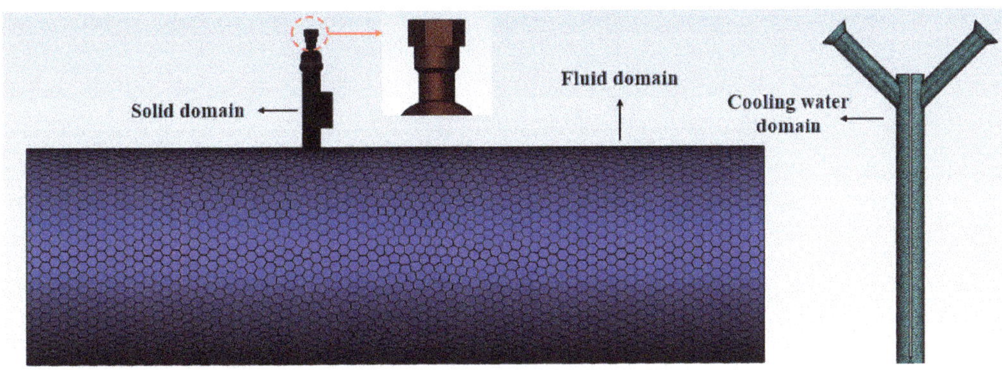

Figure 3. Computational domain mesh and distribution.

In the calculation conditions, the incoming flow Mach number within the domain is set to 0.6. The total temperature of the incoming flow is set to 2300 K, while the environmental pressure is maintained at 1.0 MPa. The cooling water flow rate is set to 1.0 kg/s. The heat transfer coefficient is 25 W/(m^2·K), and the ambient temperature is 293.15 K. The emissivity of the shield is specified as 0.85, the emissivity of the probe wire is 0.9, and the emissivity of the ball welding is also set to 0.9.

2.3. Error Analysis

The primary sources of temperature measurement error ΔT of the total temperature probe, are velocity error σ_w, thermal conductivity error σ_c and radiation error σ_r, among which the velocity error σ_w refers to the deviation between the total temperature T_0 of the air stream and the effective temperature T_g of the air stream, as shown in Equation (1):

$$\sigma_w = T_0 - T_g \tag{1}$$

Thermal conductivity error σ_c means that there is a temperature gradient between the measuring end and the support, and the heat will be conducted from the high temperature measuring end to the low temperature support, so that the indicated temperature of the sensor T_{jg} is lower than the effective temperature of the air flow T_g, and the difference between the two is called the thermal conductivity error, as shown in Equation (2):

$$\sigma_c = T_g - T_{jg} \tag{2}$$

Radiation error σ_r is only caused by the probe node and the surrounding solid wall exchanging heat through radiation, so that the temperature indicated by the sensor T_j deviates from the effective temperature of the airflow T_{jg}, and the deviation between the two is called radiation error, as shown in Equation (3) below:

$$\sigma_r = T_{jg} - T_j \tag{3}$$

The temperature measurement deviation of the total temperature probe can be expressed as the sum of velocity error, thermal conductivity error, and radiation error, or it can be expressed as the difference between the total temperature and the indicated temperature of the sensor when considering the air recovery characteristics, thermal conductivity characteristics, and radiation characteristics, namely:

$$\Delta T = \sigma_w + \sigma_c + \sigma_r = T_0 - T_j \tag{4}$$

In this paper, the deviation in temperature measurement of the total temperature probe is mainly analyzed. During the simulation, a fluid-solid conjugate heat transfer coupling is performed for the air-fluid domain, the total temperature probe solid domain, and the cooling-water fluid domain, which requires a radiation model. The simulated flow field velocity cloud images and the temperature cloud image are shown in Figures 4 and 5, respectively. The figure shows that when airflow flows from the inlet to the shield of the total temperature probe, the closer the shield is, the lower the flow rate, and the higher the static temperature. When the airflow reaches the vicinity of the ball welding, the flow rate decreases to 0, and the static temperature reaches its highest. At the same time, due to the effective heat transfer of cooling water through the total temperature probe, the surface temperature of the shield is reduced, and the radiation heat between the ball welding surface and the shield is increased, thereby reducing the surface temperature of the ball welding.

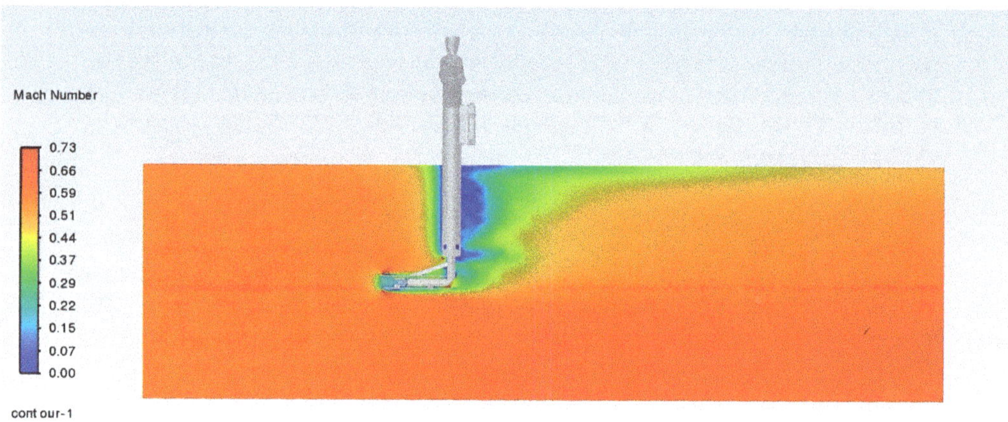

Figure 4. Flow field velocity cloud diagram.

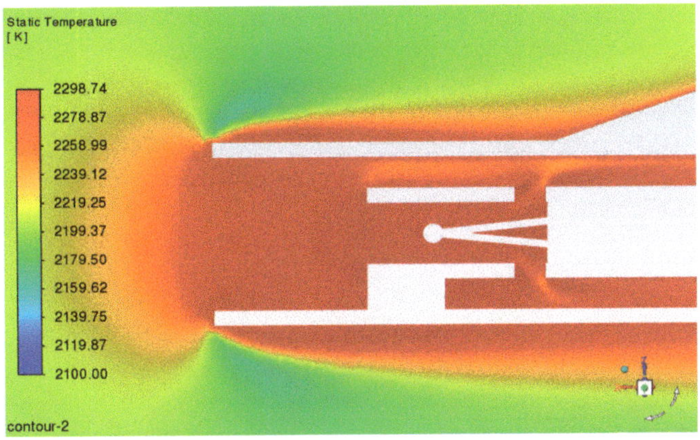

Figure 5. Flow field static temperature cloud diagram.

In the simulation, factors such as aerodynamics, the cooling water region, fluid–structure interaction, and radiation heat transfer were considered. The average temperature of bead welding obtained from the simulation is the result of combined velocity, conduction, and radiation errors. From the bead welding temperature cloud diagram (Figure 6) and the average temperature value of the bead welding surface, the average temperature of the bead welding surface is 2280.73 K. According to Equation (4), the temperature measurement deviation of the total temperature probe is calculated to be 19.27 K. It is this CFD-simulated ΔT value, derived directly from Equation (4), that serves as the objective function to be minimized in our subsequent optimization model.

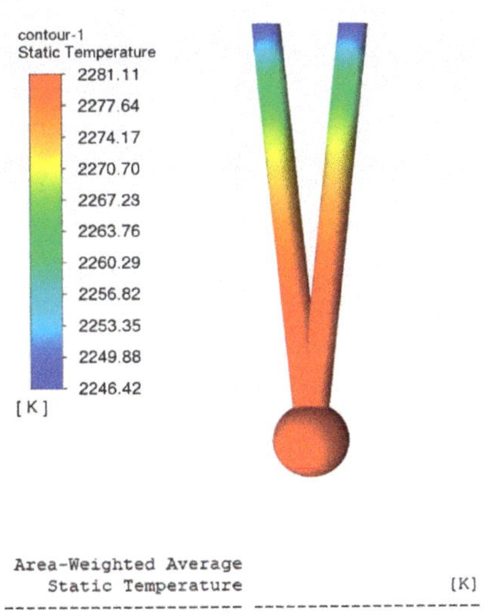

Figure 6. Total temperature probe bead welding temperature cloud diagram and average temperature values.

3. Optimization Design

The shielded total temperature probe is typically used to measure the total temperature of high-temperature, high-speed airflow. During the measurement, there is usually steady-state error, including velocity error, thermal conductivity error, and radiation error, which causes the probe's temperature to fail to accurately represent the total temperature of the incoming flow, thereby reducing the probe's temperature measurement accuracy. Several factors influence the measurement accuracy of the shielded probe, including the material and shape. The probe in this paper is made of a precious metal and is very sensitive to temperature. Optimizing the design of the probe's shielding cover is crucial for improving its temperature measurement accuracy.

3.1. Optimization Problem

3.1.1. Shield-Structure Design

The ratio of the inlet to outlet areas of the shield significantly influences thermal conductivity error by altering the internal gas flow state and velocity distribution, thereby modifying the heat transfer process. Previous studies demonstrate that reducing this area ratio increases velocity error but decreases radiation error, while also affecting thermal conductivity error [31]. An optimal ratio exists that minimizes the total steady-state error, including thermal-conductivity error, achievable by adjusting the inner shield's opening diameter.

Employing a double-shield configuration effectively increases the probe's flow-facing surface area, reducing radiant heat transfer and the temperature difference between the probe and computational domain perimeter [7]. Different shield parameters provide varying degrees of obstruction to radiant heat transfer. The synergistic effect between inner and outer shields enhances measurement accuracy in complex environments: the outer shield protects against direct mechanical damage from high-speed airflow, while the inner shield stabilizes the sensitive element and minimizes vibration from airflow impacts. For instance, in aero-engine exhaust temperature measurements, properly designed outer shield shape and size promote uniform airflow distribution around the probe, thereby reducing velocity-induced measurement errors.

The optimization process aims to minimize the deviation in the total temperature probe's temperature measurements by adjusting its structural parameters. Given the high-temperature (2300 K), high-pressure (1.0 MPa), and high-Mach number (0.6) operating environment, the primary sources of temperature measurement deviation are conduction and radiation errors. Therefore, the structural parameters selected for optimization are the diameter of the internal shield, the orifice diameter of the internal shield, the diameter of the external shield, the internal shield length, the external shield front length, and the external shield rear length, as shown in the schematic diagram of the optimized parameters in Figure 7. The initial values and ranges of these parameters are presented in Table 1.

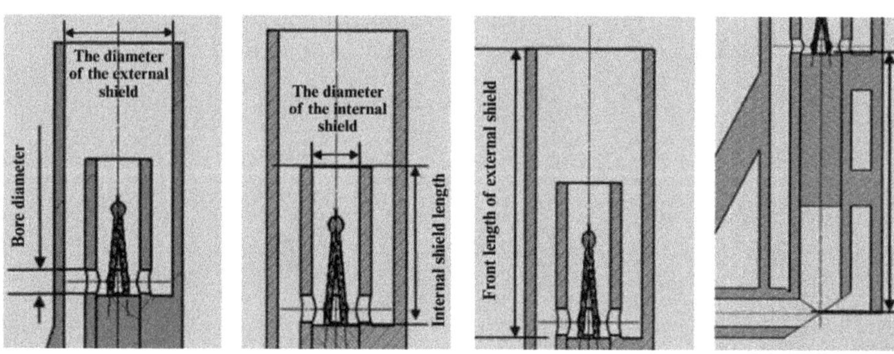

Figure 7. Structural diagram of optimized parameters for the total temperature probe.

Table 1. Initial values and ranges of variation in the optimized parameters.

Structural Parameters	The Diameter of the Internal Shield *D_in* (mm)	Bore Diameter of the Internal Shield *D* (mm)	The Diameter of the External Shield *D_ex* (mm)	Internal Shield Length *L_in* (mm)	Front Length of External Shield *L_1* (mm)	Rear Length of External Shield *L_2* (mm)
Initial value	5.00	2.00	11.00	11.60	21.50	36.70
Range of variation	5.0–7.0	1.5–2.5	10.0–12.0	9.6–13.6	18.5–21.5	28.7–36.7

This parameter selection is justified by their distinct roles: D_in and D collectively determine the inlet-to-outlet area ratio, critically influencing internal flow field structure and recovery characteristics, with literature confirming an optimal ratio exists for minimizing total steady-state error [26]. D_ex serves as the primary barrier against high-speed incoming flow, providing flow rectification and deceleration while influencing radiative heat loss. L_in governs the internal flow development length and heat conduction path, balancing velocity error reduction against conduction error. L_1 and L_2 define the external shield's geometric configuration, where L_1 guides incoming flow and affects pressure distribution, while L_2 governs flow stability and wake effects—together ensuring a stable, low-pressure-loss flow environment for the internal shield.

The objective is to optimize the structure of the total temperature probe by minimizing its temperature measurement deviation. The objective function is established as follows:

$$\begin{gathered} min\ F(D\_in, D, D\_ex, L\_in, L\_1, L\_2) \\ s.t. \begin{cases} \left(\begin{matrix} D\_in \in [\,5.0\,,\,7.0\,] \\ D \in [\,1.5\,,\,2.5\,] \end{matrix}\right) \\ \left(\begin{matrix} D\_ex \in [\,10.0\,,\,12.0\,] \\ L\_in \in [\,9.6,\,13.6\,] \end{matrix}\right) \\ \left(\begin{matrix} L\_1 \in [\,18.5\,,\,21.5\,] \\ L\_2 \in [\,28.7\,,\,36.7] \end{matrix}\right) \end{cases} \end{gathered} \tag{5}$$

The temperature-measurement deviation ΔT is governed by a six-parameter function $F(D\_in, D, D\_ex, L\_in, L\_1, L\_2)$, i.e., $\Delta T = F(D\_in, D, D\_ex, L\_in, L\_1, L\_2)$.

3.1.2. Structural Parameter Analysis

Before constructing the surrogate model and performing optimization, it is essential to quantify the influence of the six key structural parameters on the temperature measurement deviation ΔT of the total temperature probe and identify their interactions.

To ensure the reliability and robustness of the sensitivity analysis results, global sensitivity analysis based on the Sobol method was conducted using three distinct surrogate modeling approaches: grid-search-optimized SVR, Kriging, and BPNN. This multi-model comparative analysis aims to quantify the influence of the six key structural parameters on the temperature measurement deviation ΔT and identify their interactions, while verifying the consistency of sensitivity rankings across different modeling techniques.

This study employs three key sensitivity metrics: the first-order index ($S1$) quantifying individual parameter effects, the total-order index (ST) capturing comprehensive influences including all interactions, and their difference (ST-$S1$) measuring interaction strength [34].

The first-order sensitivity index $S1_i$ measures the direct contribution of the input parameter X_i to the output variance, excluding the interaction effects of this parameter with other parameters. X_i denotes the i-th parameter among the six structural parameters. $S1_i$ is calculated using the following formula [35]:

$$S1_i = \frac{V[E(Y|X_i)]}{V(Y)} \tag{6}$$

where $V[E(Y|X_i)]$ is the variance of the conditional expectation when X_i is fixed. Y is the true value of the output.

The total-order sensitivity index ST_i measures the total contribution of the input parameter X_i to the output variance. The formula for ST_i is as follows:

$$ST_i = 1 - \frac{V[E(Y|X_{\sim i})]}{V(Y)} \tag{7}$$

where $V[E(Y|X_{\sim i})]$ is the variance of the conditional expectation when other parameters is fixed. $X_{\sim i}$ is the set of all parameters except X_i.

The sensitivity rankings of parameters obtained from the three surrogate models are visually presented in Figure 8, where Figure 8a illustrates the ranking from the SVR model, Figure 8b from the Kriging model, and Figure 8c from the BPNN model. These visual comparisons provide an intuitive understanding of parameter importance across different modeling approaches. The first-order, total-order, and interaction strength Sobol indices obtained from each model are comparatively presented in Table 2.

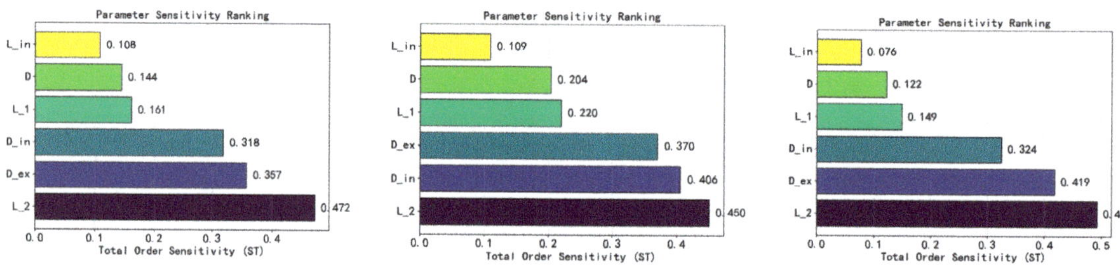

(a) (b) (c)

Figure 8. (**a**) The *ST* of the SVR model; (**b**) The *ST* of the Kriging model; (**c**) The *ST* of the BPNN model.

Table 2. Comparison of Sobol sensitivity indices from three surrogate models.

Model	Structural Parameter	S1	ST	ST-S1
SVR	D_in	0.1240	0.3182	0.1942
	D	0.0067	0.1444	0.1377
	D_ex	0.1436	0.3567	0.2130
	L_in	0.0110	0.1081	0.0970
	L_1	−0.0047	0.1609	0.1657
	L_2	0.2605	0.4723	0.2118
Kriging	D_in	0.1195	0.4059	0.2864
	D	0.0045	0.2037	0.1992
	D_ex	0.1006	0.3702	0.2697
	L_in	−0.0047	0.1089	0.1136
	L_1	0.0281	0.2202	0.1921
	L_2	0.1871	0.4502	0.2630
BPNN	D_in	0.1289	0.3244	0.1956
	D	0.0196	0.1218	0.1022
	D_ex	0.1425	0.4185	0.2761
	L_in	0.0223	0.0764	0.0541
	L_1	−0.0103	0.1490	0.1593
	L_2	0.2408	0.4926	0.2519

The Sobol sensitivity analysis results from the three surrogate models demonstrate good consistency, validating the reliability of the conclusions. As shown in Table 2, all three models identified L_2 as the most sensitive parameter, with total-order indices (ST) ranging from 0.4502 to 0.4926; D_ex and D_in ranked as the second and third most sensitive parameters, with ST values ranging from 0.3567 to 0.4185 and 0.3182–0.4059, respectively. Notably, the Kriging model showed slight differences in the ranking of D_in and D_ex compared to the other two models, but the numerical differences remain within acceptable limits. The interaction strength analysis revealed significant nonlinear coupling effects. All models indicated that L_2, D_ex, and D_in exhibit the strongest interactions (ST-$S1$ > 0.19), suggesting complex synergistic or antagonistic effects among these parameters when influencing temperature measurement deviation.

The medium-sensitivity parameters L_1 and D, with ST values in the 0.12–0.22 range, require consideration of their interaction effects with other parameters during optimization. Regarding low-sensitivity parameters, all three models consistently identified L_in as having the least influence ($ST < 0.12$), suggesting it can be assigned lower priority during the optimization process while focusing computational resources on more sensitive parameters.

Overall, the consistency in parameter sensitivity rankings and interaction strength patterns across the three models enhances the credibility of the analysis results, providing a solid theoretical foundation for subsequent probe structure optimization.

In this paper, the sample data are obtained using the numerical simulation method for the total temperature probe described in Section 2. Under the design conditions of the total temperature probe (inlet total temperature: 2300 K, inlet Mach number: 0.6, environmental pressure: 1.0 MPa), a sensitivity-analysis-based non-uniform sampling strategy was implemented for its six key structural parameters. According to the Sobol sensitivity analysis results, five levels were selected for each of the three highly sensitive parameters (L_2, D_ex, D_in), while three levels were chosen for each of the three less sensitive parameters (L_1, D, L_in). A full factorial design was employed, generating 3375 representative parameter combinations. For these sampled points, the numerical calculation method described in Section 2, along with Fluent commands, was utilized to individually perform geometric modeling, mesh generation, and numerical simulation. The initial values of the optimization objectives corresponding to the sampled points were obtained by post-processing the simulation results. The sampling strategy, guided by sensitivity analysis, ensures comprehensive coverage of the entire design space while significantly improving the efficiency and focus of data acquisition.

3.2. Surrogate Model

To address the computational challenges associated with high-fidelity numerical simulations, surrogate models have emerged as a powerful tool for efficient optimization and design. These models approximate complex systems with reduced computational cost while maintaining high accuracy. Selecting an appropriate surrogate model is critical. Given that the input is a low-dimensional, structured vector of geometric parameters and the output is a scalar temperature deviation, the problem is well-suited for regression models that excel at learning nonlinear mappings in tabular data. While advanced architectures like Convolutional or Recurrent Neural Networks are powerful for spatial or sequential data, they are not optimized for this type of structured input and may introduce unnecessary complexity. In the context of optimizing the dual-shield total temperature probe for aero-engine applications, a surrogate model based on SVR is employed to predict temperature measurement deviations under varying structural parameters.

We have N data points $X^{(i)} = \left[{D_{in}}^{(i)}, D^{(i)}, {D_{ex}}^{(i)}, {L_{in}}^{(i)}, {L_1}^{(i)}, {L_2}^{(i)}\right]$, $i = 1,2, \ldots, N$ and their corresponding outputs $y^{(i)}$, the objective is to predict the output $\hat{y}\left(X^{(new)}\right)$ for a new input point $X^{(new)} = [D\_in, D, D\_ex, L\_in, L\_1, L\_2]$.

SVR seeks to identify a hyperplane that best fits the training data while minimizing prediction error. Unlike methods that require minimizing errors for all sample points, it employs a loss function known as the ε-insensitive loss function. This function does not penalize prediction errors smaller than ε, while applying linear penalties only to deviations exceeding this threshold. Such a design enhances the model's robustness. The loss function is formally defined as follows:

$$L\left(y^{(i)},\hat{y}^{(i)}\right)=\begin{cases}0 & if \left|y^{(i)}-\hat{y}^{(i)}\right|\le\varepsilon\\ \left|y^{(i)}-\hat{y}^{(i)}\right|-\varepsilon & otherwise\end{cases}\tag{8}$$

where $y^{(i)}$ is the true value, $\hat{y}^{(i)}$ is the predicted value. This equation indicates that loss is calculated only when the difference between the predicted and actual values exceeds ε. When the error exceeds ε, the loss becomes proportional to the amount by which it exceeds this threshold.

The mathematical model of SVR can be expressed as the following optimization problem:

$$\min_{\omega,b,\xi,\xi^*}\left(\frac{1}{2}\|\omega\|^2+C\sum\nolimits_{i=1}^{N}(\xi_i+\xi_i^*)\right)\tag{9}$$

where ω is the weight vector representing model complexity. ξ_i and ξ_i^* are slack variables used to handle data points that cannot be fitted precisely. C is the regularization parameter that controls the trade-off between model complexity and error, also referred to as the penalty parameter. A larger C imposes a heavier penalty on points lying outside the margin band, causing the model to attempt to fit more data points; conversely, a smaller C results in higher tolerance for errors.

The constraints for SVR are as follows:

$$\begin{cases}y^{(i)}-\left(\omega^T X^{(i)}+b\right)\le\varepsilon+\xi_i,\\ \left(\omega^T X^{(i)}+b\right)-y^{(i)}\le\varepsilon+\xi_i^*,\\ \xi_i,\xi_i^*\ge 0 \qquad i=1,\ldots,N\end{cases}\tag{10}$$

where b is the bias term. These constraints ensure that the model's prediction errors do not exceed ε, and they allow for some flexibility through the slack variables to handle data points that are difficult to fit precisely.

SVR employs a kernel function to map the input data into a high-dimensional space, enabling the identification of a linear hyperplane for fitting the data in this space. Commonly used kernel functions include linear, polynomial, and radial basis function (RBF) kernels. The RBF kernel function $K(X^{(i)},X^{(j)})$ is defined as:

$$K(X^{(i)},X^{(j)})=\Phi\left(X^{(i)}\right)^T\cdot\Phi\left(X^{(j)}\right)=exp\left(-\gamma\left\|X^{(i)}-X^{(j)}\right\|^2\right)\tag{11}$$

where $\Phi\left(X^{(i)}\right)$ is the high-dimensional mapping of the input vector $X^{(i)}$, the parameter γ controls the shape of the kernel function.

By solving the dual problem of Equation (9), the optimal Lagrange multipliers α_i,α_i^* can be obtained. Subsequently, ω and b are calculated. Finally, the prediction for a new input point $X^{(new)}$ is:

$$\hat{y}\left(X^{(new)}\right)=\sum\nolimits_{i=1}^{N}(\alpha_i-\alpha_i^*)K\left(X^{(i)},X^{(new)}\right)+b\tag{12}$$

3.3. Genetic Algorithm Optimization

To efficiently identify the global optimal configuration of the probe's structural parameters for minimizing temperature measurement deviation, a GA was employed. GAs are a class of population-based optimization techniques inspired by the principle of natural evolution, renowned for their robustness in handling nonlinear, high-dimensional problems and their strong global search capability without requiring gradient information. This makes them particularly suitable for the present study, where the trained SVR surrogate model implicitly defines the objective function.

The selection of the Genetic Algorithm for this optimization task was motivated by several key factors that align with the problem's characteristics. Firstly, the relationship between the six structural parameters and the temperature deviation is highly nonlinear and expected to be multimodal, presenting a complex design space. GA, as a population-based global search method, is particularly adept at exploring such spaces without being trapped in local optima, a common pitfall of gradient-based algorithms. Secondly, GA operates without requiring derivative information, which is advantageous when the objective function is implicitly defined by a surrogate model, as in this study. Lastly, GA has a well-established track record of successful integration with surrogate models for the optimization of complex engineering systems, including thermal management [25,28], electromechanical design [26,29], and fluidic systems [27], providing a reliable and validated foundation for our approach.

A GA is used to optimize the probe's structural parameters to minimize the temperature measurement deviation of total temperature probe. These parameters include inner screen aperture diameter, inner screen length, external shield front length, and external shield rear length. The optimization problem can be described as follows.

$$\begin{aligned} &\min_{X} |T_{mean}(X) - T_{true}| \\ &s.t.\ \sigma_{T,\ weighted} = \sqrt{\frac{\sum_{i=1}^{n} A_i (T_i - T_{mean}(X))^2}{\sum_{i=1}^{n} A_i}} < 1 \end{aligned} \tag{13}$$

In the formula, X is the vector of structural parameters $[D\_in, D, D\_ex, L\_in, L\_1, L\_2]^T$. T_{mean} is the probe's measured value from the simulation, which corresponds to the true output value $y^{(i)}$ for that data point. T_{true} is the true total temperature (2300 K). In the constraint formula, $\sigma_{T,\ weighted}$ is the standard deviation of the surface Weighted temperature. n is the number of grid points on the thermocouple bead surface, which is 1426 in this study. T_i is the temperature at the i-th surface cell. A_i is the area of the i-th cell. $\sum_{i=1}^{N} A_i$ is the total surface area.

$\sigma_{T,\ weighted}$ directly quantifies the absolute dispersion of the local temperature from the mean value. A smaller $\sigma_{T,\ weighted}$ indicates a more uniform temperature field with smaller thermal gradients.

Imposing a constraint $\sigma_{T,\ weighted}$ guides the optimization away from designs that might have a good average temperature but suffer from severe local hot spots or cold spots. A uniform temperature distribution on the sensing element leads to a more stable and reliable measurement signal by minimizing errors induced by internal heat conduction.

As shown in Figure 9, the optimization of the total temperature probe follows these steps:

The GA was configured with careful consideration to balance exploration of the design space and convergence efficiency. The fitness function was defined as the temperature measurement deviation determined by six key structural parameters, which was approximated using the SVR surrogate model to replace computationally expensive high-fidelity simulations. A population size of 500 individuals was chosen to maintain sufficient genetic diversity. The algorithm used a blend crossover with a probability of 0.9 to recombine promising solutions, and a Gaussian mutation operator with a probability of 0.1 to introduce perturbations and prevent premature convergence. The optimization process was set to terminate after 1000 generations, with elitism used to preserve the best solution across generations.

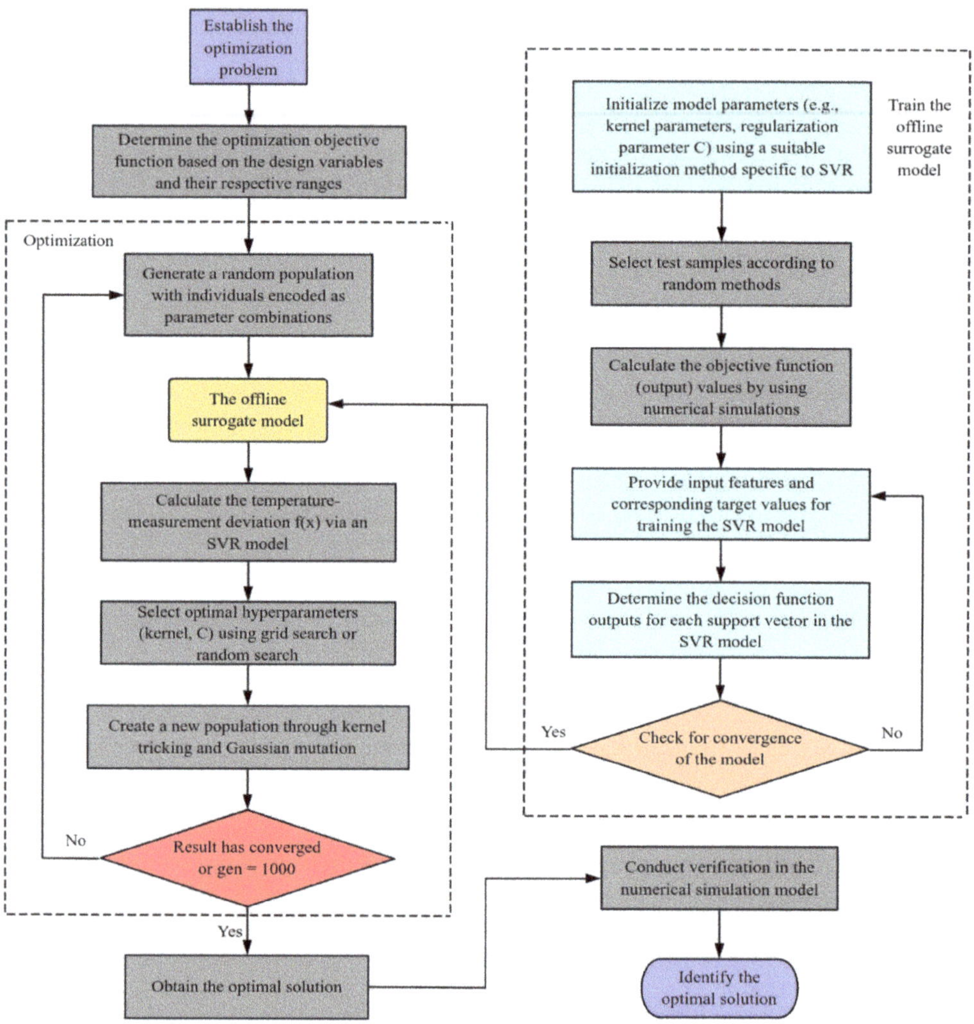

Figure 9. Schematic of the total temperature probe optimization process.

3.4. Simulation Verification

To clearly demonstrate the implementation process of the simulation verification and its position within the overall optimization framework, the comprehensive workflow is depicted in Figure 10. This verification step essentially executes the "Numerical simulation" branch of the framework, utilizing the optimal structural parameters obtained from the "Offline Model".

The specific implementation follows the detailed settings outlined in the diagram: an unstructured grid was employed for meshing, and the boundary conditions were applied. This high-fidelity simulation, conducted under the same rigorous conditions used to generate the training dataset, serves as the definitive benchmark for validating the surrogate model's predictive accuracy and the genetic algorithm's optimal solution.

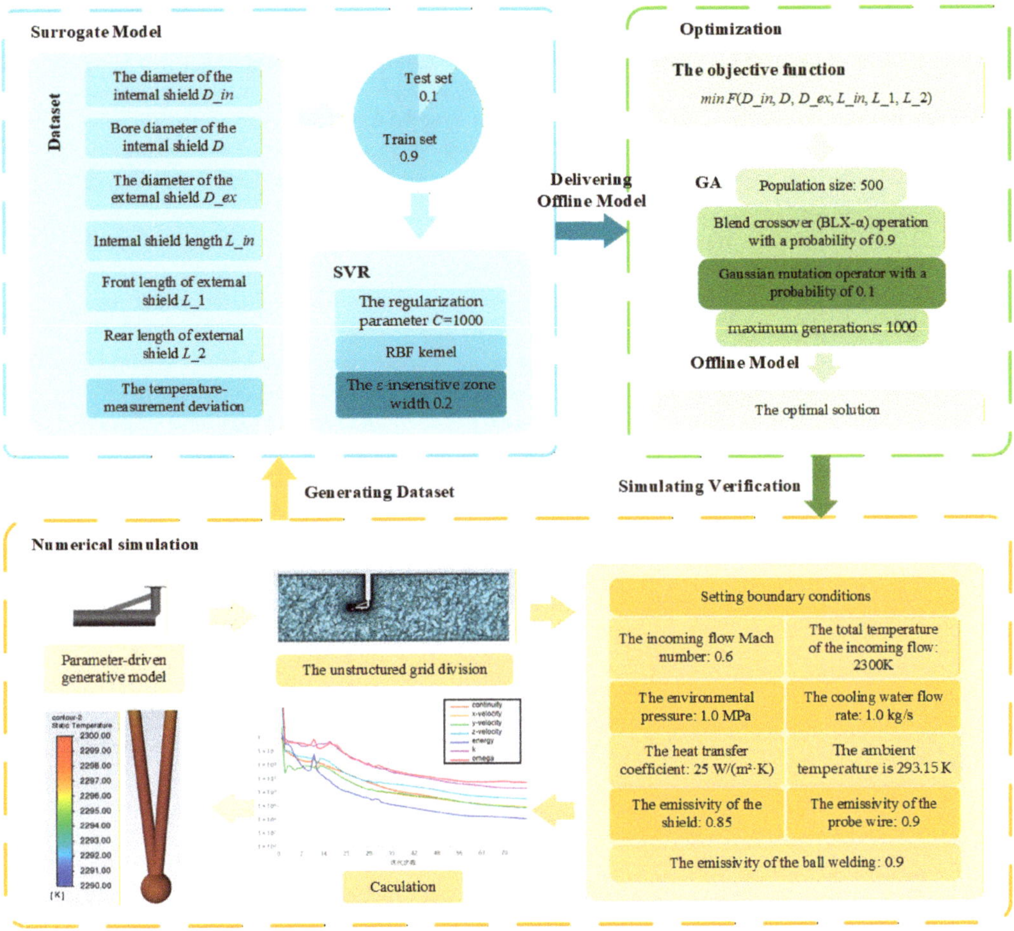

Figure 10. Framework of the surrogate model-based optimization methodology.

3.4.1. Surrogate Model Construction

The dataset was divided into training and test sets at a ratio of 9:1. The optimal parameters for the SVR model were determined through a comprehensive grid search process, considering various combinations of regularization parameter C, kernel parameter γ, and ε-insensitive zone width. The final SVR model in this study employs an RBF kernel, with the regularization parameter C set to 1000, the kernel parameter γ set to 1, and the ε-insensitive zone width set to 0.2. These parameters are chosen to balance model complexity and predictive accuracy.

The parameter C controls the trade-off between the model's complexity and its ability to fit the training data. A smaller C value results in a simpler model that allows for larger errors, potentially leading to underfitting. Conversely, a larger C value results in a more complex model that fits the training data more precisely, potentially leading to overfitting. In this study, C is set to 1000 to ensure a high level of model complexity and precise fitting of the training data.

The kernel parameter γ controls the width of the RBF kernel. A smaller γ value indicates a wider kernel, making the model less sensitive to local variations and more suitable for capturing global trends. A larger γ value indicates a narrower kernel, making the model more sensitive to local variations and better suited for capturing local features. In this study, γ is set to 1 to balance sensitivity to local and global variations in the data.

The ε-insensitive zone width ε defines the model's tolerance for errors. A smaller ε value makes the model more sensitive to errors, allowing fewer errors and thus increasing the model's complexity. A larger ε value makes the model less sensitive to errors, allowing more errors and thus reducing the model's complexity. In this study, ε is set to 0.2 to provide a moderate level of error tolerance, ensuring that the model is neither overly complex nor overly simplified.

To demonstrate the advantages of the SVR model as a surrogate model for this problem, we additionally employed Kriging and BPNN as surrogate models to approximate the target problem. The performance of these three models was evaluated under their respective optimal parameter configurations.

The relevant parameters of the Kriging model were configured as follows: the initial parameter θ was set to 0.01 to control the kernel width and balance sensitivity to local variations against overfitting risks; the squared exponential kernel function was selected for its suitability to smooth data; and a nugget parameter δ of 1×10^{-12} was applied to enhance numerical stability while preventing underfitting from excessive regularization.

The relevant parameters of the BPNN model were configured as follows: the input layer consists of 6 nodes; there are two hidden layers, the first with 128 nodes and the second with 64 nodes, both using the ReLU activation function; the output layer has one node with a linear activation function; the Adam optimizer was adopted with a learning rate of 0.02; the training was run for 2000 epochs with a batch size of 20, and the verbose setting was set to 1.

The model evaluation metric uses the coefficient of determination, R^2, which ranges from 0 to 1. A value closer to 1 indicates better model performance, while a value closer to 0 suggests worse performance. The formula is as follows:

$$R^2 = 1 - \frac{\sum_{i=1}^{N}\left(y^{(i)} - \hat{y}^{(i)}\right)^2}{\sum_{i=1}^{N}\left(y^{(i)} - \overline{y}\right)^2} \tag{14}$$

where $\hat{y}^{(i)}\,(i = 1,2,\ldots,N)$ is the predicted value for the i-th sample, $y^{(i)}\,(i = 1,2,\ldots,N)$ is the actual value for the i-th sample, $\overline{y}$ is the average value of the actual value, and N is the number of samples.

The prediction results of the three models are shown in Figure 11, where Figure 11a presents the SVR model's performance, Figure 11b shows the Kriging model's performance, and Figure 11c displays the BPNN model's results.

The SVR model achieved an R^2 value of 0.9591 and a Mean Squared Error (MSE) of 3.3869; the Kriging model attained an R^2 of 0.9086 and an MSE of 2.1594; while the BPNN model yielded an R^2 of 0.7881 and an MSE of 10.8098, as shown in Table 3.

Table 3. Comparative Performance of Three Surrogate Models.

Evaluation Metrics	The SVR Model	The Kriging Model	The BPNN Model
R^2	0.9591	0.9086	0.7881
MSE	3.3869	2.1594	10.8098

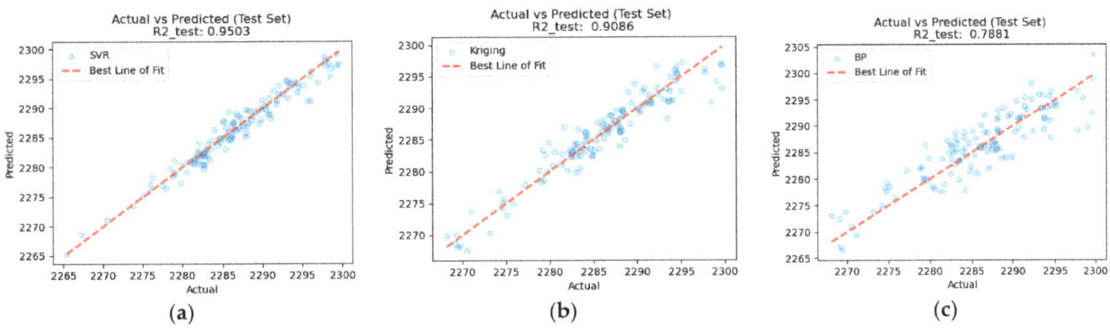

Figure 11. (**a**) The model performance of the SVR model on the testing set; (**b**) The model performance of the Kriging model on the testing set; (**c**) The model performance of the BPNN model on the testing set.

In terms of R^2, the SVR model significantly outperforms both Kriging and BPNN. As evidenced in Figure 11, the deviations between the predicted and actual values are notably smaller for the SVR model. Therefore, the SVR model is more suitable for the problem under investigation.

The complete training results of the SVR model are presented below. Figure 12 illustrates the model performance on the training set, where the R^2 is 0.9840 and the MSE is 0.7220. These metrics indicate that the model fits the training data very well. The low MSE value further suggests that the model's predictions are close to the actual values, with minimal deviation.

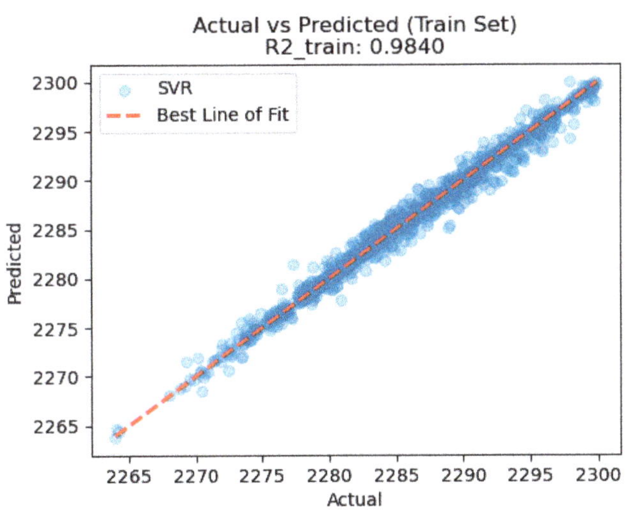

Figure 12. The model performance of the SVR model on the training set.

Figure 11a presents the model performance on the testing set, with an R^2 of 0.9503 and an MSE of 3.3869. The slightly lower R^2 value and higher MSE on the test set compared to the training set suggest that, while the model generalizes well to unseen data, it shows a modest increase in prediction error. This is expected, as models often perform better on training data due to overfitting.

Figure 13 compares prediction results. This suggests the SVR is suitable as a surrogate model for genetic algorithm optimization in this paper.

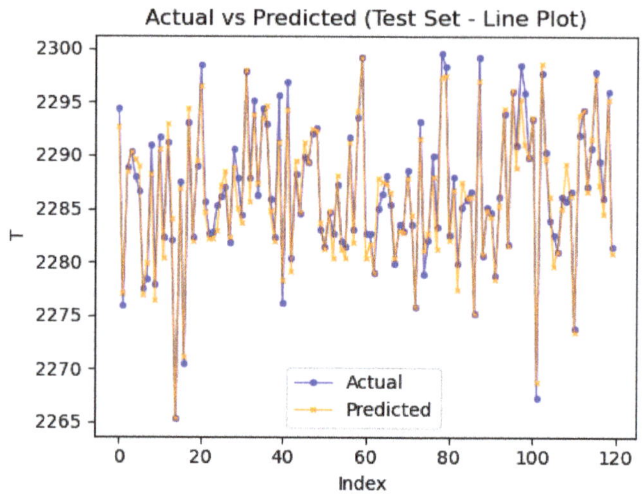

Figure 13. Comparison of prediction results.

3.4.2. Verification of Optimization Results

In Section 3.3, we discussed the basic optimization workflow and detailed the genetic algorithm's parameter settings. In this section, we validate the optimization results to demonstrate the feasibility of the proposed methodology.

The convergence behavior of the Genetic Algorithm, monitored through the evolution of the objective function (temperature deviation ΔT), is presented in Figure 14. The history shows a characteristic trend: a rapid and substantial decrease in ΔT during the initial 20 generations, as the algorithm efficiently explores the design space and identifies promising regions. This is followed by a period of refined search with diminishing returns, where only minor improvements are achieved. The population reached a stable global optimum around the 70th generation, with no further significant improvement observed thereafter.

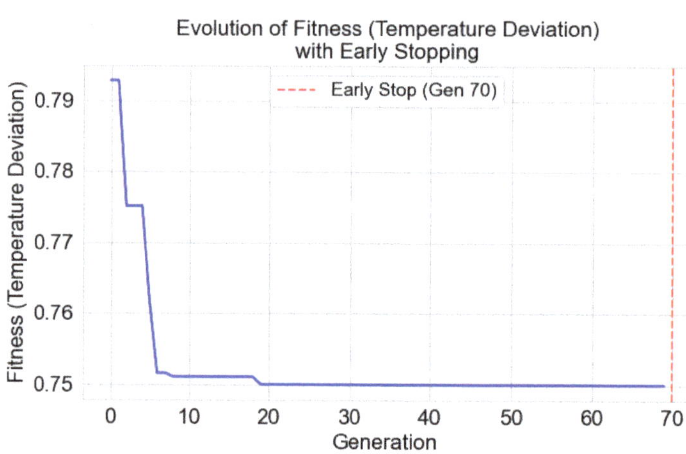

Figure 14. Evolution of cost function.

The optimal set of structural parameters identified by the GA is listed in Table 4. The temperature measurement deviation was reduced from an initial value of 2.05 K to an optimal value of 0.75 K, corresponding to a reduction of 1.30 K.

Table 4. Comparison of structural parameter dimensions before and after.

Structural Parameters	The Diameter of the Internal Shield D_in (mm)	Bore Diameter of Internal Shield D (mm)	The Diameter of the Internal Shield D_ex (mm)	Internal Shield Length L_in (mm)	Front Length of External Shield L_1 (mm)	Rear Length of External Shield L_2 (mm)
Before	5.00	2.00	11.00	11.60	21.50	36.70
After	5.90	2.07	11.92	11.77	20.36	35.39

The optimization results are both physically meaningful and align with the earlier sensitivity analysis. The most significant adjustments occurred in the most sensitive parameters: a reduction in the rear shield length (*L_2*) to stabilize the wake flow, and an increase in the shield diameters (*D_in*, *D_ex*) to enhance radiative shielding and flow recovery. These synergistic changes effectively balance the reduction in velocity, conduction, and radiation errors.

Under representative aero-engine operating conditions (total temperature: 2300 K, Mach number: 0.6, pressure: 1.0 MPa), the probe was redesigned in 3D using optimized structural parameters to verify its measurement accuracy. After extracting the computational domain, meshing, and setting the boundary conditions, high-fidelity simulations were conducted to obtain detailed temperature distributions. Figure 15a presents the simulation results for the initial design, showing a temperature deviation of 2.05 K. In contrast, the optimized probe in Figure 15b exhibits a significantly reduced deviation of approximately 0.86 K. This performance meets the stringent accuracy requirements (typically within ±1.0 K) for high-precision temperature measurement in critical aero-engine applications. Furthermore, the absolute error between this validated result and the genetic-algorithm-predicted value (0.75 K) is only 0.11 K, demonstrating the high predictive accuracy of the surrogate model-based optimization framework and its ability to meet rigorous engineering design goals.

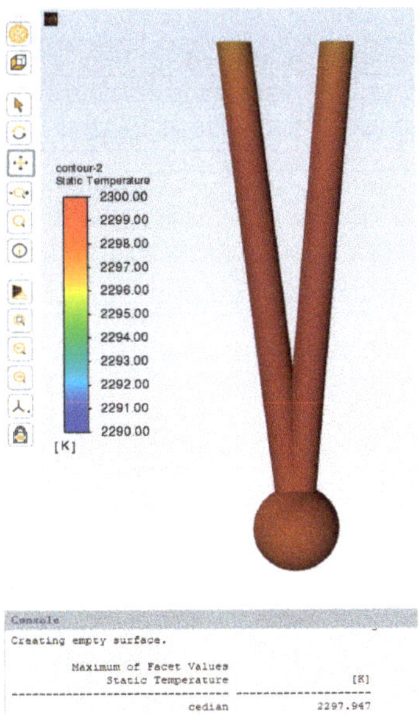

(**a**)

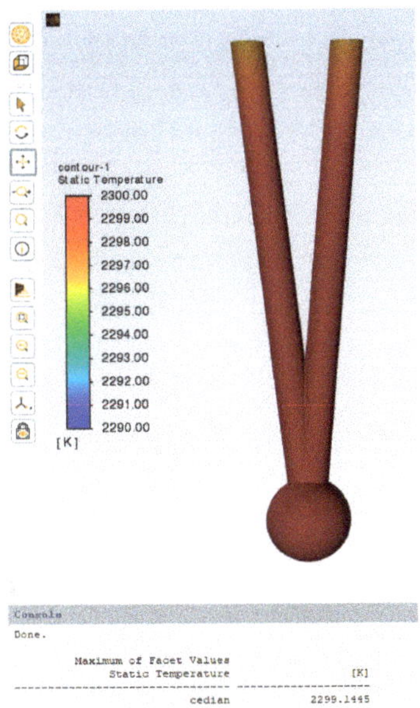

(**b**)

Figure 15. (**a**) The simulation verification results under the initial state; (**b**) Simulation verification results after optimization.

4. Conclusions

This study developed and validated an automated optimization framework integrating conjugate heat transfer CFD, Support Vector Regression surrogate modeling, and a Genetic Algorithm for the design of a dual-shield total temperature probe for aero-engine applications.

The framework effectively solves the problems of traditional design methods reliant on costly experimentation or high-fidelity simulation loops. The application of the proposed framework successfully reduced the probe's temperature measurement deviation from an initial 2.05 K to an optimized value of 0.86 K. This represents an absolute reduction of 1.19 K and a 58% relative improvement in accuracy. The optimized design meets the stringent ±1.0 K accuracy requirement for critical aero-engine total temperature measurements.

The core workflow of the developed framework is geometry-agnostic. It provides a cost-effective and generalizable strategy that can be readily adapted to the optimized design of various other temperature sensors, pressure probes, and similar aerothermodynamic components across a wide range of operating conditions, making way for high-performance, low-cost, and rapid development cycles for advanced equipment.

Despite these promising results, certain limitations remain. Firstly, the current surrogate model is constructed for a fixed set of inflow conditions. Future work will incorporate inflow Mach number, total temperature, and pressure as additional input variables to develop a condition-agnostic design tool with stronger generalization capabilities. Secondly, as problem complexity increases, both surrogate modeling and optimization methods need enhancement. We plan to explore deep learning-based modeling approaches and more advanced optimization algorithms like PSO or SSO to solve more challenging design problems. Finally, physical experimentation remains essential for validation. Our next step is to manufacture the optimized probe and conduct calibration tests in a high-temperature wind tunnel, closing the loop between digital design and physical implementation.

Author Contributions: Conceptualization, X.Z. and J.Z.; methodology, X.Z., Y.W. and J.Z.; software, X.Z. and Y.W.; validation, Y.W. and Y.A.; formal analysis, J.Z.; data curation, Y.W. and Y.A.; writing—original draft preparation, X.Z. and Y.W.; writing—review and editing, X.Z., Q.L. and Y.A.; supervision, X.Z. and Y.W. All authors have read and agreed to the published version of the manuscript.

Funding: This research received no external funding.

Data Availability Statement: The data presented in this study are subject to industry-confidentiality restrictions and are available upon reasonable request from the corresponding author.

Conflicts of Interest: The authors declare no conflicts of interest.

Abbreviations

The following abbreviations are used in this manuscript:

CFD	Computational Fluid Dynamics
SVR	Support Vector Regression
BPNN	Backpropagation Neural Network
RBF	Radial Basis Function
MSE	Mean Squared Error
GA	Genetic Algorithm

References

1. Murugan, M.; Walock, M.; Ghoshal, A.; Knapp, R.; Caesley, R. Embedded temperature sensor evaluations for turbomachinery component health monitoring. *Energies* **2021**, *14*, 852. [CrossRef]
2. Behr, T.; Kalfas, A.; Abhari, R. A probabilistic uncertainty evaluation method for turbomachinery probe measurements. *E3S Web Conf.* **2022**, *345*, 02001. [CrossRef]
3. Xue, Z.; Li, P.; Du, Z.; Yang, Y.; Zhou, Y.; Wu, X. Study on the double-shielded thermocouple probe for total temperature. *Appl. Therm. Eng.* **2025**, *267*, 125633. [CrossRef]
4. Zhao, G.; Zhao, C.; Song, L.; Tong, X. Analyses on and applications of thermocouples used for airflow temperature measurements in aircraft. *Sens. Transducers* **2014**, *179*, 234–239.
5. Dahl, A.I.; Fiock, E.F. Shielded thermocouples for gas turbines. *Trans. Am. Soc. Mech. Eng.* **1949**, *71*, 153–160. [CrossRef]
6. Frankel, J.; Chan, H. Analytical developments and experimental validation of a thermocouple model through an experimentally acquired impulse response function. *Int. J. Heat Mass Transf.* **2019**, *141*, 1301–1314. [CrossRef]
7. Wang, Y.; Zhao, J.; Zhao, R. Shape parameterization optimization of thermocouples used in aeroengines. *Aerospace* **2023**, *10*, 202. [CrossRef]
8. Markides, C.; Mastorakos, E. Experimental investigation of the effects of turbulence and mixing on autoignition chemistry. *Flow Turbul. Combust.* **2011**, *86*, 585–608. [CrossRef]
9. Manjhi, S.; Kumar, R. Performance assessment of K-type, E-type and J-type coaxial thermocouples on the solar light beam for short duration transient measurements. *Measurement* **2019**, *146*, 343–355. [CrossRef]
10. Yang, C.; Wu, W.; Xiong, Y.; Yao, Z. Calibration technology of high- temperature thermocouple for combustor exit of an aero-engine. *J. Aerosp. Power* **2016**, *31*, 769–774.
11. Ummer, Z.; Zhang, W.; Yang, W.; Zou, Z.; Zhao, J. Numerical investigation on metrological fidelity of a shielded thermocouple probe and the effects of geometrical parameters. *Int. J. Turbo Jet-Engines* **2019**, *39*, 383–401. [CrossRef]
12. Etemad, S. CFD simulation of thermocouple measurement of hot gas jets. *Int. Mech. Eng. Congr. Expo.* **2011**, *10*, 177–186. [CrossRef]
13. Put, F.; Lucherini, A.; Van Coile, R.; Merci, B. CFD-based analysis of deviations between thermocouple measurements and local gas temperatures during the cooling phase of compartment fires. *Fire Saf. J.* **2024**, *150*, 104276. [CrossRef]
14. Villafañe, L.; Paniagua, G. Aero-thermal analysis of shielded fine wire thermocouple probes. *Int. J. Therm. Sci.* **2013**, *65*, 214–223. [CrossRef]
15. Matas, R.; Sedláček, J.; Čibera, V. Preliminary study to the temperatures of the thermocouple probes affected by the environment of heated walls. *EPJ Web Conf.* **2016**, *114*, 02071. [CrossRef]
16. Wang, Z.; Ji, N.; Ma, C. Steady-state error estimation and calibration of a shielded total temperature probe for turbomachinery. *Int. J. Therm. Sci.* **2023**, *190*, 108298. [CrossRef]
17. Ali, L.F.; Humaidi, A.J. Offset Temperature and Amplitude–Frequency Effect on Convection Heat Transfer in Partially Gradient Porous Cavity with Different Outlet Port Locations. *Processes* **2025**, *13*, 2279. [CrossRef]
18. Zink, F.; Vipperman, J.; Schaefer, L. CFD simulation of thermoacoustic cooling. *Int. J. Heat Mass Transf.* **2010**, *53*, 3940–3946. [CrossRef]
19. Ghosh, S.; Mondal, S.; Kapat, J.; Ray, A. Parametric shape optimization of pin fin arrays using a multi-fidelity surrogate model based Bayesian method. *Appl. Therm. Eng.* **2024**, *247*, 122876. [CrossRef]
20. Du, P.; Zhu, X.; Wang, J.X. Deep learning-based surrogate model for three-dimensional patient-specific computational fluid dynamics. *Phys. Fluids* **2022**, *34*, 081906. [CrossRef]
21. Wilson, B.; Wakes, S.; Mayo, M. Surrogate modeling a computational fluid dynamics-based wind turbine wake simulation using machine learning. In Proceedings of the 2017 IEEE Symposium Series on Computational Intelligence, Honolulu, HI, USA, 27 November–1 December 2017; pp. 1–8. [CrossRef]
22. Elkarii, M.; Boukharfane, R.; Benjelloun, S.; Bouallou, C. A CFD-based surrogate model for predicting slurry pipe flow pressure drops. *Part. Sci. Technol.* **2023**, *41*, 432–442. [CrossRef]
23. Jeon, K.; Yang, S.; Kang, D.; Na, J.; Lee, W.B. Development of surrogate model using CFD and deep neural networks to optimize gas detector layout. *Korean J. Chem. Eng.* **2019**, *36*, 325–332. [CrossRef]
24. Morozova, N.; Trias, F.X.; Capdevila, R.; Schillaci, E.; Oliva, A. A CFD-based surrogate model for predicting flow parameters in a ventilated room using sensor readings. *Energy Build.* **2022**, *266*, 112146. [CrossRef]
25. Zhu, W.; Guo, L.; Jia, Z.; Tian, D.; Xiong, Y. A surrogate-model-based approach for the optimization of the thermal design parameters of space telescopes. *Appl. Sci.* **2022**, *12*, 1633. [CrossRef]
26. Zhang, X.; Liu, H.; Hu, M.; Zhang, Y.; Zhu, C. A multi-objective optimization study on the electromechanical system for a space mechanism based on a Catboost surrogate model and NSGA-III algorithm. *Expert Syst. Appl.* **2025**, *268*, 126312. [CrossRef]
27. Shan, X.Y.; Wang, B.C.; Xu, K.K.; Li, H.X. Surrogate model-based structure optimization of jetting system. *IEEE Trans. Compon. Packag. Manuf. Technol.* **2020**, *10*, 494–501. [CrossRef]

28. Li, C.; Li, Y.; Gao, L.; Garg, A.; Li, W. Surrogate model-based heat dissipation optimization of air-cooling battery packs involving herringbone fins. *Int. J. Energy Res.* **2021**, *45*, 8508–8523. [CrossRef]
29. Gu, J.; Hua, W.; Yu, W.; Zhang, Z.; Zhang, H. Surrogate model-based multiobjective optimization of high-speed PM synchronous machine: Construction and comparison. *IEEE Trans. Transp. Electrif.* **2022**, *9*, 678–688. [CrossRef]
30. Yang, W.; Zhang, W.; Zou, Z.; Wang, X.; Zhao, J. Steady state error estimation and modification of a shielded thermocouple. *J. Aerosp. Power* **2018**, *33*, 2784–2795.
31. Berntsson, F. An inverse heat conduction problem and improving shielded thermocouple accuracy. *Numer. Heat Transf. Part A Appl.* **2012**, *61*, 754–763. [CrossRef]
32. Zhao, Y.; Yan, C.; Wang, X.; Liu, H.; Zhang, W. Uncertainty and sensitivity analysis of SST turbulence model on hypersonic flow heat transfer. *Int. J. Heat Mass Transf.* **2019**, *136*, 808–820. [CrossRef]
33. Blazek, J. *Computational Fluid Dynamics: Principles and Applications*, 3rd ed.; Butterworth-Heinemann: Oxford, UK, 2015; pp. 84–86.
34. Soboĺ, I.M. Sensitivity estimates for nonlinear mathematical models. *Math. Model. Comput. Exp.* **1993**, *1*, 407.
35. Saltelli, A.; Annoni, P.; Azzini, I.; Campolongo, F.; Ratto, M.; Tarantola, S. Variance based sensitivity analysis of model output. Design and estimator for the total sensitivity index. *Comput. Phys. Commun.* **2010**, *181*, 259–270. [CrossRef]

mathematics

Article

GCML: A Short-Term Load Forecasting Framework for Distributed User Groups Based on Clustering and Multi-Task Learning

Junling Wan [1], Yusen Sun [2], Jianguo Fan [3], Yu Zhou [2], Rui Ye [1] and Peisen Yuan [1,*]

1 College of Artificial Intelligence, Nanjing Agricultural University, Nanjing 211800, China
2 State Grid Electric Power Research Institute, NARI Group Co., Ltd., Nanjing 211106, China
3 Chongqing Three Gorges Water Conservancy and Electric Power Co., Ltd., Chongqing 401120, China
* Correspondence: peiseny@njau.edu.cn

Abstract

Short-term load forecasting of distributed user groups is crucial for the efficient operation of electricity markets, but existing methods mainly rely on intra-group consistency while neglecting inter-group correlations, which limits the utilization of cross-group information and reduces forecasting accuracy. To overcome these limitations, this study introduces a clustering and multi-task learning-based framework for short-term load forecasting of distributed user groups. First, historical load data are clustered to form representative consumption groups. Next, a Transformer encoder is used as a hard parameter shared network for multi-task learning. Within the multi-task framework, we apply dynamic task weighting and task-specific prediction heads, which balance multi-task losses while optimizing the forecasting performance of each group. Moreover, a filter-attention mechanism and an Inception convolution module are introduced into the encoder to improve local pattern extraction and multi-scale feature fusion. Experiments conducted on two publicly available datasets show that, for the London smart meter dataset, the MAE values of the clusters are 0.2858 and 0.4312, and the RMSE values are 0.5042 and 0.5266. On different clusters of the UCI electricity load dataset, the MAE values are 0.1617, 0.1554, and 0.2608, and the RMSE values are 0.2299, 0.2130, and 0.3678, respectively. These results demonstrate that our method outperforms baseline models and significantly improves the accuracy of distributed user short-term load forecasting in electricity markets.

Keywords: clustering; distributed user group; filter-attention; multi-task learning; short-term load forecasting; Inception convolution

MSC: 68T07

1. Introduction

To accelerate the development of a unified national electricity market and ensure the high-quality operation of the new power system, it is essential to address the challenge of accurate electricity consumption [1]. Short-term power load forecasting for the distributed user aggregate is a critical process in formulating spot trading clearing strategies, and accurate load forecasting for different groups of distributed users plays a vital role in ensuring the stable operation of power systems, optimizing resource allocation, and enhancing economic efficiency [2,3].

Compared with traditional large-scale entities participating in the spot market, distributed users are numerous, with small individual loads and high heterogeneity, posing significant challenges for load forecasting [4]. In particular, different user groups exhibit distinct consumption patterns. Conventional models struggle to uncover true load–driver relationships amid strong nonlinearities and high-dimensional covariates [5,6]. There is an urgent need to develop aggregation methods for large-scale heterogeneous user resources within the electricity market environment, to identify the key factors influencing electricity consumption across various user types and time periods [7]. Moreover, traditional electricity demand forecasting approaches primarily perform system-level predictions uniformly across all users, failing to effectively account for the diversity in consumption habits and the complexity of influencing factors among different industries and user groups [8–10].

To address the higher requirements for load forecasting accuracy posed by the diversity and volatility of users' electricity consumption behaviors, in recent years, some studies have employed cluster analysis methods to capture electricity consumption differences among various user groups, thereby achieving more accurate load forecasting [11,12]. The load clustering algorithm is used to partition users into different clusters, forming corresponding resource aggregates, and further analyzing the users' electricity consumption characteristics [13]. By grouping and modeling users with similar electricity consumption patterns, such methods effectively reduce the prediction errors caused by the randomness of individual user behaviors and lay a foundation for subsequent refined load management [14].

In the scenario of multi-user collaborative prediction, how to leverage the correlations among users to improve overall prediction performance has become a research hotspot. Multi-task learning has been applied to time-series prediction for multiple users recently [15]. By sharing the underlying feature representations and model parameters, the correlations among different tasks are mined. Meanwhile, multi-task learning can study multiple tasks simultaneously during the training process and is capable of capturing a broader range of power consumption pattern features [16]. This mechanism not only enhances the model's ability to characterize complex electricity consumption patterns but also alleviates the data sparsity problem through information complementarity, making it particularly suitable for practical scenarios with a large number of users but limited individual data [17].

Although these methods are effective in most application scenarios, there are still some fundamental challenges that remain unresolved: (1) The electricity market has numerous participants with distinct consumption patterns. Therefore, making overall predictions without considering these variations may obscure group-specific characteristics, increasing prediction errors. (2) Predicting each user group separately ignores the inherent correlations in electricity consumption trends between different groups and fails to effectively integrate multi-source information to improve prediction accuracy. (3) Existing methods capture the insufficient local features of electricity load data, have poor dynamic adaptability, and struggle to balance short-term fluctuations and long-term trends within one scale.

To address the above issues, our paper proposes a short-term load forecasting framework for distributed user **G**roups based on **C**lustering and **M**ulti-task **L**earning, called **GCML**. Firstly, distributed user groups are formed by clustering load curves. Secondly, a multi-task learning framework based on the Transformer encoder is employed, combined with a dynamic weighting mechanism and lightweight prediction heads designed for specific tasks, enabling unified feature extraction and information sharing across different user groups. Finally, we employ a filter-attention mechanism and an Inception convolution module within the shared encoder to enhance the model's ability to capture local patterns and fuse multi-scale information.

The main contributions of this paper are summarized as follows:

(1) This paper proposes a novel load forecasting model, which forecasts the short-term load by segmenting electricity user groups and jointly optimizing multiple forecasting tasks, thereby improving prediction accuracy on the demand side of the electricity market.
(2) An improved multi-task learning architecture is proposed to capture correlations between distributed user groups. It uses an encoder-only approach to extract common features across clusters, introduces dynamic weighting, and assigns independent task heads for multiple forecasting tasks, overcoming the limitations of single-task modeling.
(3) The filter-attention mechanism and Inception convolution module are integrated into an encoder, significantly enhancing the model's ability to capture local patterns and fuse multi-scale features of load data.
(4) We conducted experiments on publicly available datasets, and the experimental results show that GCML outperforms existing baseline models.

2. Related Work

As a central issue in the development of trading strategies for electricity markets, the accuracy of short-term electricity load forecasting for distributed users has attracted considerable research attention [18]. However, the diversity of customer types and electricity consumption behaviors in the electricity market poses a significant challenge to achieving highly accurate forecasts; existing research has primarily focused on modeling within the group correlations and capturing complex patterns, which often neglects the variations between different distributed user groups [9,19].

Currently, the short-term electricity load forecasting for distributed users research primarily includes two approaches: (1) clustering-based load forecasting methods; (2) multi-task learning-based forecasting methods.

2.1. Clustering-Based Load Forecasting Methods

In order to identify different patterns in load data and achieve more accurate short-term load forecasting, researchers have proposed many time-series forecasting methods based on clustering. By clustering historical data and building specialized forecasting models for each group, these methods reduce the interference of complex load patterns on a single model and improve prediction performance [20]. For example, Hyojeoung et al. [21] used a time-series clustering method based on Euclidean distance and dynamic time warping distance to cluster household electricity demand before forecasting. Dalil et al. [22] extracted consumption patterns through outlier detection and replacement, followed by cluster analysis, and improved prediction accuracy. Fang et al. [23] developed a short-term time-series prediction model based on multilinear trend fuzzy information particles, employing K-Medoids clustering and novel fuzzy association rules to enhance both data characterization and semantic representation.

Existing studies mainly applied the clustering algorithms to classify users into clusters and then use prediction algorithms to predict the electricity load for each group [13,24], but these methods have some shortcomings. First, predicting each group individually ignores the possible intrinsic correlation of electricity consumption trends among different user groups, and the model can only learn the electricity consumption patterns within the clusters, which restricts the generalization ability of the model; second, the model needs to be trained individually for each type of group, which increases the complexity of the model [25].

2.2. Multi-Task Learning Methods for Time-Series Forecasting

In recent years, multi-task deep learning has been used for time-series prediction in several fields, and existing studies have proved that multi-task learning frameworks can implicitly capture the dynamic relationship between multiple time series and improve the accuracy and generalization ability of time-series prediction [26,27]. Tian et al. [28] adopted multi-task learning techniques and an end-to-end learning framework to handle multiple load forecasting tasks in parallel, achieving favorable prediction performance. Guo et al. [29] proposed a multi-task learning method based on bidirectional long short-term memory to realize the prediction of cold, heat, and electricity combined loads. Jiang et al. [30] constructed a multi-task framework of dual-level information extraction by integrating LSTM and CNN methods to realize multi-family short-term load forecasting. Zhang et al. [31] used the DBSCAN clustering algorithm to group data and proposed a multi-task graph convolutional network to learn different spatial patterns for short-term load forecasting.

However, existing multi-task learning methods still face challenges in distributed user groups, primarily due to the insufficient consideration of variations and dynamic changes between different user groups, which limits the model's adaptability and accuracy.

To address the limitations of previous studies, this paper proposes a short-term load forecasting method that integrates clustering and multi-task learning. By applying a multi-task learning framework to distributed user groups aggregated through time-series clustering, while incorporating dynamic weighting, innovative attention mechanisms, and multi-scale feature extraction methods, our approach enhances both the forecasting accuracy and the time performance.

3. Methodology

3.1. Problem Definition

The purpose of distributed user group short-term load forecasting is to simultaneously predict the future load values of M user groups over the next S time steps. Given a total of M load forecasting tasks, the historical load data of the m-th user group is represented as follows:

$$\mathbf{X}^{(m)} = \{x_{:,1}^{(m)}, \ldots, x_{:,T}^{(m)}\} \in \mathbb{R}^{n_m \times T} \tag{1}$$

where $\mathbf{X}^{(m)}$ denotes the historical load data matrix of the m-th user group, n_m is the number of measurement channels in that group, and T represents the number of time steps in the historical observation window. The forecasting target for the m-th user group is formulated as

$$\mathbf{Y}^{(m)} = \{x_{:,T+1}^{(m)}, \ldots, x_{:,T+S}^{(m)}\} \in \mathbb{R}^{n_m \times S}, \quad m = 1, 2, \ldots, M \tag{2}$$

where $\mathbf{Y}^{(m)}$ represents the predicted load matrix of the m-th user group for the next S steps. The forecasting results of all user groups are organized as follows:

$$\mathbf{Y}_{all} = \{\mathbf{Y}^{(1)}, \mathbf{Y}^{(2)}, \ldots, \mathbf{Y}^{(M)}\} \in \mathbb{R}^{M \times n_m \times S} \tag{3}$$

where $\mathbf{Y}_{all}$ denotes the unified output representation of multi-task forecasting.

3.2. Processing Model

In order to capture the power consumption differences in the load aggregates and achieve more accurate power load forecasting, this paper proposes a short-term power load forecasting model based on clustering and multi-task learning. The processing model of GCML is shown in Figure 1.

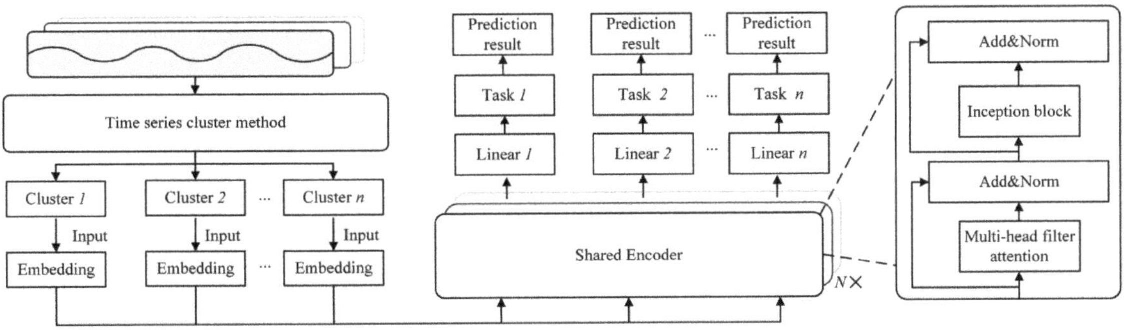

Figure 1. The processing model of GCML for short-term electricity load forecasting for distributed users.

As illustrated in Figure 1, the proposed model consists of 3 main components: (1) Distributed user clustering: the historical load data of distributed users are first clustered, with users exhibiting similar consumption patterns grouped into different categories. (2) Multi-task learning framework: a hard parameter sharing strategy is adopted, where different groups share the encoder of the Transformer to achieve joint modeling and feature extraction across groups. In addition, each group is assigned an independent linear layer as the task-specific prediction head, ensuring that group-specific load characteristics can be accurately captured based on the shared global representations. (3) Enhanced feature extraction module: An Inception convolution module and a filter-attention mechanism are incorporated into the encoder. These components collectively enhance the model's ability to represent and forecast complex time-series data.

3.3. Clustering for Distributed Users

The clustering of electricity users is based on their power consumption behaviors, grouping users with similar consumption patterns to form corresponding load aggregates. In this paper, we utilize a deep clustering algorithm to achieve the clustering of heterogeneous electricity users. Specifically, low-dimensional features of the load curves are extracted by an autoencoder [32], and then K-means [33] is applied for clustering. The set of electricity consumption of all users is $\mathbf{A} = \{\mathbf{z}_1, \mathbf{z}_2, \ldots, \mathbf{z}_N\}, \mathbf{z}_i \in R^T$, where A represents the set of historical load curves of all users, $\mathbf{z}_i$ represents the power load curve of the i-th user, and T is the number of time points.

Firstly, the low-dimensional representation of the load data is extracted through the self-encoding encoding and decoding process, as shown in Equations (4) and (5).

$$h_i = f_{\theta_{\text{enc}}}(z_i) = \sigma_{\text{enc}}(W_{\text{enc}} z_i + b_{\text{enc}}) \tag{4}$$

$$\hat{z}_i = f_{\theta_{\text{dec}}}(h_i) = \sigma_{\text{dec}}(W_{\text{dec}} h_i + b_{\text{dec}}) \tag{5}$$

where W_{enc} and b_{enc} are the encoder parameters, σ_{enc} is the activation function, W_{dec} and b_{dec} are the decoder parameters, $f_{\theta_{\text{enc}}}$ is the mapping function of the encoder, θ_{dec} denotes the parameter set of the decoder, and σ_{dec} is the output layer activation function.

Next, the low-dimensional latent vectors $h_1, h_2 \ldots h_n$ obtained by the autoencoder are used as inputs to K-means clustering, which classifies users into multiple distinct clusters. We randomly select K hidden vectors as the initial center $\{c_1, c_2 \ldots c_K\}$, assign the sample to the nearest cluster k, and update the cluster center, as shown in Equations (6) and (7).

$$k_i = \arg \min_{k \in \{1, \ldots, K\}} \|h_i - c_k\|_2^2 \tag{6}$$

$$c_k = \frac{1}{|S_k|} \sum_{i:k_i=k} h_i \tag{7}$$

where k_i is the cluster to which the ith sample belongs, $S_k = \{i|k_i = k\}$ is the sample set of the k-th cluster, and $|S_k|$ is the number of samples in the cluster.

By analyzing the consumption behaviors of distributed users, those with similar load patterns are grouped together, enabling more accurate predictions. However, forecasting the load behavior of these groups requires not only capturing the internal relationships within each cluster but also modeling the interactions between clusters of distributed users.

3.4. Multi-Task Learning

To extract useful information from correlated distributed user groups, this study adopts a multi-task learning (MTL) framework [34], treating the load forecasting tasks for each user group as distinct yet related, thus effectively capturing the inherent relationships between different clusters. The MTL enables the parallel training of multiple load forecasting tasks by leveraging shared parameters in the lower layers of the model to extract common features across tasks, thereby improving overall forecasting accuracy.

According to the parameter sharing strategy, this method is generally categorized into hard parameter sharing and soft parameter sharing [35]. In this paper, we employ a hard parameter sharing framework. The encoder serves as a shared backbone network for forecasting tasks from different clusters, while each task has its own task-specific linear prediction head. In the shared layers, all tasks use identical parameters, which effectively mitigate overfitting and enhance the model's generalization ability [36]. The multi-task learning architecture of our proposed model is illustrated in Figure 2.

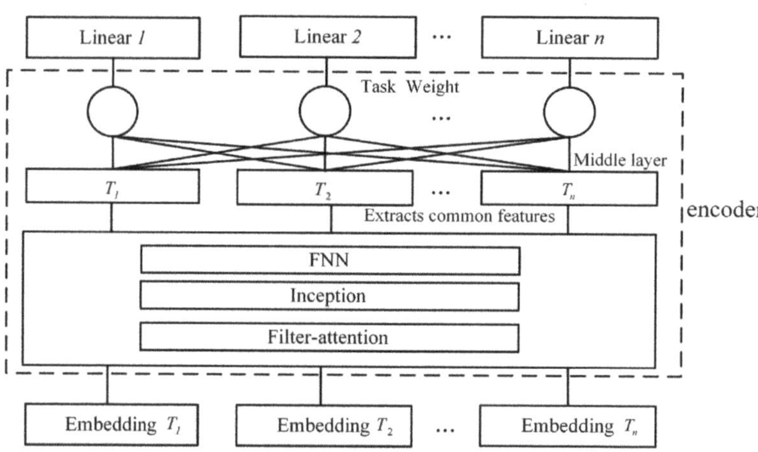

Figure 2. Encoder-only-based multi-task learning architecture for extracting inter-group shared information.

As shown in Figure 2, this paper employs an encoder-only Transformer architecture [37] as the backbone network to learn representative features of different user groups $T_1, T_2, \ldots, T_n$ and introduces a weighting mechanism. Additionally, to improve the prediction accuracy of the standard Transformer, a linear layer is designed as the prediction head. The MTL framework is trained end-to-end, with samples from all user clusters processed in parallel. During forward propagation, the shared encoder extracts common features, while task-specific heads generate forecasts for their respective clusters. Thus, the Transformer encoder serves as a unified feature extractor, enabling the model to capture both global consumption trends and cluster-specific patterns.

The overall loss in multi-task learning is typically formulated as a weighted sum of the individual task losses. To ensure balanced training, we employ a dynamic weighting strategy that adapts to each task's learning stage, inherent difficulty, and current performance [34,38]. Specifically, all clusters perform load forecasting, and the weights are dynamically adjusted according to the rate of change in each task's loss function, encouraging similar learning progress across tasks. This strategy prevents any single task from dominating the optimization and ensures that all tasks receive sufficient training. Assuming a total of n tasks, the weight for task d at iteration t, denoted as $\alpha_d(t)$, is computed according to Equations (8) and (9).

$$\alpha_d(t) = \frac{d \exp(r_d(t-1)/T)}{\sum_i \exp(r_i(t-1)/T)} \tag{8}$$

$$r_d(t-1) = \frac{Loss_d(t-1)}{Loss_d(t-2)}, r_d(t-1) > 0 \tag{9}$$

where t is the number of iterations; $Loss_d(t-1)$ and $r_d(t-1)$ are the loss function and relative decline rate of task d at iteration $t-1$, respectively; and T is a constant to control the smoothness of the task weights.

The dynamic weighting strategy adaptively adjusts task weights according to learning progress, effectively balancing training across different user groups. Compared to methods such as uncertainty weighting [39], it requires no additional learnable parameters, thereby avoiding instability in parameter estimation under small-sample or low-quality data conditions.

After sharing the encoder, an independent task-specific prediction head is designed for each forecasting task. Each head implemented as a fully connected neural network, is responsible for generating the predicted values corresponding to its respective cluster. By employing separate task heads, the model enables differentiated outputs across tasks, thereby achieving joint modeling of load data from multiple user aggregates.

3.5. *Encoder-Only-Based Shared Encoder Architecture*

In this paper, we adopt the encoder-only architecture of the Transformer [37] as the shared component in the multi-task learning framework to extract features from different users. This design reduces the number of parameters and enables faster convergence on strongly periodic electricity load data by incorporating a linear layer as the prediction head, further improving prediction accuracy. Additionally, to better capture local patterns and multi-scale features, we apply a filter-attention mechanism and an Inception convolution module into the model.

3.5.1. Filter-Attention Mechanism

The self-attention mechanism distributes the weights across the entire sequence, which limits its ability to capture the local temporal patterns [40,41]. To address the above issues, we propose a filter-attention mechanism that strengthens the model's focus on short-term dependencies.

By applying a two-dimensional convolutional filter to the attention matrix and performing filtering operations on the attention distribution, the model has enhanced the ability to capture and model local patterns. This enables the model to pay more attention to the local important information in the data when calculating the attention weights, and suppress unnecessary information interference, thereby enhancing the model's performance when dealing with complex and variable time-series data and allowing the model to capture the key features and local changes in the data more accurately. The structure of the filter-attention mechanism is illustrated in Figure 3.

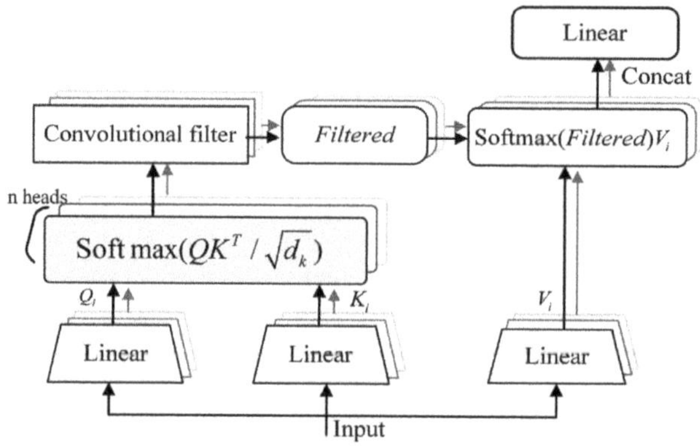

Figure 3. Multi-head filter-attention mechanism structure.

In Figure 3, the values of Q, K, and V are initially obtained through a process of linear projection, which can be mathematically expressed as follows:

$$\begin{cases} Q = \text{Linear}(X) \in \mathbb{R}^{B\times L\times H\times d_k} \\ K = \text{Linear}(X) \in \mathbb{R}^{B\times L\times H\times d_k} \\ V = \text{Linear}(X) \in \mathbb{R}^{B\times L\times H\times d_v} \end{cases} \quad (10)$$

where $d_k = d_v = d_{\text{mod}\,el}/H$, Q, K, and V represent the query, key, and value, respectively, and H is the number of attention heads.

The dot product between the query and the key is calculated and multiplied by the scaling factor to obtain the attention score as defined in Equation (11).

$$scores = \frac{QK^T}{\sqrt{d_k}} \quad (11)$$

Instead of directly proceeding with aggregation, the attention distribution is divided according to the number of heads, and a two-dimensional convolution filter with kernel size $(1, f_s)$, where f_s denotes the filter window size, is applied to the attention map of each head.

The filtered-attention maps are subsequently recombined, and the resulting matrix is then used to compute the weighted sum over the value matrices, thereby producing the final attention outputs. The process of filtered-attention can be formally defined in Equations (12) and (13),

$$A_{\text{filtered}} = \text{Conv2D}(softmax(\text{scores})); kernel = (1, f_s) \quad (12)$$

$$Attn_{out} = Linear(concat(A_{\text{filtered}}V)) \quad (13)$$

where A_{filtered} denotes the filtered-attention weight matrix, and $Attn_{out}$ represents the final attention output. The filter-attention mechanism enhances the expression ability of local patterns by applying convolution filters on the attention matrix, so that the model can pay more attention to the local important information in the data, thereby improving the performance of the model in dealing with complex time-series data.

3.5.2. Multi-Scale Information Fusion

The Inception convolution [42] module performs parallel convolution operations using kernels of various sizes, enabling the extraction of features at multiple scales. Concatenating and fusing features from different scales allows the model to analyze data from multiple perspectives and levels of granularity, enhancing its expressive power and significantly improving performance on complex datasets.

As shown in Figure 4, the parallel 1D convolution branches are set within the module, and convolution kernels of different sizes slide along the time axis, as shown in Equations (14)–(16),

$$conv1 = \mathrm{Conv1d}\left(X_{attn}^{\mathrm{T}},\ kernel = 1,\ out\_channels = d_{ff}\right) \tag{14}$$

$$conv3 = \mathrm{Conv1d}\left(X_{attn}^{\mathrm{T}}, kernel = 3,\ padding = 1,\ padding\_mode = circular\right) \tag{15}$$

$$conv5 = \mathrm{Conv1d}\left(X_{attn}^{\mathrm{T}}, kernel = 5,\ padding = 2,\ padding\_mode = circular\right) \tag{16}$$

where d_{ff} represents the number of convolution output channels, and $conv1$, $conv3$, and $conv5$, respectively, indicate the results of one-dimensional convolution operations using convolution kernels of sizes 1, 3, and 5.

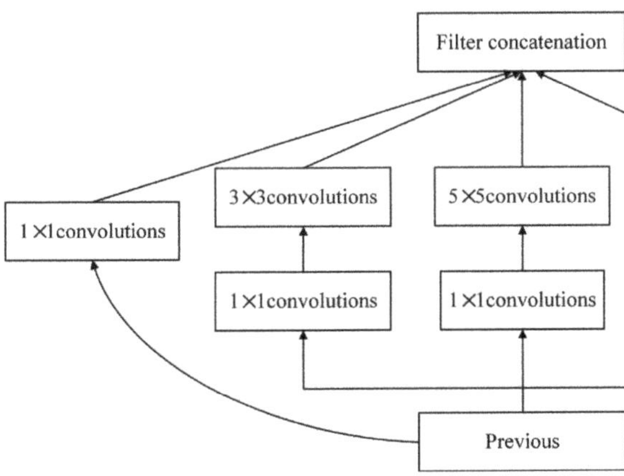

Figure 4. Inception network architecture for multi-scale information extraction.

Through the combined use of these convolution operations, the model effectively extracts both local and global features of time-series data at multiple scales while preserving sequence integrity. Next, the temporal features at different scales will be captured and concatenated to integrate multi-scale information, as described in Equation (17),

$$\begin{cases} conv_{all} = concat(conv1, conv3, conv5) \\ FFN = \mathrm{Conv1d}(ReLU(conv_{all}), kernel = 1, out\_channels = d_{model}) \end{cases} \tag{17}$$

where $conv_{all}$ denotes the fused feature obtained after concatenation, FFN refers to the output of the feedforward network, and $out\_channels$ indicates the number of output channels.

By concatenating data at multiple scales, the model is capable of not only accurately capturing local patterns within complex load data but also learning the underlying long-term trends. Therefore, the model's ability is enhanced to represent the internal structure of load data while preserving computational efficiency.

4. Experiments

4.1. Experimental Settings

4.1.1. Experimental Environment

The experimental platform is Windows Server 2019, with an Intel Xeon E5-2686 v4 CPU, 96 GB of server memory, and an NVIDIA Tesla P40 GPU equipped with 24 GB memory and configured with CUDA 11.6. The model is implemented using PyTorch 1.13.1 and Python 3.8.

4.1.2. Datasets

In this paper, we conduct experiments on publicly available datasets, using the following datasets:

(1) Dataset I: London smart meter dataset (https://www.kaggle.com/datasets/jeanmidev/smart-meters-in-london, accessed on 16 November 2025).
(2) Dataset II: UCI electricity load dataset (https://archive.ics.uci.edu/dataset/321, accessed on 16 November 2025).

Dataset I mainly contains daily and hourly electricity consumption data of 5567 London households, and this paper selects the hourly electricity consumption dataset, while dataset II includes the daily electricity load data of 321 customers with hourly electricity consumption from 2011 to 2014.

4.1.3. Data Processing

In order to solve the impact of missing data in the dataset on the experimental results and deal with the subtle differences in the time-series data, the linear interpolation [43] method is used to fill the missing values to ensure the continuity and integrity of the data. For two given data points x_1 and x_0, we perform linear interpolation to fill in period-missing values, which is calculated as Equation (18).

$$y = y_0 + \frac{(y_1 - y_0)(x - x_0)}{x_1 - x_0} \tag{18}$$

Using linear interpolation to fill in missing values preserves the continuity and smoothness of time-series data, making it particularly effective for datasets with strong temporal patterns. For each user, the missing energy values of certain days are estimated by calculating the linear interpolation between the nearest known values before and after the interval. Additionally, it reduces the risks of overfitting and noise amplification.

To further address dimensional discrepancies among different features, a standardization method is employed in this study to preprocess the data. We applied Z-score normalization to standardize the features by subtracting the mean and dividing by the standard deviation, ensuring zero mean and unit variance for each feature and thereby eliminating scale differences across features and improving the stability and convergence speed of the model training. Thereby, this enables fair comparison and evaluation of various indicators on a uniform scale and improves the reliability and validity of the subsequent analysis. Additionally, the 2 datasets were divided into a training set and a test set in an 8:2 ratio.

4.1.4. Result Evaluation

To evaluate the clustering performance of the proposed method, this paper adopts the silhouette coefficient (SC) [33] as the evaluation metric. The SC is an indicator used to evaluate clustering performance. A higher SC value closer to 1 indicates better clustering results, and its calculation formula is as Equations (19) and (20),

$$s(i) = \frac{b(i) - a(i)}{\max(a(i), b(i))} \tag{19}$$

$$SC = \frac{1}{n}\sum_{i=1}^{n} s(i), \tag{20}$$

where $a(i)$ denotes the average distance from sample point i to other points in the same cluster, and $b(i)$ denotes the average distance from sample point i to the nearest point in the other cluster. The overall silhouette coefficient is obtained by averaging the silhouette coefficient of all individual points.

To quantitatively assess the prediction accuracy of the GCML model, we adopt the Mean Absolute Error (MAE) [44], coefficient of determination (R^2) [45], and Root Mean Square Error (RMSE) [46] as evaluation metrics.

The MAE evaluates the model's performance by calculating the average absolute difference between the actual and predicted values, which is highly general and easy to compute. The RMSE highlights larger deviations while maintaining consistent dimensions, and R^2 provides a better reflection of the model's fit to the data. The calculation methods are shown in Equations (21)–(23), respectively,

$$MAE = \frac{1}{n}\sum_{i=1}^{n}|y_i - \hat{y}_i| \tag{21}$$

$$RMSE = \sqrt{\frac{1}{n}\sum_{i=1}^{n}(y_i - \hat{y}_i)^2} \tag{22}$$

$$R^2 = 1 - \frac{\sum_{i=1}^{n}(y_i - \bar{y})^2}{\sum_{i=1}^{n}(y_i - \hat{y}_i)^2} \tag{23}$$

where y_i is the true value, $\hat{y}_i$ is the predicted value, and n is the number of samples.

4.2. Comparison of Clustering Results on 2 Datasets

After preprocessing the data, we chose the silhouette coefficient (SC) as the evaluation metric, as it effectively considers both intra-cluster cohesion and inter-cluster separation, providing an intuitive and reliable measure for determining the optimal number of clusters.

By comparing the SC for different numbers of clusters, the optimal clustering solutions for datasets I and II can be identified, enabling the classification of user types. Figure 5 shows the silhouette coefficients obtained for different numbers of clusters on two datasets.

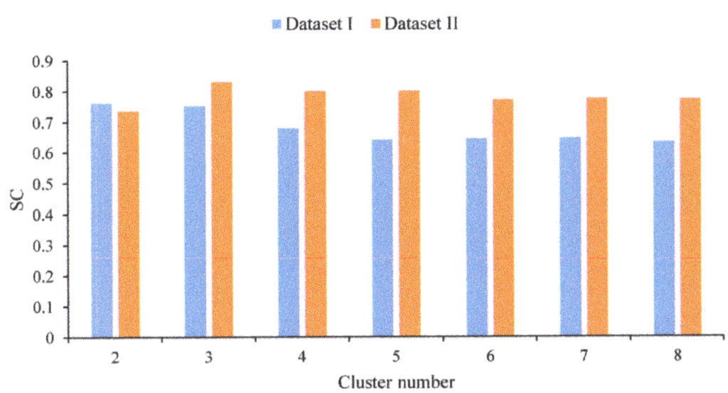

Figure 5. Comparison of SC under different number of clusters on 2 datasets.

As shown in Figure 5, dataset I achieves the highest silhouette coefficient when the number of clusters is 2, indicating that 2 is the optimal choice. For dataset II, the silhouette coefficient reaches its maximum value when the number of clusters is 3, suggesting that dividing users into 3 groups is more appropriate. After clustering the two datasets according to the optimal number of clusters, the electricity consumption patterns of typical users in each cluster are illustrated in Figure 6.

Figure 6 demonstrates the effectiveness of the clustering results in revealing distinct electricity consumption patterns among user groups. In dataset I, Cluster 0 corresponds to high-demand users with consistently high load levels, pronounced peak–valley variations, and strong temporal regularity, while Cluster 1 represents low-demand users exhibiting relatively low overall consumption and minor fluctuations. For dataset II, Cluster 1 consists of high-demand users characterized by intense electricity usage and prominent peaks; Cluster 2 represents medium-demand users with periodic load profiles; and Cluster 0 includes low-demand users whose consumption behavior is stable but less structured.

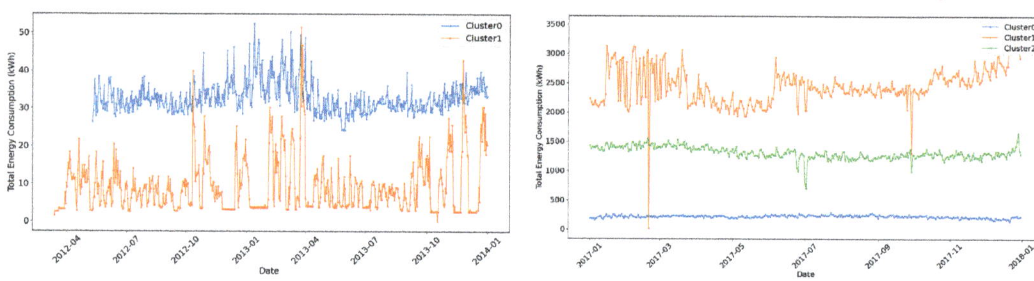

(a) (b)

Figure 6. The electricity consumption trends of typical users in each cluster after clustering. (**a**) The electricity consumption trends of typical users in each cluster after clustering on dataset I. (**b**) The electricity consumption trends of typical users in each cluster after clustering on dataset II.

By partitioning users into clusters, tailored modeling for each cluster can effectively capture group-specific temporal characteristics, mitigating biases caused by holistic modeling and significantly improving short-term load forecasting accuracy. Furthermore, in electricity market clearing, cluster-based user classification enables more accurate prediction of bidding behaviors and demand response potentials across different groups, thereby optimizing the price formation mechanism and enhancing market efficiency and resource allocation.

The clustering algorithm groups users with similar electricity consumption patterns into corresponding load aggregates, thereby reducing the number of users that need to be modeled independently. This approach enables more accurate prediction of electricity demand for different user groups, enhances the model's ability to capture and exploit patterns in the data, and contributes to the effective optimization of power market operations.

4.3. Training Parameter Tuning

The reasonable selection of training epochs is essential for preventing overfitting or underfitting, optimizing training efficiency, and ensuring prediction accuracy. As presented in Figure 7, on both dataset I and dataset II, the training and test losses of the proposed model decrease rapidly in the early stages and gradually stabilize after about 50 epochs, indicating that 50 iterations are sufficient for model convergence.

After an initial decline, the model performance stabilizes on both datasets, indicating effective learning of load data features and good generalization ability. Therefore, the number of training epochs is set to 50 in the prediction experiments on both datasets.

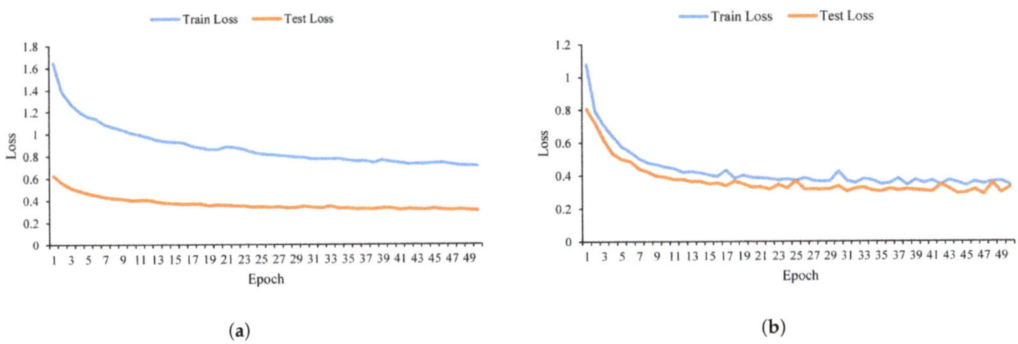

Figure 7. The change in loss in the multi-task Transformer model during training and testing. (**a**) Training loss and testing loss changes of the model when using the clusters clustered on dataset I. (**b**) Training loss and testing loss changes of the model when using the clusters clustered on dataset II.

An appropriate look-back length is crucial for short-term power load forecasting. In our paper, historical window lengths of 24, 48, 72, and 96 h are selected for training. The MAE and RMSE of the clustered data are then compared to serve as the evaluation criteria for subsequent experiments. The experimental results are demonstrated in Figure 8.

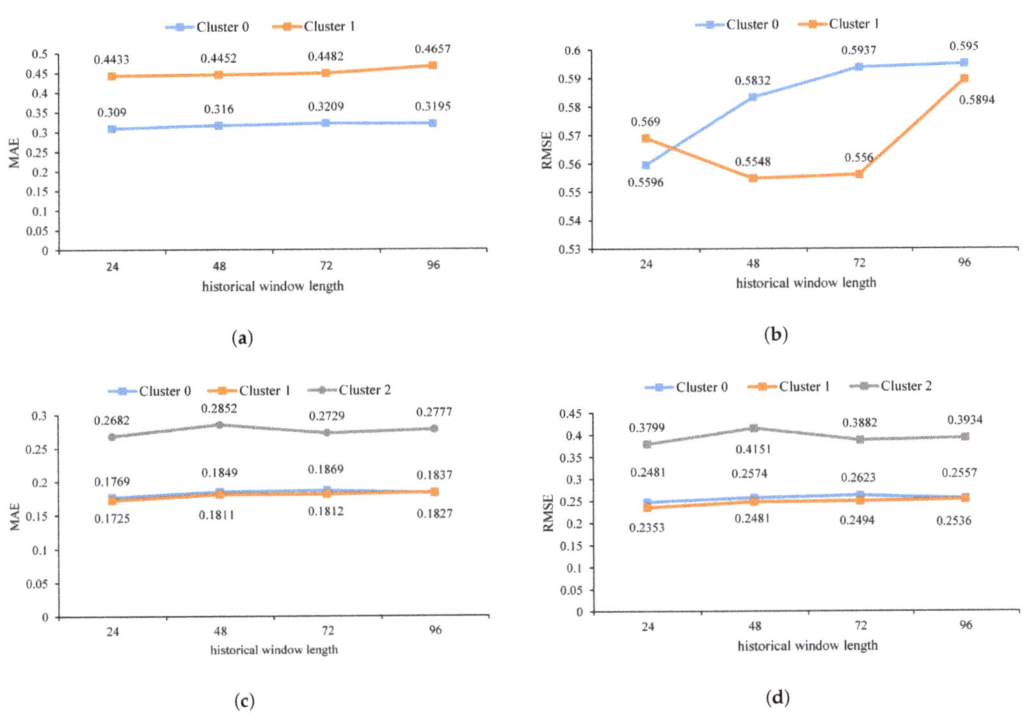

Figure 8. Comparison of forecasting results for different clusters under various historical window lengths. (**a**) Comparison of predicted MAE values for different historical window lengths on dataset I. (**b**) Comparison of predicted RMSE values for different historical window lengths on dataset I. (**c**) Comparison of predicted MAE values for different historical window lengths on dataset II. (**d**) Comparison of predicted RMSE values for different historical window lengths on dataset II.

As shown in Figure 8, with the increase in the historical window length, the MAE values obtained for different clusters in dataset I exhibit an overall upward trend, although the differences remain relatively small. At the same time, the RMSE achieves its best performance when the historical window length is 24. For dataset II, both the MAE and RMSE reach their minimum values when the historical window length is smallest, outperforming other settings. Considering the results from both datasets and the short-term electricity load forecasting scenarios in this study with prediction lengths of 12 and 24, the historical window length of 24 is selected as the optimal configuration.

In the following experiments, we set the historical input length to 24, employ the Adam optimizer with a learning rate of 1×10^{-3}, apply a dropout rate of 1×10^{-1}, and use a batch size of 32. Moreover, training runs for 50 epochs are performed on two datasets.

4.4. Effectiveness of Clustering for Short-Term Forecasting

We evaluate the effectiveness of distributed user clustering by comparing the load forecasting results of each aggregated cluster with those obtained from the original unclustered data. The results for prediction horizons of 12 and 24 steps are shown in Figure 9, where Cluster i denotes the *i*-th cluster formed after data aggregation, and Original represents the unclustered dataset.

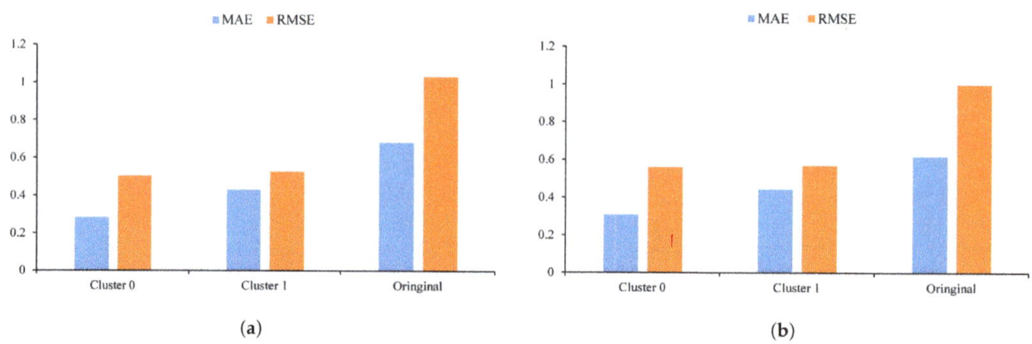

Figure 9. The prediction results of the clustered aggregates and the original data under different prediction windows. (**a**) Comparison of the predicted results between the clustered clusters and the original data when the prediction window is 12. (**b**) Comparison of the predicted results between the clustered clusters and the original data when the prediction window is 24.

As demonstrated in Figure 9, when the prediction window is 12, the proposed model achieves significantly lower MAE and RMSE values for both clustered aggregates compared to direct predictions on the original data. Similarly, at a 24-step prediction horizon, the MAE and RMSE of the clustered groups remain smaller than the original dataset. These results clearly indicate that clustering the distributed users significantly improves forecasting performance compared to direct predictions on the original dataset.

4.5. Comparison with Baseline Models

To evaluate the proposed method, we compare it with the representative methods as the baseline from both multi-task and single-task models.

(1) **Single-task models**: we adopt Timemixer [47], Convtimenet [48], Timesnet [49], ETSformer [50], Fedformer [51], and Dlinear [52].
(2) **Multi-task models**: include Multi-Transformer [53], AutoSTL [54], and Multitask-GNN [55].

4.5.1. Comparison of Experimental Results on Dataset I

Evaluation of prediction performance based on MAE and RMSE: When the prediction lengths are 12 and 24, short-term load forecasting experiments were conducted on clustered distributed users using the method proposed in this paper and baseline models on dataset I. The experimental results are summarized in Table 1.

Table 1. Comparison of short-term load forecasting performance of different models on dataset I.

Task Type	Method	Cluster 0 (12-Step)		Cluster 1 (12-Step)		Cluster 0 (24-Step)		Cluster 1 (24-Step)	
		MAE	RMSE	MAE	RMSE	MAE	RMSE	MAE	RMSE
Single-task models	Timemixer	0.5049	0.9387	0.4964	0.9749	0.5079	0.9248	0.5052	0.9929
	Convtimenet	0.5052	0.9928	0.4863	0.9764	0.5124	0.9937	0.5083	1.0245
	Timesnet	0.4860	0.8588	0.4898	0.8860	0.4483	0.8349	0.4981	0.8894
	ETSformer	0.5554	0.9029	0.6875	1.0601	0.5592	0.8992	0.7540	1.1250
	Fedformer	0.7412	1.1114	0.6924	1.1659	0.7511	1.1215	0.7424	1.1973
	Dlinear	0.4614	0.8024	0.5016	0.8830	0.4661	0.8072	0.5068	0.8853
Multi-task models	Multi-Transformer	0.3543	0.6467	0.4877	0.6750	0.3259	0.6108	0.4892	0.7109
	AutoSTL	0.4037	0.7412	0.4966	0.7635	0.4174	0.7603	0.5063	0.7940
	Multitask-GNN	0.2917	0.5323	0.5071	0.7126	0.4001	0.6246	0.4738	0.6929
	GCML	**0.2858**	**0.5042**	**0.4312**	**0.5266**	**0.3090**	**0.5596**	**0.4433**	**0.5690**

As illustrated in Table 1, in the 12-step short-term load forecasting task for distributed user groups, the proposed method achieves MAE values of 0.2858 and 0.4312 while the RMSE values are 0.5042 and 0.5266. When the forecasting horizon is extended to 24 steps, the MAE values remain as 0.3090 and 0.4433, and the RMSE values are 0.5596 and 0.5690. In both cases, the results are significantly better than those of other baseline methods, including both single-task and multi-task models.

Across all forecasting tasks, the method achieves the most favorable results: (1) Compared to DLinear, the best-performing single-task baseline, the proposed method reduces the MAE by 38.06% and 14.03%, while the RMSE is reduced by 37.16% and 40.36% in the 12-step scenario. In the 24-step scenario, the reductions are 33.71% and 12.53% for the MAE, as well as 30.67% and 35.73% for the RMSE. (2) In the 12-step case, it yields relative MAE reductions of 19.33% and 11.59% and RMSE reductions of 22.04% and 21.99% across the two clusters. (3) In the 24-step case, the method consistently surpasses the baselines; compared with the Multi-Transformer baseline, it decreases the MAE by 5.19% and 9.3% and the RMSE by 8.38% and 19.96%. These results highlight the effectiveness of the model in capturing short-term load variations and its robust generalization capability across different forecasting horizons.

Moreover, the experimental results demonstrate that the multi-task model outperforms the single-task model in both prediction horizons. This is because many single-task baseline methods fail to capture cross-cluster dependencies and struggle with complex time-series patterns and noisy data. These limitations highlight the effectiveness of multi-task learning, which leverages the correlations and complementarities between different user groups with varying distributions, thereby enhancing the model's ability to capture load variation patterns and improving forecasting performance.

Evaluation of model interpretability based on R^2: In order to more comprehensively evaluate the performance of each model in the short-term power load forecasting task, we also compare the R^2 values obtained by different models for short-term power load forecasting on dataset I, and the obtained experimental results are shown in Table 2.

Table 2. Comparison of R^2 in short-term load forecasting among different models on dataset I.

Task Type	Method	Cluster 0		Cluster 1	
		R^2 (12-Step)	R^2 (24-Step)	R^2 (12-Step)	R^2 (24-Step)
Single-task models	Timemixer	0.2595	0.2445	0.2516	0.2316
	Convtimenet	0.4211	0.3721	0.3745	0.3624
	Timesnet	0.5636	0.5516	0.5549	0.5381
	ETSformer	0.5671	0.5238	0.4553	0.4108
	Fedformer	0.3464	0.3240.	0.3266	0.3445
	Dlinear	0.6432	0.6388	0.6238	0.5812
Multi-task models	Multi-Transformer	0.5816	0.6269	0.5447	0.4945
	AutoSTL	0.4511	0.4221	0.4167	0.3706
	Multitask-GNN	0.7168	0.6908	0.4922	0.5200
	GCML	**0.7587**	**0.6958**	**0.7297**	**0.6856**

As illustrated in Table 2, our model demonstrates superior performance across different clusters and forecasting horizons, achieving the optimal prediction results. For the 12-step forecasting horizon, compared to the best-performing single-task model Dlinear, it shows improvements of 17.96% and 17.01%, respectively. Meanwhile, compared to the better-performing multi-task model Multitask-GNN, it achieves increases of 5.85% and 48.25%, respectively. Additionally, it also shows significant improvements over other models for the 24-step forecasting horizon, fully verifying the superiority of GCML in complex data distributions and multi-task scenarios.

In addition, when the prediction length is 4 steps, the MAE, RMSE, and R^2 of Cluster 0 forecasting using GCML are 0.2386, 0.4179, and 0.8254, respectively. Meanwhile, on Cluster 1, the MAE is 0.4089, RMSE is 0.4988, and R^2 is 0.7499. The proposed model outperforms other comparison methods, demonstrating superior performance in short-term load forecasting.

4.5.2. Comparison of Experimental Results on Dataset II

Evaluation of prediction performance based on MAE and RMS: The experimental results of short-term electricity load forecasting with prediction horizons of 12 steps and 24 steps, conducted on different clusters obtained from clustering dataset II using the model proposed in this study, are presented in Table 3.

Table 3. Comparison of short-term load forecasting performance of different models on dataset II.

Task Type	Method	Cluster 0 (12-Step)		Cluster 1 (12-Step)		Cluster 2 (12-Step)		Cluster 0 (24-Step)		Cluster 1 (24-Step)		Cluster 2 (24-Step)	
		MAE	RMSE	MAE	RMSE	MAE	RMSE	MAE	RMSE	MAE	RMSE	MAE	RMSE
Single-task models	Timemixer	0.2564	0.3962	0.2626	0.3997	0.3226	0.5268	0.2705	0.4200	0.2745	0.4206	0.3446	0.5674
	Convtimenet	0.3674	0.4788	0.3764	0.5436	0.5099	0.9008	0.3824	0.5332	0.4861	0.7263	0.5467	0.8592
	Timesnet	0.3664	0.4831	0.277	0.4063	0.3626	0.5922	0.3801	0.5051	0.3116	0.4678	0.4007	0.6473
	ETSformer	0.3757	0.4908	0.3596	0.4594	0.5099	0.6825	0.4185	0.5546	0.4169	0.5365	0.5884	0.7911
	Fedformer	0.4581	0.6036	0.4130	0.5515	0.5393	0.7440	0.4850	0.6440	0.4434	0.5924	0.5733	0.7843
	Dlinear	0.3771	0.5231	0.5093	0.6708	0.6293	0.8688	0.4309	0.5899	0.5576	0.7306	0.6904	0.9252
Multi-task models	Multi-Transformer	0.1883	0.2622	0.2264	0.3177	0.2792	0.3973	0.1909	0.2648	0.1888	0.2602	0.2887	0.2887
	AutoSTL	0.2445	0.3306	0.2427	0.3295	0.4258	0.5914	0.2643	0.3556	0.2675	0.3660	0.4076	0.5588
	MultiTask-GNN	0.3644	0.4586	0.3249	0.4181	0.2808	0.3932	0.3767	0.4760	0.3949	0.4823	0.2920	0.4098
	GCML	**0.1617**	**0.2299**	**0.1554**	**0.2130**	**0.2608**	**0.3678**	**0.1769**	**0.2481**	**0.1725**	**0.2353**	**0.2682**	**0.3799**

As demonstrated in Table 3, the proposed method consistently achieves the lowest MAE and RMSE values in all forecasting scenarios, showing clear improvements over the compared models: (1) In the 12-step forecasting task, the MAE values obtained for the three clusters are 0.1617, 0.1554, and 0.2608, while the corresponding RMSE values are 0.2299, 0.2130, and 0.3678. Compared with TimeMixer, which performs relatively well among the single-task models, the MAE is reduced by 37.01%, 40.82%, and 19.16%, and the RMSE is reduced by 42.00%, 46.71%, and 30.18%, respectively. (2) In the 24-step forecasting task, the MAE values for the three clusters are 0.1796, 0.1725, and 0.2682, with RMSE values of

0.2481, 0.2353, and 0.3799. Relative to TimeMixer, the MAE decreases by 34.60%, 37.16%, and 22.17%, and the RMSE decreases by 40.93%, 44.06%, and 33.05%, respectively.

In addition, the approach also shows clear advantages over advanced multi-task learning frameworks. We use AutoSTL as a representative baseline, and the method consistently outperforms across different forecasting horizons and user groups. The detailed performance in different scenarios is as follows: (1) In the 12-step forecasting task, the MAE and RMSE are reduced by 33.86% and 30.46% for Cluster 1, by 36.00% and 35.36% for Cluster 2, and by 38.75% and 37.81% for Cluster 3; (2) for the 24-step task, the reductions in the MAE are 33.07%, 35.52%, and 34.20%, with corresponding decreases in the RMSE of 30.23%, 35.71%, and 32.02% across the three clusters. These results indicate that the proposed method not only improves short-term prediction accuracy but also delivers stable gains across varying conditions.

Evaluation of model interpretability based on R^2: To evaluate the interpretability and fitting performance of different models in the short-term load forecasting task, we employed R^2 as the evaluation metric to assess their fitting performance. Table 4 presents the R^2 values of various models for the 12-step and 24-step forecasting tasks across different clusters, offering a clear comparison of their effectiveness and fitting effects at different forecasting horizons.

As shown in Table 4, our model consistently achieves higher R^2 values than the baseline models under different clustering scenarios, indicating superior fitting performance and stability. In the 12-step forecasting task, it outperforms the best-performing baseline across all clusters, with improvements ranging from about 1.7% to 6.2%. Similarly, in the 24-step task, the proposed model maintains its advantage, yielding gains of approximately 0.9% to 2.8% over the strongest baseline. These results highlight the model's ability to exploit inter-cluster correlations and enhance pattern learning through knowledge sharing, thereby improving prediction accuracy.

Table 4. Comparison of R^2 in short-term load forecasting among different models on dataset II.

Task Type	Method	Cluster 0		Cluster 1		Cluster 2	
		R^2 (12-Step)	R^2 (24-Step)	R^2 (12-Step)	R^2 (24-Step)	R^2 (12-Step)	R^2 (24-Step)
Single-task models	Timemixer	0.8798	0.8648	0.8745	0.8610	0.8745	0.8109
	Convtimenet	0.8363	0.8048	0.8251	0.7610	0.7759	0.7230
	Timesnet	0.7764	0.7556	0.8388	0.7853	0.7387	0.6750
	ETSformer	0.5554	0.9029	0.6875	1.0601	0.5592	0.8992
	Fedformer	0.7412	0.8014	0.6924	0.8059	0.7511	0.8215
	Dlinear	0.7379	0.6668	0.7465	0.6804	0.6804	0.6296
Multi-task models	Multi-Transformer	0.9313	0.9299	0.8991	0.9323	0.8421	0.8327
	AutoSTL	0.8907	0.8735	0.8914	0.8660	0.6501	0.6877
	Multitask-GNN	0.7896	0.7734	0.8252	0.7674	0.8252	0.8321
	GCML	**0.9471**	**0.9384**	**0.9546**	**0.9446**	**0.8647**	**0.8557**

To further evaluate the model's performance in short-term forecasting, we conducted experiments using a 4-step prediction horizon. The results show that for Cluster 0, the model achieved an MAE of 0.1561, an RMSE of 0.2216, and an R^2 of 0.9509. In Cluster 1, it obtained even better performance with an MAE of 0.1461, an RMSE of 0.1986, and an R^2 of 0.9605. For Cluster 3, the metrics were 0.2631, 0.3738, and 0.8603, respectively. Compared with other methods, our model demonstrates superior accuracy and stronger predictive capability across all clusters.

Experimental results on multiple datasets demonstrate that the proposed model consistently achieves superior predictive performance. By employing a multi-task learning framework with a shared encoder, the model simultaneously acquires knowledge across related tasks, thereby enhancing its generalization to unseen scenarios. In addition, the integration of a filter-attention mechanism emphasizes critical local information, while multi-scale feature extraction enables the capture of complex dynamic patterns in time-series data. The improved forecasting accuracy enables aggregators to submit more reliable bids in electricity markets and enhances the operational efficiency of power systems with high penetration of distributed energy resources.

4.6. Performance Comparison

By adopting a multi-task model, multiple forecasting tasks can be addressed simultaneously, whereas single-task models handle only one objective. The multi-task approach improves prediction accuracy, reduces redundant computation, and enhances efficiency.

To assess practicality, this study evaluates time performance by recording training and testing durations of each model, reflecting computational efficiency and real-time applicability. For fairness, the reported time of single-task models corresponds to the total duration required for predicting each cluster separately. Comparative results for the 24-step forecasting horizon are shown in Figure 10.

As illustrated in Figure 10, a comparison of time performance on the two datasets indicates that the multi-task model generally outperforms the single-task baseline models, with the only exception being the linear model DLinear. This may be attributed to the relatively simple structure and small number of parameters of DLinear, which allow it to maintain high computational efficiency even in single-task scenarios.

To sum up, the results on dataset I and dataset II demonstrate that multi-task learning not only provides advantages in forecasting accuracy but also exhibits superior efficiency and practicality in terms of time performance, further validating the feasibility and effectiveness of the proposed approach in real-world applications.

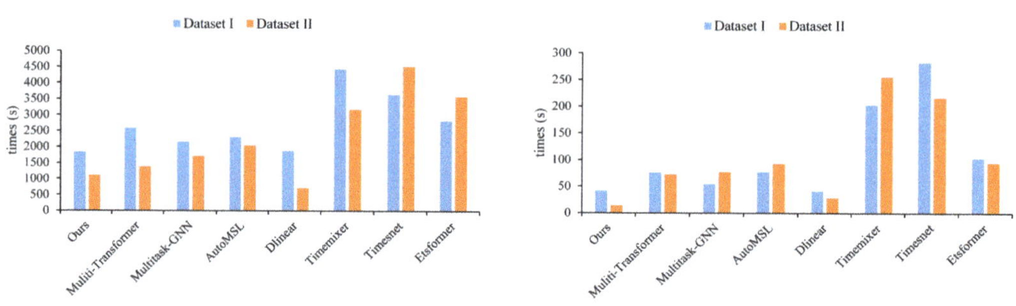

(a) (b)

Figure 10. Comparison of training and testing time of different models on 2 datasets. (**a**) Comparison of training time of different models on 2 datasets. (**b**) Comparison of testing time of different models on 2 datasets.

4.7. Ablation Experiment

In order to verify the effectiveness of each module in the multi-task model proposed in this paper, ablation experiments are carried out for comparative analysis. The model used in this paper is regarded as the benchmark network, and the following three models are obtained by removing the relevant modules in the proposed model, respectively, which are used for ablation experiments.

(1) w/o Multi-task: Instead of adopting the multi-task learning paradigm, load forecasting is performed independently for each cluster after clustering.
(2) w/ Self-attention: The filter-attention module is replaced with the vanilla self-attention module from the original Transformer architecture.

(3) w/o Inception: The Inception module is removed from the model, thus disabling multi-scale feature extraction.
(4) w/o Dy-weighting: The dynamic weighting strategy is removed from the model.
(5) w/ Un-weighting: The dynamic weighting is replaced with the uncertainty weighting.
(6) w/ InceptionSize: The number of convolutional branches in the Inception module is set to 4, with an additional branch of kernel size 7.
(7) w/ FilterSize: The window size in the filter-attention mechanism is set to 5.

The ablation experiments were conducted using the above variant models, and their results were compared with those of the proposed model. The detailed experimental findings are presented in Table 5.

Table 5. Comparison of short-term load forecasting performance of different models on dataset I.

Method	Cluster 0 (12-Step)		Cluster 1 (12-Step)		Cluster 0 (24-Step)		Cluster 1 (24-Step)	
	MAE	RMSE	MAE	RMSE	MAE	RMSE	MAE	RMSE
w/o Multi-task	0.5521	0.9515	0.6898	1.0363	0.5785	0.9714	0.6309	1.0019
w/ Self-attention	0.3372	0.6452	0.4964	0.7103	0.3218	0.6181	0.4903	0.7131
w/o Inception	0.3828	0.7067	0.5058	0.7715	0.3539	0.6853	0.5022	0.7347
w/o Dy-weighting	0.3263	0.5205	0.4601	0.5857	0.3363	0.5687	0.4984	0.6132
w/ Un-weighting	0.3058	0.5639	0.4437	0.5563	0.3257	0.6088	0.4834	0.5865
w/ InceptionSize	0.2907	0.5251	0.4452	0.5405	0.3194	0.5992	0.4834	0.5865
w/ FilterSize	0.2983	0.5565	0.4474	0.5766	0.3146	0.5893	0.4560	0.5712
GCML	**0.2858**	**0.5042**	**0.4312**	**0.5266**	**0.3090**	**0.5596**	**0.4433**	**0.5690**

As shown in Table 5, the proposed model demonstrates the following improvements across different clusters and forecasting horizons: (1) In the 12-step forecasting, compared with the experimental results of the w/o Multi-task, w/ Self-attention, w/o Inception models, w/o Dy-weighting, and w/ Un-weighting, the MAE obtained by the proposed model on Cluster 0 is reduced by 48.23%, 15.24%, 25.34%, 12.41%, 6.54%, 1.69%, and 4.19%, respectively, and the RMSE is reduced by 47.01%, 21.85%, 28.65%, 3.13%, 10.59%, 3.98%, and 9.40%, respectively; (2) for Cluster 1, the proposed model outperforms the other models, with the MAE reduced by 37.50%, 13.14%, 14.75%, 6.28%, 2.82%, 3.15%, and 3.62%, respectively, and the RMSE reduced by 49.18%, 25.86%, 31.74%, 10.09%, 5.34%, 2.57%, and 8.67%, respectively. In the 24-step forecasting scenario, the proposed model continues to yield lower values for the relevant metrics on both distributed user groups, surpassing the results of the ablation models.

The ablation experiment was conducted using the user aggregates obtained after clustering in dataset II, and the experimental results are shown in Table 6.

Table 6. Comparison of short-term load forecasting performance of different models on dataset II.

Method	Cluster 0 (12-Step)		Cluster 1 (12-Step)		Cluster 2 (12-Step)		Cluster 0 (24-Step)		Cluster 1 (24-Step)		Cluster 2 (24-Step)	
	MAE	RMSE	MAE	RMSE	MAE	RMSE	MAE	RMSE	MAE	RMSE	MAE	RMSE
w/o Multi-task	0.3542	0.4683	0.2765	0.3857	0.3329	0.5086	0.3862	0.5091	0.2907	0.4117	0.3555	0.5632
w/ Self-attention	0.1861	0.2604	0.1876	0.2649	0.3005	0.4371	0.1936	0.2683	0.1888	0.2618	0.2890	0.4109
w/o Inception	0.2144	0.2963	0.1996	0.2824	0.3149	0.4645	0.2211	0.3007	0.3007	0.2919	0.2981	0.4293
w/o Dy-weighting	0.1919	0.2682	0.1865	0.2593	0.3107	0.4461	0.2177	0.2990	0.1902	0.2612	0.4306	0.6090
w/ Un-weighting	0.1985	0.2757	0.1684	0.2321	0.3901	0.5595	0.2158	0.2972	0.2077	0.2860	0.3248	0.4652
w/ InceptionSize	0.1755	0.2346	0.1659	0.2240	0.2732	0.3880	0.1781	0.2677	0.1747	0.2867	0.2759	0.3978
w/ FilterSize	0.1695	0.2378	0.1580	0.2161	0.2644	0.3781	0.1831	0.2565	0.1946	0.2558	0.2729	0.3869
GCML	**0.1617**	**0.2299**	**0.1554**	**0.2130**	**0.2608**	**0.3678**	**0.1769**	**0.2481**	**0.1725**	**0.2353**	**0.2682**	**0.3799**

From Table 6, the proposed model demonstrates superior performance across different clusters, with the key results under the 12-step forecasting horizon summarized as follows: (1) On the aggregate obtained by Cluster 0, compared with the experimental results of the w/o Multi-task, w/ Self-attention, w/o Inception models, w/o Dy-weighting, w/ Un-weighting, w/ InceptionSize, and w/ FilterSize, the MAE of the proposed model is decreased by 54.35%, 13.11%, 24.58%, 18.64%, 15.74%, 7.86%, and 4.60%, respectively, and the RMSE is reduced by 50.91%, 11.71%, 22.41%, 14.28%, 16.61%, 2.00%, and 3.32%, respectively; (2) in the case of Cluster 1, the MAE is reduced by 43.79%, 17.17%, 22.14%, 7.72%, 16.68%, 7.17%, and 2.53%, respectively, and the RMSE is reduced by 44.78%, 19.59%, 24.58%, 7.37%, 17.86%, 4.91%, and 1.43%, respectively; and (3) on the Cluster 3 dataset, the MAE is decreased by 21.66%, 13.21%, 17.18%, 33.14%, 16.06%, 4.54%, and 1.36%, respectively, while the RMSE is diminished by 27.68%, 15.86%, 20.82%, 34.26%, 17.68%, 5.21%, and 2.72%, respectively. Meanwhile, the experimental results also indicate that the model proposed in this study outperforms the ablation models in the 24-step forecasting scenario.

The ablation experiment results demonstrate that GCML achieves superior performance across different architectural designs. By leveraging multi-task learning, the model can capture inter-group correlations and enhance generalization ability for complex load patterns. The integration of the filter-attention mechanism and Inception convolution further strengthens local feature extraction and multi-scale representation. Meanwhile, key parameters such as the window size of the filter-attention mechanism and the number of convolution kernels in the Inception module also have a certain impact on model performance.

4.8. Visualization of Prediction Results on Different Datasets

In order to better understand the characteristics of the load sequence under test, we present the visualization case of short-term power load forecasting using the proposed method in Figure 11, mainly including the results on two clusters after clustering, when the prediction length is 24 and 12, respectively. In each subfigure, the solid line represents the ground truth, while the dashed line shows the prediction value generated by the corresponding model.

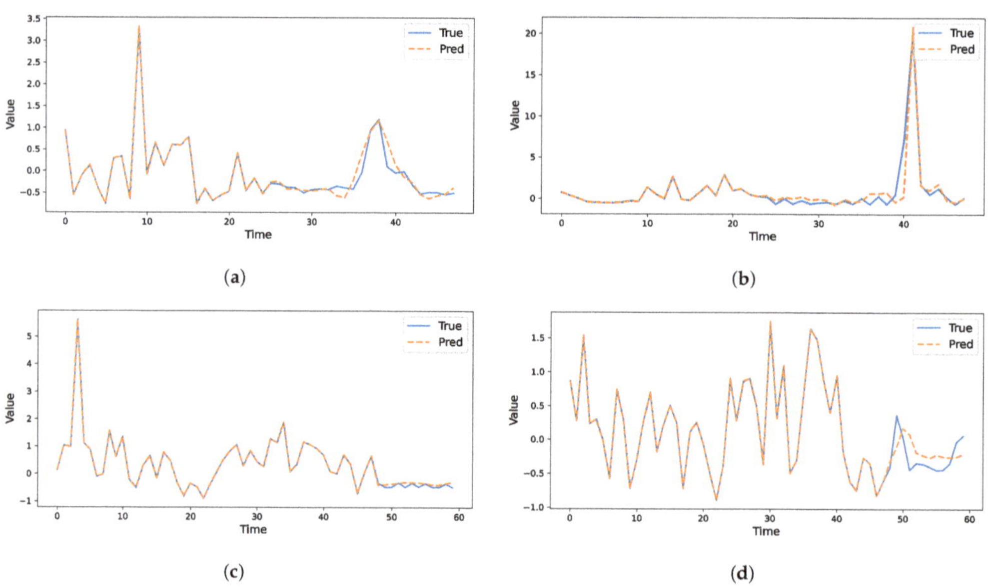

Figure 11. Visualization of prediction cases for load aggregators under different forecasting lengths on dataset I. (**a**) Visualization of the results for Cluster 0 with a prediction length of 24. (**b**) Visualization of the results for Cluster 1 with a prediction length of 24. (**c**) Visualization of the results for Cluster 0 with a prediction length of 12. (**d**) Visualization of the results for Cluster 1 with a prediction length of 12.

As shown in Figure 11, the proposed model demonstrates remarkable stability in prediction trends. For both forecasting horizons, the predicted loads for all types of users closely match the actual power values, indicating excellent performance in load forecasting. This result suggests that the model can provide valuable support for management and operation in the electricity market.

Figure 12 presents the visualization results of short-term electricity load forecasting on the three clusters obtained after clustering dataset II. From the visualization results, it can also be observed that our model exhibits excellent predictive performance. Meanwhile, it can effectively capture complex trends in different samples, which demonstrates that the proposed method has strong capability in extracting features of load data.

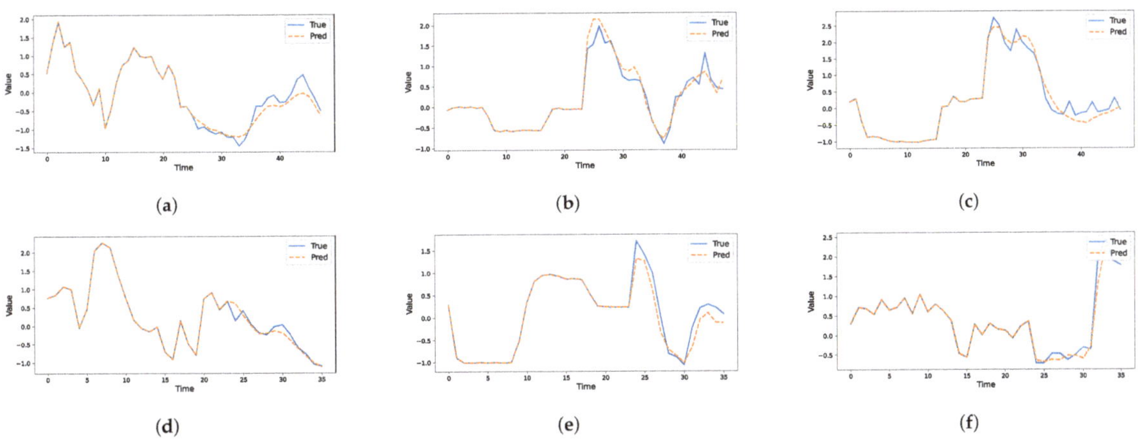

Figure 12. Visualization of prediction cases for load aggregators under different forecasting lengths on dataset II. (**a**) Visualization of the results for Cluster 0 with a prediction length of 24. (**b**) Visualization of the results for Cluster 1 with a prediction length of 24. (**c**) Visualization of the results for Cluster 2 with a prediction length of 24. (**d**) Visualization of the results for Cluster 0 with a prediction length of 12. (**e**) Visualization of the results for Cluster 1 with a prediction length of 12. (**f**) Visualization of the results for Cluster 2 with a prediction length of 12.

4.9. Results Discussion

Experiments were conducted on two publicly available power datasets to verify the effectiveness of the proposed short-term load forecasting algorithm based on clustering and multi-task learning. A comprehensive analysis of the experimental results was performed, taking into account the advantages, limitations, and comparisons with other methods.

(1) Our model combines clustering algorithms with multi-task learning to accurately classify user electricity consumption patterns while overcoming the limitations of traditional models. By learning from multiple related tasks, the model captures shared patterns across different groups, improving prediction accuracy and adaptability in complex scenarios with diverse user behaviors.

(2) Compared to other models, our approach's main advantage lies in the integration of filter-attention mechanisms and Inception convolution modules into the encoder. This combination enhances the model's ability to capture local patterns and fuse multi-scale features, resulting in improved prediction performance. By focusing on relevant features and extracting information at multiple scales, the model becomes more robust to variations in the data.

(3) The effectiveness of the proposed model is systematically validated through comparative experiments and ablation studies. Experimental analysis demonstrates that the proposed method exhibits significant advantages in prediction accuracy, with each module playing a crucial role.

5. Conclusions

To effectively utilize cross-group information between distributed user groups and improve short-term load forecasting accuracy, this research proposes a clustering and multi-task learning framework. Firstly, users are divided into consumption groups using clustering algorithms. Secondly, a shared encoder with dynamic weighting is employed for joint multi-task training, while independent linear task heads are assigned to each group. Furthermore, a filter-attention mechanism and an Inception convolution module are incorporated into the encoder to capture local patterns and extract multi-scale temporal features from load data. The experiment results demonstrate that GCML outperforms the comparison methods in load forecasting across various horizons, effectively improving prediction accuracy for distributed users. And this model can be used for diverse electricity usage scenarios and holds importance for efficient market clearing in the electricity spot market.

In the future, we can explore dynamic clustering methods for seasonal patterns to further enhance the adaptability and prediction performance of the model in scenarios where external variables are introduced, and we will investigate incremental learning strategies and lightweight model update mechanisms.

Author Contributions: Conceptualization, J.W.; Methodology, J.W.; Formal analysis, J.F.; Resources, Y.Z.; Data curation, J.F.; Writing—original draft, J.W.; Writing—review & editing, Y.S., Y.Z., R.Y. and P.Y.; Visualization, R.Y.; Supervision, P.Y.; Funding acquisition, P.Y. All authors have read and agreed to the published version of the manuscript.

Funding: This work was jointly supported by the following projects: NSFC (Grant No. 62377012) and Jiangsu Province Post graduate Practice and Innovation Program (No. SJCX240221).

Data Availability Statement: The original datasets are openly available in the following repositories: The electricity load forecasting dataset is on Kaggle [https://www.kaggle.com/datasets/jeanmidev/smart-meters-in-london, accessed on 16 November 2025] and individual household electric power consumption is from the UCI Machine Learning Repository [https://archive.ics.uci.edu/dataset/321, accessed on 16 November 2025]. These publicly accessible datasets were used to validate our proposed method, and we have properly cited them in the manuscript.

Conflicts of Interest: Authors Yusen Sun and Yu Zhou were employed by the company NARI Group Co., Ltd. Author Jianguo Fan was employed by the company Chongqing Three Gorges Water Conservancy and Electric Power Co., Ltd. The remaining authors declare that the research was conducted in the absence of any commercial or financial relationships that could be construed as a potential conflict of interest.

References

1. Fan, D.; Liu, Y.; Xu, X.; Shao, X.; Deng, X.; Xiang, Y.; Liu, J. Economic Operation of an Agent-Based Virtual Storage Aggregated Residential Electric-Heating Loads in Multiple Electricity Markets. *J. Clean. Prod.* **2024**, *454*, 142112. [CrossRef]
2. Pourdaryaei, A.; Mohammadi, M.; Mubarak, H.; Abdellatif, A.; Karimi, M.; Gryazina, E.; Terzija, V. A New Framework for Electricity Price Forecasting Via Multi-Head Self-Attention and CNN-based Techniques in the Competitive Electricity Market. *Expert Syst. Appl.* **2024**, *235*, 121207. [CrossRef]

3. Zhang, D. Optimization and Research of Smart Grid Load Forecasting Model Based on Deep Learning. *Int. J.-Low-Carbon Technol.* **2024**, *19*, 594–602. [CrossRef]
4. Eren, Y.; Kucukdemiral, I. A Comprehensive Review on Deep Learning Approaches for Short-Term Load Forecasting. *Renew. Sustain. Energy Rev.* **2024**, *189*, 114031. [CrossRef]
5. Botman, L.; Soenen, J.; Theodorakos, K.; Yurtman, A.; Bekker, J.; Vanthournout, K.; Blockeel, H.; Moor, B.D.; Lago, J. A Scalable Ensemble Approach to Forecast the Electricity Consumption of Households. *IEEE Trans. Smart Grid* **2023**, *14*, 757–768. [CrossRef]
6. Dong, H.; Zhu, J.; Li, S.; Wu, W.; Zhu, H.; Fan, J. Short-term Residential Household Reactive Power Forecasting Considering Active Power Demand Via Deep Transformer Sequence-to-sequence Networks. *Appl. Energy* **2023**, *329*, 120281. [CrossRef]
7. Qiu, D.; Wang, Y.; Wang, J.; Jiang, C.; Strbac, G. Personalized Retail Pricing Design for Smart Metering Consumers in Electricity Market. *Appl. Energy* **2023**, *348*, 121545. [CrossRef]
8. Li, K.; Li, Z.; Huang, C.; Ai, Q. Online Transfer Learning-Based Residential Demand Response Potential Forecasting for Load Aggregator. *Appl. Energy* **2024**, *358*, 122631. [CrossRef]
9. Guan, W.; Zhang, D.; Yu, H.; Peng, B.; Wu, Y.; Yu, T.; Wang, K. Customer Load Forecasting Method Based on the Industry Electricity Consumption Behavior Portrait. *Front. Energy Res.* **2021**, *9*, 742993. [CrossRef]
10. Jalalifar, R.; Delavar, M.R.; Ghaderi, S.F. SAC-ConvLSTM: A Novel Spatio-Temporal Deep Learning-Based Approach for a Short Term Power Load Forecasting. *Expert Syst. Appl.* **2024**, *237*, 121487. [CrossRef]
11. Pei, J.; Liu, N.; Shi, J.; Ding, Y. Tackling the Duck Curve in Renewable Power System: A Multi-Task Learning Model with Itransformer for Net-Load Forecasting. *Energy Convers. Manag.* **2025**, *326*, 119442. [CrossRef]
12. Sheng, Y.; Wang, H.; Yan, J.; Liu, Y.; Han, S. Short-term Wind Power Prediction Method Based on Deep Clustering-Improved Temporal Convolutional Network. *Energy Rep.* **2023**, *9*, 2118–2129. [CrossRef]
13. Yan, Q.; Lu, Z.; Liu, H.; He, X.; Zhang, X.; Guo, J. Short-term Prediction of Integrated Energy Load Aggregation Using a Bi-Directional Simple Recurrent Unit Network with Feature-Temporal Attention Mechanism Ensemble Learning Model. *Appl. Energy* **2024**, *355*, 122159. [CrossRef]
14. Zha, W.; Ji, Y.; Liang, C. Short-term Load Forecasting Method Based on Secondary Decomposition and Improved Hierarchical Clustering. *Results Eng.* **2024**, *22*, 101993. [CrossRef]
15. Tan, M.; Liao, C.; Chen, J.; Cao, Y.; Wang, R.; Su, Y. A multi-task learning method for multi-energy load forecasting based on synthesis correlation analysis and load participation factor. *Appl. Energy* **2023**, *343*, 121177. [CrossRef]
16. Xiao, J.-W.; Cao, M.; Fang, H.; Wang, J.; Wang, Y.-W. Joint Load Prediction of Multiple Buildings Using Multi-Task Learning with Selected-Shared-Private Mechanism. *Energy Build.* **2023**, *293*, 113178. [CrossRef]
17. Gao, Y.; Wu, J.; Yang, Y.; Wang, Z.; Ding, Z. Frequency-Aware Multi-Task Forecasting for Integrated Energy Systems Via Variational Mode Decomposition and Convolution-Attention Encoding. *IEEE Trans. Smart Grid* **2025**. [CrossRef]
18. Junior, M.Y.; Freire, R.Z.; Seman, L.O.; Stefenon, S.F.; Mariani, V.C.; dos Santos Coelho, L. Optimized Hybrid Ensemble Learning Approaches Applied to Very Short-Term Load Forecasting. *Int. J. Electr. Power Energy Syst.* **2024**, *155*, 109579.
19. Wang, Z.; Zhang, H.; Yang, R.; Chen, Y. Improving Model Generalization for Short-Term Customer Load Forecasting with Causal Inference. *IEEE Trans. Smart Grid* **2025**, *16*, 424–436. [CrossRef]
20. Li, Y.; Anastasiu, D.C. MC-ANN: A Mixture Clustering-Based Attention Neural Network for Time Series Forecasting. *IEEE Trans. Pattern Anal. Mach.* **2025**, *47*, 6888–6899. [CrossRef]
21. Kim, H.; Park, S.; Kim, S. Time-series Clustering and Forecasting Household Electricity Demand Using Smart Meter Data. *Energy Rep.* **2023**, *9*, 4111–4121. [CrossRef]
22. Hadjout, D.; Sebaa, A.; Torres, J.F.; Martinez-Alvarez, F. Electricity Consumption Forecasting with Outliers Handling Based on Clustering and Deep Learning with Application to the Algerian Market. *Expert Syst. Appl.* **2023**, *227*, 120123. [CrossRef]
23. Li, F.; Wang, C. Develop a Multi-Linear-trend Fuzzy Information Granule Based Short-Term Time Series Forecasting Model with K-Medoids Clustering. *Inf. Sci.* **2023**, *629*, 358–375. [CrossRef]
24. Yang, W.; Shi, J.; Li, S.; Song, Z.; Zhang, Z.; Chen, Z. A Combined Deep Learning Load Forecasting Model of Single Household Resident User Considering Multi-Time Scale Electricity Consumption Behavior. *Appl. Energy* **2022**, *307*, 118197. [CrossRef]
25. Dab, K.; Henao, N.; Nagarsheth, S.; Dube, Y.; Sansregret, S.; Agbossou, K. Consensus-based Time-Series Clustering Approach to Short-Term Load Forecasting for Residential Electricity Demand. *Energy Build.* **2023**, *299*, 113550. [CrossRef]
26. Chen, Z.; Jiaze, E.; Zhang, X.; Sheng, H.; Cheng, X. Multi-Task Time Series Forecasting with Shared Attention. In Proceedings of the Industrial Conference on Data Mining, New York, NY, USA, 15–19 July 2020; pp. 917–925.
27. Hao, S.; Bao, J.; Lu, C. A Time Series Multitask Framework Integrating a Large Language Model, Pre-Trained Time Series Model, and Knowledge Graph. *arXiv* **2025**, arXiv:2503.07682. [CrossRef]
28. Tian, Z.; Liu, W.; Zhang, J.; Sun, W.; Wu, C. EDformer Family: End-to-end Multi-Task Load Forecasting Frameworks for Day-Ahead Economic Dispatch. *Appl. Energy* **2025**, *383*, 125319. [CrossRef]

29. Guo, Y.; Li, Y.; Qiao, X.; Zhang, Z.; Zhou, W.; Mei, Y.; Lin, J.; Zhou, Y.; Nakanishi, Y. BiLSTM Multitask Learning-Based Combined Load Forecasting Considering the Loads Coupling Relationship for Multienergy System. *IEEE Trans. Smart Grid* **2022**, *13*, 3481–3492. [CrossRef]
30. Jiang, L.; Wang, X.; Li, W.; Wang, L.; Yin, X.; Jia, L. Hybrid Multitask Multi-Information Fusion Deep Learning for Household Short-Term Load Forecasting. *IEEE Trans. Smart Grid* **2021**, *12*, 5362–5372. [CrossRef]
31. Zhang, W.; Yu, Y.; Ji, S.; Zhang, S.; Ni, C. A Multitask Graph Convolutional Network with Attention-Based Seasonal-Trend Decomposition for Short-Term Load Forecasting. *IEEE Trans. Power Syst.* **2024**, *40*, 3222–3231. [CrossRef]
32. Deng, S.; Cai, Q.; Zhang, Z.; Wu, X. User Behavior Analysis Based on Stacked Autoencoder and Clustering in Complex Power Grid Environment. *IEEE Trans. Intell. Transp.* **2022**, *23*, 25521–25535. [CrossRef]
33. Michalakopoulos, V.; Sarmas, E.; Papias, I.; Skaloumpakas, P.; Marinakis, V.; Doukas, H. A Machine Learning-Based Framework for Clustering Residential Electricity Load Profiles to Enhance Demand Response Programs. *Appl. Energy* **2024**, *361*, 122943. [CrossRef]
34. Zhang, Y.; Yang, Q. A Survey on Multi-Task Learning. *IEEE Trans. Knowl. Data Eng.* **2022**, *34*, 5586–5609. [CrossRef]
35. Yang, Q.; Zhang, Y.; Dai, W.; Pan, S.J. Multi-task Learning. *Mach. Learn.* **2020**, 126–140.
36. Heng, S. Enhanced Multi-Energy Load Forecasting Via Multi-Task Learning and GRU-attention Networks in Integrated Energy Systems. *Electr. Eng.* **2025**, *107*, 7673–7683. [CrossRef]
37. Fu, Z.; Lam, W.; Yu, Q.; So, A. M.-C.; Hu, S.; Liu, Z.; Collier, N. Decoder-Only or Encoder-Decoder? Interpreting Language Model As a Regularized Encoder-Decoder. *arXiv* **2023**, arXiv:2304.04052.
38. Gao, S.; Koker, T.; Queen, O.; Hartvigsen, T.; Tsiligkaridis, T.; Zitnik, M. UniTS: A Unified Multi-Task Time Series Model. In Proceedings of the NeurIPS, Vancouver, BC, Canada, 9–15 December 2024; pp. 140589–140631.
39. Ye, C.; Xiong, W.; Gu, Q.; Zhang, T. Corruption-robust algorithms with uncertainty weighting for nonlinear contextual bandits and markov decision processes. In Proceedings of the International Conference on Machine Learning, Honolulu, HI, USA, 23–29 July 2023; pp. 39834–39863.
40. Liang, J.; Cao, L.; Madden, S.; Ives, Z.; Li, G. RITA: Group Attention is All You Need for Timeseries Analytics. In Proceedings of the ACM SIGMOD Conference, Santiago, Chile, 9–15 June 2024; pp. 62:1–62:28.
41. Ye, T.; Dong, L.; Xia, Y.; Sun, Y.; Zhu, Y.; Huang, G.; Wei, F. Differential Transformer. In Proceedings of the ICLR, Hong Kong, China, 20–22 October 2025.
42. Bueno-Barrachina, J.-M.; Ye-Lin, Y.; del Amor, F.N.; Fuster-Roig, V. Inception 1D-Convolutional Neural Network for Accurate Prediction of Electrical Insulator Leakage Current from Environmental Data During Its Normal Operation Using Long-Term Recording. *Eng. Appl. Artif.* **2023**, *119*, 105799. [CrossRef]
43. Wang, Y.; Xu, X.; Hu, L.; Fan, J.; Han, M. A time series continuous missing values imputation method based on generative adversarial networks. *Knowl.-Based Syst.* **2024**, *283*, 111215. [CrossRef]
44. Qiu, X.; Wu, X.; Lin, Y.; Guo, C.; Hu, J.; Yang, B. DUET: Dual Clustering Enhanced Multivariate Time Series Forecasting. In Proceedings of the KDD 2025, Toronto, ON, Canada, 3–7 August 2025; pp. 1185–1196.
45. Chicco, D.; Warrens, M.J.; Jurman, G. The Coefficient of Determination R-squared is More Informative Than SMAPE, MAE, MAPE, MSE and RMSE in Regression Analysis Evaluation. *PeerJ Comput. Sci.* **2021**, *7*, e623. [CrossRef] [PubMed]
46. Seo, H.; Lim, C. ST-MTM: Masked Time Series Modeling with Seasonal-Trend Decomposition for Time Series Forecasting. In Proceedings of the KDD 2025, Toronto, ON, Canada, 3–7 August 2025; pp. 1209–1220.
47. Wang, S.; Wu, H.; Shi, X.; Hu, T.; Luo, H.; Ma, L.; Zhang, J.Y.; Zhou, J. TimeMixer: Decomposable Multiscale Mixing for Time Series Forecasting. In Proceedings of the ICLR, Vienna, Austria, 7 May 2024.
48. Cheng, M.; Yang, J.; Pan, T.; Liu, Q.; Li, Z. ConvTimeNet: A Deep Hierarchical Fully Convolutional Model for Multivariate Time Series Analysis. In Proceedings of the WWW'25: Companion Proceedings of the ACM on Web Conference 2025, Sydney, Australia, 28 April–2 May 2025; pp. 171–180.
49. Wu, H.; Hu, T.; Liu, Y.; Zhou, H.; Wang, J.; Long, M. TimesNet: Temporal 2D-Variation Modeling for General Time Series Analysis. In Proceedings of the ICLR, Kigali, Rwanda, 1–5 May 2023.
50. Woo, G.; Liu, C.; Sahoo, D.; Kumar, A.; Hoi, S. ETSformer: Exponential Smoothing Transformers for Time-series Forecasting. In Proceedings of the ICLR 2023, Online, 1–5 May 2023.
51. Zhou, T.; Ma, Z.; Wen, Q.; Wang, X.; Sun, L.; Jin, R. FEDformer: Frequency Enhanced Decomposed Transformer for Long-term Series Forecasting. In Proceedings of the International Conference on Machine Learning, Pontignano, Italy, 19–22 September 2022; pp. 27268–27286.
52. Zeng, A.; Chen, M.; Zhang, L.; Xu, Q. Are Transformers Effective for Time Series Forecasting? In Proceedings of the AAAI, Washington, DC, USA, 7–14 February 2023; pp. 11121–11128.
53. Zou, S.; Yang, J.; Ruan, X.; Qin, Y.; Wu, Y.; Li, C.; Zhang, W. MSM-TFL: A Multiservice, Multitask Transformer Framework for Edge Load Prediction. *IEEE Internet Things J.* **2025**, *12*, 37790–37808. [CrossRef]

54. Zhang, Z.; Zhao, X.; Miao, H.; Zhang, C.; Zhao, H.; Zhang, J. AutoSTL: Automated Spatio-Temporal Multi-Task Learning. In Proceedings of the AAAI Conference on Artificial Intelligence, Washington, DC, USA, 7–14 February 2023; pp. 4902–4910.
55. Han, X.; Huang, Y.; Pan, Z.; Li, W.; Hu, Y.; Lin, G. Multi-Task Time Series Forecasting Based on Graph Neural Networks. *Entropy* **2023**, *25*, 1136. [CrossRef] [PubMed]

mathematics

MDPI

Article

Stochastic Optimization and Adaptive Control for Dynamic Bus Lane Management Under Heterogeneous Connected Traffic

Bo Yang [1], Chunsheng Wang [1,*], Junxi Yang [2] and Zhangyi Wang [1]

[1] School of Automation, Central South University, Changsha 410083, China; csuybo@csu.edu.cn (B.Y.)
[2] School of Traffic and Transportation Engineering, Central South University, Changsha 410083, China; 8212240307@csu.edu.cn
* Correspondence: wangcsu@csu.edu.cn

Abstract: The efficiency of intelligent urban mobility increasingly depends on adaptive mathematical models that can optimize multimodal transportation resources under stochastic and heterogeneous conditions. This study proposes a Markovian stochastic modeling and metaheuristic optimization framework for the adaptive management of bus lane capacity in mixed connected traffic environments. The heterogeneous vehicle arrivals are modeled using a Markov Arrival Process (MAP) to capture correlated and busty flow characteristics, while the system-level optimization aims to minimize total fuel consumption through discrete lane capacity allocation. To support real-time adaptation, a Hidden Markov Model (HMM) is integrated for queue-length estimation under partial observability. The resulting nonlinear and nonconvex optimization problem is solved using Genetic Algorithm (GA), Differential Evolution (DE), and Particle Swarm Optimization (PSO), ensuring robustness and convergence across diverse traffic scenarios. Numerical experiments demonstrate that the proposed stochastic–adaptive framework can reduce fuel consumption and vehicle delay by up to 68% and 65%, respectively, under high saturation and connected-vehicle penetration. The findings verify the effectiveness of coupling stochastic modeling with adaptive control, providing a transferable methodology for energy-efficient and data-driven lane management in smart and sustainable cities.

Keywords: Markov Arrival Process (MAP); stochastic queuing model; adaptive traffic control; metaheuristic optimization; hidden Markov model (HMM)

MSC: 90B20

1. Introduction

The rapid evolution of smart cities is transforming urban mobility through the integration of intelligent, connected, and sustainable transportation systems. As global urbanization accelerates, cities are increasingly challenged by congestion, excessive fuel consumption, and environmental degradation. Intelligent Transportation Systems (ITS) have therefore become a cornerstone for achieving efficient and sustainable mobility by leveraging data-driven and model-based control technologies to optimize traffic operations and energy utilization [1–3]. Public transportation, in particular, plays a pivotal role in promoting carbon neutrality and social equity, as demonstrated by recent smart transit initiatives in the United States, Australia, and China [4–6].

Among various ITS strategies, bus lane management is recognized as one of the most effective approaches to enhance transit efficiency and reliability in dense urban areas [7,8]. Conventional bus lanes (BLs), while guaranteeing priority for public transport, often suffer from inefficiencies such as unauthorized vehicle intrusion, underutilization during off-peak hours, and increased congestion in adjacent lanes during peak demand [9,10]. To overcome these limitations, Dynamic bus lane (DBL) strategies enable flexible lane capacity allocation in response to temporal traffic variations. Early models such as the Intermittent Bus Lane (IBL) [11] and Bus Lane with Intermittent Priority (BLIP) [12,13] attempted to optimize road-space usage through rule-based switching mechanisms. However, these methods exhibited limited adaptability to stochastic traffic variations and frequently failed to maintain operational stability under high saturation conditions [14,15].

Recent advances in connected vehicle (CV) technologies have created new opportunities for adaptive and cooperative management of DBL systems. Through vehicle-to-everything (V2X) communication, connected vehicles can share speed, position, and signal phase information in real time, enabling predictive traffic control and coordinated bus prioritization [16,17]. Previous studies, including those by Guler et al. [18] and Zhao and Zhou [19], demonstrated that cooperative signal control combined with dynamic bus lane activation can substantially improve intersection throughput and travel time reliability. Building upon these findings, further developments—such as dynamic or cooperative bus lane priority algorithms [20,21]—have shown the potential of CV-assisted control in enhancing efficiency and sustainability. Nevertheless, most of these studies assume deterministic or homogeneous traffic conditions, neglecting the stochastic interactions between connected and non-connected vehicles. This simplification restricts the scalability and robustness of existing models in realistic heterogeneous traffic environments.

Modeling traffic flow under mixed connected environments requires a stochastic mathematical framework capable of capturing both correlated arrivals and random variability. Queueing theory provides a rigorous foundation for describing such dynamic processes, particularly at signalized intersections [22,23]. The Markov Arrival Process (MAP), an extension of the Poisson process, is widely recognized for its ability to represent bursty and correlated traffic arrivals [24–26]. For example, Alfa and Neuts [25] and Mirzaeian et al. [26] verified that MAP-based models can effectively characterize vehicular arrival dependencies in intelligent transportation systems. More recent studies have successfully employed MAP structures to optimize traffic signal control [27] and highway toll operations [28,29]. However, their integration into bus lane capacity optimization frameworks remains largely unexplored. This research gap highlights the necessity of a stochastic–adaptive modeling approach that can represent time-varying heterogeneous flows while supporting analytical optimization and control.

In parallel, traffic state estimation under partial observability has been extensively investigated using the Hidden Markov Model (HMM) framework. HMMs are particularly suitable for reconstructing unobservable states—such as queue length and congestion level—based on incomplete probe-vehicle observations [30,31]. Hao et al. [32] and Zhao et al. [33] demonstrated that HMM-based inference can accurately estimate queue length distributions even under low connected-vehicle penetration. The fusion of HMM estimation with stochastic optimization therefore provides a promising basis for developing adaptive and data-driven control strategies. Despite these advances, only limited research has explored how real-time estimation mechanisms can be mathematically embedded within optimization frameworks for bus lane management in connected and heterogeneous environments.

While previous MAP- or HMM-based studies [27–29,32,33] have effectively modeled correlated traffic arrivals or estimated hidden queue states, they treated these two aspects separately—focusing either on stochastic arrival modeling or on real-time state estimation. In contrast, the present study integrates both MAP-based stochastic flow modeling and HMM-based adaptive estimation into a unified optimization–control framework. Moreover, unlike earlier deterministic or single-stage approaches, our model embeds metaheuristic optimization (GA/DE/PSO) directly into the stochastic–adaptive structure, allowing coordinated offline capacity allocation and online queue regulation under heterogeneous connected traffic. This coupling of stochastic theory, probabilistic estimation, and evolutionary optimization constitutes a key advancement beyond existing MAP/HMM-based traffic control studies.

To address these limitations, this study proposes an adaptive mathematical optimization–control framework for the Connected Dynamic Bus Lane (C-DBL) system at isolated intersections under heterogeneous traffic conditions. The framework integrates MAP-based stochastic queueing modeling, HMM-based real-time estimation, and metaheuristic optimization algorithms—including Genetic Algorithm (GA), Differential Evolution (DE), and Particle Swarm Optimization (PSO)—to achieve energy-efficient and adaptive lane management. Specifically, the model determines the optimal lane capacity allocation that minimizes total fuel consumption and vehicle delay while enabling online adjustments according to real-time traffic states. The proposed methodology contributes to the literature by combining stochastic modeling, adaptive control, and evolutionary optimization within a unified mathematical structure, offering a scalable solution for sustainable and intelligent urban mobility.

The main contributions of this research are fourfold:

1. A stochastic queuing model for heterogeneous connected traffic. A MAP-based queuing framework is developed to capture dynamic arrival correlations between connected and conventional vehicles in mixed traffic flows, improving the realism of traffic representation.
2. An intelligent optimization algorithm for lane capacity management. A non-linear optimization problem is formulated to minimize total fuel consumption, solved via metaheuristic techniques suited for complex and nonconvex systems.
3. An adaptive control mechanism integrating real-time estimation. The HMM-based queue estimation model enables online adjustments of the C-DBL activation and capacity according to observed traffic conditions, ensuring responsive and stable operation.

2. C-DBL System and Control Strategy

2.1. System Description

As shown in Figure 1, the C-DBL system includes a dedicated bus lane alongside adjacent general-purpose lanes (for through, left, or right turns). Its primary purpose is to provide a partially dedicated lane for CVs. CVs are required to have mutual communication capabilities to collect real-time vehicle queue data. Buses utilize global positioning systems or wireless communication features to capture their status. Roadside devices acquire and forward real-time vehicle queue and signal phase and timing (SPaT) information to a cloud server for data analysis and planning. In the C-DBL system, the trajectory of CVs after entering the system can be divided into four main segments: (1) changing lanes to enter the C-DBL; (2) queuing within the C-DBL during the red signal phase; (3) waiting to depart; and (4) accelerating to a specified speed.

Based on the description, we establish a dual-layer optimization-control framework for C-DBL, as illustrated in Figure 2. The upper layer is an optimal model based on SQM, designed to determine the optimal capacity configuration of the C-DBL under varying traffic scenarios. The lower layer is a dynamic control decision model that estimates the traffic situation in the social lane (SL) using the characteristics of connected vehicles and indicates when CVs should enter the C-DBL based on the obtained optimal capacity. Specifically, the control strategy is triggered at the start of each intersection signal cycle (C_i, $i = 1, 2, \ldots$), when the signal light turns red, the first action is to determine the number of queued vehicles V in the SL during the current signal cycle (C_i). If V reaches the optimal configuration L^*, the second action is to determine whether the last bus is within the priority access range. If it is not, the CV will then enter the C-DBL.

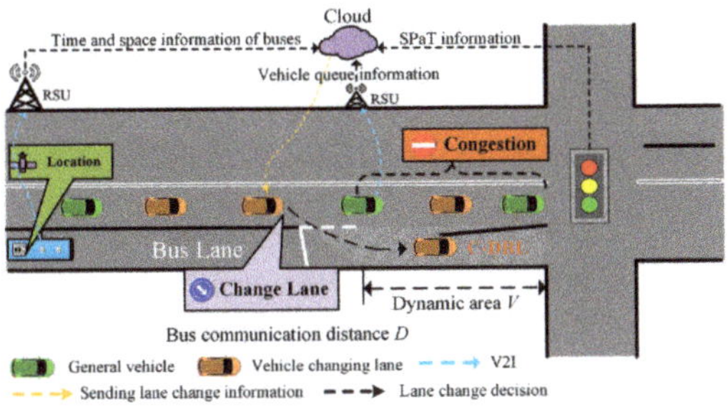

Figure 1. Overall architecture of C-DBL system.

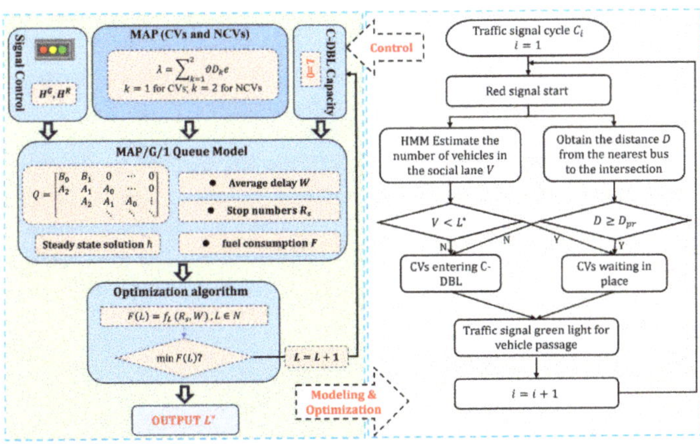

Figure 2. C-DBL system optimization and control framework (the green section for Modeling & Optimization, the yellow section for C-DBL Control Strategy, and other functional modules).

In the proposed C-DBL system, the lane prioritization policy is designed as a hierarchical structure. Under normal conditions, the C-DBL maintains bus priority to ensure reliable public transport operation to ensure public transport reliability. However, during non-bus phases or when the bus headway exceeds a threshold, the C-DBL can be adaptively shared with connected vehicles (CVs) from adjacent social lanes. The access decision is governed by the real-time queue state estimated via the HMM-based module, ensuring that shared use by CVs does not interfere with scheduled bus operations. Therefore, the lane prioritizes buses first while conditionally admitting CVs when capacity permits.

2.2. Vehicle Queue Detection Using HMM

In connected vehicle environments, probe vehicle data can be used to estimate queue lengths at signalized intersections. This process is modeled using an HMM, where the queue lengths are treated as hidden states, and the stopping positions of probe vehicles serve as observations.

The sequence of queue lengths $V = \{V_1, V_2, \ldots, V_C\}$ follows a time-homogeneous Markov process, with the transition probabilities describing how queue lengths evolve between cycles. The observations $q = \{q_1, q_2, \ldots, q_C\}$ represent the partial queues observed by probe vehicles, with the emission probabilities relating these observations to the underlying queue lengths.

The emission probability $P(q_i \mid V_i)$ for a given cycle is defined by

$$P(q_i \mid V_i) = \begin{cases} p^{n_i}(1-p)^{V_i-n_i} & if\ V_i \geq |q_i| \\ 0 & if\ V_i \leq |q_i| \end{cases} \tag{1}$$

where n_i is the number of probe vehicles in cycle i, and p is the penetration rate of probe vehicles.

To estimate queue lengths cycle-by-cycle, we apply the Maximum Likelihood Estimation (MLE) using the Viterbi algorithm. This approach finds the most probable sequence of queue lengths given the observed data by maximizing the likelihood of the sequence. The transition probabilities, emission probabilities, and initial state probabilities are required for this estimation process. For details on the HMM, please refer to the literature [32,33].

2.3. Transit Priority Communications Range

A networked environment facilitates the direct transmission of real-time data to the traffic signal control system. To ensure seamless execution of prioritized access, the control system must determine the minimum upstream distance required to initiate prioritization decisions. This distance is referred to as the minimum communication range D_{pr}.

Unlike traditional fixed-position detection systems [18], this distance is variable within a connected environment. Therefore, the activation range for priority should be dynamically adjusted based on real-time bus kinematics and current traffic conditions. Let us assume that the signal cycle duration at the target intersection is c, with a green light duration of g, a red-light duration of r, and that the allowable throughput capacity of the C-DBL is L^* (in pcu/cycle). According to traffic flow theory, the required activation distance can be expressed as follows

$$D_{pr}(i) \geq L^*(i) + \max\{r_{re}(i)L^*(i)\frac{k_{jam}g}{r}, v_{bus}r_{re}\} \tag{2}$$

where k_{jam} denotes traffic density, r_{re} denotes the remaining red-light duration after the last CV enters during the i-th signal cycle, and v_{bus} indicates the speed of the connected bus. Additionally, the capacity $L^*(i)$ of the C-DBL during the i-th signal cycle will be discussed in the following section.

2.4. Traffic Flow Modeling in Heterogeneous and Connected Environments

We consider the arrival process of hybrid traffic flow, comprising both connected vehicles (CVs) and conventional vehicles (NCVs), within a networked environment. The arrival process of these vehicles is modelled using a MAP, which effectively captures the correlation and heterogeneity of vehicle arrivals in intelligent transportation systems [25,26].

Let the state of the underlying Markov process governing the vehicle arrivals be denoted as v_t, $t \geq 0$, and the state space is $\{0, 1, \ldots, M\}$. The dynamics of the process v_t follow an irreducible continuous-time Markov chain with transition rates defined by the infinitesimal generator D. For two vehicle types, the MAP is completely characterized by the state space of the underlying process and the corresponding transition matrices D_k for each type of vehicle, where $k = 1, 2$ with D_0 representing the rate matrix when no vehicle arrives.

The vehicle arrival rates for each type k (with $k = 1$ for CVs and $k = 2$ for NCVs) are computed as

$$\lambda_k = \vartheta D_k e,\ k = 1,2 \tag{3}$$

where ϑ is the steady-state probability vector of the underlying Markov process v_t, and e is a column vector of ones. The total arrival rate of vehicles, λ, is the sum of the individual rates

$$\lambda = \lambda_1 + \lambda_2 \tag{4}$$

The variance of the inter-arrival times for vehicles of type k is expressed as

$$v(k) = 2\vartheta(-D_0 - D_k)^{-1}e - \left(\frac{1}{\lambda_k}\right)^2,\ k = 1,2 \tag{5}$$

The correlation coefficient $c(k)$ between consecutive inter-arrival times for vehicles of type k is given by

$$cor(k) = \frac{[\vartheta(D_0 + D_k)^{-1}\lambda_k D_k (D_0 + D_k)^{-1}e - \frac{1}{\lambda_i^2}]}{v(k)} \tag{6}$$

Detailed definitions of the abbreviations and mathematical symbols covered in this study can be found in the Abbreviations.

3. Stochastic Queuing Model and Performance Index

3.1. System State

To construct a theoretical model of the queuing process at a signalized intersection under the C-DBL system. Let us define two phase matrices, H^G and H^R, representing the system states during the green and red phases, respectively. Each matrix encodes the active duration of its corresponding signal phase within one complete cycle. Specifically, $H^G \in \mathbb{R}^{(g+r)\times g}$, $H^R \in \mathbb{R}^{(g+r)\times r}$, where g and r denote the number of discrete time steps (or phase units) of the green and red lights, respectively. For the matrix H^G, the elements are defined as follows: if $i = 1,2,\ldots,g-1$ or $i = r, j = 1$, then $H^G_{(i,j+1)} = 1$; otherwise, $H^G_{(i,j)} = 0$. For the matrix H^R, the elements are defined as follows: if $i = 0,1,\ldots,r-1$, then $H^R_{(g+i,j+1)} = 1$; otherwise, $H^R_{(g+i,j)} = 0$.

At time n, let L_n represent the number of vehicles in the normal lanes and K_n denote the number of vehicles in the C-DBL. Additionally, H_n refer to the values of the green and red phases, respectively, and J_n indicate the state of the MAP. Thus, the system state can be characterized by a Markov chain $\{L_n, K_n, S_n, J_n, n > 0\}$ with a state space

Let l and k denote the number of social vehicles in the social lane and C-DBL, respectively, and s denote the signal state at time t_n, where $l \geq 0,\ 0 \leq k \leq V$. The state space $\varnothing$ of the process $\{L_n, K_n, S_n, n > 0\}$ can be represented as

$$\begin{aligned}\varnothing = \{(l,0,s,j), l \geq 0,\ 1 \leq s \leq g+r, 1 \leq j \leq M\} \\ \cup \left\{\begin{matrix}(l,k,s,m), 0 \leq l \leq V, 1 \leq k \leq min(k,V), \\ V-l \leq s \leq V-k\end{matrix}\right\} \\ \cup \left\{\begin{matrix}(l,k,s,m), l \geq V, 1 \leq k \leq min(k,V), \\ 1 \leq s \leq V-k\end{matrix}\right\} \\ \cup \left\{\begin{matrix}(l,k,s,m), l \geq V, 1 \leq k \leq min(k,V), \\ g+l \leq s \leq c\end{matrix}\right\}\end{aligned} \tag{7}$$

The state $\varnothing$ is arranged in lexicographic order, and the infinitesimal generator of the Markov chain $\{L_n, K_n, S_n, J_n, n > 0\}$ exhibits the following block structure

$$Q = \begin{bmatrix} B_0 & B_1 & 0 & \cdots & 0 & 0 \\ A_2 & A_1 & A_0 & \cdots & 0 & 0 \\ & A_2 & A_1 & A_0 & \vdots & 0 \\ & & \ddots & \ddots & \ddots & \vdots \\ 0 & 0 & \cdots & A_2 & A_1 & A_0 \\ 0 & 0 & 0 & \cdots & A_1 & A_0 \end{bmatrix} \tag{8}$$

where

$$B^0_{i,j} = \begin{cases} \left[0, H^R \otimes D_1\right] & 0 \le i \le V-1; j = i+1 \\ \left[H^G \otimes D_0, 0\right] & 1 \le i \le V; j = i-1 \\ H^G \otimes D_0, H^R \otimes D_0] & i = j = 0 \\ \left[0, H^R \otimes D_0\right] & 1 \le i = j \le V \end{cases};$$

$$B^1_{i,i} = diag\{\left[H^G \otimes (D_1 + D_2), H^R \otimes D_2\right]\} \quad 1 \le i \le V$$

$$A^0_{i,i} = diag\left\{\left[0, H^R \otimes D_2\right] \quad 1 \le i \le V\right\}$$

$$A^2_{i,j} = \begin{cases} \left[H^G \otimes D_0, 0\right] & 1 \le i \le V; j = i-1 \\ \left[H^G \otimes D_0, 0\right] & i = j = 0 \end{cases}$$

$$A^1_{i,j} = \begin{cases} \left[0, H^R \otimes D_1\right] & 0 \le i \le V-1; j = i+1 \\ \left[H^G \otimes (D_1 + D_2)\ H^R \otimes D_0\right] & 1 \le i = j \le V \end{cases}$$

3.2. Model Solution

Assume that the Markov process $\{L_n, K_n, S_n, J_n, n > 0\}$ is irreducible and defined within a finite state space. Consequently, for any specified set of system parameters, there exists a unique stationary distribution $\hbar$ associated with the process.

$$\hbar Q = 0; \hbar e = 1 \tag{9}$$

where e is the unit column vector, $\hbar = (\hbar_0, \hbar_1, \hbar_{2,} \ldots)$ and $\hbar^i_j = \left(\hbar^i_{j1}, \hbar^i_{j2}, \ldots, \hbar^i_{jV}\right)$.

As shown in Equation (9), the stationary distribution $\hbar Q = 0$, which can be solved using standard linear algebra methods. However, solving high-dimensional systems becomes challenging due to constraints on computational memory and processing speed. To resolve these issues, a specialized stable algorithm is recommended. Algorithm 1 summarizes the computational procedure based on the matrix-geometric method to obtain the stationary distribution and key performance metrics.

The solution process for the stochastic queueing model is summarized in Algorithm 1, which is based on the matrix-geometric method for level-dependent quasi-birth-and-death (QBD) processes. The goal of this algorithm is to derive the stationary probability vector $\hbar$ and the rate matrix R, which describe the steady-state behavior of the system under heterogeneous traffic arrivals modeled by the MAP structure. The main inputs, intermediate computations, and outputs are detailed step-by-step below.

Algorithm 1. Solving Process for Random Queueing Models

Step	Description
Input: Block matrices $\{B_0, B_1, A_0, A_1, A_2\}$ from the infinitesimal generator of the MAP/QBD system; convergence threshold ε. **Output:** Steady-state probability vectors $\hbar$ and the rate matrix R.	
Step 1. Initialization	Import the block matrices $\{B_0, B_1, A_0, A_1, A_2\}$ representing transitions among boundary and internal levels. Set iteration counter $k = 0$ and initialize $R^{(0)} = 0$
Step 2. Ergodicity Check and Base Probability	Compute the stationary vector $\hbar$ satisfying $\hbar\sum_{i=0}^{2} A_i = \hbar; \pi e = 1$. The stability (ergodicity) condition $\hbar A_0 e < \hbar A_2 e$ is verified to ensure that the system converges to a steady state.
Step 3. Computation of the Rate Matrix R	Iteratively solve R from the nonlinear matrix equation $A_0 + RA_1 + R^2 A_1 = 0$. Using the functional iteration $R[k+1] = -(A_0 + R^2 A_1){A_2}^{-1}$, repeat until $\|R(k+1) - R(k)\| < \varepsilon$.
Step 4. Boundary Probability Computation	Form the boundary-level blocks $(\hbar_0, \hbar_1)$ by solving $(\hbar_0, \hbar_1) = \begin{pmatrix} B_0 & B_1 \\ A_2 & A_1 + RA_2 \end{pmatrix}$, together with the normalization condition $\hbar_0 e + \hbar_1 (I - R)^{-1} e = 1$
Step 5. Computation of Level Probabilities	Obtain the stationary probability vectors for higher levels as $\hbar_n = \hbar_1 R^{n-1}, n \geq 1$ for, $n \geq 1$. This step yields the limiting distribution of queue states under steady conditions.
Step 6. Performance Metric Evaluation	Based on $\{\hbar_n\}$, compute expected queue length, average delay, and fuel consumption as given in Equations (10)–(15).

3.3. *Performance Metrics*

3.3.1. Vehicle Average Queue Length and Delay

The average queue length and delay are computed according to Equations (10) and (11), respectively, which link the expected number of vehicles to the system's service rate.

$$\overline{L} = \sum_{l+k=0}^{\infty} (l+k) \sum_{s=1}^{g+r} \sum_{j=1}^{M} \hbar_{l,k,s,j} \tag{10}$$

$$W = \frac{E(L)}{\lambda} = \frac{\sum_{l+k=0}^{\infty} (l+k) \sum_{s=1}^{g+r} \sum_{j=1}^{M} \hbar_{l,k,s,j}}{\sum_{k=1}^{2} \vartheta D_k e} \tag{11}$$

3.3.2. Queuing of Vehicles in SL

The number of queued vehicles in the SL can serve as a straightforward indicator of the effectiveness of C-DBL system, compared against the average total queue length. Let's denote $\overline{L}_S$ as the number of vehicles in the social lane.

$$\overline{L}_S = \sum_{l=0}^{\infty} \sum_{k=0}^{V} \sum_{s=1}^{g+r} \sum_{j=1}^{M} k\hbar_{l,k,s,j} \quad (12)$$

3.3.3. Maximum Queue Length for Vehicles

Let us designate $\overline{L}_{max}$ as the maximum total number of social vehicles at signalized intersection and $\overline{L}_{sl-max}$ as the maximum number of vehicles in the social lane.

$$\overline{L}_{max} = \sum_{l+k=0}^{\infty} (l+k) \sum_{j=1}^{M} \hbar_{l,k,(g+r),j} \quad (13)$$

$$\overline{L}_{sl-max} = \sum_{l=0}^{\infty} \sum_{k=0}^{V} k \sum_{j=1}^{M} \hbar_{l,k,(g+r),j} \quad (14)$$

3.3.4. Fuel Consumption of Vehicles in a Cycle

Depending on the state of travel of the vehicle at the intersection (acceleration, deceleration, idling, constant speed). The total fuel consumption of the vehicle can be calculated using the formula provided by Wu et al. [34].

$$F = \sum_{i=1}^{\lambda T(g+r)} F_i = \lambda(g+r)(\overline{\mathcal{R}}_a \bar{t}_a + \overline{\mathcal{R}}_d \bar{t}_d + \overline{\mathcal{R}}_i \bar{t}_i + \overline{\mathcal{R}}_c \bar{t}_c) \quad (15)$$

where F represents the total fuel consumption of all vehicles passing through the intersection; F_i represents the fuel consumption of vehicle i passing through the signalized intersection; $\overline{\mathcal{R}}_a$, $\overline{\mathcal{R}}_d$, $\overline{\mathcal{R}}_i$, $\overline{\mathcal{R}}_c$ denote the average fuel consumption rate of the vehicle under acceleration, deceleration, idling, and constant speed, respectively; and $\bar{t}_a$, $\bar{t}_d$, $\bar{t}_i$, $\bar{t}_c$ represent the duration of the vehicle under acceleration, deceleration, idling, and constant speed, respectively.

Define the number of stranded vehicles $\overline{L}_g$ at the moment of the end of the green light by the following equation

$$\overline{L}_g = \sum_{l+k=0}^{\infty} (l+k) \sum_{j=1}^{M} \hbar_{l,k,g,j} \quad (16)$$

Thus, the total number of vehicles stops under the C-DBL system is divided into the following two scenarios.

- Non-Congested $(L_g < V)$

In this scenario, the intersection is in a non-congested state. Social vehicles will not receive the information to enter the BL. The total number of stops N_1 can be calculated using the following equation

$$N_1 = \overline{L}_{sl-max} + min\left(\frac{\overline{L}_{sl-max}\lambda}{1-\lambda}, \lambda g\right) \quad (17)$$

- Congested $(L_g \geq V)$

In this situation, the signalized intersection is in a congested state, and the C-DBL provides passage for social vehicles. At this time, the total number of stops N_2 can be expressed as

$$N_2 = 2(\overline{L}_g - V) + min\{\frac{min[(\overline{L}_g - V), \overline{L}_{sl-max}]\lambda}{1-\lambda}, \lambda g\} \quad (18)$$

Therefore, the number of stops under non-congested and congested conditions are described by Equations (17) and (18), and the stopping rate per vehicle is calculated by Equation (19).

$$R_s = \frac{N_1 + N}{(g+r)\lambda} \tag{19}$$

The total vehicle fuel consumption through signalized intersection can be expressed as

$$F = \lambda(g+r)\left[\left(\overline{\mathcal{R}}_a + \overline{\mathcal{R}}_d\right)\cdot R_s\cdot \bar{t}_d + \overline{\mathcal{R}}_i\cdot W\right] \tag{20}$$

where $\bar{t}_d$ is the average time for each acceleration and deceleration of the vehicle.

4. Optimal Capacity Allocation

4.1. Problem Definition

The optimization problem is formulated in Equation (21), where the nonlinear objective function $F(L)$ in Equation (22) minimizes total fuel consumption derived from Equation (20).

$$\begin{gathered} F(L^*) = \min\frac{F(L)-F(0)}{F(0)} \\ s.t.\ 0 \le L \le L_{max},\ L \in N \end{gathered} \tag{21}$$

where $F(L)$ denotes the total fuel consumption of all vehicles under lane configuration L, and $F(0)$ represents the baseline fuel consumption when no C-DBL control is implemented. The normalization by $F(0)$ allows for a dimensionless performance index, facilitating comparison across different traffic demand levels or arrival modes.

The fuel consumption function $F(L)$ is a non-linear, non-convex function of L, where changes in the allocated bus lane volume result in variations in the traffic flow dynamics and fuel consumption of vehicles. The objective function is often expressed in the form of

$$F(L) = C_s\cdot R_s(L)\cdot \bar{t}_d + C_d\cdot W(L) \tag{22}$$

where C_s denotes the fuel consumption of the vehicle at the intersection due to acceleration and deceleration and C_d denotes the fuel consumption of the vehicle at the intersection due to idling.

4.2. Solution Methodology

The high-dimensional stochastic system is solved using the matrix-geometric method summarized in Algorithm 1 to solve the optimization problem, three well-known optimization algorithms—Differential Evolution (DE), Genetic Algorithm (GA), and Particle Swarm Optimization (PSO)—are employed. These algorithms are adapted for discrete optimization by ensuring that the bus lane allocation V is treated as an integer variable., Algorithm 2 shows the pseudo code for solving the optimal C-DBL volume. The solution methodology is as follows:

- Initialization: Define a population of candidate solutions (individuals or particles), randomly initialized within the feasible solution space for L (i.e., $L_{min} \le L \le L_{max},\ L \in N$).
- Fitness Evaluation: Evaluate the fitness of each candidate solution by computing the objective function $F(L)$. The fitness is based on minimizing the fuel consumption over time, which depends on the lane allocation L.

$$Fitness\ (L_i) = F(L_i) \tag{23}$$

Algorithm 2. GA pseudo-code for solving the optimal C-DBL volume

INPUT: Objective function $F(L)$
OUTPUT: The optimal bus lane capacity L^* that minimizes fuel consumption $F(L)$
Initialize:

- Set the number of generations $t = 0$.
- Generate an initial population $P(t)$ randomly within $L_{min} \leq L \leq L_{max}$.

Evaluate: Evaluate the population $P(t)$ using the objective function $F(L)$
while termination criterion is not satisfied **do**

$$t = t + 1$$

Choose users to assemble $P(t)$ from $P(t-1)$ based on their fitness.
Alter users of $P(t)$ by applying crossover and mutation operations.

- Apply mutation and crossover to generate new individuals (solutions for L)
- Ensure that L remains a discrete integer after mutation and crossover operations

end while
Return the optimal bus lane capacity L that minimizes the fuel consumption $F(L)$, which corresponds to the best solution found during the evaluation.

5. Validation

5.1. Comparison with Existing Research

To demonstrate the feasibility of the C-DBL strategy, this paper conducted a numerical comparison with existing literature, including a DBL design proposed by Zhao and Zhou [19] to regulate the allowance of left-turning buses into the opposite dedicated bus lane, a pre-signal strategy proposed by He et al. [35] to reduce vehicle delay, and a DBL control strategy proposed by Shan et al. [36] in a partially connected vehicle environment, Wu et al. [17] developed and evaluated bus lanes with intermittent and dynamic priority in connected vehicle environments. All papers provide detailed data analysis of their respective systems.

As shown in Figure 3a, under varying traffic saturation levels (0.2–1.0), the proposed C-DBL strategy demonstrates significant improvement in reducing traffic delays compared to three state-of-the-art DBL methods. At low saturation levels (0.2–0.4), the C-DBL strategy achieves a 12–18% improvement over the model proposed by Wu et al. [17]. For medium saturation levels (0.6–0.8), it surpasses the rule-based strategy developed by Zhao and Zhou [19] by 22–27%. Under high saturation conditions (V/C = 1.0), the C-DBL strategy reduces delays by 35%, highlighting its advantage in congested scenarios compared to He et al.'s [35] traffic-responsive system. Figure 3b highlights the energy efficiency comparison between C-DBL and Shan et al.'s [36] hybrid DBL framework. Under peak hour conditions, the proposed strategy reduces fuel consumption by 40.55%, outperforming Shan et al.'s [36] benchmark by 19.13%. The comparative analysis confirms that the C-DBL strategy is a technically feasible and environmentally beneficial solution for modern transportation systems.

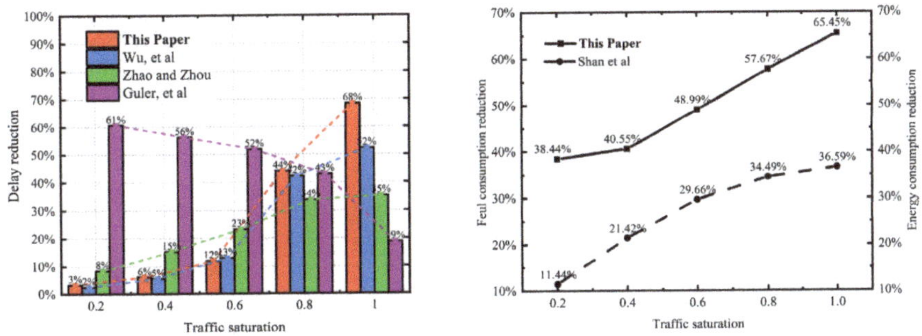

(**a**) (**b**)

Figure 3. Comparison results with existing research (**a**) Reduction in delay [17–19]. (**b**) Reduction in energy consumption [36].

5.2. Simulation

To validate the effectiveness of the proposed methodology, we developed four representative traffic scenarios through the SUMO simulation platform. A comprehensive comparative analysis was conducted among three approaches: (1) the baseline SUMO simulation, (2) HMM with varying connected vehicle penetration rates (10%, 50%, 90%), and (3) the proposed method, with particular focus on vehicle queue length estimation performance.

As illustrated in Figure 4a,b, The proposed method demonstrates remarkable consistency with SUMO simulation results in vehicle queue length estimation, while exhibiting significantly lower estimation errors compared to traditional HMM approaches. Quantitative error metrics reveal that our method achieves an RMSE of 3.33, maintaining minimal deviation from the SUMO baseline. This performance substantially outperforms HMM implementations with 10% penetration rate (RMSE = 47.8981) and 50% penetration rate (RMSE = 5.4231), while approaching the accuracy level of HMM-90% implementation (RMSE = 2.8825). In terms of MAPE metric, the proposed method achieves 0.55%, demonstrating clear advantages over HMM-10% (6.08%) and HMM-50% (0.70%), with only marginal difference compared to HMM-90% (0.46%). These quantitative findings collectively demonstrate that the proposed MAP-based SQM effectively characterizes traffic flow performance in connected environments, showing strong agreement with simulation benchmarks. The results validate the method's generalization capability and engineering applicability for real-world implementations.

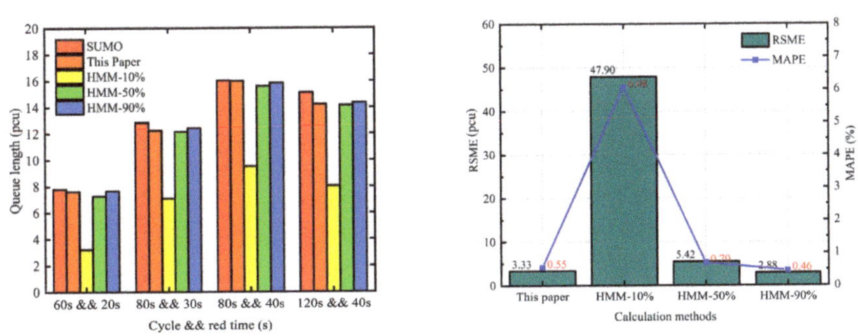

(**a**) (**b**)

Figure 4. Comparison with simulation benchmarks, "&&" representing the signal cycle and red light duration (s). (**a**) Queue length (pcu) over saturation levels. (**b**) Estimation errors—RMSE (veh) and MAPE (%) under different HMM penetration rates.

6. Numerical Experiment

To ensure the reproducibility and transparency of the proposed experiments, the simulation configuration is summarized in Table 1. The model integrates the MAP-based stochastic traffic flow generation, HMM-based queue estimation, and GA/DE/PSO under heterogeneous connected traffic environments.

Table 1. Simulation Settings for the C-DBL Numerical Experiments.

Category	Parameter/Description	Value/Setting
Simulation Environment	Platform	SUMO 1.19.0 (for microscopic traffic simulation) + MATLAB 2023a (for optimization and analysis)
	Processor and Memory	Intel Core i5-9300H (2.4 GHz), 16 GB RAM (Intel Corporation, Santa Clara, CA, USA)
Signal Control Parameters	Signal cycle length (C)	100 s
	Green phase duration (g)	50 s
	Red phase duration (r)	50 s
Road Configuration	Intersection layout	1 through lanes + 1 C-DBL
Traffic Composition	Vehicle types	CVs, NCVs and Buses
	Proportion	30% CVs, 60% NCVs, 10% Buses
Arrival Scenarios	Traffic saturation levels	0.3 (low), 0.6 (medium), 0.9 (high)
	Arrival modes	(i) Steady (M); (ii) Busty NCV (MAP1); (iii) busty CV (MAP2)
Optimization Parameters	Algorithms	GA, DE, PSO
	Population size	50
	Maximum generations	100
	Mutation/Crossover settings	Empirically tuned for convergence stability
Validation Setup	Simulation runs	30 independent runs per scenario with random seeds

6.1. Optimal Capacity Configuration

To analyze the numerical results of the C-DBL optimal capacity allocation experiments for different traffic saturation and arrival modes, we evaluate the performance of three optimization algorithms (GA, DE and PSO) in terms of the optimal capacity L^* and the associated fuel consumption $F(L^*)$.

As shown in Table 2, the experiments consider three traffic saturation levels (I: 0.3; II: 0.6; III: 0.9) and three vehicle arrival modes: stable arrival (M), conventional vehicle burst arrival (MAP1) and CVs burst arrival (MAP2).

From Table 3, it can be observed that as the saturation level increases or as the arrival pattern transitions from steady to busty, the optimal capacity shows an increasing trend. The improvement in fuel consumption is particularly significant under high saturation or high variability arrival patterns. The optimization effects of the three algorithms are generally similar; however, slight differences exist in certain scenarios, indicating that the capacity configuration problem proposed in this study, C-DBL, exhibits good adaptability to various evolutionary algorithms.

Table 2. Experimental parameter.

	M	MAP1	MAP2
I	$D_0 = -0.025$ $D = 0.025$	$D_0 = \begin{bmatrix} -0.065 & 0.024 \\ 0.008 & -0.028 \end{bmatrix}$ $D = \begin{bmatrix} 0.04 & 0 \\ 0 & 0.02 \end{bmatrix}$	$D_0 = \begin{bmatrix} -0.065 & 0.024 \\ 0.008 & -0.028 \end{bmatrix}$ $D = \begin{bmatrix} 0.04 & 0 \\ 0 & 0.02 \end{bmatrix}$
II	$D_0 = -0.1$ $D = 0.1$	$D_0 = \begin{bmatrix} -0.542 & 0.203 \\ 0.027 & -0.095 \end{bmatrix}$ $D = \begin{bmatrix} 0.339 & 0 \\ 0 & 0.068 \end{bmatrix}$	$D_0 = \begin{bmatrix} -0.086 & 0.032 \\ 0.092 & -0.323 \end{bmatrix}$ $D = \begin{bmatrix} 0.054 & 0 \\ 0 & 0.231 \end{bmatrix}$
III	$D_0 = -0.225$ $D = 0.225$	$D_0 = \begin{bmatrix} -0.438 & 0.164 \\ 0.008 & -0.281 \end{bmatrix}$ $D = \begin{bmatrix} -0.274 & 0 \\ 0 & -0.201 \end{bmatrix}$	$D_0 = \begin{bmatrix} -0.274 & 0.104 \\ 0.114 & -0.399 \end{bmatrix}$ $D = \begin{bmatrix} 0.171 & 0 \\ 0 & 0.285 \end{bmatrix}$

Table 3. Optimal capacity allocation results.

Saturation Level	Arrival Mode	Optimization Algorithm	Optimal Capacity L^* (pcu/cycle)	FC Reduction (%)
0.3	Steady (M)	GA	2	0.143
		DE	2	0.143
		PSO	2	0.143
	Burst (MAP1)	GA	2	0.042
		DE	2	0.042
		PSO	2	0.042
	Connected Burst (MAP2)	GA	2	0.896
		DE	2	0.896
		PSO	2	0.896
0.6	Steady (M)	GA	2	2.322
		DE	2	2.322
		PSO	2	2.322
	Burst (MAP1)	GA	4	1.436
		DE	4	1.436
		PSO	4	1.436
	Connected Burst (MAP2)	GA	3	18.599
		DE	3	18.599
		PSO	3	18.599
0.9	Steady (M)	GA	5	27.858
		DE	5	27.858
		PSO	5	27.858
	Burst (MAP1)	GA	5	27.027
		DE	5	27.027
		PSO	5	27.027
	Connected Burst (MAP2)	GA	5	50.766
		DE	5	50.766
		PSO	5	50.766

It is noteworthy that under a saturation level of 0.9 and a bursty arrival pattern (especially MAP2), the maximum reduction in fuel consumption can exceed 50%. This finding validates that a reasonable configuration of lane capacity can effectively reduce queuing and idling energy consumption, thereby significantly alleviating the energy waste and emission pressure associated with congestion. Overall, the experimental results provide strong evidence for the feasibility and robustness of capacity optimization based on C-DBL across diverse traffic scenarios, offering substantial support for energy savings and emission reductions in intelligent transportation systems operating in high-traffic or highly variable environments.

6.2. Results of the C-DBL Control Strategy

This section analyzes the effect of adaptive C-DBL and fixed-capacity C-DBL strategies on vehicle fuel consumption reduction under different traffic saturation levels, based on experimental results with a penetration rate of 0.9 (Figure 5a) and 0.3 (Figure 5b) for connected vehicles, respectively. As shown in Figure 5, the adaptive C-DBL consistently outperforms the fixed-capacity C-DBL as the traffic saturation increases. Notably, at a traffic saturation of 1.2, the adaptive C-DBL achieves a fuel consumption reduction of about 67%, which is more than that of the fixed-capacity scheme (57%), demonstrating its excellent adaptability under high saturation and high penetration conditions.

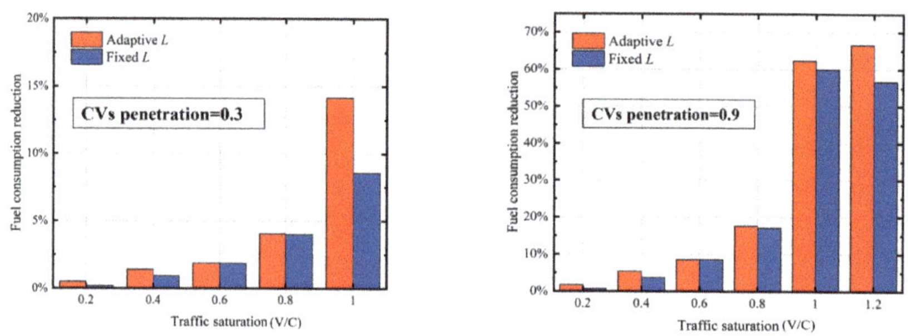

(a) (b)

Figure 5. Comparison of two C-DBL control strategies (**a**) CVs penetration = 0.3. (**b**) CVs penetration = 0.9.

In Figure 5, the adaptive C-DBL shows an advantage even though the overall fuel consumption reduction is small. At a traffic saturation of 1, the adaptive strategy reduces fuel consumption by 15%, while the fixed capacity approach reduces fuel consumption by 9%. Together, these results validate that the adaptive C-DBL control strategy can reduce fuel consumption more effectively than the fixed-capacity scheme at different traffic saturation levels, regardless of whether the penetration of connected vehicles is high or low.

7. Sensitivity Analysis

7.1. Sensitivity to Random Traffic Flows

This study evaluates the impact of the C-DBL strategy on traffic performance across varying saturation levels (0.1 to 0.9). Figure 6 illustrates the key effects on vehicle delay, fuel consumption, and the number of stops. The data presented in Figure 6a clearly demonstrate that C-DBL outperforms the C-DBL control strategy across all metrics at different saturation levels. At a saturation level of 0.1, the optimization improvements for C-DBL in terms of delay, fuel consumption, and the number of stops is 0.47%, 0.18%, and 0.10%, respectively. As saturation increases to 0.9, CDBL achieves a delay of 34.75%, showing significant optimization compared to DBL in terms of reduced delay, fuel consumption, and the number of stops.

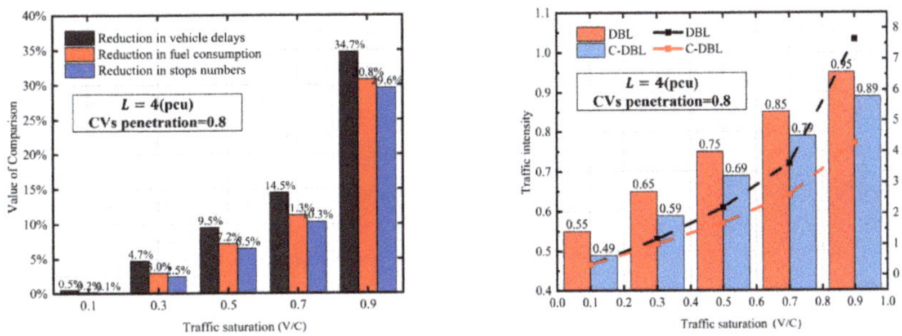

(a) (b)

Figure 6. Sensitivity analysis to traffic saturation (V/C = 0.3–0.9) for the proposed C-DBL system with MAP2 arrivals. (**a**) overall performance (Average delay (s/veh); FC (mL/cycle); stops (pcu/cycle)); (**b**) traffic intensity and queue length (pcu). Optimization performed with GA, DE, and PSO (N_p = 50, G_{max} = 100).

C-DBL consistently exhibits stronger performance than DBL in alleviating congestion, reducing fuel consumption, and minimizing stops across the entire traffic volume range, with particularly pronounced improvements at higher traffic volumes. Figure 6b further indicates that the performance enhancements of C-DBL relative to DBL in terms of traffic intensity and vehicle queue length significantly increase with rising saturation levels. This suggests that C-DBL possesses greater adaptability and cooperative control advantages under high-flow and even oversaturated conditions, effectively reducing vehicle queuing and significantly alleviating congestion while lowering energy consumption.

7.2. Sensitivity to CVs Penetration

To evaluate the applicability and robustness of the proposed C-DBL strategy under varying CV penetration, we conduct numerical experiments at 10%, 20%, 40%, 60%, 80%, and 100% CV market shares. As shown in Figure 7a, when the CV penetration is only 10%, C-DBL reduces vehicle delays, fuel consumption, and number of stops by approximately 11.9%, 9.3%, and 9.3%, respectively, compared with the conventional DBL approach. As the penetration rate increases to 100%, these improvements further rise to 56.1%, 51.3%, and 59.3%, respectively, indicating that higher CV penetration enables C-DBL to leverage vehicle connectivity and real-time information sharing more fully for significant performance gains.

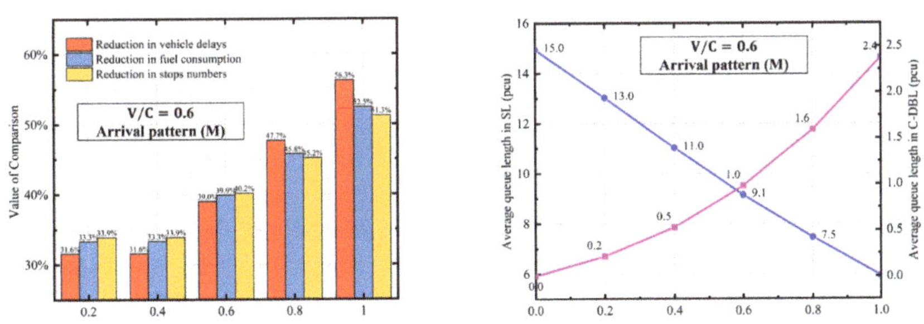

(a) (b)

Figure 7. Impact of CV penetration rate (10–100%) on system performance under MAP2 arrival pattern and V/C = 0.6. (**a**) overall performance; (**b**) queue length in SL (blue line) and C-DBL (pink line).

Figure 7b provides additional insight into C-DBL's sensitivity to CV penetration by examining queue lengths. Specifically, as the CV penetration rate increases from 10% to 100%, the queue length of social vehicles (i.e., non-connected vehicles) decreases markedly from approximately 14.95 NCVs units (pcu) to 5.94 pcu. Meanwhile, the queue length of connected vehicles increases from near 0.0 pcu to about 2.37 pcu. This redistribution of queues highlights C-DBL's ability to dynamically balance congestion between social and connected vehicles in mixed traffic settings. Overall, these findings confirm the robustness and adaptability of C-DBL across a wide range of CV penetration levels, demonstrating its potential to enhance network-wide efficiency in evolving connected and automated transportation systems.

7.3. Sensitivity to the C-DBL Capacity

To comprehensively assess the applicability of the C-DBL strategy under varying traffic congestion conditions, this study conducts numerical research based on four key performance indicators: vehicle delay, fuel consumption, number of stops, and queue length in SL. The analysis spans saturation levels from 0.1 to 0.9 and congestion levels from 1 to 7.

As illustrated in Figure 8a, the optimal lane-capacity configurations converge stably across increasing traffic saturation levels under GA, DE, and PSO. For instance, under low saturation (0.1) and mild congestion (congestion level 1), the optimization is only 0.54%. In contrast, at high saturation (0.9) and severe congestion (capacity level 7), the optimization reaches 41.81%. These results indicate that the C-DBL strategy is more effective at reducing vehicle delays when the road network is under high load. Furthermore, at the same saturation level (0.9), the optimization exhibits a nonlinear variation with increasing capacity of C-DBL (initially rising from 6.37% to a peak of 43.39%, then declining to 37.57%), suggesting that C-DBL requires the integration of other control mechanisms to maintain stability under moderate to high congestion conditions. Figure 8b shows that total fuel consumption decreases monotonically as the allocated capacity approaches its optimum, but improves significantly when saturation is $\geq$0.5 and congestion level is $\geq$3 (increasing from 5.32% to 31.41%).

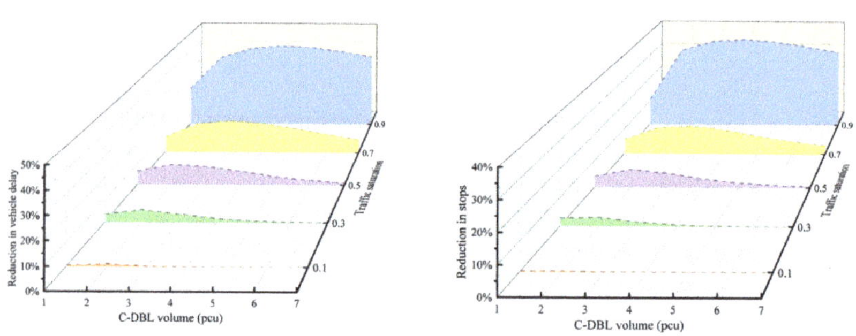

Figure 8. Optimization results for C-DBL capacity allocation under heterogeneous arrivals and saturation levels V/C = 0.3, 0.6, 0.9. (**a**) Convergence of GA, DE, and PSO algorithms for optimal lane capacity (pcu). (**b**) Fuel consumption (L/100 km) versus capacity showing monotonic decrease toward the optimum.

The results presented in Figure 9a demonstrate a positive correlation between fuel consumption optimization and saturation levels. Under low congestion (congestion levels 1 to 2), the optimization of fuel consumption increases gradually with saturation, while under high congestion (congestion levels 6 to 7), the optimization effect improves significantly, indicating a strong dependency of C-DBL's fuel consumption optimization performance on traffic volume thresholds. Figure 9b further highlights the optimization advantage of C-DBL regarding societal lane queue length, achieving an optimization rate of 50.48% under a saturation level of 0.9 and moderate congestion (congestion level 4), demonstrating the significant role of dynamic lane allocation in mitigating congestion spillover in bottleneck areas.

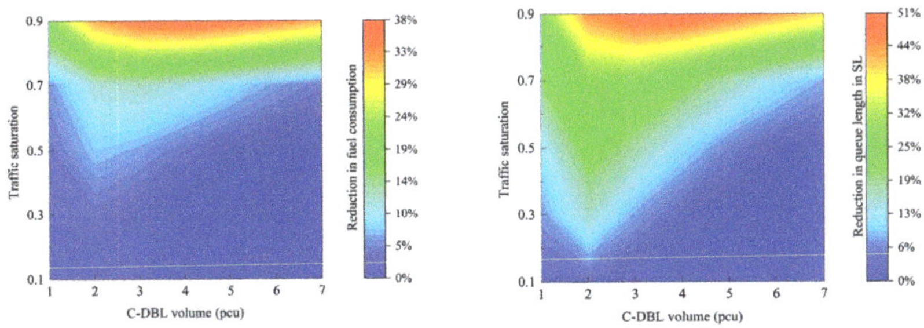

(a) (b)

Figure 9. Sensitivity to C-DBL capacity for different saturation levels (V/C = 0.3, 0.6, 0.9) under M arrivals. (**a**) Fuel consumption (mL/cycle). (**b**) Queue length (pcu). The proposed optimization achieves balanced performance between energy efficiency and traffic delay.

Overall, the response of the C-DBL strategy to congestion levels exhibits notable nonlinear characteristics. Under high saturation and severe congestion conditions, the strategy excels in reducing vehicle delays and alleviating societal lane queue lengths; however, its optimization effects are limited by activation thresholds in low saturation or mild congestion scenarios.

7.4. Sensitivity to Traffic Flow Heterogeneity

This section analyzes the sensitivity of C-DBL performance to traffic flow heterogeneity, considering Poisson arrivals, MAP I, and MAP II. As shown in Figure 10a, under high traffic saturation (0.9), system idleness is highly sensitive to traffic heterogeneity. For MAP I, SL exhibits a relatively low inter-arrival time variance (0.692) and moderate correlation (2.127), whereas CV presents a significantly higher variance (4.255) and stronger correlation (2.375). This stark contrast results in generally lower idleness, primarily due to the bursty arrivals of CV, which increase C-DBL utilization. In contrast, MAP II balances variance (SL: 1.257; CV: 3.121) while maintaining stable correlation (~1.9–2.3), leading to a relatively higher idleness compared to MAP I. The Poisson model demonstrates the least sensitivity, with idleness decreasing by only 1.5% (from 0.447 to 0.44), as its inherent randomness mitigates the impact of saturation-driven resource contention.

As shown in Figure 10b, at low saturation (0.3), reduced congestion leads to stable system idleness across all traffic models. Despite the higher variance of vehicle 2 (5.891), MAP I maintains a relatively low idleness (decreasing by 2.5%, from 0.161 to 0.166), as resource redundancy compensates for sporadic arrivals. MAP II further highlights its resilience, with moderate variance (SL: 2.161; CV: 2.337) and reduced correlation (~1.67–1.98), resulting in a slight idleness decrease (1.0%, from 0.312 to 0.309). The Poisson model remains stable (idleness: 0.447 to 0.44), underscoring its robustness under low-density conditions.

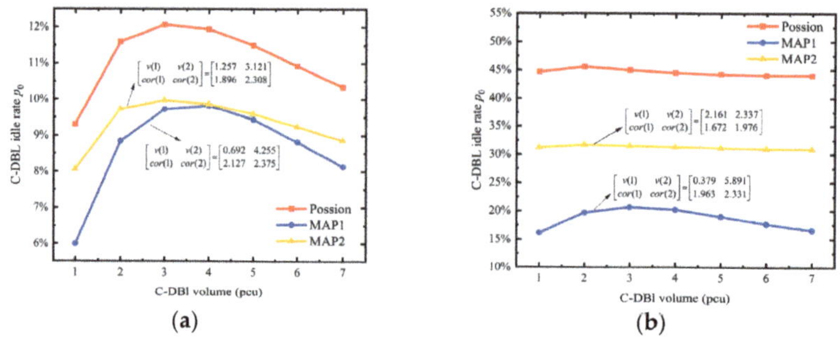

Figure 10. Sensitivity to C-DBL capacity: (**a**) traffic saturation = 0.9; (**b**) traffic saturation = 0.3.

8. Discussion

This study developed a stochastic–adaptive optimization framework for Connected Dynamic Bus Lane (C-DBL) systems, integrating MAP-based stochastic queue modeling, HMM-based real-time estimation, and metaheuristic optimization to achieve coordinated lane capacity management in heterogeneous connected traffic. Compared with previous MAP-or HMM-based traffic control studies [27–29,32,33], the proposed framework establishes a closed-loop stochastic–adaptive mechanism that simultaneously captures correlated arrivals (via MAP) and real-time hidden-state feedback (via HMM), which were previously treated as independent sub-problems. This integration enables adaptive bus-lane capacity management under realistic heterogeneous connected environments.

The results reveal that the proposed C-DBL strategy effectively reduces intersection delay and fuel consumption—achieving up to 68.3% reduction in fuel use and 65.5% reduction in average delay—while maintaining system stability across varying traffic saturations and connected-vehicle penetration rates. The integration of MAP and HMM enables accurate representation of stochastic and partially observable traffic dynamics, while the application of GA, DE, and PSO ensures robust global optimization in nonconvex solution spaces.

From a broader perspective, this research contributes a generalizable stochastic–adaptive control paradigm applicable to other intelligent transportation systems. The combination of probabilistic modeling, real-time estimation, and evolutionary optimization offers a scalable approach for managing uncertainty, enhancing energy efficiency, and supporting sustainable urban mobility planning.

Author Contributions: Conceptualization, B.Y. and C.W.; methodology, B.Y.; software, B.Y. and J.Y.; validation, B.Y. and Z.W.; writing—original draft preparation, B.Y.; writing—review and editing, B.Y., C.W. and J.Y.; visualization, B.Y. and Z.W.; project administration, C.W.; funding acquisition, B.Y. All authors have read and agreed to the published version of the manuscript.

Funding: Graduate Student Innovation Project of Central South University, grant number 2024ZZTS0448.

Data Availability Statement: The raw data supporting the conclusions of this article will be made available by the authors on request.

Acknowledgments: The authors acknowledge the constructive feedback provided by the anonymous reviewers. All content has been reviewed and confirmed by the authors.

Conflicts of Interest: The authors declare no conflict of interest.

Abbreviations

The following abbreviations are used in this manuscript:

BLIP	Bus Lane with Intermittent Priority
C-DBL	Connected Dynamic Bus Lane
CV	connected vehicles
DE	Differential Evolution
HMM	Hidden Markov Model
ITS	Intelligent Transportation Systems
GA	Genetic Algorithm
MAP	Markov Arrival Process
MAPE	Mean Absolute Percentage Error
MLE	Maximum Likelihood Estimation
NCV	non-connected vehicle
PSO	Particle Swarm Optimization
RMSE	Root Mean Square Error
SL	social lane
SPaT	signal phase and timing
A_i, B_i	Block matrices of the infinitesimal generator Q of the Markov chain ($i = 0.1\ldots$).
C_i	Signal cycle of the intersection ($i = 1,\ 2,\ \ldots$).
c	Signal cycle duration at the target intersection.
C_s	Fuel consumption coefficient due to vehicle acceleration and deceleration
C_d	Fuel consumption coefficient due to vehicle idling
$cor(k)$	Correlation coefficient between consecutive inter-arrival times for vehicles.
D_0, D_1	Transition rate matrices of the MAP
F_i	Fuel consumption of the ith vehicle passing through the signalized intersection
g, r	Duration of green and red phases at signalized intersection
$[H^G, H^R]$	Matrix representing green and red light duration
J_n	State of the MAP at time n
K_{jam}	Traffic density
K_n	Number of vehicles in the C-DBL at time n
L	Average total queue length of vehicles
p	Penetration rate of probe vehicles
π	Steady-state probability vector of underlying Markov chain
Q	Infinitesimal generator of the Markov chain
R_a, R_d, R_i, R_c	Average fuel consumption rate under acceleration, deceleration, idling, and cruising
R	Matrix solved iteratively in the model solution process
$v(k)$	Variance of inter-arrival times for vehicles
λ	Total vehicle arrival rate
$\hbar$	Unique stationary distribution of the Markov chain

References

1. Rahmani, A.M.; Naqvi, R.A.; Yousefpoor, E.; Yousefpoor, M.S.; Ahmed, O.H.; Hosseinzadeh, M.; Siddique, K. A Q-learning and fuzzy logic-based hierarchical routing scheme in the intelligent transportation system for smart cities. *Mathematics* **2022**, *10*, 4192. [CrossRef]
2. Kuo, Y.-H.; Leung, J.M.; Yan, Y. Public transport for smart cities: Recent innovations and future challenges. *Eur. J. Oper. Res.* **2022**, *306*, 1001–1026. [CrossRef]
3. Bittencourt, J.C.N.; Jesus, T.C.; Peixoto, J.P.J.; Costa, D.G. The Road to Intelligent Cities. *Smart Cities* **2025**, *8*, 77. [CrossRef]
4. Mees, P. A centenary review of transport planning in Canberra, Australia. *Prog. Plan.* **2014**, *87*, 1–32. [CrossRef]
5. Karner, A.; Levine, K. Equity-advancing practices at public transit agencies in the United States. *Transp. Res. Rec. J. Transp. Res. Board* **2021**, *2675*, 1431–1441. [CrossRef]
6. Shi, F.; Cao, L.; Dong, Y.; Sun, Z. Utilization Rate of Bus-only Lanes on the Main Roads in Beijing. *Int. J. High Sch. Res.* **2023**, *5*, 69–76. [CrossRef]

7. Qiao, W.; Yang, Z.; Peng, B.; Cai, X.; Zhang, Y. Integrated Evaluation Method of Bus Lane Traffic Benefit Based on Multi-Source Data. *Mathematics* **2024**, *12*, 2664. [CrossRef]
8. Vest, A.; McMahon, P.J.; Cuellar, J. Developing dedicated bus lane screening criteria in Baltimore, Maryland. *Transp. Res. Rec. J. Transp. Res. Board* **2018**, *2672*, 52–63. [CrossRef]
9. Li, S.G.; Ju, Y.F. Evaluation of bus-exclusive lanes. *IEEE Trans. Intell. Transp. Syst.* **2009**, *10*, 236–245. [CrossRef]
10. Lin, Y.; Zhang, N.; Dong, H. Capability of intermittent bus lane utilization for regular vehicles. *J. Adv. Transp.* **2022**, *2022*, 4799497. [CrossRef]
11. Viegas, J.; Lu, B. The intermittent bus lane signals setting within an area. *Transp. Res. Part C Emerg. Technol.* **2004**, *12*, 453–469. [CrossRef]
12. Currie, G.; Lai, H. Intermittent and dynamic transit lanes: Melbourne, Australia, experience. *Transp. Res. Rec.* **2008**, *2072*, 49–56. [CrossRef]
13. Eichler, M.; Daganzo, C.F. Bus lanes with intermittent priority: Strategy formulae and an evaluation. *Transp. Res. Part B Methodol.* **2006**, *40*, 731–744. [CrossRef]
14. Tumminello, M.L.; Zare, N.; Macioszek, E.; Granà, A. Assaying Traffic Settings with Connected and Automated Mobility Channeled into Road Intersection Design. *Smart Cities* **2025**, *8*, 86. [CrossRef]
15. Wu, D.; Han, X. A Two-Lane Cellular Automaton Model to Evaluate the Bus Lane with Intermittent Priority. *J. Adv. Transp.* **2022**, *2022*, 9028212. [CrossRef]
16. Zhang, L.; Zhang, L. Distributed traffic signal optimization at V2X intersections. *Mathematics* **2024**, *12*, 773. [CrossRef]
17. Wu, W.; Head, L.; Yan, S.; Ma, W. Development and evaluation of bus lanes with intermittent and dynamic priority in connected vehicle environment. *J. Intell. Transp. Syst.* **2018**, *22*, 301–310. [CrossRef]
18. Guler, S.I.; Gayah, V.V.; Menendez, M. Bus priority at signalized intersections with single-lane approaches: A novel pre-signal strategy. *Transp. Res. Part C Emerg. Technol.* **2016**, *63*, 51–70. [CrossRef]
19. Zhao, J.; Zhou, X. Improving the operational efficiency of buses with dynamic use of exclusive bus lane at isolated intersections. *IEEE Trans. Intell. Transp. Syst.* **2018**, *20*, 642–653. [CrossRef]
20. Gao, Z.; Long, K.; Li, C.; Wu, W.; Han, L.D. Bus Priority Control for Dynamic Exclusive Bus Lane. *Comput. Mater. Contin.* **2019**, *61*, 345–361. [CrossRef]
21. Hounsell, N.; Shrestha, B. A new approach for co-operative bus priority at traffic signals. *IEEE Trans. Intell. Transp. Syst.* **2011**, *13*, 6–14. [CrossRef]
22. Elbaum, Y.; Novoselsky, A.; Kagan, E. A Queueing Model for Traffic Flow Control in the Road Intersection. *Mathematics* **2022**, *10*, 3997. [CrossRef]
23. Wu, Z.; Waterson, B. Waterson Urban intersection management strategies for autonomous/connected/conventional vehicle fleet mixtures. *IEEE Trans. Intell. Transp. Syst.* **2021**, *23*, 12084–12093. [CrossRef]
24. Pankratova, E.; Moiseeva, S.; Farkhadov, M. Infinite-server resource queueing systems with different types of Markov-modulated Poisson process and renewal arrivals. *Mathematics* **2022**, *10*, 2962. [CrossRef]
25. Alfa, A.S.; Neuts, M.F. Modelling vehicular traffic using the discrete time Markovian arrival process. *Transp. Sci.* **1995**, *29*, 109–117. [CrossRef]
26. Mirzaeian, N.; Cho, S.-H.; Scheller-Wolf, A. A queueing model and analysis for autonomous vehicles on highways. *Manag. Sci.* **2021**, *67*, 2904–2923. [CrossRef]
27. Yang, B.; Wang, C.; Cao, Y.; Yang, Q. Modeling and evaluating the impact of variable bus lane on isolated signal intersection performance. *Phys. A Stat. Mech. Its Appl.* **2024**, *643*, 129786. [CrossRef]
28. Wang, P.; Zhao, J.; Gao, Y.; Sotelo, M.A.; Li, Z. Lane work-schedule of toll station based on queuing theory and PSO-LSTM model. *IEEE Access* **2020**, *8*, 84434–84443. [CrossRef]
29. Petrović, A.; Nikolić, M.; Bugarić, U.; Delibašić, B.; Lio, P. Lio Controlling highway toll stations using deep learning, queuing theory, and differential evolution. *Eng. Appl. Artif. Intell.* **2022**, *119*, 105683. [CrossRef]
30. An, C.; Shen, H.; Xu, Y.; Lu, Z.; Xia, J. Hidden mixture vehicle discharge state inference at signalized intersection using vehicle travel time and discharge headway data. *IEEE Trans. Intell. Transp. Syst.* **2022**, *23*, 21700–21711. [CrossRef]
31. Wang, S.; Zhang, X.; Li, F.; Yu, P.S.; Huang, Z. Efficient traffic estimation with multi-sourced data by parallel coupled hidden markov model. *IEEE Trans. Intell. Transp. Syst.* **2018**, *20*, 3010–3023. [CrossRef]
32. Hao, P.; Ban, X.J.; Guo, D.; Ji, Q. Cycle-by-cycle intersection queue length distribution estimation using sample travel times. *Transp. Res. Part B Methodol.* **2014**, *68*, 185–204. [CrossRef]
33. Zhao, Y.; Shen, S.; Liu, H.X. A hidden Markov model for the estimation of correlated queues in probe vehicle environments. *Transp. Res. Part C Emerg. Technol.* **2021**, *128*, 103128. [CrossRef]
34. Wu, L.; Ci, Y.; Wang, Y.; Chen, P. Fuel consumption at the oversaturated signalized intersection considering queue effects: A case study in Harbin, China. *Energy* **2020**, *192*, 116654. [CrossRef]

35. He, H.; Guler, S.I.; Menendez, M. Adaptive control algorithm to provide bus priority with a pre-signal. *Transp. Res. Part C Emerg. Technol.* **2016**, *64*, 28–44. [CrossRef]
36. Shan, X.; Wan, C.; Hao, P.; Wu, G.; Barth, M.J. Developing a novel dynamic bus lane control strategy with eco-driving under partially connected vehicle environment. *IEEE Trans. Intell. Transp. Syst.* **2024**, *25*, 5919–5934. [CrossRef]

mathematics

MDPI

Article

Emission-Constrained Dispatch Optimization Using Adaptive Grouped Fish Migration Algorithm in Carbon-Taxed Power Systems

Kai-Hung Lu [1,2,*], Xinyi Jiang [1] and Sang-Jyh Lin [3]

[1] School of Electronic and Electrical Engineering, Minnan University of Science and Technology, Quanzhou 362700, China
[2] Key Laboratory of Industrial Automation Control Technology and Application of Fujian Higher Education, Quanzhou 362700, China
[3] Department of Electronic Communication Engineering, National Kaohsiung University of Science and Technology, Kaohsiung 811213, Taiwan
* Correspondence: khluphd@gmail.com

Abstract: With increasing global pressure to decarbonize electricity systems, particularly in regions outside international carbon trading frameworks, it is essential to develop adaptive optimization tools that account for regulatory policies and system-level uncertainty. An emission-constrained power dispatch strategy based on an Adaptive Grouped Fish Migration Optimization (AGFMO) algorithm is proposed. The algorithm incorporates dynamic population grouping, a perturbation-assisted escape strategy from local optima, and a performance-feedback-driven position update rule. These enhancements improve the algorithm's convergence reliability and global search capacity in complex constrained environments. The proposed method is implemented in Taiwan's 345 kV transmission system, covering a decadal planning horizon (2023–2033) with scenarios involving varying load demands, wind power integration levels, and carbon tax schemes. Simulation results show that the AGFMO approach achieves greater reductions in total dispatch cost and CO_2 emissions compared with conventional swarm-based techniques, including PSO, GACO, and FMO. Embedding policy parameters directly into the optimization framework enables robustness in real-world grid settings and flexibility for future carbon taxation regimes. The model serves as decision-support tool for emission-sensitive operational planning in power markets with limited access to global carbon trading, contributing to the advanced modeling of control and optimization processes in low-carbon energy systems.

Keywords: carbon emission constraints; adaptive grouped fish migration optimization (AGFMO); renewable energy integration; power dispatch optimization; low-carbon energy transition

MSC: 90C90; 91B76; 49M37

1. Introduction

As climate change mitigation efforts accelerate, carbon trading schemes have become essential instruments for incentivizing low-carbon transitions in energy systems. By assigning economic value to greenhouse gas emissions, these markets encourage utilities and industrial actors to invest in cleaner technologies and reduce their carbon footprint [1,2]. Their widespread adoption has significantly reshaped dispatch strategies and long-term planning in the power sector [3,4].

https://doi.org/10.3390/math13172722

However, not all regions benefit from participation in such mechanisms. Taiwan, for instance, remains excluded from international carbon markets due to geopolitical constraints [5,6]. This exclusion poses a structural challenge: without access to carbon pricing signals or international offsetting mechanisms, Taiwan must pursue decarbonization through internally driven, policy-compatible dispatch strategies.

Despite recent growth in wind and solar deployment, Taiwan's power system remains predominantly fossil-fueled, with coal and natural gas accounting for the bulk of generation [7]. The intermittency of renewables adds further complexity, making it difficult to reconcile emission goals with grid reliability [8,9]. Although Taiwan's renewable energy development includes both solar PV and wind energy, this study focuses primarily on wind power for several reasons. First, Taiwan's government has designated offshore wind as a core strategy in its long-term decarbonization plan, with substantial capacity expansion planned through to 2030. Second, wind energy exhibits greater resilience during extreme weather events, as evidenced by continued wind turbine operation during Typhoon Danas in 2025, while PV installations suffered widespread damage. Third, due to land and geographical constraints, PV expansion is expected to plateau, making wind energy a more viable long-term lever for carbon reduction. As such, this paper focuses on wind-based dispatch modeling to provide policy-relevant insights and can serve as a reference for similar regions globally.

Existing research offers limited guidance for such non-market contexts. For example, Qiu and Entchev [10] and De Carne et al. [11] focus on renewable variability within market-integrated systems, while Wu et al. [12] and Leal Filho et al. [13] emphasize the role of carbon pricing in reshaping fossil-fuel usage—an option unavailable in Taiwan.

More broadly, the literature assumes the presence of carbon markets, leaving a strategic and methodological gap for regions without such mechanisms. Hameed et al. [14] present optimization models embedded within market structures, and Bechara and Alnouri [15] explore carbon-constrained planning but stop short of addressing renewable-induced dispatch volatility. Han et al. [16] consider demand response and storage, yet do not examine how fossil-fuel-heavy systems maintain dispatch feasibility during energy transitions. Likewise, studies by Russo et al. [17] and Gao et al. [18] address renewable integration in island contexts but do not grapple with the policy isolation that defines Taiwan's case.

In addition, while optimization techniques such as PSO, NSGA-II, and MOPSO have been applied to emission-constrained dispatch [19–24], they often rely on problem structures and parameter regimes that presume market participation. For example, Li et al. [21] and Li and Liu [22] model trading environments or microgrids, but their solutions are poorly suited to national-scale, policy-constrained systems. Liu et al. [23] discuss AI-driven decarbonization without tailoring methods to the technical dynamics of grid-scale fossil–renewable coexistence. Qin et al. [25] offer low-carbon dispatch models but do not tackle algorithmic robustness under volatile load and fuel-price scenarios.

These gaps are addressed through a tailored dispatch optimization method based on an Adaptive Grouped Fish Migration Optimization (AGFMO) algorithm. Designed specifically for systems operating outside of carbon market frameworks, AGFMO integrates genetic recombination strategies with grouped migration dynamics to improve global search capacity and solution adaptability. The proposed method is implemented within a dispatch model that reflects Taiwan's energy mix, renewable growth projections, and carbon taxation policies.

The contributions of this work are threefold:

(1) Algorithmic innovation: AGFMO is extended the traditional fish migration model through adaptive dynamic grouping and local disturbance mechanisms, enhancing exploration capacity in constrained, high-renewable scenarios. It addresses the convergence limitations often observed in PSO-based dispatch models.
(2) Context-specific dispatch framework: The model is explicitly developed for fossil-fuel-dependent grids operating without international market access. It provides actionable strategies for emission-aware dispatch and renewable integration under isolated policy regimes.
(3) Scalable application for isolated or developing regions: While tailored to Taiwan, the framework is designed to be flexible enough to be adapted to other regions facing similar geopolitical or infrastructural constraints. The framework offers a viable carbon reduction pathway that complements international climate objectives without requiring full market integration.

By addressing both methodological and contextual gaps, this study contributes to the global dialog on low-carbon energy transitions in policy-constrained environments. It offers both a robust optimization tool and a replicable dispatch strategy for achieving meaningful emission reductions in systems that fall outside conventional carbon pricing mechanisms.

Following this introduction, Section 2 uses data mining techniques to develop wind power output forecasts and analyze installed capacity utilization, providing a data-driven foundation for the emission-constrained dispatch model formulated in Section 3. Section 3 defines the optimal power flow framework under carbon emission constraints on Taiwan's 345 kV system, establishing the context-specific dispatch optimization problem addressed in this work. Section 4 details the design of the proposed AGFMO algorithm and its enhancements over the standard fish migration approach, highlighting how this algorithmic innovation improves global search and convergence for the dispatch optimization. Section 5 presents the simulation studies and results, including scenario analyses under various carbon tax and renewable integration levels. The efficacy of the proposed approach and its advantages over conventional methods are demonstrated by these findings, illustrating the method's viability and scalability for emission-constrained dispatch planning. Finally, Section 6 provides a summary of key insights and a critical analysis, linking the outcomes back to the contributions and discussing implications for low-carbon power system operation.

2. Application of Data Mining in Wind Power Output and Installed Capacity Forecasting

2.1. Application of Data Mining in Wind Power Forecasting

Forecasting wind power output is notoriously difficult, largely due to the inherent variability caused by shifting weather patterns, seasonal dynamics, and local geographical features. Taiwan, with its growing portfolio of wind energy installations, faces an urgent need to improve the predictability of wind power output (WPO) and installed capacity (WIC) to manage grid stability and ensure efficient power dispatch [26].

To address this challenge, data mining was adopted—not merely as a statistical tool, but as a means to uncover hidden regularities and inform smarter decision-making. Drawing on several years of historical data in Taiwan, a forecasting model was developed that is designed to support day-ahead power dispatch [27,28].

The analysis revealed patterns that, while not unexpected, are highly actionable; once cleaned and processed, these patterns can reveal insights beyond what raw intuition can provide.

(1) Data Collection and Cleaning:

The dataset spanned multiple years and included site-level data such as wind speed, power output, temperature, and installed capacity. Basic preprocessing was applied: obvious outliers were removed, and missing values imputed based on local regression. While the dataset was relatively clean, some anomalies were still identified and manually verified.

(2) Feature Selection and Modeling:

Using multivariate regression analysis, wind speed, ambient temperature, and month of the year were identified as the most predictive variables. The resulting model (see below) offers a practical baseline for regional wind output estimation:

$$P_{wind} = \alpha_0 + \alpha_1 \cdot Wind_{speed} + \alpha_2 \cdot Temperature + \alpha_3 \cdot Season + \epsilon \tag{1}$$

where P_{wind} represents the predicted wind power generation, and α_1, α_2, α_3 are regression coefficients. The residual term ϵ captures the deviation between the observed and predicted values, accounting for random fluctuations and other external factors not explicitly modeled. By applying multivariate regression, this model captures the relationships between wind power output and various influencing factors.

(3) Construction of the wind power forecasting model

Based on the results of the regression analysis, a forecasting model for wind power generation was developed. This model not only reflects patterns in historical data but also dynamically adjusts forecasts using current meteorological data. The forecasting model can be expressed as follows:

$$\hat{P}_{wind} = f\left(Wind_{speed}, \ Temperature, \ Season, \ Variation \ldots\right) \tag{2}$$

The model is used to predict wind power output under different meteorological conditions, providing a reliable input for optimizing future power dispatch [27,28].

2.2. Relationship Between Data Mining and Installed Capacity

Beyond forecasting wind power generation, this study also investigates how installed wind capacity relates to actual generation efficiency. Understanding how effectively installed capacity is utilized—especially under varying operational and environmental conditions—provides insight into overall system performance. To this end, data mining techniques were applied to uncover trends and correlations that would otherwise remain hidden in the raw data [28].

(1) Installed capacity analysis:

Data were collected from both onshore and offshore wind farms across Taiwan, including variables such as nameplate capacity, maintenance schedules, downtime records, and actual generation figures. By comparing output under different load conditions, the effective utilization rate of installed capacity was estimated. Notably, offshore installations showed greater variability during seasonal transitions, likely due to harsher environmental exposure [26].

(2) Modeling the Efficiency Relationship:

To quantify this relationship, a regression-based model was constructed in which generation efficiency was treated as the dependent variable and installed capacity as the key predictor. The model can be expressed as:

$$Ef_{wind} = \beta_0 + \beta_1 \cdot S_{installed} + \beta_2 \cdot T_D + \beta_3 \cdot M_w + \rho \tag{3}$$

where Ef_{wind} represents generation efficiency, $S_{installed}$ denotes the installed capacity, β_0, β_1, β_2, β_3 are regression coefficients. T_D stands for the transmission distance from the wind farm to the nearest grid connection point (km), M_w is the site's average wind speed (m/s), and ρ is the error term. This model enables the prediction of generation efficiency under varying installed capacity conditions [28]. According to the regression analysis conducted in [28], the estimated values of the coefficients are $\beta_0 = 0.35$, $\beta_1 = 0.0024$, $\beta_2 = -0.0018$, and $\beta_3 = 0.045$, which reflect the empirical influence of capacity size, grid distance, and wind conditions on generation performance.

(3) Integrating forecast and optimization:

The insights obtained through data mining are directly fed into the power dispatch optimization framework. By anticipating shifts in demand and generation potential, resources can be allocated more effectively and dispatch can be scheduled more efficiently. For instance, knowing that offshore capacity drops by 12–15% during typhoon season enables preemptive load rerouting or reserve activation by operators. These predictive components, when integrated into the AGFMO-based optimization (detailed in the next section), enhance not only dispatch precision but also the resilience of the system under carbon emission constraints [29].

By analyzing wind power output in relation to installed capacity through data mining methods, this chapter establishes a data-driven foundation for optimizing power dispatch. The insights gained here—particularly the predictive understanding of utilization rates—will inform the optimization strategy presented in the next section where the design of the AGFMO algorithm and its application to achieving optimal dispatch under carbon emission constraints are presented.

3. Optimal Power Flow (OPF) with Carbon Emission Constraints

To enhance the clarity of the solution framework, an integrated flowchart is provided in Figure 1. This diagram illustrates the main procedural steps of the emission-constrained OPF model, highlighting its integration with the wind utilization prediction module developed in Section 2. Specifically, the forecasted wind availability is treated as a constraint within the OPF formulation. The AGFMO algorithm employs the dispatch of fossil-fuel generators, taking into account both fuel costs and carbon taxation schemes. The resulting outputs include optimal power generation schedules and associated carbon cost metrics. This integration enables a practical low-carbon dispatch strategy suited to policy-constrained energy systems to be developed.

The traditional OPF formulation is extended by incorporating carbon dioxide emission constraints. Using the 345 kV transmission system of the Taiwan Power Company, carbon emission control is simulated under various load conditions for 2023, 2028, and 2033, covering off-peak, average, and peak loads. The objective is to determine whether Taiwan's carbon emission cap can be met under actual power generation costs, or to estimate the excess emissions if the cap is exceeded. The study also integrates independent power producers (IPPs) for optimal emission control and evaluates the impact of renewable energy investments. To simplify comparing emissions and fuel costs, carbon pricing from international carbon markets is used to convert emissions into the same currency as fuel costs for analysis.

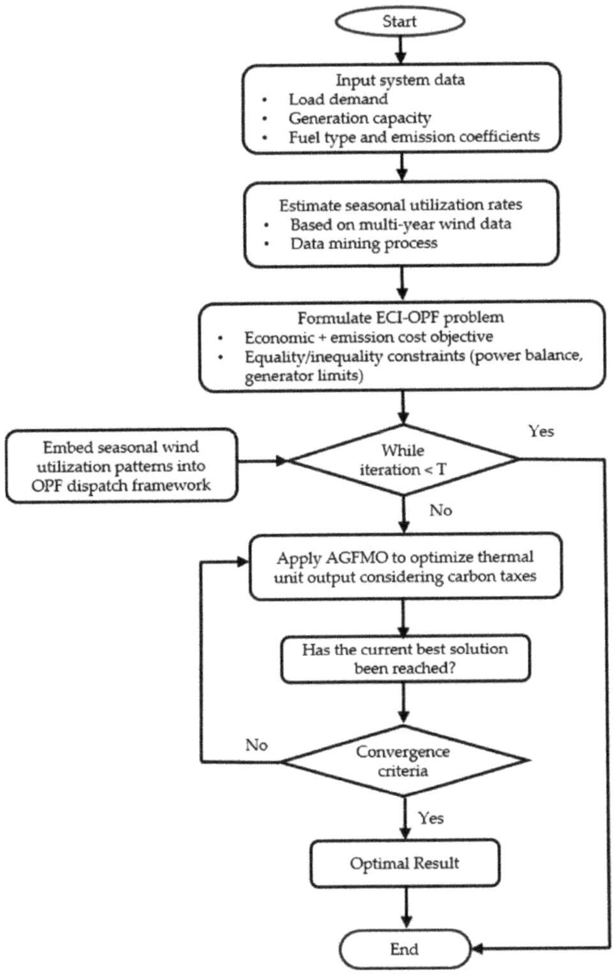

Figure 1. Flowchart of the emission-constrained optimal power flow (OPF) model integrating wind utilization forecasts and AGFMO-based dispatch optimization.

3.1. Objective Equation

The following equations were developed to minimize the cost of fuel dispatch in a power system considering carbon dioxide emissions.

$$C_{gen} = \sum_{k=1}^{N} a_k + b_k P_k + c_k P_k^2 \tag{4}$$

$$C_{CO_2} = \left(\sum_{k=1}^{N} \alpha_k + \beta_k P_k + \gamma_k P_k^2 \right) \cdot \lambda_{CO_2} \tag{5}$$

$$\text{Min}\,(C_{total}) = \min\,(C_{gen} + C_{CO_2}) \tag{6}$$

where N represents the total number of generators in the system, while P_k denotes the power output of the k-th generator. The cost structure includes several components: a_k refers to the fixed cost associated with operating the k-th generator, b_k is the linear fuel cost coefficient that indicates how fuel costs increase proportionally with the power output, and

c_k captures the quadratic fuel cost coefficient, accounting for the non-linear increase in fuel consumption as the generator output increases. On the emissions side, λ_{CO_2} represents a flat-rate carbon cost per ton of CO_2, which, when combined with generator-specific emission factors, determines the total emission-related cost. This modeling approach reflects a fixed carbon tax scenario, in line with Taiwan's current situation where no official carbon pricing mechanism has been implemented, and policy development remains in discussion. The inclusion of λ_{CO_2} within the objective function enables direct incorporation of carbon-related penalties into dispatch optimization. Specifically, α_k represents the fixed carbon emissions from the k-th generator, while the linear and quadratic components of carbon emissions are described by β_k and γ_k, respectively, reflecting how emissions vary with power output.

The coefficients a_k, b_k, c_k and α_k, β_k, γ_k are parameterized according to the typical characteristics of fossil-fueled generators in Taiwan. Coal-fired units are modeled with higher baseline cost and emission levels, where $a_k = 510$, $b_k = 14.3$, and $c_k = 0.0045$, while the corresponding emission coefficients are set as $\alpha_k = 0.215$, $\beta_k = 0.0038$, and $\gamma_k = 0.000012$. For gas-fired units, the operational cost is relatively lower in fixed and quadratic terms, with $a_k = 780$, $b_k = 19.6$, and $c_k = 0.0078$, and emissions are accordingly reduced with coefficients $\alpha_k = 0.172$, $\beta_k = 0.0025$, and $\gamma_k = 0.000009$. Oil-fired units, characterized by their higher carbon intensity and cost, are represented by $a_k = 1200$, $b_k = 36.5$, and $c_k = 0.0102$, alongside emission coefficients of $\alpha_k = 0.26$, $\beta_k = 0.0045$, and $\gamma_k = 0.000015$. These parameter values are selected with reference to the Taiwan Power Company's public disclosures and national emission factor databases [26], ensuring that the dispatch and emission cost modeling is grounded in realistic, region-specific data.

3.1.1. Equality Constraints

The equality constraints ensure that the total power generated by the main generator buses, along with the wind turbine output, must be equal to the total load demand plus transmission losses. The load balance equation can be formulated as follows:

$$\sum_{k=1}^{N} P_{gen,\,k} + \sum_{j=1}^{y} P_{wind,\,j} = \sum_{i=1}^{x} P_{load,\,k} + P_{loss} \tag{7}$$

where $P_{gen,k}$ represents the power output of the k-th generator bus, while $P_{wind,\,j}$ indicates the power produced by the j-th wind turbine bus. The total load at the i-th load bus is denoted by $P_{load,k}$ and P_{loss} accounts for the total transmission losses within the system. Additionally, the variables N, y, and x correspond to the total number of generator buses, wind turbine buses, and load buses, respectively.

3.1.2. Inequality Constraints

The inequality constraints reflect the operational limits of the system, including generation capacity bounds, bus voltage ranges, wind power output limits, and overall carbon emission caps. These constraints ensure that the power system operates safely, efficiently, and within the boundaries of environmental regulations. The mathematical formulation of these inequality conditions is as follows:

$$\underline{P_{gen,\,k}} \le P_{gen,\,k} \le \overline{P_{gen,\,k}} \tag{8}$$

$$\underline{U_e} \le U_e \le \overline{U_e} \tag{9}$$

$$0 \le P_{wind} \le \overline{P_{wind}} \tag{10}$$

$$S_d \le \overline{S_d} \tag{11}$$

$$\sum_{k=1}^{N} CO_{2,k} \leq \overline{CO_{2,k}} \quad (12)$$

The system operates under several constraints. The generation limits for each generator bus, denoted by $\underline{P_{gen,\,k}}$ and $\overline{P_{gen,\,k}}$, set the minimum and maximum allowable power output, while the voltage at each bus e must remain within the bounds $\underline{U_e}$ and $\overline{U_e}$. The total number of buses in the system is represented by N. For wind turbines, their generation is capped at $\overline{P_{wind}}$. Additionally, transmission line d has a capacity limit defined by $\overline{S_d}$. Regarding environmental considerations, the carbon emissions from the k-th generator bus, denoted as $CO_{2,k}$, must not exceed the annual carbon emission limit, $\overline{CO_{2,k}}$.

In this study, all wind energy generated is directly dispatched without curtailment. Photovoltaic sources are not considered in the optimization model due to focus on wind-based dispatch, which is consistent with Taiwan's long-term offshore wind policy emphasis. Battery energy storage systems (BES) are not included in the current formulation, as the study focuses on direct dispatch optimization under renewable uncertainty and fossil balancing, reflecting real-world operational constraints in Taiwan.

3.2. The ECI for Power Flow Solution

The Equivalent Current Injection (ECI) method is employed [30,31] for solving the power flow, as it provides faster convergence compared to the Newton-Raphson method, especially in systems with complex load conditions. Load scenarios are evaluated for short-term (2023), medium-term (2028), and long-term (2033) with the integration of onshore and offshore wind turbines. The focus is on minimizing the power system's fuel dispatch cost while considering carbon dioxide emissions. The procedure for the equivalent current injection (ECI) method can be described as follows:

Step 1: The process begins with defining the allowable error threshold, typically set below 10^{-6}.

Step 2: Import the system data required for analysis, which includes bus data, transmission line details, as well as predefined voltage settings and real/reactive power values.

Step 3: Formulate the admittance matrix (Y_{Bus}) for the power system.

Step 4: Check for the presence of any voltage-controlled buses (PV Bus) in the system.

If present, proceed to Step 5;
If absent, move to Step 6.

Step 5: Make necessary adjustments to the Jacobian matrix before moving to Step 6.

Step 6: Perform LU decomposition on the Jacobian matrix.

Step 7: Compute the equivalent current injection at load buses and calculate the error values for the real and imaginary components of the generator bus voltage.

Step 8: Use the computed voltage error values to update the voltage values.

Step 9: Check if the computed error falls within the acceptable range (error $\leq$ tolerance). If so, the process concludes; otherwise, return to Step 5 for further iterations.

A detailed derivation of the ECI method can be found in [32]. This method's ability to handle complex and dynamic load conditions, while minimizing fuel and carbon costs, highlights its suitability for modern power systems with integrated renewable energy sources.

4. Adaptive Grouped Fish Migration Optimization (AGFMO) with Carbon Emission Constraints

4.1. AGFMO

The Fish Migration Optimization (FMO) algorithm draws inspiration from the natural behaviors of fish, particularly their migratory patterns in search of food, breeding grounds, and favorable environmental conditions [32]. These biologically driven behaviors are abstracted into a computational framework capable of addressing complex numerical optimization problems.

Building upon the standard FMO, an improved variant, termed Adaptive Grouped Fish Migration Optimization (AGFMO), is proposed. The core enhancement lies in the integration of an adaptive dynamic population grouping strategy (ADGPS), which facilitates a more effective balance between global exploration and local exploitation throughout the optimization process. Specifically, AGFMO partitions the fish population into subgroups based on their fitness values, allowing different search behaviors to emerge dynamically during the algorithm's evolution. This design enables the algorithm to more efficiently navigate multi-objective and constrained optimization landscapes—such as power dispatch problems under carbon emission limits.

The original FMO relies on a simplified bioenergetic model to describe energy consumption during fish migration. This is represented mathematically as:

$$E = a \cdot t + a \cdot U_s^x \quad (13)$$

where E represents the energy consumption, t is the time spent, U_s is the swimming speed of the fish, and a, b, and x are constants related to metabolic rate, energy use scaling, and swimming speed, respectively. In this study, the parameter values were adopted from existing literature on fish bioenergetics modeling, with $a = 0.6$, $b = 1.2$, and $x = 2.0$, reflecting typical metabolic scaling observed in similar agent-based or population-based models [32]. These constants ensure that the model realistically captures the trade-off between exploration and exploitation in the fish migration process, as adapted in the original FMO framework.

In AGFMO, the population of fish is dynamically divided into subgroups based on their fitness values. This strategy allows the algorithm to switch between global exploration and local exploitation, increasing the chances of finding a global optimum while still refining local solutions.

The steps of the AGFMO algorithm with ADGPS are as follows:

(1) Initialization: The initial fish population is generated by randomly assigning positions and velocities within predefined bounds. Each fish's position P_i represents a candidate solution to the optimization problem (e.g., generator dispatch levels), and is initialized as:

$$P_i = P_{min} + rand() \cdot (P_{max} - P_{min}) \quad (14)$$

where P_{min} and P_{max} represent the lower and upper bounds of the search space.

(2) Fitness function: Each fish is evaluated using a fitness function that accounts for both economic and environmental objectives. Specifically:

$$\text{Fitness}(P_i) = \omega_1 C_{gen}(P_i) + \omega_2 C_{CO2}(P_i) \quad (15)$$

where $C_{gen}(P_i)$ is the power generation cost of solution P_i, $C_{CO2}(P_i)$ is the carbon emission cost of the same solution, ω_1 and ω_2 are weight factors representing the relative importance of generation cost and carbon emissions, respectively.

(3) Swim process: In each iteration, every fish evaluates multiple candidate positions within its movement range before selecting the best one. The swimming distance is governed by its velocity Us and a time t parameter:

$$d = U_s \cdot t \quad (16)$$

The energy consumption during swimming is given by:

$$E = a \cdot U_s^x \tag{17}$$

After evaluating all candidates, the fish moves to the position with the highest fitness. The parameters for the energy model are adopted based on standard bioenergetic formulations, where $a = 0.6$ and $x = 2.0$, consistent with metabolic scaling observed in previous fish migration optimization literature [32]. The swimming time t is normalized to 1 for simplicity, allowing U_s to directly represent the movement range in each iteration.

(4) Dynamic grouping: The population is dynamically divided into two groups based on fitness:
    (1) Local search group: Fish with higher fitness values perform fine-tuned local exploitation around known optima.
    (2) Global search group: Lower-performing individuals explore under-sampled regions of the search space to maintain population diversity and avoid premature convergence.

(5) Migration process: Fish that fail to improve their fitness through local search are reallocated to new global positions, a process aimed at escaping local optima. Their updated position is calculated using a velocity-based rule inspired by social best guidance:

$$P_i(t+1) = P_i(t) + U_i(t) \tag{18}$$

where $P_i(t)$ is the current position, and $U_i(t)$ is the updated velocity based on the fish's best position and the global best position found so far.

Cooperative evolution: At each generation, cooperative crossover allows individuals from different groups to exchange information. The offspring position is generated using:

$$P_{new} = \beta \cdot P_{partent1} + (1 - \beta) \cdot P_{partent2} \tag{19}$$

where β is a parameter controlling the contribution of each parent, and $P_{parent1}$ and $P_{parent2}$ are selected from different groups.

4.2. AGFMO for Solving the Power Dispatch Problem with Carbon Emission Constraints

As formulated in Section 3, the carbon-constrained optimal power flow (OPF) problem aims to minimize the total generation cost and associated CO_2 emissions while adhering to a set of operational and environmental constraints. These include generator output limits, transmission line capacities, and regulatory caps on carbon emissions. Equation (4) defines the multi-objective cost function, integrating both economic and environmental components.

To solve this non-linear and high-dimensional optimization problem, the AGFMO algorithm is applied. AGFMO is well-suited for the carbon-constrained dispatch setting, as it combines adaptive subgrouping, cooperative search dynamics, and bio-inspired movement strategies to balance convergence and diversity.

Within the AGFMO framework, each fish is used to represent a candidate dispatch vector $P = \{P_1, P_2, \ldots, P_n\}$, corresponding to the power outputs of all generating units. The fitness function evaluates each fish based on a weighted sum of fuel cost and CO_2 emissions:

$$\min \left(\omega_1 \cdot C_{gen} \cdot P_i(t) + \omega_2 \cdot C_{CO_2} \cdot P_i(t) \right) \tag{20}$$

where ω_1 and ω_2 are weights that reflect the importance of generation cost and carbon emissions, respectively.

The Adaptive Grouped Fish Migration Optimization (AGFMO) algorithm addresses the constrained optimization problem by iteratively guiding a population of candidate solutions—represented as individual "fishes"—toward the optimal power dispatch configuration. The algorithm proceeds through the following steps:

Step 1: Initialization

(1) Population Initialization: Each fish is randomly initialized within permissible generation bounds, where its position P_i corresponds to a specific generation schedule across all units.
(2) Velocity Initialization: Each fish is also assigned an initial velocity vector U_i, representing its search direction in the solution space.

Step 2: Fitness Evaluation

Each fish is evaluated based on a composite fitness function that integrates both fuel generation cost and carbon emission penalties.

Step 3: Dynamic grouping

Using the ADGPS, the population is split into two subgroups based on fitness:

(1) Local search group: Fish with better fitness values perform local exploitation, refining the solutions in their immediate neighborhood.
(2) Global search group: Fish with lower fitness values explore new regions of the search space, ensuring diversity and preventing premature convergence.

Step 4: Local search (swimming process)

For fish in the local search group, a local search is applied within a smaller range. Each fish evaluates potential new positions by updating its position and velocity based on its current best-known position and the global best solution.

The velocity update is influenced by the fish's personal best position P_{best} and the global best position P_{global_best}:

$$U_i(t+1) = \omega \cdot U_i(t) + c_1 \cdot r_1(P_{best} - P_i(t)) + c_2 \cdot r_2\left(P_{global\_best} - P_i(t)\right) \tag{21}$$

where ω is the inertia weight, c_1 and c_2 are cognitive and social coefficients, r_1 and r_2 are random numbers between 0 and 1.

Step 5: Global search (migration process)

For fish in the global search group, a migration step is performed to explore the global search space.

Step 6: Cooperative evolution

Periodically, the fish in the local and global groups exchange information through cooperative evolution. This exchange enables the global group to benefit from the knowledge of the local group and vice versa.

Step 7: Update fitness and selection

New candidate positions are evaluated. If a fish's new position yields improved fitness, it is retained; otherwise, the fish reverts to its previous best-known solution.

Step 8: Termination

The algorithm halts when either the maximum number of iterations is reached or when improvements in the global best solution fall below a predefined threshold over successive generations.

Step 9: Return the Optimal Dispatch Solution

Upon convergence, the fish with the best fitness value is taken to represent the optimal dispatch configuration that minimizes both cost and emissions while satisfying all system constraints.

The following Algorithm 1 outlines the AGFMO pseudocode for solving the power dispatch problem:

Algorithm 1. Pseudocode of the AGFMO algorithm.

```
Initialize parameters:
Set population size N, maximum iterations T, velocity limits, and generator output bounds.
Initialize fish population:
P ← Random positions P_i within bounds for each fish;
U ← Random initial velocities U_i for each fish;
Evaluate initial fitness:
For each fish Pi in population:
    Compute fitness: (P_i)= ω1·C_gen·P_i(t) + ω2·C_CO2·P_i(t)
    Store personal best position: P_best_i ← P_i
Set global best: G_best ← best(P_best_i)
While iteration < T do:
    Sort fish by fitness F(P_i)
    Divide population into two groups:
        Local search group: top-performing fish;
        Global search group: remaining fish;
    For each fish in local search group:
        Update velocity;
        Update position;
        Apply bounds to P_i;
        Re-evaluate fitness F(P_i);
        If F(P_i) < F(P_best_i):
            P_best_i = P_i
    For each fish in global search group:
        Migrate to a new random position within bounds;
        Re-evaluate fitness F(P_i);
        If F(P_i) < F(P_best_i):
            P_best_i = P_i
        Apply cooperative evolution across groups;
        Update fish positions and velocities across all dimensions;
        If stopping criteria met (e.g., max iterations or no fitness improvement):
            Break loop;
    Return:
        Return best-found solution P_best
```

5. Case Analysis and Discussion

The Taiwan 345 kV power system, shown in Figure 1, was analyzed using the ECI method for power flow and the AGFMO algorithm to optimize system parameters, minimizing carbon emissions and operational costs. This approach effectively handles the complexity of the 345 kV system. Each test case considered varying load conditions and renewable energy integration, providing insights into system performance. Tests were conducted using MATLAB 2016b on a PC with a 2.9-GHz Intel processor and 16 GB memory.

5.1. The Model of Taipower's 345 kV High-Voltage Transmission System

The Taipower 345 kV system is the core network used for Taiwan's power transmission [26], as shown in Figure 2. It uses high-voltage transmission lines to deliver electricity generated by nuclear, thermal, hydroelectric power plants, and renewable energy sources such as wind and solar power to substations across Taiwan. The electricity is then stepped down and supplied to users. This system encompasses key components such as power plants, transmission lines, and substations, ensuring stable and efficient power transmission. It also incorporates redundancy designs and protection measures to handle faults and ensure the safety and reliability of the power grid.

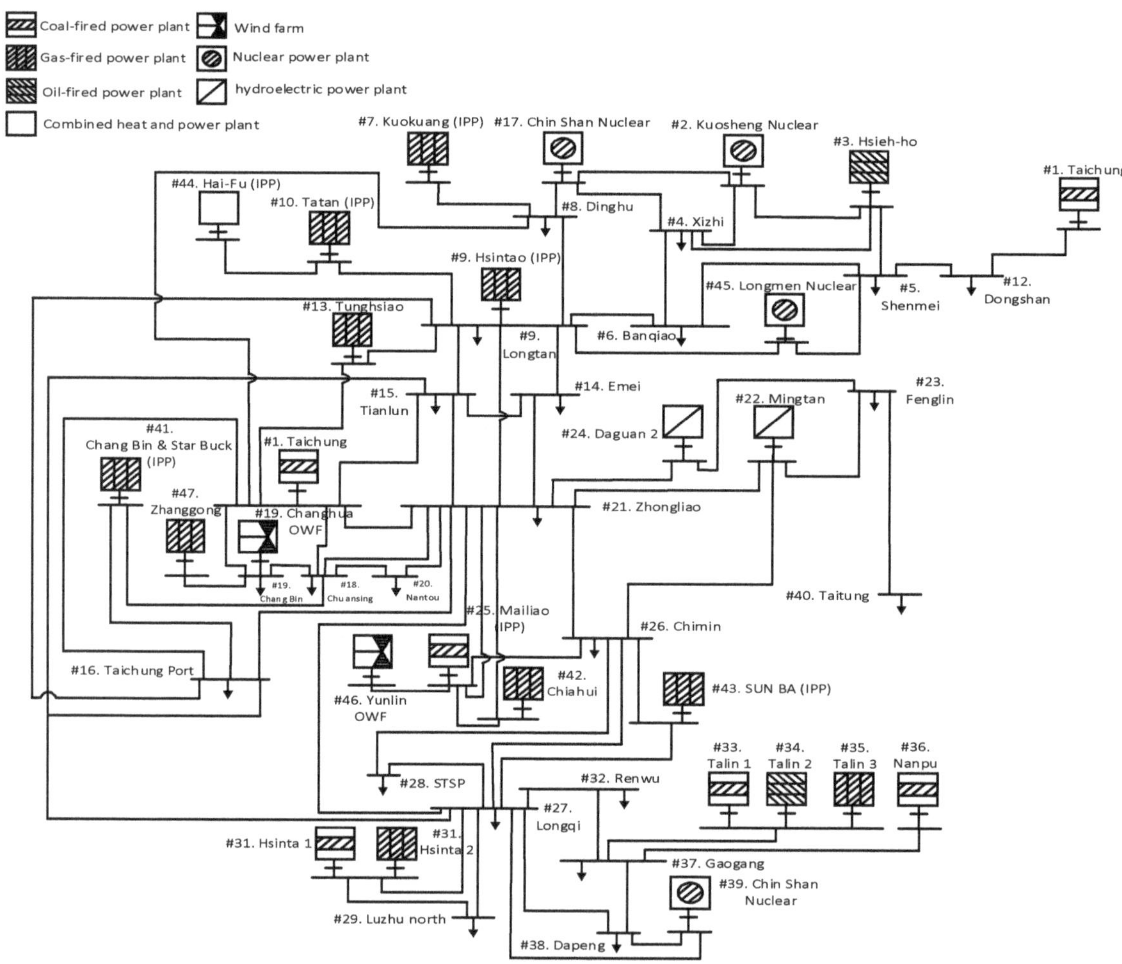

Figure 2. Taiwan power grid structure diagram.

The system's total load for each year in the cases is referenced from the study [33]. In 2023, the peak load was 33,927 MW, the annual average load was 24,816 MW, and the off-peak load was 15,706 MW. For 2028 and 2033, the load growth estimates are based on Taipower's projections for the next decade [34]. In 2028, the peak load is expected to reach

40,263 MW, with an annual average load of 29,451 MW and an off-peak load of 18,337 MW. By 2033, the peak load is forecasted to rise to 47,033 MW, with an annual average load of 34,403 MW and an off-peak load of 20,465 MW.

As highlighted in related studies [35], the proportion of different power generation capacities in Taiwan correlates with load growth forecasts. In 2023, the total installed capacity was approximately 38,446 MW, with small hydropower and solar power plants excluded due to their negligible impact on overall capacity. This adjustment, consistent with common modeling practices, slightly reduces the total compared to the Taiwan Power Company's official data but maintains the key trends needed for macro-level analysis.

Looking ahead, Taiwan Power Company's 2022 development plan projects a steady increase in generation capacities over the next decade [34]. The projected expansions include renewable energy, conventional hydropower, thermal power, and nuclear power, reflecting the Taiwan's strategic focus on diversifying its energy sources and increasing capacity to meet future load demands. By aligning with the latest expected commercial operation years, this study provides a forward-looking analysis that captures dynamic shifts in Taiwan's power system and offers valuable insights for future energy planning.

5.2. Utilizing Data Mining for the Assessment of Wind Power Output and Installed Capacity

Using data mining and multivariate regression analysis, a cyclical pattern in load fluctuations was identified, with low-load periods in February, average loads in May and October, and peak loads in July (as shown in Table 1), reflecting seasonal power demand shifts. As Taiwan plans to expand offshore wind power, onshore and offshore wind generation are evaluated separately. Onshore data cover Taiwan's main island, while offshore data are based on estimates from islands like Penghu and Kinmen [36]. A regression model was used to calculate average hourly power generation per kilowatt of installed capacity under different load conditions. During peak loads, generation averages 11.67 kWh per kW, 42.05 kWh during average loads, and 52.97 kWh during low loads. Lower generation rates are typically associated with malfunctions or maintenance [36]. Wind power analysis under seasonal and monthly load changes provides insights into wind output under varying conditions.

Table 1. Comprehensive statistics of wind power generation in Taiwan's power system.

Metric	Year Peak	Year Average	Year Low
Rep. month	7	10	2
Wind power generation (kWh)	23,167,537	8,265,104	100,165,267
Operating hours (H)	108,579.55	104,333.1	105,411.15
Downtime (H)	10,489.66	14,706.91	5948.85
Avg. hourly generation (kWh)	31,139.52	111,377.83	134,630.74
Fault-free avg. hourly generation (kWh)	33,536.25	120,778.67	151,114.34
Onshore net gen./capacity (%)	11.66	42.04	52.97
Offshore net gen./capacity (%)	13.82	61.55	65.83
Monthly availability (%)	91.22	87.53	94.7

In addition, Table 2 shows a significant increase in both onshore and offshore wind power generation from 2023 to 2033. Offshore wind, which has no contribution in 2023, is projected to rise significantly by 2033, highlighting its growing importance in Taiwan's energy mix. This approach not only explains and predicts complex systems, as shown in the tables, but also lays a solid foundation for future power scheduling and wind energy development.

Table 2. Yearly wind power generation evaluation results.

Year	Onshore Wind (MWh)	Offshore Wind (MWh)	Total Wind (MWh)
2023	1,468,670.42	0	1,468,670.42
2028	2,317,986.21	1,088,886.33	3,406,872.54
2033	3,090,528.53	2,750,002.32	5,840,530.85

5.3. Minimization of Fuel Dispatch Costs and Emissions Under Carbon Tax Scenarios

The AGFMO algorithm was used to obtain the results presented in Tables 3–5 for dispatch cost and CO_2 emissions under varying carbon tax levels. Each table corresponds to a different planning year—2023, 2028, and 2033—evaluated using the same optimization model described in Section 3, with updated load and capacity data. The findings reveal a clear pattern: while increasing carbon taxes substantially raises dispatch costs, the corresponding reductions in emissions are relatively modest.

Table 3. Minimization of fuel dispatch cost under carbon emission pricing in 2023.

Metric		Carbon Tax (NTD) 500	1500	2500
Dispatch cost (NTD)	Peak (20%)	137,341,336	150,594,559	172,301,044
	Avg (65%)	73,819,293	90,000,017	104,131,988
	Low (15%)	41,299,501	46,504,288	52,340,511
Total cost (NTD)		713,713,208,005	831,270,998,730	962,388,054,661
Avg cost (NTD/MWh)		3233.01	3770.75	4247.43
Carbon emissions (tons)	Peak (20%)	19,001	18,521	18,759
	Avg (65%)	13,950	14,121	13,487
	Low (15%)	4694	4613	4673
Total emissions (tons)		122,079,250	117,758,501	115,991,850
Emissions (tons/MWh)		0.53	0.52	0.51

Table 4. Minimization of fuel dispatch cost under carbon emission pricing in 2028.

Metric		Carbon Tax (NTD) 500	1500	2500
Dispatch cost (NTD)	Peak (20%)	167,182,804	183,251,821	211,410,310
	Avg (65%)	82,240,770	91,441,180	102,483,167
	Low (15%)	1,566,809,501,147	1,720,687,815,156	1,870,560,887,881
Total cost (NTD)		5847.21	6402.41	7021.08
Avg cost (NTD/MWh)		21,791	21,751	21,897
Carbon emissions (tons)	Peak (20%)	17,451	17,007	15,907
	Avg (65%)	7081	7351	6752
	Low (15%)	148,012,721	145,670,911	143,819,537
Total emissions (tons)		0.55	0.54	0.53
Emissions (tons/MWh)		292,001,901	314,174,027	345,627,781

In 2023 (Table 3), with a carbon tax of 500 NTD/ton, the dispatch cost during the peak period is 137,341,336 NTD, and annual CO_2 emissions total 122,079,250 tons. When the tax increases to 2500 NTD/ton, the dispatch cost escalates dramatically to 962,388,054,661 NTD, while emissions drop only slightly to 115,991,850 tons. This suggests a non-linear relationship where emission reductions taper off despite a steep rise in cost.

A similar trend is observed in 2028 (Table 4). At 500 NTD/ton, dispatch costs are 1.57 trillion NTD, with emissions at 148 million tons. At 2500 NTD/ton, costs rise to nearly

1.87 trillion NTD, yet emissions only decline to 143.8 million tons. These results imply that the marginal effectiveness of carbon taxes in reducing emissions diminishes over time as the energy system matures.

Table 5. Minimization of fuel dispatch cost under carbon emission pricing in 2033.

Metric		Carbon Tax (NTD) 500	1500	2500
Dispatch cost (NTD)	Peak (20%)	333,370,429	361,553,285	405,567,495
	Avg (65%)	158,657,560	145,566,522	160,612,670
	Low (15%)	3,179,699,580,483	3,311,754,575,311	3,588,500,497,124
Total cost (NTD)		9801.21	10,528.36	11,507.33
Avg cost (NTD/MWh)		29,720	29,598	29,512
Carbon emissions (tons)	Peak (20%)	24,702	24,501	23,052
	Avg (65%)	10,021	8587	8981
	Low (15%)	204,311,588	201,302,527	193,521,851
Total emissions (tons)		0.64	0.64	0.62
Emissions (tons/MWh)		560,526,821	582,511,836	605,521,781

The trend continues in 2033 (Table 5). Even with a high carbon tax of 2500 NTD/ton, emissions fall only slightly—from 204.3 million tons to 193.5 million tons—while dispatch costs climb sharply to 3.59 trillion NTD. This indicates that without structural changes in fuel usage, carbon taxes alone yield limited emission reduction benefits, despite increasing economic costs.

Table 6 illustrates changes in the fuel mix under different carbon tax levels. In 2023, coal accounted for 62.21% and gas 35.25% of total electricity generation under a 500 NTD/ton tax. With a tax of 2500 NTD/ton, coal's share declines marginally to 57.50%, while gas rises to 40.36%. However, even in 2033 under the same high tax rate, coal still makes up 62.28% of generation—indicating little progress toward decarbonization. These results suggest that without complementary policy interventions, carbon pricing alone is insufficient to significantly reduce coal dependence.

Table 6. Analysis of carbon tax and fuel mix by year.

Year	Carbon Tax (NTD)	Total Generation (MW)	Coal Generation (MW)	Coal Mix (%)	Oil Generation (MW)	Oil Mix (%)	Gas Generation (MW)	Gas Mix (%)
2023	500	17,811.20	11,081.11	62.21	450.21	2.52	6279.88	35.25
	1500	18,001.05	10,840.53	58.84	251.81	1.39	7160.52	39.77
	2500	17,765.50	10,237.036	57.50	377.03	2.12	7171.88	40.36
2028	500	22,362.27	12,957.07	57.82	709.39	3.17	8721.69	39.00
	1500	22,262.65	12,545.19	56.23	731.19	3.28	9011.33	40.47
	2500	22,350.35	10,956.77	48.92	1157.14	5.17	10258.32	45.89
2033	500	27,793.71	19,440.05	69.80%	511.44	1.84	7881.06	28.35
	1500	27,454.14	18,955.15	68.90%	376.90	1.37	8159.95	29.72
	2500	27,473.60	17,146.30	62.28%	758.88	2.76	7171.88	34.95

Although higher carbon taxes shift generation marginally toward gas, low-cost coal remains dominant. For example, in 2023, the AGFMO-optimized dispatch results in 11,081.11 MW of coal generation and 6279.88 MW of gas. At 2500 NTD/ton, coal generation falls to 10,237.04 MW and gas increases to 7171.88 MW. Despite these changes, the system remains constrained by its reliance on coal, limiting the effectiveness of carbon pricing in driving down emissions.

Overall, while the AGFMO algorithm effectively minimizes costs under given constraints, the results highlight a critical insight: carbon taxes alone do not lead to significant emission reductions unless accompanied by broader structural reforms in the energy system. Long-term decarbonization will require complementary policies beyond price signals—such as fuel switching incentives, renewable energy mandates, or stricter emissions caps.

5.4. Balancing Cost and Carbon: Dispatch Optimization Under Emission Limits

The results point to an increasingly evident trend in energy system planning: carbon emission constraints are becoming central to dispatch decisions—not just technically, but politically and ethically as well. The AGFMO algorithm, in its dynamic OPF form, attempts to reconcile these layers of complexity. Yet, as seen in the 2023 simulation (Table 7), the presence of a carbon cap did not really change the outcome. Why? Because emissions were already within policy limits that year, meaning cost minimization and compliance essentially coincided.

Table 7. Results of 2023 cost minimization analysis with carbon emission constraints.

Metric		Carbon Tax (NTD) 500	1500	2500
Dispatch cost (NTD)	Peak (20%)	141,838,709	156,131,118	175,651,393
	Avg (65%)	76,247,689	88,157,397	104,580,690
	Low (15%)	42,287,502.8	48,534,629	52,611,982
Total cost (NTD)		734,161,332,165	851,213,119,090	980,934,218,911
Avg cost (NTD/MWh)		3157.36	3734.95	4313.99
Carbon emissions (tons)	Peak (20%)	19,431	18,217	19,097
	Avg (65%)	14,549	14,425	13,310
	Low (15%)	4931	4917	4831
Total emissions (tons)		122,008,876	119,537,619	116,607,114
Emissions (tons/MWh)		0.53	0.52	0.51

That alignment does not hold in 2028 (Table 8) or 2033 (Table 9). The rising load demand starts to push the system up against those same carbon thresholds. For example, Taiwan's 2035 target is 139.1 million tons of CO_2—a 25–28% reduction from 2005 levels. In 2028, even with a steep carbon tax of 2500 NTD/ton, emissions still clock in at 139,328,479 tons. Close, but not quite. By 2033 (Table 9), the goal is still exceeded unless carbon abatement mechanisms are significantly tightened. It is a clear tension: reducing emissions while keeping systems cost-efficient becomes harder as demand rises.

And it is not just about emissions. Table 7 shows that dispatch costs, surprisingly, stay in a fairly tight range across tax levels. This raises a different kind of question: if cost does not vary much, why is carbon not falling faster? The answer seems to lie in structural inertia—namely, coal. Even with tax pressure, it does not exit the mix easily.

The AGFMO model adapts dispatch in response to cost and carbon signals. In 2023, under a 500 NTD/ton tax, emissions hit 122 million tons, and the dispatch cost lands at 734.2 billion NTD. At higher tax levels, emissions nudge downward, but not dramatically. The signal is there, but the system is not pivoting fast enough.

This all points to a broader insight: carbon pricing helps, but it will not carry the whole decarbonization load. Without complementary policy moves—fuel switching mandates, capacity caps, or technology subsidies—progress stalls. Carbon taxes can shape the direction, but structural reform is what gets you there.

Table 8. Results of 2028 cost minimization analysis with carbon emission constraints.

Metric		Carbon Tax (NTD) 500	1500	2500
Dispatch cost (NTD)	Peak (20%)	296,721,83	310,584,094	345,069,350
	Avg (65%)	179,164,910	192,945,169	202,292,615
	Low (15%)	94,600,393	96,617,308	103,659,348
Total cost (NTD)		1,654,241,780,591	1,738,198,483,069	1,897,727,342,301
Avg cost (NTD/MWh)		6038.39	6460.29	7076.44
Carbon emissions (tons)	Peak (20%)	22,614	22,419	23,202
	Avg (65%)	15,526	15,712	15,578
	Low (15%)	6406	6850	6735
Total emissions (tons)		139,023,194	138,564,127	139,328,479
Emissions (tons/MWh)		0.51	0.52	0.51

Table 9. Results of 2033 cost minimization analysis with carbon emission constraints.

Metric		Carbon Tax (NTD) 500	1500	2500
Dispatch cost (NTD)	Peak (20%)	629,145,597	646,260,891	688,809,335
	Avg (65%)	524,092,942	547,841,323	520,853,527
	Low (15%)	207,220,315	212,196,309	216,637,323
Total cost (NTD)		4,325,948,476,247	4,439,729,682,009	4,473,557,069,706
Avg cost (NTD/MWh)		13,348.43	13,962.43	14,090.23
Carbon emissions (tons)	Peak (20%)	26,075	26,086	26,681
	Avg (65%)	14,687	14,878	14,740
	Low (15%)	7095	7041	7034
Total emissions (tons)		141,207,615	140,531,437	140,919,598
Emissions (tons/MWh)		0.44	0.44	0.43

As shown in Table 10, in 2023, without the addition of new renewable energy, the system's carbon emissions reached approximately 140,919,598 tons, exceeding the policy limit of 139,000,000 tons. By integrating 2500 MW of wind power, emissions were reduced to 139,466,684 tons, successfully meeting the emissions target.

Table 10. Cost minimization under wind power increment and carbon emission constraints in 2023.

Metric		Carbon Tax (NTD) 500	1500	2500
Dispatch cost (NTD)	Peak (20%)	620,480,292	611,651,084	688,949,738
	Avg (65%)	494,575,870	494,948,891	475,215,728
	Low (15%)	203,415,678	204,225,477	218,363,863
Total cost (NTD)		4,139,911,890,922	4,160,944,758,703	4,213,821,810,374
Avg cost (NTD/MWh)		12,640.65	12,916.99	13,269.20
Carbon emissions (tons)	Peak (20%)	25,877	25,906	27,117
	Avg (65%)	14,311	14,455	14,185
	Low (15%)	7705	7602	7513
Total emissions (tons)		138,466,684	138,690,758	138,102,927
Emissions (tons/MWh)		0.43	0.43	0.42

Under a carbon tax of 500 NTD/ton, the total dispatch cost was reduced to 4,139,911,890,922 NTD, with an average generation cost of 12,640.65 NTD/MWh. When the carbon tax increased to 1500 NTD/ton, the total dispatch cost rose slightly to 4,160,944,758,703 NTD, with an average generation cost of 12,916.99 NTD/MWh. At the highest carbon tax of 2500 NTD/ton, the dispatch cost increased further to 4,213,821,810,374 NTD, while emissions remained controlled at 138,102,927 tons, staying within the target.

The integration of wind power led to significant cost reductions across different carbon tax levels. For a 500 NTD/ton tax, generation costs were reduced by 186,036,585,325 NTD; for a 1500 NTD/ton tax, the reduction was 278,784,923,306 NTD; and under a 2500 NTD/ton tax, the cost was reduced by 259,735,259,332 NTD compared to scenarios without renewable energy integration. To maintain cost efficiency, the optimal purchase price for wind energy should not exceed 16,172 NTD/MWh at a 500 NTD/ton carbon tax, 17,987.9 NTD/MWh at a 1500 NTD/ton tax, and 22,789 NTD/MWh at a 2500 NTD/ton tax. Ensuring that renewable energy purchase prices remain below these levels would prevent excessive increases in generation costs, making wind power integration both environmentally and economically viable.

This analysis highlights the importance of integrating renewable energy, such as wind power, to meet emissions targets while keeping generation costs manageable. Carbon pricing alone is insufficient to achieve these goals, underscoring the need for renewable energy expansion to ensure long-term sustainability.

5.5. Performance Evaluation of AGFMO

To achieve the most precise cost analysis and evaluation, as illustrated in Tables 3–10, the AGFMO algorithm is utilized. Compared to other algorithms, AGFMO demonstrates superior accuracy in minimizing dispatch costs across a variety of constrained scenarios, making it the optimal solution for handling complex optimization tasks under multiple constraints.

To further demonstrate AGFMO's outstanding performance, this section evaluates its application under wind power increments and carbon tax constraints. Figures 3–5 illustrate the convergence of dispatch costs under carbon taxes of 500, 1500, and 2500 NTD, with an annual average rate of 65%. The results indicate that AGFMO is highly effective in managing multi-constraint optimization problems, particularly over long-term iterations where its convergence continues to improve. In contrast, other algorithms like PSO [23], genetic ant colony optimization (GACO) [37] and FMO [32], although showing faster initial convergence, tend to plateau early and exhibit limited effectiveness in cost minimization under stricter conditions.

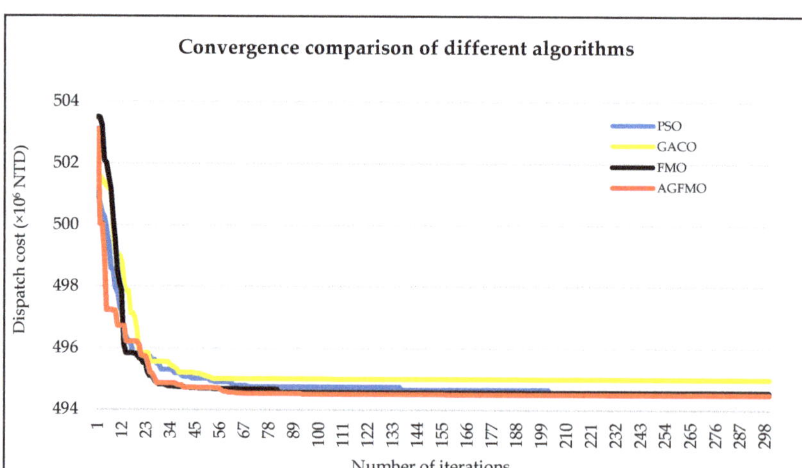

Figure 3. Dispatch cost convergence under wind power and carbon tax constraints (500 NTD, 65% annual average).

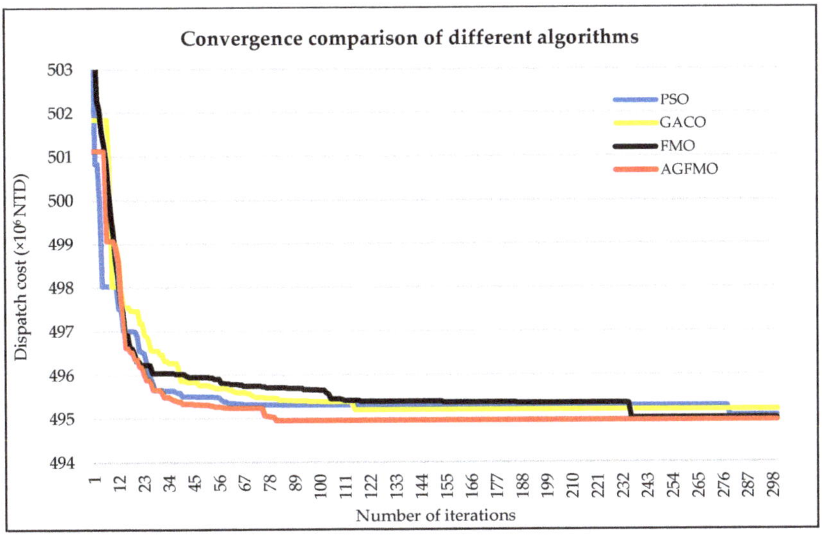

Figure 4. Dispatch cost convergence under wind power and carbon tax constraints (1500 NTD, 65% annual average).

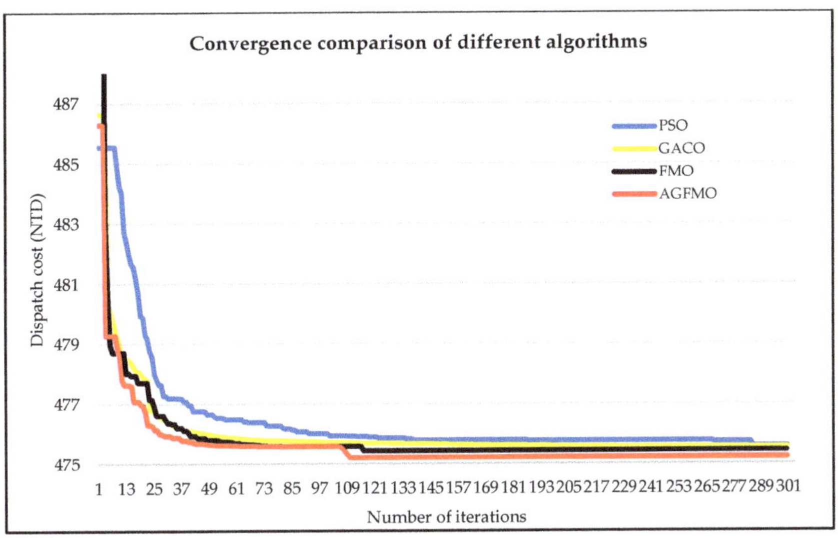

Figure 5. Dispatch cost convergence under wind power and carbon tax constraints (2500 NTD, 65% annual average).

The quantitative comparison in Table 11 provides further evidence for these observations. Across all carbon tax scenarios, AGFMO consistently achieves lower total dispatch costs, converges in fewer iterations or with more stable patterns, maintains a higher success rate, and preserves greater population diversity (measured by average Euclidean distance) compared to the original FMO. These metrics were obtained from 30 independent simulation runs for each scenario, with success defined as achieving a final cost within 0.1% of the best-known solution. This confirms that the adaptive grouping strategy in AGFMO not only improves convergence speed but also enhances solution robustness and stability under varying policy constraints.

Table 11. Comparative performance of AGFMO and FMO under different carbon tax scenarios (65% annual average wind utilization).

Carbon Tax (NTD)	Algorithm	Total Cost (NTD)	Iterations to Converge	Success Rate	Avg. Euclidean Distance
500	FMO	495,583,410	83	88.9%	0.136
	AGFMO	494,575,870	93	96.7%	0.182
1500	FMO	495,001,915	236	86.7%	0.129
	AGFMO	494,948,891	81	93.3%	0.176
2500	FMO	475,443,854	116	90.0%	0.141
	AGFMO	475,215,728	110	96.7%	0.185

Note: Success rate is calculated based on 30 independent runs for each scenario, with success defined as achieving a final cost within 0.1% of the best-known solution.

To further validate the general optimization capability of AGFMO beyond the power dispatch context, the algorithm was also evaluated on selected CEC2020 benchmark functions under a 15-dimensional (15D) search space. Due to space constraints, three representative functions—F1 (unimodal), F5 (hybrid), and F9 (composition)—were selected to cover diverse optimization landscapes. The results, summarized in Table 12, show that AGFMO achieves mean fitness values close to the ideal optima, with low standard deviations and small relative errors, indicating high stability and accuracy. In particular, the algorithm demonstrates consistent convergence behavior across unimodal and multimodal functions, as illustrated in Figure 6 for the F9 case. These findings confirm that AGFMO's adaptive grouping mechanism is effective not only in complex, real-world dispatch problems but also in generalized benchmark scenarios.

Table 12. AGFMO performance on selected CEC2020 benchmark functions (15D).

Function	Ideal Value	Mean Fitness Value	STD	Relative Error
F1	100	101.6114	0.02	1.6114%
F5	1700	1755.845	25.48	3.2856%
F9	2400	2516.537	10.63	4.8557%

AGFMO's superior performance can be attributed to its adaptive mechanism, which allows it to flexibly explore the solution space and reduce the likelihood of becoming trapped in local optima. This adaptability is especially valuable when managing complex energy systems, where balancing fluctuating renewable energy sources with strict carbon emission limits is crucial. The results not only demonstrate AGFMO's capability to optimize dispatch costs but also highlight its robustness and reliability in addressing real-world energy challenges.

In summary, AGFMO provides both the highest precision in cost evaluation and long-term stability, making it an ideal tool for future energy systems that must meet increasing environmental and regulatory demands.

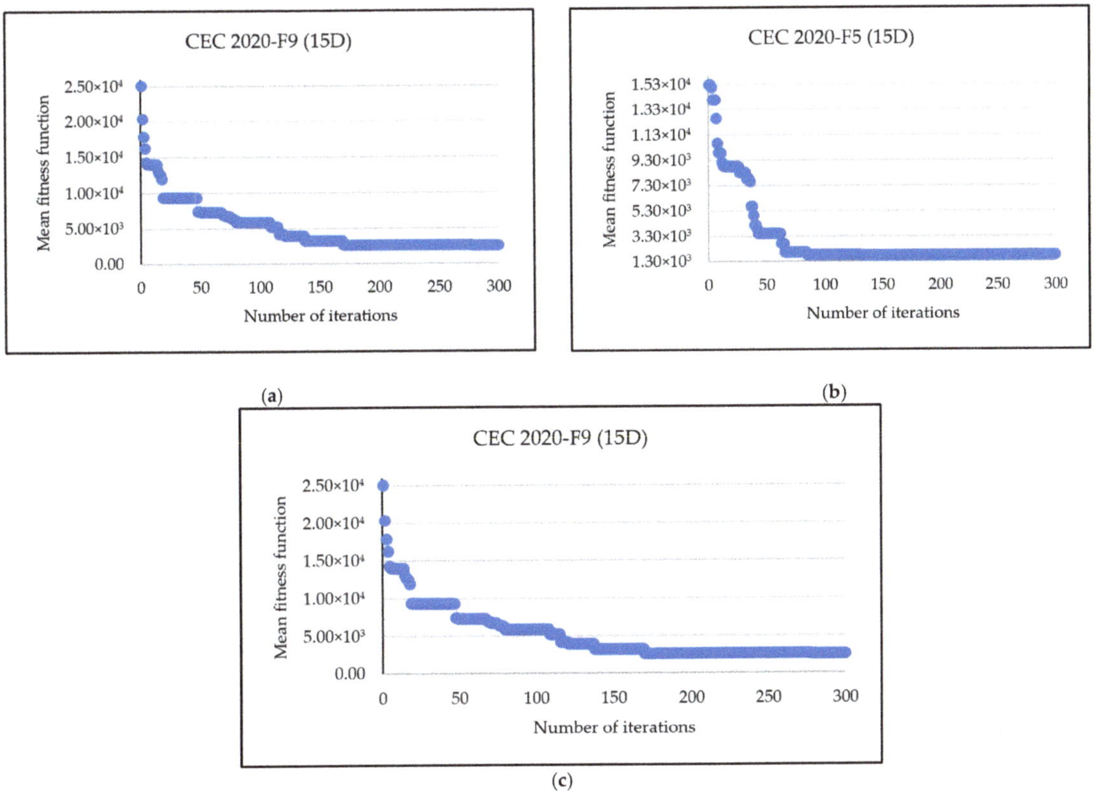

Figure 6. Dispatch cost convergence under wind power and carbon tax constraints (2500 NTD, 65% annual average).

6. Conclusions and Critical Analysis

This study introduced an Adaptive Grouped Fish Migration Optimization (AGFMO) algorithm to address the complex challenge of optimizing power dispatch in carbon-constrained environments, using Taiwan as a representative case. In the absence of access to international carbon trading mechanisms, the results show that meaningful emissions reductions are still achievable through internal, algorithm-driven dispatch strategies. By incorporating projected renewable energy development and fluctuating carbon tax scenarios, the proposed framework offers a realistic pathway toward meeting Taiwan's national targets by 2033.

From a methodological standpoint, the AGFMO algorithm extends conventional metaheuristics by incorporating adaptive grouping, recombination, and disturbance strategies that enhance global search behavior and mitigate premature convergence. These features have proven critical in navigating the non-linear, multi-constraint dispatch landscape associated with high renewable penetration and emission limits. The comparative performance gains over traditional methods underscore AGFMO's potential as a flexible optimization engine for energy systems facing structural constraints.

On the practical front, the findings carry broader implications beyond the Taiwan case. Many regions—whether politically isolated or institutionally underdeveloped—face similar challenges in balancing fossil-fuel dependence with decarbonization mandates. The AGFMO-based framework offers a scalable, market-independent solution for dispatch planning, capable of adapting to local resource availability, policy settings, and operational uncertainties. Importantly, it offers a viable strategy for aligning domestic energy planning with broader climate goals, even in the absence of external market incentives.

In summary, advanced algorithmic design can play a pivotal role in enabling low-carbon transitions within constrained environments. AGFMO not only delivers technical improvements over existing optimization methods but also addresses a critical policy gap by enabling emission reductions in systems excluded from global trading regimes. Its adaptability and robustness position it as a strong candidate for application across a wider range of energy planning contexts in the era of deep decarbonization.

Author Contributions: K.-H.L. conceptualized the research framework, defined the primary research objectives, and designed the optimization model for emission-constrained power dispatch. He supervised the entire research process, ensured the integration of carbon tax policy considerations, and provided critical revisions to enhance the academic rigor of the manuscript. X.J. developed the simulation models, performed data processing, and conducted detailed algorithmic analyses using the AGFMO method. She was responsible for running the case studies, analyzing the computational results, and interpreting the impact of carbon emission constraints on system performance. S.-J.L. carried out the comprehensive literature review, established the theoretical background on carbon tax policies and emission reduction strategies, and assisted in validating the simulation outcomes. He also contributed to preparing visual illustrations and improving the overall clarity and presentation of the manuscript. All authors have read and agreed to the published version of the manuscript.

Funding: The project was supported by the Fujian Provincial Education Research Projects for Young and Middle-Aged Teachers (No. JAT241182) and the Technology Innovation Team of Minnan University of Science and Technology (No. 23XTD112).

Data Availability Statement: All data supporting the reported results are included in the article.

Conflicts of Interest: The authors declare no conflicts of interest.

References

1. Zhang, W.; Ji, C.; Liu, Y.; Hao, Y.; Song, Y.; Cao, Y.; Qi, H. Dynamic Interactions of Carbon Trading, Green Certificate Trading, and Electricity Markets: Insights from System Dynamics Modeling. *PLoS ONE* **2024**, *19*, e0304478. [CrossRef]
2. Zhao, X.; Chen, H.; Hu, S.; Zhou, Y. The Impact of Carbon Quota Allocation and Low-Carbon Technology Innovation on Carbon Market Effectiveness: A System Dynamics Analysis. *Environ. Sci. Pollut. Res.* **2023**, *30*, 28943–28955. [CrossRef] [PubMed]
3. Liu, Z.; Deng, Z.; He, G.; Wang, H.; Zhang, X.; Lin, J.; Qi, Y.; Liang, X.; Davis, S.J. Challenges and Opportunities for Carbon Neutrality in China. *Nat. Rev. Earth Environ.* **2022**, *3*, 141–155. [CrossRef]
4. Huang, S.; Du, C.; Jin, X.; Zhang, D.; Wen, S.; Jia, Z. The Impact of Carbon Emission Trading on Renewable Energy: A Comparative Analysis Based on the CGE Model. *Sustainability* **2023**, *15*, 12649. [CrossRef]
5. National Development Council, Taiwan. Taiwan's Pathway to Net-Zero Emissions by 2050. Available online: https://www.ndc.gov.tw/en/Content_List.aspx?n=B154724D802DC488 (accessed on 3 November 2024).
6. Global Taiwan Institute. On the Path to Net Zero: Will Taiwan Reach Its Goal? Available online: https://globaltaiwan.org/2023/08/on-the-path-to-net-zero-will-taiwan-reach-its-goal/ (accessed on 3 November 2024).
7. International Energy Agency (IEA). Chinese Taipei—IEA Country Profile. Available online: https://www.iea.org/countries/chinese-taipei (accessed on 3 November 2024).
8. Ang, T.-Z.; Salem, M.; Kamarol, M.; Das, H.S.; Nazari, M.A.; Prabaharan, N. A Comprehensive Study of Renewable Energy Sources: Classifications, Challenges and Suggestions. *Energy Strategy Rev.* **2022**, *43*, 100939. [CrossRef]
9. Hassan, Q.; Algburi, S.; Sameen, A.Z.; Salman, H.M.; Jaszczur, M. A Review of Hybrid Renewable Energy Systems: Solar and Wind-Powered Solutions: Challenges, Opportunities, and Policy Implications. *Results Eng.* **2023**, *20*, 101621. [CrossRef]
10. Qiu, K.; Entchev, E. Modeling, Design and Optimization of Integrated Renewable Energy Systems for Electrification in Remote Communities. *Sustain. Energy Res.* **2024**, *11*, 10. [CrossRef]
11. De Carne, G.; Maroufi, S.M.; Beiranvand, H.; De Angelis, V.; D'Arco, S.; Gevorgian, V.; Waczowicz, S.; Mather, B.; Liserre, M.; Hagenmeyer, V. The Role of Energy Storage Systems for a Secure Energy Supply: A Comprehensive Review of System Needs and Technology Solutions. *Electr. Power Syst. Res.* **2024**, *236*, 110963. [CrossRef]
12. Wu, Y.-H.; Dai, H.; Xie, Y.; Masui, T. The Efforts of Taiwan to Achieve NDC Target: An Integrated Assessment on the Carbon Emission Trading System. *Nat. Hazards* **2019**, *99*, 1295–1310. [CrossRef]

13. Leal Filho, W.; Balogun, A.-L.; Surroop, D.; Lange Salvia, A.; Narula, K.; Li, C.; Hunt, J.D.; Gatto, A.; Sharifi, A.; Feng, H.; et al. Realising the Potential of Renewable Energy as a Tool for Energy Security in Small Island Developing States. *Sustainability* **2022**, *14*, 4965. [CrossRef]
14. Hameed, G.; Nair, P.S.B.; Tan, R.R.; Foo, D.C.Y.; Short, M. A Novel Mathematical Model to Incorporate Carbon Trading and Other Emission Reduction Techniques within Energy Planning Models. *Sustain. Prod. Consum.* **2023**, *40*, 571–589. [CrossRef]
15. Bechara, C.A.; Alnouri, S.Y. Energy Assessment Strategies in Carbon-Constrained Industrial Clusters. *Energy Convers. Manag.* **2022**, *254*, 115204. [CrossRef]
16. Han, H.; Wei, T.; Wu, C.; Xu, X.; Zang, H.; Sun, G.; Wei, Z. A Low-Carbon Dispatch Strategy for Power Systems Considering Flexible Demand Response and Energy Storage. *Front. Energy Res.* **2022**, *10*, 883602. [CrossRef]
17. Russo, M.A.; Carvalho, D.; Martins, N.; Monteiro, A. Forecasting the Inevitable: A Review on the Impacts of Climate Change on Renewable Energy Resources. *Sustain. Energy Technol. Assess.* **2022**, *52*, 102283. [CrossRef]
18. Gao, L.; Yang, S.; Chen, N.; Gao, J. Integrated Energy System Dispatch Considering Carbon Trading Mechanisms and Refined Demand Response for Electricity, Heat, and Gas. *Energies* **2024**, *17*, 4705. [CrossRef]
19. Pierri, E.; Hellkamp, D.; Thiede, S.; Herrmann, C. Enhancing Energy Flexibility through the Integration of Variable Renewable Energy in the Process Industry. *Procedia CIRP* **2021**, *98*, 7–12. [CrossRef]
20. Hadi, M.B.; Moeini-Aghtaie, M.; Khoshjahan, M.; Dehghanian, P. A Comprehensive Review on Power System Flexibility: Concept, Services, and Products. *IEEE Access* **2022**, *10*, 99257–99267. [CrossRef]
21. Li, H.; Han, Y.; Wang, X.; Wen, F. Optimal Strategies of Power Generation Companies and Electricity Customers Participating in Electricity Retailing Trading. *IEEE Access* **2023**, *11*, 129660–129670. [CrossRef]
22. Li, P.; Liu, Q. Optimizing Energy Management Strategies for Microgrids through Chaotic Local Search and Particle Swarm Optimization Techniques. *Heliyon* **2024**, *10*, e36669. [CrossRef]
23. Liu, Z.; Sun, Y.; Xing, C.; Liu, J.; He, Y.; Zhou, Y.; Zhang, G. Artificial Intelligence Powered Large-Scale Renewable Integrations in Multi-Energy Systems for Carbon Neutrality Transition: Challenges and Future Perspectives. *Energy AI* **2022**, *10*, 100195. [CrossRef]
24. Cheraghi, R.; Jahangir, M.H. Multi-Objective Optimization of a Hybrid Renewable Energy System Supplying a Residential Building Using NSGA-II and MOPSO Algorithms. *Energy Convers. Manag.* **2023**, *294*, 117515. [CrossRef]
25. Qin, M.; Yang, Y.; Zhao, X.; Xu, Q.; Yuan, L. Low-Carbon Economic Multi-Objective Dispatch of Integrated Energy System Considering the Price Fluctuation of Natural Gas and Carbon Emission Accounting. *Prot. Control Mod. Power Syst.* **2023**, *8*, 1–18. [CrossRef]
26. Taiwan Power Company. About Us. Available online: https://www.taipower.com.tw (accessed on 3 November 2024).
27. Fan, W.; Fu, Y.; Zheng, S.; Bian, J.; Zhou, Y.; Xiong, H. DEWP: Deep Expansion Learning for Wind Power Forecasting. *ACM Trans. Knowl. Discov. Data* **2024**, *18*, 71. [CrossRef]
28. Khan, M.I. Data Mining and Statistical Review of Optimization Techniques of Hybrid Renewable Energy Systems. *Int. J. Innov. Technol. Explor. Eng.* **2020**, *10*, 181–192. [CrossRef]
29. Zhao, Y.; Zhang, C.; Zhang, Y.; Wang, Z.; Li, J. A Review of Data Mining Technologies in Building Energy Systems: Load Prediction, Pattern Identification, Fault Detection and Diagnosis. *Energy Built Environ.* **2020**, *1*, 149–164. [CrossRef]
30. Lin, W.M.; Huang, C.H.; Zhan, T.S. A Hybrid Current-Power Optimal Power Flow Technique. *IEEE Trans. Power Syst.* **2008**, *23*, 177–185. [CrossRef]
31. Lu, K.-H.; Qian, W.; Jiang, Y.; Zhong, Y.-S. The Calibrated Safety Constraints Optimal Power Flow for the Operation of Wind-Integrated Power Systems. *Processes* **2024**, *12*, 2272. [CrossRef]
32. Pan, J.-S.; Hu, P.; Chu, S.-C. Binary Fish Migration Optimization for Solving Unit Commitment. *Energy* **2021**, *226*, 120329. [CrossRef]
33. Bureau of Energy, Ministry of Economic Affairs, Taiwan. Official Website. Available online: https://www.moeaea.gov.tw (accessed on 3 November 2024).
34. Ministry of Environment, Taiwan. Official Website. Available online: https://www.moenv.gov.tw (accessed on 3 November 2024).
35. Yang, C.-H.; Chen, B.-H.; Wu, C.-H.; Chen, K.-C.; Chuang, L.-Y. Deep Learning for Forecasting Electricity Demand in Taiwan. *Mathematics* **2022**, *10*, 2547. [CrossRef]
36. Lin, Y.-C. Taiwan's Electricity Demand under the COVID-19 and Supply Chain Disruption. *Emerg. Mark. Financ. Trade* **2024**, *60*, 688–703. [CrossRef]
37. Chen, G.; Li, Z.; Zhang, Z.; Li, S. An Improved ACO Algorithm Optimized Fuzzy PID Controller for Load Frequency Control in Multi Area Interconnected Power Systems. *IEEE Access* **2020**, *8*, 6429–6447. [CrossRef]

mathematics

MDPI

Article

Combined Framework for State of Charge Estimation of Lithium-Ion Batteries: Optimized LSTM Network Integrated with IAOA and AUKF

Jing Han [1,2], Yaolin Dong [2] and Wei Wang [2,*]

[1] China Aluminum Ningxia Energy Group Co., Ltd., Yinchuan 750004, China; 254602072@csu.edu.cn
[2] School of Automation, Central South University, Changsha 410083, China; dyl0812@csu.edu.cn
[*] Correspondence: wangwei729@csu.edu.cn

Abstract: The State of Charge (SOC) is vital for battery system management. Enhancing SOC estimation boosts system performance. This paper presents a combined framework that improves SOC estimation's accuracy and stability for electric vehicles. The framework combines a Long Short-Term Memory (LSTM) network with an Adaptive Unscented Kalman Filter (AUKF). An Improved Arithmetic Optimization Algorithm (IAOA) fine-tunes the LSTM's hyperparameters. Its novelty lies in its adaptive iteration algorithm, which adjusts iterations based on a threshold, optimizing computational efficiency. It also integrates a genetic mutation strategy into the AOA to overcome local optima by mutating iterations. Additionally, the AUKF's adaptive noise algorithm updates noise covariance in real-time, enhancing SOC estimation precision. The inputs of the proposed method include battery current, voltage, and temperature, then producing an accurate SOC output. The predictions of LSTM are refined through AUKF to obtain reliable SOC estimation. The proposed framework is firstly evaluated utilizing a public dataset and then applied to battery packs on actual engineering vehicles. Results indicate that the Root Mean Square Errors (RMSEs) of the SOC estimations in practical applications are below 0.6%, and the Maximum Errors (MAX) are under 3.3%, demonstrating the accuracy and robustness of the proposed combined framework.

Keywords: adaptive unscented Kalman filter; arithmetic optimization algorithm; Lithium-ion batteries; State of Charge; long short-term memory network

MSC: 68T05; 68T07

1. Introduction

Batteries are a crucial energy carrier in diverse fields such as consumer electronics, electric vehicles, smart grids, and others [1–4]. Currently, the commonly used types of batteries include Lead–Acid, Nickel–Metal Hydride, and Lithium-ion batteries [5–8]. Lithium-ion batteries are highly sought after due to their extended lifespan and exceptional energy density [9–12].

In battery systems, the SOC is a crucial indicator that represents a battery's available capacity [13]. However, the SOC is difficult to measure directly due to the battery's chemical complexity, nonlinear response, and potential measurement errors [14,15]. Inaccurate estimation of the SOC can result in overcharging or over-discharging of the battery, potentially leading to thermal runaway, fire, or even explosion in severe scenarios [16–18].

Various methods for SOC estimation have been discussed. Traditional SOC estimation method includes the Coulomb counting (CC) method [19] and the open-circuit voltage (OCV) method [20]. The CC method involves integrating the current over time. However, current measurement errors can lead to cumulative errors with this approach, reducing estimation accuracy. The OCV method establishes a look-up table, allowing for a precise SOC estimate to be obtained by matching the measured OCV with the corresponding SOC value in the table. However, during operation, the value of OCV is difficult to measure or calculate due to varying currents [20].

The model-based filtering method is a reliable approach, with several methods available such as sliding mode observer [21], H-infinity observer [22,23], Kalman filter (KF) [24,25], and others. The KF is widely used among these methods due to its excellent autoregressive and state estimation ability. However, the standard KF is limited to linear models, while battery models exhibit nonlinearity. To overcome this limitation, an extended Kalman filter (EKF) has been proposed and employed in SOC estimation [24]. However, the EKF ignores high-order terms of the system, which leads to decreased filtering accuracy. Therefore, an unscented Kalman filter (UKF) has sometimes been adopted as a substitute. However, the fixed initial noise set by the algorithm does not adjust with the battery's operational dynamics, which can lead to significant fluctuations in the estimation results. To update the noise adaptively, Wang et al. [25] employed an adaptive algorithm that allows noise to vary with the battery's operation. The validation conducted on a third-order resistance–capacitance model showed that this method achieved improved accuracy and robustness than UKF. Currently, various modifications and adaptations of model-based filtering methods are proposed to enhance the robustness of results. However, building an accurate and universal battery model is challenging because of the inherent complexity of chemical reactions and dynamic environments within batteries [26].

Compared to the model-based filtering method, data-driven approaches utilize extensive relevant data to establish mathematical relationships between SOC and input parameters, avoiding the necessity for constructing intricate mechanistic models [27]. Common data-driven methods include support vector machines [28], neural networks [29–33], and enhanced networks [34]. For instance, Deng et al. [30] proposed a data-driven approach utilizing Gaussian Process Regression (GPR) to address SOC estimation challenges in battery packs. The results verified that the proposed model has better SOC estimation performance than the regular model. Chaoui et al. [31] and Hong et al. [33] applied a recurrent neural network (RNN) and LSTM network in online electric vehicle battery analysis. Results demonstrated that the LSTM network exhibited more strong and efficient prediction capabilities. To achieve optimal performance in deep learning methods, optimization algorithms are used to optimize the network. Mao et al. [34] utilized particle swarm optimization to optimize the neural network, aiming to enhance the precision of SOC estimations. However, the results obtained by this approach did not meet the desired expectations. It was evident that employing a more effective optimization algorithm could yield superior outcomes. Abualigah et al. [35] introduced the AOA and evaluated its performance on actual engineering issues.

Existing data-driven methods primarily rely on neural networks for SOC estimation, enhancing estimation accuracy through optimization algorithms. By employing suitable networks and optimization algorithms, improved estimations can be achieved. However, data-driven methods rely on a substantial amount of data, and noise in the dataset can cause significant errors in the estimation results [36]. In response to this situation, researchers have designed hybrid methods that leverage the advantages of various methods. Common hybrid methods include segmented models that combine traditional SOC estimation methods with model-based filtering methods [37] and fusion models that integrate data-driven methods with model-based filtering methods [38–41]. For instance, Misyris et al. [37] combined the OCV method with a linear Kalman filter to achieve both short-term and long-term SOC estimation. However, this method relies on an accurate equivalent battery model and struggles to estimate the SOC of nonlinear battery systems effectively. Charkhgard et al. [38] presented a hybrid model that combined a neural network (NN) and extended Kalman filter (EKF). In this model, the NN was employed to perform an initial SOC estimation using historical battery data, while the EKF was utilized to refine the SOC estimations based on the battery's terminal voltage. This approach offered improved estimation accuracy and reduced disturbances compared to estimating the SOC using either an NN or EKF alone. However, the extent of improvement was limited by the methods employed in the hybrid method. The traditional NN had difficulty predicting time-series data effectively, and the EKF faced challenges in achieving high-precision filtering for nonlinear systems like batteries. Therefore, He et al. [39] and Cui et al. [40] developed a hybrid method utilizing a combination of neural networks and UKF. However, the neural networks used in [39,40] fail to fully exploit historical data to enhance the relationship between input data and the SOC. Moreover, fixed-noise statistical characteristics of the UKF determined based on prior knowledge can potentially cause filtering failure, leading to errors in system state estimation. Zhang et al. [41] employed an LSTM network optimized by an attentional mechanism algorithm combined with the KF for SOC estimation. The LSTM network was effective at handling time-series data, and the attentional mechanism algorithm improved the correlation between input data in the model. Finally, the KF was used to achieve higher-precision SOC estimation. However, this model requires manual tuning of the LSTM network hyperparameters, which is highly time-consuming. In summary, existing hybrid methods typically combine neural networks with Kalman filtering algorithms. However, current research lacks suitable algorithms for optimizing network hyperparameters. The employed filtering algorithms need to be adaptable to nonlinear systems while ensuring adaptive noise adjustment. As a result, there is a demand for a combined framework that achieves two goals: optimizing the initial hyperparameters of the data-driven method and adaptively updating noise to ensure precise and consistent SOC estimation.

In this paper, a combined framework is presented, which combines an LSTM network optimized by an Improved Arithmetic Optimization Algorithm (IAOA) and Adaptive Unscented Kalman Filter (AUKF) algorithm. The combined framework aims to address the challenges of optimizing LSTM hyperparameters, ensuring the applicability of nonlinear systems, and adapting to noise covariance, thus facilitating accurate SOC estimation. The LSTM network is utilized for preliminary SOC estimation, with the IAOA determining the optimal hyperparameters of the network and the AUKF providing the final SOC estimations. The main contributions are summarized as follows:

(a) This study presents a hybrid framework that combines a data-driven approach (LSTM) with a model-based filtering (AUKF) method for estimating the State of Charge (SOC). The framework automates the time-consuming hyperparameter tuning process and combines the predictive strength of deep learning with the error correction strength of AUKF. This results in an efficient and robust solution for high-accuracy SOC estimation that does not require complex battery modeling.

(b) An IAOA is incorporated within the proposed framework to efficiently optimize the LSTM network's hyperparameters. The IAOA enhances the standard Arithmetic Optimization Algorithm (AOA) in two key aspects: an adaptive iteration mechanism that improves computational efficiency by terminating early when a fitness threshold is met, and a genetic mutation strategy that helps the algorithm escape local optima, thereby enhancing its global search capability.

(c) The AUKF can adaptively update its noise covariance in real-time based on the battery's operational state; thus, the estimation errors are adaptively reduced. The integration of the AUKF further improves the accuracy and robustness of the estimation, especially under the complex and dynamic conditions found in real-world applications.

(d) The proposed framework is rigorously validated not only on a public dataset under various standard conditions but also on operational data from two distinct real-world electric vehicle battery packs, confirming its practical effectiveness and generalization capability.

The subsequent structure is as follows. Section 2 provides a detailed description of the proposed method. Section 3 analyzes its performance and practicality. Finally, Section 4 summarizes the paper.

2. Methodology

Figure 1 depicts the combined framework for SOC estimation. It comprises three main components: LSTM construction, IAOA for parameter optimization, and AUKF correction. The IAOA is utilized to determine the initial hyperparameters for the LSTM network. The SOC estimation from the optimized LSTM network serves as the output of the measurement function, while the SOC estimates from Coulomb counting (CC) are selected as the output of the state function. By incorporating the AUKF and combining these two outputs, an accurate SOC estimation is ultimately obtained.

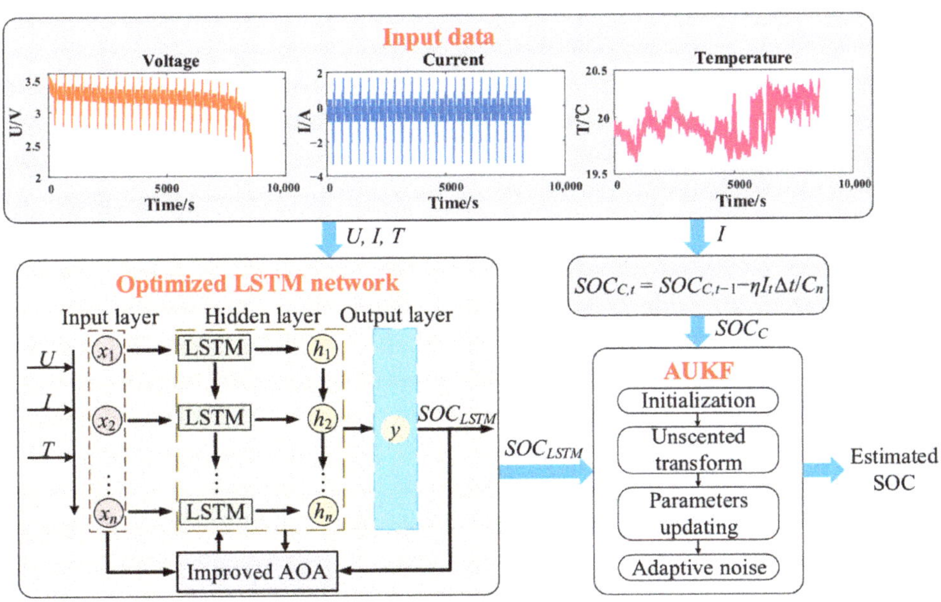

Figure 1. The proposed combined framework for SOC estimation.

2.1. Structure of the LSTM Network

To address the modeling issues of a series of serialized data with nonlinear features over the time scale, the RNN has been widely applied. However, the RNN struggles to handle long-term dependencies within time series data, and training failures may occur. The LSTM has been developed as an enhanced version of the RNN to overcome this challenge, specifically developed to handle long-term dependencies.

The structure of an LSTM cell is depicted in Figure 2. The LSTM network comprises three main components: the forget gate, input gate, and output gate. These components collaborate to determine whether to retain or forget newly received information. Specifically, the input gate decides how much of the current input data should be saved to the cell state; the forget gate determines how much of the previous cell state should be retained in the current cell state; and the output gate controls how much of the current cell state should be passed on as the current output value. The mathematical expressions of the LSTM unit are as given by (1).

$$\begin{cases} i_t = \text{sig}(w_{xi}x_t + w_{hi}h_{t-1} + b_i) \\ f_t = \text{sig}\left(w_{xf}x_t + w_{hf}h_{t-1} + b_f\right) \\ c_t = f_t c_{i-1} + i_t \cdot \tanh(w_{xc}x_t + w_{hc}h_{t-1} + b_c) \\ o_t = \text{sig}(w_{xo}x_t + w_{ho}h_{t-1} + b_o) \\ h_t = o_t \tanh(c_t) \end{cases} \quad (1)$$

where w and b represent weights and bias, x_t, h_t, and c_t denote the input sequence, output data, and memory of hidden cell at time t, and sig() means the sigmoid activation function.

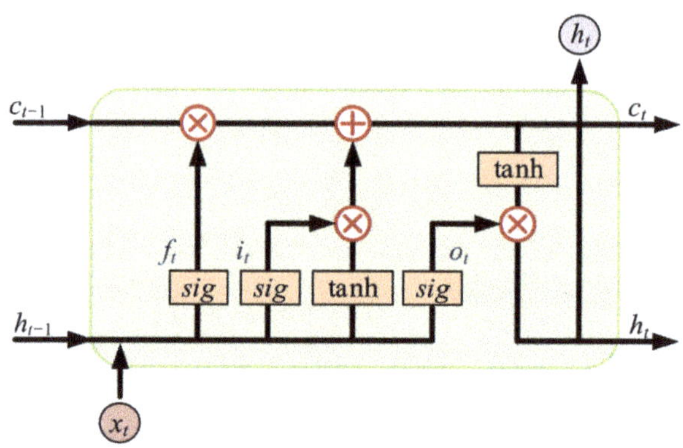

Figure 2. Structure of an LSTM cell. The '×' and '+' symbols represent element-wise multiplication and addition, respectively.

Within the LSTM unit, the input data x_t is combined with the output data h_{t-1} from the previous neuron. Each is multiplied by their respective weights and added with biases to obtain the forget gate factor f_t. The forget gate factor is responsible for generating a new memory cell c_t based on the memory cell c_{t-1} from the previous neuron, influencing the output data h_t of the current neuron accordingly.

Simultaneously, the input gate factor i_t is involved in the update of the memory cell, allowing the memory cell c_t to be influenced by both the previous memory cell c_{t-1} and the current input factor i_t. Finally, the output gate factor o_t is responsible for adjusting the value of the output data h_t.

The LSTM network takes battery voltage, current, and temperature data as inputs, represented as $x_t = [V_t, I_t, T_t]$, and outputs the corresponding SOC value SOC_t. To enhance the utilization of historical information in the input data, an information enhancement unit was designed, with its architecture illustrated in Figure 3. This unit employs a sliding window technique with a window size of s, reconstructing the input as $[x(t), x(t-s), \ldots, x(t-s \times k)]$, where k represents the number of time steps.

To fully leverage the capabilities of LSTM for accurate SOC estimation, several hyperparameters require careful configuration during the training process. These critical hyperparameters include the number of hidden layers, the number of neurons, the maximum epoch, the initial learning rate, and the dropout rate. It is noteworthy that while increasing the number of hidden layers can enhance LSTM performance to some extent, this improvement comes at the cost of exponential growth in computational complexity and increased risk of overfitting. To maintain a balance between computational efficiency and overfitting prevention, a single hidden layer is chosen.

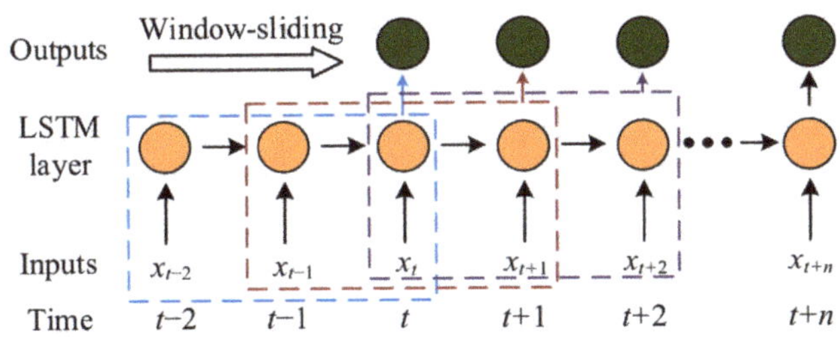

Figure 3. The information enhancement unit.

Regarding the optimization of remaining hyperparameters, manual tuning through repetitive experiments proves to be time-consuming and unlikely to yield optimal configurations. To address this challenge, we have designed IAOA to systematically search for and identify the optimal combination of these hyperparameters, thereby enhancing the overall efficiency of the LSTM network.

2.2. Improved Arithmetic Optimization Algorithm

The AOA is a meta-heuristic optimization approach that leverages arithmetic operators to achieve global optimization. It possesses notable advantages such as rapid convergence speed and high precision.

The standard AOA's optimization process primarily consists of three stages: initialization, exploration, and development. Initially, a math optimizer accelerated (MOA) is initialized to determine a search stage and set a math optimizer probability (MOP) to identify the optimal position. The calculations for MOA and MOP are defined by Equations (2) and (3), respectively.

$$\mathrm{MOA}(C_t) = L + C_t \times (\frac{U - L}{M_t}) \tag{2}$$

$$MOP(C_t) = 1 - \frac{C_t^{1/\mu}}{M_t^{1/\mu}} \tag{3}$$

where C_t represents the current iteration, M_t represents the maximum iterations, L and U represent the lower and upper bounds of the MOA, and μ denotes the sensitive parameter defining the convergence accuracy during the iterative process.

Next, a random number r_1 is generated within the range of 0 and 1 to determine whether the algorithm should proceed to the exploration or development stage. During the exploration stage, the AOA conducts a global search within the search interval and employs different search strategies based on division and multiplication. On the other hand, the development stage focuses on high-precision calculations using subtraction and addition operations, which are suitable for local area search. In both stages, random numbers r_2 and r_3 are utilized to determine whether multiplication, division, addition, or subtraction operations should be employed.

Lastly, a fitness function is utilized to assess each individual's optimality during each current iteration. After M_t iterations, the optimal individual can be determined as the combination of the hyperparameters (the number of neurons, the maximum epoch, the initial learning rate, and the dropout rate). In the case of AOA, the RMSE is adopted as the fitness function as given by (4).

$$\text{RMSE} = \sqrt{\frac{1}{S}\sum_{i=1}^{S} (SOC_{act}(i) - SOC_{est}(i))^2} \tag{4}$$

where S represents the data sample size, i represents the current individual number, SOC_{est} represents the estimated SOC value, and SOC_{act} represents the actual SOC value.

However, the standard AOA has two notable issues. Firstly, the AOA requires iterating until C_t reaches M_t, even if the fitness function value is already sufficiently small. This will result in additional computational costs. Secondly, the standard AOA may encounter the problem of converging to a local optimal value during the iteration process, which can lead to the optimal individual failing to meet the desired requirements. To address these two problems, some approaches have been introduced to enhance the standard AOA. Firstly, an adaptive iteration method is employed to dynamically adjust the number of iterations based on the convergence status. This helps to reduce unnecessary computation and improve efficiency. Secondly, a genetic mutation technique is integrated into the AOA, enhancing its capability and mitigating the risk of becoming trapped in local optima.

In contrast to the standard iteration process, the adaptive iteration approach employs the optimal fitness function (O_{FF}) to determine whether to terminate the iteration before C_t reaches M_t. If the value of O_{FF} drops below the fitness function threshold, the iteration is concluded early. Conversely, if the value of O_{FF} does not meet the termination criterion, the iteration continues until C_t reaches M_t. This adaptive iteration strategy enables the rapid acquisition of the optimal individual. To avoid premature termination of the iteration without achieving optimal results, it is crucial to set a small fitness function threshold FF. The value of FF is typically set to a target optimum value to ensure the iteration continues until an acceptable level of optimization is reached. This prevents premature convergence to suboptimal solutions.

To prevent the algorithm from becoming trapped in local optima, a genetic mutation operator is incorporated into the AOA. This operator introduces random variations by occasionally reinitializing individuals during the update process. Such a mechanism enables the algorithm to explore new regions of the search space, thereby increasing the probability of discovering globally superior solutions.

In summary, the IAOA is employed to optimize the remaining hyperparameters for the LSTM network. The parameter search ranges were set to [32, 50, 0.001, 0.1] for the lower bounds and [256, 300, 0.01, 0.5] for the upper bounds, corresponding to the number of neurons, maximum epochs, initial learning rate, and dropout rate, respectively. The process involves initializing the parameters, updating individuals using four operators, and calculating fitness function values. Additionally, the O_{FF} is continuously updated during the iteration and compared to a predefined threshold to determine whether to terminate the iteration. At the end of each iteration, the individual undergoes genetic mutation using the genetic mutation algorithm. The value of the optimal individual is then assigned to the desired hyperparameters, completing the construction of the LSTM network. The operational procedure of the IAOA is detailed in Algorithm 1.

Algorithm 1 Improved Arithmetic Optimization Algorithm

Input: Current iteration and maximum iterations C_t, M_t, fitness function threshold FF, upper and lower limits of hyperparameters UB, LB, sensitive parameter α, and initial individual x.
Output: Optimal individual x_{best}.

While $O_{FF} > FF$ && $C_t < M_t$ % adaptive iteration
    Calculate the updated MOA and MOP.
    for i = 1: size(x, 1)
        for j = 1: size(x, 2)
            Set random numbers r_1, r_2, r_3.
            if $r_1 > MOA$
                Entering the exploration stage.
                Choose multiplication or division based on r_2.
            else
                Entering the development stage.
                Choose addition or subtraction based on r_3.
            end
        end
        Determine and update the optimal individual.
    end
    $C_t = C_t + 1$
    Genetic mutation algorithm.
end

2.3. *Adaptive Unscented Kalman Filter*

In UKF, noise covariances are treated as constant. However, the noise calculated by prior knowledge may not accurately represent the actual noise generated during battery operation, which can vary over time. Estimating the system state using constant noise can lead to significant errors. To address this issue and improve estimation accuracy, an adaptive noise covariance method is employed. Firstly, initialize system parameters and compute the mean and covariance of the state variables. Then, sample the state variables using a sigma sampling strategy and calculate the updated parameters through the unscented transformation. Subsequently, update the cross-covariance $P_{xy,t}$ and Kalman gain $K_{kal,t}$ based on the modified parameters. Finally, flexibly tune the model's noise variance to better match the observed noise characteristics during battery operation. By incorporating the adaptive noise covariance method into the UKF framework, the AUKF aims to improve accuracy by considering the time-varying characteristics of the noise.

In this paper, the initial estimation of the SOC is conducted using the IAOA-LSTM method, resulting in a set of measured values. Subsequently, the AUKF is employed to refine the measured values, integrating the Coulomb counting method, thereby achieving high-precision estimation. The proposed model is given by (5).

$$\begin{cases} SOC_{C,t} = SOC_{C,t-1} - \eta \frac{I_t \Delta t}{C_n} + w_t \\ y_t = SOC_{LSTM,t} + v_t = LSTM(I_t, U_t, T_t) + v_t \end{cases} \tag{5}$$

where η indicates coulomb efficiency, and I_t, U_t, and T_t represent current, voltage, and temperature at time t, respectively. Δt denotes the sampling interval, C_n is the nominal capacity, w_t and v_t are the process and measurement noises with variances Q_t and R_t, and $SOC_{C,t}$ and $SOC_{LSTM,t}$ represent the calculated SOC of Coulomb counting and the measured SOC by the AOA-LSTM network, respectively.

Then, the UT is utilized to obtain new state variables and joint covariance through point transformation. Sigma points are constructed for the state variables $SOC_{C,t-1}$ and $SOC_{LSTM,t-1}$, and updated sigma points are generated for the state variable $SOC_{C,t}$ and the output variable y_t. Subsequently, the joint covariance $P_{xy,t}$ and the Kalman gain $K_{kal,t}$ of the state and output variables are calculated as given by (6) and (7).

$$P_{xy,t} = \sum_{i=0}^{2N} W_{c,i}(SOC_i - \overline{SOC_i})(y_i - \overline{y_i})^T \tag{6}$$

$$K_{kal,t} = P_{xy,t}(P_{y,t})^{-1} \tag{7}$$

where N represents the sample number, W_c represents the covariance weight, $\overline{y_i}$ represents the mean of the output variable, and $P_{y,t}$ indicates the covariance of the output variable.

Finally, online correction of the covariance of noises is conducted using the error sequence H_t between the actual output and measurement output, as given by (8)–(10). The calculated noise covariances are incorporated into the state space model. The flow of AUKF can be expressed as Algorithm 2.

$$H_t = \frac{1}{N}\sum_{i=t-N+1}^{t} (y_i - \overline{y_i})(y_i - \overline{y_i})^T \tag{8}$$

$$Q_t = K_{kal,t} H_t K_{kal,t}^T \tag{9}$$

$$R_t = H_t + \sum_{i=1}^{2N} W_{c,i}(y_i - \overline{y_i})(y_i - \overline{y_i})^T \tag{10}$$

The above analysis shows that the SOC calculated using the Coulomb counting method is treated as a state vector and is involved in the unscented transformation, yielding an estimated value. This estimated value is then combined with the measured value obtained from the LSTM network to update the Kalman gains, state vector, and covariance, resulting in an improved SOC estimation.

Algorithm 2 Adaptive Unscented Kalman Filter

Input: Initial value of state variable x_0, and number of samples n.
Output: State after filtering X_{new}.
1: Building the state space model.
2: Calculate state mean x_0 and covariance $P_{0|x}$.
3: for $t = 1: n-1$
4: Sampling sigma points.
5: Unscented transform.
6: Calculate joint covariance $P_{xy,t}$ and Kalman gain $K_{kal,t}$.
7: Update state variable $X_{new,t} = x_t$, and state covariance $P_{x,t}$.
8: Noise variances Q_t and R_t adaptive correction.
9: Update noise $w(t)$ and $v(t)$.
10: end

3. Experiment Results and Analysis

This section provides a comprehensive description of the collected experimental data, encompassing a public battery test dataset and a set of operational data from batteries in practical engineering applications. Based on the experimental data, we have designed a series of comparative experiments to rigorously validate the superiority and generalizability of the proposed framework.

3.1. Datasets and Parameters Setting

The experimental data consists of two parts: the first part uses a public battery cell dataset to verify the predictive performance of the method, and the second part uses the battery pack data from actual engineering vehicles to verify the robustness and generalization performance of the method.

The battery cell dataset is derived from the A123 battery subset within the University of Maryland open source battery dataset [42], with detailed information available at https://calce.umd.edu/battery-data#INR (accessed on 13 December 2023). The A123 battery cell dataset encompasses comprehensive voltage, current, and temperature measurements under various operating conditions at multiple temperatures (0 °C, 20 °C, 30 °C, and 50 °C). The dataset includes diverse operational profiles, specifically the Dynamic Stress Test (DST), US06 (United States Government's Light Vehicle Drive Cycle) and Federal Urban Driving Schedule (FUDS). This dataset is utilized to validate the effectiveness of the proposed framework across different operating conditions. The dataset was partitioned into training, validation, and test sets in a 50%/10%/40% split.

The battery pack dataset is derived from the operational data of two distinct engineering vehicles. The dataset includes current, voltage, and temperature measurements from two vehicle battery packs in Shanghai and Hefei. The dataset collects data from different months of the year to simulate the effectiveness of the method under different temperature conditions. The historical data from electric vehicles is used as the training/validation set, while the data in August 2022, December 2022, and April 2023 are utilized as the test set, respectively. Table 1 summarizes the fundamental parameters of the battery cells and packs in the datasets. Additionally, Table 2 lists the initial parameters of the algorithms employed in the proposed combined framework, and their settings were determined based on the following consideration:

1. Sliding Window Parameters (s and k): The sliding window interval (s = 4) and the number of time steps (k = 30) were chosen to provide the LSTM network with sufficient historical context for accurate time-series prediction. These values represent a trade-off between capturing long-term battery dynamics and maintaining manageable computational complexity.
2. IAOA Parameters (M_t, FF, μ and P_m): The maximum number of iterations (M_t = 100) was set to ensure the IAOA had adequate opportunity to converge to an optimal solution without incurring excessive computational time. The fitness function threshold (FF = 0.01) serves as an early stopping criterion, allowing the optimization to terminate if a sufficiently low error (RMSE < 1%) is achieved, thereby improving efficiency. The mutation probability (P_m = 0.1) is set to maintain sufficient diversity for escaping local optima, without compromising the algorithm's convergence due to excessive mutation. The sensitive parameter (μ = 5) is a standard value recommended by the algorithm, chosen to maintain a proper balance between the algorithm's exploration and exploitation phases.

Table 1. Parameters of cells and packs.

Parameters	Cells in A123 Dataset	Pack1	Pack2
Cell Chemistry	$LiFePO_4$	$LiFePO_4$	$LiFePO_4$
Nominal Capacity	1.1 Ah	405 Ah	206 Ah
Cell Voltage	3.2 V	3.2 V	3.2 V
Maximum Voltage	3.6 V	-	-
Number of Series-Parallel Cells	-	26 Series and 2 Parallel	8 Series and 1 Parallel
Pack Nominal Voltage	-	83.2 V	25.6 V
Pack Nominal Current	-	400 A	206 A

Table 2. Parameters of the proposed method.

Parameter	Meaning	Value
s	Sliding Window Interval	4
k	Time Step of Sliding Window	30
M_t	Maximum Number of Iterations	100
FF	Fitness Function Threshold	0.01
μ	Sensitive Parameter	5
P_m	Mutation Probability	0.1

To improve convergence, enhance model performance, prevent numerical overflow, and reduce the risk of overfitting, the data is converted into the range of $[-1, 1]$ with the normalization formula as given by (11).

$$x_{nor} = \frac{2(x_i - x_{avg})}{x_a - x_b} \tag{11}$$

where x_a and x_b denote the maximum and minimum values of the data, x_{avg} denotes the average value, and x_i denotes the individual data point.

RMSE and MAX are selected as the performance indicators. The equations of RMSE and MAX are as given by (4) and (12), respectively.

$$MAX = max(|\ SOC_{act} - SOC_{est}\ |) \tag{12}$$

3.2. SOC Estimation with the IAOA-LSTM Network

In this subsection, the US06, FUDS, and DST datasets of A123 battery cells are used to validate the accuracy of the method. The results under the US06 cycle are depicted in Figure 4. In this study, it is assumed that the discharge processes begin at 100% SOC. Additionally, considering the precision of the measuring instrument and data preprocessing, the actual SOC values can be calculated using the CC method.

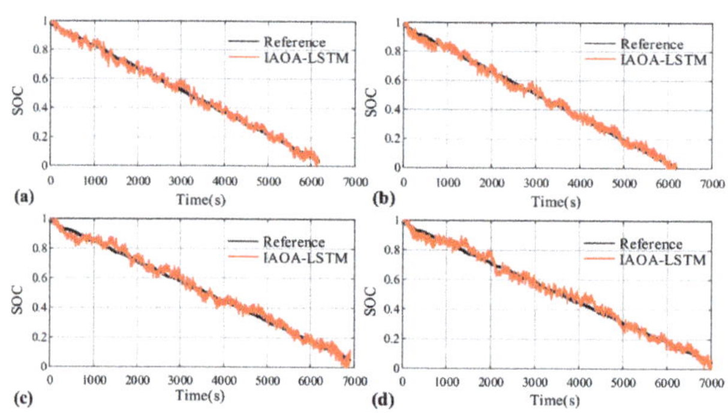

Figure 4. Results of the IAOA-LSTM network for US06 condition at (a) 0 °C, (b) 20 °C, (c) 30 °C, and (d) 50 °C.

The results demonstrate that the IAOA-LSTM network can generally estimate the SOC trend with an RMSE of around 2.5%. However, the MAX of the results for both testing cycles is within the range of 7% to 10%. This indicates that while the IAOA-LSTM network can achieve SOC estimation to a certain extent, there is room for improving the results' precision and resilience. To tackle this challenge, the proposed method incorporates AUKF to mitigate fluctuations and enhance the precision of the results.

3.3. SOC Estimation with the Proposed Combined Framework

AUKF, which incorporates adaptive noise correction and compensates for UKF's limitations, is utilized to enhance the outcomes of the IAOA-LSTM network. The results of the proposed method under the US06 cycle are illustrated in Figure 5. It is apparent that the proposed method achieves precise SOC estimation across different temperatures, yielding smooth results. The comparative experimental results are summarized in Tables 3–5.

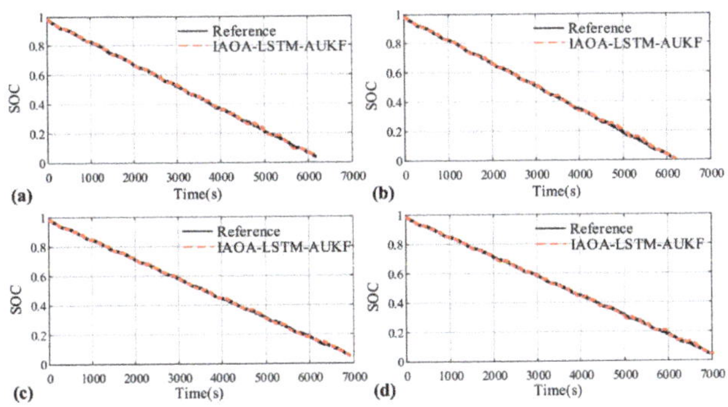

Figure 5. Results of the proposed IAOA-LSTM-AUKF method for US06 condition at (**a**) 0 °C, (**b**) 20 °C, (**c**) 30 °C, and (**d**) 50 °C.

Table 3. SOC estimation results for US06 condition at 0 °C, 20 °C, 30 °C, and 50 °C.

US06	RMSE (%)				MAX (%)			
	0 °C	20 °C	30 °C	50 °C	0 °C	20 °C	30 °C	50 °C
IAOA-LSTM	2.31 ± 0.32	2.36 ± 0.27	2.75 ± 0.23	2.69 ± 0.31	9.78	8.33	9.06	9.74
IAOA-LSTM-UKF	1.32 ± 0.10	1.19 ± 0.07	1.09 ± 0.16	1.30 ± 0.14	8.73	5.40	4.22	5.05
AOA-LSTM-AUKF	0.68 ± 0.04	0.58 ± 0.06	0.55 ± 0.03	0.63 ± 0.06	1.94	1.99	2.35	2.46
Proposed method	0.58 ± 0.03	0.53 ± 0.07	0.53 ± 0.01	0.61 ± 0.02	1.83	1.89	2.19	2.27

Table 4. SOC estimation results for FUDS condition at 0 °C, 20 °C, 30 °C, and 50 °C.

FUDS	RMSE (%)				MAX (%)			
	0 °C	20 °C	30 °C	50 °C	0 °C	20 °C	30 °C	50 °C
IAOA-LSTM	1.76 ± 0.19	2.19 ± 0.22	3.14 ± 0.19	2.26 ± 0.12	7.07	8.27	11.37	8.50
IAOA-LSTM-UKF	1.17 ± 0.10	1.29 ± 0.11	1.60 ± 0.10	1.24 ± 0.09	5.02	6.52	7.31	5.32
AOA-LSTM-AUKF	0.54 ± 0.02	0.51 ± 0.07	0.51 ± 0.10	0.66 ± 0.04	2.13	2.34	2.28	1.89
Proposed method	0.45 ± 0.03	0.43 ± 0.03	0.47 ± 0.07	0.49 ± 0.04	1.99	2.02	2.21	1.52

Table 5. SOC estimation results for DST condition at 0 °C, 20 °C, 30 °C, and 50 °C.

DST	RMSE (%)				MAX (%)			
	0 °C	20 °C	30 °C	50 °C	0 °C	20 °C	30 °C	50 °C
IAOA-LSTM	2.12 ± 0.21	2.31 ± 0.18	3.01 ± 0.19	2.77 ± 0.12	9.54	8.56	8.89	10.17
IAOA-LSTM-UKF	1.41 ± 0.14	1.27 ± 0.17	1.26 ± 0.11	1.42 ± 0.09	7.89	5.68	6.41	6.64
AOA-LSTM-AUKF	0.64 ± 0.04	0.56 ± 0.04	0.57 ± 0.03	0.60 ± 0.05	2.05	2.16	2.26	2.56
Proposed method	0.54 ± 0.02	0.44 ± 0.03	0.43 ± 0.02	0.55 ± 0.04	1.89	1.77	1.80	2.11

The results indicate that the proposed method achieves significantly lower values of both RMSE and MAX for SOC estimation compared to the other three methods. The proposed combined method exhibits significant improvements compared to the IAOA-LSTM-UKF method. Under the US06 cycle at 30 °C, the RMSE is reduced from 1.09% to

0.53%, and under the FUDS cycle at 30 °C, it decreases from 1.60% to 0.47%. The MAX is significantly reduced from 4.22% to 2.19% under the US06 cycle at 30 °C and from 7.31% to 2.21% under the FUDS cycle at 30 °C. Overall, the proposed combined method maintains an RMSE within 0.7% and a MAX within 2.5% for SOC estimation. It exhibits high accuracy in SOC estimation for battery cells.

To evaluate the proposed model's estimation performance, it is compared with some advanced existing methods, including LSTM-EKF [43], LTG-SABO-GRU [44], RNN with small sequence [45], and unidirectional LSTM [46]. Table 6 shows the RMSE of various models on the FUDS test condition at 20 °C.

Table 6. SOC estimation results of some advanced methods for FUDS.

Methods	RMSE (%)	Parameter Optimization	Denoising Algorithm
LSTM-EKF [43]	0.72	No	Yes
LTG-SABO-GRU [44]	0.62	Yes	No
RNN with small sequence [45]	0.82	Yes	No
Unidirectional LSTM [46]	0.73	Yes	No
Proposed method	0.43	Yes	Yes

It can be observed that the proposed IAOA-LSTM-AUKF exhibits the best estimation performance with an RMSE of 0.43%. The proposed model synergistically integrates an optimization algorithm, a data-driven method, and a model-based filtering method, amalgamating the advantages of these two types of hybrid models. Moreover, it optimizes the hyperparameters of the data-driven model and exhibits superiority in handling nonlinear problems. As a result, it demonstrates superior performance in SOC estimation compared to other methods.

3.4. Discussion for Computational Burden

While the proposed method can significantly enhance SOC estimation accuracy, it is essential to avoid incurring an excessive computational burden in the process. To evaluate the computational load of the proposed model, it is compared with LSTM and LSTM-UKF. All experiments were conducted on a desktop workstation with the following hardware configuration. The system was equipped with an Intel Core i7-8700K CPU operating at 3.70 GHz, 32 GB of DDR4 RAM, and an NVIDIA GeForce GTX 1050 Ti GPU with 4 GB of VRAM. Table 7 presents the results for SOC estimation under FUDS condition. The results contain the estimation errors and computation times of the BPNN, LSTM, IAOA-LSTM, LSTM-UKF, and proposed IAOA-LSTM-AUKF methods. Compared to the LSTM network, the proposed method exhibits superior performance with highly accurate results, albeit requiring a longer computation time. At 30 °C, the LSTM network yields estimation results that exhibit significant fluctuations, as evidenced by an RMSE of 2.77%. In contrast, the proposed hybrid method delivers highly accurate and smooth results, with an RMSE of only 0.48%. Although the proposed method takes less than twice the computation time of the LSTM network, it produces errors that are 4–5 times smaller. Overall, the proposed model demonstrates better performance than the BPNN, LSTM, IAOA-LSTM and LSTM-UKF regarding the RMSE while still maintaining an acceptable computation time.

Table 7. Computation burden results for FUDS under various temperature conditions.

Temperature	RMSE (%)				Computation Time (s)			
	0 °C	20 °C	30 °C	50 °C	0 °C	20 °C	30 °C	50 °C
BPNN	7.17	5.94	4.52	3.91	0.52	0.53	0.59	0.57
LSTM	2.97	2.56	2.77	2.79	0.44	0.42	0.48	0.45
IAOA-LSTM	1.87	2.19	3.14	2.26	0.47	0.48	0.53	0.49
LSTM-UKF	1.17	1.29	1.60	1.24	0.79	0.82	0.86	0.88
IAOA-LSTM-AUKF	0.45	0.43	0.47	0.49	0.90	0.92	0.98	0.97

3.5. Assessment of the Convergence Rate

To estimate SOC utilizing the CC method in AUKF, it is difficult to obtain a precise initial SOC value. However, in practical applications, obtaining such a value can be challenging as the measured initial SOC may be influenced by temperature and sensor performance, leading to errors. Therefore, a reliable SOC estimation method should quickly correct any errors in the initial value. In this subsection, the initial SOC is initialized to 70% and 50% under US06 cycle at 20 °C, whereas the actual remains 100%. Figure 6 displays the SOC estimation results obtained using the proposed method. In the figure, the solid line represents the actual SOC values, gradually decreasing from 100% to 0%. The dashed line, on the other hand, represents the estimated SOC values, starting from either 70% or 50% and gradually fitting to the actual values, eventually reaching 0%.

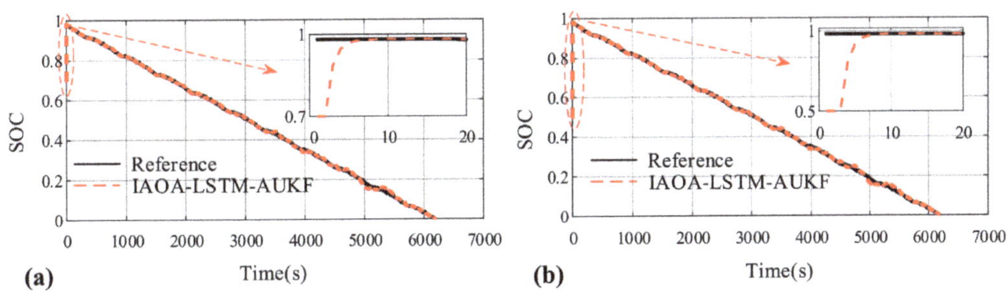

Figure 6. Results of proposed IAOA-LSTM-AUKF method under different initial SOC values: (**a**) 70%; (**b**) 50%.

It is shown that with the proposed method, regardless of the initial SOC being configured at 70% or 50%, the SOC converges rapidly to its actual value within 10 s. This demonstrates the adaptability of the proposed method in correcting initial noise. Even if there are significant changes or errors in the initial SOC due to environmental or other factors, the proposed method exhibits excellent convergence ability and accurately estimates the true SOC value.

3.6. Verification by Electric Vehicle Battery Pack

In practical engineering applications, batteries are typically deployed as battery packs in electric vehicles. To validate the effectiveness of the proposed method in applications, actual performance data from electric vehicles is utilized for testing purposes. In this subsection, the practicality of the proposed framework in real-world scenarios is evaluated by collecting operation data from two electric aerial lift vehicle (EALV) battery packs, as illustrated in Figure 7. The operating conditions of battery pack 1 and pack 2 from EALV models G01BB03 and G01JB01 are illustrated in Figures 8 and 9, respectively. The operating condition data are collected on the basis of the complete battery pack assembly. While minor inconsistencies between individual cells can create a small self-balancing current (100–300 mA), its effect on SOC estimation is negligible. Given that the rated current of the packs exceeds 200 A, this balancing current accounts for less than 0.15% of the total current and does not significantly impact the results.

Figure 7. Electric vehicle and battery pack.

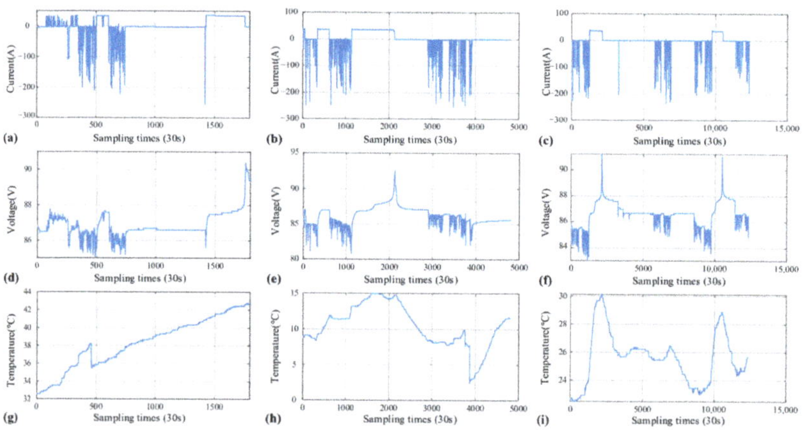

Figure 8. Operating conditions of battery pack 1. (**a**,**d**,**g**) are current, voltage, and temperature in August 2022. (**b**,**e**,**h**) are current, voltage, and temperature in December 2022. (**c**,**f**,**i**) are current, voltage, and temperature in April 2023.

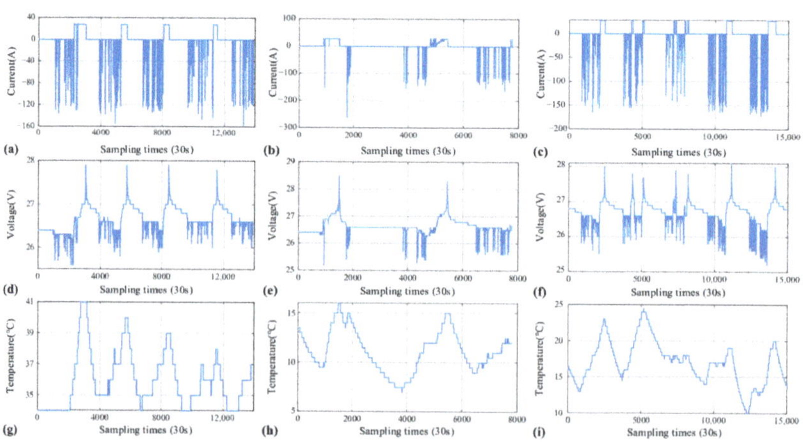

Figure 9. Operating conditions of battery pack 2. (**a**,**d**,**g**) are current, voltage, and temperature in August 2022. (**b**,**e**,**h**) are current, voltage, and temperature in December 2022. (**c**,**f**,**i**) are current, voltage, and temperature in April 2023.

The results and errors obtained from the experimental testing are presented in Figures 10 and 11, while a summary is provided in Tables 8 and 9. For battery pack1, the proposed method demonstrates superior accuracy compared to the other two methods, with an RMSE of 0.6% and MAX of 3.05% in December 2022, and an 0.31% RMSE of 0.31% and MAX of 1.82% in April 2023. Regarding battery pack 2, the proposed method attains remarkable precision, reflecting an RMSE of 0.24% and a MAX of 2.25% for the actual battery SOC estimation, demonstrating its excellent applicability. These results demonstrate that the proposed method can provide accurate SOC estimations of battery packs across various temperature conditions throughout the year.

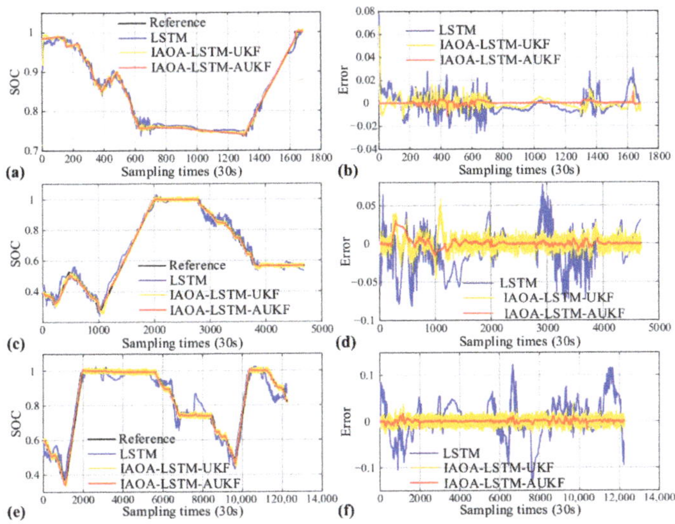

Figure 10. Results and errors for battery pack 1 in (**a**) August 2022, (**b**) errors of (**a**), (**c**) December 2022, (**d**) errors of (**c**), (**e**) April 2023, (**f**) errors of (**e**).

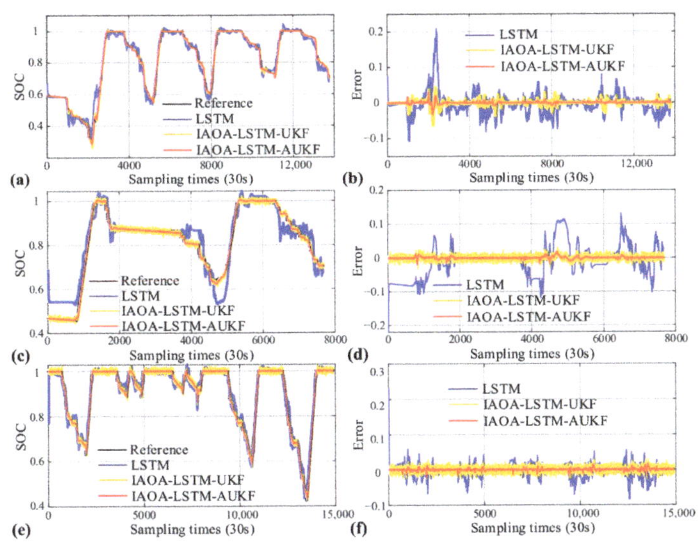

Figure 11. Results and errors for battery pack 2 in (**a**) August 2022, (**b**) errors of (**a**), (**c**) December 2022, (**d**) errors of (**c**), (**e**) April 2023, (**f**) errors of (**e**).

Table 8. SOC estimation results for battery pack 1.

DST	RMSE (%)			MAX (%)		
	IAOA-LSTM	IAOA-LSTM-UKF	Proposed Method	IAOA-LSTM	IAOA-LSTM-UKF	Proposed Method
August 2022	0.87	0.48	0.38	7.76	6.74	2.01
December 2022	2.62	0.99	0.60	8.14	5.92	3.05
April 2023	4.06	0.74	0.31	12.76	3.99	1.82

Table 9. SOC estimation results for battery pack 2.

DST	RMSE (%)			MAX (%)		
	IAOA-LSTM	IAOA-LSTM-UKF	Proposed Method	IAOA-LSTM	IAOA-LSTM-UKF	Proposed Method
August 2022	3.07	0.87	0.32	20.94	6.39	3.26
December 2022	4.88	0.72	0.33	21.96	3.18	3.06
April 2023	1.72	0.71	0.24	22.97	3.01	2.25

The results demonstrate that the proposed method excels in accurately and smoothly estimating the SOC of battery cells. The proposed method effectively corrects errors arising from the initial SOC offset and achieves exceptional SOC estimation for actual electric vehicle battery packs. These findings highlight the potential of the proposed method for practical applications. Accurate SOC estimation using the proposed method is essential for optimizing battery management and improving the overall performance and reliability of electric vehicle systems.

4. Conclusions

This research presents a combined framework combining an optimized Long Short-Term Memory (LSTM) network with an Adaptive Unscented Kalman Filter (AUKF) for State of Charge (SOC) estimation. The method is designed to harness the predictive power of LSTM and the refinement capabilities of AUKF to enhance estimation accuracy and precision. The LSTM network is fine-tuned using an Improved Arithmetic Optimization Algorithm (IAOA) to ascertain the most effective hyperparameters, ensuring the network's optimal operation. The AUKF is then employed to refine the LSTM's initial estimates, with a dynamic noise algorithm rectifying the inaccuracies inherent in standard Unscented Kalman Filter (UKF) noise assumptions, thereby boosting the SOC estimation's precision and robustness.

The method's efficacy is validated through SOC estimations of battery cells under standard conditions. Comparative analysis reveals that this method surpasses IAOA-LSTM, IAOA-LSTM-UKF, and AOA-LSTM-AUKF methods in accuracy metrics, recording a Root Mean Square Error (RMSE) and Maximum error (MAX) of less than 0.6% and 3.3%, respectively. Further evaluations using battery pack datasets confirm the method's capability to precisely predict SOC in electric vehicles under real operating conditions, achieving an RMSE of 0.31% and an MAX of 1.82%.

Author Contributions: Conceptualization, J.H. and Y.D.; methodology, J.H.; software, Y.D.; validation, J.H.; formal analysis, Y.D.; investigation, J.H.; resources, Y.D.; data curation, J.H.; writing—original draft preparation, Y.D.; writing—review and editing, W.W.; visualization, Y.D.; supervision, W.W.; project administration, W.W.; funding acquisition, W.W. All authors have read and agreed to the published version of the manuscript.

Funding: The authors wish to express their gratitude for the support provided by the National Natural Science Foundation of China (NNSF) (Grant No. 62103443), Hunan Natural Science Foundation (Grant No. 2022JJ40630).

Data Availability Statement: The original contributions presented in this study are included in the article; further inquiries can be directed to the corresponding author.

Conflicts of Interest: Authors Jing Han, Yaolin Dong and Wei Wang were employed by the company China Aluminum Ningxia Energy Group Co., Ltd. The authors declare no conflict of interest.

Abbreviations

The following abbreviations are used in this manuscript:

SOC	State of Charge
LSTM	Long Short-Term Memory
AUKF	Adaptive Unscented Kalman Filter
IAOA	Improved Arithmetic Optimization Algorithm
CC	Coulomb Counting
RMSE	Root Mean Square Errors
MAX	Maximum Errors
OCV	Open-circuit Voltage
MOA	Math Optimizer Accelerated
MOP	Math Optimizer Probability
DST	Dynamic Stress Test
FUDS	Federal Urban Driving Schedule
US06	United States Government's Light Vehicle Drive Cycle
EALV	Electric Aerial Lift Vehicle

References

1. Wang, C.; Li, F.; Liao, Y.; Cao, Y. Flyback Converter Based Charge Balancing Control with Cell-Load and Cell-Cell Operation Modes in Battery System. *Appl. Energy* **2025**, *394*, 126181. [CrossRef]
2. Jung, S.-W.; An, Y.-Y.; Suh, B.; Park, Y.; Kim, J.; Kim, K.-I. Multi-Agent Deep Reinforcement Learning for Scheduling of Energy Storage System in Microgrids. *Mathematics* **2025**, *13*, 1999. [CrossRef]
3. Cao, Y.; Liao, Y.; Chen, L.; Wang, C.; Hu, Y. A Wireless Power Feedback-Based Battery Equalizer with Multiple-Receiver. *IEEE Trans. Transp. Electrif.* **2025**, *11*, 9332–9345. [CrossRef]
4. Tran, M.-K. A Comprehensive Equivalent Circuit Model for Lithium-Ion Batteries, Incorporating the Effects of State of Health, State of Charge, and Temperature on Model Parameters. *J. Energy Storage* **2021**, *43*, 103252. [CrossRef]
5. Calborean, A.; Murariu, T.; Morari, C. Optimized Lead-Acid Grid Architectures for Automotive Lead-Acid Batteries: An Electrochemical Analysis. *Electrochim. Acta* **2021**, *372*, 137880. [CrossRef]
6. Silvestri, L.; Forcina, A.; Arcese, G.; Bella, G. Recycling Technologies of Nickelemetal Hydride Batteries: An LCA Based Analysis. *J. Clean. Prod.* **2020**, *273*, 123083. [CrossRef]
7. Seo, M.; Song, Y.; Kim, J.; Paek, S.W.; Kim, G.-H.; Kim, S.W. Innovative Lumped-Battery Model for State of Charge Estimation of Lithium-Ion Batteries under Various Ambient Temperatures. *Energy* **2021**, *226*, 120301. [CrossRef]
8. Wang, C.; Li, F.; Cao, Y. Dual-Frequency Dual-Type-Output Wireless Power Transfer System with Independent Adjustable Outputs. *IEEE J. Emerg. Sel. Topics Power Electron.* 2025; *early access*. [CrossRef]
9. Al-Rahamneh, A.; Izco, I.; Serrano-Hernandez, A.; Faulin, J. Machine Learning-Based State-of-Health Estimation of Battery Management Systems Using Experimental and Simulation Data. *Mathematics* **2025**, *13*, 2247. [CrossRef]
10. Guo, R.; Shen, W. Online State of Charge and State of Power Co-Estimation of Lithium-Ion Batteries Based on Fractional-Order Calculus and Model Predictive Control Theory. *Appl. Energy* **2022**, *327*, 120009. [CrossRef]
11. Wang, C.; Cao, M.; Cao, Y. Battery Aging Estimation Algorithm with Active Balancing Control in Battery System. *J. Energy Storage* **2025**, *108*, 115055. [CrossRef]
12. Dong, Y.; Wang, W.; Cao, Y.; Cao, M.; Zhou, X.; Hou, X. An Improved Data-Driven Approach and a Voltage Integral Indicator for Remaining Useful Life Estimation of Proton Exchange Membrane Fuel Cells. *J. Power Sources* **2025**, *640*, 236726. [CrossRef]
13. Wang, C.; Cui, N.; Cui, Z.; Yuan, H.; Zhang, C. Fusion Estimation of Lithium-Ion Battery State of Charge and State of Health Considering the Effect of Temperature. *J. Energy Storage* **2022**, *53*, 105075. [CrossRef]
14. Wei, M.; Liu, Y.; Wang, H.; Yuan, S.; Hu, J. State of Charge Prediction for Electric Vehicles Based on Integrated Model Architecture. *Mathematics* **2025**, *13*, 2197. [CrossRef]
15. Wang, C.; Li, R.; Cao, Y.; Li, M. A Hybrid Model for State of Charge Estimation of Lithium-Ion Batteries Utilizing Improved Adaptive Extended Kalman Filter and Long Short-Term Memory Neural Network. *J. Power Sources* **2024**, *620*, 235272. [CrossRef]
16. Hu, X.; Feng, F.; Liu, K.; Zhang, L.; Xie, J.; Liu, B. State Estimation for Advanced Battery Management: Key Challenges and Future Trends. *Renew. Sustain. Energy Rev.* **2019**, *114*, 109334. [CrossRef]

17. Cao, Y.; Abu Qahouq, J.A. Evaluation of Bi-directional Single-inductor Multi-input Battery System with State-of-charge Balancing Control. *IET Power Electron.* **2018**, *11*, 2140–2150. [CrossRef]
18. Hong, J.; Wang, Z.; Qu, C.; Zhou, Y.; Shan, T.; Zhang, J.; Hou, Y. Investigation on Overcharge-Caused Thermal Runaway of Lithium-Ion Batteries in Real-World Electric Vehicles. *Appl. Energy* **2022**, *321*, 119229. [CrossRef]
19. Huang, S.; Kang, J.; Zhao, B.; Wu, O.; Wang, J.V. A SOC Correction Method Based on Unsynchronized Full Charge and Discharge Control Strategy in Multi-Branch Battery System. *Energies* **2023**, *16*, 6287. [CrossRef]
20. Bian, X.; Wei, Z.G.; Li, W.; Pou, J.; Sauer, D.U.; Liu, L. State-of-Health Estimation of Lithium-Ion Batteries by Fusing an Open-Circuit-Voltage Model and Incremental Capacity Analysis. *IEEE Trans. Power Electron.* **2021**, *37*, 2226–2236. [CrossRef]
21. El Mejdoubi, A.; Oukaour, A.; Chaoui, H.; Gualous, H.; Sabor, J.; Slamani, Y. State-of-Charge and State-of-Health Lithium-Ion Batteries' Diagnosis According to Surface Temperature Variation. *IEEE Trans. Ind. Electron.* **2016**, *63*, 2391–2402. [CrossRef]
22. Kim, I.-S. The Novel State of Charge Estimation Method for Lithium Battery Using Sliding Mode Observer. *J. Power Sources* **2006**, *163*, 584–590. [CrossRef]
23. Yu, Q.; Xiong, R.; Lin, C.; Shen, W.; Deng, J. Lithium-Ion Battery Parameters and State-of-Charge Joint Estimation Based on H-Infinity and Unscented Kalman Filters. *IEEE Trans. Veh. Technol.* **2017**, *66*, 8693–8701. [CrossRef]
24. Jiang, C.; Wang, S.; Wu, B.; Fernandez, C.; Xiong, X.; Coffie-Ken, J. A State-of-Charge Estimation Method of the Power Lithium-Ion Battery in Complex Conditions Based on Adaptive Square Root Extended Kalman Filter. *Energy* **2021**, *219*, 119603. [CrossRef]
25. Wang, H.; Sun, C.; Zhou, G.; Zhu, Y.; Hu, D. SOC Estimation of Lithium Battery Based on AUKF Algorithm of Third-Order RC Model. In Proceedings of the 2022 25th International Conference on Electrical Machines and Systems (ICEMS), Chiang Mai, Thailand, 29 November–2 December 2022; pp. 1–6.
26. She, C.; Zhang, L.; Wang, Z.; Sun, F.; Liu, P.; Song, C. Battery State-of-Health Estimation Based on Incremental Capacity Analysis Method: Synthesizing From Cell-Level Test to Real-World Application. *IEEE J. Emerg. Sel. Topics Power Electron.* **2023**, *11*, 214–223. [CrossRef]
27. Chemali, E.; Kollmeyer, P.J.; Preindl, M.; Emadi, A. State-of-Charge Estimation of Li-Ion Batteries Using Deep Neural Networks: A Machine Learning Approach. *J. Power Sources* **2018**, *400*, 242–255. [CrossRef]
28. Pan, C.; Peng, Z.; Yang, S.; Wen, G.; Huang, T. Adaptive Neural Network-Based Prescribed-Time Observer for Battery State-of-Charge Estimation. *IEEE Trans. Power Electron.* **2023**, *38*, 165–176. [CrossRef]
29. Wang, C.; Li, M. A Novel Neural Network Model with Cascaded Structure for State-of-Charge Estimation in Lithium-Ion Batteries. *CSEE J. Power Energy Syst.* **2024**, *99*, 1–12.
30. Deng, Z.; Hu, X.; Lin, X.; Che, Y.; Xu, L.; Guo, W. Data-Driven State of Charge Estimation for Lithium-Ion Battery Packs Based on Gaussian Process Regression. *Energy* **2020**, *205*, 118000. [CrossRef]
31. Chaoui, H.; Ibe-Ekeocha, C.C. State of Charge and State of Health Estimation for Lithium Batteries Using Recurrent Neural Networks. *IEEE Trans. Veh. Technol.* **2017**, *66*, 8773–8783. [CrossRef]
32. Chemali, E.; Kollmeyer, P.J.; Preindl, M.; Ahmed, R.; Emadi, A. Long Short-Term Memory Networks for Accurate State-of-Charge Estimation of Li-Ion Batteries. *IEEE Trans. Ind. Electron.* **2018**, *65*, 6730–6739. [CrossRef]
33. Hong, J.; Wang, Z.; Chen, W.; Yao, Y. Synchronous Multi-Parameter Prediction of Battery Systems on Electric Vehicles Using Long Short-Term Memory Networks. *Appl. Energy* **2019**, *254*, 113648. [CrossRef]
34. Mao, X.; Song, S.; Ding, F. Optimal BP Neural Network Algorithm for State of Charge Estimation of Lithium-Ion Battery Using PSO with Levy Flight. *J. Energy Storage* **2022**, *49*, 104139. [CrossRef]
35. Abualigah, L.; Diabat, A.; Mirjalili, S.; Abd Elaziz, M.; Gandomi, A.H. The Arithmetic Optimization Algorithm. *Comput. Methods Appl. Mech. Eng.* **2021**, *376*, 113609. [CrossRef]
36. Vidal, C.; Malysz, P.; Naguib, M.; Emadi, A.; Kollmeyer, P.J. Estimating Battery State of Charge Using Recurrent and Non-Recurrent Neural Networks. *J. Energy Storage* **2022**, *47*, 103660. [CrossRef]
37. Misyris, G.S.; Doukas, D.I.; Papadopoulos, T.A.; Labridis, D.P.; Agelidis, V.G. State-of-Charge Estimation for Li-Ion Batteries: A More Accurate Hybrid Approach. *IEEE Trans. Energy Convers.* **2019**, *34*, 109–119. [CrossRef]
38. Charkhgard, M.; Farrokhi, M. State-of-Charge Estimation for Lithium-Ion Batteries Using Neural Networks and EKF. *IEEE Trans. Ind. Electron.* **2010**, *57*, 4178–4187. [CrossRef]
39. He, W.; Williard, N.; Chen, C.; Pecht, M. State of Charge Estimation for Li-Ion Batteries Using Neural Network Modeling and Unscented Kalman Filter-Based Error Cancellation. *Int. J. Electr. Power Energy Syst.* **2014**, *62*, 783–791. [CrossRef]
40. Cui, Z.; Kang, L.; Li, L.; Wang, L.; Wang, K. A Combined State-of-Charge Estimation Method for Lithium-Ion Battery Using an Improved BGRU Network and UKF. *Energy* **2022**, *259*, 124933. [CrossRef]
41. Zhang, X.; Huang, Y.; Zhang, Z.; Lin, H.; Zeng, Y.; Gao, M. A Hybrid Method for State-of-Charge Estimation for Lithium-Ion Batteries Using a Long Short-Term Memory Network Combined with Attention and a Kalman Filter. *Energies* **2022**, *15*, 6745. [CrossRef]
42. Pecht, M. *Battery Data Set*; CALCE Battery Research Group: Maryland, MD, USA, 2017; Available online: https://calce.umd.edu/battery-data#INR (accessed on 13 December 2023).

43. Liu, X.; Xia, W.; Li, S.; Lin, M.; Wu, J. State of Charge Estimation for Lithium-Ion Battery Pack With Selected Representative Cells. *IEEE Trans. Transp. Electrific.* **2024**, *10*, 4107–4118. [CrossRef]
44. Xiao, Y.; Song, W.; Liu, W.; Wan, F. Estimation of Lithium Battery State of Charge Using the LTG-SABO-GRU Model. *Meas. Sci. Technol.* **2024**, *35*, 115106. [CrossRef]
45. Zhao, Y.; Li, Y.; Cao, Y.; Jiang, L.; Wan, J.; Rehtanz, C. An RNN With Small Sequence Trained by Multi-Level Optimization for SOC Estimation in Li-Ion Battery Applications. *IEEE Trans. Veh. Technol.* **2023**, *72*, 11469–11481. [CrossRef]
46. Du, Z.; Zuo, L.; Li, J.; Liu, Y.; Shen, H.T. Data-Driven Estimation of Remaining Useful Lifetime and State of Charge for Lithium-Ion Battery. *IEEE Trans. Transp. Electrific.* **2022**, *8*, 356–367. [CrossRef]

mathematics

MDPI

Article

Energy Optimization Strategy for Wind–Solar–Storage Systems with a Storage Battery Configuration

Yufeng Wang [1], Haining Ji [1,2,*], Runteng Luo [1], Bin Liu [1,2] and Yongzi Wu [1]

1 School of Physics and Optoelectronics, Xiangtan University, Xiangtan 411105, China
2 Hunan Engineering Laboratory for Microelectronics, Optoelectronics and System on a Chip, Xiangtan University, Xiangtan 411105, China
* Correspondence: sdytjhn@xtu.edu.cn

Abstract: With the progressive advancement of the energy transition strategy, wind–solar energy complementary power generation has emerged as a pivotal component in the global transition towards a sustainable, low-carbon energy future. To address the inherent challenges of intermittent renewable energy generation, this paper proposes a comprehensive energy optimization strategy that integrates coordinated wind–solar power dispatch with strategic battery storage capacity allocation. Through the development of a linear programming model for the wind–solar–storage hybrid system, incorporating critical operational constraints including load demand, an optimization solution was implemented using the Artificial Fish Swarm Algorithm (AFSA). This computational approach enabled the determination of an optimal scheme for the coordinated operation of wind, solar, and storage components within the integrated energy system. Based on the case study analysis, the AFSA optimization algorithm achieves a 1.07% reduction in total power generation costs compared to the traditional Simulated Annealing (SA) approach. Comparative analysis reveals that the integrated grid-connected operation mode exhibits superior economic performance over the standalone storage microgrid system. Additionally, we conducted a further analysis of the key factors contributing to the enhancement of economic benefits. The strategy proposed in this paper significantly enhances power supply stability, reduces overall costs and promotes the large-scale application of green energy.

Keywords: wind–solar energy storage microgrid system; energy optimization strategy; artificial fish swarm algorithm; simulated annealing; joint operation

MSC: 68W50

1. Introduction

The ongoing global energy transition has been significantly accelerated by remarkable advancements in renewable energy technologies [1]. In parallel, the dual challenge of optimizing cost-effectiveness while ensuring reliable energy supply has emerged as a critical strategic imperative for the development of sustainable low-carbon economies [2,3]. A dual-phase energy transition strategy has been established by Chinese government, with ambitious targets of achieving a 20% share of non-fossil energy in primary consumption by 2030, followed by carbon neutrality by 2060 [4,5]. To accomplish this objective, the implementation of wind–solar–storage microgrid model becomes particularly crucial, boasting advantages such as environmental friendliness, reduced reliance on fossil fuels, and enhanced utilization efficiency of renewable energy. Nevertheless, this model also faces several challenges, including high initial investment costs, energy losses, and lifespan constraints. According to the latest research data released by the International Renewable Energy Agency (IRENA) [6], global renewable energy capacity additions are projected to experience a substantial surge in 2024, with annual installations anticipated to rise by 25% compared to current levels, surpassing the 700 GW threshold. Notably, solar photovoltaic (PV) technology demonstrates particularly robust momentum within this expansion framework, with its annual newly installed capacity projected to achieve a year-on-year increase of approximately 30%. Accounting for approximately 550 GW of the total additions, solar PV installations are expected to represent nearly 80% of the annual capacity expansion, further solidifying their status as the principal driving force in global clean energy transition initiatives. However, China remains the main driving force behind the increase in installed capacity of renewable energy worldwide. In 2024, the newly added photovoltaic capacity exceeded 340 GW, an increase of 30% compared to 2023, while the newly added wind energy capacity was 80 GW, unchanged from last year. (Figure 1).

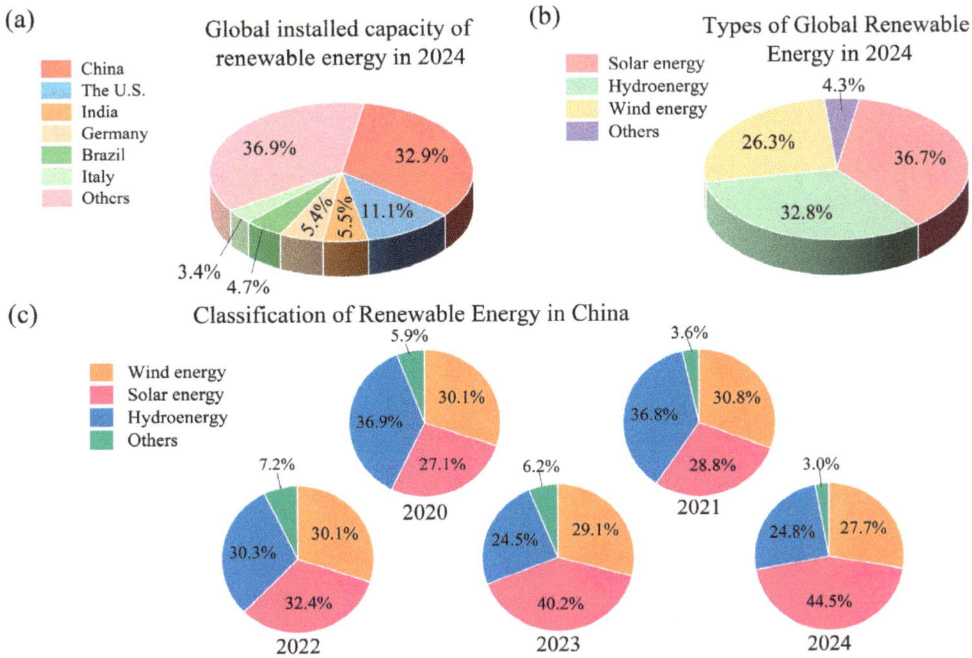

Figure 1. (**a**) Global installed capacity of renewable energy in 2024, (**b**) Global distribution of renewable energy types in 2024 and (**c**) Classification of renewable energy in China.

Battery energy storage systems have garnered significant research attention due to their crucial role in maintaining grid stability through peak shaving and valley filling operations [7]. These systems effectively mitigate the inherent intermittency of renewable energy generation while enhancing grid flexibility and dispatchability [8]. The key to improving the stability and economic benefits of distributed renewable energy system is not only in optimizing the configuration scheme of energy storage system and ensuring efficient and reasonable dispatching, but also in optimizing the operation mode of power system [9,10]. Although numerous studies have explored the impact of integrating solar and wind energy into power systems, a systematic solution to the grid operation challenges caused by intermittency and volatility has yet to be established [11].

Recently, extensive research has been conducted on the wind–solar–storage microgrid scheduling optimization. Huang et al. developed an energy optimization scheduling model for wind–solar–storage microgrids incorporating comprehensive cost factors with a specific focus on minimizing demand response costs [12]. In a related study, Ma et al. implemented a particle swarm optimization (PSO) algorithm for capacity allocation in wind–solar–storage systems within smart microgrids. However, this solution process was often found to converge to local optima [13]. To enhance the accuracy of search direction and prevent convergence to local optima, Zhang et al. developed an enhanced artificial fish swarm algorithm (AFSA). This improved version incorporates a decay factor and introduces regional search uncertainty, effectively mitigating repetitive search patterns and improving optimization performance [14]. Additionally, Zhang et al. proposed an innovative hybrid optimization approach combining modified genetic algorithms (GAs) with ant colony optimization (ACO) to enhance the reliability of sustainable energy systems by addressing key challenges including renewable energy variability, energy storage limitations, and residential demand fluctuations [15]. Simultaneously, Maklewa Agoundedemba et al. used the combined genetic algorithm (GA) and model predictive control (MPC) to size and optimize the hybrid renewable energy system (PV/Wind/FC/Battery), subject to certain constraints on the power flow and battery state of charge [16]. Furthermore, Parastegari et al. investigated the optimal scheduling problem for both joint operation (JO) and uncoordinated operation (UO) of wind farms and pumped storage power stations, which was systematically verified to enhance the system's profitability through JO implementation [17].

Although extensive research has been conducted on wind–solar–storage microgrid systems and battery capacity optimization, encompassing diverse technical perspectives, the joint operational mechanisms of microgrid systems remain significantly underexplored in current literature. Meanwhile, the existing fossil fuel-based power generation models are plagued by issues such as environmental pollution, resource depletion, and price volatility [18], whereas independently operated power grid models face challenges like energy wastage and limited anti-interference capabilities. Particularly in the context of China's comprehensive requirements for energy security assurance and economic performance enhancement [19], several critical research gaps persist. These include the optimization of environmental benefits and the development of advanced operational strategies for storage-integrated microgrid systems, which warrant comprehensive investigation.

This paper explores the optimization of wind–solar–storage configuration schemes. By integrating renewable energy and energy storage technologies for rational configuration and joint operation of multiple power grids, it effectively overcomes the environmental problems of fossil energy generation, while improving the flexibility and anti-interference ability of the power grid. The proposed model incorporates critical system operational constraint condition, particularly focusing on safety and stability requirements. Through comparative performance analysis on the artificial fish swarm algorithm (AFSA) and the conventional Simulated Annealing (SA) approach, an optimal energy storage configuration scheme and energy management strategy are derived, demonstrating significant economic benefits while simultaneously enhancing renewable energy integration and optimizing resource utilization.

2. The Wind–Solar–Storage Microgrid Model

The wind–solar–storage microgrid system structure is illustrated in Figure 2, consisting of a 275 kW wind turbine model, 100 kW photovoltaic model, lithium iron phosphate battery, and user load. When power demand is not fully met, electricity can be obtained from the main grid or supplied by the battery storage system. During periods of excess power, surplus energy is directed to the storage system rather than fed back to the main grid, thereby minimizing grid fluctuations. The symbol list in this model is shown in Table 1.

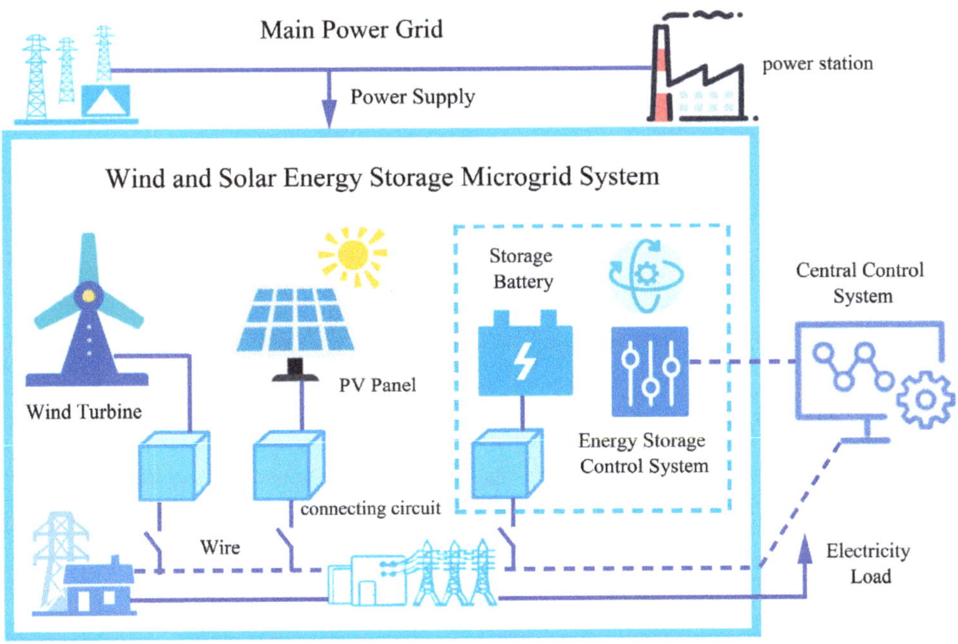

Figure 2. Structural diagram of wind–solar-energy storage microgrid system.

Table 1. Basic list of symbols.

Symbols	Meaning
P_W	the output power of the fan
P_R	the rated power of the fan
v_c, v_R, v_F	the cut-in, rated, cut-off wind speed
C_{wind}	the unit cost of wind power generation
P_a	the annual average output power
C_{solar}	the unit cost of photovoltaic power generation
C_p	the installation cost
y_p	lifespan years
$R_{op}, P_{loan}, P_{intr}$	operating rates, loan ratio and loan interest rate
H_{fp}	the equivalent annual power generation hours
$P_{ess,t}$	the charging and discharging power of the energy storage system at time t
SOC_t, SOC_{t+1}	the state of charge before and after the battery respectively
$E_{storage}$	the rated capacity of the energy storage system
C_{bat}	the life loss cost of lithium iron phosphate battery
C_{invest}	the total investment cost of lithium iron phosphate battery

2.1. The Wind Turbine Model

The relationship between wind turbine output power and wind speed has been demonstrated to be representable through a piecewise function, as shown in numerous studies [20].

$$P_W = \begin{cases} P_R \; for \; v_R < v \leq v_F \\ P_R \frac{v - v_c}{v_R - v_c} \; for \; v_c \leq v \leq v_R \\ 0 \; otherwise \end{cases} \quad (1)$$

In which P_W is the output power of the fan, P_R is the rated power of the fan, v_c is the cut-in wind speed, v_R is the rated wind speed, v_F is the cut-off wind speed. According to the manufacturer's data, the fan utilized in this study has a rated power of 275 kW, a cut-in wind speed of 4 m/s, a rated wind speed of 12 m/s, a cut-off wind speed of 20 m/s, and a design life of 20 years.

A unit power generation cost calculation model is established in this paper, based on the equal distribution of total generation costs over the wind farm's entire expected lifespan [21].

$$C_{wind} = \frac{r(1+r)^{y_w}}{(1+r)^{y_w} - 1} \cdot \left[\frac{Q}{8760F} \right] \tag{2}$$

$$F = \frac{P_a}{P_R} \tag{3}$$

In which C_{wind} is the unit cost of wind power generation, r is the annual interest rate of investment loans, y_w refers to the payback time of the investment in the construction of the plant, Q is the unit investment cost of plant construction, F is the capacity factor, P_a is the annual average output power. By consulting the reference [22], the parameters of the cost model for wind power generation are shown in Table 1: The parameters of the economic cost model for wind turbine power generation are provided in Table 2.

Table 2. Parameters of economic cost model of wind turbine power generation.

Parameter Type	r (%)	y_w (Years)	Q ($/kW)	F
numeric value	10	20	1142	0.5

2.2. The PV Battery Model

In order to facilitate practical application, the steady-state power output of PV batteries can be simplified as follows, and the formula of PV output power is [23]:

$$P_{PV} = P_{STC} G_{AC} [1 + k(T_c - T_\tau)] / G_{STC} \tag{4}$$

In which G_{AC} is the light intensity, P_{STC} and G_{STC} are the maximum test power and light intensity under standard test conditions respectively, k is the power temperature coefficient, T_c is the working temperature of the battery panel, T_τ is the reference temperature and its value is 25 °C. The cost of photovoltaic power generation is primarily determined by installation costs, system efficiency, policy and financing conditions, operational lifespan, and maintenance expenses. Based on these factors, the PV unit generation cost model can be established [22].

$$C_{solar} = C_p (1/y_p + R_{op} + P_{loan} \cdot P_{intr}) / H_{fp} \tag{5}$$

In which C_{solar} and C_p are the unit cost of photovoltaic power generation and the installation cost, y_p is lifespan years, R_{op} is operating rates, P_{loan} and P_{intr} are loan ratio and loan interest rate, and H_{fp} is the equivalent annual power generation hours. The parameters of the economic cost model for photovoltaic power generation were obtained by consulting reference [22], as shown in Table 3.

Table 3. Parameters of the economic cost model for PV power generation.

Parameter Type	C_p ($)	y_p (Years)	R_{op}	P_{loan}	P_{intr}	H_{fp} (h)
numeric value	1651	20	2%	70%	7%	1600

2.3. The Battery Charging and Discharging Model

2.3.1. Battery State of Charge

The state of charge (SOC), a critical parameter for indicating remaining battery capacity, must be maintained consistent between the start and end of each dispatch cycle to ensure continuous operation. The simplified SOC update formula for the energy storage system can be expressed as [24–26]:

$$SOC_{t+1} = SOC_t + \frac{P_{ess,t} \cdot \triangle t}{E_{storage}} \tag{6}$$

$$SOC_0 = SOC_n \tag{7}$$

In which $P_{ess,t}$ is the charging and discharging power of the energy storage system at time t, SOC_t and SOC_{t+1} are the state of charge before and after the battery respectively, $E_{storage}$ is the rated capacity of the energy storage system, $\triangle t$ is the time interval of each time period of the energy storage system, n is the last time value of a scheduling cycle of the energy storage system.

2.3.2. Battery Discharge Cost

We compared batteries with other energy storage methods in terms of working principle, energy storage time, cycle life, recycling capacity, and cost by consulting a large number of references, as shown in Table 4. Overall, batteries have significant advantages [27–30]. The lithium iron phosphate ($LiFePO_4$) batteries utilized in this study has its discharge cost determined by its lifecycle, which is influenced by factors such as charge–discharge cycles, depth of discharge, and operating temperature. The equivalent economic loss cost of lithium iron phosphate batteries is expressed as follows [31]:

$$C_j = \frac{C_{invest}}{N_{ESS}} \tag{8}$$

$$C_{bat} = \sum_{j=0}^{N_b} C_j \tag{9}$$

Table 4. Performance comparison of various energy storage methods.

	Battery	Pumped-Storage	Supercapacitors	RSOC System
Working principle	electrochemical reaction	Potential energy storage	Electrostatic energy storage	Reversible electrochemistry
Energy storage duration	4–5 h	4–24 h	<30 min	>12 h
cycle life	>3000 times	>50 years	>500,000 times	20,000 h
resources sustainability	Rich in iron and phosphorus	Water resource dependence	Carbon materials are abundant	Ceramic materials are abundant
Recycling capacity	Low	The equipment can be reused	The material can be 100% recycled	Ceramic components can be recycled
Costs	Low	Medium	Average	High

In which C_{bat} and C_{invest} are respectively the life loss cost and total investment cost of lithium iron phosphate battery, C_j is the cost corresponding to the battery charge and discharge depth of d_j, N_b and N_{ESS} are the charge and discharge times in a scheduling cycle and the maximum charge and discharge times in the life cycle of the battery. According to the literature [32], $LiFePO_4$ batteries are employed in this study, with the detailed parameters presented in Table 5:

Table 5. Relevant parameters of $LiFePO_4$ battery.

Parameter Type	$P_{charge,t(max)}$ (kW)	$P_{discharge,t(max)}$ (kW)	SOC_{max}	SOC_{min}	η_{charge}	$\eta_{discharge}$
numeric value	12	12	10%	90%	95%	95%

2.4. The Joint Grid Energy Storage Configuration Model

The joint grid model, as illustrated in Figure 3, is designed to effectively interconnect multiple power grids and energy storage systems, enabling optimal resource allocation and sharing across different regions. This approach has been demonstrated to enhance overall operational efficiency while reducing operational costs of storage facilities, thereby improving economic performance. Additionally, the system's flexibility is enhanced to better accommodate the stochastic variability of renewable energy generation.

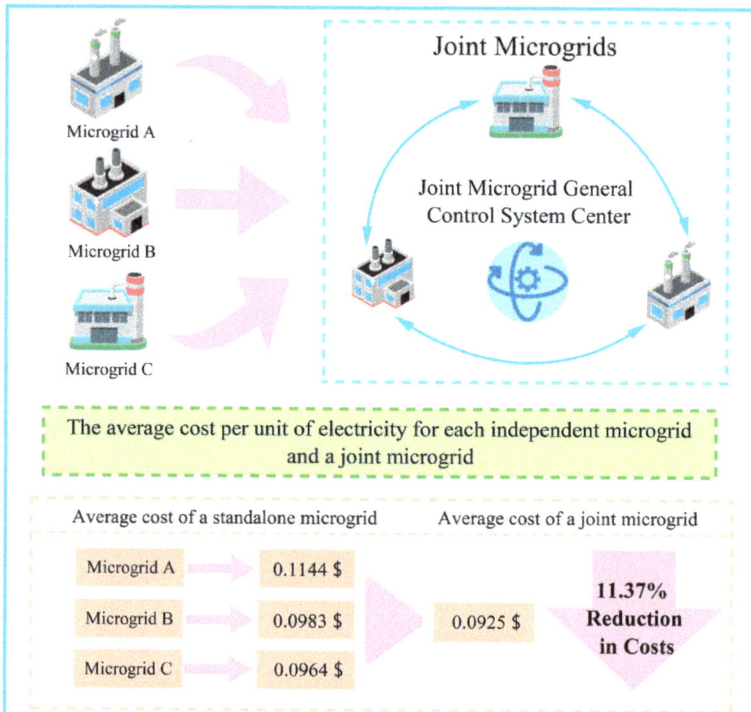

Figure 3. United grid energy storage configuration system diagram.

2.5. Operating Costs and Power Purchase Costs

In wind–solar–storage systems, annual equipment replacement costs and operational maintenance expenses are identified as significant components of operational expenditures [33]. At the same time, in the power purchase pricing system, differences between summer and winter are primarily reflected during peak demand periods. On weekdays, peak electricity rates are typically observed during morning and dusk hours, while off-peak electricity rates are typically observed during night hours. Furthermore, weekend rates are generally lower than those on weekdays [34,35]. The power purchase pricing system and peak/off-peak periods are shown in Figure 4.

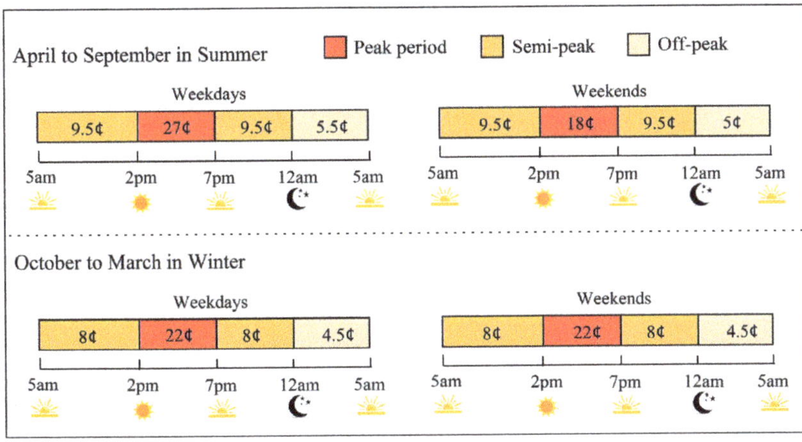

Figure 4. The time-of-use power purchase pricing system and the peak/off-peak periods diagram.

3. Energy Optimization and Algorithm Solving

3.1. Energy Optimization Strategy

The system energy optimization in this strategy is achieved through a time-segmented dynamic regulation mechanism and the specific workflow is structured as follows: Initial wind–solar–storage power values are collected in real-time and dynamically matched with user load demands for supply-demand analysis. Predefined differentiated energy dispatch strategies are automatically triggered when integrated generation deviates from load requirements. Then, the daily cycle is then divided into 24 equal intervals, during which programmed algorithms are executed to perform dynamic regulation of charge/discharge power, real-time tracking and adjustment of battery state-of-charge (SOC), among other operational tasks. The operational strategies and electricity procurement plans for the energy storage system are ultimately derived, as illustrated in Figure 5.

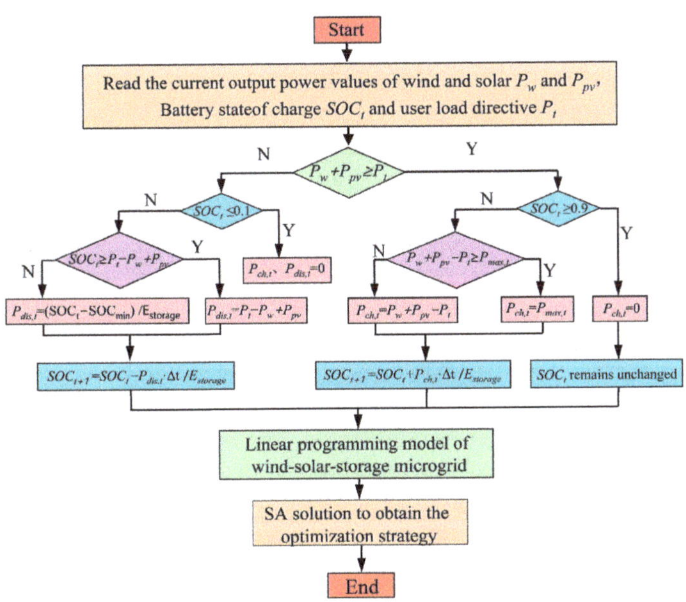

Figure 5. System operation judgment strategy chart.

Initially, the system reads the initial parameters and evaluates whether satisfies the load demand. When the conditions are met, first determine whether the SOC exceeds the upper limit (90%). If exceeded, charging is prohibited. Otherwise, the system evaluates whether the remaining power exceeds the rated charging power of the battery. If exceeded, the battery will be charged at its maximum rated power. On the contrary, if it is below this threshold, the battery will absorb the remaining available power.

When the power generation is insufficient, if the SOC is below 10%, the battery will neither charge nor discharge. If it has not been reached yet, continue to determine whether the remaining capacity meets the demand gap. If satisfied, the battery will discharge at the required power; Otherwise, discharge according to the remaining capacity power. Then update the battery charging status.

3.2. The Linear Programming Model of Wind–Solar Energy Storage Microgrid

To address the linear programming problem in energy management strategies for the wind–solarenergy storage microgrid, an objective function needs to be established for the linear programming model of the wind–solar–storage microgrid.

$$minC_{total} = P_W \cdot C_{wind} \cdot T + P_{PV} \cdot C_{solar} \cdot T + C_{bat} \cdot P_{discharge,t} \cdot T + f \cdot P_{grid,t} \cdot T \quad (10)$$

In which C_{total} is the total operation cost of the microgrid, f is the power purchase price, $P_{discharge,t}$ and $P_{grid,t}$ are the discharge power of the energy storage system at time t and the power purchased from the main grid.

An objective function is formulated to minimize the total operational costs of the microgrid, while simultaneously accounting for critical constraints such as generation capacity limits, charge–discharge power balance, battery state-of-charge limitations, and climbing rate constraint [36].

3.2.1. The Charge–Discharge Power Balance

$$P_W + P_{PV} + P_{ess,t} + P_{grid,t} = P_t + P_{curtailment,t} \quad (11)$$

In which $P_{curtailment,t}$ is the amount of abandoned wind and solar power of the energy storage system at the moment.

3.2.2. The Generation Capacity Limits

$$-P_{max,t} \ll P_{ess,t} \ll P_{max,t} \quad (12)$$

$$P_{W,min} \ll P_W \ll P_{W,max} \quad (13)$$

$$P_{PV,min} \ll P_{PV} \ll P_{PV,max} \quad (14)$$

In which $P_{max,t}$ is the maximum charging and discharging power of the energy storage at the moment, $P_{W,min}$ and $P_{W,max}$ are the minimum and maximum values of fan output power respectively, $P_{PV,min}$ and $P_{PV,max}$ are the minimum and maximum values of photovoltaic output power.

3.2.3. The Battery State-of-Charge Limitations

$$SOC_{min} \leq SOC_t \leq SOC_{max} \quad (15)$$

This constraint can prevent overcharging and overdischarging of the battery and increase its service life.

3.2.4. The Climbing Rate Constraint

$$\triangle P_W \leq P_{W,control} \quad (16)$$

$$\triangle P_{PV} \leq P_{PV,control} \quad (17)$$

In which $\triangle P_W$ and $\triangle P_{PV}$ are the difference between the current and previous given values of wind turbine and photovoltaic output, respectively, $P_{W,control}$ and $P_{PV,control}$ are the constraint values for wind turbine and photovoltaic output, respectively.

3.3. The Simulated Annealing Optimization Algorithm (SA)

Given the presence of exceedingly complex constraint condition inherent in this study, we ultimately decided to employ the simulated annealing algorithm The simulated annealing optimization algorithm (SA), a robust global optimization method based on stochastic search, is inspired by the annealing process in solid-state physics [37,38]. This algorithm demonstrates distinctive advantages through the effective escape from local optima to approach global optimal or superior solutions, thereby facilitating the discovery of global or near-global optimal solutions. This algorithm is widely implemented in practical engineering domains including manufacturing scheduling, network optimization, and path planning scenarios. These optimization problems are characterized by multiple local optima, where traditional methods are easily trapped in local solutions, resulting in suboptimal outcomes [39–41].

3.4. AFSA Based on Hybrid Mutation Operator and SA

In addition, we introduce another artificial fish swarm optimization algorithm (AFSA), which demonstrates significant advantages in directional search guidance and local optimum avoidance. However, its convergence performance is significantly compromised under two specific operational scenarios. (1) random individual fish movements that disrupt systematic search patterns, and (2) excessive aggregation phenomena at suboptimal solutions. These limitations ultimately lead to reduced optimization accuracy and compromised solution quality [42–44]. A genetic algorithm-inspired mutation operation is introduced to enhance algorithm diversity and adaptability in this paper. Through this method, the exploratory capability of AFSA in complex optimization problems is effectively enhanced, thereby improving global optimum identification. The overall process is structured as follows: Initially, a global search is conducted using the AFSA with mutation operators for optimal solution identification in the solution space. Subsequently, the simulated annealing algorithm is applied to perform a localized refinement search on the optimal artificial fish individuals, achieving local optimization [45]. The optimal near-exact extreme value is ultimately achieved through this process. The fundamental workflow of the AFSA based on hybrid mutation operator and SA is illustrated in Figure 6.

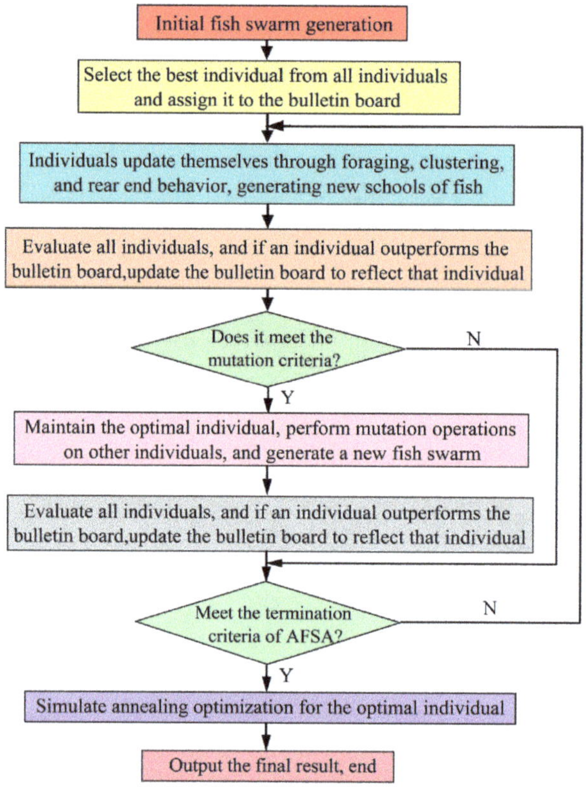

Figure 6. Flow chart of AFSA based on mutation operator and SA.

4. Example Analysis and Discussion

Three independent park-level wind–solar microgrid systems (Park A, B, C) are analyzed in this study. The only variation between systems is assumed to be in wind turbine and PV cell quantity, and battery energy storage system configurations. The parameters of various components such as wind turbines, PV cells, and batteries are shown in Tables 1–3 above.

4.1. Independent Operation and Energy Storage Configuration of Each Park

According to the equipment manual and analysis of numerous case results, independent park-level storage systems employ $LiFePO_4$ batteries with the following technical and economic parameters: a discharge cost of 110.12 \$/kWh, an operational SOC range of 10–90%, charge/discharge efficiency of 95%, and a projected lifespan of 10 years. Subsequently, based on the formula of the wind solar discharge cost model mentioned earlier, the purchase cost of renewable energy was calculated to be 0.0688 USD/kWh for wind energy and 0.0551 USD/kWh for solar energy. Table 6 comprehensively presents three key performance metrics for each park: operational costs, optimal battery configurations obtained through SA algorithm, and average unit electricity supply costs.

Table 6. Comparison table of basic parameters of each park.

	Microgrid A	Microgrid B	Microgrid C
Operating costs (\$)	5506	6882	6194
Battery configuration scheme	100 kW/150 kWh	100 kW/230 kWh	80 kW/150 kWh
Average cost (\$/kW)	0.1144	0.0983	0.0964

4.2. Joint Park Operation Energy Storage Configuration

When the aggregate power generation of the three parks matches the total load demand, an integrated joint operation system is established, whose architectural configuration is illustrated in Figure 3. The joint operation maintains consistent renewable energy procurement costs at 0.0688 $/kWh for wind power and 0.0551 $/kWh for solar energy, with the energy storage system configuration remaining identical to individual park operations. The total operational cost is calculated as 18,583 $, while an additional cost of 4,129 $ is required for joint system coordination and inter-park electricity transmission. In addition, other costs are ignored. The optimal battery configuration for the joint park is determined to be 182.48 kW/405 kWh through energy storage optimization performed using the simulated annealing optimization algorithm (SA). Among them, a 0.0925 $/kWh average unit electricity supply cost is achieved for the joint park system, 11.37% lower than the average cost of standalone park operations. Figure 7 provides a comprehensive temporal analysis of energy flow characteristics throughout a 24-h period, illustrating three key parameters for both individual and joint park operations: daily load profiles, electricity procurement from the main grid, and abandoned wind/solar power due to generation overcapacity. Table 7 presents a comprehensive comparison of key operational metrics between standalone and joint operation modes, including: (1) total electricity procurement from the grid, (2) cumulative energy curtailment, (3) aggregate power supply expenditures, and (4) mean unit electricity costs.

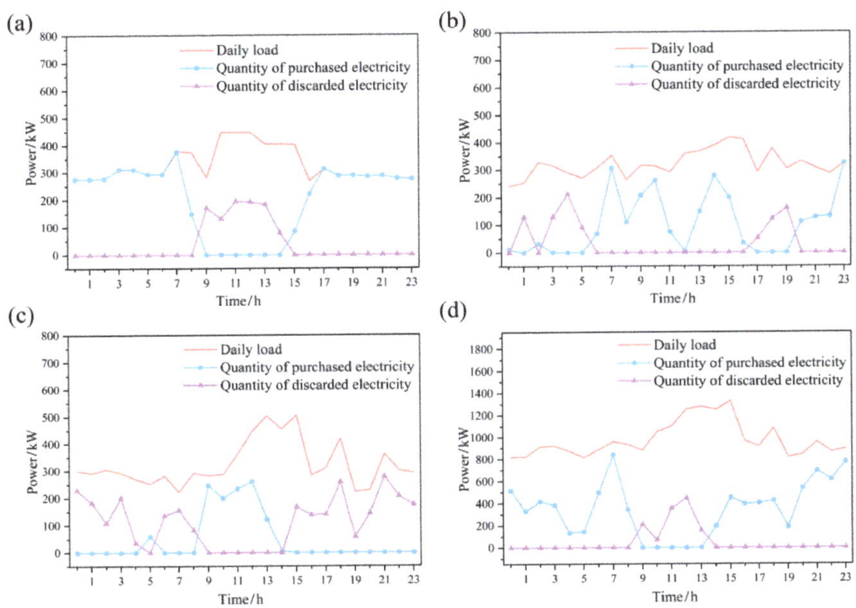

Figure 7. Daily load, power purchase and waste conditions of each park: (**a**) Park A, (**b**) Park B, (**c**) Park C and (**d**) Joint Park.

Table 7. Comparison table of corresponding parameters of independent operation and joint operation.

	Microgrid A	Microgrid B	Microgrid C	Joint Microgrids
Total purchased (kW)	4879.30	2570.00	2699.39	8823.55
Total abandoned (kW)	1098.65	676.70	1128.02	1578.23
Total cost ($)	898.54	754.13	753.26	1841.84
Average cost ($/kW)	0.1144	0.0983	0.0964	0.0925

From the comprehensive analysis of Figure 7 and Table 5, it can be seen that: The total purchased electricity for independent operation is 10,148.68 kW, and through joint park operation, power resource sharing and optimized scheduling have been achieved. The total purchased electricity is 8823.55 kW, which has been significantly reduced. This change not only highlights the advantages of resource sharing, but also reflects the effectiveness of joint operation in reducing the dependence on the main power grid. By optimizing load balancing and sharing power resources in joint operations, the total abandoned power of the joint park is 1578.23 kW, which significantly reduces power waste and abandonment compared to the total abandoned power of 2903.63 kW of independent parks, thereby improving overall power utilization efficiency. Additionally, internal power demand is effectively balanced by the shared use of energy storage systems across multiple parks or regions. During periods of low electricity prices, energy is stored in the energy storage system and later released during peak price periods, thereby reducing the need to purchase high-priced electricity. This dispatching strategy not only leads to a reduction in enterprise electricity procurement expenditures but also results in decreased production costs, shortened payback period, and enhanced economic efficiency. The joint operation model demonstrates remarkable potential in optimizing energy utilization, particularly through two key aspects: significant minimization of energy waste and substantial improvement in electricity utilization efficiency, establishing it as a promising solution for industrial energy management.

Furthermore, the joint microgrid is optimized through AFSA integrated with mutation operators and SA, resulting in an average power supply cost of 0.0913 $/kWh, which is 1.07% lower than that achieved by the traditional SA. The energy storage configuration for the joint park operation under the two dispatching optimization methods is illustrated in Figure 8. Based on the analysis, the following conclusions can be drawn:

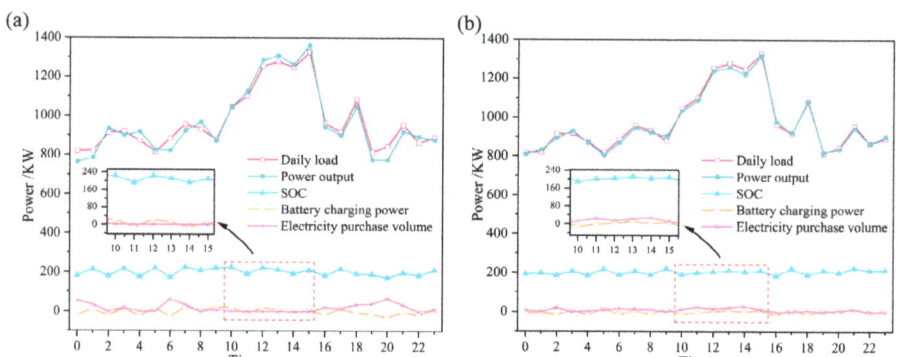

Figure 8. Optimal scheduling process of two algorithms for joint Park: (**a**) Simulated annealing algorithm, (**b**) Artificial Fish Swarm Algorithm.

(1) The optimization algorithm outperforms the traditional algorithm in guiding the search trajectory, allowing it to escape local optima and identify superior configuration solutions. (2) Throughout a given day, the optimization algorithm more closely aligns the daily load curve with the power output curve, leading to a significant reduction in total electricity purchased and wasted. In contrast, between 4:00 and 8:00, the curves under the traditional algorithm show a lower degree of coincidence, likely because the algorithm becomes trapped in a local optimum during the search process. (3) Traditional algorithms often charge and discharge batteries between 10:00 and 14:00, which may have a negative impact on their lifespan. In contrast, the optimization algorithm primarily relies on power procurement from the main grid, resulting in a significant reduction in the number of charge–discharge cycles for the joint system's battery. This helps extend the

battery's lifespan while achieving cost savings. During this period, which coincides with the off-peak electricity pricing, purchasing power from the main grid is more cost-effective compared to obtaining electricity from the battery storage system. (4) The scheduling results of optimization algorithms are superior to traditional algorithms and the SOC curve of the optimization algorithm exhibits narrower fluctuations, with less variation in the depth of battery charge and discharge, which contributes to the deceleration of battery aging. As a consequence, the frequency of replacements and maintenance costs are reduced, ultimately lowering overall production costs and improving the equipment's economic efficiency and sustainable development.

5. Conclusions

In conclusion, this study establishes a linear programming model for wind–solar–storage integrated microgrid systems addressing the stochastic variability of renewable energy and the coordination capabilities of $LiFePO_4$ battery storage systems, while comprehensively considering various constraints, including load demand, grid limitations, and battery capacity. The solution is achieved through an enhanced AFSA, which incorporates a genetic algorithm-inspired mutation operator to improve population diversity and adaptive search capabilities. This algorithmic enhancement enables more effective global optimum exploration, ultimately yielding an optimized configuration scheme for coordinated wind–solar–storage system operation. On this basis, this study proposes a joint microgrid energy storage configuration model. A comparative case analysis shows that: (1) The joint operation mode achieves significant economic advantages by reducing the total purchased electricity from 10,148.68 kW in independent operation to 8823.55 kW. (2) The system curtailment is considerably reduced from 2903.63 kW to 1578.23 kW representing a 45.7% reduction in energy waste and a corresponding improvement in energy utilization efficiency. (3) In the joint microgrid, compared with traditional strategies, the optimization strategy proposed in this study reduces the total power generation cost by 1.07%. The proposed strategy offers practical guidance for short-term dispatch operations in wind–solar–storage microgrids while informing future research directions, particularly in further improving the economic optimization scheduling model, considering the impact of factors such as weather changes and labor costs.

Author Contributions: Conceptualization, Y.W. (Yufeng Wang) and R.L.; methodology, Y.W. (Yufeng Wang); software, Y.W. (Yufeng Wang); validation, Y.W. (Yufeng Wang), H.J. and B.L.; formal analysis, Y.W. (Yufeng Wang); investigation, Y.W. (Yufeng Wang); resources, Y.W. (Yongzi Wu); data curation, Y.W. (Yongzi Wu); writing—original draft preparation, Y.W. (Yufeng Wang); writing—review and editing, Y.W. (Yufeng Wang) and H.J.; visualization, Y.W. (Yufeng Wang); supervision, H.J.; project administration, Y.W. (Yufeng Wang); funding acquisition, H.J. All authors have read and agreed to the published version of the manuscript.

Funding: This work was financially supported by the National Natural Science Foundation of China (No. 51902276, 62005234), the Natural Science Foundation of Hunan Province (No. 2019JJ50583, 2023JJ30585), the Scientific Research Fund of Hunan Provincial Education Department (No. 21B0111), and the Hunan Provincial Innovation Foundation for Postgraduate (No. QL20220158).

Data Availability Statement: Data will be made available on request.

Conflicts of Interest: The authors declare no conflicts of interest.

References

1. Hassan, Q.; Viktor, P.; Al-Musawi, T.J.; Ali, B.M.; Algburi, S.; Alzoubi, H.M.; Al-Jiboory, A.K.; Sameen, A.Z.; Salman, H.M.; Jaszczur, M. The renewable energy role in the global energy Transformations. *Renew. Energy Focus* **2024**, *48*, 100545. [CrossRef]
2. Yan, J.; Jie, Q. Mechanisms of policy intervention for China's transformation of the low-carbon economy. *J. Clean. Prod.* **2025**, *487*, 144550. [CrossRef]
3. Onabowale, O. Energy policy and sustainable finance: Navigating the future of renewable energy and energy markets. *World J. Adv. Res. Rev.* **2024**, *25*, 2235–2252. [CrossRef]
4. Hepburn, C.; Qi, Y.; Stern, N.; Ward, B.; Xie, C.; Zenghelis, D. Towards carbon neutrality and China's 14th Five-Year Plan: Clean energy transition, sustainable urban development, and investment priorities. *Environ. Sci. Ecotechnol.* **2021**, *8*, 100130. [CrossRef]
5. Liu, Q.; Wang, Q.; Hong, Q. China's Energy Transition with the Scenario of Carbon Neutrality, Outlook by 2060. In *Annual Report on China's Petroleum, Gas and New Energy Industry (2021)*; Springer: Berlin/Heidelbeg, Germany, 2022; pp. 25–44.
6. The International Renewable Energy Agency. Available online: https://www.irena.org (accessed on 22 April 2025).
7. Faisal, M.; Hannan, M.A.; Ker, P.J.; Hussain, A.; Mansor, M.B.; Blaabjerg, F. Review of energy storage system technologies in microgrid applications: Issues and challenges. *IEEE Access* **2018**, *6*, 35143–35164. [CrossRef]
8. Elalfy, D.A.; Gouda, E.; Kotb, M.F.; Bureš, V.; Sedhom, B.E. Comprehensive review of energy storage systems technologies, objectives, challenges, and future trends. *Energy Strat. Rev.* **2024**, *54*, 101482. [CrossRef]
9. Wang, H.; Huang, J. Joint investment and operation of microgrid. *IEEE Trans. Smart Grid* **2015**, *8*, 833–845. [CrossRef]
10. Meng, Q.; Tong, X.; Hussain, S.; Luo, F.; Zhou, F.; He, Y.; Liu, L.; Sun, B.; Li, B. Enhancing distribution system stability and efficiency through multi-power supply startup optimization for new energy integration. *IET Gener. Transm. Distrib.* **2024**, *18*, 3487–3500. [CrossRef]
11. Ejuh Che, E.; Roland Abeng, K.; Iweh, C.D.; Tsekouras, G.J.; Fopah-Lele, A. The Impact of Integrating Variable Renewable Energy Sources into Grid-Connected Power Systems: Challenges, Mitigation Strategies, and Prospects. *Energies* **2025**, *18*, 689. [CrossRef]
12. Huang, J.; Wu, K. Energy Optimal Scheduling Method of Microgrid with Wind and Solar Storage Based on Demand Response. In *Journal of Physics: Conference Series*; IOP Publishing: Bristol, UK, 2023; p. 012017.
13. Ma, X.; Fang, X.; Lv, L.; Ling, K.; Shi, Y. Optimal Allocation of Wind and Solar Storage Capacity in Smart Microgrid Based on Particle Swarm Optimization Algorithm. In Proceedings of the 2024 International Conference on Smart City and Information System, Kuala Lumpur, Malaysia, 17–19 May 2024; pp. 93–98.
14. Zhang, C.; Zhang, F.-M.; Li, F.; Wu, H.-S. Improved artificial fish swarm algorithm. In Proceedings of the 2014 9th IEEE Conference on Industrial Electronics and Applications, Hangzhou, China, 9–11 June 2014; IEEE: Piscataway, NJ, USA, 2014; pp. 748–753.
15. Zarate-Perez, E.; Sebastian, R. Assessment and Optimization of Residential Microgrid Reliability Using Genetic and Ant Colony Algorithms. *Processes* **2025**, *13*, 740. [CrossRef]
16. Agoundedemba, M.; Kim, C.K.; Kim, H.-G.; Nyenge, R.; Musila, N. Modelling and optimization of microgrid with combined genetic algorithm and model predictive control of PV/Wind/FC/battery energy systems. *Energy Rep.* **2025**, *13*, 238–255. [CrossRef]
17. Parastegari, M.; Hooshmand, R.-A.; Khodabakhshian, A.; Forghani, Z. Joint operation of wind farms and pump-storage units in the electricity markets: Modeling, simulation and evaluation. *Simul. Model. Pract. Theory* **2013**, *37*, 56–69. [CrossRef]
18. Ebhota, W.S.; Jen, T.C. Fossil fuels environmental challenges and the role of solar photovoltaic technology advances in fast tracking hybrid renewable energy system. *Int. J. Precis. Eng. Manuf. Technol.* **2020**, *7*, 97–117. [CrossRef]
19. Fang, D.; Shi, S.; Yu, Q. Evaluation of sustainable energy security and an empirical analysis of China. *Sustainability* **2018**, *10*, 1685. [CrossRef]
20. Borowy, B.S.; Salameh, Z.M. Methodology for optimally sizing the combination of a battery bank and PV array in a wind/PV hybrid system. *IEEE Trans. Energy Convers.* **1996**, *11*, 367–375. [CrossRef]
21. Amr, M.; Petersen, H.; Habali, S. Assessment of windfarm economics in relation to site wind resources applied to sites in Jordan. *Sol. Energy* **1990**, *45*, 167–175. [CrossRef]
22. LiXue, C.; Fang, F. Energy Optimization Management of Microgrid System with Wind, Solar, and Storage Considering Battery Life. *Mod. Electr. Power* **2018**, *35*, 62–69.
23. Gavanidous, E.; Bakirtzis, A. Design of a stand alone system with renewable energy sources using trade off methods. *IEEE Trans. Energy Convers.* **1992**, *7*, 42–48. [CrossRef]
24. Ma, X.; Chen, J.; Yu, S.; Li, S.; Lu, W. Optimal Research of User-Side Energy Storage Systems Considering Capacity Market Participation. *Trans. China Electrotech. Soc.* **2020**, *35*, 4028–4037.
25. Pandžić, H.; Bobanac, V. An accurate charging model of battery energy storage. *IEEE Trans. Power Syst.* **2018**, *34*, 1416–1426. [CrossRef]
26. Teng, J.-H.; Luan, S.-W.; Lee, D.-J.; Huang, Y.-Q. Optimal charging/discharging scheduling of battery storage systems for distribution systems interconnected with sizeable PV generation systems. *IEEE Trans. Power Syst.* **2012**, *28*, 1425–1433. [CrossRef]

27. Rahman, M.M.; Oni, A.O.; Gemechu, E.; Kumar, A. Assessment of energy storage technologies: A review. *Energy Convers. Manag.* **2020**, *223*, 113295. [CrossRef]
28. Amladi, A.G.; Resink, F.; el Tambouli, O.; Venkataraman, V.; Woudstra, T.; Aravind, P.V. Reversible Solid Oxide Cells for Energy Storage in the Netherlands: Thermodynamics and Fuel Selection. *ECS Trans.* **2023**, *111*, 1803. [CrossRef]
29. Javeed, A.; Rehman, F.; Draz, U.; Rehman, Z.U.; Farooq, N.; Karami, A.M.; Hussain, S. Structural and electrochemical studies of triple conducting nanocomposites for energy conversion devices. *Solid State Ion.* **2024**, *407*, 116499. [CrossRef]
30. Calise, F.; Cappiello, F.L.; Cimmino, L.; d'Accadia, M.D.; Vicidomini, M. Renewable smart energy network: A thermoeconomic comparison between conventional lithium-ion batteries and reversible solid oxide fuel cells. *Renew. Energy* **2023**, *214*, 74–95. [CrossRef]
31. Vrettos, E.I.; Papathanassiou, S.A. Operating policy and optimal sizing of a high penetration RES-BESS system for small isolated grids. *IEEE Trans. Energy Convers.* **2011**, *26*, 744–756. [CrossRef]
32. Question A: Coordinated and Optimized Configuration of Wind, Solar and Energy Storage in Microgrids in Industrial Parks. Available online: https://blog.csdn.net/weixin_44209907/article/details/139181308 (accessed on 20 January 2025).
33. Mathew, S.; Kennedy, D. A strategy for optimal equipment replacement. *Prod. Plan. Control.* **2003**, *14*, 571–577. [CrossRef]
34. Sepúlveda-Mora, S.B.; Hegedus, S. Making the case for time-of-use electric rates to boost the value of battery storage in commercial buildings with grid connected PV systems. *Energy* **2021**, *218*, 119447. [CrossRef]
35. Yang, P.; Tang, G.; Nehorai, A. A game-theoretic approach for optimal time-of-use electricity pricing. *IEEE Trans. Power Syst.* **2012**, *28*, 884–892. [CrossRef]
36. Qi, W.; Liu, J.; Chen, X.; Christofides, P.D. Supervisory predictive control of standalone wind/solar energy generation systems. *IEEE Trans. Control. Syst. Technol.* **2010**, *19*, 199–207. [CrossRef]
37. Aarts, E.H.L.; Van Laarhoven, P.J.M. Simulated annealing: An introduction. *Stat. Neerl.* **1989**, *43*, 31–52. [CrossRef]
38. Rutenbar, R. Simulated annealing algorithms: An overview. *IEEE Circuits Devices Mag.* **1989**, *5*, 19–26. [CrossRef]
39. Suman, B.; Kumar, P. A survey of simulated annealing as a tool for single and multiobjective optimization. *J. Oper. Res. Soc.* **2006**, *57*, 1143–1160. [CrossRef]
40. Li, X.-G.; Wei, X. An improved genetic algorithm-simulated annealing hybrid algorithm for the optimization of multiple reservoirs. *Water Resour. Manag.* **2008**, *22*, 1031–1049. [CrossRef]
41. Ekren, O.; Ekren, B.Y. Size optimization of a PV/wind hybrid energy conversion system with battery storage using simulated annealing. *Appl. Energy* **2010**, *87*, 592–598. [CrossRef]
42. Azizi, R. Empirical study of artificial fish swarm algorithm. *arXiv* **2014**, arXiv:1405.4138.
43. Luan, X.-Y.; Li, Z.-P.; Liu, T.-Z. A novel attribute reduction algorithm based on rough set and improved artificial fish swarm algorithm. *Neurocomputing* **2016**, *174*, 522–529. [CrossRef]
44. Pourpanah, F.; Wang, R.; Lim, C.P.; Wang, X.-Z.; Yazdani, D.J. A review of artificial fish swarm algorithms: Recent advances and applications. *Artif. Intell. Rev.* **2023**, *56*, 1867–1903. [CrossRef]
45. Jiang, M.; Cheng, Y. Simulated Annealing Artificial Fish Swarm Algorithm. In Proceedings of the 2010 8th World Congress on Intelligent Control and Automation, Jinan, China, 7–9 July 2010; IEEE: Piscataway, NJ, USA, 2010; pp. 1590–1593.

mathematics

MDPI

Article

Stability and Performance Analysis of Single-Step FCS-MPC System Based on Regional ISS Theory

Weiguang Hu *, Long Chen and Zhangyi Wang

School of Automation, Central South University, Changsha 410083, China; 234611001@csu.edu.cn (L.C.); 8207220504@csu.edu.cn (Z.W.)
* Correspondence: 184606028@csu.edu.cn

Abstract: In recent years, finite-control-set model predictive control (FCS-MPC) has attracted significant attention in power electronic converter control, resulting in substantial research advancements. However, no formal method currently exists to prove the stability of FCS-MPC systems. Additionally, many application studies have yet to adequately address the relationship between the selection of design parameters and system performance. To address the lack of stability and performance guarantees in FCS-MPC system design, this paper investigates a class of single-step FCS-MPC systems. The analysis is based on regional input-to-state stability (ISS) theory. Sufficient conditions for ensuring regional stability are derived, and a method for estimating the system's domain of attraction and ultimate bounded region is developed. Simulation experiments validated the analytical results and revealed the relationships between the domain of attraction and system stability, as well as between the ultimate bounded region and steady-state performance. The results indicate that appropriate parameter design can ensure system stability. Furthermore, the proposed method elucidates how changes in design parameters affect system stability and steady-state performance, providing a theoretical foundation for designing a class of FCS-MPC systems.

Keywords: finite-control-set model predictive control (FCS-MPC); stability analysis; performance analysis; regional input-to-state stability (ISS); power converter

MSC: 93D23; 93D30; 93C10

1. Introduction

Finite-control-set model predictive control (FCS-MPC) is a special form of model predictive control (MPC) characterized by restricting control inputs to a discrete set with a finite number of elements. Besides the general advantages of MPC, the most remarkable feature of FCS-MPC is its ability to solve optimization problems using the enumeration search algorithm. This makes the formulation of FCS-MPC strategies extremely simple and intuitive, and also results in a relatively low computational complexity under a short prediction horizon [1–3]. In recent years, FCS-MPC has attracted significant attention in the field of power electronic converter control, driving numerous research advancements [4–7]. Despite the extensive application and research on FCS-MPC algorithms in recent years, some issues still remain to be fully resolved. First, to date, there is no formal method available to prove the stability of FCS-MPC algorithms. Second, the relationship between system parameters and performance has not been adequately explored [8–10]. These issues undoubtedly hinder the further development of FCS-MPC.

In applied research, several novel design schemes aiming to ensure stability have been proposed [11–14]. These schemes rely on the Lyapunov direct method. Specifically, this method either introduces additional Lyapunov functions or uses the Lyapunov function itself as the cost function. System stability is ensured by guaranteeing a non-positive change in the Lyapunov function during the optimization process. However, due to the limitation of control inputs to a finite set, it is not always possible to find a feasible control input from this set during system operation to ensure a non-positive change in the Lyapunov function. This lack of necessary theoretical support has been a major constraint in the application of these methods.

In the initial development stage of FCS-MPC, some pioneering theoretical studies focusing on its stability were carried out. References [15,16] proposed a method to express the closed-loop solution of FCS-MPC systems. Based on this, reference [17] presented the stability results for linear time-invariant (LTI) systems with finite constraint sets. However, these results are only applicable to open-loop stable systems, and the finite control set must contain the origin. Reference [18] analyzed the stability of the FCS-MPC system using the regional input-to-state stability (ISS) theory, extending the analysis to open-loop unstable systems. Nevertheless, the obtained results were overly conservative. Subsequently, references [19,20] employed the practical stability theory to reduce the conservatism of the results through direct analysis. However, these methods are only applicable to single-input systems without constraints, and the theoretical derivation processes in these references are incomplete. The above-mentioned studies jointly constitute the analysis framework based on LTI systems with quantized inputs. Nevertheless, there are still some urgent problems to be solved within this framework. Unfortunately, after these initial studies, the theoretical research on the stability of FCS-MPC stagnated for a long time. In recent years, references [21–23] introduced a new analysis framework based on affine switching systems, providing new ideas for the stability research of FCS-MPC. However, compared with the earlier framework, these methods can only guarantee stability near a few equilibrium points determined by the discrete control set, which limits their practical applicability.

In summary, although the affine switching system provides an interesting new perspective, considering the potential for practical application, we chose to continue the theoretical research within the earlier framework. First, to address the issues such as the narrow applicability of the analysis methods and the incomplete theoretical derivations in the existing research under this framework, we analyzed the closed-loop model of the FCS-MPC system in detail. Following the approach in references [19,20], we modeled the effect of the finite control set as a quantization error. On this basis, we proposed a more general method for calculating the quantization error, which enables the analysis to be extended to multi-input systems, thus broadening the applicability of the method. Subsequently, by applying the ISS theory, we fully derived the sufficient conditions for system stability, provided a complete theoretical derivation and proof, and established the relationship between quantization error and system performance. At the same time, to address the issue of the unclear relationship between system parameters and performance to some extent, based on the above-derived theoretical results, we developed an iterative algorithm that can be used to estimate the system's domain of attraction and ultimate convergence region. This method can intuitively demonstrate the stability characteristics and steady-state performance of the system under the current parameters, filling a gap in the current research within this framework, and thus providing a theoretical reference for controller design. Finally, simulation examples were used to verify the correctness of the theoretical results and demonstrate the reference value of the proposed method for controller design.

The rest of this paper is organized as follows. Section 2 presents the mathematical model of the studied system. Section 3 introduces the key concepts of the regional ISS theory. Section 4 analyzes the stability of the system and proposes a method for estimating the domain of attraction and ultimate bounded region. Section 5 validates the proposed method through simulation examples. Section 6 summarizes the main research findings and concludes the paper.

Notation and Basic Definitions: The sets of real numbers, integers, non-negative real numbers, non-negative integers, n-dimensional real vectors and $n \times m$-dimensional real matrices are denoted by $\mathbb{R}$, $\mathbb{Z}$, $\mathbb{R}_{\geq 0}$, $\mathbb{Z}_{\geq 0}$, $\mathbb{R}^n$ and $\mathbb{R}^{n\times m}$ respectively. The Euclidean norm of a vector or matrix is denoted by $|\cdot|$. Given a signal w, $\mathbf{w} \triangleq \{w_0, w_1, \ldots\}$ denotes the signal's sequence; $||\mathbf{w}|| \triangleq \sup_{k\geq 0}\{|w_k|\}$ and $\mathcal{M}_W$ denote the set of $\mathbf{w}$ where the values of w are limited to a compact set $W \in \mathbb{R}^m$. Given a matrix $A \subseteq \mathbb{R}^{n\times n}$, the maximum and minimum eigenvalues of A are denoted by $\lambda_{\max}(A)$ and $\lambda_{\min}(A)$ respectively. Given closed sets $A \subseteq \mathbb{R}^n$ $B \subseteq \mathbb{R}^n$, where $B \subseteq A$, then $A \backslash B \triangleq \{x | x \in A, x \notin B\}$. If function $f(x) : \mathbb{R}_{\geq 0} \to \mathbb{R}_{\geq 0}$ is continuous, strictly increasing and positive definite, it is said to be a $\mathcal{K}$-function. If for each fixed $k \geq 0$, $f(x,k) : \mathbb{R}_{\geq 0} \to \mathbb{R}_{\geq 0}$ is a $\mathcal{K}$-function, for each fixed $x \geq 0$, $f(x,k) : \mathbb{Z}_{\geq 0} \to \mathbb{R}_{\geq 0}$ is a non-increasing function, and $\lim_{k\to\infty} f(x,k) = 0$; then, function $f(x,k) : \mathbb{R}_{\geq 0} \times \mathbb{Z}_{\geq 0} \to \mathbb{R}_{\geq 0}$ is said to be a $\mathcal{K}_{\mathcal{L}}$-function.

2. Mathematical Model of Single-Step FCS-MPC System

2.1. Mathematical Model of the Controlled Plant

In the application research of FCS-MPC, one class of systems is the LTI system [2,3], which can be represented by the following dynamic equation:

$$x_{k+1} = Ax_k + Bu_k, \tag{1}$$

where $k \in \mathbb{Z}_{\geq 0}$, $x_k \in \mathbb{R}^n$ and $u_k \in \mathbb{R}^m$ are the state vector and control input vector, respectively; $A \in \mathbb{R}^{n\times n}$ and $B \in \mathbb{R}^{n\times m}$ are constant matrices. The system is subject to the following state and control constraints:

$$x_k \in \mathcal{X}, \forall k \in \mathbb{Z}_{\geq 0}, \tag{2}$$

$$u_k \in \mathcal{U} = \{\overline{u}_1, \overline{u}_2, \ldots, \overline{u}_p\}, \forall k \in \mathbb{Z}_{\geq 0}, \tag{3}$$

where $\mathcal{X}$ is a compact set and $\mathcal{U}$ is a known finite set; the subscript $p \in \mathbb{Z}_{\geq 0}$ is a constant indicating the number of control candidates.

Let the reference value be denoted by $x_k{}^*$, which represents either a fixed point in the state space or a periodic state trajectory, satisfying

$$x_{k+1}{}^* = Ax_k{}^* + Bu_k{}^*, \tag{4}$$

where $u_k{}^*$ denotes the steady-state control input, which may be a constant or a periodic value depending on the reference trajectory. Therefore

$$u_k{}^* \in \mathcal{U}^*, \forall k \in \mathbb{Z}_{\geq 0}, \tag{5}$$

where $\mathcal{U}^*$ is a known finite set. Let $\varepsilon_k = x_k - x_k{}^*$, and the error dynamics can then be expressed as

$$\varepsilon_{k+1} = A\varepsilon_k + B(u_k - u_k{}^*), \tag{6}$$

The control objective is to drive ε_k to zero.

2.2. Control Law of Single-Step FCS-MPC

Based on the discrete-time LTI system with state and finite-control-set constraints introduced in Section 2.1, this section presents the fundamental features of the single-step FCS-MPC algorithm applied to the aforementioned system. In Section 2.3, we will further formulate the mathematical model of the closed-loop system composed of the controlled plant and the FCS-MPC controller.

The general form of the FCS-MPC cost function is given by

$$J(\varepsilon_k, u_k, u_k{}^*) = \varepsilon_k{}^T Q \varepsilon_k + (u_k - u_k{}^*)^T R (u_k - u_k{}^*) + \hat{\varepsilon}_{k+1}^T P \hat{\varepsilon}_{k+1}, \tag{7}$$

where $\hat{\varepsilon}_{k+1}$ denotes the predicted state error calculated according to (6), and $P \in \mathbb{R}^{n\times n}$, $Q \in \mathbb{R}^{n\times n}$ and $R \in \mathbb{R}^{m\times m}$. Since the main idea of the FCS-MPC controller is to minimize a cost function related to the state error, matrix P must be positive definite, while Q and R are required to be positive semidefinite, as they may be zero in practical applications. For simplicity and clarity, the weighting matrices Q and R are often chosen to be diagonal.

The structure of the single-step FCS-MPC system is illustrated in Figure 1.

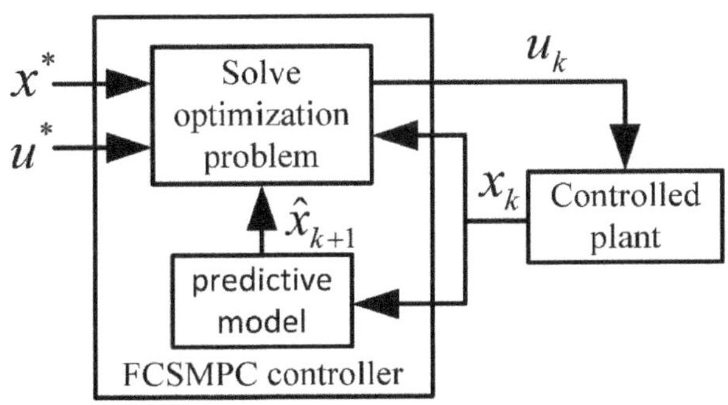

Figure 1. Structure of the single-step FCS-MPC system.

The single-step FCS-MPC algorithm can thus be formulated as the following optimization problem:

$$\min_{u_k} J(\varepsilon_k, u_k, u_k{}^*) = \varepsilon_k{}^T Q \varepsilon_k + (u_k - u_k{}^*)^T R (u_k - u_k{}^*) + \hat{\varepsilon}_{k+1}^T P \hat{\varepsilon}_{k+1} \tag{8}$$

subject to the following:

(1) The dynamic Equation (6);

(2) The state constraint (2) and the discrete control constraints (3).

Let the solution to the above optimization problem be denoted by $u^{opt}(\varepsilon_k, u_k{}^*)$. Then, the closed-loop form of the FCS-MPC system can be expressed as

$$\varepsilon_{k+1} = A\varepsilon_k + B(u^{opt}(\varepsilon_k, u_k{}^*) - u_k{}^*). \tag{9}$$

According to Refs. [17,24], $u^{opt}(\varepsilon_k, u_k{}^*)$ is a piecewise function. Depending on the number of candidate inputs in the control set, the number of segments can be extremely large, making direct analysis of system (9) challenging.

Given that the control input is constrained to a finite set, if the state region under investigation is bounded such that all admissible inputs selected from the control set cannot drive the system state outside the constraint set, the state constraints can be neglected. Consequently, we consider the optimal control law without state constraints, which will be derived below.

Equation (7) can be transformed into the following form:

$$J(\varepsilon_k, u_k, u_k^*) = (H^{1/2}u_k - H^{1/2}(K\varepsilon_k + u_k^*))^T (H^{1/2}u_k - H^{1/2}(K\varepsilon_k + u_k^*)) + d(\varepsilon_k), \quad (10)$$

where $H = R + B^T PB$, $K = -H^{-1}B^T PA$ and $d(x_k) = \varepsilon_k{}^T(Q + A^T PA - K^T HK)\varepsilon_k$. The optimal control vector without state constraints can be expressed as [15,16]

$$u_k{}^{of} = K\varepsilon_k + u_k{}^* + H^{-1/2}w(\varepsilon_k, u_k{}^*) \quad (11)$$

where $w(\varepsilon_k, u_k{}^*) = (q_{\mathbb{V}}(H^{1/2}(K\varepsilon_k + u_k{}^*)) - H^{1/2}(K\varepsilon_k + u_k{}^*))$, $\mathbb{V} = H^{1/2}\mathcal{U}$, $q_{\mathbb{V}}(\ )$ denotes the Euclidean quantifier, which is defined as follows.

Definition 1 [Euclidean Vector Quantizer]. *Consider a set $A \subseteq R^n$ and a countable (not necessarily finite) set $B \triangleq \{b_i\} \subset \mathbb{R}^n$, $i \in I \subseteq \mathbb{Z}_{\geq 0}$, which satisfies that $\exists \varepsilon > 0 : |b_i - b_j| \geq \varepsilon, \forall i,j \in I$. If function $q_B(\cdot) : A \to B$ satisfies that $q_B(a) = b_i \in B$, where $|a - b_i| \leq |a - b_j|$, hold for $\forall b_j \neq b_i$; then, $q_B(\cdot)$ is a Euclidean vector quantizer.*

2.3. Closed-Loop System Model in Positively Invariant Set

If there exists an invariant set of system (6) with respect to the control law (11), and this set lies within the state constraint set $\mathcal{X}$, then (11) represents the optimal solution to the optimization problem (8) within this invariant set. Consequently, the closed-loop form of system (9) can be established for further analysis. To compute this invariant set in the following discussion, the controlled system is assumed to satisfy the following condition.

Assumption 1. *There exists a feedback control law $\widetilde{K} \in \mathbb{R}^{m\times n}$, as well as a symmetric positive definite matrix $Q_P \in \mathbb{R}^{n\times n}$, such that the matrices P and R in the cost function (7) satisfy the following relationship:*

$$P = (A + B\widetilde{K})^T P(A + B\widetilde{K}) + (Q_P + \widetilde{K}^T R\widetilde{K}). \quad (12)$$

This assumption is not overly restrictive, as it can be satisfied whenever system (1) is stabilizable.

If **Assumption 1** holds, the following properties of the system matrices can be derived, which are essential in the subsequent analysis. It is straightforward to obtain

$$P - Q = (A + B\widetilde{K})^T P(A + B\widetilde{K}) + \widetilde{K}^T R\widetilde{K}. \quad (13)$$

This implies that $(P - Q)$ is positive definite, and hence

$$\lambda_{\max}(P) - \lambda_{\min}(Q) > 0, \quad (14)$$

Furthermore, similar to the derivation of (10), we have

$$A^T PA - P + Q - K^T HK = -(\widetilde{K} - K)^T H(\widetilde{K} - K), \quad (15)$$

which implies that $(A^T PA - P + Q - K^T HK)$ is negative semidefinite.

Based on (10) and (15), for the unconstrained optimal control law (11) applied to system (6), we derive

$$f(\varepsilon, u^{of}, u^*)^T Pf(\varepsilon, u^{of}, u^*) - \varepsilon^T P\varepsilon \leq -\varepsilon^T Q\varepsilon - (u^{of} - u^*)^T R(u^{of} - u^*) + |w|^2 \quad (16)$$

and therefore, the set $\Xi \triangleq \{\varepsilon | \varepsilon^T P\varepsilon \leq d, d \in \mathbb{R}_{>0}\}$ is a candidate invariant set.

To determine the conditions under which Ξ becomes invariant, we analyze the boundedness of $|w(\varepsilon_k, u_k{}^*)|$ over $\Xi \times \mathcal{U}^*$. Its upper bound can be computed as follows:

(1) Compute the set $U_h(u_k{}^*)$:

Define

$$U_h(u_k{}^*) \triangleq \left\{ H^{1/2}K\varepsilon_k + H^{1/2}u_k{}^* \middle| \varepsilon_k \in \Xi \right\} \tag{17}$$

Let $u_h = H^{1/2}K\varepsilon_k + H^{1/2}u_k{}^*$. Since $H^{1/2}K \in \mathbb{R}^{m\times n}$, by augmenting it with $n-m$ linearly independent row vectors $\widetilde{k}_1, \ldots, \widetilde{k}_{n-m}$, we obtain a nonsingular matrix:

$$\widetilde{K}_h \triangleq \left[H^{1/2}K; \widetilde{k}_1; \ldots; \widetilde{k}_{n-m} \right] \tag{18}$$

Then, we have

$$\widetilde{U}_h^* \triangleq \left\{ \widetilde{u}_h^* | \widetilde{u}_h^{*T} (\widetilde{K}_h^{-1})^T P \widetilde{K}_h^{-1} \widetilde{u}_h^* \le d \right\}, \tag{19}$$

where $\widetilde{u}_h^* = [u_h{}^*; \widetilde{u}_1; \ldots; \widetilde{u}_{n-m}]$, $u_h{}^* = u_h - H^{1/2}u_k{}^*$, and $\widetilde{u}_1, \ldots, \widetilde{u}_{n-m}$ are auxiliary variables to be eliminated.

Let

$$\widetilde{f}_h(\widetilde{u}_h^*) \triangleq \widetilde{u}_h^{*T} (\widetilde{K}^{-1})^T P \widetilde{K}^{-1} \widetilde{u}_h^*, \tag{20}$$

and by setting the partial derivatives of $\widetilde{f}_h(\widetilde{u}_h)$ with respect to the auxiliary variables to zero and solving the resulting equations, we obtain

$$[\widetilde{u}_1; \ldots; \widetilde{u}_{n-m}]^T = \widetilde{A} u_h{}^*. \tag{21}$$

Substituting $\widetilde{u}_h^* = \left[I; \widetilde{A} \right] u_h{}^*$ into the inequality $\widetilde{f}_h(\widetilde{u}_h) \le d$ leads to

$$U_h{}^* \triangleq \left\{ u_h{}^* | u_h{}^{*T} \begin{bmatrix} I \\ \widetilde{A} \end{bmatrix}^T (\widetilde{K}^{-1})^T P \widetilde{K}^{-1} \begin{bmatrix} I \\ \widetilde{A} \end{bmatrix} u_h{}^* \le d \right\}. \tag{22}$$

As illustrated in Figure 2, this set is the projection of $\widetilde{U}_h^*$ onto the m-dimensional hyperplane where $u_h{}^*$ resides.

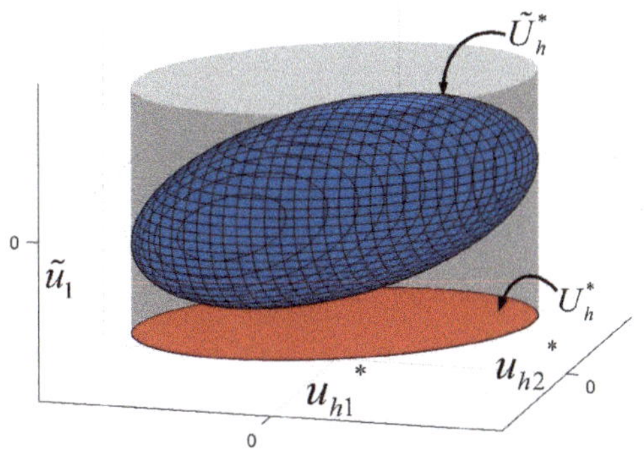

Figure 2. Illustration for relationship between $\widetilde{U}_h^*$ and $U_h{}^*$ with $n = 3, m = 2$.

Thus,

$$U_h(u_k{}^*) \triangleq \left\{ u_h | (u_h - H^{1/2}u_k{}^*)^T \begin{bmatrix} I \\ \widetilde{A} \end{bmatrix}^T (\widetilde{K}^{-1})^T P \widetilde{K}^{-1} \begin{bmatrix} I \\ \widetilde{A} \end{bmatrix} (u_h - H^{1/2}u_k{}^*) \le d \right\}. \tag{23}$$

As shown in Figure 3, for each $u_k{}^*$, $\mathcal{U}_h$ is obtained by translating $\mathcal{U}_h{}^*$ in the hyperplane.

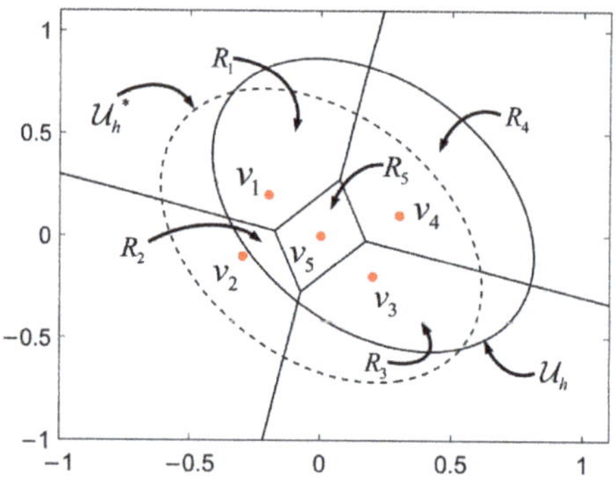

Figure 3. Illustration for relationship between U_h and $U_h{}^*$, and the optimal space R_i corresponding to each discrete control vector with $m = 2$, $p = 5$. The solid and dashed ellipses correspond to U_h and $U_h{}^*$, respectively.

(2) Calculate the upper bound of $|w(\varepsilon_k, u_k{}^*)|$ on $\Xi \times \mathcal{U}^*$:

For each discrete control value $v_i \in H^{1/2}\mathcal{U}$, define the region [17]:

$$\begin{aligned} \widetilde{R}_i &\triangleq \left\{ x \middle| (v_i - x)^T (v_i - x) \le (v_j - x)^T (v_j - x), j \ne i \right\} \\ &= \left\{ x | 2({v_j}^T - {v_i}^T)x \le {v_j}^T v_j - {v_i}^T v_i, j \ne i \right\} \end{aligned}, \tag{24}$$

so that $q_{\mathbb{V}}(x) = v_i$ for $x \in \widetilde{R}_i$.

Define

$$R_i(u_k{}^*) = \widetilde{R}_i \cap U_h(u_k{}^*). \tag{25}$$

For each fixed $u_k{}^* \in \mathcal{U}^*$, solving the optimization problem

$$\max_{x \in R_i(u_k{}^*)} f_w(x) = (v_i - x)^T (v_i - x) \tag{26}$$

over all regions $R_i(u_k{}^*)$ yields the upper bound of $|w(\varepsilon_k, u_k{}^*)|$ over $\Xi \times \mathcal{U}^*$, denoted as

$$\Delta q \triangleq \max_{\varepsilon \in \Xi, u_k{}^* \in \mathcal{U}^*} \left| q_{\mathbb{V}}(H^{1/2}(K\varepsilon_k + u_k{}^*)) - H^{1/2}(K\varepsilon_k + u_k{}^*) \right|. \tag{27}$$

As shown in Figure 3, for each fixed $u_k{}^*$, (26) is a quadratic optimization problem with linear and quadratic inequality constraints, which can be solved using standard optimization tools.

Assumption 2. *Suppose that there exists a constant d, such that $d > \frac{\Delta q^2 \lambda_{max}(P)}{\lambda_{min}(Q)}$, and for all $\varepsilon \in \Xi$, the corresponding state $x \in \mathcal{X}$.*

If **Assumption 2** holds, then from (14) and (16), for any $\varepsilon \in \Xi$ $u_k{}^* \in \mathcal{U}^*$, we have

$$f(\varepsilon, \hat{u}^{of}(\varepsilon, u^*), u^*)^T P f(\varepsilon, \hat{u}^{of}(\varepsilon, u^*), u^*) < d. \tag{28}$$

Hence, Ξ is an invariant set of system (6) with respect to (11). When $x_k \in \Xi$ and $u_k{}^* \in \mathcal{U}^*$, the solution of (8) is

$$u^{opt}(x_k) = u^{of}(x_k) = K\varepsilon_k + u_k{}^* + H^{-1/2} w(\varepsilon_k, u_k{}^*). \tag{29}$$

By treating $w(\varepsilon_k, u_k{}^*)$ as a disturbance and denoting it as w_k, we have

$$w_k \in \{x||x| \le \Delta q\},\ \forall k \in \mathbb{Z}_{\ge 0}, \tag{30}$$

And

$$||\mathbf{w}|| = \Delta q. \tag{31}$$

Thus, the closed-loop system (9) on the set Ξ becomes

$$\varepsilon_{k+1} = F(\varepsilon_k, w_k) = A\varepsilon_k + B(K\varepsilon_k + H^{-1/2}w_k). \tag{32}$$

3. Regional ISS Theory

ISS theory is an important tool to analyze the relationship between state trajectories and inputs of nonlinear systems. This concept was first proposed in [25] and has since been extended in various directions by subsequent researchers. In practical model predictive control (MPC) applications, state and input constraints are typically present, rendering global ISS results less applicable. To address this limitation, a regional version of ISS was proposed in [26], which allows for stability analysis within a restricted domain. This concept makes it feasible to apply ISS theory to constrained MPC systems. To characterize the stability properties of the FCS-MPC system studied in this paper, we adopt the definition of regional ISS presented in [27]:

Consider a discrete-time autonomous system of the following form:

$$x_{k+1} = F(x_k, w_k),\ k \in \mathbb{Z}_{\ge 0}, \tag{33}$$

where $x_k \in \mathbb{R}^n$ is the state, $w_k \in \mathbb{R}^q$ represents an unknown disturbance, and the transition map $F(x_k, w_k)$ may be discontinuous. Given an initial state $\overline{x}$ and a disturbance sequence $\mathbf{w}$, the state trajectory of the system is denoted as $x(k, \overline{x}, \mathbf{w})$.

Assumption 3.

(1) *For system (33), the origin is an equilibrium point.*

(2) *The disturbance w_k satisfies $w_k \in W$ for $\forall k \in \mathbb{Z}_{\ge 0}$, where W is a compact set containing the origin.*

Definition 2 [Robust Positively Invariant Set (RPIS)]. *Suppose that* **Assumption 3** *holds; $\Xi \subseteq \mathbb{R}^n$ is an RPIS for system (33) if $F(x, w) \in \Xi$ holds for $\forall w \in W$ and $\forall x \in \Xi$.*

Definition 3 [Regional Input-to-State Stability (ISS)]. *Suppose that* **Assumption 3** *is satisfied. Given a compact set $\Xi \subseteq \mathbb{R}^n$ containing the origin as an interior point, if Ξ is an RPIS for system (33), and there exists a $\mathcal{K}_\mathcal{L}$-function β and a $\mathcal{K}$-function γ , such that*

$$|x(k, \overline{x}, w)| \le \beta(|\overline{x}|, k) + \gamma(||\mathbf{w}||), \forall k \ge 0, \forall \overline{x} \in \Xi. \tag{34}$$

Then the system (33) is said to be regional ISS with $\mathbf{w} \in \mathcal{M}_W$ in Ξ.

4. Analysis of System Stability and Performance

If **Assumption 1** and **Assumption 2** hold, then system (9) can be represented by (32) within the set Ξ. Moreover, system (32) satisfies **Assumption 3**, and Ξ is an RPIS for (32). The following proof establishes the ISS property of system (32) in Ξ.

4.1. ISS Proof

Theorem 1. *Suppose that **Assumption 1** and **Assumption 2** hold; then, system (32) is ISS in Ξ with respect to the disturbance sequence $w \in \mathcal{M}_W$.*

Proof of Theorem 1. To facilitate the proof, we define several parameters and functions. Let $a_1 = \lambda_{\min}(P)$, $a_2 = \lambda_{\max}(P)$, $a_3 = \lambda_{\min}(Q)$, $a_4 = a_3 a_2{}^{-1}$, $a_5 = a_2 a_3{}^{-1} b^{-1}$,

$$V(\varepsilon) \triangleq \varepsilon^T P \varepsilon, \tag{35}$$

$$\Theta \triangleq \left\{\varepsilon \middle| V(\varepsilon) \leq a_5 ||\mathbf{w}||^2 \right\}, \mathbf{w} \in \mathcal{M}_W, \tag{36}$$

where $b \in \mathbb{R}_{(0,1]}$. Using these definitions, the set Ξ can be rewritten as

$$\Xi \triangleq \{\varepsilon : V(\varepsilon) \leq d\}. \tag{37}$$

It is straightforward to obtain

$$V(\varepsilon_k) \geq a_1 |\varepsilon_k|^2, \forall \varepsilon_k \in \Xi, \tag{38}$$

$$V(\varepsilon_k) \leq a_2 |\varepsilon_k|^2, \forall \varepsilon_k \in \Xi. \tag{39}$$

From inequality (16), we know that

$$\Delta V(\varepsilon_k) = \varepsilon_{k+1}{}^T P \varepsilon_{k+1} - \varepsilon_k{}^T P \varepsilon_k \leq -a_3 |\varepsilon_k|^2 + |w_k|^2, \forall \varepsilon_k \in \Xi \tag{40}$$

By **Assumption 2**, there exists a constant $b \in \mathbb{R}_{(0,1]}$ such that $a_5 \Delta q < d$, and thus $\Theta \subset \Xi$. If $x_k \in \Theta$, from (39), (40), and (14), we obtain

$$V(\varepsilon_{k+1}) \leq (1 - a_4) V(\varepsilon_k) + ||\mathbf{w}||^2 \leq a_5 ||\mathbf{w}||^2. \tag{41}$$

which implies that $\varepsilon_{k+1} \in \Theta$. Therefore, once the state trajectory enters Θ, it remains inside.

If $\varepsilon_k \in \Xi \backslash \Theta$, from (39) and (40), it follows that there exists a constant $c > 0$ such that

$$\Delta V(\varepsilon_k) \leq -a_4 V(\varepsilon_k) + ||\mathbf{w}||^2 \leq -c. \tag{42}$$

As Ξ is an RPIS containing the origin as an interior point for system (32), and $V(\varepsilon)$ is upper bounded on Ξ, for any initial condition $\bar{\varepsilon} \in \Xi$, there exists a finite time index

$$j_0 = \min\{k \in \mathbb{Z}_{\geq 0} : \varepsilon(k, \bar{\varepsilon}, w) \in \Theta\} \tag{43}$$

For $k < j_0$, we must have $V(\varepsilon(k, \bar{\varepsilon}, \mathbf{w})) > a_5 ||\mathbf{w}||^2$. From (39) and (40), it follows that

$$V(\varepsilon(k, \bar{\varepsilon}, \mathbf{w})) \leq (1 - (1-b) a_4) V(\varepsilon(k-1, \bar{\varepsilon}, \mathbf{w})), \tag{44}$$

and iteratively

$$V(\varepsilon(k, \bar{\varepsilon}, \mathbf{w})) \leq (1 - (1-b) a_4)^k V(\bar{\varepsilon}). \tag{45}$$

Thus, we have

$$V(\varepsilon(k, \bar{\varepsilon}, \mathbf{w})) \leq \max\left\{\beta_a(V(\bar{\varepsilon}), k), a_5 ||\mathbf{w}||^2 \right\}, \bar{\varepsilon} \in \Xi, k \in \mathbb{Z}_{\geq 0}, \tag{46}$$

where $\beta_a(\varepsilon, r) = (1 - (1-b) a_4)^r \varepsilon$, which is a $\mathcal{K}_{\mathcal{L}}$-function.

From inequality (38), it follows that

$$|\varepsilon(k,\bar{\varepsilon},\mathbf{w})| \leq \max\left\{\sqrt{a_1{}^{-1}\beta_a(a_2|\bar{\varepsilon}|^2,k)}, \sqrt{a_1{}^{-1}a_5||\mathbf{w}||^2}\right\}, \bar{\varepsilon} \in \Xi, k \in \mathbb{Z}_{\geq 0}. \tag{47}$$

Finally, define

$$\beta(\varepsilon,r) = \sqrt{a_1{}^{-1}\beta_a(a_2|\varepsilon|^2,r)}, \tag{48}$$

$$\gamma(\varepsilon) \triangleq \sqrt{a_1{}^{-1}a_5\varepsilon^2}. \tag{49}$$

It can be verified that $\beta(\varepsilon,s)$ is a $\mathcal{K}_{\mathcal{L}}$-function and $\gamma(\varepsilon)$ is a $\mathcal{K}$-function. Therefore, the system (32) is ISS in Ξ with respect to the disturbance sequence $\mathbf{w} \in \mathcal{M}_W$. □

4.2. Performance Estimation

This section presents a computational procedure for estimating the domain of attraction and the ultimate bounded region of the system state trajectories, based on the results established in Sections 2.3 and 4.1. In Section 5.1, the proposed method will be illustrated through simulation examples, where we demonstrate the relationship between the domain of attraction and system stability, as well as between the ultimate bounded region and steady-state performance.

According to inequality (46), the state trajectories originating from Ξ will asymptotically approach and eventually enter the set Θ. Specifically, we have

$$\lim_{k\to\infty} \varepsilon(k,\bar{\varepsilon},\mathbf{w})^T P \varepsilon(k,\bar{\varepsilon},\mathbf{w}) \leq a_5 \Delta q^2, \forall \overline{x} \in \Xi. \tag{50}$$

Once the state trajectory enters Θ, the feasible set of optimal control values changes, leading to a corresponding update in Δq. If the new value of Δq recalculated over Θ still satisfies **Assumption 2**, then ISS analysis can be iteratively applied on the newly defined region Θ. This process can continue until **Assumption 2** is no longer satisfied.

Based on this idea, the following iterative algorithm (Algorithm 1) is proposed for estimating the domain of attraction and the ultimate bounded region of system (9):

Algorithm 1 Calculation of Domain of Attraction and Ultimate Bounded Region

Input the parameters d, a_4 and the number of iterations n. Let $d_{MPC} = d$.
Extend $H^{1/2}K \in \mathbb{R}^{m\times n}$ to obtain $\widetilde{K}_h \in \mathbb{R}^{n\times n}$.
Set the partial derivative of Equation (20) with respect to the auxiliary control variable to zero, and solve the system of equations to obtain Equation (21).
Obtain $U_h(u_k{}^*)$ according to Equation (23).
for i = 1: n
    For each $u_k{}^*$ in $\mathcal{U}^*$, partition $U_h(u_k{}^*)$ into $R_i(u_k{}^*)$ according to (25).
    Use the optimization tool to calculate the maximum value of $|w(\varepsilon_k, u_k{}^*)|$ on all $R_i(u_k{}^*)$and record it in Δq.
    if $d > a_4{}^{-1}\Delta q$
        $d = a_4{}^{-1}\Delta q$
    else
        Record the value of d that last satisfies $d > a_4{}^{-1}\Delta q$ as d_f.
        Break the loop.
    end if
end for
if i = 1
    The system is unstable on $\mathcal{X}_{MPC}$.
else
    The system is stable on $\mathcal{X}_{MPC}$ and ultimately converges to Θ_f.
end if

Then, the domain of attraction and the ultimate bounded region of system (9) can be expressed as

$$\mathcal{X}_{MPC} = \left\{ \varepsilon | \varepsilon^T P \varepsilon \leq d_{MPC} \right\}, \tag{51}$$

$$\Theta_f = \left\{ \varepsilon | \varepsilon^T P \varepsilon \leq d_f \right\}. \tag{52}$$

Remark 1. *The number of iterations n is introduced to limit the computational time. By setting a maximum number of iterations within an acceptable range, a more accurate estimate of the ultimate bounded region Θ_f can be obtained without excessive computational burden.*

Remark 2. *According to [28], it is generally permissible for the state to temporarily exceed the constraint limits. This is because, as long as Θ_f is within the state constraint bounds, the state trajectory will quickly converge back within the state constraints.*

5. Simulation Experiment

Two models are considered in this section. The first is an open-loop unstable mathematical model with a fixed reference value, and the second is a three-phase inverter simulation model with a periodic reference signal. In both cases, the controller parameters are designed based on the procedures described in the previous sections. The stability and performance of the system are then analyzed, and the accuracy of the theoretical analysis is verified through simulations.

5.1. Illustrative Mathematical Example

The plant model is defined as

$$A = \begin{bmatrix} 0.2 & 0 \\ 0.2 & 1.1 \end{bmatrix}, B = \begin{bmatrix} 0.3 & 0.4 \\ 0.5 & 0.2 \end{bmatrix};$$

The state constraint set and the finite control set are

$$\mathcal{X} = \left\{ x : \begin{bmatrix} 1 & -1 & 0 & 0 \\ 0 & 0 & 1 & -1 \end{bmatrix}^T x \leq \begin{bmatrix} 3.8 & -0.2 & 3.2 & -0.4 \end{bmatrix}^T \right\}, \tag{53}$$

$$\mathcal{U} = \left\{ \begin{bmatrix} -3.6361 \\ 7.0134 \end{bmatrix}, \begin{bmatrix} -4.3848 \\ 7.3378 \end{bmatrix}, \begin{bmatrix} -3.5010 \\ 6.5765 \end{bmatrix}, \begin{bmatrix} -4.2496 \\ 6.9009 \end{bmatrix} \right\}, \tag{54}$$

The weighting matrices are

$$Q = \begin{bmatrix} 1 & 0 \\ 0 & 1 \end{bmatrix}, R = \begin{bmatrix} 0.1 & 0 \\ 0 & 0.1 \end{bmatrix}, P = \begin{bmatrix} 1.0138 & 0.0374 \\ 0.0374 & 1.5926 \end{bmatrix},$$

where P is obtained by solving the discrete Riccati equation. The reference state is $x^* = \begin{bmatrix} 2 & 1.8 \end{bmatrix}^T$, and the corresponding steady-state control is $u^* = \begin{bmatrix} -3.9429 & 6.9571 \end{bmatrix}^T$.

Using **Algorithm 1**, the domain of attraction and ultimate bounded region are calculated as shown in Figure 4.

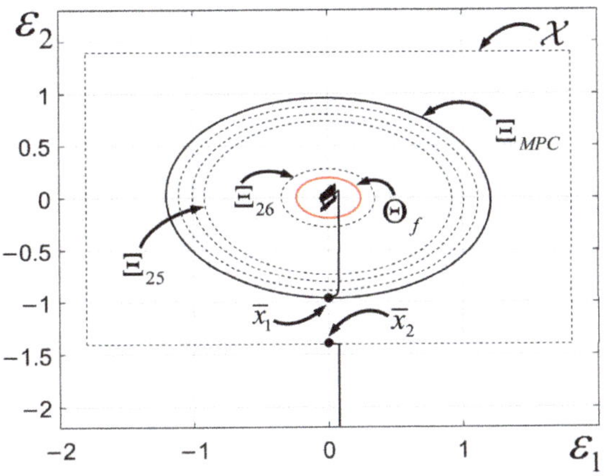

Figure 4. Calculation results of the system's domain of attraction and convergence region, and the state error trajectories. ε_1, ε_2 represent the two components of the error vector ε. The black solid circle represents the domain of attraction, and the red circle indicates the convergence region. The black dashed circles illustrate the intermediate iterations in **Algorithm 1**, and the black dashed box denotes the imposed state constraints.

$$\Xi_{MPC} = \left\{ \varepsilon | \varepsilon^T P \varepsilon \leq 1.47 \right\}, \tag{55}$$

and after 30 iterations, the estimated ultimate bounded region becomes

$$\Theta_f = \left\{ \varepsilon | \varepsilon^T P \varepsilon \leq 0.0585 \right\}. \tag{56}$$

From the discussion in Section 4.1, it can be concluded that the domain of attraction represents the region within which the system stability is guaranteed. If the initial state error belongs to Ξ_{MPC}, the error trajectory will converge to Θ_f and remain within Ξ_{MPC} in this process. Otherwise, it may diverge.

For example, with initial error $\overline{x}_1 = \begin{bmatrix} 2 & 0.8393 \end{bmatrix}^T$, the trajectory converges to Θ_f. However, for $\overline{x}_2 = \begin{bmatrix} 2 & 0.41 \end{bmatrix}^T$, the system diverges, as shown in Figures 4 and 5, verifying the regional ISS property.

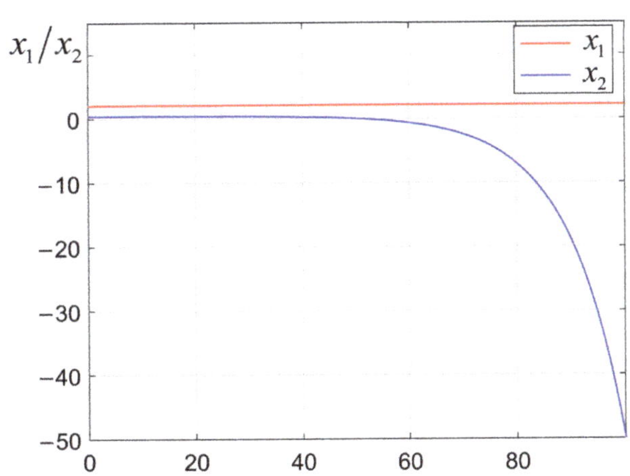

Figure 5. System state trajectories starting from $\overline{x}_2 = \begin{bmatrix} 2 & 0.41 \end{bmatrix}^T$.

According to the definition of Θ_f, the Euclidean norm of the steady-state error satisfies

$$\lim_{k\to\infty} |\varepsilon(k,\bar{\varepsilon},\mathbf{w})| \leq \sqrt{d_f/\lambda_{\min}(P)} = 0.2405. \tag{57}$$

Therefore, the size of ultimate bounded region represents the steady-state error of the system. The norm of the state error starting from $\bar{x}_1$ is shown in Figure 6. As shown in Figure 6, this bound aligns with simulation results. The state waveform is illustrated in Figure 7.

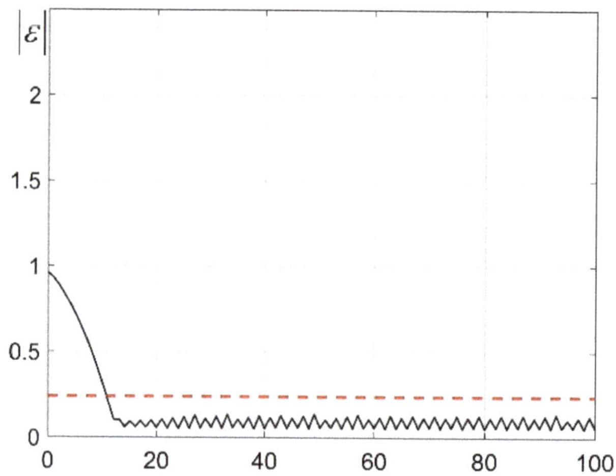

Figure 6. Estimated performance results and norm of state error starting from $\bar{x}_1$. The black solid line represents the Euclidean norm of the state error trajectory starting from $\bar{x}_1$, and the red dashed line indicates the estimated upper bound of the steady-state error norm.

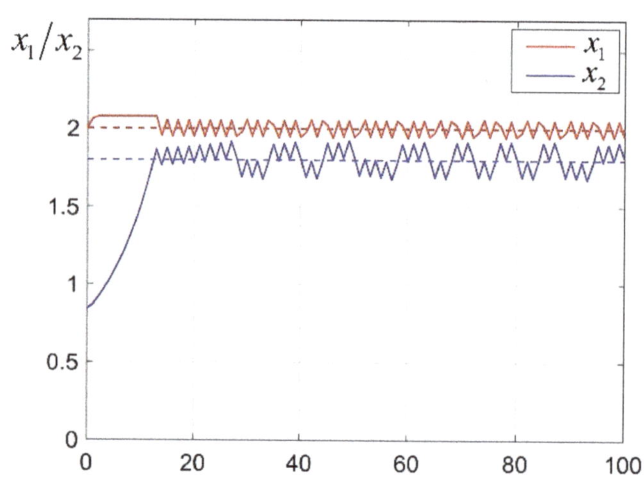

Figure 7. System state waveform starting from $\bar{x}_1$. The red and blue dashed lines indicate the reference values of x_1 and x_2.

5.2. Two-Level Inverter Simulation Model

The circuit is shown in Figure 8, with parameters $V_{dc} = 80$ V, $r = 5\ \Omega$ and $L = 17$ mH.

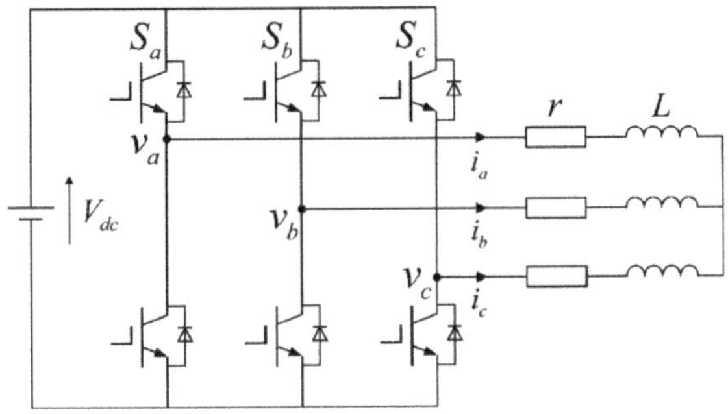

Figure 8. Two-level inverter topology. The arrows indicate the reference directions of phase currents i_a, i_b and i_c.

In the two-phase rotating coordinate system, the continuous-time model is

$$\begin{bmatrix} \frac{di_\alpha}{dt} & \frac{di_\beta}{dt} \end{bmatrix}^T = A_c \begin{bmatrix} i_\alpha & i_\beta \end{bmatrix}^T + B_c \begin{bmatrix} u_\alpha & u_\beta \end{bmatrix}^T, \tag{58}$$

where

$$A_c = \begin{bmatrix} -\frac{r}{L} & 0 \\ 0 & -\frac{r}{L} \end{bmatrix}, B_c = \begin{bmatrix} \frac{1}{L} & 0 \\ 0 & \frac{1}{L} \end{bmatrix}.$$

Using zero-order hold with sampling time $T = 75\ \mu s$, we discretize the system

$$A = e^{A_c T}, \tag{59}$$

$$B = (e^{A_c T} - I)A_c^{-1} B_c. \tag{60}$$

Based on the circuit structure, the finite control set can be represented as

$$\mathcal{U} = U_{dc} \left\{ \begin{bmatrix} 0 \\ 0 \end{bmatrix}, \begin{bmatrix} -1/3 \\ -1/\sqrt{3} \end{bmatrix}, \begin{bmatrix} -1/3 \\ 1/\sqrt{3} \end{bmatrix}, \begin{bmatrix} -2/3 \\ 0 \end{bmatrix}, \begin{bmatrix} 2/3 \\ 0 \end{bmatrix}, \begin{bmatrix} 1/3 \\ -1/\sqrt{3} \end{bmatrix}, \begin{bmatrix} 1/3 \\ 1/\sqrt{3} \end{bmatrix}, \begin{bmatrix} 0 \\ 0 \end{bmatrix} \right\}. \tag{61}$$

To simplify analysis, the state constraints are rewritten in terms of error

$$\mathcal{X} = \left\{ x \middle| \begin{bmatrix} 1 & -1 & 0 & 0 \\ 0 & 0 & 1 & -1 \end{bmatrix}^T \varepsilon \leq \begin{bmatrix} 5.5 & 5.5 & 5.5 & 5.5 \end{bmatrix}^T \right\}, \tag{62}$$

which indicates that the state variables do not exceed a certain range from the reference value.

The cost matrices are

$$Q = \begin{bmatrix} 1 & 0 \\ 0 & 1 \end{bmatrix}, R = \begin{bmatrix} 0.001 & 0 \\ 0 & 0.001 \end{bmatrix}, P = \begin{bmatrix} 5.1165 & 0 \\ 0 & 5.1165 \end{bmatrix}$$

where P is obtained by solving the discrete Riccati equation. The reference is $x_k{}^* = \begin{bmatrix} 5\cos(100\pi kT) & 5\sin(100\pi kT) \end{bmatrix}^T$, and the steady-state control is $u_k{}^* = B^{-1}(x_{k+1}{}^* - Ax_k{}^*)$.

Using **Algorithm 1**, as shown in Figure 9, we obtain the following:

$$\Xi_{MPC} = \left\{ \varepsilon | \varepsilon^T P \varepsilon \leq 64.2328 \right\}. \tag{63}$$

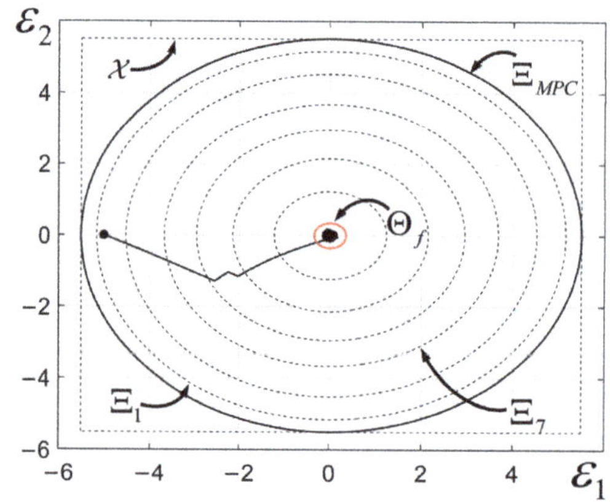

Figure 9. Calculation results of the system's domain of attraction and convergence region, and the state error trajectories. ε_1, ε_2 represent the two components of the error vector ε. The black solid circle represents the domain of attraction, and the red circle indicates the convergence region. The black dashed circles illustrate the intermediate iterations in **Algorithm 1**, and the black dashed box denotes the imposed state constraints.

After iterations,

$$\Theta_f = \left\{ \varepsilon | \varepsilon^T P \varepsilon \leq 0.263 \right\}. \quad (64)$$

For initial value $\overline{x} = \begin{bmatrix} 0 & 0 \end{bmatrix}^T$, the error state trajectory, as shown in Figure 9, converges to Θ_f.

According to the definition of Θ_f, the Euclidean norm of the steady-state error satisfies

$$\lim_{k \to \infty} |\varepsilon(k, \overline{\varepsilon}, \mathbf{w})| \leq 0.3520. \quad (65)$$

as shown in Figure 10, aligning with the performance estimation results. Additionally, the state waveform is illustrated in Figure 11.

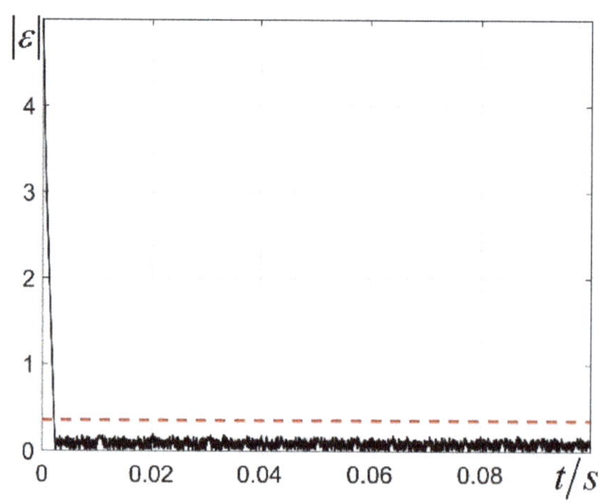

Figure 10. Estimated performance results and norm of state error starting from $\overline{x}$. The black solid line represents the Euclidean norm of the state error trajectory starting from $\overline{x}$, and the red dashed line indicates the estimated upper bound of the steady-state error norm.

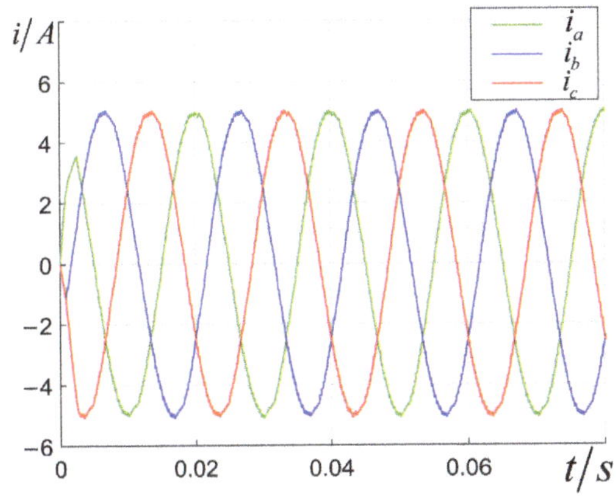

Figure 11. System state trajectories starting from $\overline{x}$.

Through the analysis of the mathematical model and circuit model, the specific calculation process of **Algorithm 1** is elucidated, and the relationship between the domain of attraction and system stability, as well as the relationship between the ultimate bounded region and steady-state performance of the system, is shown. Additionally, the results of the analysis have been validated, proving the effectiveness of the analysis method and its applicability to a class of power electronic converters.

6. Conclusions

In this paper, we first conducted a detailed analysis of the closed-loop model of the single-step FCS-MPC system. Based on the relevant concepts of regional input-to-state stability (ISS) theory, we derived sufficient conditions to ensure the regional ISS of the system, established the relationship between quantization error and system performance, and provided a complete theoretical derivation and proof. On this basis, an iterative algorithm was proposed for estimating the system's domain of attraction and ultimate bounded region. Finally, simulation experiments were carried out to verify the correctness of the theoretical analysis, which also demonstrated the relationship between the domain of attraction and system stability, as well as between the ultimate bounded region and steady-state performance. The results indicate that appropriate parameter design can provide stability assurance for the system, and the proposed method enables an intuitive illustration of the stability characteristics and steady-state performance under different parameter settings, thereby offering theoretical guidance for the design of a class of FCS-MPC systems. Compared with existing studies, this paper presents a more general quantization error calculation method, which extends the analysis from previously studied single-input systems to multi-input systems with state constraints. Furthermore, we provide a complete derivation of the sufficient conditions for ISS under certain conditions, thereby addressing the incomplete theoretical proofs observed in some earlier works within the same analytical framework. In addition, the iterative algorithm proposed in this study serves as an effective tool for exploring the relationship between system parameters and performance, filling a gap in the current research within this framework.

Author Contributions: W.H.: conceptualization, methodology, writing—original draft. L.C.: data curation, formal analysis, writing—review and editing. Z.W.: software, visualization, writing—review and editing. All authors have read and agreed to the published version of the manuscript.

Funding: This research was funded by the National Natural Science Foundation of China (NNSF) (grant no. 62103443) and the Hunan Natural Science Foundation (grant no. 2022JJ40630).

Data Availability Statement: The original contributions of the study are included in the article. Requests for additional information can be directed to the corresponding author.

Conflicts of Interest: The authors declare that no commercial or financial relationships were present during the course of the research that might constitute a potential conflict of interest.

References

1. Rodriguez, J.; Garcia, C.; Mora, A.; Flores-Bahamonde, F.; Acuna, P.; Novak, M.; Zhang, Y.; Tarisciotti, L.; Davari, S.A.; Zhang, Z.; et al. Latest Advances of Model Predictive Control in Electrical Drives—Part I: Basic Concepts and Advanced Strategies. *IEEE Trans. Power Electron.* **2022**, *37*, 3927–3942. [CrossRef]
2. Rodriguez, J.; Garcia, C.; Mora, A.; Davari, S.A.; Rodas, J.; Valencia, D.F.; Elmorshedy, M.; Wang, F.; Zuo, K.; Tarisciotti, L.; et al. Latest Advances of Model Predictive Control in Electrical Drives—Part II: Applications and Benchmarking with Classical Control Methods. *IEEE Trans. Power Electron.* **2022**, *37*, 5047–5061. [CrossRef]
3. Karamanakos, P.; Geyer, T. Guidelines for the Design of Finite Control Set Model Predictive Controllers. *IEEE Trans. Power Electron.* **2020**, *35*, 7434–7450. [CrossRef]
4. Gulbudak, O.; Gokdag, M. Finite Control Set Model Predictive Control Approach of Nine Switch Inverter-Based Drive Systems: Design, Analysis, and Validation. *ISA Trans.* **2021**, *110*, 283–304. [CrossRef] [PubMed]
5. Saberi, S.; Rezaie, B. Robust Adaptive Direct Speed Control of PMSG-Based Airborne Wind Energy System Using FCS-MPC Method. *ISA Trans.* **2022**, *131*, 43–60. [CrossRef] [PubMed]
6. Wu, W.; Wang, D.; Peng, Z.; Liu, X. Model Predictive Direct Power Control for Modular Multilevel Converter under Unbalanced Conditions with Power Compensation and Circulating Current Reduction. *ISA Trans.* **2020**, *106*, 318–329. [CrossRef]
7. Ayala, M.; Doval-Gandoy, J.; Rodas, J.; Gonzalez, O.; Gregor, R. Current Control Designed with Model Based Predictive Control for Six-Phase Motor Drives. *ISA Trans.* **2020**, *98*, 496–504. [CrossRef]
8. Vazquez, S.; Rodriguez, J.; Rivera, M.; Franquelo, L.G.; Norambuena, M. Model Predictive Control for Power Converters and Drives: Advances and Trends. *IEEE Trans. Ind. Electron.* **2017**, *64*, 935–947. [CrossRef]
9. Quevedo, D.E.; Aguilera, R.P.; Geyer, T. Predictive Control in Power Electronics and Drives: Basic Concepts, Theory, and Methods. In *Advanced and Intelligent Control in Power Electronics and Drives*; Orłowska-Kowalska, T., Blaabjerg, F., Rodríguez, J., Eds.; Springer International Publishing: Cham, Switzerland, 2014; pp. 181–226, ISBN 978-3-319-03401-0. [CrossRef]
10. Karamanakos, P.; Liegmann, E.; Geyer, T.; Kennel, R. Model Predictive Control of Power Electronic Systems: Methods, Results, and Challenges. *IEEE Open J. Ind. Appl.* **2020**, *1*, 95–114. [CrossRef]
11. Akter, M.P.; Mekhilef, S.; Mei Lin Tan, N.; Akagi, H. Modified Model Predictive Control of a Bidirectional AC–DC Converter Based on Lyapunov Function for Energy Storage Systems. *IEEE Trans. Ind. Electron.* **2016**, *63*, 704–715. [CrossRef]
12. Makhamreh, H.; Trabelsi, M.; Kükrer, O.; Abu-Rub, H. A Lyapunov-Based Model Predictive Control Design with Reduced Sensors for a PUC7 Rectifier. *IEEE Trans. Ind. Electron.* **2021**, *68*, 1139–1147. [CrossRef]
13. Komurcugil, H.; Guler, N.; Bayhan, S. Weighting Factor Free Lyapunov-Function-Based Model Predictive Control Strategy for Single-Phase T-Type Rectifiers. In Proceedings of the IECON 2020 The 46th Annual Conference of the IEEE Industrial Electronics Society, Singapore, 18–21 October 2020; pp. 4200–4205. [CrossRef]
14. Guler, N.; Komurcugil, H. Energy Function Based Finite Control Set Predictive Control Strategy for Single-Phase Split Source Inverters. *IEEE Trans. Ind. Electron.* **2022**, *69*, 5669–5679. [CrossRef]
15. Quevedo, D.E.; Doná, J.A.D.; Goodwin, G.C. RECEDING HORIZON LINEAR QUADRATIC CONTROL WITH FINITE INPUT CONSTRAINT SETS. *IFAC Proc. Vol.* **2002**, *35*, 183–188. [CrossRef]
16. Quevedo, D.E.; De Dona, J.A.; Goodwin, G.C. On the Dynamics of Receding Horizon Linear Quadratic Finite Alphabet Control Loops. In Proceedings of the 41st IEEE Conference on Decision and Control, 2002, Las Vegas, NV, USA, 10–13 December 2002; Volume 3, pp. 2929–2934. [CrossRef]
17. Quevedo, D.E.; Goodwin, G.C.; De Doná, J.A. Finite Constraint Set Receding Horizon Quadratic Control. *Int. J. Robust Nonlinear Control* **2004**, *14*, 355–377. [CrossRef]
18. Aguilera, R.P.; Quevedo, D.E. On the Stability of MPC with a Finite Input Alphabet. *IFAC Proc. Vol.* **2011**, *44*, 7975–7980. [CrossRef]
19. Aguilera, R.P.; Quevedo, D.E. Stability Analysis of Quadratic MPC with a Discrete Input Alphabet. *IEEE Trans. Autom. Control* **2013**, *58*, 3190–3196. [CrossRef]
20. Aguilera, R.P.; Quevedo, D.E. Predictive Control of Power Converters: Designs with Guaranteed Performance. *IEEE Trans. Ind. Inform.* **2015**, *11*, 53–63. [CrossRef]
21. Xu, D.; Lazar, M. Finite Control Set Model Predictive Control with Limit Cycle Stability Guarantees. *arXiv* **2024**, arXiv:2407.07615. Available online: http://arxiv.org/abs/2407.07615 (accessed on 22 April 2025).

22. Xu, D.; Damsma, S.; Lazar, M. On the Steady-State Behavior of Finite-Control-Set MPC with an Application to High-Precision Power Amplifiers. In Proceedings of the 2022 European Control Conference (ECC), London, UK, 12–15 July 2022; pp. 820–825. Available online: https://ieeexplore.ieee.org/abstract/document/9838191 (accessed on 22 April 2025).
23. Egidio, L.N.; Daiha, H.R.; Deaecto, G.S. Global Asymptotic Stability of Limit Cycle and H2/H∞ Performance of Discrete-Time Switched Affine Systems. *Automatica* **2020**, *116*, 108927. [CrossRef]
24. Bemporad, A.; Morari, M.; Dua, V.; Pistikopoulos, E.N. The Explicit Linear Quadratic Regulator for Constrained Systems. *Automatica* **2002**, *38*, 3–20. [CrossRef]
25. Sontag, E.D. Smooth Stabilization Implies Coprime Factorization. *IEEE Trans. Autom. Control* **1989**, *34*, 435–443. [CrossRef]
26. Nesic, D.; Laila, D.S. A Note on Input-to-State Stabilization for Nonlinear Sampled-Data Systems. *IEEE Trans. Autom. Control* **2002**, *47*, 1153–1158. [CrossRef]
27. Raimondo, D.M. Nonlinear Model Predictive Control: Stability, Robustness and Applications. Ph.D. Thesis, Università degli Studi di Pavia, Pavia, Italy, 2009. Available online: http://sisdin.unipv.it/labsisdin/raimondo/publications.php (accessed on 18 February 2025).
28. Preindl, M. Robust Control Invariant Sets and Lyapunov-Based MPC for IPM Synchronous Motor Drives. *IEEE Trans. Ind. Electron.* **2016**, *63*, 3925–3933. [CrossRef]

Σ mathematics

MDPI

Article

Data-Driven Voltage Control Method of Active Distribution Networks Based on Koopman Operator Theory

Zhaobin Du, Xiaoke Lin *, Guoduan Zhong, Hao Liu and Wenxian Zhao

School of Electric Power Engineering, South China University of Technology, Guangzhou 510641, China; epduzb@scut.edu.cn (Z.D.); epzgd2024@mail.scut.edu.cn (G.Z.); 202420113635@mail.scut.edu.cn (H.L.); epzhouwx@mail.scut.edu.cn (W.Z.)

* Correspondence: 202221015082@mail.scut.edu.cn

Abstract: The advent of large-scale distributed generation (DG) has introduced several challenges to the voltage control of active distribution networks (ADNs). These challenges include the heterogeneity of control devices, the complexity of models, and their inherent fluctuations. To maintain ADN voltage stability more economically and quickly, a data-driven ADN voltage control scheme is proposed in this paper. Firstly, based on the multi-run state sensitivity matrix, buses with similar voltage responses are clustered, and critical buses are selected to downsize the scale of the model. Secondly, a linear voltage-to-power dynamics model in high-dimensional state space is trained based on the offline data of critical bus voltages, DGs, and energy storage system (ESS) outputs, utilizing the Koopman theory and the Extended Dynamic Mode Decomposition (EDMD) method. A linear model predictive voltage controller, which takes ADN stability and control cost into account, is also proposed. Finally, the effectiveness and applicability of the method are verified by applying it to an improved 33-bus ADN system. The proposed control method can respond more quickly and accurately to the voltage fluctuation problems caused by source-load disturbances and short-circuit faults.

Keywords: active distribution networks; voltage control; Koopman operator theory; data-driven; model predictive control; partition

MSC: 37M10

1. Introduction

The vigorous development of DG, such as wind power and photovoltaic power generation, to facilitate the decarbonization of distribution networks is a crucial goal for the development of future energy and power systems [1]. The uncertainty associated with DG may result in more frequent and rapid voltage fluctuations [2], which places higher demands on the performance of the ADN voltage control method.

Currently, most ADN voltage control modes and methods inherit the "hierarchical" control system of the transmission network. The traditional timescales for the action of steady-state ADN voltage control are on the order of minutes and above [3], with the optimal control solutions based on accurate models of each action typically requiring more time to compute [4]. Papers [5,6] propose multi-stage voltage control strategies that integrate resources such as plug-in electric vehicles (PEVs), DGs, and on-load tap changers (OLTC), using predictive or robust control methods to manage voltage regulation under high renewable penetration and uncertainty. Papers [7,8] present coordinated voltage/VAR control methods that utilize multiple devices across different timescales to mitigate voltage fluctuations in high renewable penetration scenarios, incorporating uncertainties in load and generation and leveraging real-time simulations for validation. These approaches focus on voltage control within timescales of minutes or longer. On timescales of milliseconds, ADNs remain vulnerable to risky conditions caused by unforeseen events such as rapid changes in DG outputs and large-capacity load casting [9,10], which in turn lead to unacceptable voltage fluctuations for sensitive users, such as the semiconductor industry [11]. Therefore, faster and more accurate voltage control methods are needed to improve the voltage reliability and safety of ADNs.

Simultaneously, novel types of resources and devices, including DGs and ESS, are being utilized extensively on the ADN, thereby creating a sophisticated operational environment characterized by frequent alterations in device status and topology information [12]. Papers [13,14] propose model predictive control (MPC)-based voltage optimization techniques that coordinate the operation of DGs, OLTC, and capacitor banks to improve voltage regulation and minimize energy loss, while considering uncertainties and various load behaviors in distribution networks. The traditional model-based voltage control methods are confronted with two major challenges: (1) The control method is predicated on the assumption that the precise dynamic models and parameters are known, which is often impractical in real-world applications [15,16]. (2) These models, typically based on offline data, lack the requisite adaptability needed to cope with evolving system dynamics and substantial unpredictability [17].

The recent digitization of ADNs has provided the wide availability of a substantial volume of real-time operational data [18], which encompasses valuable insights such as user behavioral characteristics and system state alterations [19]. Consequently, data-driven control methodologies have attracted considerable attention as a solution to the challenge presented by inadequate precise model parameters. Data-driven control methods for power systems can be classified into two categories, depending on whether the dynamic models are explicitly mapped. Approaches such as Deep Reinforcement Learning (DRL) typically do not necessitate acquiring an analytical dynamics model. In nature, DRL constructs the control method through direct interaction with input data. Paper [17] proposes a novel dual timescale DRL-based voltage control framework for fast control of photovoltaic (PV) inverters in the ADN that does not require a physical model. However, DRL-based methods hardly capture the nonlinear features, and the training process is time-consuming. This makes it difficult to adapt quickly to the rapid state changes of the ADN [11].

Another data-driven approach focuses on linearizing the nonlinear system to derive an approximate linearized model for state prediction and controller design. To illustrate, Floquet theory addresses the time evolution of periodically driven systems [11]. Alternatively, Koopman operator theory provides a promising method for deriving high-dimensional linear approximate models directly from data [20]. The lifting process employs nonlinear basis functions, and an approximation of the original nonlinear dynamics is obtained when the lifted linear dynamical system is projected into the original space [21]. Paper [22] develops a large-signal linear microgrid model using Koopman for voltage control, while paper [23] introduces an online adaptive Koopman operator optimal control (AKOOC) method for secondary voltage and frequency control, demonstrating improved stability and adaptiveness under varying conditions. However, most existing studies concentrate solely on the transient process of the transmission network [24] and microgrid, and have not fully explored the potential of Koopman operator theory in addressing the voltage control challenge in ADNs. Furthermore, their methodologies entail the necessity for comprehensive state measurements, which places considerable demands on the reliability of sensor configurations and communication infrastructure.

The extensive utilization of distributed resources has reduced the efficiency and precision of the traditional centralized voltage control mechanisms in ADNs [13]. The large-scale installation of sensors throughout ADNs presents significant economic and engineering challenges. In contrast, Koopman-based controllers can achieve stable voltage control across the full area with less state-measurement information, provided that the critical buses are selected reasonably [24]. The critical step involves clustering buses with analogous voltage response characteristics into the same partition. The majority of existing studies employ Euclidean distance or cosine similarity to quantify the similarity between two bus sensitivity vectors. Paper [25] uses modified cosine similarity to cluster nodes with similar voltage fluctuations and selects critical measurements from each cluster to reduce measurement requirements while ensuring optimal control. However, Euclidean distance solely measures the straight-line distance between two vectors, neglecting directionality and correlation. Similarly, cosine similarity prioritizes directional similarity between vectors, yet it does not fully utilize magnitude information.

To address the aforementioned issues, this paper presents a novel approach to ADN voltage control, grounded in Koopman operator theory. The main contributions are as follows:

(1) A novel partitioning and critical bus selection method for active distribution networks (ADNs) based on Mahalanobis distance. This method utilizes the local monotonicity and directional characteristics of voltage distribution. The Mahalanobis distance-based partitioning and critical bus selection approach captures both the magnitude and directional sensitivity of voltage-to-power responses. It enables the more precise identification of critical buses while reducing the computational burden on controllers and minimizing the measurement requirements for state estimation.

(2) The rapid construction of a high-dimensional linear state-space model of ADN voltage-to-power dynamics using Koopman operator theory and the Extended Discrete Multivariate Decomposition (EDMD) method. By leveraging partitioning, the system's strong time-domain dependencies, and the fact that voltage control strategies typically do not undergo drastic changes, the Koopman operator efficiently linearizes the system's dynamics. This approach captures the time-varying nonlinear characteristics of voltage changes in ADNs without relying on network topology or parameters during training or voltage control. This model significantly reduces the response time of optimal control strategies, demonstrating strong practical potential for mitigating voltage fluctuations in future power systems.

The remainder of this paper is structured as follows: Section 2 outlines the ADN partitioning and critical bus selection methodology. Section 3 presents a data-driven linearization method for the voltage-to-power dynamics model. Section 4 presents the design of the ADN model predictive voltage controller based on the aforementioned linearized model. Section 5 validates the effectiveness and applicability of the control algorithm based on the improved 33-bus ADN. Section 6 concludes the paper. The framework of the proposed voltage control strategy is depicted in Figure 1.

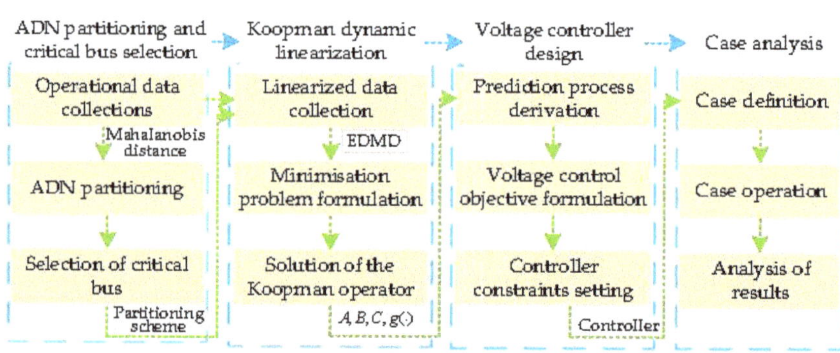

Figure 1. Framework of the proposed voltage control strategy.

2. ADN Partitioning and Critical Bus Selection

The voltage-to-power sensitivity reflects the voltage response characteristics of the buses. In this section, the improved Mahalanobis distance is employed to measure the similarity between bus sensitivity matrices. The Mahalanobis distance accounts for the correlation between variables by incorporating the covariance matrix. This method combines magnitude and direction information, increasing accuracy in high-dimensional space and enhancing the applicability of the analysis of complex systems.

2.1. Similarity Metric Quantization of Bus Voltage Response Characteristics

Taking bus i in an ADN containing N_m buses as example, the similarity between the voltage response characteristics of bus i and the other buses can be quantified using the Mahalanobis distance:

$$d(M_i, M_j) = \sqrt{(M_i - M_j)^T S_{ij}^{-1} (M_i - M_j)} \tag{1}$$

where $d(M_i, M_j)$ denotes the sensitivity similarity between bus i and bus j. M_i and M_j represent the sensitivity matrices of bus i and j, respectively. S_{ij} is the covariance matrix of the sensitivity matrices of bus i and j, indicating the correlation between the sensitivities of the bus:

$$\begin{aligned} S_{ij} &= \frac{1}{N_m \times N_s - 1}(\widetilde{M}_i \widetilde{M}_i^T + \widetilde{M}_j \widetilde{M}_j^T) \\ \widetilde{M}_i &= vec(M_i(n_s) - \mu_i) \\ \widetilde{M}_j &= vec(M_j(n_s) - \mu_j) \\ \mu_i &= \frac{1}{N_m \times N_s} \sum_{n_s=1}^{N_s} \sum_{i=1}^{N_m} M_i(n_s) \\ \mu_j &= \frac{1}{N_m \times N_s} \sum_{n_s=1}^{N_s} \sum_{j=1}^{N_m} M_j(n_s) \end{aligned} \tag{2}$$

where μ_i and μ_j represent the average values of the elements in the similarity matrices M_i and M_j at bus i and j, respectively. N_s denotes the number of typical scenarios. $vec(\cdot)$ refers to a function that converts a matrix into a column vector by stacking its columns sequentially.

The sensitivity matrix M_i for bus i can be derived from a review of historical data or the execution of simulations:

$$\begin{aligned} & M_i = [M_{P,i}\ M_{Q,i}], M_i \in \mathbb{R}^{N_m \times 2N_s} \\ & M_{P,i} = \begin{bmatrix} P_{i,1}(1) & \dots & P_{i,1}(n_s) & \dots & P_{i,1}(N_s) \\ \dots & & \dots & & \dots \\ P_{i,N_m}(1) & \dots & P_{i,N_m}(n_s) & \dots & P_{i,N_m}(N_s) \end{bmatrix} \quad i,j \in \{1,2,\dots,N_m\}, n_s \in \{1,2,\dots,N_s\} \\ & M_{Q,i} = \begin{bmatrix} Q_{i,1}(1) & \dots & Q_{i,1}(n_s) & \dots & Q_{i,1}(N_s) \\ \dots & & \dots & & \dots \\ Q_{i,N_m}(1) & \dots & Q_{i,N_m}(n_s) & \dots & Q_{i,N_m}(N_s) \end{bmatrix} \quad i,j \in \{1,2,\dots,N_m\}, n_s \in \{1,2,\dots,N_s\} \end{aligned} \tag{3}$$

where $P_{i,j}(n_s)$ represents the voltage-active power sensitivity between bus i and j in scene n_s, while the value of $Q_{i,j}(n_s)$ denotes the voltage-reactive power sensitivity:

$$\begin{aligned} P_{i,j}(n_s) &= \Delta U_i(n_s) / \Delta P_j(n_s) \\ Q_{i,j}(n_s) &= \Delta U_i(n_s) / \Delta Q_j(n_s) \end{aligned} \tag{4}$$

2.2. Partitioning and Critical Bus Selection

The number of sets is not a predefined parameter in the division of buses. Once the similarity between the buses has been quantified, the buses whose Mahalanobis distance is below a predefined value σ can be divided into the partitioned set H_n:

$$i,j \in H_n,\ if\ \ d(M_i, M_j) < \sigma \tag{5}$$

Since the number of partitions directly influences the required number of sensors and thus the associated costs, the selection of σ must balance precision and practicality. Moreover, historical partitioning data can provide valuable insights, serving as a reference for setting an appropriate threshold that aligns with prior successful implementations while ensuring system efficiency and cost-effectiveness.

The similarity between the buses within H_n can then be expressed as:

$$\Phi_n = \begin{bmatrix} d(M_i, M_i) & \dots & d(M_i, M_j) \\ \dots & \dots & \dots \\ d(M_j, M_i) & \dots & d(M_j, M_j) \end{bmatrix} i, j \in H_n \tag{6}$$

The critical bus dominant index c_i is defined as follows:

$$c_i = \sum_{b_i=1}^{m} \Phi_n(a_i, b_i), i \in H_n \tag{7}$$

where m represents the number of buses in H_n, while $\Phi_n(a_i, b_i)$ denotes the a_ith column element of the b_ith row of the matrix.

The buses within H_n are ordered according to c_i, with the bus exhibiting the highest index designated as the critical bus.

In existing ADNs, if the historical operational data of each bus are available, the unit voltage-to-power sensitivity matrix can be calculated. If the historical data are insufficient, it can be obtained through an offline power flow calculation based on the state estimation and simulation model of the ADN, or by inverting the Jacobi matrix.

3. Koopman High-Dimensional Dynamic Linearization of ADN Voltage-to-Power Dynamics Models

The voltage control system of an ADN can be conceptualized as a multiple-input multiple-output discrete-time nonlinear dynamical system [26]:

$$\begin{aligned} x(k+1) &= f(x(k), \Delta u(k)) \\ y(k) &= Dx(k) \end{aligned} \tag{8}$$

where $x(k)$ is the system state at time step k. $y(k)$ is the system output and the dimension is the number of critical buses. $\Delta u(k)$ represents the control input change. $f(\cdot)$ is a nonlinear function describing the input–output relationship of the system.

Remark: *While the Koopman operator method does not strictly require the nonlinear function $f(\cdot)$ to satisfy local Lipschitz continuity, such a condition is often desirable to ensure the existence of a well-defined Koopman operator and to facilitate the convergence of numerical approximation methods such as EDMD. Moreover, since the dynamical model $f(\cdot)$ originates from an actual physical system, its nonlinear relationships are typically expected to satisfy local Lipschitz continuity.*

Due to the fact that voltage control strategies in power systems typically do not undergo drastic changes, and that the system's historical states (e.g., previous voltage and power conditions) significantly influence voltage variations, the system can be adjusted in a relatively stable manner, which provide Koopman operator theory with enhanced adaptability. Based on Koopman operator theory [20,26,27], the above model is approximated as the following dynamical model in the form of a high-dimensional linear state space:

$$\begin{aligned} Z(k) &= g(x(k), \Delta u(k)) \\ Z(k+1) &= AZ(k) + B\Delta u(k) \\ x(k) &= CZ(k) \\ y(k) &= Dx(k) \end{aligned} \tag{9}$$

where $Z(k)$ represents the state of the linear dynamical system after lifting, $Z \in R^{N_l}$, N_l is contingent upon the dimensions of nonlinear observation functions. $Z(k+1)$ denotes the state at the $k+1$ predicted from the previous step. $g(\cdot)$ is the observable function. Under the approximation provided by the EDMD method, A, B, and C are all constant linear matrices. The matrices A and B facilitate the prediction of high-dimensional linear state variables comprising control inputs. The C matrix maps the high-dimensional state back to the original low-dimensional state space of the original system. Figure 2 shows a schematic of linearization.

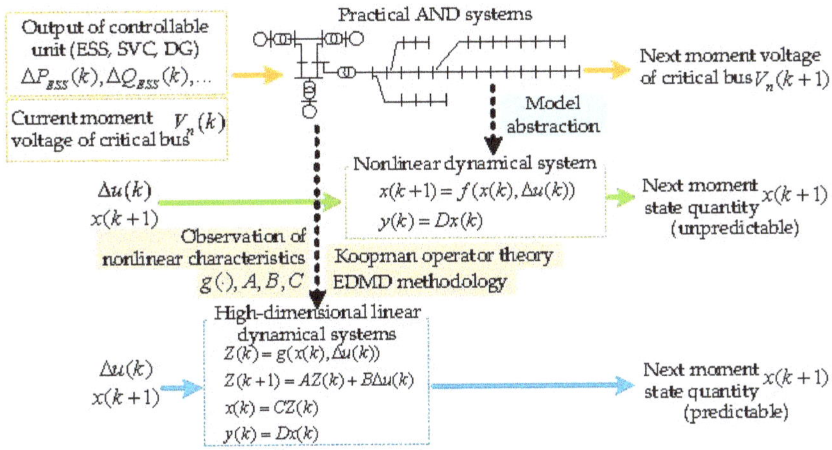

Figure 2. Schematic of linearization of voltage-power dynamics model.

Combine the system state variables $x(k)$ and the control inputs $\Delta u(k)$ into the extended state variables:

$$\chi(k+1) = F(\chi) = \begin{bmatrix} f(x(k), \Delta u(k)) \\ \Delta u(k+1) \end{bmatrix} \tag{10}$$

Then the corresponding Koopman operator $\mathcal{K}$ is defined as:

$$(\mathcal{K}g)(\chi) = g \cdot F(\chi) \tag{11}$$

As $\mathcal{K}$ is infinite-dimensional and cannot be realized in practical control systems, a finite-dimensional approximation $\mathcal{K}_f$ is obtained by EDMD:

$$\begin{gathered} \min_{\mathcal{K}_f} \frac{1}{2} \sum_{k=0}^{N_k-1} \left\| \psi(\chi(k+1)) - \mathcal{K}_f \psi(\chi(k)) \right\|^2 \\ \psi(\chi) = [\psi_1(\chi), \psi_2(\chi), \ldots, \psi_N(\chi), a], a \in R^m \end{gathered} \tag{12}$$

where a is a constant term. N_k represents the total sampling point. $\psi_i(x)$ is the chosen observation function, and the first item of Equation (9) is rewritten as:

$$Z = g(\chi) = [\chi, \psi(\chi)] \tag{13}$$

According to Equation (12), the collected state data $\{x_1, x_2, \ldots, x_p\}$ and control data $\{\Delta u_1, \Delta u_2, \ldots, \Delta u_p\}$ satisfy:

$$\begin{gathered} y_i = f(x_i, \Delta u_i), i = 1, 2, \ldots, p \\ y_i = x_{i+1} \end{gathered} \tag{14}$$

By decomposing the first N_k elements of $\mathcal{K}_f$ as $\overline{\mathcal{K}_f} = [A_k \quad B_k]$, the optimization problem Equation (12) can be transformed into:

$$\min_{\mathcal{K}_f} \frac{1}{2} \sum_{k=0}^{N_k-1} \| \psi(\chi(k+1)) - A_k \psi(\chi(k)) - B_k \Delta u(k) \|^2 \tag{15}$$

Under the given observation function space and dataset, Equation (15) constitutes a convex optimization problem. Solving the above minimization problem yields the A_k and B_k matrices. The matrix C_k can be found using the least squares method:

$$\min_{C_k} \frac{1}{2} \sum_{k=0}^{N_k-1} \|x(k+1) - C_k \psi(x(k))\|^2 \tag{16}$$

4. Voltage Control Scheme Based on Voltage-to-Power High-Dimensional Linearization Model

MPC is a widely utilized linear control method that optimizes current control decisions by predicting future behavior [28]. In the case of nonlinear systems, this can be approximated by utilizing a local linearization method in the vicinity of the equilibrium point, which is then integrated into a linear MPC strategy. However, this approach is typically effective within a limited region around the equilibrium point [29]. For the ADNs with multi-heterogeneous power access, the reliability of relying solely on multi-step model projections to mitigate the inaccuracies introduced by local linearization is significantly limited [30].

This section presents a new voltage control scheme for ADN, which employs the MPC strategy on a high-dimensional linear state-space model. This approach not only captures the nonlinear characteristics of the system but also enables rapid and precise voltage control by considering the dynamic constraints and uncertainties of the system throughout the control process.

4.1. Controller Design

The state variables for the voltage controller include the rotor angle δ_g and rotor speed of the measurable synchronous machine relative to the standard frequency deviation value $\Delta\omega_g$ and the voltage of each critical bus V_n, $x(k) = [\delta_1, \ldots, \delta_g, \Delta\omega_1, \ldots, \Delta\omega_g, V_1, \ldots, V_b]$. g is the number of observable synchronous machines and b is the number of critical buses. The control variables of the voltage controller are the power output of all controllable units in the area that are capable of meeting the requisite fast-response requirements, including ESS, reactive power compensation equipment, controllable DG, and other similar devices. Figure 3 shows the framework of the proposed control method.

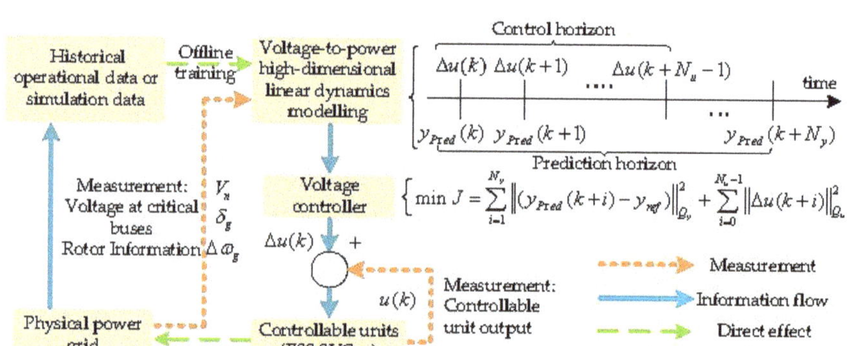

Figure 3. Framework of voltage controller based on the high-dimensional model and MPC.

The prediction and control horizons of the MPC are N_y and N_u, respectively. The prediction and control step lengths are N_y/t_c and N_u/t_c, respectively, where t_c denote the control period. The length of N_y is generally equal to or greater than the length of N_u. For the case $i > N_u$, let $\Delta u(k+i) = 0$. It is assumed that there is a communication infrastructure available for information flow in the system. The set of predicted input and output variables at each moment is denoted by Δu and y_{Pred}:

$$\Delta u = \left[\Delta u(k)^T \, \Delta u(k+1)^T \, \ldots \, \Delta u(k+N_u-1)^T\right]^T \tag{17}$$

$$y_{Pred} = \left[y_{Pred}(k+1)^T \, y_{Pred}(k+2)^T \, \ldots \, y_{Pred}(k+N_y)^T\right]^T \tag{18}$$

The state prediction can be calculated sequentially by Equation (19):

$$\begin{aligned} y_{Pred}(k+1) &= Dx_{Pred}(k+1) = CDZ_{Pred}(k+1) \\ &= CD[AZ(k) + B\Delta u(k)] \\ &= CDAg(x(k), \Delta u(k)) + CDB\Delta u(k) \end{aligned} \tag{19}$$

Alterations in system dynamics or external disruptions lead to the updated predicted values at each stage, which are then treated as new state inputs and expanded over the horizon N_y:

$$y_{Pred} = \psi g(x(k), \Delta u(k)) + \phi \Delta u \tag{20}$$

where ψ, ϕ are the coefficient matrices:

$$\psi = \begin{bmatrix} CDA & CDA^2 & \ldots & CDA^{N_y} \end{bmatrix}^T \tag{21}$$

$$\phi = \begin{bmatrix} CB & 0 & 0 & 0 \\ CAB & CB & 0 & 0 \\ \ldots & \ldots & \ldots & \ldots \\ CA^{N_u-1}B & CA^{N_u-2}B & \ldots & CB \\ \ldots & \ldots & \ldots & \ldots \\ CA^{N_y-1}B & CA^{N_y-2}B & \ldots & CA^{N_y-N_u}B \end{bmatrix} \tag{22}$$

The relationship between $u(k)$ and $\Delta u(k)$ can be expressed as follows:

$$u(k) = u(k-1) + \Delta u(k) \tag{23}$$

$$u(k+1) = u(k) + \Delta u(k+1) = u(k-1) + \Delta u(k) + \Delta u(k+1) \tag{24}$$

Expand further to N_u:

$$u(k) = \varphi u(k-1) + \theta \Delta u(k) \tag{25}$$

where φ and θ are the additional coefficient matrices, which can be expressed by the identity matrix I:

$$\begin{aligned} \varphi &= [II \ldots I]^T \\ \theta &= \begin{bmatrix} I & 0 & 0 & 0 \\ I & I & 0 & 0 \\ \ldots & \ldots & \ldots & \ldots \\ I & I & I & I \end{bmatrix} \end{aligned} \tag{26}$$

The objective of the MPC is to minimize the discrepancy between the predicted voltage and the rated voltage over the horizon N_y:

$$\min J = (y_{Pred} - y_{ref})^T Q_y (y_{Pred} - y_{ref}) \tag{27}$$

where Q_y is the matrix of weight coefficients for the control error of the voltage of the bus, $Q_y \in \mathbb{R}^{n \times n}$, and n is the number of state variable dimensions. The rated voltage y_{ref} is taken at the last sample before the controller is triggered.

To achieve optimal performance, it is essential to minimize the control cost, which allows Equation (27) to be reformulated as a quadratic programming problem:

$$\min J = \sum_{i=1}^{N_y} \left\| (y_{Pred}(k+i) - y_{ref}) \right\|_{Q_y}^2 + \sum_{i=0}^{N_u-1} \|\Delta u(k+i)\|_{Q_u}^2 \tag{28}$$

where Q_u is the matrix of cost coefficients for the control output, $Q_u \in \mathbb{R}^{m \times m}$, and m is the number of control variable dimensions. The objective of the MPC can be adjusted by modifying the weighting matrices.

4.2. Voltage Controller Constraints and Output Corrections

The state constraints are:

$$x^{\min} \le x(k+i) \le x^{\max} \tag{29}$$

where $u^{\min}$ and $x^{\max}$ are the boundary constraints of the state variables, for V_n set 0.95 p.u. and 1.05 p.u., $\Delta\omega_g$ set -0.1 p.u. and 0.1 p.u., and δ_g set 0 rad and 1 rad.

The control constraints are:

$$\begin{aligned} &\delta^{k+i}\Delta u^{\min} \le \Delta u(k+i) \le \delta^{k+i}\Delta u^{\max} \\ &u^{\min} \le u(k+i) \le u^{\max} \end{aligned} \tag{30}$$

where δ^{k+i} is the available state vector of the control object, with elements that are 0–1 binary variables. If the control object is in an uncontrollable state, the available state flag of the device is assumed to be zero. By incorporating δ^{k+i}, the model can adaptively capture the dynamic constraints, thereby providing a more accurate and flexible representation of the system's control behavior. $u^{\min}$, $u^{\max}$, $\Delta u^{\min}$ and $\Delta u^{\max}$ represent the boundaries of the control inputs and the boundaries of the amount of control change, respectively. Due to the limited timescale of voltage control, the controller does not consider constraints on the charge state of ESS.

Control correction:

As illustrated by Equation (28), the controller exhibits the distinctive attribute of real-time correction. It is possible that during the voltage stabilization period and at the outset of the control, the estimation of the controller may exhibit a degree of deviation, which could result in the oscillation of the ADN voltage. To address this issue, it is necessary to implement corrective measures to the control inputs:

$$u(k+1) = Mu(k) \ if \left| y_{Pred}(k) - y_{ref}(k) \right| < \varepsilon \tag{31}$$

where M is the identity diagonal matrix and ε is the control trigger positive constant.

4.3. Robustness Derivation of Voltage Controllers

Considering the high-security requirements of ADNs, the high-dimensional lifting of the state in the mapping linear space needs to be robust to input uncertainty.

Proposition 1. *If a bounded voltage noise perturbation input is present, and provided that the ADN state volume satisfies $x^{min} \le x(k+i) \le x^{max}$ and the control input satisfies $\Delta u^{min} \le \Delta u(k+i) \le \Delta u^{max}$, it can be demonstrated that the perturbation of the predicted state is also bounded in the Koopman lifting space.*

Proof of Proposition 1. For a given input state and current control, the lifted state in the high-dimensional linear space can be expressed as follows:

$$Z = g(\chi) = [\chi, \psi(\chi)] \tag{32}$$

From Equation (10) it follows that the augmented state χ_i satisfies the boundedness condition when $x^{\min} \leq x(k+i) \leq x^{\max}$ and $\Delta u^{\min} \leq \Delta u(k+i) \leq \Delta u^{\max}$ are satisfied. Therefore, it is only necessary to discuss the boundedness of the following parts:

$$\tilde{z} = \psi(\chi) = \|M\chi + D\|_2 \tag{33}$$

where $M \in N$ is the state variable weight matrix, which is non-negative, $M \in \mathbb{R}^{N\times(n+m)}$. D is the deviation vector, and $\|\cdot\|_2$ is the quadratic form.

Since the quadratic form is a convex function and the augmented state variables are non-negative, the bounds of the lifted state can be obtained as follows:

$$\begin{array}{l} \tilde{z}_{\min} \leq \tilde{z} \leq \tilde{z}_{\max} \\ \tilde{z}_{\max} = \|M_x x_{\max} + M_u|\Delta u|_{\max} + D\|_2 \\ \tilde{z}_{\min} = \|M_x x_{\min} + D\|_2 \end{array} \tag{34}$$

where M_x and M_u are the state variable and control input weight matrices, respectively. $M_x \in \mathbb{R}^{N\times n}$, $M_u \in \mathbb{R}^{N\times m}$. The boundedness of $\|M\chi + D\|_2$ is ensured by the finite-dimensional nature of M and the constraints on χ. The maximum and minimum values exist within the feasible region and can be determined either numerically or through eigenvalue analysis, regardless of whether M is positive semidefinite [30].

Then, the lifted state variable in the prediction time domain can be determined from $Z(k+1) = AZ(k) + B\Delta u(k)$. Matrices A and B satisfy $A_{ij} > 0, \forall i,j$ and $B_{ij} > 0, \forall i,j$. Therefore, the lifted state will be bounded within the following limits:

$$AZ_{\min} + B\Delta u^{\min} \leq Z^+ \leq AZ_{\max} + B\Delta u^{\max} \tag{35}$$

where Z^+ is the state vector in the high-dimensional linear space in the prediction time domain. $Z_{\min}$, $Z_{\max}$ are the boundaries in the prediction time domain.□

Accordingly, when transferring the ADN state variables from the initial nonlinear space to the elevated linear space, the impact of noise or disturbance remains constrained within the complete prediction horizons. This indicates that the proposed voltage controller, based on the high-dimensional linearized model, is resilient to noise and disturbance.

4.4. ADN Voltage Control Program

The voltage control scheme of the ADN based on the Koopman operator can be implemented through the following steps.

Step 1: Partition the ADN and identify critical buses.

Divide the ADN into regions and select the critical bus in each region for monitoring and control.

Step 2: Collect data from measurements.

Gather the voltage data from the critical buses, along with the active and reactive power outputs of the distributed generators (DG) and energy storage systems (ESS).

Step 3: Check for necessary corrections.

Determine if the control inputs require correction. If a correction is necessary, initiate the procedure outlined in Equation (31). Otherwise, the subsequent step is undertaken.

Step 4: State prediction and MPC optimization.

Predict the state at N_y. Solve the MPC optimization problem to determine the optimal control sequence for each prediction step. The control variables for the first prediction step are then applied.

Step 5: Repeat the process.

Repeat Steps 2 through 4 in a loop. Once the stopping criterion $\sum_{n=0}^{N} (y_{Pred}(k-n) - y_{ref})^2 < \varepsilon$ is satisfied, the control process is complete.

5. Case Analysis

5.1. Case Settings

To validate the ADN critical bus selection scheme and voltage control scheme proposed in the paper, simulation calculations are carried out in the improved 33-bus ADN system. To simplify the analysis, the transmission grid is modeled as a standard 3-machine, 9-bus system. The ADN is equipped with four distributed wind turbines (WTs) located at buses 3, 16, 23, and 31, and eight ESSs located at buses B1, B3, 3, 7, 11, 18, 25, and 27. The distributed WTs operate with a power factor of not less than 0.95. The capacity of the ESSs in the ADN is 400 kW·h, with an upper limit of 400 kW for charging and discharging power and an upper limit of 200 kVar for reactive power output. The ESS in the transmission grid has a power capacity of 30% of the nominal value of the corresponding synchronous generators, respectively [31]. The sampling time of the voltage sensor is 0.01 s, and both the response time and communication delay of the ESS are assumed to be 0.01 s.

5.2. Partitioning and Selection of Critical Buses

The voltage-to-power sensitivity of each bus is calculated under different operating state scenarios. As an example, the sensitivity of buses 2, 5, 15, and 20 in varying operational scenarios is illustrated in Figure 4. Following the methodology outlined in Section 2.1, the ADN is divided into five regions.

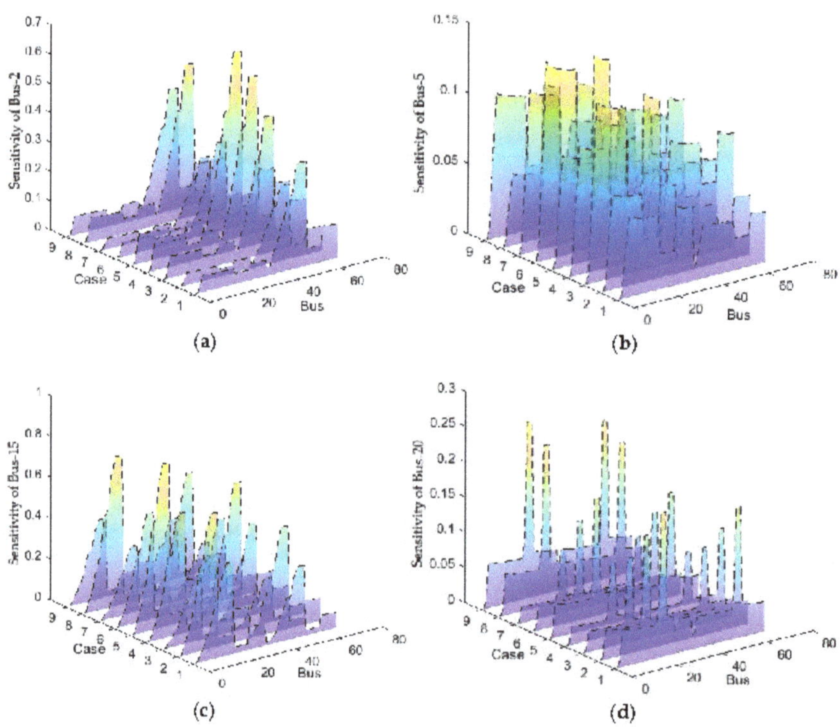

Figure 4. Multi-operation state sensitivity schematic. (**a**) Sensitivity of bus-2; (**b**) sensitivity of bus-5; (**c**) sensitivity of bus-15; (**d**) sensitivity of bus-20.

Following the critical bus selection method outlined in Section 2, it is established that the critical buses encompass [2,15,21,26,32]. The ADN topology, device locations, and critical bus locations are illustrated in Figure 5.

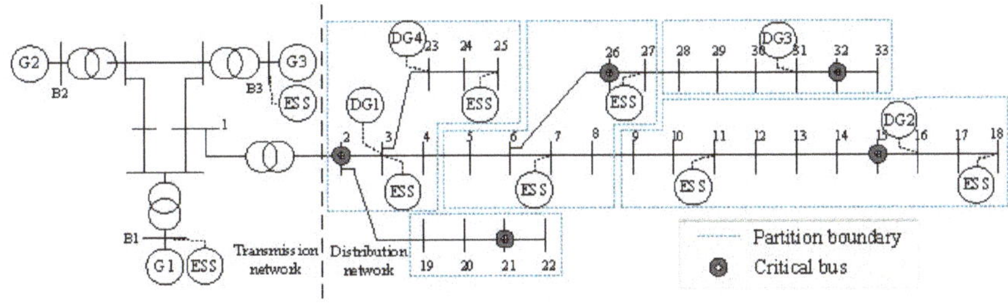

Figure 5. Schematic diagram of ADN partitioning and critical bus selection.

5.3. Selection of Optimal Lifting Dimension and Verification of Linearization

In this subsection, the control input data and the voltage state data are processed to obtain the high-dimension model and to validate the model's accuracy through the EDMD method. The specific data collection methods are detailed in the Appendix. The analysis reveals that a lifting dimension of 3 achieves the best balance between model accuracy and computational efficiency. This result is further supported by a comparison of the model's accuracy across different lifting dimensions.

The initial state is that of an 11-dimensional space. The selected lifting dimensions are tested in the range of 0–50. As illustrated in Figure 6, the root mean square error (RMSE) results exhibit a notable increase when the number of lifting dimensions is in the range of 10–25. Outside this range, whether in lower or higher numbers of lifting dimensions, the model demonstrates relatively high accuracy. The results demonstrate that the accuracy is not directly proportional to the number of lifting dimensions. The selection of the optimal dimensions should balance the computational cost and the desired level of accuracy.

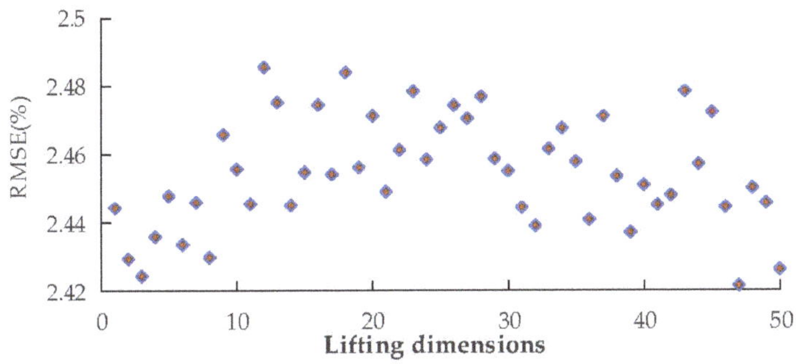

Figure 6. Prediction of RMSE in different lifting dimensions.

To verify the advantage of the Koopman-base model relative to the voltage-to-power sensitivity model [29], a set of the sampled data is selected for the comparison of the prediction effect. Under the same initial state, the RMSE of the predicted and actual state variable curves are calculated separately as in Table 1.

Table 1. RMSE under different methods of prediction.

Methods of Prediction	Koopman Lifting 3 Dimensions	Koopman Lifting 13 Dimensions	Sensitivity Matrix
RMSE	0.0236	0.0248	0.0297

The Koopman model demonstrates superior prediction accuracy in the presence of diverse parameter fluctuations. In contrast, the predictor based on the sensitivity matrix is less effective when the operating state changes, since linearization is only conducted at

x_0. This may result in suboptimal solutions. Meanwhile, the single Koopman linearization process is completed in a mere 0.38 s, demonstrating impressive training efficiency and the capability to effectively cope with the rapid state changes of the ADN.

5.4. Voltage Control Case Comparison

The control performance of the coordinated voltage control method based on the MPC of the Koopman linearized system is validated in the improved 33-bus system and evaluated in comparison with alternative voltage control methodologies.

Scheme 1: K-VMPC-based predictive control of voltage of ADN (lifting 3 dimensions) (K-VMPC-3).

Scheme 2: K-VMPC-based predictive control of voltage of ADN (lifting 13 dimensions) (K-VMPC-13).

Scheme 3: voltage control based on one-step optimal control (VOPC) [32].

Scheme 4: MPC voltage control based on sensitivity matrix (S-MPC) [28].

Scheme 5: no voltage control (No-Control).

5.4.1. ADN Power Fluctuation

(1) DG output plummet

Within t = 3 s - 3.1 s , the DG at bus-16 in the ADN is set to plummet by 150 MW in a relatively short period, resulting in an overall voltage drop. Voltage control is initiated at t = 3.05 s to facilitate the coordinated response of all fast-response units to mitigate the impact of the perturbation. The voltage change of the critical bus under each scheme is illustrated in Figure 7. As the degree of voltage fluctuation of bus-2 is not significant, only the voltage change of buses 15, 21, 26, and 32 is depicted.

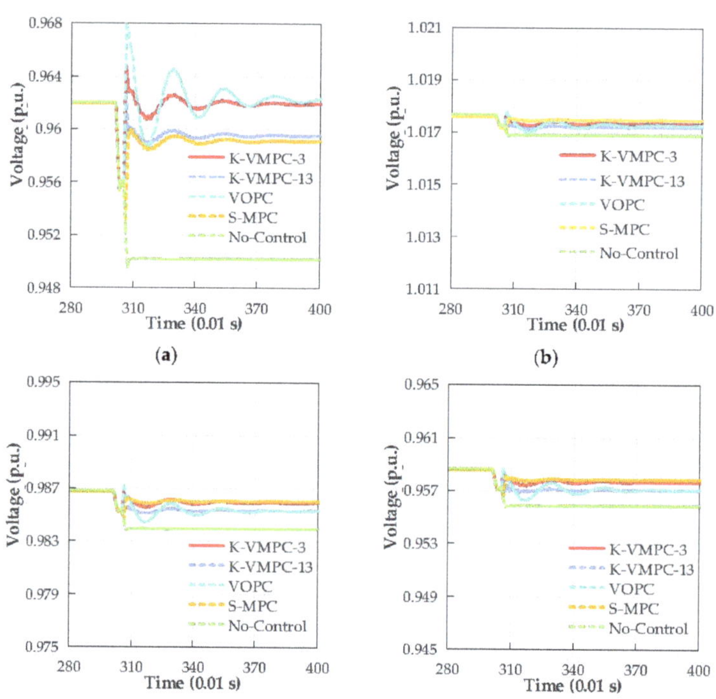

Figure 7. Variation of voltage magnitude at each critical bus under different control schemes. (**a**) Voltage at bus-15; (**b**) voltage at bus-21; (**c**) voltage at bus-26; (**d**) voltage at bus-32.

(2) Load demand increase

Within t = 3 s - 3.1 s, a 140 kW load is connected to the grid in the ADN at bus-14. This results in an overall voltage drop, which in turn triggers the voltage control at t = 3.05 s. Figure 8 illustrates the variation of the critical bus voltage under each control scheme.

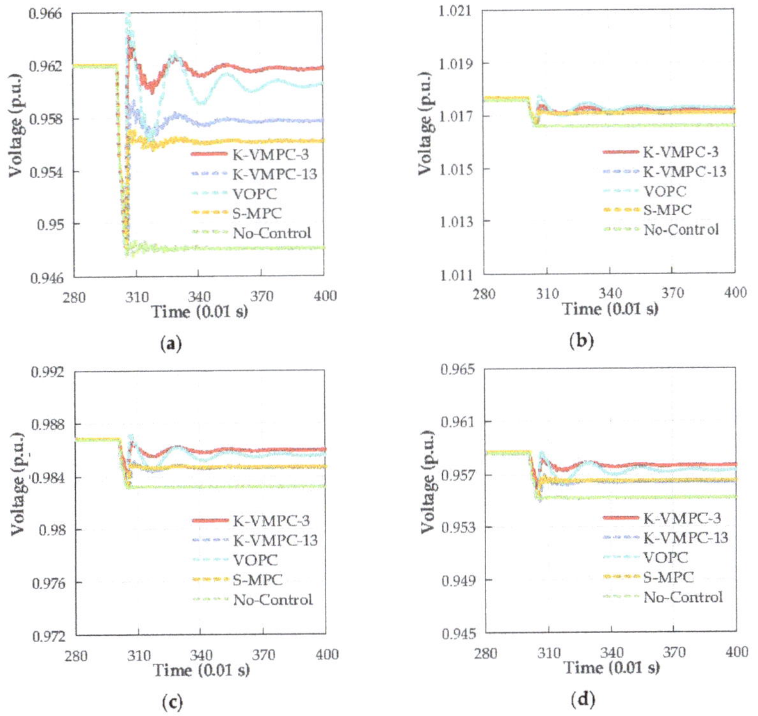

Figure 8. Variation of voltage magnitude at each critical bus under different control schemes. (**a**) Voltage at bus-15; (**b**) voltage at bus-21; (**c**) voltage at bus-26; (**d**) voltage at bus-32.

As illustrated in Figures 7 and 8, fluctuations in regional voltage are observed when there is an abrupt change in DG or when a significant load is connected to the grid. In some instances, the voltage at critical buses drops below 0.95 p.u., resulting in voltage over-limit and deterioration in power quality at the customer side. When the voltage fluctuation meets the criteria for triggering the controller, the adjustable resources in the regional grid are activated to address the power quality degradation. The VOPC method is capable of accurately restoring the voltage, but it requires time to restore the voltage operation to its state before the disturbance. The S-MPC method struggles to adapt to changes in the system state, thereby preventing it from accurately restoring the voltage to its pre-disturbance level. The K-VMPC-13 method also exhibits limitations in accurately controlling the voltage restoration effect in certain scenarios. Consequently, a comparison of prediction accuracies based on test data is crucial for the selection of lifting dimensions.

The K-VMPC-3 method exhibits a single optimal voltage recovery control solution time of 0.05 ms to 0.2 ms, a markedly shorter interval than that required to meet the criteria for a rapid solution. Furthermore, it rapidly determines the optimal output for each controllable unit and demonstrates superior rapid and precise regulation capabilities in comparison to conventional voltage control methodologies.

5.4.2. Three-Phase Short-Circuit Faults

A three-phase short-circuit fault is scheduled to occur at bus-6 at t = 2 s, and it is anticipated to be removed at t = 2.15 s. This is expected to result in voltage dips and fluctuations in the transmission grid and ADN, which will in turn trigger voltage control. A coordinated control strategy is employed to regulate the response of all fast-response units to mitigate the impact of this disturbance. Figure 9 illustrates the ADN's voltage variation under each control scheme.

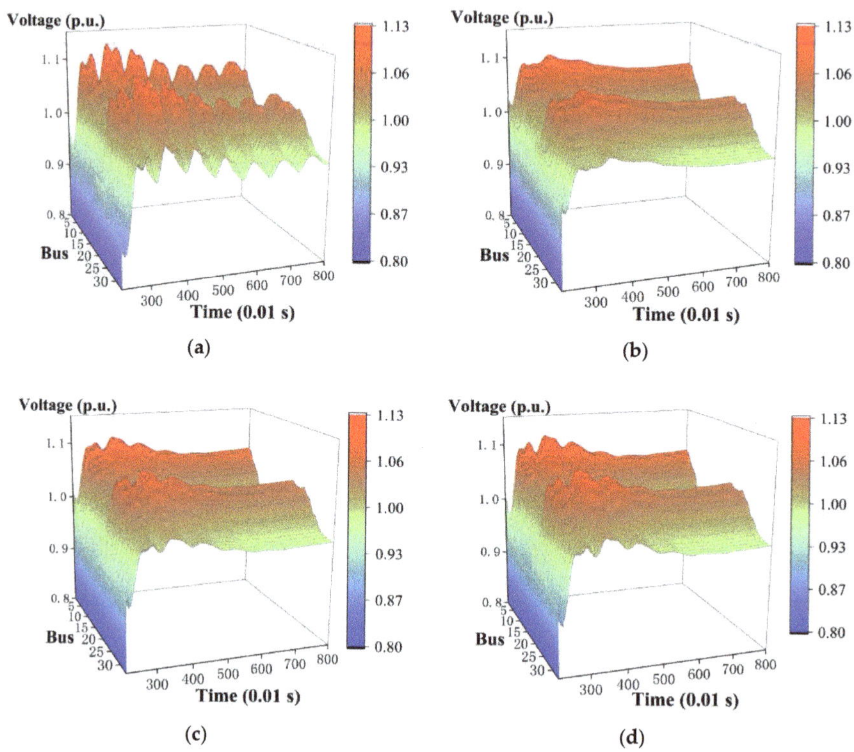

Figure 9. Variation of ADN voltage amplitude under different control schemes. (**a**) No-control; (**b**) K-VMPC-3; (**c**) K-VMPC-13; (**d**) S-MPC.

From Figure 9, it is evident that the overall voltage can be restored to the normal level after adopting the control method because the ADN operating state is unchanged before and after the fault, but there are differences in the voltage recovery effect among different control methods. The voltage under the K-VMPC-3 voltage control method proposed in this paper is shown in Figure 9b, which shows faster voltage restoration with the least overall fluctuation compared with the K-VMPC-13 and S-MPC methods shown in Figure 9c,d.

Under the scenario of a short-circuit fault, the K-VMPC-based ADN voltage control scheme is also able to quickly solve the optimal output of each controllable unit to realize the rapid recovery of the overall voltage and has a faster and more accurate performance compared with other traditional voltage control schemes.

6. Conclusions

To address the voltage recovery needs that arise from fluctuations in load and energy sources in the ADN, this paper presents a data-driven voltage control method, which is based on Koopman operator theory. The conclusions are as follows:

1. A methodology for the partitioning and selection of critical buses based on the Mahalanobis distance is proposed. The method ensures voltage control performance in incomplete state-measurement scenarios while reducing the stringent requirements for measurement and communication, thereby it enhances the economic feasibility of the control method.

2. A data-driven control method is employed to achieve the mapping of the high-dimensional linear space of the voltage-to-power dynamics system. This approach enables lifting linearization without information about the actual ADN voltage control model.

3. Considering the associated costs of ESS and DG, a voltage MPC law is devised based on linearized voltage-to-power dynamics. The controller developed in this paper significantly reduces the solution time of the optimal control method in comparison to traditional controllers based on the real model.

4. Conducting multi-scenario simulations and comparisons of the efficiency of voltage control schemes on the improved IEEE 33-bus distribution system, the proposed controller is less demanding regarding system parameter accuracy. Furthermore, it is capable of effectively supporting the voltage stability of the entire system during periods of significant fluctuations in sources or loads and the recovery from three-phase faults. This ensures the full consumption of new energy while maintaining the security and stability of loads in the ADN.

Moreover, the interconnection between the source, network, load, and storage components of the power system deepens and the scope of demand-side response and integrated energy systems expands. The ability to adaptively select nonlinear observation functions for Koopman operation is identified as a pivotal area of inquiry for subsequent research.

Author Contributions: Conceptualization, X.L. and Z.D.; methodology, X.L. and Z.D.; software, X.L.; validation, Z.D., X.L., G.Z., H.L., and W.Z.; formal analysis, X.L.; investigation, G.Z., H.L., and W.Z.; resources, Z.D.; data curation, X.L.; writing—original draft preparation, X.L.; writing—review and editing, X.L. and Z.D.; visualization, G.Z., H.L., and W.Z.; supervision, Z.D.; project administration, X.L.; funding acquisition, Z.D. All authors have read and agreed to the published version of the manuscript.

Funding: This research work was supported by the National Natural Science Foundation of China (grant no. U22B6007).

Data Availability Statement: The data used to support the findings of this study can be obtained through the sample construction method described in Sections 3 and 4 and Appendix A.

Acknowledgments: The authors would like to express our sincere gratitude to the anonymous referees for providing valuable suggestions and comments that have significantly contributed to the improvement of our manuscript.

Conflicts of Interest: The authors declare no conflicts of interest.

Appendix A

Linearized data collection methods:

The linearization of the Koopman model necessitates a substantial quantity of system input and output data, including current state data, control input data, and output data about the subsequent moment in time. The dataset should satisfy the following criteria: it should contain as much of the nonlinear dynamics of the system as possible. Accordingly, the data collection process should be designed to maximize randomness and facilitate the expansion of the system state across its entire operational range.

Following the aforementioned analysis, this section collates data from 60 distinct sets of random initial states, comprising the voltage value of the low-voltage side of the transformer connected to the upper grid, the load at each bus, and the line impedance. Each set of initial states is matched with a sequence of randomly generated control inputs to a controllable unit of length 1400. The current input state of the ADNs that are controlled in each step (a total of 1400) is collected, as well as the voltage value of each bus. The data are collected with a fixed sampling period of 0.01 ms. The randomly generated LV-side voltages of the upper transformer are situated within the interval [1.02 p.u., 1.05 p.u.]. The ADN parameters are located within the interval [0.98 p.u., 1.02 p.u.] to simulate parameter uncertainties and state variations in the real situation.

The generation of the stochastic control sequence is contingent upon the initial determination of the range of output signals of the controllable unit. To illustrate, in the case of an ESS installed in the distribution network, the capacity of S is 400 kW-h, the upper limit of the charging/discharging power is 400 kW, and the upper limit of the reactive power output is 200 kVar. In light of the aforementioned range of the control volume stochastic matrix, designated as $\{U^{ESS}\}$, and the vector of the kth column in the matrix, denoted as U_k^{ESS}, the interval time T_u between every two vectors in this ESS output sequence is selected. T_u must be considerably longer than the sampling time Δt of the system during the experiment to guarantee the smoothness of the control signal. In this case, $T_u = 0.5s$ is chosen.

The principle of determining the ith (total I) random control output value at the current moment is that if t is an integer multiple of the interval time T_u, such as k times, then the kth column vector U_k^{ESS} in the random control output sequence $\{U^{ESS}\}$ is taken as the output value at the current moment. Otherwise, if t is between kT_u and $(k+1)T_u$, the voltage value at the current moment is obtained according to the linear interpolation method by using U_k^{ESS} and U_{k+1}^{ESS}. The expression is shown in Equation (36), in which $ceil(\cdot)$ is the upward rounding function.

$$\begin{aligned} &k = ceil(t/T_u) \\ &u_i(t) = \frac{U_{k+1,i}^{ESS} - U_{k,i}^{ESS}}{T_u}(t-(k-1)T_u) + U_{k,i}^{ESS}, i = 1,2,\ldots,I \end{aligned} \tag{A1}$$

References

1. Chen, X.; Mcelroy, M.B.; Wu, Q.; Shu, Y.; Xue, Y. Transition towards higher penetration of renewables: An overview of interlinked technical, environmental and socio-economic challenges. *J. Mod. Power Syst. Clean Energy* **2019**, *7*, 1–8. [CrossRef]
2. Zhao, C.; Guan, Y. Data-driven stochastic unit commitment for integrating wind generation. *IEEE Trans. Power Syst.* **2015**, *31*, 2587–2596. [CrossRef]
3. Zhu, X.; Wang, J.; Lu, N.; Samaan, N.; Huang, R.; Ke, X. A Hierarchical VLSM-Based Demand Response Strategy for Coordinative Voltage Control Between Transmission and Distribution Systems. *IEEE Trans. Smart Grid* **2019**, *10*, 4838–4847. [CrossRef]
4. Sun, X.; Qiu, J. Hierarchical voltage control strategy in distribution networks considering customized charging navigation of electric vehicles. *IEEE Trans. Smart Grid* **2021**, *12*, 4752–4764. [CrossRef]
5. Azzouz, M.A.; Shaaban, M.F.; El-Saadany, E.F. Real-time optimal voltage regulation for distribution networks incorporating high penetration of PEVs. *IEEE Trans. Power Syst.* **2015**, *30*, 3234–3245. [CrossRef]
6. Maharjan, S.; Khambadkone, A.M.; Peng, J.C.H. Robust constrained model predictive voltage control in active distribution networks. *IEEE Trans. Sustain. Energy* **2020**, *12*, 400–411. [CrossRef]
7. Xu, Y.; Dong, Z.Y.; Zhang, R.; Hill, D.J. Multi-timescale coordinated voltage/var control of high renewable-penetrated distribution systems. *IEEE Trans. Power Syst.* **2017**, *32*, 4398–4408. [CrossRef]
8. Singh, S.; Pamshetti, V.B.; Singh, S.P. Time horizon-based model predictive Volt/VAR optimization for smart grid enabled CVR in the presence of electric vehicle charging loads. *IEEE Trans. Ind. Appl.* **2019**, *55*, 5502–5513. [CrossRef]
9. Park, C.H.; Jang, G. Systematic method to identify an area of vulnerability to voltage sags. *IEEE Trans. Power Deliv.* **2016**, *32*, 1583–1591. [CrossRef]
10. Li, Y.; Wang, Y.; Ye, H.; Xie, W.; Hua, B.; Lu, C. An integrated dynamic voltage control strategy in active distribution network based on improved model predictive control. *IET Gener. Transm. Distrib.* **2023**, *17*, 993–1006. [CrossRef]
11. Li, C.; Liu, X.; Sun, K.; Cao, Y.; Ma, F.; Zhou, B. A hybrid control strategy to support voltage in industrial active distribution networks. *IEEE Trans. Power Deliv.* **2018**, *33*, 2590–2602. [CrossRef]
12. Li, Y.; Lu, C.; Tang, Y.; Fang, C.; Cui, Y. Dynamic Control and Time-Delayed Channel Scheduling Co-Design for Voltage Control in Active Distribution Networks. *IEEE Trans. Smart Grid* **2024**, *15*, 1837–1848. [CrossRef]
13. Wang, Z.; Wang, J.; Chen, B.; Begovic, M.M.; He, Y. MPC-based voltage/var optimization for distribution circuits with distributed generators and exponential load models. *IEEE Trans. Smart Grid* **2014**, *5*, 2412–2420. [CrossRef]
14. Dutta, A.; Ganguly, S.; Kumar, C. Model predictive control-based optimal voltage regulation of active distribution networks with OLTC and reactive power capability of PV inverters. *IET Gener. Transm. Distrib.* **2020**, *14*, 5183–5192. [CrossRef]
15. Wang, Z.; Liu, J.; Zhu, X.; Li, X.; Li, G.; Bai, L. Model-Free Distributed Voltage Control for Distribution Networks Based on State Space Mapping and Super-Linear Feedback. *IEEE Trans. Power Syst.* **2024**, *39*, 6290–6304. [CrossRef]
16. Li, Y.; Zhang, P.; Althoff, M.; Yue, M. Distributed formal analysis for power networks with deep integration of distributed energy resources. *IEEE Trans. Power Syst.* **2018**, *34*, 5147–5156. [CrossRef]

17. Cao, D.; Zhao, J.; Hu, W.; Yu, N.; Ding, F.; Huang, Q.; Chen, Z. Deep reinforcement learning enabled physical-model-free two-timescale voltage control method for active distribution systems. *IEEE Trans. Smart Grid* **2021**, *13*, 149–165. [CrossRef]
18. Wang, W.; Yu, N.; Gao, Y.; Shi, J. Safe off-policy deep reinforcement learning algorithm for volt-var control in power distribution systems. *IEEE Trans. Smart Grid* **2019**, *11*, 3008–3018. [CrossRef]
19. Bai, L.; Xue, Y.; Xu, G.; Dong, J.; Olama, M.M.; Kuruganti, T. A data-driven network optimisation approach to coordinated control of distributed photovoltaic systems and smart buildings in distribution systems. *IET Energy Syst. Integr.* **2021**, *3*, 285–294. [CrossRef]
20. Koopman, B.O. Hamiltonian Systems and Transformation in Hilbert Space. *Proc. Natl. Acad. Sci. USA* **1931**, *17*, 315–318. [CrossRef] [PubMed]
21. Williams, M.O.; Kevrekidis, I.G.; Rowley, C.W. A data–driven approximation of the koopman operator: Extending dynamic mode decomposition. *J. Nonlinear Sci.* **2015**, *25*, 1307–1346. [CrossRef]
22. Ma, Z.; Wang, Z.; Cheng, R. Analytical large-signal modeling of inverter-based microgrids with koopman operator theory for autonomous control. *IEEE Trans. Smart Grid* **2023**, *15*, 1376–1387. [CrossRef]
23. Gong, X.; Wang, X.; Joos, G. An online data-driven method for microgrid secondary voltage and frequency control with ensemble Koopman modeling. *IEEE Trans. Smart Grid* **2022**, *14*, 68–81. [CrossRef]
24. Korda, M.; Susuki, Y.; Mezić, I. Power grid transient stabilization using Koopman model predictive control. *IFAC-PapersOnLine* **2018**, *51*, 297–302. [CrossRef]
25. Huo, Y.; Li, P.; Ji, H.; Yu, H.; Yan, J.; Wu, J.; Wang, C. Data-driven coordinated voltage control method of distribution networks with high DG penetration. *IEEE Trans. Power Syst.* **2022**, *38*, 1543–1557. [CrossRef]
26. Zhao, T.; Wang, J.; Lu, X.; Du, Y. Neural Lyapunov control for power system transient stability: A deep learning-based approach. *IEEE Trans. Power Syst.* **2021**, *37*, 955–966. [CrossRef]
27. Abraham, I.; Murphey, T.D. Active Learning of Dynamics for Data-Driven Control Using Koopman Operators. *IEEE Trans. Robot.* **2019**, *35*, 1071–1083. [CrossRef]
28. Gupta, R.; Sossan, F.; Paolone, M. Grid-aware distributed model predictive control of heterogeneous resources in a distribution network: Theory and experimental validation. *IEEE Trans. Energy Convers.* **2020**, *36*, 1392–1402. [CrossRef]
29. Valverde, G.; Van Cutsem, T. Model predictive control of voltages in active distribution networks. *IEEE Trans. Smart Grid* **2013**, *4*, 2152–2161. [CrossRef]
30. Hossain, R.R.; Adesunkanmi, R.; Kumar, R. Data-driven linear Koopman embedding for networked systems: Model-predictive grid control. *IEEE Syst. J.* **2023**, *17*, 4809–4820. [CrossRef]
31. Ping, Z.; Yin, Z.; Li, X.; Liu, Y.; Yang, T. Deep Koopman model predictive control for enhancing transient stability in power grids. *Int. J. Robust Nonlinear Control* **2021**, *31*, 1964–1978. [CrossRef]
32. Guo, Y.; Wu, Q.; Gao, H.; Chen, X.; Ostergaard, J.; Xin, H. MPC-based coordinated voltage regulation for distribution networks with distributed generation and energy storage system. *IEEE Trans. Sustain. Energy* **2018**, *10*, 1731–1739. [CrossRef]

mathematics

MDPI

Article

Economic Load Dispatch Problem Analysis Based on Modified Moth Flame Optimizer (MMFO) Considering Emission and Wind Power

Hani Albalawi [1,2], Abdul Wadood [1,2,*] and Herie Park [3,*]

1 Renewable Energy and Environmental Technology Center, University of Tabuk, Tabuk 47913, Saudi Arabia; halbala@ut.edu.sa
2 Electrical Engineering Department, Faculty of Engineering, University of Tabuk, Tabuk 47913, Saudi Arabia
3 Department of Electrical Engineering, Dong-A University, Busan 49315, Republic of Korea
* Correspondence: wadood@ut.edu.sa (A.W.); bakery@donga.ac.kr (H.P.)

Abstract: In electrical power system engineering, the economic load dispatch (ELD) problem is a critical issue for fuel cost minimization. This ELD problem is often characterized by non-convexity and subject to multiple constraints. These constraints include valve-point loading effects (VPLEs), generator limits, emissions, and wind power integration. In this study, both emission constraints and wind power are incorporated into the ELD problem formulation, with the influence of wind power quantified using the incomplete gamma function (IGF). This study proposes a novel metaheuristic algorithm, the modified moth flame optimization (MMFO), which improves the traditional moth flame optimization (MFO) algorithm through an innovative flame selection process and adaptive adjustment of the spiral length. MMFO is a population-based technique that leverages the intelligent behavior of flames to effectively search for the global optimum, making it particularly suited for solving the ELD problem. To demonstrate the efficacy of MMFO in addressing the ELD problem, the algorithm is applied to four well-known test systems. Results show that MMFO outperforms other methods in terms of solution quality, speed, minimum fuel cost, and convergence rate. Furthermore, statistical analysis validates the reliability, robustness, and consistency of the proposed optimizer, as evidenced by the consistently low fitness values across iterations.

Keywords: economic load dispatch; wind power; emission; nature-inspired optimization; modified technique; moth flame optimizer

MSC: 68T20

1. Introduction

Growing power demand has significantly increased the generation costs. Hence, there is an increasing need to economically disengage the power in order to reduce fuel expenses and ensure the consistent functioning of the power grid [1,2]. To minimize fuel costs and adhere to all system and producing unit constraints, the economic load dispatch (ELD) problem primarily seeks to organize the output of power generation units to meet the needed load demand in a logical manner. Newton–Raphson, lambda iteration, dynamic programming, and gradient methods are some of the well-established procedures that have been suggested in the literature as appropriate ways to address this particular issue. However, as shown in [3], the gradient approach demonstrates a sluggish rate of convergence and has difficulties when faced with constraints related to inequality. The convergence characteristics of Newton's approach are subject to the influence of the initial estimation, which might potentially hinder its effectiveness in obtaining an optimal solution if the initialization is wrong. The linear programming approach is plagued by inaccuracies and the approximation of piece-wise linear costs. Additionally, as mentioned in [3], the application of quadratic programming to the piece-wise quadratic cost approximation demonstrates inefficiency if the step size is not appropriately chosen. The interior point approach, although commonly seen as more computationally efficient, may not yield a realistic solution for non-linear objective functions [4]. Furthermore, it is important to acknowledge that these traditional approaches need the utilization of incremental fuel cost curves, which demonstrate a consistent upward trend or incremental linear trend. The ELD problem demonstrates input–output features that are non-convex, non-linear, and non-smooth [5]. In order to get beyond the limitations of conventional methods, several soft computing approaches have been proposed in the literature.

In [5], an innovative methodology for oppositional pigeon-inspired optimization has been proposed to address the prevalent problem of premature convergence in the case of power system problem optimization. A chameleon swarm algorithm is proposed in [6] to address the ELD problem. In addition, a comprehensive exploitation phase is carried out to tackle the problem of ELD using quasi-quadratic programming for smart building [7]. In [8], a Q-learning-based search optimization was used to solve the ELD problem for different IEEE benchmark functions. The ELD problem is solved as multi-objective economic load dispatch (MELD) considering generation cost and transmission losses in [9] using the Particle Swarm Optimization (PSO) algorithm. In [10], the modified version of PSO was used for the utilization of adaptive acceleration constants. This strategy helps in determining the most suitable value for the acceleration constant in the evaluation of fitness function values. In [11], a hybrid approach was utilized consisting of bacteria foraging (BSA) and PSO to deal with the non-convex ELD problem considering the influence of valve-point effects. This inclusion aims to decrease the degree of unpredictability in the search procedure and improve the collective behavior of the optimizer. The ELD problem has been solved utilizing the application of invasive weed optimization [12] while considering the effects of valve-point loading effect and prohibited operation zones. In order to best solve the ELD problem, grey wolf optimizer (GWO) has been used for different IEEE test systems [13]. In [14], an ant lion optimizer was recalled to solve the ELD problem on four compact test systems keeping in view the valve-point effect scenario. A novel hybrid methodology was designed in [15] by combining the PSO with pattern search to solve the ELD problem formulation. In [16], a combination of the Big Bang–Big Crunch (BB-BC) and PSO optimization techniques has been suggested for solving the ELD problem in a more resilient and efficient way. Artificial bee colony (ABC) optimization has been utilized in [17] to solve the ELD problem considering the valve-point effects for different IEEE test systems, i.e., IEEE three, thirteen, and forty systems.

In [18], the authors explore the possibility of improving the ELD problem solution by the deployment of a hybrid algorithm that combines a genetic algorithm (GA) and differential evolution (DE) with a dynamically coordinated PS algorithm considering the valve-point loading effect. In order to best solve the ELD problem including the valve-point effects, a new variant of PSO known as catfish PSO has been utilized in [19]. In [20], the authors examined the conventional ELD problem and proposed a novel approach that involves the elimination of inefficient generators through the utilization of the differential evolution (DE) technique. The implementation of this methodology has resulted in a reduction of 19.88% in the overall fuel cost in comparison to conventional methods. In [21], a comparative analysis of five soft computing approaches, specifically DE, PSO, evolutionary programming (EP), genetic algorithm (GA), and simulated annealing (SA), has been utilized to solve the dynamic ELD problem. This comparative analysis takes into account several constraints, including limitations on the generator ramp rate. In [22], an improved version of teaching–learning-based optimization with incorporation of quasi-oppositional-based learning has been proposed to enhance the exploration and convergence characteristics of the proposed optimizer in order to best solve the ELD problem. To tackle the ELD problem, a modified version of the DE approach is suggested in [23]. The proposed optimizer entails the incorporation of a tournage-best vector during the mutation phase.

The generation of electrical energy from fossil fuel-based thermal power stations has led to an increase in the emission of harmful pollutants, including oxides of nitrogen (NOx), sulfur oxides (SO), and carbon monoxide (CO). To address these environmental issues, computational methods have been developed to optimize power generating efficiency while reducing hazardous emissions. The integration of renewable energy sources (RESs), such as wind and solar power, has significantly alleviated the challenges related to rising generating prices and harmful fossil emissions [23]. The assimilation of energy from RESs into thermal power systems has necessitated alterations to the traditional quadratic equation utilized for calculating the cost of fuel. These enhancements include the incorporation of Beta and Weibull distribution functions, which account for the probabilistic fluctuations in the supply of solar and wind energy [24], respectively. PSO is a global methodology inspired by metaheuristic principles used to achieve optimal results in ELD integrated with wind power for the development of hybrid energy generating systems [25]. The enhancement of wind power availability, in conjunction with thermal power generation units, has been accomplished by a unique optimization technique known as HIC-SQP [26]. The aim is to optimize direct costs, inflated costs, and underestimated costs to reduce both power generating expenses and hazardous gas emissions. In [27], an exchange market algorithm (EMA) has been recalled to solve the ELD problem with wind power integration.

The optimization of the ELD problem is crucial for effective power grid management due to rising global energy demands and power generation costs as well as with integration of renewable energies Conventional approaches have difficulties with restrictions and non-convexity in ELD to handle the inherent unpredictability and non-linear dynamics resulting in unsatisfactory solutions The aforementioned research indicates that a majority of the techniques [5–25] require the adjustment of a significant amount of control parameters. Therefore, in order to obtain an optimal solution, it is necessary to accurately adjust the control settings, a process that can be both time-consuming and laborious. The moth flame optimization (MFO) algorithm [28] is a recently developed methodology that draws inspiration from the migration patterns of moths in relation to moonlight. The moth employs a mechanism called transverse orientation to enhance its movement [29]. This technique has demonstrated rapid convergence and effective utilization in tackling diverse engineering design issues. However, in the conventional MFO approach, in the last step of iterative optimization, the majority of individuals are concentrated in a limited terrestrial area surrounding the present ideal individual [30–33]. If sophisticated multimodal global optimization problems are being addressed, it is possible for the entire population to quickly achieve the local optimum [31] and be prone to early convergence.

This paper proposes the modified version of MFO known as MMFO. The MMFO technique entails incorporating the idea of the Archimedean spiral into the conventional MFO; employing these modifications has led to improvements in the resilience, precision, and search efficiency of the optimizer while also drastically lowering the number of iterations needed to obtain the best solution. This Archimedean spiral enables moths to perform adaptive movements, which ensures a balanced exploration of the search space early in the optimization process and a more focused exploitation near the optimal solutions in later stages. This study presents the MMFO methodology as a potential resolution for the ELD problem.

The key contribution of this paper is expressed as follows:

1. A novel metaheuristic optimization algorithm referred to as MMFO that aims to improve the exploration capacity of the traditional MFO to the ELD problem.
2. The proposed MMFO is successfully applied to four well-known IEEE ELD test systems as well as on 11 benchmark functions to verify the MMFO.
3. The proposed approach is validated in independent runs using various statistical illustrations, including minimal fitness value quantile plots, boxplots, histograms, standard normal plots, and cumulative distribution function plots for each distinct case study for accuracy, robustness, and stability.

The subsequent sections of this paper are organized in the following manner. The problem formulation of the ELD problem is presented in Section 2. The methods for solving the problem are elaborated in Section 3. The findings and subsequent statistical analysis are discussed in Sections 4 and 5.

2. Mathematical Modeling of Problem Formulation

The ELD problem is an optimization problem with constraints that seeks to streamline the allocation of total power to different generating units by optimizing the overall fuel and emission costs. Within the framework of the ELD problem, specific limitations are considered, including the equilibrium of power in the presence and absence of transmission line losses, the maximum capacity for production, and the influence of valve-point loading [22].

2.1. Objective Function

Minimizing the overall amount of fuel used and the amount of pollution from power plants is the main goal of the ELD problem. Therefore, as shown below, the objective function is created by adding the fuel prices of individual dedicated generating units and the emissions from fossil-fueled thermal units, weighted by their respective contributions.

$$F_1 = \sum_{i=1}^{N} C_i(P_i) + \sigma \times \sum_{i=1}^{N} E_i(P_i) \tag{1}$$

For the sake of this discussion, we will use the notation $E_i(P_i)$ to indicate emissions, $C_i(P_i)$ to indicate fuel cost, N to denote the number of generating units, and P_i to indicate active power generated by the i-th generating unit, while σ denotes $C(p_i)^{max}$ and $E(p_i)^{min}$.

2.1.1. Characteristics of a Smooth Cost Function

The quadratic function is used to express the smooth fuel cost characteristic function in the standard ELD problem, as explained in reference [22].

$$\sum_{i=1}^{N} C_i(P_i) = \sum_{i=1}^{N} a_i + b_i P_i + c_i P_i^2 \tag{2}$$

The coefficients representing the fuel cost of the i-th unit are represented by a_i, b_i, and c_i.

2.1.2. Characteristics of Non-Smooth Cost Functions

The output power of the generating unit is regulated via several valves in thermal power plants. Incoming steam flow is mostly controlled by these valves. Thus, the steam valves are opened in response to rising power demand, which causes a spike in losses and changes in the cost curve's shape. The effect that has been described is sometimes called a valve-point loading effect. Considering the numerous non-differential scores and non-smooth features in the cost curve, this phenomenon of valve-point loading [22] is important. Here, we show how the existence of valve-point effects transforms the objective function of the ELD problem into a non-convex quadratic and sinusoidal function.

$$F_2 = \sum_{i=1}^{N} C_i(P_i) = \sum_{i=1}^{N} a_i + b_i P_i + c_i P_i^2 + \left|e_i sin\left(f_i\left(P_i^{min} - P_i\right)\right)\right| \tag{3}$$

The cost coefficients, denoted as e_i and f_i, are used to illustrate the effects of valve-point loading. Additionally, P_i^{min} is employed to show the minimal active power generation limit of the i-th generator.

2.1.3. Characteristics of Non-Smooth Emission Functions

Fossil fuel generating units are primarily responsible for emitting two main pollutants, namely SOx and NOx. The mathematical expression that represents the functionality of the overall pollutant emissions is as follows.

$$\sum_{i=1}^{N} E_i(P_i) = \sum_{i=1}^{N} \alpha_i + \beta_i P_i + \gamma_i P_i^2 + \eta_i \exp(\delta_i P_i) \tag{4}$$

The emission coefficients of the i-th generator are denoted by α_i, β_i, γ_i, η_i, and δ_i. The equation presented above demonstrates that the pollutant emission function has a high degree of non-linearity, mostly attributed to the inclusion of both quadratic and exponential terms.

2.1.4. Wind Power Generation Availability Cost Function

A significant advantage in electrical power generation with regard to cost-effectiveness and environmental sustainability is the incorporation of wind power into thermal power producing units. Several models aim to explain the scheduling of operational generating cost and real power generation in power generation systems that include both wind and thermal power units. Given the unpredictable nature of wind speed, the power generation operator is unsure about the availability of wind power. Given the discrepancy between the actual and predicted power output, it is possible that there was an overestimation of the wind power availability. This could have resulted in the need to purchase additional electricity to meet the load requirements. Occasionally, there may be surplus power resulting from underestimating the availability of wind power. This surplus power is then utilized to compensate the wind power suppliers for the costs incurred from underutilizing all of the available wind power. The following model can be used to show the total cost of generating wind electricity [33].

$$C_3 = \sum_{n=1}^{wg} \left[\left(C_{W.P(DIR,n)} + C_{W.P(OE,n)} \right) + C_{W.P(UE,n)} \right] \tag{5}$$

The entire number of wind power generating units is denoted by wg, and the variable C_3 stands for the aggregate cost of wind power generation. Here, $C_{W.P(DIR,n)}$ refers to the direct cost, $C_{W.P(OE,n)}$ to the overestimated cost, and $C_{W.P(UE,n)}$ to the underestimated cost as they relate to wind power generating units. A direct proportionality exists between CW and the output of wind power generation. In terms of mathematics, the nth wind power generating unit can be expressed as $P\ (DIR, n)$.

$$C_{W.P(DIR,n)} = \sum_{n=1}^{wg} (q_n \times W.P_n) \tag{6}$$

The coefficient qn in Equation (6) represents the direct electrical energy cost from the nth wind power generating unit, measured in dollars per megawatt-hour (MWh). On the other hand, W represents the true electrical output power, measured in megawatts (MW), from the nth wind power producing unit. The variable C_W represents the unbalanced overestimated cost resulting from an overestimation of wind power availability. In response to a lack of electrical power from wind power generating units, more real power in megawatts (MW) is obtained. This can be mathematically represented as follows:

$$C_{W.P(OE,n)} = \sum_{n=1}^{wg} (C_{rw,n} \times X(V_{oe,n})) \tag{7}$$

The cost coefficient for overestimation for each wind power generating unit is represented by $C_{rw,n}$ and is measured in dollars per megawatt-hour (MWh), whereas $X(V_{OE,n})$

represents the predicted value of wind power overestimation for the nth wind power generating unit, as demonstrated in Equation (8).

$$X(V_{OE,n}) = W.P_n\left[\ 1-\exp\left(-\frac{V_{IN,n}^{K_n}}{C_n^{K_n}}\right)+\exp\left(-\frac{V_{OUT,n}^{K_n}}{C_n^{K_n}}\right)\ \right]+\left(\ \frac{W.P_{r,n}\times V_{IN,n}}{V_{r,n}-V_{IN,n}}+W.P_n\ \right).\left[\ \exp\left(-\frac{V_{IN,n}^{K_n}}{C_n^{K_n}}\right)-\exp\left(-\frac{V_{1,n}^{K_n}}{c_n^{km}}\right)\ \right]+ \left(\frac{W.P_{r,n}\times C_n}{V_{r,n}-V_{IN,n}}\right)\left\{\ \Gamma\left[1+\frac{1}{K_n},\left(\frac{V_{1,n}}{c_n}\right)^{K_n}\right]-\Gamma\left[1+\frac{1}{K_n},\left(\frac{V_{IN,n}}{C_n}\right)^{K_n}\right]\ \right\} \tag{8}$$

The cut-in, cut-out, and rated wind speeds are represented by the variables V_{IN}, V_{OUT}, and *Vr*, respectively, and are expressed in meters per second. One way to represent the intermediary parameter is as $V_1 = V_{IN} + (Vr - V_{IN}) \times W.P_1/W.Pr$. The coefficients C_n and K_n represent the size and shape factor, respectively, for the nth wind power generating unit in the Weibull distribution. In megawatts (MW), *W.Pn* and *W.Pr* denote the electrical power produced and rated for the nth wind power producing unit, respectively. Additionally, the following mathematical expression can be used to describe the gamma function, which is defined by its incompleteness and limited parameter count of two [33].

$$\Gamma(p,c) = 1/\Gamma(c) \times \int_0^p t^{c-1}e^{-t}dt \tag{9}$$

A typical gamma function consists of a solitary parameter that is expressed as follows:

$$\Gamma(p) = \int_0^p t^{p-1}e^{-p}dt \tag{10}$$

The penalty cost, denoted as $C_{W.P(UE,n)}$, arises from the underestimation of wind power availability, wherein the actual active power generated by wind power producing units exceeds the forecast active power. Compensation is offered to cover the costs incurred by wind power suppliers in this context.

$$C_{W.P(UE,n)} = \sum_{n=1}^{wg}(C_{ew,n} \times Y(V_{UE,n})) \tag{11}$$

$C_{ew,n}$ represents the cost coefficient for underestimate in dollars per megawatt-hour (MWh) for the nth wind power producing unit. Equation (12) mathematically represents the expected value of wind power underestimate for the nth wind power producing unit, denoted as $Y_{(VUE,n)}$.

$$Y(V_{UE,n}) = (W.P_{r,n}-W.P_n)\left[\ \exp\left(-\frac{V_{r,n}^{K_n}}{C_n^{K_n}}\right)-\exp\left(-\frac{V_{OUT,n}^{K_n}}{C_n^{K_n}}\right)\ \right]+\left(\ \frac{W.P_{1,n}\times V_{IN,n}}{V_{r,n}-V_{IN,n}}+W.P_n\ \right).\left[\ \exp\left(-\frac{V_{r,n}^{K_n}}{C_n^{K_n}}\right)-\exp\left(-\frac{V_{1,n}^{K_n}}{c_n^{kn}}\right)\ \right]+ \left(\frac{W.P_{r,n}\times C_n}{V_{r,n}-V_{IN,n}}\right)\left\{\ \Gamma\left[1+\frac{1}{K_n},\left(\frac{V_{1,n}}{c_n}\right)^{K_n}\right]-\Gamma\left[1+\frac{1}{K_n},\left(\frac{V_{r,n}}{C_n}\right)^{K_n}\right]\ \right\} \tag{12}$$

To model the objective function, one can combine the quadratic fuel cost function, which includes V.P.L.E (Equation (3)), with the wind power generation availability cost function (Equation (5)). This combination results in the total generating cost (*TGC*) in dollars per hour:

$$TGC = \sum_{m=1}^{tg}\left[\begin{array}{l} A_m + B_mP_m + C_mP_m^2 + \\ abs(E_m\sin(F_m(P_{m,\min}-P_m))) \end{array}\right] + \sum_{n=1}^{wg}\left[\begin{array}{l} (q_n \times W.P_n) + (C_{rw,n} \times X(V_{oe,n}) + \\ (C_{ew,n} \times Y(V_{UE,n}) \end{array}\right] \tag{13}$$

2.2. Constraint Functions

2.2.1. Constraint on Power Balance

As stated in reference [22], it is expected that the aggregate power produced by dedicated generators will be equal to the combined value of the load demand (PD) and the entire losses incurred during transmission.

$$\sum_{i=1}^{N} P_i - P_D - P_L = 0 \tag{14}$$

The symbol P_L represents the overall transmission loss, and P_D is the load demand. The calculation of losses associated with the transmission of electricity from the producing station to the load is often performed by load flow analysis or by utilizing Kron's loss coefficients, as outlined below.

$$P_L = \sum_{i=1}^{N}\sum_{j=1}^{N} P_i B_{ij} P_j + \sum_{i=1}^{N} P_i B_{0i} + B_{00} \tag{15}$$

The variables B_{ij}, B_{0i}, and B_{00} represent the loss B coefficients and constants under typical operational circumstances.

2.2.2. Constraints on Generation Limits

The maximum Pmax and minimum Pmin restrictions, as indicated in reference [22], and the active power-generated output of each producing unit must meet the specified requirements.

$$P_i^{min} \leq P_i \leq P_i^{max}, f \text{ or } i = 1, 2, 3, \ldots, N. \tag{16}$$

2.2.3. Ramp Rate Limit Constraints

The power outputs of thermal power units are limited by the ramp rate restrictions due to their inertia. This limitation is beneficial for prolonging the service life of the units and is characterized as follows:

$$\begin{cases} P_{t,i} - P_{t-1,i} \leq UR_i \\ P_{t-1,i} - P_{t,i} \leq DR_i \end{cases} \tag{17}$$

3. Design Methodology Using MMFO

3.1. Moth Flame Optimization

A new swarm intelligence optimization technique called the moth flame optimization (MFO) algorithm was introduced by Seyedali Mirjalili in 2015 [28]. It takes its cue from the nighttime spiral flight of a moth, which changes its direction of flight in response to the moon. However, in the case of artificial flame which is very close as compared to the moon, moths would eventually form a spiral flight path toward the flame, keeping their angle with the artificial light constant. The MFO is capable of exploring many solution spaces and has excellent parallel optimization abilities. For multimodal and non-convex problems where there is the possibility of many local optimum points, the MFO is more suitable.

3.1.1. Initialize Parameters

The MFO is fundamentally a swarm intelligence optimization algorithm. In the ELD problem, the candidate solutions are represented by m, where m refers to the moths. Moths navigate either in a one-dimensional or multi-dimensional space within the feasible domain, with their flight paths defining the range of possible solutions. The population of moths, M, is described as follows:

$$M = \begin{bmatrix} m_{1,1} & m_{1,2} & \cdots & m_{1,d} \\ m_{2,1} & m_{2,2} & \cdots & m_{2,d} \\ \vdots & \vdots & \ddots & \vdots \\ m_{n,1} & m_{n,2} & \cdots & m_{n,d} \end{bmatrix} \tag{18}$$

Here, d is dimension size, where n represent the number of moths.

Every moth in the MFO has a matching flame, and the moth updates its position by flying along the flame. The flame that the dimension represents as F is matched by the moth. The flame's position is stated as follows:

$$F = \begin{bmatrix} F_{1,1} & F_{1,2} & \cdots & F_{1,d} \\ F_{2,1} & F_{2,2} & \cdots & F_{2,d} \\ \vdots & \vdots & \ddots & \vdots \\ F_{n,1} & F_{n,2} & \cdots & F_{n,d} \end{bmatrix} \tag{19}$$

The search space's upper bound (ub) and lower bound (lb) are as follows:

$$ub = [ub_1, ub_2, ub_3, \cdots\cdots, ub_{n-1}, ub_n] \tag{20}$$

$$lb = [lb_1, lb_2, lb_3, \cdots\cdots, lb_{n-1}, lb_n] \tag{21}$$

3.1.2. The Moth's Location Updating

The logarithmic spiral function (S) that the moth flies according to is constructed as follows:

$$S(K_i, F_j) = d_i \times e^{at} \times cos(2\pi t) + F_j \tag{22}$$

where the symbol K_i indicates the i-th moth and designates a spiral function, and F_j signifies the location of the j-th flame. The constant a represents the value required to preserve the shape of the logarithm spiral. The distance between the j-th flame and the i-th moth is denoted as d_i. The random integer t is the distance parameters. The computation of the value of d_i is performed by employing Equation (20), defined as a value between -1 and +1.

$$d_i = |F_j - K_i| \tag{23}$$

The variable Ki represents the position of the i-th flame, F_j represents the position of the j-th moth, and the distance between the j-th flame and the i-th moth is represented by i and is updated by the following:

$$flame\ number = round\left((N - L) \times \frac{N-1}{T}\right) \tag{24}$$

where N indicates the upper limit of flames, T marks the upper limit of iterations, and L represents the current number of iterations. The adjustment of the position of each moth in relation to a flame is determined by the following equation.

3.2. Modified Moth Flame Optimizer

The MMFO is an enhanced version of the moth flame optimization (MFO) algorithm, where the movement of moths is based on the Archimedean spiral rather than the logarithmic spiral used in the standard MFO. The flight paths of the moths toward flames follow a spiral trajectory, providing better exploration and exploitation of the search space.

The position update formula for the MMFO using the Archimedean spiral is mathematically expressed as follows:

$$M_i^{t+1} = F_i + D.e^{b.l} \times cos(2\pi l) \quad (25)$$

where M_i^{t+1} is the updated position of the moth iii at iteration $t + 1$, F_i is the position of the flame i (the best solution found so far), D is the distance between the moth and the flame, b controls the shape of the spiral, and l is a random number in the range [−1,1].

This Archimedean spiral enables moths to perform adaptive movements, which ensures a balanced exploration of the search space early in the optimization process and a more focused exploitation near the optimal solutions in later stages.

Archimedean Spiral Motion

The core idea of the MMFO is to update the position of each moth based on the Archimedean spiral toward a flame. This spiral is given by the following:

$$M_i^{t+1} = F_i + D.l \quad (26)$$

Here, $D = \left|M_i^{t+1} - F_i\right|$ is the Euclidean distance between the moth and the flame. The Archimedean spiral is described mathematically as follows:

$$S(\theta) = r(\theta).(cos\theta, sin\theta) \quad (27)$$

where $r(\theta) = a + b.\theta)$ defines the radius of the spiral as a function of the angle θ, and a and b are constants controlling the growth of the spiral. For the MMFO, this translates to the following:

$$M_i^{t+1} = F_i + (a + b.\theta).(cos\theta, sin\theta) \quad (28)$$

where a controls the initial radius of the spiral, b defines how fast the spiral expands or contracts, and θ is a random value determining the angle of the spiral. Also, the coordinate for the Archimedean spiral could be found in [34,35].

This equation ensures that moths follow a spiral trajectory toward the flames, where they explore the search space in wide arcs initially (exploration) and tighten their paths as they converge toward the best solutions (exploitation). The pseudocode summary and graphical abstract of the proposed MMFO is given in Algorithm 1 and Figure 1.

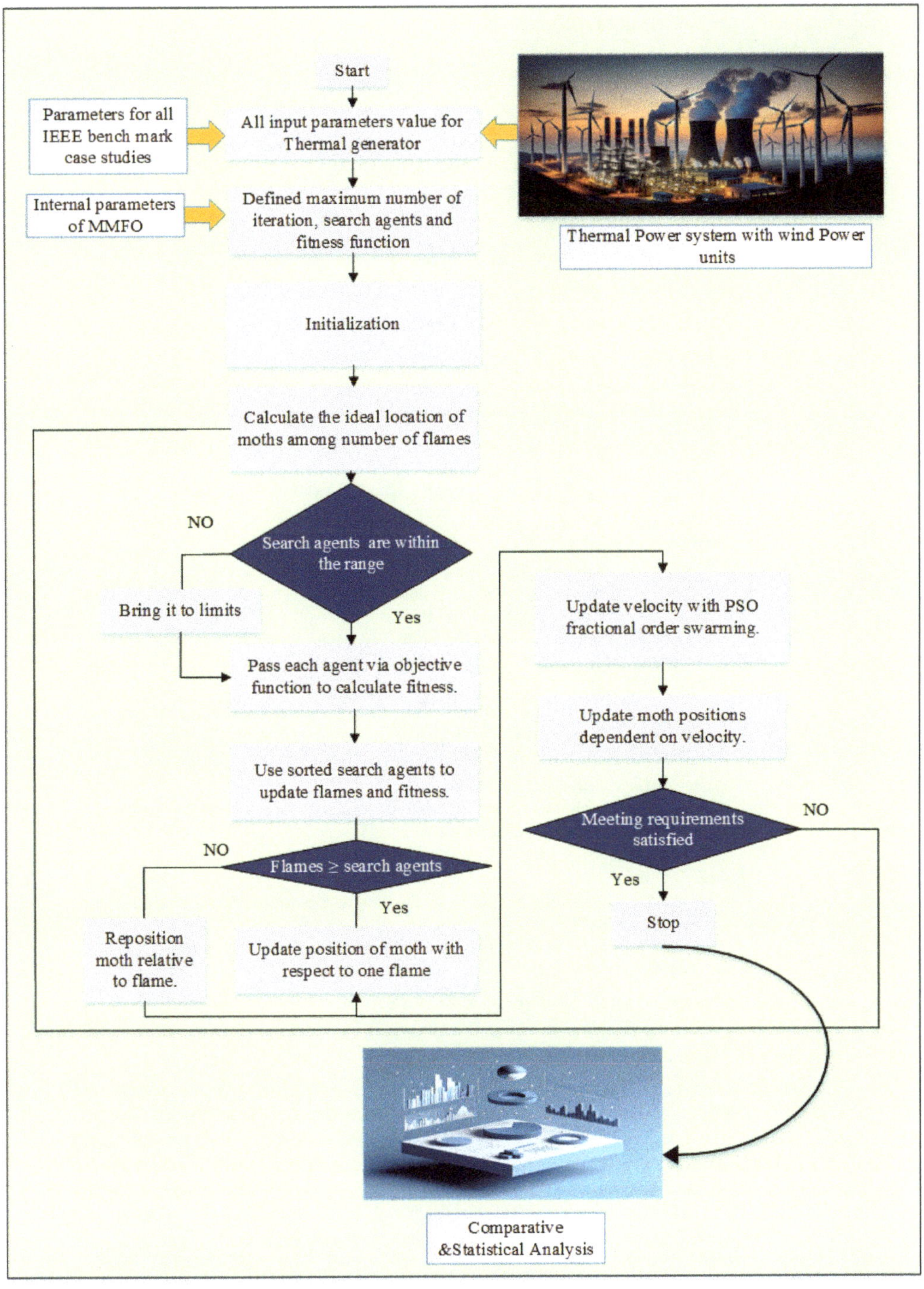

Figure 1. Graphical abstract of the proposed methodology.

Algorithm 1: Pseudocode of MMFO

1. Initialize parameters:
   Number of moths (N);
   Maximum number of iterations (MaxIter);
   Search space bounds (LB, UB);
   Moths' positions (M) randomly within the search space;
   Number of flames (F), initially equal to N.
2. Initialize flames (best solutions):
   Set the initial positions of flames (F) as the top N moths' positions.
3. Evaluate the fitness of all moths:
   For each moth Mi, evaluate the fitness using the objective function.
4. Sort moths based on fitness:
   Rank moths from best to worst based on fitness values.
   The best moths are selected as flames (F).
5. Loop through iterations (t = 1 to MaxIter):
   a. Update number of flames dynamically:
      Reduce the number of flames as iterations progress.
      Flame_no = round $(N - t \times (N - 1)/\text{MaxIter})$
   b. For each moth Mi (i = 1 to N):
      i. Select the corresponding flame F_i:
         If $i \leq$ Flame_no, select the i-th flame;
         If $i >$ Flame_no, select the last flame.
      ii. Calculate distance between the moth and the flame: $D = |F_i - M_i|$
      iii. Update moth position using Archimedean spiral:
         $M_i^{t+1} = F_i + D.l$
         where l is a random number in the range $[-1, 1]$, determining the spiral movement's direction and distance.
      iv. Ensure the updated moth position is within search bounds (LB, UB).
   c. Evaluate the fitness of updated moths:
      For each updated moth Mi, calculate its fitness using the objective function.
   d. Sort moths based on their updated fitness:
      Rank all moths based on fitness values.
   e. Update flames:
      Select the top Flame_no moths as the new flames for the next iteration.
   f. Check stopping criteria:
      If the maximum number of iterations is reached or the convergence condition is met, exit the loop.
6. Return the best flame (optimal solution) as the result.

4. Results and Discussion

The effectiveness of the proposed MMFO approach in solving the constraint optimization problem is assessed by initially applying it on a standard benchmark function. The most effective way for evaluating optimization techniques is to employ to standard unimodal and multimodal benchmark functions. The optimizer with the lowest error is regarded as a good optimizer [30,31]. For a fair comparison of performances of the proposed MMFO and other competing algorithms in solving the benchmark, common and default settings for all and individual algorithms are shown in Table 1.

Table 1. Common and default settings for all algorithms.

Algorithm	Common Setting		Default Setting
	Population Size	Number of Iterations	
PSO	30	1000	Inertia weight = 0.7, cognitive C_1 = 2, Social (C_2) = 2
GSA	30	1000	Gravitational constant (G) = 1
BA	30	1000	Loudness (A) = 0.5, pulse rate = 0.5
MFO	30	1000	Spiral function parameter (b) = 1
MMFO	30	1000	b = 1 + 0.5 × (1 − Iteration/Max_iteration);

In order to evaluate different optimization methods across different contexts, this paper uses a complete set of 11 benchmark functions. Unimodal functions are the first seven functions (F1–F7), whereas multimodal functions are the last four functions (F8–F11). All these benchmark functions have been taken from [28]. The MMFO achieves an optimum result in all different test scenarios. The results are tabulated in Table 2 which shows the performance of MMFO in terms of average fitness value over 100 independent runs with other state-of-the-art solvers, and it has been observed that the MMFO surpasses other optimization techniques in terms of average fitness value. To further demonstrate the superiority of our proposed optimizer, it has been also applied to a set of 10 benchmark functions consisting of different multimodal multi-objective optimization functions. The mathematical formulation and function details could be found in reference [36]. From Table 3, it has been realized that the MMFO outperforms the conventional MFO in terms of best, median, mean, and worst value and optimizes it up to optimum values. The results shown in Table 4 present statistically significant differences between MMFO and MFO in all metrics, with p-values below 0.05 using the Wilcoxon test. This indicates that MMFO exhibits a distinct optimization performance compared to MFO, suggesting that the modifications in MMFO have a substantial impact on the optimization outcomes. The consistent differences across metrics highlight the different behaviors of these two methods. In Table 4, it has been further concluded that the null hypothesis (H0) is rejected in all scenarios which indicates that our proposed MMFO differed significantly and outperformed its counterpart MFO.

In order to further validate the performance of the MMFO approach, it is first applied on the conventional ELD problem, which entails minimizing fuel cost. This assessment is carried out utilizing two practical benchmark IEEE testing systems. The subsequent content is presented as follows.

Case study 1 examines a small test system including three thermal units, each supporting a load requirement of 850 MW. The second case study focuses on a medium-sized test system consisting of 13 thermal generating units having a load demand of 1800 MW.

After validating the performance to solve the traditional ELD problem, the suggested technique minimizes fuel cost and emission by taking into consideration VPLEs, transmission line loss generator limitations of a standard IEEE benchmark system consisting of six power units for emission, and forty power units for wind power.

Table 2. MMFO comparison with other solvers for unimodal and multimodal benchmark functions.

Functions	Dim	MFO [28]		PSO [28]		GSA [28]		BA [28]		MMFO	
		Mean	STD	Mean	STD	Mean	STD	Mean	STD	Mean	STD
$F_1(x) = \sum_{i=1}^{n} x_i^2$	100	0.000117	0.00015	1.32115	1.15388	608.232	464.654	20792.4	5892.40	0.0039	0.0031
$F_2(x) = \sum_{i=1}^{n} \lvert x_i\rvert + \prod_{i=1}^{n} \lvert x_i\rvert$	100	0.000639	0.000877	7.71556	4.13212	22.7526	3.36513	89.785	41.9577	0.0040	0.0014
$F_3(x) = \sum_{i=1}^{n} \left(\sum_{j-1}^{i} x_j\right)^2$	100	696.730	188.527	736.393	361.781	135,760	48,652.6	62,481.3	29,769.1	1.4061×10^3	1.6103×10^3
$F_4(x) = \max_i \{\lvert x_i\rvert, 1 \leqslant i \leqslant n\}$	100	70.6864	5.27505	12.9728	2.63443	78.7819	2.81410	49.7432	10.14363	31.6315	10.5376
$F_5(x) = \sum_{i=1}^{n-1} \left[100(x_{i+1} - x_i^2)^2 + (x_i - 1)^2\right]$	100	139.148	120.260	77,360.83	51,156.15	741.003	781.2393	199,512	125,238	83.1924	109.3115
$F_6(x) = \sum_{i=1}^{n} ([x_i + 0.5])^2$	100	0.00011	9.87×10^{-5}	286.651	107.079	3080.96	898.635	17,053.4	4917.56	0.0037	0.0027
$F_7(x) = \sum_{i=1}^{n} ix_i^4 + \text{random}[0,1)$	100	0.091155	0.04642	1.037316	0.310315	0.112975	0.037607	6.045055	3.045277	0.0211	0.0064
$F_8(x) = \sum_{i=1}^{n} -x_i \sin\left(\sqrt{\lvert x_i\rvert}\right)$	100	8496.78	725.8737	−3571	430.7989	−2352.32	382.167	65,535	0	-9.4023×10^3	585.8782
$F_9(x) = \sum_{i=1}^{n} [x_i^2 - 10\cos(2\pi x_i) + 10]$	100	84.600	16.1665	124.29	14.2509	31.0001	13.6605	96.2152	19.5875	74.9637	22.3468
$F_{10}(x) = -20\exp\left(-0.2\sqrt{\frac{1}{n}\sum_{i=1}^{n} x_i^2}\right) - \exp\left(\frac{1}{n}\sum_{i=1}^{n} \cos(2\pi x_i)\right) + 20 + e$	100	1.2603	0.72956	9.1679	1.56898	3.74098	0.17126	15.9460	0.77495	0.0958	0.4038
$F_{11}(x) = \frac{1}{4000}\sum_{i=1}^{n} x_i^2 - \prod_{i=1}^{n} \cos\left(\frac{x_i}{\sqrt{i}}\right) + 1$	100	0.0190	0.02173	12.418	4.16583	0.04978	0.04978	220.281	54.7066	0.0165	0.0143

Table 3. MMFO vs. MFO comparison for CEC2020 benchmark functions.

Function	Best		Median		Mean		Std		Worst	
	MMFO	MFO	MMFO	MFO	MMFO	MFO	MMFO	MFO	MMFO	MFO
F1	7.5000×10^{-1}	7.5605×10^{-1}	7.5000×10^{-1}	7.8610×10^{-1}	7.5004×10^{-1}	8.0100×10^{-1}	4.9873×10^{-4}	2.9151×10^{-3}	8.0952×10^{-1}	1.0502×10^{0}
F2	7.5000×10^{-1}	1.4078×10^{0}	7.5000×10^{-1}	1.4673×10^{0}	7.5251×10^{-1}	1.5807×10^{0}	1.1347×10^{-2}	2.6191×10^{-3}	1.9372×10^{0}	3.2955×10^{0}
F3	1.0000×10^{0}	1.0789×10^{0}	1.0000×10^{0}	1.0975×10^{0}	1.0002×10^{0}	1.1002×10^{0}	1.0677×10^{-3}	5.8074×10^{-5}	1.1315×10^{0}	1.1488×10^{0}
F4	7.5000×10^{-1}	1.5865×10^{0}	7.5000×10^{-1}	1.6938×10^{0}	7.5008×10^{-1}	1.7240×10^{0}	9.0085×10^{-4}	3.3394×10^{-3}	8.4823×10^{-1}	2.1179×10^{0}
F5	1.7559×10^{0}	7.4318×10^{-1}	1.7559×10^{0}	7.6418×10^{-1}	1.7560×10^{0}	7.6312×10^{-1}	4.5372×10^{-4}	1.4216×10^{-4}	1.8116×10^{0}	7.8235×10^{-1}
F6	1.0000×10^{0}	4.3480×10^{-4}	1.0000×10^{0}	2.2378×10^{-1}	1.0003×10^{0}	2.8438×10^{-1}	2.6533×10^{-3}	2.4468×10^{-3}	1.2731×10^{0}	8.6231×10^{-1}
F7	1.3603×10^{0}	1.8459×10^{0}	1.3603×10^{0}	2.0237×10^{0}	1.3607×10^{0}	2.0365×10^{0}	5.0828×10^{-3}	2.6639×10^{-4}	2.0788×10^{0}	2.4668×10^{0}
F8	2.0373×10^{0}	4.4031×10^{0}	2.0373×10^{0}	4.5035×10^{0}	2.0375×10^{0}	4.5165×10^{0}	2.7515×10^{-3}	1.3499×10^{-4}	2.4898×10^{0}	4.7865×10^{0}
F9	9.5950×10^{-1}	1.2183×10^{0}	9.5950×10^{-1}	1.2426×10^{0}	9.5975×10^{-1}	1.2480×10^{0}	2.5713×10^{-3}	6.9523×10^{-5}	1.2761×10^{0}	1.3536×10^{0}
F10	2.9160×10^{0}	1.3471×10^{1}	2.9160×10^{0}	1.3637×10^{1}	2.9161×10^{0}	1.3695×10^{1}	2.8887×10^{-4}	5.7093×10^{-4}	2.9544×10^{0}	1.4400×10^{1}

Table 4. Statistical comparison of MMFO and MFO performance using Wilcoxon signed-rank test.

Test Metric	*p*-Value	Test Statistic (W)	Conclusion (Reject H0)
Best value	0.0001	116866.0000	Yes
Median value	0.0000	116867.0000	Yes
Mean value	0.0001	116884.0000	Yes
Std	0.0000	423354.0000	Yes
Worst value	0.0000	129714.0000	Yes

4.1. Case 1. Three Thermal Generating Units with a Load Demand of 850 MW

The purpose of this case study is to assess the performance of the proposed MMFO and MFO with a load demand of 850 MW using a three-unit producing system, taking into account the valve-point loading impact. The parameters for fuel cost and the upper and lower limits for generators have been sourced from references [17,33,37–42]. The findings derived from the use of MMFO and MFO are presented in Table 5, alongside the findings documented in the existing literature. Table 6 illustrates the distribution of powers among several generators in response to a specified load demand of 850 MW. The suggested MMFO algorithm demonstrates superior performance, achieving a total cost of 8194.48008 USD/h, in comparison to MFO and other state-of-the-art algorithms.

Table 5. Optimum results for case 1 with other optimization techniques.

Algorithm	P1 (MW)	P1 (MW)	P1 (MW)	PG (MW)	Cost (USD/h)
GSA [39]	300.210	149.795	399.995	850	8234.1
PSO-SQP [38]	300.3	400	149.7	850	8234.1
PSO [38]	300.3	400	149.7	850	8234.1
GA [38]	398.7	399.6	50.1	848.4	8222.1
GA-PS-SQP [38]	300.30	400	149.70	850	8234.10
QOPO [43]	300.25	400	149.75	850	8234.07
MFO	358.0935	365.7145	126.192	850	8198.2314
MMFO	396.769	328.4747	124.7563	850	8194.4800

Table 6. Comparison of total fuel cost with up-to-date algorithms for case 1.

Method	Minimum Cost (USD/h)
GWO [13]	8253.11
GA [37]	8234.419
EP [37]	8234.1357
SA [37]	8234.1355
GA-PS-SQP [38]	8234.1
CPSO-SQP [41]	8234.07
NDS [44]	8234.07
MFEP [40]	8234.08
NSS [37]	8234.08
CPSO [41]	8234.07
GSA[39]	8234.1
iBA [42]	8234.07
GAB [40]	8234.08
QOPO [43]	8234.07
MFO	8198.23141
MMFO	8194.48008

Moreover, the findings are succinctly presented in Table 6 and juxtaposed with alternative comparison methodologies proposed in the existing literature. The proposed method yields superior outcomes compared to previous procedures. It has been seen that the proposed method achieved a superior solution and minimized the overall fuel cost to the optimal level, demonstrating the superiority of the suggested technique over other state-of-the-art algorithms in terms of total net gain in cost (USD/h). Figure 2 displays the convergence characteristic graph of MMFO vs. MFO, illustrating a more rapid convergence and the achievement of the lowest fuel cost within a reduced number of iterations as compared to MFO. Figure 3 shows the statistical analysis of MMFO vs MFO using cumulative distribution function (CDF), histograms, boxplot and fitness propagation obtained during the course of simulation

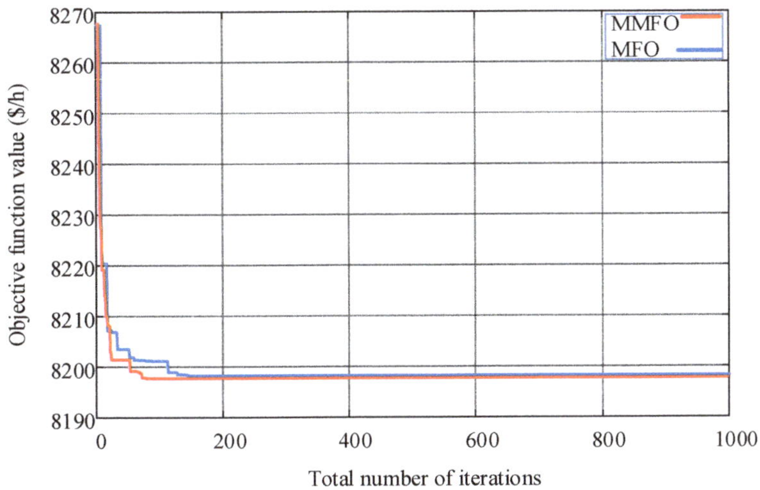

Figure 2. MMFO vs. MFO convergence characteristics curve for case 1.

4.2. Case 2. Thirteen Thermal Generating Units with 1800 MW Load Demands

This case study examines the efficacy of the suggested MMFO with load requirements of 1800 MW using the system of 13 generating units, taking into account the valve-point loading effect. The parameters for fuel cost and the upper and lower limits for generators have been sourced from references [8,17,38,40,43,45,46]. The outcomes derived using MMFO and MFO are presented in Table 7 for load demands of 1800 MW, in addition to the findings reported in the literature. Table 7 depicts the distribution of power among various generators in response to load demands of 1800 MW. The suggested MMFO demonstrates superior outcomes, with a total expenditure of 17,960.14253 USD/h. The data presented in Table 8 clearly demonstrate that the suggested method outperforms other strategies, including conventional Fast EP (FEP), EP (CEP), MFEP, enhanced FEP (IFEP), and PSO. With the expansion of the system to 13 units, the suggested technique has demonstrated a significant cost reduction of at least USD per hour in comparison to the Fast EP (FEP), MFEP, and PSO techniques for a load requirement of 1800 MW. The aforementioned results demonstrate the efficacy of the suggested MMFO approach. Figure 4 indicates that the MMFO and MFO convergence characteristic allows it to reach the global optimal solution with fewer iterations. When compared to other methods discussed in the relevant literature, the suggested MMFO has shown to be more effective. Optimal fuel cost and enhanced convergence rate have improved the solution's overall quality. Figure 5 shows the complete statistical analysis of the proposed MMFO VS MFO consisting of CDF, histogram, boxplot and fitness propagation demonstrating the reliability consistency of MMFO over MFO.

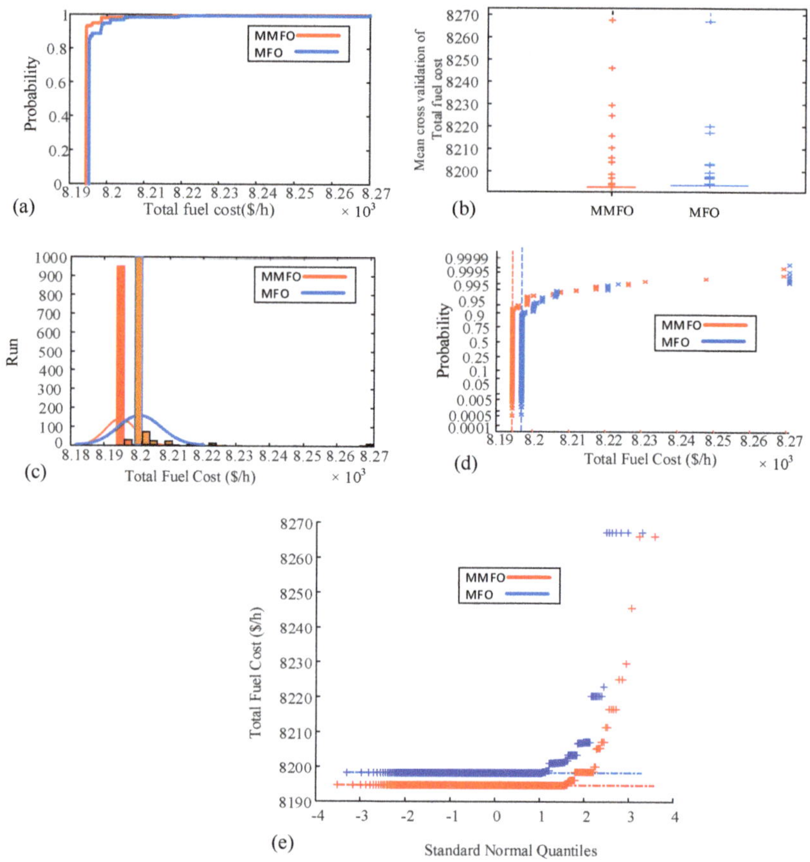

Figure 3. MMFO vs. MFO comparison during total fuel cost minimization for 3 thermal generating units: (**a**) CDF, (**b**) boxplot illustration, (**c**) histogram, (**d**) probability plot for normal distribution, and (**e**) quantile–quantile plot.

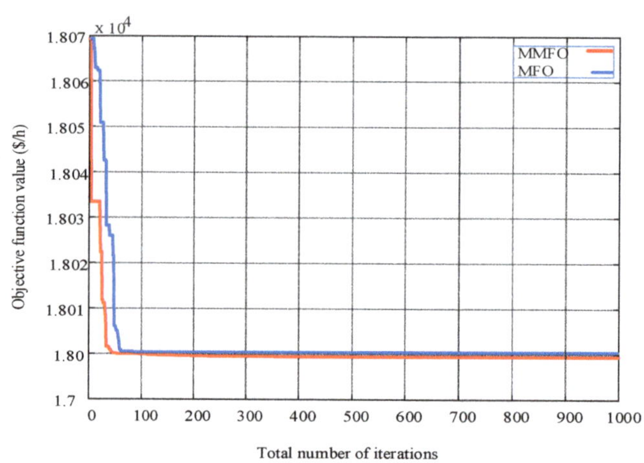

Figure 4. Convergence characteristic of MMFO vs. MFO for 13-unit system.

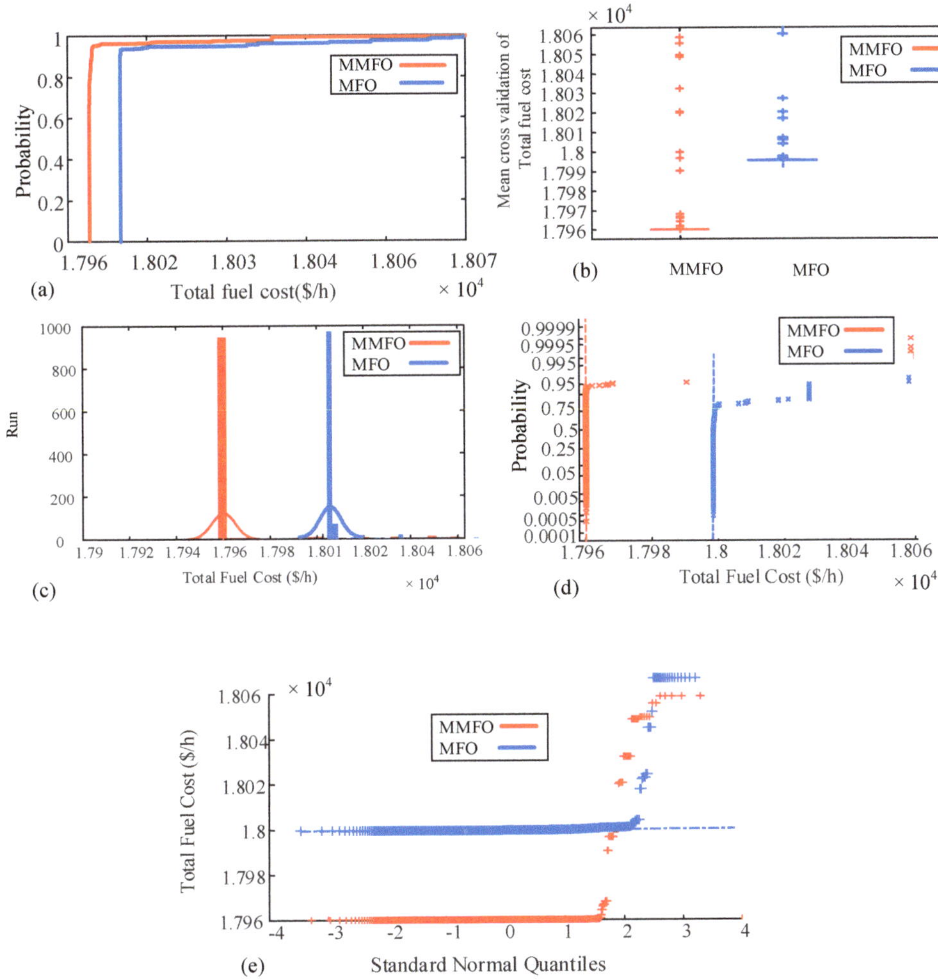

Figure 5. MMFO vs. MFO comparison during total fuel cost minimization for 13 thermal generating units: (**a**) CDF, (**b**) boxplot illustration, (**c**) histogram, (**d**) probability plot for normal distribution, and (**e**) quantile–quantile plot.

Table 7. Optimum power distribution for 13 generator units with other algorithms.

Unit	GWO [13]	NN-EPSO [13]	MFO	MMFO
1	807.1247	490	532.6321	481.7726
2	144.869	189	305.1329	194.1905
3	297.9434	214	89.01453	244.7307
4	60	160	117.7604	116.1982
5	60	90	117.7238	117.4941
6	60	120	122.1081	132.1647
7	60	103	60	77.94045

Table 7. *Cont.*

Unit	GWO [13]	NN-EPSO [13]	MFO	MMFO
8	60	88	99.69107	125.2659
9	60.0362	104	92.019	92.16435
10	40	13	40	40
11	40.0267	58	48.91808	43.26936
12	55	66	120	78.6438
13	55	55	55	56.16537
TG (MW)	1800	1750	1800	1800
Total Cost (USD/h)	18,051.11	18,442.59	18,008.89	17,960.14

Table 8. Comparison of total fuel cost with up-to-date algorithms for case 2.

Technique	Total Fuel Cost (USD/h)
MFEP [40]	18,028.09
FEP [40]	18,018.00
PSO [43]	18,030.72
CEP [40]	18,048.21
MFO	18,008.89
MMFO	17,960.14253

4.3. Case 3. Six Generating Units with 1000 MW Load Demand with Emission

A small test system has been used in this scenario to assess its efficacy in delivering a more efficient and precise solution for high load demand. The generator maximum and lowest limitations, emission coefficients, and fuel cost coefficients have been extracted from references [43,47–50]. Table 9 displays the optimal solutions obtained by MMFO, which includes the power generating output of each unit for the economic emission dispatch (EELD) problem. This study examines the outcomes obtained utilizing the scalar factor w. It has been noticed that when w is set to 0.5, the desired balance values are reached. In this situation, the EELD problem obtained with a weight (w) of 0.5, as shown in the table, has been selected for further investigation and comparison [4]. Table 10 presents a comparison of the solutions obtained by MMFO and other previously published approaches for minimizing fuel cost (FC) in ELD and minimizing emissions (E) in the economic emission issue. Based on the table, MMFO has produced lower results for the lowest fuel cost compared to other algorithms. The acquired findings are compared with nine distinct strategies that have been suggested in the literature and sourced from [43] The simulation results indicate that the suggested MMFO approach offers superior fuel cost compared to other strategies but with somewhat higher emissions compared to NGPSO. The emission level is significantly elevated owing to the significant reduction in fuel cost of 51,337.3323 USD/h, which is 15,201.0077 USD/h lower than NGPSO. In addition, the suggested MMFO approach has been shown to provide both the lowest fuel cost and the lowest pollution cost when compared to other strategies. The graph in Figure 6 illustrates the convergence characteristic of total fuel cost when using various scaling factors. It reveals that the convergence is rapid and achieves the optimal solution in a reduced number of iterations. Thus, it can be said that the suggested MMFO offers a superior and better compromised solution.

Table 9. Optimum power allocation among 6 units for different values of w.

w	P1	P2	P3	P4	P5	P6	Total Load	Fuel Cost (USD/h)	Emission (tons/h)
0	103.652	99.53047	154.1789	159.767	246.1043	236.7673	1000	52,009.8943	801.4391
0.1	103.652	99.53047	154.1789	159.767	246.1043	236.7673	1000	51,796.5424	807.0951
0.2	103.652	99.53047	154.1789	159.767	246.1043	236.7673	1000	51,812.7033	806.5594
0.3	103.652	99.53047	154.1789	159.767	246.1043	236.7673	1000	51,616.4886	813.7519
0.4	103.652	99.53047	154.1789	159.767	246.1043	236.7673	1000	51,347.5181	824.8128
0.5	103.652	99.53047	154.1789	159.767	246.1043	236.7673	1000	51,337.3323	824.4148
0.6	103.652	99.53047	154.1789	159.767	246.1043	236.7673	1000	51,048.3607	842.7160
0.7	103.652	99.53047	154.1789	159.767	246.1043	236.7673	1000	51,023.9795	845.2482
0.8	103.652	99.53047	154.1789	159.767	246.1043	236.7673	1000	50,824.5949	862.3027
0.9	103.652	99.53047	154.1789	159.767	246.1043	236.7673	1000	50,508.2147	910.1253
1	103.652	99.53047	154.1789	159.767	246.1043	236.7673	1000	50,385.4867	986.7312

Table 10. Comparison of results of six-unit system with other algorithms.

Unit	1	2	3	4	5	6	C	E
QOTLBO	107.3101	121.497	206.501	206.5826	304.9838	304.6036	64,912	1281
TLBO	107.8651	121.5676	206.1771	205.1879	306.5555	304.1423	64,922	1281
MODE	108.6284	115.9456	206.7969	210	301.8884	308.4127	64,843	1286
PDE	107.3965	122.1418	206.7536	203.7047	308.1045	303.3797	64,920	1281
NSGA	113.1259	116.4488	217.4191	207.9492	304.6641	291.5969	64,962	1281
SPEA	104.1573	122.9807	214.9553	203.1387	316.0302	289.9396	64,884	1285
MOGA	108.9318	123.1808	205.1513	206.67	304.8553	302.6093	64,838.57	1285.49
OGHS	105.7331	119.0825	205.2976	204.7772	305.8042	308.9128	64,722.74	1281.349
NGPSO	144.0425	150	190.507	192.9285	284.9083	288.0456	66,538.34	1228.365
QOPO	82.83027	82.61994	197.7722	202.2269	317.4203	317.6234	61,197.88	1238.819
MMFO	103.652	99.53047	154.1789	159.767	246.1043	236.7673	51,337.3323	824.4148

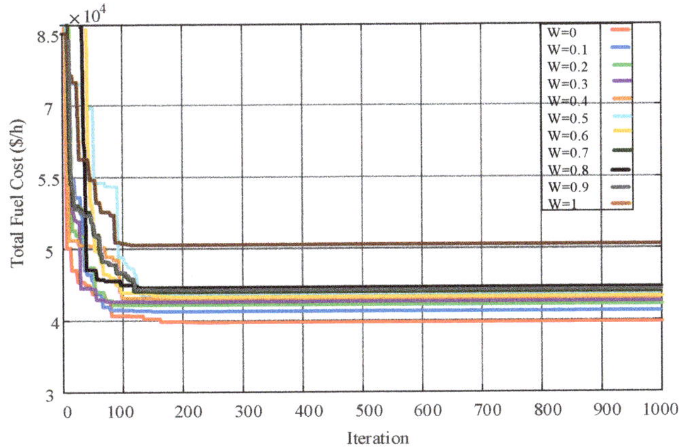

Figure 6. MMFO convergence graphs for IEEE six-generator system with different scaling.

4.4. Case 4. Thirty-Seven Thermal Generating Units and Three Wind Power Units with Demand of 10,500 MW

This scenario investigates a modified case study of ELD-VPLE, focusing on a total of 40 generators. Specifically, the analysis includes thirty-seven thermal power generating units and three units of wind power producing units, which are examined for the bi-objective function. The integration of ELD-VPLE with wind power is achieved by employing the system model formulation of Equation (3). Equation (5) is used to include the total cost of generation. The dataset containing information on thermal and wind power generating units has been sourced from references [27,45,46,51,52]. Table 11 depicts the distribution of power among various generators in response to load demands of 10,500 MW. Table 12 presents the optimal overall cost value in dollars per hour when compared to alternative algorithms. Furthermore, it has been shown that the suggested MMFO exhibits strong performance in the context of bi-objective functions, thereby reducing the overall fuel cost to an optimal level. Furthermore, it has significantly enhanced the overall quality of the solution in terms of achieving the most efficient fuel cost, faster convergence rate, and improved dependability. As shown in Figure 7, the minimum fitness value is obtained in a fewer number of iterations; furthermore, it has been observed that the convergence process is expedited, resulting in a shorter number of iterations to obtain the global optimum solution.

Table 11. Optimum power allocation for 40-unit test system (37 thermal and 3 wind power units).

Power Units	MFO	MMFO	Power Units	MFO	MMFO
1	114	112.2146	21	523.2265	534.9080
2	110.782043	85.7714	22	345.1678	519.7360
3	97.35768193	88.2117	23	523.2798	461.0149
4	179.853732	180.9641	24	550	532.9676
5	47	82.4790	25	523.2365	532.8027
6	140	139.9986	26	522.6056	541.2884
7	300	300	27	47	80.9368
8	300	289.7228	28	163.3979	112.6556
9	285.1041	288.4185	29	169.6291	126.9149
10	130	200.5044	30	190	158.8551
11	318.0878	289.2551	31	172.465	199.9890
12	94	243.7934	32	166.535	172.3346
13	216.8874	304.4608	33	90	90
14	484.0405941	390.7212	34	65.63347	86.84495
15	500	500	35	110	57.10207
16	500	353.3224	36	110	72.98398
17	500	313.0460	37	511.2403	500.4913
18	220	421.2108	38	18	19.85508
19	511.4687	495.8544	39	46	46.0001
20	550	518.3697	40	54	54
Total cost MFO 139,576.3965			Total cost MMFO 138,155.7853		

Table 12. Comparison of total fuel cost for 40-unit test system with wind power units.

Method	Minimum Cost (USD/h)
Best Compromise [51]	143,587.90
PSO [52]	139,000.03
DWTED2 [51]	154,993.00
PWTED2 [51]	156,878.97
EMA [27]	144,356.00
GAEPSO [27]	146,035.00
PSO [27]	142,068.00
COOT [52]	139,000.63
MFO	139,576.3965
MMFO	138,155.7853

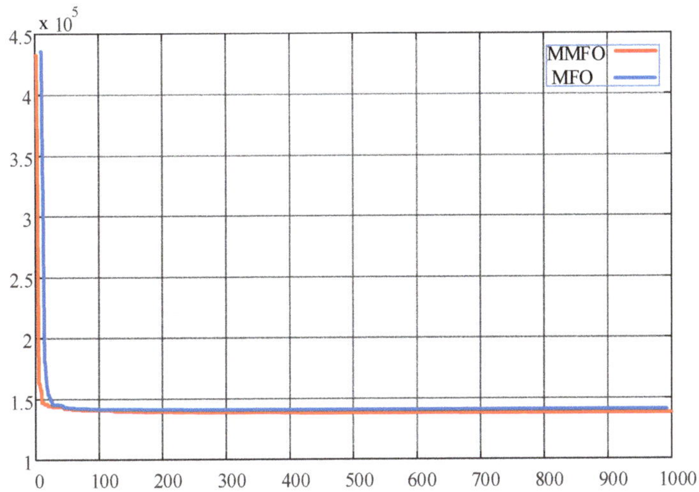

Figure 7. Convergence characteristic of MMFO vs. MFO for 40-unit system with wind power.

5. Comparative and Statistical Analysis

The proposed MMFO was applied to solve the ELD problem for the IEEE benchmark systems comprising three, six, eleven, and forty generating units, incorporating wind power effects. The results obtained by the proposed optimizer were aligned with and superior to those reported in references [13,27,37–46,51,52]. The MMFO successfully achieved optimal solutions for addressing the ELD problem while considering both emission constraints and wind power factors. The findings confirm that MMFO outperforms other optimization methods in solving this non-convex, non-linear, and complex optimization problem, offering a faster convergence rate. In comparison with methods cited in the literature, the MMFO demonstrated superior performance under similar boundary conditions and characteristics. Convergence graphs from the simulations across all case studies highlight MMFO's faster convergence and ability to find optimal solutions in fewer iterations. As evidenced in Tables 6, 8, 10, and 12, the proposed MMFO achieved a significant reduction in total fuel cost, demonstrating a clear advantage over state-of-the-art techniques. The results show that MMFO consistently improves solution quality and minimizes total cost to its optimal value. A comprehensive statistical analysis was conducted on the test systems to ensure the dependability, consistency, and stability of the proposed method. A total of 100 independent simulations were performed, with the median outcome serving as a benchmark for determining the best solution. Figures 3, 5 and 8 provide a quantitative analysis using the empirical cumulative distribution function (CDF), histograms, boxplots, and fitness progressions in each independent run. Figures 3a, 5a, and 8a demonstrate that MMFO significantly increases the probability of finding the optimal solution compared to traditional MFO. Figures 3b, 5b and 8b reveal that MMFO consistently achieves a lower median of the final solution in 100 trials compared to MFO, while Figures 3c, 5c, and 8c show the histogram indicating minimal fitness after multiple trials. Moreover, Figures 3d, 5d and 8d reflect the probability distribution for normality, indicating that MMFO has a higher likelihood of solving the ELD and EELD problems more efficiently than conventional MFO. Finally, Figures 3e, 5e and 8e show that MMFO exhibits a favorable minimum fitness relative to the quantiles of the normal distribution. Based on these visual and graphical analyses, it is evident that incorporating the Archimedean spiral into the optimization framework significantly enhances MMFO's performance and serves as a robust mathematical tool for developing new variants of traditional optimization techniques.

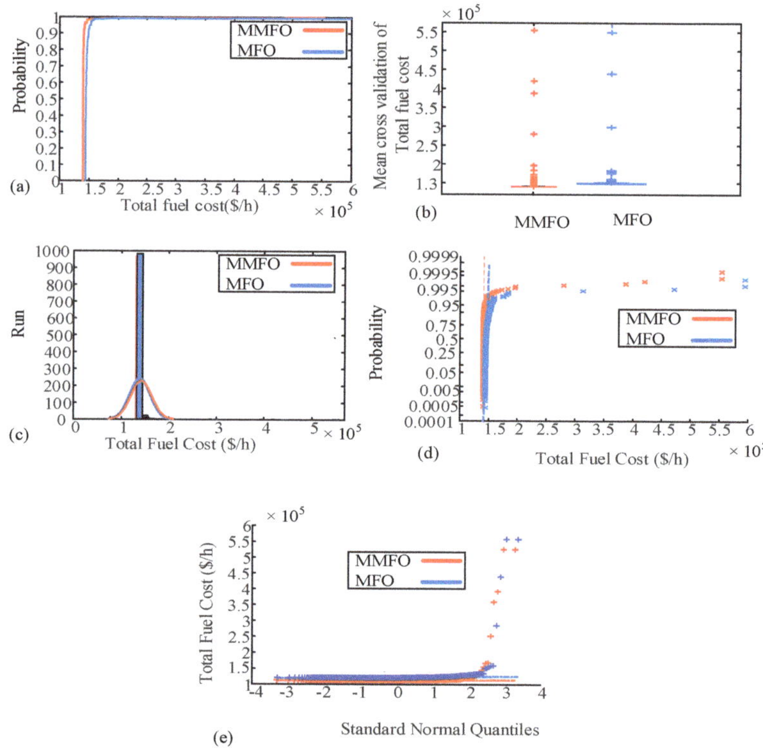

Figure 8. MMFO vs. MFO statistical analysis during total fuel cost minimization for 37 thermal generating units and 3 wind power: (**a**) CDF, (**b**) boxplot illustration, (**c**) histogram, (**d**) probability plot for normal distribution, and (**e**) quantile–quantile plot.

6. Conclusions

This study introduces a novel variant of the moth flame optimization algorithm, termed MMFO, designed to address the complex ELD and EELD problems, which are characterized by non-linearity, non-convexity, and non-smoothness. The proposed MMFO method is initially validated through its application to a wide range of generating units, from small systems with three units to large-scale systems with up to forty units, demonstrating its capability to deliver reliable and competitive solutions.

The effectiveness and performance of the MMFO approach are assessed across various scales, including small (three units and six units with emission), medium (thirteen units), and large (forty units) generating systems consisting of thirty-seven thermal and three wind power units. The evaluation considers fuel cost, emission cost, and wind power cost under different load demands and constraints. Comparative results highlight the efficacy of the proposed method in solving simple ELD problems, EELD and ELD with wind power scenarios, by achieving the lowest cost and emissions in power generation across all unit sizes in distinct case studies.

For case 1, the proposed MMFO reveals an improvement in percentages of 0.71% for GWO, 0.485% for GA, and 0.48% over EP, SA, GA-PS-SQP, NDS, MEEP, NSS, HCPSO, GSA, iBA, GAB, QOPO, and MFO in total fuel cost in dollars per hour, keeping in view it is a very small system. For case 2, the optimal setting determined by MMFO with MEEP, FEP, PSO, CEP, and MFO shows an improvement in percentages of 0.3768%, 0.3211%, 0.3914, 0.4879%, and 0.2706%, respectively, in dollars per hour.

For case 3, the MMFO again has superiority in net improvement in percentage over other state-of-the-art solvers in both fuel cost and emission. There were observed net improvements in percentages in fuel cost of 20.912%, 20.924%, 20.828%, 20.922%, 20.973%, 20.878%, 20.822%, 20.681%, 22.845%, and 16.112% with QOTLBO, TLBO, MODE, PDE, NSGA, SPEA, MOGA, OGHS, NGPSO, and QOPO, respectively, while in the case of emission reduction, there was an improvement of 35.64% with QOTLBO and TLBO, 35.893% with MODE, 35.64 with PDE and NSGA, and 35.84%, 35.867%, 35.860%, and 35.88% with SPEA, MOGA, OGHS, NGPSO, and QOPO, respectively.

For case 4 consisting of thirty-seven thermal units and three wind power units, a net improvement in percentage in total fuel cost was obtained that corresponds to 3.783%, 0.6073%, 10.863%, 11.934%, 4.295%, 2.753%, 0.6077%, and 1.017%.

Furthermore, the method's reliability, robustness, and consistency are confirmed through statistical analyses, including cumulative distribution function (CDF) plots, lowest objective function values, normal distribution probabilities, and histogram representations across independent runs. The results reveal that incorporating the Archimedean spiral within the MFO framework significantly enhances the optimizer's convergence speed. The obtained results provide strong evidence of MMFO's efficiency in discovering superior and optimal solutions for the EELD problem, establishing MMFO as a highly effective tool for combined economic and emission optimization as well as for the ELD problem with wind power. Additionally, the proposed approach requires less computational effort and demonstrates superior convergence properties, achieving optimal trade-offs more efficiently than alternative methods.

In the future, the proposed MMFO will be implemented for real-time load dispatch in smart grids for fuel costs and emission optimization with the integration of more complex constraints in real-time power dispatch.

Author Contributions: Conceptualization, H.A., A.W. and H.P.; methodology, H.A., A.W. and H.P.; writing—original draft, H.A. and A.W.; writing—review and editing, A.W. and H.P.; supervision, A.W.; funding acquisition, H.A. and A.W. All authors have read and agreed to the published version of the manuscript.

Funding: This article is derived from a research grant funded by the Research, Development, and Innovation Authority (RDIA)—Kingdom of Saudi Arabia—with grant number (13385-Tabuk-2023-UT-R-3-1-SE).

Data Availability Statement: The original contributions presented in the study are included in the article, further inquiries can be directed to the corresponding author.

Acknowledgments: The authors extend their appreciation to the Research, Development, and Innovation Authority (RDIA), Saudi Arabia, for funding this work through grant number (13385-Tabuk-2023-UT-R-3-1-SE).

Conflicts of Interest: The authors declare that there are no conflicts of interest.

References

1. Arul, R.; Ravi, G.; Velusami, S. An improved harmony search algorithm to solve economic load dispatch problems with generator constraints. *Electr. Eng.* **2014**, *96*, 55–63. [CrossRef]
2. Yu, J.; Kim, C.-H.; Rhee, S.-B. Clustering cuckoo search optimization for economic load dispatch problem. *Neural Comput. Appl.* **2020**, *32*, 16951–16969. [CrossRef]
3. Walters, D.C.; Sheble, G.B. Genetic algorithm solution of economic dispatch with valve point loading. *IEEE Trans. Power Syst.* **1993**, *8*, 1325–1332. [CrossRef]
4. Ismaeel, A.A.; Houssein, E.H.; Khafaga, D.S.; Abdullah Aldakheel, E.; AbdElrazek, A.S.; Said, M. Performance of osprey optimization algorithm for solving economic load dispatch problem. *Mathematics* **2023**, *11*, 4107. [CrossRef]
5. Ramalingam, R.; Karunanidy, D.; Alshamrani, S.S.; Rashid, M.; Mathumohan, S.; Dumka, A. Oppositional Pigeon-Inspired Optimizer for Solving the Non-Convex Economic Load Dispatch Problem in Power Systems. *Mathematics* **2022**, *10*, 3315. [CrossRef]
6. Said, M.; El-Rifaie, A.M.; Tolba, M.A.; Houssein, E.H.; Deb, S. An efficient chameleon swarm algorithm for economic load dispatch problem. *Mathematics* **2021**, *9*, 2770. [CrossRef]
7. Chen, K.; Zhu, Z.; Wang, J. Economic dispatch for smart buildings with load demand of high volatility based on quasi-quadratic online adaptive dynamic programming. *Mathematics* **2022**, *10*, 4701. [CrossRef]
8. Hsieh, Y.-Z.; Su, M.-C. A Q-learning-based swarm optimization algorithm for economic dispatch problem. *Neural Comput. Appl.* **2016**, *27*, 2333–2350. [CrossRef]
9. Jain, N.K.; Nangia, U.; Jain, A. PSO for Multiobjective Economic Load Dispatch (MELD) for Minimizing Generation Cost and Transmission Losses. *J. Inst. Eng. Ser. B* **2016**, *97*, 185–191. [CrossRef]
10. Jain, N.K.; Nangia, U.; Jain, J. Economic Load Dispatch Using Adaptive Social Acceleration Constant Based Particle Swarm Optimization. *J. Inst. Eng. Ser. B* **2018**, *99*, 431–439. [CrossRef]
11. Jayabarathi, T.; Bahl, P.; Ohri, H.; Yazdani, A.; Ramesh, V. A hybrid BFA-PSO algorithm for economic dispatch with valve-point effects. *Front. Energy* **2012**, *6*, 155–163. [CrossRef]
12. Jayabarathi, T.; Yazdani, A.; Ramesh, V. Application of the invasive weed optimization algorithm to economic dispatch problems. *Front. Energy* **2012**, *6*, 255–259. [CrossRef]
13. Kamboj, V.K.; Bath, S.K.; Dhillon, J.S. Solution of non-convex economic load dispatch problem using Grey Wolf Optimizer. *Neural Comput. Appl.* **2016**, *27*, 1301–1316. [CrossRef]
14. Kamboj, V.K.; Bhadoria, A.; Bath, S.K. Solution of non-convex economic load dispatch problem for small-scale power systems using ant lion optimizer. *Neural Comput. Appl.* **2016**, *28*, 2181–2192. [CrossRef]
15. Labbi, Y.; Ben Attous, D. A hybrid particle swarm optimization and pattern search method to solve the economic load dispatch problem. *Int. J. Syst. Assur. Eng. Manag.* **2014**, *5*, 435–443. [CrossRef]
16. Labbi, Y.; Ben Attous, D. A Hybrid Big Bang–Big Crunch optimization algorithm for solving the different economic load dispatch problems. *Int. J. Syst. Assur. Eng. Manag.* **2017**, *8*, 275–286. [CrossRef]
17. Labbi, Y.; Ben Attous, D.; Mahdad, B. Artificial bee colony optimization for economic dispatch with valve point effect. *Front. Energy* **2017**, *8*, 449–458. [CrossRef]
18. Mahdad, B.; Srairi, K. Solving practical economic dispatch using hybrid GA–DE–PS method. *Int. J. Syst. Assur. Eng. Manag.* **2014**, *5*, 391–398. [CrossRef]
19. Murali, K.; Jayabarathi, T. Solution to economic dispatch problem with valve-point loading effect by using catfish PSO algorithm. *Front. Energy* **2014**, *8*, 290–296. [CrossRef]
20. Nascimento, M.H.R.; Nunes, M.V.A.; Rodríguez, J.L.M.; Leite, J.C. A new solution to the economical load dispatch of power plants and optimization using differential evolution. *Electr. Eng.* **2017**, *99*, 561–571. [CrossRef]
21. Pattanaik, J.K.; Basu, M.; Dash, D.P. Dynamic economic dispatch: A comparative study for differential evolution, particle swarm optimization, evolutionary programming, genetic algorithm, and simulated annealing. *J. Electr. Syst. Inf. Technol.* **2019**, *6*, 1. [CrossRef]
22. Prakash, T.; Singh, V.P.; Singh, S.P.; Mohanty, S.R. Economic load dispatch problem: Quasi-oppositional self-learning TLBO algorithm. *Energy Syst.* **2018**, *9*, 415–438. [CrossRef]
23. Yu, X.; Yu, X.; Lu, Y.; Sheng, J. Economic and emission dispatch using ensemble multi-objective differential evolution algorithm. *Sustainability* **2018**, *10*, 418. [CrossRef]
24. Jiang, S.; Ji, Z.; Wang, Y. A novel gravitational acceleration enhanced particle swarm optimization algorithm for wind–thermal economic emission dispatch problem considering wind power availability. *Int. J. Electr. Power Energy Syst.* **2015**, *73*, 1035–1050. [CrossRef]
25. Pandit, M.; Chaudhary, V.; Dubey, H.M.; Panigrahi, B. Multi-period wind integrated optimal dispatch using series PSO-DE with time-varying Gaussian membership function based fuzzy selection. *Int. J. Electr. Power Energy Syst.* **2015**, *73*, 259–272. [CrossRef]
26. Morshed, M.J.; Asgharpour, A. Hybrid imperialist competitive-sequential quadratic programming (HIC-SQP) algorithm for solving economic load dispatch with incorporating stochastic wind power: A comparative study on heuristic optimization techniques. *Energy Convers. Manag.* **2014**, *84*, 30–40. [CrossRef]

27. Hagh, M.T.; Kalajahi, S.M.S.; Ghorbani, N. Solution to economic emission dispatch problem including wind farms using Exchange Market Algorithm Method. *Appl. Soft Comput.* **2020**, *88*, 106044. [CrossRef]
28. Mirjalili, S. Moth-flame optimization algorithm: A novel nature-inspired heuristic paradigm. *Knowl. Based Syst.* **2015**, *89*, 228–249. [CrossRef]
29. Chang, C.C.W.; Ding, T.J.; Han, W.; Chai, C.C.; Yam, C.M.; Yian, H.C.; Xin, L.H. Moth flame optimization for the maximum power point tracking scheme of photovoltaic system under partial shading conditions. *Energy Rep.* **2023**, *9*, 374–379. [CrossRef]
30. Wadood, A.; Park, H. A Novel Application of Fractional Order Derivative Moth Flame Optimization Algorithm for Solving the Problem of Optimal Coordination of Directional Overcurrent Relays. *Fractal Fract.* **2024**, *8*, 251. [CrossRef]
31. Wadood, A.; Ahmed, E.; Rhee, S.B.; Sattar Khan, B. A Fractional-Order Archimedean Spiral Moth–Flame Optimization Strategy to Solve Optimal Power Flows. *Fractal Fract.* **2024**, *8*, 225. [CrossRef]
32. Nadimi-Shahraki, M.H.; Zamani, H.; Fatahi, A.; Mirjalili, S. MFO-SFR: An enhanced moth-flame optimization algorithm using an effective stagnation finding and replacing strategy. *Mathematics* **2023**, *11*, 862. [CrossRef]
33. Khan, B.S.; Raja, M.A.Z.; Qamar, A.; Chaudhary, N.I. Design of moth flame optimization heuristics for integrated power plant system containing stochastic wind. *Appl. Soft Comput.* **2021**, *104*, 107193. [CrossRef]
34. Hammer, Ø. *The Perfect Shape: Spiral Stories*; Springer: Berlin/Heidelberg, Germany, 2016.
35. Guo, M.; Wang, J.S.; Zhu, L.; Guo, S.S.; Xie, W. Improved ant lion optimizer based on spiral complex path searching patterns. *IEEE Access* **2020**, *8*, 22094–22126. [CrossRef]
36. Liang, J.J.; Qu, B.; Gong, D.W.; Yue, C. *Problem Definitions and Evaluation Criteria for the CEC 2019 Special Session on Multimodal Multiobjective Optimization*; Computational Intelligence Laboratory, Zhengzhou University: Zhengzhou, China, 2019; pp. 353–370.
37. Tsai, M.-T.; Gow, H.-J.; Lin, W.-M. A novel stochastic search method for the solution of economic dispatch problems with non-convex fuel cost functions. *Int. J. Electr. Power Energy Syst.* **2011**, *33*, 1070–1076. [CrossRef]
38. Alsumait, J.S.; Sykulski, J.K.; Al-Othman, A.K. A hybrid GA–PS–SQP method to solve power system valve-point economic dispatch problems. *Appl. Energy* **2010**, *87*, 1773–1781. [CrossRef]
39. Duman, S.; Güvenç, U.; Yörükeren, N. Gravitational search algorithm for economic dispatch with valve-point effects. *Int. Rev. Electr. Eng.* **2010**, *5*, 2890–2895.
40. Sinha, N.; Chakrabarti, R.; Chattopadhyay, P.K. Evolutionary programming techniques for economic load dispatch. *IEEE Trans. Evol. Comput.* **2003**, *7*, 83–94. [CrossRef]
41. Cai, J.; Li, Q.; Li, L.; Peng, H.; Yang, Y. A hybrid CPSO–SQP method for economic dispatch considering the valve-point effects. *Energy Convers. Manag.* **2012**, *53*, 175–181. [CrossRef]
42. Al-Betar, M.A.; Awadallah, M.A. Island bat algorithm for optimization. *Expert Syst. Appl.* **2018**, *107*, 126–145. [CrossRef]
43. Basetti, V.; Rangarajan, S.S.; Shiva, C.K.; Pulluri, H.; Kumar, R.; Collins, R.E.; Senjyu, T. Economic emission load dispatch problem with valve-point loading using a novel quasi-oppositional-based political optimizer. *Electronics* **2021**, *10*, 2596. [CrossRef]
44. Lin, W.-M.; Gow, H.-J.; Tsai, M.-T. Combining of Direct Search and Signal-to-Noise Ratio for economic dispatch optimization. *Energy Convers. Manag.* **2011**, *52*, 487–493. [CrossRef]
45. Wadood, A.; Sattar Khan, B.; Albalawi, H.; Alatwi, A.M. Design of the Novel Fractional Order Hybrid Whale Optimizer for Thermal Wind Power Generation Systems with Integration of Chaos Infused Wind Power. *Fractal Fract.* **2024**, *8*, 379. [CrossRef]
46. Wadood, A.; Khan, B.S.; Khurshaid, T.; Kim, K.C.; Rhee, S.B. Chaos-infused wind power integration in the grey wolf optimal paradigm for combine thermal-wind power plant systems. *Front. Energy Res.* **2024**, *12*, 1301700. [CrossRef]
47. Wadood, A.; Ghani, A. An application of Gorilla troops optimizer in solving the problem of economic load dispatch considering valve point loading effect. *Eng. Res. Express* **2024**, *6*, 015310.
48. Reddy, A.S.; Vaisakh, K. Shuffled differential evolution for large scale economic dispatch. *Electr. Power Syst. Res.* **2013**, *96*, 237–245. [CrossRef]
49. Zou, D.; Li, S.; Li, Z.; Kong, X. A new global particle swarm optimization for the economic emission dispatch with or without transmission losses. *Energy Convers. Manag.* **2017**, *139*, 45–70. [CrossRef]
50. Hassan, M.H.; Kamel, S.; Abualigah, L.; Eid, A. Development and application of slime mould algorithm for optimal economic emission dispatch. *Expert Syst. Appl.* **2021**, *182*, 115205. [CrossRef]
51. Azizipanah-Abarghooee, R.; Niknam, T.; Roosta, A.; Malekpour, A.R.; Zare, M. Probabilistic multiobjective wind-thermal economic emission dispatch based on point estimated method. *Energy* **2021**, *37*, 322–335. [CrossRef]
52. Khan, B.S.; Qamar, A.; Wadood, A.; Almuhanna, K.; Al-Shamma, A.A. Integrating economic load dispatch information into the blockchain smart contracts based on the fractional-order swarming optimizer. *Front. Energy Res.* **2024**, *12*, 1350076. [CrossRef]

mathematics

MDPI

Article

Machine Learning Prediction of Fuel Cell Remaining Life Enhanced by Variational Mode Decomposition and Improved Whale Optimization Algorithm

Zerong Huang [1], Daxing Zhang [1], Xiangdong Wang [1], Xiaolong Huang [1], Chunsheng Wang [2], Liqing Liao [2], Yaolin Dong [2], Xiaoshuang Hou [2], Yuan Cao [2] and Xinyao Zhou [2,*]

[1] Huizhou Power Supply Bureau, Guangdong Power Grid Corporation, Huizhou 516000, China
[2] School of Automation, Central South University, Changsha 410083, China; wangcsu@csu.edu.cn (C.W.)
* Correspondence: zhouxinyao@csu.edu.cn

Abstract: In predicting the remaining lifespan of Proton Exchange Membrane Fuel Cells (PEMFC), it is crucial to accurately capture the multi-scale variations in cell performance. This study employs Variational Mode Decomposition (VMD) to decompose performance data into intrinsic modes, elucidating critical multi-scale dynamics vital for understanding the complex degradation processes in fuel cells. In addition to VMD, this research utilizes an Improved Whale Optimization Algorithm (IWOA) to optimize a Back Propagation (BP) Neural Network. The IWOA focuses on precise adjustments of weights and biases, enabling the BP network to effectively interpret complex nonlinear relationships within the dataset. This optimization enhances the predictive model's reliability and stability. Extensive experimental evaluations demonstrate that the integration of VMD, and the learning capabilities of the IWOA-optimized BP network significantly improves the model's accuracy and stability across multiple predictions, thereby increasing the reliability of lifespan predictions for PEMFCs. This methodology offers a robust framework for extending the operational life and efficiency of fuel cells.

Keywords: proton exchange membrane fuel cells; variational mode decomposition; back propagation neural network; degradation prediction

MSC: 62M20

1. Introduction

In recent years, the continuous increase in global energy consumption has led to the gradual exposure of issues such as resource depletion and environmental pollution associated with traditional fossil fuels. The energy crisis has become a key factor constraining the sustainable development of society [1]. Against this backdrop, clean and renewable energy technologies have garnered unprecedented attention. Proton Exchange Membrane Fuel Cells (PEMFC) are widely recognized for their high energy conversion efficiency, low emissions [2], and extensive applications, particularly in transportation [3,4]. However, their long-term operational stability and lifespan pose significant challenges [5–7], as performance degradation often occurs over time [8]. During operation, PEMFC undergo performance degradation, which manifests in the degradation of the membrane and deactivation of the catalyst [9]. Conducting research on the prediction of PEMFC degradation is of significant importance for reducing maintenance costs and facilitating the commercialization of this technology [10].

PEMFCs are complex nonlinear systems, the specific mechanisms of which are yet to be thoroughly investigated. Current primary degradation prediction methods can be categorized into model-based, data-driven, and hybrid forecasting approaches [11]. Model-based predictive methods rely on a deep understanding of the degradation mechanisms of PEMFC [12]. These methods utilize mathematical models to describe the physicochemical processes underlying the performance decay of the fuel cells. Mlakar et al. [13] developed a semi-empirical model that accounts for the performance degradation of PEMFCs during operation. The model, which integrated degradation effects, utilized data derived from accelerated stress tests. Khan et al. [14] introduced a dynamic semi-empirical aging model for PEMFCs, incorporating time-based elements to predict the degradation of the fuel cells. This model calculated the membrane water content in PEMFCs, enabling the diagnosis of membrane drying and flooding faults. Additionally, the model parameters were optimized using the Butterfly Optimization Algorithm. Semi-empirical models can also be integrated with filtering algorithms. Song et al. [15] proposed an online prediction method for the remaining useful life of power fuel cells, based on an Adaptive Extended Kalman Filter (AEKF). This method accounted for the degradation characteristics of vehicular fuel cells under actual operating conditions. Also, it dynamically updated the weights of operational and environmental factors utilizing AEKF, thereby enhancing prediction accuracy. Model-based predictive methods offer an intuitive understanding of the aging process and allow predictions to be made without extensive experimental data [16]. However, the accuracy of these models may be constrained by oversimplification or the failure to account for all relevant factors [17].

Data-driven approaches, particularly machine learning techniques, predict outcomes by learning patterns from historical data. These methods do not necessitate an in-depth physical understanding of the aging mechanisms but instead directly extract features from the data [18]. Among these techniques, the Back Propagation Neural Network (BPNN) has been extensively applied to the prediction of fuel cell aging. Huang et al. [19] analyzed the voltage characteristics of the start–stop process of PEMFC buses in actual traffic environments and proposed an Organic Grey BP Neural Network Model (OGNNM) to predict the start–stop voltage of PEMFCs. It provided a foundation for performance optimization and lifespan prediction of fuel cell vehicles. Commonly, optimizing BPNN parameters with optimization algorithms enhances model efficacy [20]. Chen et al. [21] proposed a predictive model that integrates a Back Propagation Neural Network (BPNN) with optimization algorithms. The model takes into account the impact of PEMFC current, hydrogen pressure, temperature, and relative humidity on the aging of PEMFCs. The optimization of the model parameters was carried out utilizing the Mind Evolutionary Algorithm (MEA), Particle Swarm Optimization (PSO), and Genetic Algorithm (GA). Similarly, Zhao et al. [22] developed a Time Convolutional Network (TCN) model optimized with GA, which demonstrated strong accuracy, robustness, and adaptability in predicting PEMFC performance degradation. The advantages of data-driven methods include powerful pattern recognition capabilities, the ability to handle large datasets, and adaptability to complex nonlinear relationships [23,24].

Hybrid models, which combine the advantages of mechanistic models and data-driven approaches, provide more accurate predictions in certain application scenarios. Tian et al. [25] introduced a method that integrated a voltage recovery model with multi-kernel relevance vector machines. To further enhance prediction accuracy, Bayesian optimization algorithms were employed to optimize the weight coefficients of the kernel functions. This approach has been verified to achieve a prediction accuracy of up to 95.35%. Similarly, Wang et al. [26] combined a semi-empirical model of voltage loss with a machine learning method based on a sliding window approach. This integration utilized the predictions from the semi-empirical model to correct inputs to the machine learning method, effectively suppressing fluctuations in long-term forecasting. However, the complexity of hybrid models may increase the risk of overfitting, particularly when data availability is limited. In contrast, focusing solely on data-driven methods might be more advantageous for the rapid development and deployment of effective predictive models.

In response to the aforementioned challenges, this paper presents a VMD-IWOA-BP predicting method, with the following main innovations:

(1) PEMFC stack voltage data are analyzed using Variational Mode Decomposition (VMD) to extract multi-scale features, enhancing the prediction of degradation by capturing subtle aging changes more effectively than traditional methods.

(2) This study employs the Improved Whale Optimization Algorithm (IWOA) combined with a Back Propagation (BP) Neural Network to optimize network parameters, improving learning efficiency and fitting complex nonlinear relationships.
(3) A comprehensive VMD-IWOA-BP prediction model has been developed, integrating multi-scale data analysis, parameter optimization, and neural network prediction. This approach enhances the model's accuracy, reliability, and adaptability across different operating conditions and aging stages.

By employing this integrated approach, this paper offers a novel technical avenue for the prediction of PEMFC degradation, with the potential to achieve improved forecasting outcomes in practical applications. The structure of this paper is as follows: Section 2 initially presents the experimental data utilized, followed by the proposal of a PEMFC degradation prediction method based on VMD-IWOA-BP. Section 3 provides the experimental predictions of the presented method, with conclusions drawn in Section 4.

2. Predictive Model Construction

2.1. The Working Principle of PEMFC

PEMFCs efficiently convert chemical energy into electrical energy utilizing electrochemistry [27]. As shown in Figure 1, hydrogen is supplied to the anode and oxygen to the cathode. At the anode, hydrogen is split into protons and electrons. The protons pass through the Proton Exchange Membrane (PEM) to the cathode, while the electrons flow through an external circuit, generating electricity. At the cathode, protons, electrons, and oxygen react to produce water, the only emission, making the process environmentally friendly and highly efficient [28,29].

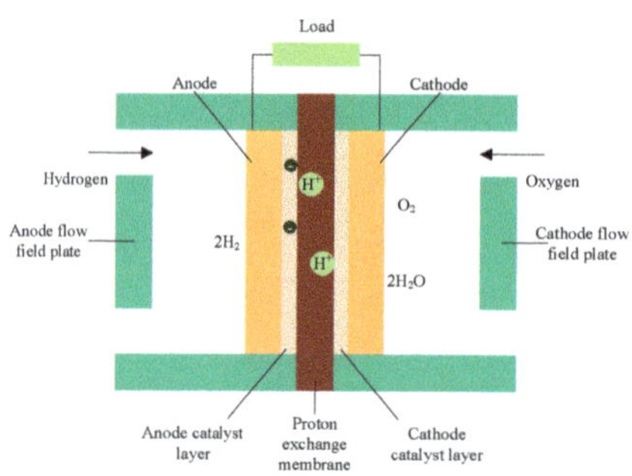

Figure 1. Schematic diagram of the working principle of PEMFC.

In this study, the RUL of the PEMFC is indirectly predicted by focusing on voltage degradation over time. The model is designed to forecast voltage decay utilizing historical operational data, with voltage decline serving as a key indicator of fuel cell health. As voltage decreases below a defined threshold, it signals the end of the fuel cell's RUL, making it a reliable proxy for estimating the remaining operational lifespan.

2.2. Basic Principles

2.2.1. Variational Mode Decomposition (VMD)

VMD [30] is an adaptive signal processing technique utilized for decomposing complex signals into intrinsic oscillatory modes that span various time scales. The essence of VMD lies in the use of a complete set of sinusoidal basis functions, allowing the signal to be represented as a linear combination of these sinusoidal waves. This process enables the decomposition of the signal across multiple scales, facilitating multi-scale signal analysis.

VMD decomposes the voltage signal $U(t)$ into K sub-signals $\{u_k\}_{k=1}^{K}$, with each sub-signal represented as an intrinsic mode function (IMF).

$$u_k = A_k(t)\cos(\phi_k(t)) \quad (1)$$

Each IMF is characterized by an amplitude $A_k(t)$, time variable t, and phase $\phi_k(t)$. VMD's decomposition principle is grounded in the minimization of the following variational problem:

$$\begin{cases} \min\limits_{\{u_k\},\{w_k\}} \{\sum_{k=1}^{K} \left\| \partial_k \left(\delta(t) + \frac{j}{\omega_k} \right) u_k(t) e^{-j\omega_k t} \right\|_2^2 \} \\ s.t. \sum_{i=1}^{K} u_k(t) = f(t) \end{cases} \tag{2}$$

Each sub-signal u_k is modulated around a specific central frequency ω_k, involving the Dirac function $\delta(t)$, imaginary unit j, and partial derivative ∂_k. To ensure effective decomposition, VMD requires the sum of all modes to equate the original voltage signal $U(t)$:

$$\sum_{k=1}^{K} u_k(t) = U(t) \tag{3}$$

The method addresses the variational model by introducing a Lagrange multiplier $\lambda(t)$ and a regularization parameter α, ensuring the decomposition aligns with the original signal dynamics:

$$\begin{aligned} L(u_k, \omega_k, \lambda) &= \alpha \sum_{k=1}^{K} \left\| \partial_k \left(\delta(t) + \frac{j}{\omega_k} \right) u_k(t) e^{-j\omega_k t} \right\|_2^2 \\ &+ \left\| U(t) - \sum_{k=1}^{K} u_k(t) \right\|_2^2 + \left\langle \lambda(t), U(t) - \sum_{k=1}^{K} u_k(t) \right\rangle \end{aligned} \tag{4}$$

Compared to traditional Empirical Mode Decomposition (EMD), VMD exhibits greater robustness to noise and disturbances. The adaptive mechanism of VMD ensures that each mode has a concentrated and finite bandwidth. This adaptability renders VMD highly flexible and accurate in processing nonlinear and non-stationary signals.

2.2.2. Improved Whale Optimization Algorithm (IWOA)

The Whale Optimization Algorithm (WOA) is a metaheuristic algorithm inspired by the social behavior of humpback whales, as introduced by Mirjalili et al. [31]. Similar to other heuristic algorithms, the essence of WOA primarily lies in the update of the whale positions or solutions. WOA is mathematically modeled on the unique bubble-net feeding behavior of humpback whales:

1. Encircling prey

$$\vec{D} = \left| C \cdot \vec{X^*}(t) - \vec{X}(t) \right| \tag{5}$$

$$\vec{X}(t+1) = \vec{X^*}(t) - A \cdot \vec{D} \tag{6}$$

In the WOA, the current best solution position, denoted as $\vec{X^*}(t)$, is updated with each iteration. Here, the target prey of the humpback whale is modeled as the optimal solution to the problem at hand, where t represents the current iteration number. The coefficients A and C are vector coefficients, and $\vec{D}$ is the displacement vector moving towards the optimal solution. The formulas for calculating A and C are as follows:

$$A = 2ar_1 - a \tag{7}$$

$$C = 2r_2 \tag{8}$$

In the iterative process, the coefficient a linearly decreases from 2 to 0. The variables r_1 and r_2 are random numbers generated within the interval $[0,\ 1]$.

2. Bubble-net attacking method (exploitation phase)

$$\vec{X}(t+1) = \begin{cases} \vec{X^*}(t) - A\cdot\vec{D}, p < 0.5 \\ \vec{X^*}(t) + \vec{D}\cdot e^{bl}\cdot\cos(2\pi l), p \geq 0.5 \end{cases} \tag{9}$$

In the model, p is a random number within the range [0, 1], l is a random number within the range [−1, 1], and b is a constant defining the logarithmic spiral shape. The mathematical modeling encompasses two types of humpback whale hunting behaviors: the shrinking encircling mechanism and the spiral updating mechanism. Since these behaviors coexist in actual predation, the parameter p is utilized to randomly select the updating mechanism.

3. Bubble-net attacking method (exploitation phase)

When $A \geq 1$, it indicates that the humpback whale is outside the encircling ring, and thus, a random search update is employed.

$$\vec{D} = \left| C\cdot\vec{X}_{rand}(t) - \vec{X}(t) \right| \tag{10}$$

$$\vec{X}(t+1) = \vec{X}_{rand}(t) - A\cdot\vec{D} \tag{11}$$

In the model, $\vec{X}_{rand}(t)$ is the position of a randomly selected whale. Additionally, when $A < 1$, the spiral encircling mechanism is employed.

Although widely utilized for its simplicity in structure, minimal parameter configuration, and ease of understanding and implementation, WOA faces certain limitations in practical applications. These include instability in the quality of the initial solutions and a tendency to become trapped in local optima. To address these issues, the following enhancement strategies are proposed in this paper:

1. Improvement in initial population generation: The incorporation of chaos mapping techniques is introduced for generating the initial population. Among various chaos mappings, the Tent map is selected for its remarkable chaotic properties and ergodicity. The mathematical expression of the Tent map is defined as follows:

$$x_{i+1} = \begin{cases} 2x_i, & 0 \leq x_i < 0.5 \\ 2(1-x_i), & 0.5 \leq x_i < 1 \end{cases} \tag{12}$$

This mapping generates a chaotic and highly random sequence of values within the interval [0, 1]. By repeatedly applying the Tent map, the initial population $\vec{X}(0)$ for the WOA is generated.

$$\vec{X}(0) = \{x_i\}_{i=1}^{N} \tag{13}$$

The population size N facilitates the Tent map's ability to exhibit strong chaotic behavior for most initial values, offering an effective mechanism to help the algorithm escape local minima and explore the search space more comprehensively. Additionally, the Tent map evenly covers the entire available state space, thereby enhancing the diversity of the initial population in the WOA.

2. Enhancement of global search capability: Simulated Annealing (SA) is employed to accept suboptimal solutions with a certain probability, preventing the algorithm from prematurely converging to local minima. Integrating the principles of SA into the WOA enhances its global search capabilities by allowing the acceptance of inferior solutions under controlled probabilities.

$$\vec{X'}(t+1) = \vec{X}(t+1) + \in \cdot\Delta \tag{14}$$

A random perturbation is applied to generate a new position, where $\in$ represents a small random number and Δ indicates the direction of the random vector. The difference in the objective function, $\Delta m(t+1)$, is calculated to determine the change in solution quality:

$$\Delta m(t+1) = m(\overrightarrow{X}'(t+1)) - m(\overrightarrow{X}(t+1)) \tag{15}$$

In the optimization process, the objective function values for the solutions, $m(\overrightarrow{X}'(t+1))$ and $m(\overrightarrow{X}(t+1))$, are evaluated. If $\Delta m(t+1) < 0$, it indicates that the new solution $\overrightarrow{X}'(t+1)$ is superior to the original solution $\overrightarrow{X}(t+1)$, thus $\overrightarrow{X}'(t+1)$ is accepted as the new current solution. Conversely, if the change in the objective function value is not favorable, a suboptimal solution may still be accepted based on the Metropolis criterion, with an acceptance probability P_{t+1}.

$$P_{t+1} = e^{\frac{\Delta m(t+1)}{T_{t+1}}} \tag{16}$$

In this context, T represents the temperature in SA, which decreases with each iteration, progressively reducing the probability of accepting inferior solutions:

$$T_{t+1} = T_t \cdot \alpha \tag{17}$$

This reduction follows an exponential decay function, where α, a constant, controls the rate of temperature decline to prevent the algorithm from cooling too rapidly and potentially settling into a local optimum (see Algorithm 1).

Algorithm 1 Improved Whale Optimization Algorithm

procedure IWOA
    Initialize the parameters a, A, C, l, p
    Generate initial population $\overrightarrow{X}(0)$ utilizing Tent chaos map with Equations (12) and (13)
    Calculate the fitness of each search agent
    $\overrightarrow{X}^*$: the best search agent
    t: 0
    while (t < MaxIterations) do
        foreach search agent $\rightarrow$ Ps do
            Update a, A, C, l, p
            if (p < 0.5) then
                if ($|A| < 1$) then /* Shrinking encircling mechanism */
                    Update the position of the current agent with Equations (5) and (6)
                else /* Search randomly for prey */
                    Select a random search agent $\overrightarrow{X}_{rand}(t)$
                    Update the position of the current agent with Equations (10) and (11)
                end if
            else /* Spiral updating mechanism */
                $\overrightarrow{X}(t+1) = \overrightarrow{D} \cdot e^{bl} \cdot \cos(2\pi l) + \overrightarrow{X}^*(t)$
            end if
        end for
        Generate a new position with Equation (14)
        Calculate the fitness of each search agent
        Calculate the difference $\Delta m(t+1)$ with Equation (15)
        if ($\Delta m(t+1) < 0$) then
            Update the best search agent
        else
            Acceptance of inferior solutions under controlled probabilities with Equations (15)–(17)
        $t = t+1$
    end while
    return $\overrightarrow{X}^*$ (MaxIterations)
end procedure

2.2.3. Back Propagation (BP) Neural Network

The Back Propagation (BP) algorithm is a commonly utilized supervised learning technique that optimizes neural network weights through gradient descent. Errors are minimized by adjusting weights and biases based on the gradients of the loss function relative to the network parameters. As shown in Figure 2, a basic neural network is often referred to as a multi-layer perceptron (MLP) or artificial neural network (ANN). It consists of three layers. The input layer receives the data. The hidden layer processes the data using weighted sums and nonlinear activation functions. Finally, the output layer generates the prediction or decision.

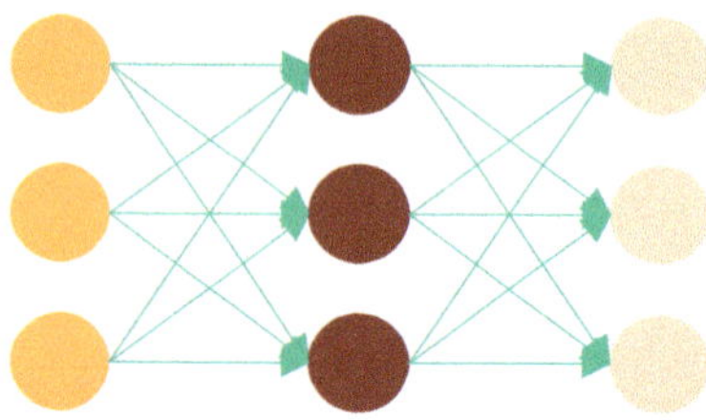

Figure 2. A basic neural network model.

The BP algorithm adjusts the connection weights between layers utilizing stochastic gradient descent (SGD), allowing the network to learn the mapping between input and output data. Through training with historical data, the network can predict the aging state of new input data, providing valuable insights for fuel cell maintenance and lifespan prediction. This method captures complex nonlinear patterns in fuel cell degradation, enhancing both accuracy and reliability in aging predictions.

2.3. VMD-IWOA-BP Predictive Method

This paper presents a VMD-IWOA-BP-based prediction methodology for the remaining useful life (RUL) of PEMFC. This comprehensive approach integrates signal processing, algorithm optimization, and predictive analysis, significantly enhancing the accuracy and robustness of prediction outcomes. The detailed implementation process is illustrated in Figure 3.

As depicted in the green box of Figure 3, the input data, after being processed by VMD, is decomposed into several sets of Intrinsic Mode Functions (IMF), denoted as IMF_K. These IMFs not only capture the multi-scale characteristics of the original data but also provide abundant information for the subsequent prediction model. Subsequently, the IMFs are partitioned into training and testing sets according to a predetermined ratio, providing data support for the training and validation of the BP neural network model. During the model training process, as indicated by the red box in the figure, the IWOA is introduced to optimize the weights and thresholds of the BP neural network. In this context, the Mean Squared Error (MSE) is employed as the fitness function $m(\vec{X}(t)$, serving as a measure to evaluate the efficacy of the solution vector $\vec{X}(t)$ within the optimization process:

$$\begin{cases} m(\vec{X}(t) = \frac{1}{n_t}\sum_{i=1}^{n_t}(U_{p_t-i} - U_{m_t-i})^2 \\ \vec{X}(t) = [W, b] \end{cases} \tag{18}$$

In this study, the weights W and biases b of the BP neural network are integrated into the population $\vec{X}(t)$ of the WOA. Also, n_t represents the number of the predicted output voltage in the train set. U_{p_t-i} denotes the predicted output voltage of train set, and U_{m_t-i} is the actual output voltage from the train set. The optimized BP model is trained on historical data to predict future output voltage components. Finally, the predicted voltage components are superimposed to obtain a comprehensive prediction result. This prediction process not only enhances the model's ability to capture the degradation trends in PEMFC performance but also improves the accuracy and reliability of the prediction outcomes.

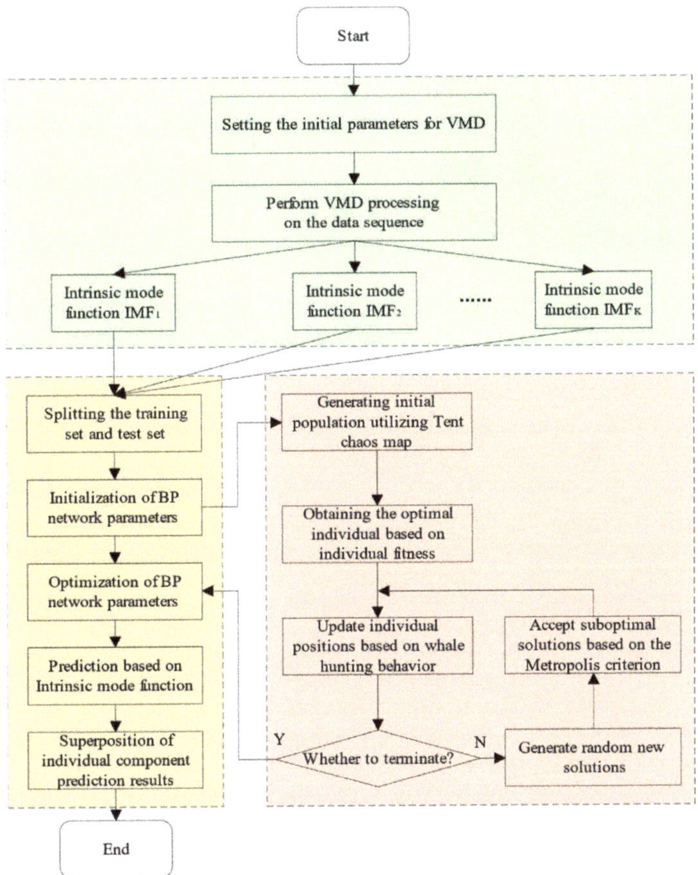

Figure 3. VMD-IWOA-BP flowchart.

3. Results and Discussion

To validate the predictive accuracy of the proposed VMD-IWOA-BP method, publicly accessible datasets were selected as the basis for experimentation. The experimental process was conducted on the Matlab R2022b software platform, leveraging its robust computational and visualization capabilities to complete the simulation training. The methodological design of this study aims to provide a scientific and precise analytical tool for PEMFC remaining useful life prediction through rigorous experimental validation.

3.1. Data Sources and Evaluation Metrics

The dataset utilized in this study comes from the IEEE PHM 2014 Data Challenge, focusing on PEMFC durability analysis. As shown in Figure 4, the experiments involved two PEMFC stacks, each with five cells. The first stack, FC1, was tested under static conditions at a constant 70A current, while the second, FC2, underwent dynamic tests with high-frequency triangular waveform current variations around 70A. Weekly experiments, including polarization curve measurements and Electrochemical Impedance Spectroscopy

(EIS), were conducted to monitor PEMFC performance changes, providing essential data for model construction and validation.

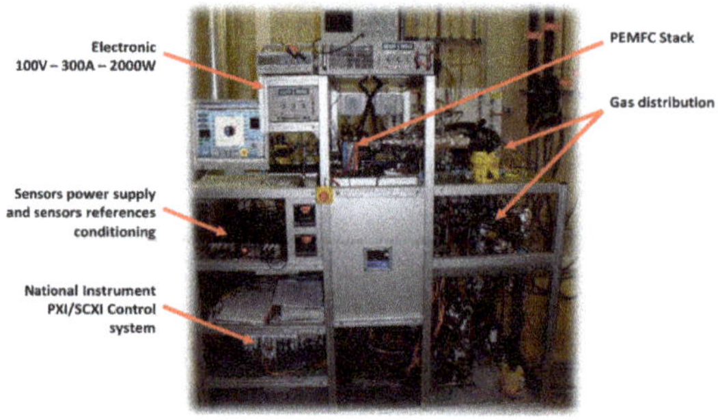

Figure 4. PEMFC fuel cell test bench [32].

To verify the predictive accuracy of the proposed method, Root Mean Square Error (RMSE) and Mean Absolute Error (MAE) are adopted as evaluation metrics for prediction performance. The corresponding formulas are as follows:

$$\text{RMSE} = \sqrt{\frac{1}{n}\sum_{i=1}^{n}\left(U_{p-i} - U_{m-i}\right)^2} \tag{19}$$

$$\text{MAE} = \frac{1}{n}\sum_{i=1}^{n}\left|U_{p-i} - U_{m-i}\right| \tag{20}$$

Here, n represents the number of data points in the test set, U_{p-i} denotes the predicted output voltage of test set, and U_{m-i} is the actual output voltage from the test set. RMSE measures the standard deviation of the differences between predicted and actual values, reflecting the magnitude of prediction errors and imposing a heavier penalty on larger errors. Consequently, it serves as a more stringent performance evaluation metric. MAE, on the other hand, represents the average of the absolute values of prediction errors, which is unaffected by the direction of the errors, providing an unbiased measure of error. Together, these two indicators comprehensively assess the predictive accuracy of the model. Generally, smaller values of RMSE and MAE indicate better prediction performance of the model.

3.2. Data Processing and Decomposition

In conducting data analysis and model prediction, ensuring the quality of raw data is paramount. Given that the original dataset contains noticeable noise and outliers, these factors can adversely impact the accuracy of model predictions. To enhance data usability and precision, this study adopts various data preprocessing techniques, including the moving average algorithm, to optimize the dataset.

As depicted in Figure 5, the preprocessed data, when compared to the raw data, exhibits a clearer and smoother curve while preserving the original degradation trends. This processing not only improves data readability but also provides a more robust foundation for subsequent model construction and prediction. Notably, Figure 5 reveals that FC1 exhibits a relatively gradual decay trend, whereas FC2 demonstrates a steeper downward trend accompanied by more extreme values that deviate from the overall trend to some extent. These observations underscore the pivotal role of data preprocessing in uncovering inherent data patterns and enhancing the performance of predictive models.

The VMD method is applied to the preprocessed data to extract its IMFs. During the VMD process, the modal number K is set to 8, decomposing the data into eight sets of IMFs. These IMFs not only capture the multi-scale characteristics of the data but also provide abundant information for model training and validation. To further optimize model performance, these IMFs are meticulously partitioned into training and testing sets. Subsequently, to effectively mitigate the interference of outliers and enhance the model's generalization ability, a normalization process is performed on the IMFs. Normalization serves as a crucial step, unifying the numerical scales across different IMFs, which not only improve computational efficiency but also optimize algorithm performance. Additionally, normalization contribute to bolstering the model's generalization capabilities, mitigating biases that might arise from improper data initialization during model training.

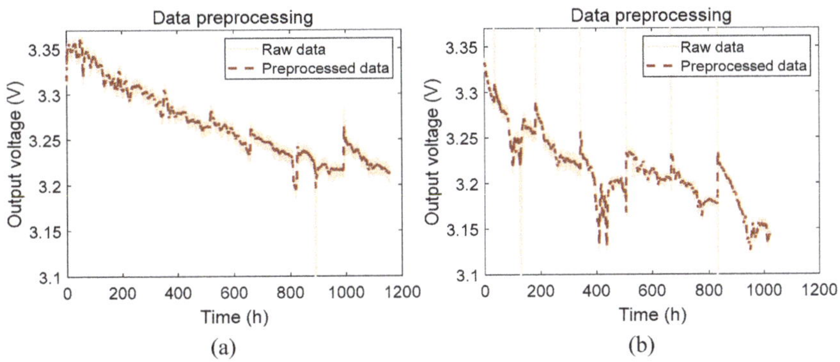

Figure 5. Data preprocessing (**a**) FC1 (**b**) FC2.

Taking FC1 as an example, Figure 6 presents the normalized voltage IMF components of the test set. As shown in Figure 6, the normalized IMF components retain their original trends while demonstrating a more consistent numerical distribution. This results in a more reliable data foundation for subsequent model training and prediction, improving the overall accuracy and stability of the model's performance.

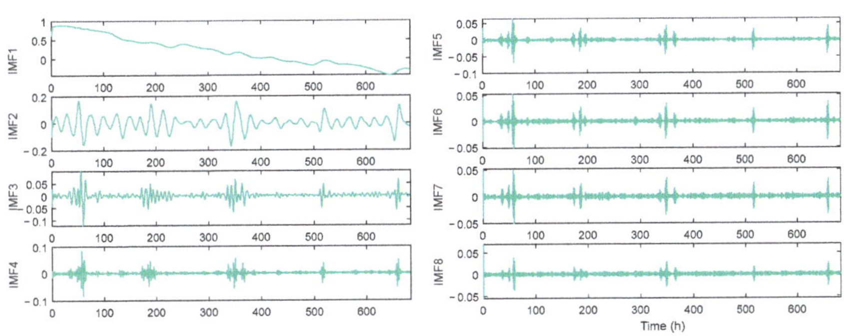

Figure 6. VMD component results.

As observed in Figure 6, each component exhibits distinct characteristics and behaviors. Specifically, IMF_1, acting as the trend component, demonstrates relatively stable fluctuations, primarily reflecting the overall trend in voltage variation in fuel cell FC1. This indicates that IMF_1 captures the long-term changes and primary trends within the data, providing crucial information for understanding the macro-level variations in fuel cell performance.

In contrast, IMF_2 through IMF_8 exhibits significantly larger fluctuations, primarily reflecting short-term variations and high-frequency changes within the data. These high-frequency components may be associated with instantaneous load changes, environmental factors, or microscopic reactions within the fuel cell during operation. Their variations may be more intricate and difficult to predict, yet they offer abundant detailed information for a profound understanding of the dynamic characteristics of fuel cell performance.

A meticulous analysis of these IMF components enables a more comprehensive grasp of the multi-scale features of fuel cell performance variations. This multi-scale approach facilitates the development of more accurate prediction models for battery performance degradation and provides a scientific basis for fuel cell health management and lifetime prediction.

3.3. Degradation Prediction under Different Predictive Methods

The structure of the BP network utilized in this study is shown in Table 1. The network consists of five input layers, ten hidden neurons, and one output layer. The hidden layer utilizes a sigmoid activation function to capture nonlinear relationships. A learning rate of 0.01 ensures steady learning and stable convergence, balancing model performance and preventing overfitting.

Table 1. Parameters of BP network.

Parameters	Value
Learning rate	0.01
Activation	sigmoid
Number of input layers	5
Number of hidden layers	10
Number of output layers	1

Table 2 compares various prediction models and their applications. The presented VMD-IWOA-BP model is specifically designed for the complex task of fuel cell aging prediction, which requires capturing long-term degradation and nonlinear dynamics. In contrast, models like the Dendritic Neuron Model (DNM) [33] are designed for general prediction tasks. Single Dendrite Neuron (SDN) [34], which utilizes Seasonal-Trend Decomposition (STD), is more suitable for handling seasonal data. The FD3 framework [35], utilizing Complete Ensemble Empirical Mode Decomposition (CEEMD), is applied to carbon emissions prediction. These models are more suited for simpler, short-term prediction tasks. While SDN and FD3 utilize decomposition techniques, they focus on short-term trends and lack global optimization, limiting their ability to handle the complexity of fuel cell degradation. By combining VMD for multi-scale feature extraction with IWOA for global optimization, the VMD-IWOA-BP model offers superior accuracy and adaptability for long-term fuel cell prediction.

Table 2. Comparison of different prediction models.

Feature	This Paper	DNM [33]	SDN [34]	FD3 Framework [35]
Problem domain	Fuel cell aging, RUL prediction	General prediction and classification	Greenhouse time series, seasonal prediction	Carbon emissions prediction
Model	BP	DNM	SDN	DNM
Decomposition	VMD	None	STD	CEEMD
Optimization algorithm	IWOA	BBO\PSO\GA \ACO\ES\PBIL	None	None

The WOA is selected for this study due to its superior performance, as shown by the experimental results. As illustrated in Figure 7, WOA consistently demonstrates faster convergence and achieves lower fitness values when compared to other optimization methods such as Genetic Algorithm (GA), Differential Evolution (DE), and Particle Swarm Optimization (PSO). These findings indicate that WOA is particularly effective in identifying optimal solutions early in the iteration process, resulting in a quicker convergence.

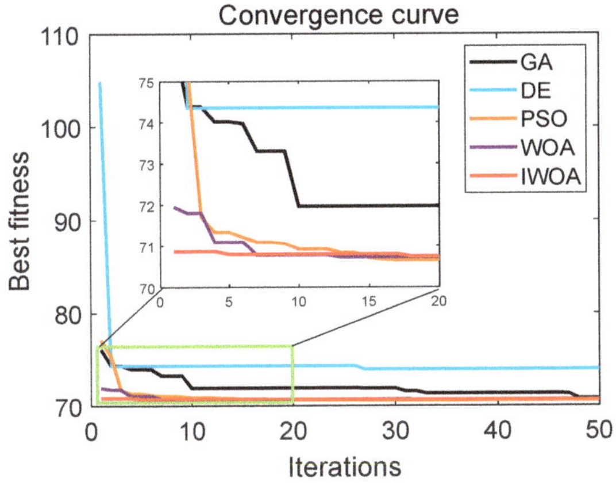

Figure 7. Convergence curve.

Figure 7 reveals that the initial fitness value of the IWOA is lower compared to WOA. This is attributed to the application of chaotic mapping in IWOA, which ensures a more uniform distribution of the initial population. By enhancing the diversity of the population, chaotic mapping allows the algorithm to start closer to optimal solutions, thereby accelerating the convergence process from the very beginning.

The results in Table 3 demonstrate that under the same experimental settings, WOA outperforms other traditional optimization algorithms in terms of prediction accuracy. Therefore, WOA is selected as the preferred optimization algorithm for this task due to its superior performance.

Table 3. RMSE of different optimization algorithms.

Dataset	VMD-GA-BP	VMD-DE-BP	VMD-PSO-BP	VMD-WOA-BP	VMD-IWOA-BP
FC1	0.0112	0.0120	0.0110	0.0102	0.0021
FC2	0.0066	0.0081	0.0038	0.0030	0.0024

Simulations are conducted utilizing BP, VMD-BP, VMD-WOA-BP, and VMD-IWOA-BP models, with the same dataset trained on 60% of the data as shown in Figure 8. The results from Figure 8 reveal that the predictive errors of the VMD-IWOA-BP model are significantly lower than those of the other methods, demonstrating its superior predictive capabilities. In the comparison depicted in Figure 8, the conventional BP network exhibits relatively large prediction errors due to the lack of effective data preprocessing and parameter optimization mechanisms. Although the VMD-BP model utilizes VMD technology to decompose the data, enhancing its representation capability, it still employs traditional methods for parameter optimization, which do not fully exploit its potential.

Tables 4 and 5 demonstrate the superior performance of the VMD-IWOA-BP model compared to other models, as evidenced across two distinct datasets. This discrepancy highlights the model's robust adaptability and versatility. Particularly notable is the model's performance on the FC1 dataset, where there was a significant reduction in prediction errors, with RMSE decreasing by 91% and MAE by 93%. Such improvements represent a substantial leap in predictive accuracy.

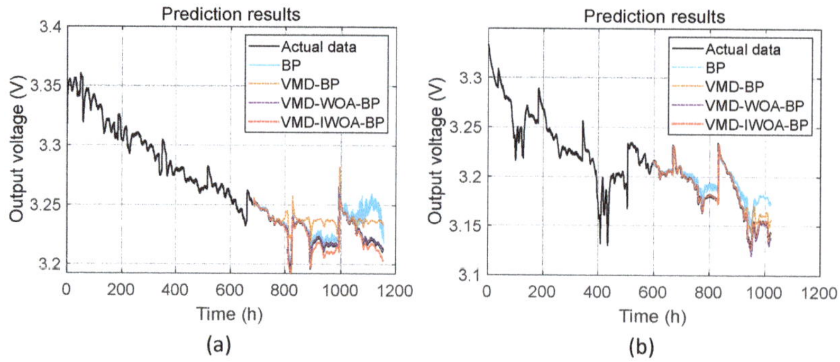

Figure 8. Prediction results: (**a**) FC1, (**b**) FC2.

Table 4. Prediction performance metrics of FC1.

Method	RMSE	MAE	Time (s)
BP	0.0237	0.0139	0.9062
VMD-BP	0.0136	0.0106	8.7393
VMD-WOA-BP	0.0102	0.0073	48.9033
VMD-IWOA-BP	0.0021	0.0009	56.9953

Table 5. Prediction performance metrics of FC2.

Method	RMSE	MAE	Time (s)
BP	0.0125	0.0082	0.9354
VMD-BP	0.0065	0.0034	7.8048
VMD-WOA-BP	0.0030	0.0015	43.8735
VMD-IWOA-BP	0.0024	0.0009	56.9243

On the FC2 dataset, the model also demonstrated superior predictive capabilities, with reductions in RMSE and MAE by 81% and 91%, respectively. This further confirms the robust performance of the VMD-IWOA-BP model in processing various types of fuel cell data.

In this study, both IWOA and WOA are set with the same maximum number of iterations (50). However, the function evaluations differ due to the introduction of the Simulated Annealing (SA) mechanism in IWOA. This mechanism allows for additional evaluations between the optimal and suboptimal solutions, enhancing the global search capability by preventing the algorithm from becoming trapped in local optimum. The analysis shows that while the VMD-IWOA-BP model offers the best accuracy, it comes at a higher computational cost, with runtimes increasing from under 1 s (BP) to approximately 57 s. However, the significant reduction in RMSE (from 0.0237 to 0.0021 for FC1) justifies the increased computational time in applications where precise predictions are critical. The time increase from VMD-WOA-BP (48 s) to VMD-IWOA-BP (57 s) is moderate. This results in a substantial boost in accuracy, making the added computational cost worthwhile when balancing accuracy with processing time. Thus, for high-accuracy demands, the improved model's efficiency remains reasonable.

To better validate the effectiveness of the presented IWOA, an ablation study was conducted. Based on the VMD-WOA-BP model, two modifications are tested separately: the addition of Tent mapping (WOA-Tent) and the inclusion of Simulated Annealing (WOA-SA). The RMSE results from these variations are presented in Table 6.

Table 6. RMSE of ablation study.

Setup	FC1	FC2
WOA	0.0102	0.0030
WOA-Tent	0.0055	0.0028
WOA-SA	0.0040	0.0027
WOA-Tent-SA	0.0021	0.0024

The results of the ablation study clearly illustrate the impact of incorporating the Tent map and SA into the WOA. The baseline WOA model shows high RMSE values of 0.0102 for FC1 and 0.0030 for FC2, indicating its limitations in accurately capturing the complex degradation patterns. Adding the Tent map (WOA-Tent) leads to a significant reduction in RMSE, particularly for FC1 (0.0055), by improving the diversity of the initial population and enhancing the exploration process. Similarly, the use of Simulated Annealing (WOA-SA) further reduces the RMSE, with FC1 achieving 0.0040, demonstrating that SA enhances global search capabilities and prevents premature convergence.

To more clearly demonstrate the advantages of the method presented in this paper, Table 7 presents the RMSE metrics from various studies, where the training set constitutes 60% of the data. Among the comparative approaches, the AEKF-NARX hybrid method [36] combines the strengths of both model-based and data-driven techniques. By leveraging the physical degradation characteristics of fuel cells and the capability of neural networks to process nonlinear time series data, this approach effectively predicts both overall degradation trends and finer details. The Transformer-LSTM hybrid method [11] integrates a Wiener process to model stochastic degradation trends with a Transformer network for capturing long-term dependencies and patterns in the data. Monte Carlo dropout is employed to quantify prediction uncertainty, offering a confidence interval for the results. This combination enables a more robust and adaptable approach to degradation prediction, capturing both global trends and local fluctuations in performance.

Table 7. Performance compared with published methods.

Method	FC1	FC2
AEKF-NARX [36]	0.0095	0.0085
Transformer-LSTM [11]	0.0038	0.0041
VMD-IWOA-BP	0.0021	0.0024

The comparative analysis in Table 7 demonstrates the superior prediction accuracy of the VMD-IWOA-BP model. For FC1, the RMSE decreases from 0.0095 with AEKF-NARX and 0.0038 with Transformer-LSTM to 0.0021 with the proposed model. Similarly, for FC2, the RMSE drops from 0.0085 (AEKF-NARX) and 0.0041 (Transformer-LSTM) to 0.0024. These results highlight the model's ability to capture both long-term degradation trends and finer-scale fluctuations, outperforming other methods in accuracy.

4. Conclusions

This study employs VMD technology to extract multi-scale features from historical data of PEMFC, providing a detailed revelation of the subtle changes occurring during the PEMFC aging process. Compared to traditional single-scale analysis methods, this technique significantly enriches the data foundation for aging prediction. Additionally, the IWOA is utilized to optimize the parameters of the BP neural network. This combined strategy not only enhances the network's learning efficiency but also significantly improves the model's ability to fit complex nonlinear relationships. By integrating the global search capability of IWOA with the learning mechanism of the BP neural network, an effective method for parameter adjustment and network training is provided for the PEMFC aging prediction model. Furthermore, by developing a comprehensive VMD-IWOA-BP prediction model, this research effectively combines multi-scale data analysis, parameter optimization, and neural network prediction. This innovative approach to model construction not only increases the accuracy and reliability of aging predictions but also enhances the model's adaptability to different operational conditions and aging stages. Experimental results demonstrate that the model achieves RMSE of 0.0021 and 0.0024 under dynamic and static conditions, respectively, showcasing its substantial potential for practical applications.

Although this study demonstrates the efficacy of the VMD-IWOA-BP model, certain limitations need to be addressed. The model's performance heavily depends on the quality and quantity of the input data, and in scenarios where data are limited, the risk of overfitting may increase. Future research could focus on mitigating this risk by incorporating more advanced regularization techniques and exploring transfer learning to leverage data from related systems.

Additionally, the computational cost of combining VMD with IWOA may pose challenges for real-time applications. Future work should investigate more efficient algorithms or hybrid models to reduce the computational load while maintaining high accuracy. Broader implications of this research include the potential to adapt the model to other fuel cell types or energy storage systems, extending its applicability across various fields.

Author Contributions: Conceptualization, Z.H. and X.Z.; methodology, X.Z.; software, D.Z.; validation, X.W., X.H. (Xiaolong Huang) and L.L.; formal analysis, C.W.; investigation, Y.D.; resources, X.H. (Xiaoshuang Hou); data curation, Z.H.; writing—original draft preparation, Z.H. and X.Z.; writing—review and editing, Y.C.; visualization, D.Z.; supervision, X.W.; project administration, Z.H.; funding acquisition, Y.C. All authors have read and agreed to the published version of the manuscript.

Funding: This research was supported by the Science and Technology Project of Huizhou Power Supply Bureau, Guangdong Power Grid Corporation. (project number: 031300KC23030008, contract number: 0313002023030103B200031).

Data Availability Statement: The original contributions presented in the study are included in the article, further inquiries can be directed to the corresponding author.

Conflicts of Interest: Authors Zerong Huang, Daxing Zhang, Xiangdong Wang and Xiaolong Huang were employed by Guangdong Power Grid Corporation. The remaining authors declare that the research was conducted in the absence of any commercial or financial relationships that could be construed as a potential conflict of interest.

References

1. Guo, R.; Chen, D.; Li, Y.; Wu, W.; Hu, S.; Xu, X. Anode Nitrogen Concentration Estimation Based on Voltage Variation Characteristics for Proton Exchange Membrane Fuel Cell Stacks. *Energies* **2023**, *16*, 2111. [CrossRef]
2. Ao, Y.; Chen, K.; Laghrouche, S.; Depernet, D. Proton exchange membrane fuel cell degradation model based on catalyst transformation theory. *Fuel Cells* **2021**, *21*, 254–268. [CrossRef]
3. Meng, X.; Mei, J.; Tang, X.; Jiang, J.; Sun, C.; Song, K. The Degradation Prediction of Proton Exchange Membrane Fuel Cell Performance Based on a Transformer Model. *Energies* **2024**, *17*, 3050. [CrossRef]
4. Liu, Z.; Xu, S.; Zhao, H.; Wang, Y. Durability estimation and short-term voltage degradation forecasting of vehicle PEMFC system: Development and evaluation of machine learning models. *Appl. Energy* **2022**, *326*, 119975. [CrossRef]
5. Zhang, Q.; Harms, C.; Mitzel, J.; Gazdzicki, P.; Friedrich, K.A. The challenges in reliable determination of degradation rates and lifetime in polymer electrolyte membrane fuel cells. *Curr. Opin. Electrochem.* **2021**, *31*, 100863. [CrossRef]
6. Wilk, A.; Węcel, D. Measurements Based Analysis of the Proton Exchange Membrane Fuel Cell Operation in Transient State and Power of Own Needs. *Energies* **2020**, *13*, 498. [CrossRef]
7. Gómez, G.; Argumosa, P.; Correro, A.; Maellas, J. Proposal of a New Technique to Obtain Some Fuel Cell Internal Parameters Using Polarization Curve Tests and EIS Results. *Energies* **2021**, *14*, 7161. [CrossRef]
8. Li, K.; Hong, J.; Zhang, C.; Liang, F.; Yang, H.; Ma, F.; Wang, F. Health state monitoring and predicting of proton exchange membrane fuel cells: A review. *J. Power Sources* **2024**, *612*, 234828. [CrossRef]
9. Tian, Z.; Wei, Z.; Wang, J.; Wang, Y.; Lei, Y.; Hu, P.; Muyeen, S.M.; Zhou, D. Research Progress on Aging Prediction Methods for Fuel Cells: Mechanism, Methods, and Evaluation Criteria. *Energies* **2023**, *16*, 7750. [CrossRef]
10. Zhang, C.; Zhang, Y.; Wang, L.; Deng, X.; Liu, Y.; Zhang, J. A health management review of proton exchange membrane fuel cell for electric vehicles: Failure mechanisms, diagnosis techniques and mitigation measures. *Renew. Sustain. Energy Rev.* **2023**, *182*, 113369. [CrossRef]
11. Hu, Y.; Zhang, L.; Jiang, Y.; Peng, K.; Jin, Z. A Hybrid Method for Performance Degradation Probability Prediction of Proton Exchange Membrane Fuel Cell. *Membranes* **2023**, *13*, 426. [CrossRef] [PubMed]

12. Chen, S.; Hao, M.; Hu, Y.; Liu, K.; Li, Y. Insight into the evolution of membrane chemical degradation in proton exchange membrane fuel cells:From theoretical analysis to model developing. *J. Power Sources* **2024**, *599*, 234238. [CrossRef]
13. Stropnik, R.; Mlakar, N.; Lotrič, A.; Sekavčnik, M.; Mori, M. The influence of degradation effects in proton exchange membrane fuel cells on life cycle assessment modelling and environmental impact indicators. *Int. J. Hydrogen Energy* **2022**, *47*, 24223–24241. [CrossRef]
14. Khan, S.S.; Shareef, H.; Kandidayeni, M.; Boulon, L.; Amine, A.; Abdennebi, E.H. Dynamic Semiempirical PEMFC Model for Prognostics and Fault Diagnosis. *IEEE Access* **2021**, *9*, 10217–10227. [CrossRef]
15. Song, K.; Wang, Y.; Hu, X.; Cao, J. Online Prediction of Vehicular Fuel Cell Residual Lifetime Based on Adaptive Extended Kalman Filter. *Energies* **2020**, *13*, 6244. [CrossRef]
16. Li, M.; Wu, J.; Chen, Z.; Dong, J.; Peng, Z.; Xiong, K.; Rao, M.; Chen, C.; Li, X. Data-Driven Voltage Prognostic for Solid Oxide Fuel Cell System Based on Deep Learning. *Energies* **2022**, *15*, 6294. [CrossRef]
17. Ren, X.; Zhang, X.; Teng, T.; Li, C. Research on Estimation Method of Fuel Cell Health State Based on Lumped Parameter Model. *Energies* **2020**, *13*, 6425. [CrossRef]
18. Gibey, G.; Pahon, E.; Zerhouni, N.; Hissel, D. Diagnostic and prognostic for prescriptive maintenance and control of PEMFC systems in an industrial framework. *J. Power Sources* **2024**, *613*, 234864. [CrossRef]
19. Huang, R.; Peng, Y.; Yang, J.; Xu, X.; Deng, P. Correlation analysis and prediction of PEM fuel cell voltage during start-stop operation based on real-world driving data. *Energy* **2022**, *260*, 124930. [CrossRef]
20. Chen, K.; Laghrouche, S.; Djerdir, A. Health state prognostic of fuel cell based on wavelet neural network and cuckoo search algorithm. *ISA Trans.* **2020**, *113*, 175–184. [CrossRef]
21. Chen, K.; Laghrouche, S.; Djerdir, A. Aging prognosis model of proton exchange membrane fuel cell in different operating conditions. *Int. J. Hydrogen Energy* **2020**, *45*, 11761–11772. [CrossRef]
22. Zhao, Z.; Shen, S.; Wang, Z. Performance degradation trend prediction of proton exchange membrane fuel cell based on GA-TCN. *Meas. Sci. Technol.* **2024**, *35*, 076007. [CrossRef]
23. Ma, T.; Xu, J.; Li, R.; Yao, N.; Yang, Y. Online Short-Term Remaining Useful Life Prediction of Fuel Cell Vehicles Based on Cloud System. *Energies* **2021**, *14*, 2806. [CrossRef]
24. Zhang, X.; Yu, Z.; Chen, W. Life Prediction Based on D-S ELM for PEMFC. *Energies* **2019**, *12*, 3752. [CrossRef]
25. Tian, Q.; Chen, H.; Ding, S.; Shu, L.; Wang, L.; Huang, J. Remaining Useful Life Prediction Method of PEM Fuel Cells Based on a Hybrid Model. *Electronics* **2023**, *12*, 3883. [CrossRef]
26. Wang, Y.; Wu, K.; Zhao, H.; Li, J.; Sheng, X.; Yin, Y.; Du, Q.; Zu, B.; Han, L.; Jiao, K. Degradation prediction of proton exchange membrane fuel cell stack using semi-empirical and data-driven methods. *Energy AI* **2023**, *11*, 100205. [CrossRef]
27. Gu, H.; Yin, B.; Yu, Y.; Sun, Y. Energy Management Strategy Considering Fuel Economy and Life of Fuel Cell for Fuel Cell Electric Vehicles. *J. Energy Eng.* **2023**, *149*, 04022054. [CrossRef]
28. Madhav, D.; Wang, J.; Keloth, R.; Mus, J.; Buysschaert, F.; Vandeginste, V. A Review of Proton Exchange Membrane Degradation Pathways, Mechanisms, and Mitigation Strategies in a Fuel Cell. *Energies* **2024**, *17*, 998. [CrossRef]
29. Li, B.; Wan, K.; Xie, M.; Chu, T.; Wang, X.; Li, X.; Yang, D.; Ming, P.; Zhang, C. Durability degradation mechanism and consistency analysis for proton exchange membrane fuel cell stack. *Appl. Energy* **2022**, *314*, 119020. [CrossRef]
30. Dragomiretskiy, K.; Zosso, D. Variational mode decomposition. *IEEE Trans. Signal Process.* **2013**, *62*, 531–544. [CrossRef]
31. Mirjalili, S.; Lewis, A. The whale optimization algorithm. *Adv. Eng. Softw.* **2016**, *95*, 51–67. [CrossRef]
32. Gouriveau, R.; Hilairet, M.; Hissel, D.; Jemei, S.; Jouin, M.; Lechartier, E.; Morando, S.; Pahon, E.; Pera, M.C.; Zerhouni, N. IEEE phm 2014 data challenge: Outline, experiments, scoring of results, winners. In Proceedings of the IEEE Conference on Prognostics and Health Management, Cheney, WA, USA, 22–25 June 2014; pp. 1–6.
33. Gao, S.; Zhou, M.; Wang, Y.; Cheng, J.; Yachi, H.; Wang, J. Dendritic Neuron Model with Effective Learning Algorithms for Classification, Approximation, and Prediction. *IEEE Trans. Neural Networks Learn. Syst.* **2018**, *30*, 601–614. [CrossRef] [PubMed]
34. Li, Q.; He, H.; Xue, C.; Liu, T.; Gao, S. A Seasonal-Trend Decomposition and Single Dendrite Neuron-Based Predicting Model for Green-house Time Series. *Environ. Model. Assess.* **2024**, *29*, 427–440. [CrossRef]
35. He, H.; Liu, T.; Li, Q.; Yang, J.; Wang, R.-L.; Gao, S. A Novel FD3 Framework for Carbon Emissions Prediction. *Environ. Model. Assess.* **2023**, *29*, 455–469. [CrossRef]
36. Pan, R.; Yang, D.; Wang, Y.; Chen, Z. Performance degradation prediction of proton exchange membrane fuel cell using a hybrid prognostic approach. *Int. J. Hydrogen Energy* **2020**, *45*, 30994–31008. [CrossRef]

MDPI AG
Grosspeteranlage 5
4052 Basel
Switzerland
Tel.: +41 61 683 77 34

Mathematics Editorial Office
E-mail: mathematics@mdpi.com
www.mdpi.com/journal/mathematics

www.ingramcontent.com/pod-product-compliance
Lightning Source LLC
Chambersburg PA
CBHW061831210926
51850CB00006B/861
* 9 7 8 3 7 2 5 8 7 4 4 4 6 *